THE
CAMBRIDGE
MEDIEVAL HISTORY

VOLUME IV. PART II

THE
CAMBRIDGE
MEDIEVAL HISTORY

VOLUME IV

THE BYZANTINE EMPIRE

PART II

GOVERNMENT, CHURCH AND
CIVILISATION

EDITED BY

J.M.HUSSEY

WITH THE EDITORIAL ASSISTANCE OF

D.M.NICOL AND G.COWAN

CAMBRIDGE
AT THE UNIVERSITY PRESS
1967

PUBLISHED BY
THE SYNDICS OF THE CAMBRIDGE UNIVERSITY PRESS

Bentley House, 200 Euston Road, London, N.W. 1
American Branch: 32 East 57th Street, New York, N.Y. 10022

©

CAMBRIDGE UNIVERSITY PRESS

1967

Printed in Great Britain at the University Printing House, Cambridge
(Brooke Crutchley, University Printer)

LIBRARY OF CONGRESS CATALOGUE
CARD NUMBER: 30-24288

PREFACE

This new edition is in a very real sense the outcome of N. H. Baynes' work for Byzantine studies in England and it is fitting that my acknowledgements should begin with a tribute to the distinguished scholar who continued the work of J. B. Bury, the original architect of the *Cambridge Medieval History*. The actual volumes would have been prepared with Baynes' help had not illness made this impossible. But in its early stages the project to replan the Byzantine volume in this series was long discussed with him and owes much to his guiding wisdom and discerning scholarship.

This is essentially the corporate enterprise of an international team of scholars and I am much indebted to their forbearance and generosity, particularly in undertaking the revision necessitated by unavoidable delays and in coming to the rescue in the face of unforeseen crises. When Professor Henri Grégoire was incapacitated by illness Professor R. J. H. Jenkins finished his chapter. One contributor withdrew at the last moment and Dr D. M. Nicol filled the gap at very short notice. Two contributors did not live to see their chapters in print and thanks are due to Professor R. J. H. Jenkins for his help with the proofs of the late Mr H. St L. B. Moss (chapter I) and to Father Joseph Gill, S.J., who dealt with those of the late Father Emil Herman, S.J. (chapter XXIII). I wish to record my special gratitude to Dr Janet Sondheimer. She translated a number of chapters, which in some cases had to be considerably adapted to reduce them to the required length, and she made many valuable comments on the text.

During the later stages of the work I was fortunate in being able to draw on Dr D. M. Nicol's expert advice and he gave most generous assistance in preparing the chapters for press and in many other ways. To Miss G. Cowan I am particularly indebted for help in proof reading both text and bibliographies and for making the Index; her wide knowledge and constant vigilance did much to reduce the errors and inconsistencies which so easily creep into a work of this complexity.

I have to thank Professor C. Toumanoff for drawing the maps of Armenia and Georgia (maps 10, 11 and 12), Professor D. Obolensky for help with the Slav territories (maps 8 and 9), and Professor B. Lewis and the late Dr D. E. Pitcher for suggestions in connection with Islamic lands and the eastern frontier (maps 13, 14 and 15).

I am also grateful to Dr D. M. Nicol for his general assistance in preparing the maps.

Among scholars who have assisted with the illustrations special thanks are due to Professor A. Grabar who was mainly responsible for their selection. I am most grateful for the advice which I have had from Professor H. Buchthal, Dr Alison Frantz, the late Mr H. St L. B. Moss, Dr D. M. Nicol, Professor D. Talbot Rice and Professor P. Underwood. Mr P. D. Whitting has generously provided the notes on the coins which were selected by him. For permission to publish I wish to thank the American School of Classical Studies at Athens, the Byzantine Institute of America, the Warburg Institute, the Dumbarton Oaks Research Library, the Agora Museum, the Corinth Museum, the British Museum, the Musée du Louvre, the Victoria and Albert Museum, Professor H. Buchthal, Dr Alison Frantz, Professor A. Grabar and Professor D. Talbot Rice.

Many other colleagues and friends have helped at all stages. I should like to record my gratitude to Mr J. S. F. Parker for editorial work on the first drafts, Dr D. I. Polemis for assistance with genealogies and proof reading, Professor P. Orgels for his work in connection with Professor Grégoire's chapter, Professor E. H. Sondheimer for help in translating the chapter on Byzantine Science, the late Dr C. M. Ady, Dr D. A. Bullough and Dr J. F. Fearns for advice on Italian history, the Rev. D. J. Chitty for a preview of his Birkbeck lectures and Dr A. D. Stokes for help with the transliteration of Slav words. And for various reasons I am also much indebted to the following: Dr E. Bickersteth, Mr P. Grierson, Miss J. L. Hurn, Professor D. M. Lang, Professor B. Lewis, Miss M. Pemberton, Professor K. M. Setton, Dr G. J. Whitrow and Miss A. Williams. I am most grateful to the secretariat of my own college for expert assistance in dealing during the past twelve years with an intractable mass of typescript. Finally it is a particular pleasure to acknowledge my debt to those of the staff of the Cambridge University Press who have helped with this enterprise, especially Mr P. G. Burbidge, whose magnificent efforts have made it possible to produce these volumes in the face of unending obstacles.

In accordance with the practice of this series, the Latin form of Greek names has generally been used, except for personal names where there is a familiar English version. In territories variously occupied by different races the same place-name may appear in more than one form, but it is hoped that the uninitiated will find some clue to such variants in the Index.

The typescript of both parts went to press in the autumn of 1961 and only a few bibliographical additions were possible after this date. The bibliographies vary in scope according to the subject-matter and the wishes of contributors. Those on Byzantium, the main concern of these volumes, may be supplemented by reference to the works cited in the General Bibliography.

J. M. H.

July 1964

INTRODUCTION

'Constantine sitting amongst the Christian bishops at the oecumenical council of Nicaea is in his own person the beginning of Europe's Middle Age.'[1] Baynes thus recognised the significance of the fourth century in the history of the Roman Empire and of Europe. Probably few scholars would still consider 717 to be the best starting point for a history of the Byzantine Empire. But unfortunately the original volume IV of the *Cambridge Medieval History* (*The Eastern Roman Empire 717–1453*) had to be revised in isolation without any foreseeable possibility of including volumes I and II which at present deal with early Byzantine history to 717 along with that of western Europe. Therefore the limiting dates of Bury's plan had to be adhered to. The most that could be done for the new volume IV was to provide two introductory chapters covering the vital years from Constantine the Great to the accession of Leo III in 717 and to ensure that such subjects as the secular church and monasticism, art and architecture, as well as political and administrative topics where necessary, included some reference to the formative period of the fourth to the seventh centuries.

Byzantine history is still in process of being written. Even so, work done since 1923 when the original volume IV appeared makes expansion possible and re-orientation inevitable. For this reason the old volume IV has been entirely replanned and rewritten (even though there could be no radical change in the limiting dates 717–1453). It was with great regret that it was decided to part with some of the brilliant contributions in the earlier volume IV, notably those of Charles Diehl on Byzantine civilisation and William Miller on the Latins in the Aegean. These still stand as memorials to Diehl's pioneer work in the Byzantine field and to Miller's historical insight based on his first-hand knowledge of Greece and the Aegean. But each generation must write its own histories: hence the complete abandonment of the old volume IV, except for J. B. Bury's Introduction.

The main emphasis in the two new volumes is placed on the history of Byzantium itself. Chapters have been added on administration, the church (including music), art, social life, literature and science, and the influence of Byzantium. Greater space has been given to the political history of the Empire. At the same time it has been possible to include (as before) a brief account of some of the near neighbours of Constantinople and their relations with Byzantium. The Balkan

[1] *CAH*, XII, p. 699.

and the Islamic countries of the near and middle East appear as in
the 1923 volume; Hungary and the Caucasian lands, vital factors in
the Byzantine political world, are all included. Venice, so closely
linked with East Rome, has been retained as previously. On the
other hand, Italy and the western European countries receive full
attention in their own right in the other volumes of this series,
though, as will be apparent, they do in fact impinge on the Byzantine story rather more than Bury would allow.

Perhaps the most marked advances of this century in Byzantine
research have been in the field of music and in administrative and
economic history. In Part II of these volumes music, with its close
liturgical associations, is treated as an integral part of secular and
ecclesiastical life. Administration is now shown to be a flexible
system capable of organic development and adaptation, and the
ancillary sciences, as for instance, numismatics, have contributed
towards filling out administrative and prosopographical details.
Even so, scholars are still reconstructing the work and personalities
of Byzantine administrators and officials, and the full fruit of such
investigations will not come in this generation. Another achievement
of comparatively recent research is fuller knowledge of Byzantine
land ownership and of various other aspects of economic life. As a
result it is necessary to modify Bury's attribution of the Byzantine
downfall to the evil effects of the Fourth Crusade.[1] Even before 1204,
signs of internal difficulties were apparent. The development of vast
landed estates threatened the central authority, while the marked
antagonism between the civil aristocracy centred in Constantinople
and the military landed magnates of the provinces was a feature of
the Byzantine economy fully in evidence by the eleventh century.
This threat to effective central control was certainly heightened by
the disintegration of the Empire after 1204, but it must be admitted
that Byzantine power had already been considerably weakened when
this occurred, and was subsequently further undermined by civil
wars, particularly during the fourteenth century.

Byzantium played an important role in the trade and industry of
the medieval world, at least before it was supplanted by the Italian
cities after 1204. The contribution of its merchants and its craftsmen
is not however treated here in its own right. When these volumes were
planned it was understood that this particular aspect of Byzantine
life would be fully covered in the *Cambridge Economic History*,
though this has in fact not proved to be the case. Economic, like
administrative, history is still in process of investigation, but even
so it is to be regretted that these volumes do not contain at least an

[1] See below, p. xvi.

interim report on commerce and industry. It also proved impractic-
able to provide chapters on military and naval defence and on the
influence of geographical factors as had originally been intended.

The case for including some indication of the relations of Byzantium with its Caucasian, Muslim and Slav neighbours is self-evident.
Both the Armenian and the Georgian principalities were near neighbours, and individual Armenians played a particularly significant role
in the internal life of Byzantium. There were economic, and often
cultural, relations with the Muslims, whether Umayyads, Abbasids,
Fatimids or others. The Slavs in the Balkans also had specially close
relations with Constantinople and although one might now hesitate
to go as far as Bury did in saying that they 'owed absolutely everything' to the Empire,[1] their debt to Byzantium in many aspects of
their medieval life is generally recognised.

Byzantium had its own integrated civilisation which was continuous throughout the middle ages, but it is being increasingly realised
that the East Roman Empire cannot be viewed in isolation. Contacts were often casual and came about by chance, as in the case of
Greek monks who settled in western communities and *vice versa*.
Diplomatic and commercial intercourse was carefully regulated, but
many other channels of communication existed. The manuscript or
ivory which found its way into some royal or episcopal western
treasury, or the active theological discussions between Latin and
Greek theologians or the Greek tutors sent to the west to instruct
some Byzantine bride-elect, all served to bring about exchange of
knowledge and experience of different traditions. In the crusading
period and the later middle ages contacts were perforce closer, and
not always as hostile as is often imagined. Byzantium, though
proudly aware of its former power, may have been only a pawn in the
diplomatic game, but in other ways its influence was by no means
negligible. The westerners who settled in Byzantine lands after the
Fourth Crusade put down roots in Greek soil and came to know
something of its civilisation. In the midst of what had once been
Greek strongholds, Chios still bears witness to the Genoese occupation, and the Venetian Castro of Naxos to the Italian families who
long flourished there. At the same time deeper knowledge of the
classical and Hellenistic and Byzantine traditions passed to the West,
where after many vicissitudes there has eventually grown up a fuller
understanding of medieval Greek civilisation and the role of Byzantium, so that by now this has almost dispelled the myth of Gibbon's
long and continuous decline and fall.   J.M.H.

---

[1] See below, p. xvi.

J.B.Bury's Introduction to the original volume IV published in 1923[1]

The present volume carries on the fortunes of a portion of Europe to the end of the Middle Ages. This exception to the general chronological plan of the work seemed both convenient and desirable. The orbit of Byzantium, the history of the peoples and states which moved within that orbit and always looked to it as the central body, giver of light and heat, did indeed at some points touch or traverse the orbits of western European states, but the development of these on the whole was not deeply affected or sensibly perturbed by what happened east of Italy or south of the Danube, and it was only in the time of the Crusades that some of their rulers came into close contact with the Eastern Empire or that it counted to any considerable extent in their policies. England, the remotest state of the West, was a legendary country to the people of Constantinople, and that imperial capital was no more than a dream-name of wealth and splendour to Englishmen, except to the few adventurers who travelled thither to make their fortunes in the Varangian guards. It is thus possible to follow the history of the Eastern Roman Empire from the eighth century to its fall, along with those of its neighbours and clients, independently of the rest of Europe, and this is obviously more satisfactory than to interpolate in the main history of Western Europe chapters having no connexion with those which precede and follow.

Besides being convenient, this plan is desirable. For it enables us to emphasise the capital fact that throughout the Middle Ages the same Empire which was founded by Augustus continued to exist and function and occupy even in its final weakness a unique position in Europe—a fact which would otherwise be dissipated, as it were, and obscured amid the records of another system of states with which it was not in close or constant contact. It was one of Gibbon's services to history that the title of his book asserted clearly and unambiguously this continuity.

We have, however, tampered with the correct name, which is simply *Roman Empire*, by adding *Eastern*, a qualification which although it has no official basis is justifiable as a convenient mark of distinction from the Empire which Charlemagne founded and which lasted till the beginning of the nineteenth century. This Western

[1 This is reprinted as a tribute to the distinguished Byzantinist who planned the *Cambridge Medieval History*. It remains unaltered except for the omission of Bury's references to chapters in the 1923 volume and the addition of editorial comments in square brackets. Ed.]

Empire had no good claim to the name of Roman. Charlemagne and those who followed him were not legitimate successors of Augustus, Constantine, Justinian, and the Isaurians, and this was tacitly acknowledged in their endeavours to obtain recognition of the imperial title they assumed from the sovrans of Constantinople whose legitimacy was unquestionable.

Much as the Empire changed after the age of Justinian, as its population became more and more predominantly Greek in speech, its descent from Rome was always unmistakably preserved in the designation of its subjects as Romans (Ῥωμαῖοι). Its eastern neighbours knew it as Rūm. Till the very end the names of most of the titles of its ministers, officials, and institutions were either Latin or the Greek translations of Latin terms that had become current in the earliest days of the Empire.[1] Words of Latin derivation form a large class in medieval Greek. The modern Greek language was commonly called *Romaic* till the middle of the nineteenth century. It is only quite recently that *Roumelia* has been falling out of use to designate territories in the Balkan peninsula. Contrast with the persistence of the Roman name in the East the fact that the subjects of the Western Empire were never called Romans and indeed had no common name as a whole; the only 'Romans' among them were the inhabitants of the city of Rome. There is indeed one district in Italy whose name still commemorates the Roman Empire—*Romagna*; but this exception only reinforces the contrast. For the district corresponds to the Exarchate of Ravenna, and was called Romania by its Lombard neighbours because it belonged to the Roman Emperor of Constantinople. It was at the New Rome, not at the Old, that the political tradition of the Empire was preserved. It is worth remembering too that the greatest public buildings of Constantinople were originally built, however they may have been afterwards changed or extended—the Hippodrome, the Great Palace, the Senatehouses, the churches of St Sophia and the Holy Apostles—by Emperors of Latin speech, Severus, Constantine, Justinian.

On the other hand, the civilisation of the later Roman Empire was the continuation of that of ancient Greece. Hellenism entered upon its second phase when Alexander of Macedon expanded the Greek world into the east, and on its third with the foundation of Constantine by the waters where Asia and Europe meet. Christianity, with

---

[1] Examples: (1) ἀσηκρῆτις (*a secretis*), δούξ, κόμης, μάγιστρος, πατρίκιος, δομέστικος, πραιπόσιτος, πραίτωρ, κουαίστωρ, κουράτωρ; ἰδίκτον, πάκτον; κάστρον, φοσσάτον, παλάτιον, βῆλον (*velum*); ἀπληκεύειν = (*castra*) *applicare*, παιδεύειν, δηριγεύειν; μοῦλτος = (*tu*)*multus*; (2) (ancient equivalents of Latin terms) βασιλεύς, αὐτοκράτωρ (*imperator*), σύγκλητος (*senatus*), ὕπατος (*consul*), ἀνθύπατος (*proconsul*), ὕπαρχος (*praefectus*), δρόμος (*cursus publicus*).

its dogmatic theology and its monasticism, gave to this third phase its distinctive character and flavour, and *Byzantine* civilisation, as we have learned to call it, is an appropriate and happy name....The continuity which links the fifteenth century A.D. with the fifth B.C. is notably expressed in the long series of Greek historians, who maintained, it may be said, a continuous tradition of historiography. From Critobulus, the imitator of Thucydides, and Chalcocondyles, who told the story of the last days of the Empire, we can go back, in a line broken only by a dark interval in the seventh and eighth centuries, to the first great masters, Thucydides and Herodotus.

The development of 'Byzantinism' really began in the fourth century. The historian Finlay put the question in a rather awkward way by asking, When did the Roman Empire change into the Byzantine? The answer is that it did not change into any other Empire than itself, but that some of the characteristic features of Byzantinism began to appear immediately after Constantinople was founded. There is, however, a real truth in Finlay's own answer to his question. He drew the dividing line at the accession of Leo the Isaurian, at the beginning of the eighth century. And, in fact, Leo's reign marked the consummation of a rapid change which had been going on during the past hundred years. Rapid: for I believe anyone who has studied the history of those centuries will agree that in the age of the Isaurians we feel much further away from the age of Justinian than we feel in the age of Justinian from the age of Theodosius the Great. Finlay's date has been taken as the starting point of this volume; it marks, so far as a date can, the transition to a new era.[1]

The chief function which *as a political power* the Eastern Empire performed throughout the Middle Ages was to act as a bulwark for Europe, and for that civilisation which Greece had created and Rome had inherited and diffused, against Asiatic aggression. Since the rise of the Sasanid power in the third century, Asia had been attempting, with varying success, to resume the role which it had played under the Achaemenids. The arms of Alexander had delivered for hundreds of years the Eastern coasts and waters of the Mediterranean from all danger from an Asiatic power. The Sasanids finally succeeded in reaching the Mediterranean shores and the Bosphorus. The roles of Europe and Asia were again reversed, and it was now for Byzantium to play on a larger stage the part formerly played by Athens and Sparta in a struggle for life and death. Heraclius proved himself not only a Themistocles but in some measure an Alexander. He not only checked the victorious advance of the enemy; he completely destroyed the power of the Great King and made him his vassal. But within ten

[1 For another view see above, p. ix. Ed.]

years the roles were reversed once more in that amazing transformation scene in which an obscure Asiatic people which had always seemed destined to play a minor part became suddenly one of the strongest powers in the world. Constantinople had again to fight for her life, and the danger was imminent and the strain unrelaxed for eighty years. Though the Empire did not succeed in barring the road to Spain and Sicily, its rulers held the gates of Europe at the Propontis and made it impossible for them to sweep over Europe as they had swept over Syria and Egypt. Centuries passed, and the Comnenians guarded Europe from the Seljuqs. The Ottomans were the latest bearers of the Asiatic menace. If the Eastern Empire had not been mortally wounded and reduced to the dimensions of a petty state by the greed and brutality of the Western brigands who called themselves Crusaders, it is possible that the Turks might never have gained a footing in Europe. Even as it was, the impetus of their first victorious advance was broken by the tenacity of the Palaeologi—assisted it is true by the arms of Timur. They had reached the Danube sixty years before Constantinople fell. When this at length happened, the first force and fury of their attack had been spent, and it is perhaps due to this delay that the Danube and the Carpathians were to mark the limit of Asiatic rule in Europe and that St Peter's was not to suffer the fate of St Sophia. Even in the last hours of its life, the Empire was still true to its traditional role of bulwark of Europe.

As a civilised state, we may say that the Eastern Empire performed three principal functions. As in its early years the Roman Empire laid the foundations of civilisation in the West and educated Celtic and German peoples, so in its later period it educated the Slavs of eastern Europe. Russia, Bulgaria, and Serbia owed it everything[1] and bore its stamp. Secondly, it exercised a silent but constant and considerable influence on western Europe by sending its own manufactures and the products of the East to Italy, France, and Germany. Many examples of its embroidered textile fabrics and its jewellery have been preserved in the West. In the third place, it guarded safely the heritage of classical Greek literature which has had on the modern world a penetrating influence difficult to estimate. That we owe our possession of the masterpieces of Hellenic thought and imagination to the Byzantines everyone knows, but everyone does not remember that those books would not have travelled to Italy in the fourteenth and fifteenth centuries, because they would not have existed, if the Greek classics had not been read habitually by the educated subjects of the Eastern Empire and therefore continued to be copied.

[1] This appears to do less than justice to the native contributions of these countries. Ed.]

Here we touch on a most fundamental contrast between the Eastern Empire and the western European states of the Middle Ages. The well-to-do classes in the West were as a rule illiterate, with the exception of ecclesiastics; among the well-to-do classes in the Byzantine world education was the rule, and education meant not merely reading, writing, and arithmetic, but the study of ancient Greek grammar and the reading of classical authors. The old traditions of Greek education had never died out. In court circles at Constantinople everyone who was not an utter parvenu would recognise and understand a quotation from Homer. In consequence of this difference, the intellectual standards in the West where book-learning was reserved for a particular class, and in the East where every boy and girl whose parents could afford to pay was educated, were entirely different. The advantages of science and training and system were understood in Byzantine society.

The appreciation of method and system which the Byzantines inherited both from the Greeks and from the Romans is conspicuously shewn in their military establishment and their conduct of war. Here their intellectuality stands out in vivid contrast with the rude dullness displayed in the modes of warfare practised in the West. Tactics were carefully studied, and the treatises on war which the officers used were kept up to date. The tacticians apprehended that it was stupid to employ uniform methods in campaigns against different foes. They observed carefully the military habits of the various peoples with whom they had to fight—Saracens, Lombards, Franks, Slavs, Hungarians—and thought out different rules for dealing with each. The soldiers were most carefully and efficiently drilled. They understood organisation and the importance of not leaving details to chance, of not neglecting small points in equipment. Their armies were accompanied by ambulances and surgeons. Contrast the feudal armies of the West, ill-disciplined, with no organisation, under leaders who had not the most rudimentary idea of tactics, who put their faith in sheer strength and courage, and attacked all antagonists in exactly the same way. More formidable the Western knights might be than Slavs or Magyars, but in the eyes of a Byzantine officer they were equally rude barbarians who had not yet learned that war is an art which requires intelligence as well as valour. In the period in which the Empire was strong, before it lost the provinces which provided its best recruits, its army was beyond comparison the best fighting machine in Europe. When a Byzantine army was defeated, it was always the incompetence of the general or some indiscretion on his part, never inefficiency or cowardice of the troops, that was to blame. The great disaster of Manzikert (1071), from which perhaps the decline of the Eastern Empire may be dated, was caused by the

imbecility of the brave Emperor who was in command.[1] A distinguished student of the art of war has observed that Gibbon's dictum,
'the vices of Byzantine armies were inherent, their victories acci-
dental', is precisely the reverse of the truth. He is perfectly right.

Military science enabled the Roman Empire to hold its own for
many centuries against the foes around it, east and west and north.
Internally, its permanence and stability depended above all on the
rule of Roman law. Its subjects had always 'the advantage of
possessing a systematic administration of justice enforced by fixed
legal procedure'; they were not at the mercy of caprice. They could
contrast their courts in which justice was administered with a systematic observance of rules, with those in which Mohammedan lawyers
dispensed justice. The feeling that they were much better off under
the government of Constantinople than their Eastern neighbours
engendered a loyal attachment to the Empire, notwithstanding what
they might suffer under an oppressive fiscal system.[2]

The influence of lawyers on the administration was always great,
and may have been one of the facts which account for the proverbial
conservatism of Byzantine civilisation. But that conservatism has
generally been exaggerated, and even in the domain of law there was
a development, though the foundations and principles remained those
which were embodied in the legislation of Justinian.

The old Roman law, as expounded by the classical jurists, was in
the East considerably modified in practice here and there by Greek
and oriental custom, and there are traces of this influence in the laws
of Justinian. But Justinianean law shows very few marks of ecclesiastical influence which in the seventh and following centuries led to
various changes, particularly in laws relating to marriage. The law-
book of the Isaurian Emperor, Leo III, was in some respects revolutionary, and although at the end of the ninth century the Macedonian
Emperors, eager to renounce all the works of the heretical Isaurians,
professed to return to the pure principles of Justinian, they retained
many of the innovations and compromised with others. The principal
reforms of Leo were too much in accordance with public opinion to be
undone. The legal status of concubinate for instance was definitely
abolished. Only marriages between Christians were recognised as
valid. Marriages between first and second cousins were forbidden.
Fourth marriages were declared illegal and even third were dis-
countenanced. It is remarkable however that in the matter of
divorce, where the differences between the views of State and
Church had been sharpest and where the Isaurians had given effect

[1] This judgement on Romanus IV Diogenes appears open to question. Ed.]
[2] Compare Finlay, *History of Greece*, II, 22–4; I, 411–12.

to the un-Roman ecclesiastical doctrine that marriage is indissoluble, the Macedonians returned to the common-sense view of Justinian and Roman lawyers that marriage like other contracts between human beings may be dissolved. We can see new tendencies too in the history of the *patria potestas*. The Iconoclasts substituted for it a parental *potestas*, assigning to the mother rights similar to those of the father....

In criminal law there was a marked change in tendency. From Augustus to Justinian penalties were ever becoming severer and new crimes being invented. After Justinian the movement was in the direction of mildness. In the eighth century only two or three crimes were punishable by death. One of these was murder and in this case the extreme penalty might be avoided if the murderer sought refuge in a church. On the other hand penalties of mutilation were extended and systematised. This kind of punishment had been inflicted in much earlier times and authorised in one or two cases by Justinian. In the eighth century we find amputations of the tongue, hand, and nose part of the criminal system, and particularly applied in dealing with sexual offences. If such punishments strike us today as barbaric (though in England, for instance, mutilation was inflicted little more than two centuries ago), they were then considered as a humane substitute for death, and the Church approved them because a tongue-less or nose-less sinner had time to repent. In the same way, it was a common practice to blind, instead of killing, rebels or unsuccessful candidates for the throne. The tendency to avoid capital punishment is illustrated by the credible record that during the reign of John Comnenus there were no executions.

The fact that in domestic policy the Eastern Empire was far from being obstinately conservative is also illustrated by the reform of legal education in the eleventh century, when it was realised that a system which had been in practice for a long time did not work well and another was substituted....That conception of the later Empire which has made the word Byzantine almost equivalent to Chinese was based on ignorance, and is now discredited. It is obvious that no State could have lasted so long in a changing world, if it had not had the capacity of adapting itself to new conditions. Its administrative machinery was being constantly modified by capable and hardworking rulers of whom there were many; the details of the system at the end of the tenth century differed at ever so many points from those of the eighth. As for art and literature, there were ups and downs, declines and renascences, throughout the whole duration of the Empire. It is only in quite recent years that Byzantine literature and Byzantine art have been methodically studied; in these wide fields of research Krumbacher's *Byzantine Literature* and Strzygowski's *Orient oder*

Rom were pioneer works marking a new age. Now that we are getting to know the facts better and the darkness is gradually lifting, we have come to see that the history of the Empire is far from being a monotonous chronicle of palace revolutions, circus riots, theological disputes, tedious ceremonies in a servile court, and to realise that, as in any other political society, conditions were continually changing and in each succeeding age new political and social problems presented themselves for which some solution had to be found. If the chief interest in history lies in observing such changes, watching new problems shape themselves and the attempts of rulers or peoples to solve them, and seeing how the characters of individuals and the accidents which befall them determine the course of events, the story of the Eastern Empire is at least as interesting as that of any medieval State, or perhaps more interesting because its people were more civilised and intellectual than other Europeans and had a longer political experience behind them. On the ecclesiastical side it offers the longest and most considerable experiment of a State-Church that Christendom has ever seen.

The Crusades were, for the Eastern Empire, simply a series of barbarian invasions of a particularly embarrassing kind, and in the present volume they are treated merely from this point of view and their general significance in universal history is not considered. The full treatment of their causes and psychology and the consecutive story of the movement are reserved for Vol. v.

But the earlier history of Venice has been included in this volume. The character of Venice and her career were decided by the circumstance that she was subject to the Eastern Emperors before she became independent. She was extra-Italian throughout the Middle Ages; she never belonged to the Carolingian Kingdom of Italy. And after she had slipped into independence almost without knowing it—there was never a violent breaking away from her allegiance to the sovrans of Constantinople—she moved still in the orbit of the Empire; and it was on the ruins of the Empire, dismembered by the criminal enterprise of her Duke Dandolo, that she reached the summit of her power as mistress in the Aegean and in Greece. She was the meeting-place of two civilisations, but it was eastern not western Europe that controlled her history and lured her ambitions. Her citizens spoke a Latin tongue and in spiritual matters acknowledged the supremacy of the elder Rome, but the influence from new Rome had penetrated deep, and their great Byzantine basilica is a visible reminder of their long political connection with the Eastern Empire.

TABLE OF CONTENTS

CHAPTER XX

THE GOVERNMENT AND ADMINISTRATION
OF THE BYZANTINE EMPIRE

By the late W. ENSSLIN, *Emeritus Professor of
Ancient History in the University of Erlangen*

CHAPTER XXI

BYZANTINE LAW

By H. J. SCHELTEMA, *Professor of Roman Law
in the University of Groningen*

CHAPTER XXII

SOCIAL LIFE IN THE BYZANTINE EMPIRE

By R. J. H. JENKINS, *Professor of Byzantine History and Literature,
Dumbarton Oaks, Center for Byzantine Studies,
Trustees for Harvard University*

CHAPTER XXIII

THE SECULAR CHURCH

By the late EMIL HERMAN, S.J., *Emeritus Professor of
Oriental Canon Law in the Pontifical Oriental Institute, Rome*

CHAPTER XXIV

BYZANTINE MUSIC AND LITURGY

By E. Wellesz, *Sometime Reader in Byzantine Music
in the University of Oxford*

CHAPTER XXV

BYZANTINE MONASTICISM

By J. M. Hussey, *Professor of History in
the University of London*

CHAPTER XXVI

BYZANTINE THEOLOGICAL SPECULATION AND SPIRITUALITY

By J. M. HUSSEY and T. A. HART

CHAPTER XXVII

BYZANTINE LITERATURE

By F. DÖLGER, *Emeritus Professor of Byzantine Studies and Modern Greek Philology and Director of the Institute for Byzantine Studies and Modern Greek Philology in the University of Munich*

CHAPTER XXVIII

BYZANTINE SCIENCE

By K. VOGEL, *Professor of the History of Science
in the University of Munich*

CHAPTER XXIX

BYZANTINE ARCHITECTURE AND ART

By A. GRABAR, *Professor of Paleochristian and Byzantine Archaeology at the Collège de France and the Ecole des Hautes Etudes, Paris*

CHAPTER XXX

THE PLACE OF BYZANTIUM IN THE MEDIEVAL WORLD

By S. RUNCIMAN, *Sometime Fellow of Trinity College, Cambridge*

BIBLIOGRAPHIES

LIST OF MAPS

DESCRIPTION OF THE PLATES

The plates are bound in between pages 336 and 337

1. Constantinople. The land walls.

The fortification walls of Constantinople built in the reign of Theodosius II (408–50) remain as the earliest surviving examples of what may properly be termed Byzantine architecture. On the landward and most vulnerable side of the city they stood about a mile to the west of the first fortifications erected by Constantine, and extended from the Sea of Marmora to the Golden Horn. They consisted of an inner wall built by the Praetorian Prefect Anthemius in 413 and an outer wall built by the Prefect Constantine Cyrus in 447 after the original works had been seriously damaged by earthquake. Between the two walls ran a terrace some twenty yards wide. The inner wall was guarded by ninety-six towers or battlements each about sixty feet high and evenly spaced along its length. The outer wall had ninety-two towers of varied shape, and beyond it lay a broad, deep moat surmounted on its inward side by another terrace and traversed by bridges which gave access to the several gates of the city.

2. Constantinople. Church of St John of Studius.

The monastery church of St John the Baptist, called 'of Studius', is the oldest surviving church in Constantinople and stands in the district of Psamathia in the south-west corner of the city not far from the Golden Gate. It was founded in 463 by the patrician Studius who had been consul nine years before. It is a basilica in plan, with an apse, narthex and atrium, though almost square in its dimensions. A fire in 1782 and an earthquake in 1894 contributed to its ruin; but the mosaic pavement (later) and north colonnade of the nave as well as the sculptured entablature of the narthex, supported on four Corinthian columns, still stand.

3. Daphni. The monastery church.

The monastery church at Daphni, seen here from the south side, is one of the best-known Byzantine churches in Greece, standing near the road between Athens and Eleusis. It was built towards the end of the eleventh century and is constructed on the cross-in-square plan, with its large dome supported not on pendentives but on four squinches, a method of construction which, though less common, gives a greater sense of spaciousness to the central portion of the interior of the building. The church is now entered through a narthex at its west end, to which was joined an exonarthex with pointed arches (recently restored) added by the French Cistercians who gained possession of the monastery in 1207. The church is celebrated for the mosaics (probably *c.* 1100) which decorate the dome, squinches, vaults and upper walls of the sanctuary, nave and inner narthex.

4. Constantinople. The palace of Tekfour Serai.

The ruins of the building known as Tekfour Serai provide the only substantially surviving example of Byzantine palace architecture in Constantinople. It is in the district of Blachernae at the northern corner of the city, an oblong structure of three storeys with an open arcade at ground level. The building has been variously assigned to the tenth century (and sometimes called 'the Palace of Constantine Porphyrogenitus'), or to the reign of Manuel I Comnenus or to the Palaeologan period. It was most probably built as an extension to the Blachernae Palace in the time of the Palaeologi, since the decorative motifs of the brickwork between the windows in the upper part of the façade appear to indicate a date later than the twelfth century. The building as a whole provides valuable evidence about the general style of secular architecture in Byzantine Constantinople.

5 and 6. Constantinople. Church of St Sophia (Hagia Sophia).

St Sophia (Hagia Sophia), church of the Holy Wisdom, or the Great Church, was built by Justinian between the years 532 and 537. The architects were Anthemius of Tralles and Isidore of Miletus. It was partially rebuilt in 562 after the dome had collapsed. Its present form is substantially that of the sixth century, except for certain structural additions and for the disappearance of the atrium which was demolished in Turkish times. The great central nave beneath the dome is separated by piers and columns from the side aisles. The dome is supported on pendentives; and galleries run above the aisles and narthex. The immense buttresses on the exterior were added in the fourteenth century and later; and the minarets that now stand at each of the four corners of the building were put up in the fifteenth and sixteenth centuries after its conversion into a mosque. The true orientation of the interior is distorted at its eastern end by the oblique setting of the sanctuary steps and the Turkish *mihrab*, intended to direct the faithful towards Mecca.

7. Thessalonica. Apostle. Mosaic in St Sophia (Hagia Sophia).

One of the figures of the Apostles from the mosaic of the Ascension which decorates the upper part of the dome of the church of St Sophia in Thessalonica. The central medallion is occupied by the figure of the seated Christ surrounded by angels, while in the lower zone stands the Virgin flanked by two angels and the twelve Apostles. The artist has tried to correct the optical distortion of his figures by presenting them in elongated form, with long legs and small heads. The placing of the Ascension rather than the more conventional Pantocrator in the central position in the dome may be due to the fact that the work is provincial in character. It belongs to the end of the ninth century.

8. Ravenna. Justinian and his retinue. Mosaic in San Vitale.

The wall mosaics in the church of San Vitale in Ravenna were executed before 547 by artists trained in the Constantinopolitan style of the early sixth century. The detail here illustrated comes from the north wall of the choir and shows portraits of the Emperor Justinian together with the Archbishop Maximian and a senator. The Empress Theodora and her ladies-in-waiting are portrayed in the mosaic on the opposite wall of the choir.

9. Thessalonica. Ezekiel's Vision. Mosaic in Hosios David.

The mosaic in the central apse of the little monastery church of Hosios David or Christ of the Latomos (the stone-mason) in Thessalonica dates from the fifth century. It shows Ezekiel's vision of Christ in glory. Christ is portrayed as a youthful and beardless figure seated on a rainbow and offset by a circular glory, which partially conceals the emerging figures of the four symbols of the Evangelists, the man of St Matthew, the eagle of St John, the lion of St Mark and the ox of St Luke. The corners of the composition are occupied by the figures of Habakkuk (or perhaps Zechariah) on the right and Ezekiel himself on the left. Below are depicted Jordan, the Four Rivers of Paradise and the figure of a pagan river god.

10 and 11. Constantinople. Mosaic in the Great Palace.

The mosaic decoration of which Plates 10 and 11 are details formed a double border covering the floor on the four sides of a peristyle courtyard in the Great Palace of the Emperors in Constantinople. It was the work of several artists and the subjects are secular in character, some being derived from classical sources, others modelled on scenes from the hunting field, the circus or country life; scenes with animals predominate. Scholars range from the fifth to the sixth century in their dating of these mosaics. Plate 10 shows an eagle struggling with a snake and Plate 11 a boy with a donkey.

12. Vladimir. Detail from Last Judgement.
 Fresco from the church of St Demetrius.

This head is from the fresco of the Last Judgement in the church of St Demetrius in Vladimir about 100 miles east of Moscow. The frescoes date from the late twelfth century and are outstanding for their sensitive and realistic figures.

13. Constantinople. Constantine IX. Mosaic in St Sophia (Hagia Sophia).

Plates 13 and 14 give two of the figures in a wall panel situated in the south gallery of the church of St Sophia in Constantinople. It shows Christ enthroned between the standing figures of the Emperor Constantine IX Monomachus (1042–55) and the Empress Zoe, whose third husband he was. The evident amendment to the inscription over the figure of the Emperor suggests that it had been altered because it referred to a portrait of one of his predecessors, Zoe's first husband, Romanus III Argyrus (1028–34). The mosaic setting shows that the portrait head of the new Emperor was substituted at the same time.

14. Constantinople. The Empress Zoe. Mosaic in St Sophia (Hagia Sophia).

The Macedonian Empress Zoe reigned from 1028 to 1050. This portrait of her comes from the mosaic described in Plate 13, where she is shown with her third husband, Constantine IX Monomachus (1042–55).

15. Constantinople. Joseph's departure. Mosaic in Kariye Camii.

The mosaics covering the roof vaults and upper walls of the inner and outer narthex of the monastery church of St Saviour in Chora or Kariye Camii in Constantinople were executed under the patronage of Theodore Metochites (see Plate 16) about the years 1303–20. Together with the contemporary frescoes in the side chapel of the same church they are among the finest expressions of the artistic revival of the Palaeologan age. The detail reproduced here is from one of the lunettes in the inner narthex of the church, where the theme of the decoration is the Life of the Virgin.

16. Constantinople. Theodore Metochites. Mosaic in Kariye Camii.

Theodore Metochites, the Grand Logothete of Andronicus II, was the patron and latter-day founder of the church of St Saviour in Chora, in whose monastery he himself died in 1331. In this panel, above the door leading from the inner narthex into the nave of the church, he is portrayed wearing fourteenth-century ceremonial court robes and head-dress and presenting a model of his church to Christ.

17. Constantinople. Virgin and Child. Mosaic in Kariye Camii.

Mosaic on the south-east pier of the side chapel of the monastery of St Saviour in Chora or Kariye Camii. The representation of the Virgin is of the type known as Hodegetria, in which the Virgin points to the Child as the Way. The inscription—ἡ χώρα τοῦ ἀχωρήτου—is similar to that which accompanies the figure of Christ in the scene of the presentation of the church by Theodore Metochites (Plate 16). It suggests a play on words, indicating the metaphysical connotation of the word Chora, the name early applied to the monastery to describe its position in the fields or suburbs of the city.

18. Greece. The Washing of the Feet. Mosaic in Hosios Loukas.

The mosaics in the monastery church of Hosios Loukas in central Greece date from the very beginning of the eleventh century if not from the end of the tenth. Although the work is provincial and monastic in character it shows signs of the trend towards a more supple and less rigid style. The detail here reproduced, showing Christ washing the feet of St Peter, decorates one of the two semicircular niches in the narthex of the church. The artist has skilfully accommodated his picture to the space available and corrected the optical illusions of the concave surface by the disposition and postures of the figures on each side of his composition.

19. Cappadocia. The Last Supper. Fresco in Karanlik (Qaranleq).

The wall-paintings in the numerous rock-cut churches of Cappadocia date mainly from the post-iconoclastic age. They reflect, though in a provincial style, the artistic tastes of Constantinople in the tenth, eleventh and twelfth centuries. The scene of the Last Supper here illustrated comes from the nave of the church known as Karanlik (Qaranleq) Kilisse, which is carved out of the side of a hill at Guereme. Its Turkish name means 'the dark church', since the building is lit by only one small window; but its walls are covered with frescoes. In this fresco of the Last Supper John is seated next to Christ, Judas is in the middle stretching out his hand, and Peter is sitting on a low divan on the extreme right. The embroidered table-cloth is set with knives and forks. (Cf. G. de Jerphanion, *Les églises rupestres de Cappadoce*, I, ii (Paris, 1932), 413, and *Planches*, II (1928), plate 101, no. 2.)

20. Macedonia. Pietà. Fresco at Nerezi.

The frescoes in the church of St Panteleimon at Nerezi, near Skoplje in southern Yugoslavia, were painted in 1164 by a gifted artist whose work reflects the Constantinopolitan style of the twelfth century. This scene of the Lamentation, one of a series showing the Life and Passion of Christ, is in bright colours against a blue background. The delicacy and expression of the figures typify the restrained feeling and humanist quality that characterise the surviving paintings of the period.

21. Cappadocia. Scenes from the Life of the Virgin.
    Fresco in Kiliclar (Qeledjlar).

These frescoes in the rock church of Kiliclar (Qeledjlar) on the east side of the south arm of the cross show the Proof of the Virgin and the Visitation. In the Proof the virginity of Mary is tested by asking her to drink a cup of water which is supposed to turn to poison in the event of her guilt. The tall figure of Zachariah is offering the cup to her, while Joseph watches on the far right. On the left Mary and Elizabeth are seen greeting each other while a maidservant watches through an open door in the background. Though in general these frescoes have been described by G. de Jerphanion as of the archaic type, he remarks that they sometimes (as here) reveal something of the austere elegance found in imperial art. (Cf. G. de Jerphanion, *op. cit.* I, i (Paris, 1925), chapter 7 and *Planches*, I (1925), plates 46, no. 1, and 56.)

22. Constantinople. Descent into Hell. Fresco in Kariye Camii.

This scene of the Anastasis or Day of Resurrection, symbolised in the traditional Byzantine fashion by the Descent of Christ into Hell, adorns the upper portion of the apse of the large parecclesion or mortuary chapel adjoining the south side of the church of St Saviour in Chora (Kariye

Camii) in Constantinople. Much of the walls and ceiling of the chapel were covered with frescoes of exceptional beauty by a single artist at the time of the reconstruction of the church in the early fourteenth century.

23. Mistra. The Raising of Lazarus. Fresco in the Pantanassa.

The monastery church of the Virgin called Pantanassa at Mistra in the Peloponnese was built in 1428 by the *protostrator* John Frangopoulos, first minister of the Despot Theodore II Palaeologus. The surviving frescoes inside the church are contemporary with its foundation. The painting of the Raising of Lazarus here illustrated is one of a series of scenes from the Life of Christ on the western end of the vault of the nave. The artist's work is characterised by his evident enjoyment of detail, not least in the architectural backgrounds of his pictures, and by his subtle use of vivid colours. The figures in this scene are dressed in bright green, blue and purple clothes; the lid of the sarcophagus is grained like red marble; and the whole composition is set against a gay yellow background.

24. Macedonia. Girl with pitcher. Fresco at Peć.

This detail of a girl carrying a pitcher is from the wall-painting of the Nativity of the Virgin in the church of St Demetrius at Peć in southern Yugoslavia. It illustrates the style of an early fourteenth-century artist of singular talent interpreting the traditional forms of Byzantine art in a provincial idiom. The head of the girl is almost realistic enough to be taken as a portrait; and the work as a whole demonstrates the 'academic' attitude to art characteristic of the many and varied local schools and styles of the time, whose artists were rediscovering the methods of the past but also incorporating the experimental ideas of their Byzantine predecessors.

25. Miniature from a treatise on Veterinary Medicine.

A miniature from the treatise entitled *Hippiatrica* or *On the Treatment of Horses*. The manuscript is in the Bibliothèque Nationale in Paris (Cod. gr. 2244, f. 54^r) and dates from the fourteenth century.

26. Miniature. The Conversion of St Paul.

This miniature painting of the conversion of St Paul shows the saint at various stages of his progress from Jerusalem to Damascus, first being blinded by the light from heaven and finally having his sight restored by Ananias. It comes from the oldest surviving manuscript of the *Christian Topography* of Cosmas Indicopleustes (Vatican MS gr. 699), which probably dates from the ninth century. The illustrations in it no doubt followed the original sixth-century prototypes fairly closely; and the biblical scenes, selected to demonstrate the unity between the Old and New Testaments, are in a grave and monumental style.

27. Miniature from a monastic typicon.

This late fourteenth-century manuscript, which contains the typicon of the Convent of the All-Holy Theotokos of Good Hope in Constantinople, was probably made by order of Euphrosyne, a grand-niece of the Emperor Michael VIII Palaeologus, and daughter of the foundress. The miniature shows the entire community of the convent. Other illustrations in the typicon portray the foundress and her relatives, and the Mother of God of Good Hope. The manuscript belongs to Lincoln College, Oxford, and is in the Bodleian Library (Bodl. gr. 35, f. 12^r).

28. Miniature. The Emperor John VI.

One of the four full-page illustrations from a manuscript copied for the ex-Emperor John VI Cantacuzenus between the years 1370 and 1375. He is shown here as Emperor enthroned and presiding over the assembly of monks and bishops at the Church Council which he convened in Constantinople in 1351. The manuscript is in the Bibliothèque Nationale in Paris (Cod. gr. 1242).

29. Silk shroud of St Germain at Auxerre.

The so-called shroud of St Germain in the church of St Eusebius at Auxerre is one of the finest examples of Byzantine textile work. It was made in Constantinople in the late tenth century. The motifs are eagles and rosettes worked in gold against a purple ground and on a generous scale, each of the eagles being almost two feet in height.

30. Ivory casket. Troyes.

The front panel of an ivory casket measuring 14 cm by 26 cm and showing hunters attacking a lion with bow and sword. It is Constantinopolitan work of the eleventh century now in the Treasury of the Cathedral at Troyes; it is said to have been brought there by the chaplain to the Bishop of Troyes after the capture of Constantinople by the Latin crusaders in 1204.

31. Ivory triptych. Palazzo Venezia, Rome.

The inside of an ivory triptych in the Palazzo Venezia in Rome. It measures 24 cm in height. The central panel is carved with the scene of the Deesis, the figure of Christ with John the Baptist on the left and the Virgin on the right; below are Sts James, John, Peter, Paul and Andrew. The side panels each have four saints arranged in pairs, the pattern being repeated on the outer faces of these panels. The outside surface of the central panel bears an ornamental cross. The metrical inscription carved on the inside of the central panel asks for divine help for one Constantine, who has been variously identified as Constantine VII, VIII, IX, X and even the last Emperor Constantine (1449–53). But comparison with the similar Harbaville triptych in the Louvre, and with another in the Vatican, suggests that this work belongs to the mid-tenth century. The Constantine in question would then be Constantine VII (913–59).

32. Marble relief. The Virgin. Istanbul.

A fine example of large-scale relief sculpture (2·01 metres in height) executed in Constantinople in the eleventh century. It was found in the district of the Mangana Palace and is now in the Archaeological Museum in Istanbul. The Virgin is shown in the Orans attitude standing on a decorated footstool. The holes in the fragment of the halo and in the two rectangular mountings on each side were probably dowel holes for the attachment of metal pieces now lost.

33. Copper relief. Virgin and Child. London.

Plaque of gilded copper (21·5 cm high) now in the Victoria and Albert Museum in London. It came from Torcello, although it was most probably made in Constantinople and may be dated to the twelfth century. The Virgin is of the Hodegetria type, pointing to the Child. The lower inscription on either side refers to an unidentified Bishop Philip.

34. Silver reliquary lid. The Women at the Tomb. Paris.

This is the larger of two plaques from a reliquary in embossed silver belonging most probably to the twelfth century, though earlier dates have been proposed. It shows the two Marys at the Sepulchre with the Angel pointing to the empty grave and winding sheet. The inscription round the frame of the picture is part of a liturgical text. The legends within the picture are texts from the Gospels. The reliquary, once in the Treasury of the Sainte-Chapelle, is now in the Louvre in Paris.

35. Enamel book-cover. The Archangel Michael. Venice.

One of several Gospel-covers enriched with enamels and precious stones in the Treasury of St Mark's in Venice. The central figure of the Archangel Michael is repoussé work with the face enamelled. The enamelled plaques in the frame on either side depict the soldier saints of the Byzantine Church. The work is probably to be assigned to the twelfth century.

36. Enamelled icon. The Entry into Jerusalem. Venice.

This enamelled icon is one of several framed in the reredos known as the Pala d'Oro in St Mark's in Venice. They are of various dates and varied workmanship. Those in the upper series, to which this icon of Christ's entry into Jerusalem belongs, are probably of the eleventh century. They show scenes from the Gospels and may have come from an iconostasis in Constantinople.

37. Enamels from the Crown of Constantine IX. Budapest.

Ten of the enamelled plaques which originally made up the crown of the Emperor Constantine IX Monomachus (1042–55) are now in the National Museum in Budapest. One portrays the Emperor himself, another his Empress Zoe, and a third her sister Theodora. The four plaques here illustrated show dancing girls in the centre (a motif doubtless inspired by some oriental work of art); on the left is the female personification of Humility, and on the right that of Truth. The work is Constantinopolitan and the crown was probably given to King Andrew I of Hungary (1046–60) by Constantine IX.

38. Silver dish. Silenus and maenad. Leningrad.

This silver dish, parts of which are gilded, was found in Russia and is now in the Hermitage Museum in Leningrad. On the left a maenad is seen dancing away with, on the right, the figure of Silenus prancing after her, holding a wineskin round his shoulders. In the exergue below are a bunch of grapes and what may be a wine-container and cup. The work is Constantinopolitan and probably to be assigned to the reign of Heraclius, between the years 610 and 629, since his monogram with the bust of a bearded Emperor appears among the five control stamps on the back of the dish.

39. Silver plate. Marriage of David. Nicosia.

This is one of a hoard of silver plates, several bearing scenes from the Life of David, discovered near Kyrenia in Cyprus in 1902. They can be dated by their control stamps to the early part of the reign of Heraclius, between 610 and 629. On the plate here illustrated the priest is seen standing between David and his bride with musicians on either side. There are wine flasks and a basket of bread in the foreground, and behind stands a portico supported on four Corinthian columns.

40. Incised plate. Corinth.

The scene on this plate found at Corinth and now in the Corinth Museum (no. 1685) may be identified with an episode in the epic of Digenis Akritas and demonstrates the popularity of the Akritan cycle as a source of illustration for Byzantine potters. A man with long curly hair is shown sitting on a low stool, with a princess sitting on his lap. The scene probably represents what was evidently a favourite episode, Digenis Akritas discovering and comforting the princess Haplorabdis after she had been abandoned in the desert by her lover. The plate, like other fragments of similar type and decoration, may be dated to the twelfth century. (Cf. A. Frantz, *B*, xv (1940–1), 90–1.)

41. Sgraffito plate. Athens.

A fragment of one of a number of plates of the twelfth and early thirteenth centuries found in the Agora at Athens and now in the Agora Museum (no. 9396). It appears to illustrate the exploits of Digenis Akritas, showing the epic hero armed with shield and club and with a falcon beside him. His round face, luxuriant curly hair and peaked cap tally with the descriptions of Digenis Akritas in the epic and songs. The dragon coiled round the plate is put in as an attribute of the hero as the famous dragon-killer. (Cf. A. Frantz, *Hesperia*, VII (1938), 464.)

42. Coins (selection and notes by P. D. Whitting).

1 Solidi of Constantius II (top) and Justinian I. The three-quarters facing, armoured bust with lance over shoulder type was used continuously until in 539 Justinian I adopted the facing bust. The earlier type reappears under Constantine IV (perhaps a conscious invocation) and Tiberius III.

2 Solidi of Phocas: as consul (top) in December 603, and wearing paludamentum over armour (bottom) the normal issue of the reign.

3 (Top) Reverse of Phocas consular solidus with St Michael advancing holding long cross in right hand. This type took the place of a similar Victory advancing, under Justin I. (Bottom) Reverse of Heraclius, solidus showing change to cross-on-steps type.

4 (Top) Solidus of Heraclius and Heraclius Constantine, period 613–29, perhaps from an Italian mint. (Bottom) Solidus of Heraclius, period 610–13, the obverse of 3 above.

5 (Top) Solidus of Heraclius and Heraclius Constantine, period 629–31. The clearly differentiated obverse types in this reign are an indication of portraiture. (Bottom) Solidus of Leontius, 695–8, with naturalistic portrait: the reverse has a cross-on-steps. This may be contrasted with 9 below with its iconoclastic stylised bust and reverse bearing another family bust.

6 Solidus of Justinian II, period 692–5: (top) obverse with bust of Christ for the first time, perhaps intended to support the Quinisextum Council's canon that Christ should be represented in human form rather than as a lamb; (bottom) the Emperor is placed alongside the earlier cross-on-steps reverse type, thus beginning what was to become a standard practice of putting the Emperor on the reverse.

7 Solidus of Justinian II, period 705–6, showing obverse (top) and reverse: perhaps issued as a gesture of rapprochement to the West which had rejected the decrees of the Quinisextum Council of 691.

8 Solidus of Leo III at the beginning of his reign: the obverse (top) shows a naturalistic approach to portraiture and the reverse returns to a pre-Justinian II type.

9 Solidus of Leo III, period 726–41: showing the iconoclastic style with portrait formalised and the reverse occupied by a family portrait (his son, Constantine V) instead of the cross-on-steps.

10 Solidus of Michael III, Theodora and Thecla: first issue of the reign, with iconoclastic ideas still controlling both the content of the designs and the style of portraiture.

11 Solidus of Michael III and Theodora, period *c.* 852–6: the obverse is copied exactly from that of Justinian II (no. 6 above) as though there had been no iconoclastic interlude. The reverse shows no such obvious movement from iconoclastic ideas of portraiture.

12 Solidus of Michael III, period 856–66. The obverse shows a noticeable decline in the standard of copying from Justinian II's original.

13 Tetarteron and solidus of Nicephorus II, having the same obverse type. (Top) Tetarteron: Nicephorus II and Basil II showing the iconoclastic style still persisting. (Bottom) Nicephorus II portrayed naturalisticly: the obverse shown belongs to this solidus.

14 Scyphate nomisma of Michael IV, obverse (top) and reverse. Under Basil II the fabric of the solidus was spread into a larger and thinner coin of the same weight and standard, usually called a nomisma, and later an hyperperon. It quickly came to be minted in cup-shaped form. Michael IV was the first Emperor to debase the $23\frac{1}{2}$ carat standard of gold, the process being carried on in successive issues by Constantine IX until it reached $17\frac{1}{2}$ carat.

15 Scyphate hyperperon of Alexius I, obverse (top) and reverse. The debasement reached its nadir of 8–6 carat under Nicephorus III and Alexius I. Alexius undertook in 1092 a comprehensive reform of the coinage in all metals and re-established a 21 carat standard of gold in the hyperperon. This coin is probably from the Thessalonica mint.

16 Silver piece of Andronicus II and Andronicus III, period 1325–8: it copies the Venetian *grosso* in type, weight and standard.

17 Scyphate hyperperon of Andronicus II, obverse only. The Virgin is seen enclosed within the walls and towers of Constantinople. The Palaeologan dynasty, at a time of outstanding achievement in the arts, produced a series of remarkably original and complex designs, generally using this obverse type: the coins were usually badly struck and debased to 5–11 carat.

18 Silver 'hyperperon' of Andronicus IV, *circa* 1376–9, reverse only. The obverse has a debased version of the bust of Christ (no. 14 above). The type was derived from the *gros tournois* popular in the West. It was equivalent in value to 4 Venetian *grossi*. These silver pieces and their fractions virtually took the place of gold currency until the end of the Empire.

All the coins are of gold and of the Constantinople mint unless stated otherwise: all are photographed from casts of pieces in the British Museum.

ACKNOWLEDGEMENTS

Grateful acknowledgement is made to the following persons and organizations for assistance in obtaining illustrations and for permission to reproduce copyright material.

For Plates 1 and 2   To Professor Max Hirmer, Hirmer Fotoarchiv; to Professor D. Talbot Rice; and to Messrs Thames and Hudson Ltd (from D. Talbot Rice, *The Art of Byzantium*).

3   To Dr Alison Frantz.

4   To Professor D. Talbot Rice.

5   To Professor Max Hirmer; and to Professor D. Talbot Rice.

6   To Professor Max Hirmer; to Professor D. Talbot Rice; and to Messrs Thames and Hudson Ltd (from D. Talbot Rice, *The Art of Byzantium*).

7   To Mr Georges K. Lykides.

8   To Professor Max Hirmer; to Professor D. Talbot Rice; and to Messrs Thames and Hudson Ltd (from D. Talbot Rice, *The Art of Byzantium*).

9   To Mr Georges K. Lykides.

10   To Professor Max Hirmer; and to Professor D. Talbot Rice.

11   To Professor D. Talbot Rice; and to the Walker Trustees.

12   To the Bibliothèque Byzantine, L'Ecole Nationale des Langues Orientales Vivantes, Paris.

13–17   To the Byzantine Institute of America.

18   To Professor Hugo Buchthal, the Warburg Institute.

19   To Professor Hugo Buchthal; and to Messrs Paul Geuthner, Librairies Orientales, Paris (from G. de Jerphanion, *Les églises rupestres de Cappadoce*).

20 and 21   To Professor A. Grabar, Collection Chrétienne et Byzantine, Ecole des Hautes Etudes, Sorbonne, Paris.

22   To the Byzantine Institute of America.

23   To Professor Hugo Buchthal.

24   To the Directors of *Art et Style* (from *L'art médiéval Yougoslave: Art et Style* 15).

25   To the Bibliothèque Nationale, Paris.

26   To Professor A. Grabar, Collection Chrétienne et Byzantine.

27 and 28 To Professor Max Hirmer; to Professor D. Talbot Rice; and to Messrs Thames and Hudson Ltd (from D. Talbot Rice, *The Art of Byzantium*).

29–31 To Messrs Giraudon; and to Professor A. Grabar, Collection Chrétienne et Byzantine.

32 To Professor Max Hirmer; to Professor D. Talbot Rice; and to Messrs Thames and Hudson Ltd (from D. Talbot Rice, *The Art of Byzantium*).

33 To the Victoria and Albert Museum (Crown Copyright).

34 To the Musée du Louvre, Paris.

35 To Mr Osvaldo Böhm; and to Professor A. Grabar, Collection Chrétienne et Byzantine.

36 To Mr Osvaldo Böhm; and to Professor A. Grabar, Collection Chrétienne et Byzantine.

37–39 To Professor Max Hirmer; to Professor D. Talbot Rice; and to Messrs Thames and Hudson Ltd (from D. Talbot Rice, *The Art of Byzantium*).

40 To Dr Alison Frantz; and to the American School of Archaeology, Corinth.

41 To Miss Alison Frantz; and to the American School of Classical Studies at Athens.

42 To Mr Philip D. Whitting; and to the Trustees of the British Museum.

CHAPTER XX

THE GOVERNMENT
AND ADMINISTRATION OF
THE BYZANTINE EMPIRE

I

In the Byzantine Empire the conception of the supremacy of monarchical power was more deeply rooted and less contested than anywhere else in medieval Europe. For more than eleven centuries the autocratic absolutism of the Byzantine Emperors was the essential feature and the chief support of that state which throughout the whole of its long and vicissitudinous history proudly retained the Roman name, although its territory was from an early date restricted to the Greek-speaking East. The tradition of the later Roman Empire, as embodied in a Diocletian and with the Christian stamp it acquired from the time of Constantine, kept itself tenaciously alive. The bitter experiences of the late third and early fourth centuries had made men content to set their hopes on a monarchy whose will should be the supreme authority in every department of public life. Executive organs stood ready to carry out the commands of the imperial will: for internal affairs a well-organised bureaucracy, for external matters the army and diplomatic corps. External pressure admittedly varied over the centuries, but it was never relaxed for long, thus ensuring that the need for accepting an autocratic ruler and his organs of government was never fundamentally challenged by his subjects, though there might be occasional opposition to individual Emperors.

Heraclius was the first Emperor to be officially designated Basileus,[1] a title which had long been current in the unofficial usage of the Greek world, and which now, with the gradual disuse of the former imperial title of Imperator Caesar Augustus, became part of official protocol. It was not until some time later that the designation of the Empress was changed from Augusta to Basilissa. Augustus was retained as a title on coins until the tenth century, and even later in certain types of documents, for example edicts and letters addressed to foreigners. After the imperial coronation of Charlemagne and his subsequent recognition as Basileus by Michael I Rangabe in 812, the Eastern

---

[1] Ἡράκλειος καὶ Ἡράκλειος νέος Κωνσταντῖνος πιστοὶ ἐν Χριστῷ βασιλεῖς (Zepos, *Jus graeco-romanum*, I, 36. Zachariae von Lingenthal, *Jus graeco-romanum*, III, 44 and 48, *nov.* xxv).

Emperors took the style 'Emperor of the Romans' (Βασιλεὺς Ῥωμαίων), a formula for which there was also an occasional precedent. This title the Byzantines reserved for themselves and in so doing emphasised, particularly *vis-à-vis* the West, the superiority of the one true Emperor of the Romans in Constantinople; at the same time, by the use of this symbol, they underlined the inalienable nature of their claim to world dominion as heirs of the ancient *Imperium Romanum*. The earlier title of Autocrator, used as a translation of Imperator, came to have the special meaning of senior Emperor,[1] though this was at first unofficial; it was later used as an appellation, and later still entered the official style, as, for an early example, on the coins of Alexander, the uncle of Constantine VII Porphyrogenitus.[2] Autocrator was reserved as a special title for the senior or sole Emperor until the time of the Palaeologi. The fact that the Bulgarian rulers, after a vain attempt by Symeon to win the title Βασιλεὺς Ῥωμαίων with its connotation of world dominion, did at least achieve in 927 the title of Basileus, may have contributed to the consolidation of the title of Autocrator. Apart from its use as a title, it remained the expression used to describe absolute power, hence our word autocracy. The autocratic ruler was being addressed as *Despotes* (δεσπότης) as early as the time of Constantine; under Justinian I this became the prescribed form of address and remained the appellative style of the Byzantine rulers until the late Comnenian period; it was indeed even retained on coins and seals under the Palaeologi until the fourteenth century, when *Despotes* had become a special title in the system of succession.[3]

All this constantly reminded the Byzantine Emperors that they were the successors of the Roman Emperors. There was however also another inheritance from Rome which was equally enduring, namely, the manner in which the ruler was appointed. The Empire was in principle elective, and remained so. Moreover, in a world converted to Christianity, there was support for the idea that the electors, in the act of election, were doing the will of God and that the person so chosen was, as it were, called to the imperial dignity by the grace of God. In both the non-Christian and the Christian periods, when the throne fell vacant, the aristocracy, who had taken the place of the senate, together with the army and people, were qualified to act as electors. Their accord was at once a condition of the validity of the

[1] First found in Nicephorus, p. 29 (ed. C. de Boor): αὐτοκράτωρ τῆς βασιλείας ἀναγορεύεται Ἡράκλειος.

[2] N. A. Mušmov, *B*, VI (1931), 99 f.; G. Ostrogorsky, *History of the Byzantine State*, p. 101.

[3] On the development of the imperial title cf. F. Dölger, *Studies presented to David Moore Robinson*, II (1953), 985 ff.; *BZ*, XXXVI (1936), 123 ff.

election and a manifestation of the will of God. By their acclamation, the electors handed over to the person chosen the sovereignty which had again devolved on them in the absence of an Emperor. And this right was also kept alive down to the time of the Palaeologi.[1] To the acclamation, which was the decisive act in appointing the Emperor, there was added the ceremony of coronation. The first Emperor to be crowned by the Patriarch of Constantinople was Leo I (457–74);[2] from the seventh century it became usual for the ceremony to be performed in St Sophia. The coronation of the Western Emperors had given the Papacy the opportunity, of which full advantage had been taken, of forging from it one of the most important rights of the Church; in contrast with this, in the East the Patriarch at first acted as the representative not of the Church but of the electors, and his participation was not regarded as an essential element in making an imperial election constitutionally valid. Later, however, as the whole ceremonial took on an increasingly ecclesiastical complexion, the coronation ceremony, which always took place in the ambo of St Sophia,[3] gained in significance, influenced as it was by the need of the Church for a guarantee of Orthodoxy and of her rights, and it came increasingly to be regarded as a usage sanctified by custom. But despite this, according to a later interpretation, the act of coronation performed by the representative of the Church still remained nothing more than an act of ecclesiastical consecration of the sovereign when he was already in full possession of the imperial power. And indeed the coronation oath, which can be traced back to the ninth century, by which the new ruler bound himself to maintain the faith and the traditions of the Church, was still taken by him as Emperor at quite a late date.[4] Anointing was added to coronation only in the twelfth century, a period when liturgical influences were especially strong. But even anointing was regarded as declaratory rather than constitutive in significance, a mark of the especially close relationship existing between God and the ruler, who had in fact always been paid the special honour due to the Lord's Anointed.

It is of course true that only a relatively small number of the long line of Byzantine Emperors came to the throne as the result of an election of the kind just described. For in accordance with ancient custom, a sovereign appointed in this way had the right of determining the succession during his own lifetime by the appointment of one

---

[1] Pseudo-Codinus, *De officiis*, XVII, p. 86, 6 ff. (*CSHB*).

[2] W. Ensslin, *Zur Frage nach der ersten Kaiserkrönung durch den Patriarchen und zur Bedeutung dieses Aktes im Wahlzeremoniell* (Würzburg, 1948), pp. 14 ff.

[3] *De cerim.* I, 38, p. 411 (*CSHB*; ed. A. Vogt, II, p. 2); Ps.-Codinus, XVII, pp. 89 f.

[4] Ps.-Codinus, *De off.* XVII, p. 86, 11 ff.; cf. F. Dölger, *BZ*, XLIII (1950), 146.

or more co-Emperors whom he chose at his own discretion. In such cases the coronation was usually performed by the Emperor himself, as it invariably was whenever an Empress—an Augusta—was crowned. The Emperor in possession of undivided sovereignty entrusted the imperial dignity to the co-Emperor by transferring the diadem to him as a symbol. If, on occasion, the Emperor permitted the Patriarch to perform this act of coronation, then the Patriarch was acting under the orders of his imperial master. Otherwise, the participation of the Patriarch in the coronation of a co-Emperor or Augusta was restricted to the offering of a prayer and the blessing of the insignia.[1] It was only in the time of the Palaeologi that the coronation of a co-Emperor came to be performed by the senior Emperor and Patriarch together.[2]

For a long period after the seventh century, the position of 'co-Emperor' did not imply any active participation in the government. It is true that even after the seventh century there was often more than one Basileus, each of whom shared in the imperial honours, but only one of them, the senior Emperor, possessed the imperial power, which after his death passed automatically to his successor. It was not until the time of the Palaeologi that a genuine co-rule re-emerged, vested in the first of the co-Emperors as heir presumptive to the throne, who was then permitted, with the assent of the senior Emperor, to bear the title of Autocrator in addition to that of Basileus.[3] The Emperors frequently crowned their own sons. Thus, despite the survival of the elective monarchy, it was possible to found a dynasty, an ambition which from the earliest days of the Roman Principate had always formed part of the intentions and plans of energetic rulers. A glance at the list of Byzantine Emperors reveals the continual growth of claims to legitimacy associated with such dynasties. The house of Heraclius was followed by the Syrian, or so-called Isaurian, dynasty, starting with Leo III; then came the particularly noteworthy Macedonian dynasty, founded by Basil I and remaining in power for a hundred and eighty-nine years; the Comneni followed from 1081 to 1185, with their successors in Trebizond from 1204 until 1461, and finally the Palaeologi (1261–1453). Legitimist sentiment, already widely rooted in popular feeling even under the houses of Constantine and Theodosius, acquired its particular significance under the Macedonians. The fact that Basil I crowned three of his sons while the fourth became Patriarch of Constantinople was interpreted by

---

[1] The first instance is the crowning of Leo II by his grandfather Leo I. *De cerim.* I, 94, p. 432, 7 ff. (*CSHB*); I, 38, p. 194, 7 ff. and 40, p. 203, 1 ff.

[2] Ps.-Codinus, *De off.* XVII, p. 90, 19 ff.

[3] *Ibid.* p. 86, 14 f.

his grandson and biographer, Constantine VII, as proof of his intention to provide stronger roots for the imperial power.[1] The Porphyrogeniti, that is to say the children of the reigning sovereign who were born in the Purple Chamber of the Palace, were increasingly regarded as the legitimate heirs to the throne. Finally, at the expressed wish of the ruler the succession could be made over to a scion of the imperial house without any preceding coronation, as it was to Manuel I, the successor of John II.

When the new ruler was a minor or was deficient in the qualities necessary in a ruler, means were found of entrusting power to a co-Emperor. Government was then carried on either by the co-Emperor alone or else by a council of regency; as an instance of this, the minority of Constantine VII Porphyrogenitus may be cited, though on this occasion the original regency council fell into the background before the forceful personality of Romanus Lecapenus, the young Emperor's future father-in-law. In certain circumstances the Dowager Empress (the mother of the reigning Emperor) might also partake in the regency, as is shown by the case of Theodora, the widow of Theophilus and mother of Michael III. During the interim, however, the title of the legitimate heir was preserved. All the same, it was readily understandable if the individual entrusted with the government acquired some sort of claim to legitimate membership of the imperial house by marriage with the Dowager Empress or with a daughter of the Emperor, as for example Nicephorus Phocas and Romanus III Argyrus did. Firmly established legitimist sentiment and loyalty to the dynasty were powerful enough to set even imperial princesses on the throne; in 1042 after the blinding of her adopted son Michael V, Zoe, together with her sister Theodora, the last legitimate descendants of the Macedonian house, were accorded the right of reigning in their own names.[2] Their brief reign also provides an exceptional example of a joint government and of a sharing of the supreme power. When Zoe in the same year married Constantine IX Monomachus the interlude of petticoat government came to an end; but it was revived for a while after the death of Constantine on 11 January 1055, this time with Theodora as sole ruler, until the Macedonian dynasty became extinct with her death at the beginning of September 1056. In this connection the Empress Irene also comes to mind. She transformed her regency for her son Constantine VI into a co-rule, and after his deposition and blinding (797) governed the Empire as sole ruler. Her sovereignty aroused no opposition, although the anomaly is apparent from her official title, in which she

---

[1] *Vita Basilii*, Theophanes Cont., p. 264 (*CSHB*).
[2] Psellus, VI, 1 (ed. E. Renauld, I, p. 117).

appears not as Empress or Basilissa, but as Emperor or Basileus.[1] But such cases are exceptional. Moreover, despite the strength of legitimist sentiment, no law of succession was ever evolved, and the legitimate successor, even though he had already been crowned, was often forced to take precautions to secure his throne.

Once an Emperor had lawfully acquired the throne, there was no constitutional method of deposing him. If his rule in any way provoked justified unrest, the final resource of his subjects lay in revolution, a weapon which was in fact abused at many periods. A new Emperor was then proclaimed; if the *coup d'état* miscarried, he suffered the dishonourable death of a usurper; if it succeeded, victory was a sign that the grace of God had departed from the deposed Emperor. Not a few Emperors were forced to abdicate and met a violent death on the battlefield or in the palace as a result of revolution. Revolution was legitimised by success. Thus Mommsen's description of the Principate is also applicable, in a somewhat modified sense, to the Byzantine Empire: it was 'an autocracy, tempered by the legal right of revolution'.[2]

Another remark of Mommsen's in the same connection is no less relevant here; starting from the fact that the people could by their will both bring the Princeps to the throne and also depose him, he writes: 'the consummation of popular sovereignty is also its self-destruction'. For, once he had been recognised, the Emperor was the only repository of sovereign power. Regardless of the ways and means by which the Emperor had reached the throne, the idea that his sovereignty descended directly from God was kept constantly alive. He was the ruler crowned by God (θεοστεφής or θεόστεπτος) and was acclaimed as such.[3] Writing to Louis the Pious, Michael II (820–9) speaks of having his power from God,[4] and Basil I, who ascended to the throne from humble origins, wrote in his Exhortation to his son Leo: 'the crown you receive at my hands comes to you from God',[5] a statement fully consonant with a remark once made by Justin II to Tiberius, whom he had raised to the dignity of Caesar: 'it is God, and not I, who entrusts this dignity to your keeping'.[6] It is then understandable that this Emperor by the grace of God actually gave

---

[1] Zepos, *Jus graeco-romanum*, I, 45; Zachariae von Lingenthal, *Jus graeco-romanum*, III, 55: Εἰρήνη πιστὸς βασιλεύς; cf. Theophanes, p. 466, 25 (ed. C. de Boor).

[2] *Römisches Staatsrecht*, II, p. 1077.

[3] *De cerim.* I, 9, p. 59, 10–p. 60, 1 (*CSHB*); cf. I, 38, p. 195, 10ff.; I, 96, p. 438, 21ff. App. I, p. 456, 11ff., and the Title of Constantine Porphyrogenitus, *DAI*, I, p. 44: Πρὸς...Ῥωμανὸν τὸν θεοστεφῆ...βασιλέα; Psellus, *Epp.* (ed. E. Kurtz and F. Drexl), p. 7, 8; p. 5, 23; p. 179, 19.

[4] Mansi, XIV, 417.   [5] *Exhortatio ad filium*, *MPG*, CVII, 32.

[6] Theophylact Simocatta, III, 11, 8 (ed. C. de Boor, p. 132).

expression to the conception that his rule proceeded from God.[1] The Emperor even pronounced the words of Institution at the consecration of a Patriarch: 'by the grace of God and by our imperial power which proceeds from God's grace this man is appointed Patriarch of Constantinople'.[2] Throughout the whole Byzantine period there recur formulae which express the idea that the whole being and activity of the Emperor rested in God. The Emperor and his rule are regarded as being sent down from the celestial sphere and are included within the divine orbit, so that they are themselves thought of as being ἔνθεος.[3] It is thus not surprising that the Byzantines saw in the imperial power the terrestrial image of the power of God. This idea is as old as the Christian Empire itself; it was voiced as early as the fourth century by Eusebius of Caesarea.[4] Constantine Porphyrogenitus saw in the rhythm and order of the imperial power the image of the harmony of the creation and the government of all things by their Creator.[5] Nicetas Choniates in the late twelfth century saw no distinction between the power of God and the power of the Emperors, since the Emperors had their power from God and nothing stood between them and God.[6] They were governed and guided by God.[7] Their rule was a joint rule with God or Christ[8]—indeed the monarch could speak of 'God who rules together with us'.[9] Just as between friends everything is held in common, and since a pious Emperor was the friend of God, God and the Emperor shared together in the government of the world.[10] It is no wonder that the Emperor appeared to his subjects as the representative of God on earth and, particularly in later periods, the ceremonial of the life of the ruler in his palace was modelled on the pattern of the life of Christ.[11]

Christianity, the one fruitful source of strength to the Byzantine

---

[1] *De cerim.* II, 3, p. 526, 18; II, 4, p. 528, 11; Leo VI, *Nov.* 2: ἡ οὖν ἐκ θεοῦ βασιλεία ἡμῶν (ed. P. Noailles and A. Dain, p. 19).

[2] *De cerim.* II, 14, p. 565, 1f.: ἡ θεία χάρις καὶ ἡ ἐξ αὐτῆς βασιλεία ἡμῶν προβάλλεται ...τοῦτον πατριάρχην Κωνσταντινουπόλεως.

[3] *De cerim.* I, 2, p. 36, 2; I, 5, p. 49, 11–p. 50, 10; I, 63, p. 280, 6–22.

[4] N. H. Baynes, 'Eusebius and the Christian Empire', *AIPHO*, II (1934), 13ff. (reprinted in *Byzantine Studies and Other Essays*, pp. 168ff.).

[5] *De cerim.* I, pr., p. 5, 6ff.; cf. E. Barker, *Social and Political Thought in Byzantium* (Oxford, 1957), pp. 103–4.

[6] Nicetas Choniates, p. 583 (*CSHB*).

[7] Cf. *De cerim.* I, 77, p. 372, 21; II, 19, p. 611, 19, and II, 43, p. 649, 17 (θεοκυβέρνητοι); *ibid.* II, 3, p. 527, 2 and 7; II, 5, p. 513, 3 (θεόθεν ὁδηγηθέντες). O. Treitinger, *Die oströmische Kaiser- und Reichsidee*, p. 43.

[8] *De cerim.* I, 5, p. 47, 6; I, 76, p. 372, 5f.; I, 77, p. 373, 8f.; II, 19, p. 612, 4f.; II, 43, p. 650, 4 and 22.

[9] *MPG*, XCVIII, 1014.

[10] Theophylact of Ochrida cited by K. Prächter, *BZ*, I (1892), 402.

[11] A. Heisenberg, *Aus der Geschichte und Literatur der Palaiologenzeit* (*SBAW*, 1920), p. 83.

conception of imperial authority, had bestowed on Constantine himself the exalted title of Equal of the Apostles[1] (ἰσαπόστολος), which his successors always retained. This title contained an assertion and a claim: the office of ruler counted as an Apostolate, and the Emperor was thought of by his subjects as the wisest of the heralds of the Faith, an Apostle Paul, who, with Christ as breastplate, could deflect the weapons of the enemy, and was therefore powerful, ruling as the Anointed of the Lord.[2] Or the task of the Emperor might be compared to that of the Apostle Peter, to whom Christ had entrusted his flock to feed.[3] With all this, it is not surprising that the Christian Autocrator continued to be included in the sphere of the superhuman and sanctified, nor that his person and all that went with it could be for so long described as divine (θεῖος), thus providing a link with the late Roman ruler-cult. From the ninth century this designation gradually came to be excluded from protocol, though whether this was the result of western criticism or of Studite reforms remains unknown.[4] However, the expression is still to be found, used by way of adulatory apostrophising, in the letters of Psellus.[5] Θεῖος used in the sense of '*divus*' in speaking of an apotheosised Emperor is also found applied to John Vatatzes. The sanctity of the Emperor, on the other hand, was and continued to be a familiar theme in the acclamations; the word used, ἅγιος, was a recognised ecclesiastical expression and also a sign of the increasing influence of the Church on ceremonial. The *Trisagion* or threefold 'Holy' which was the acclamation of the people at the crowning and which was repeated after the anointing, marked out the Emperor as chosen of the Lord and consecrated to him.[6] Leo I, after his elevation as Emperor and coronation, could speak of accepting 'a holy and felicitous governance',[7] and the ἁγία βασιλεία occupied a conspicuous place in the acclamations of the people, particularly in their prayers for a long reign.[8] As the chosen

[1] A. Baumstark, 'Konstantiniana aus syrischer Kunst und Liturgie', *Konstantin der Grosse und seine Zeit*, ed. F. J. Dölger (Freiburg i. Br., 1913), 248 ff.; Agathe Kaniuth, *Die Beisetzung Konstantins des Grossen* (Breslau, 1941), p. 43; O. Treitinger, *op. cit.* p. 130.

[2] *De cerim.* I, 73, p. 368, 2 ff.

[3] *MPG*, CXIII, 456.

[4] Cf. W. Ensslin, *Gottkaiser und Kaiser von Gottes Gnaden* (*SBAW*, 1943), p. 71 ff.; L. Bréhier and L. Battifol, *Les survivances du culte impérial romain* (Paris, 1920), pp. 49 f.

[5] Psellus, *Epp.* I, p. 1, 4; p. 2, 18; p. 6, 3; p. 33, 2; p. 38, 3 (ed. E. Kurtz and F. Drexl).

[6] *De cerim.* I, 38, p. 193, 3; Ps.-Codinus, *De off.* XVII, p. 90, 11 ff.

[7] *De cerim.* I, 91, p. 412, 12.

[8] *De cerim.* I, 2, p. 36, 11 f.; p. 37, 6; I, 3, p. 43, 18; I, 9, p. 61, 2: πολυχρόνιον ποιήσει ὁ θεὸς τὴν ἁγίαν βασιλείαν; Ps.-Codinus, *De off.* VI, p. 46, 5 f. and 8 f.: πολυχρόνιον ποιήσει ὁ θεὸς τὴν θεοπρόβλητον θεόστεπτον καὶ θεοφρούρητον κραταιὰν καὶ ἁγίαν βασιλείαν σας εἰς πολλὰ ἔτη. Cf. O. Treitinger, *op. cit.* p. 42, note 58.

of the Trinity, the Autocrator could thus be apostrophised as ἅγιε,[1] since he reigned by the grace of God and in accordance with his will.

But the will of God could only be that the Christian world should be ruled by a Christian sovereign. Thus it was a necessary condition for a successor to the throne that he should belong not only to the Empire but equally to the Orthodox Church, and in addition that he should be in full possession of his physical and mental powers. A lawfully appointed Autocrator was not only heir to the idea of a universal Emperor but was at the same time representative of Christendom, which was conceived as being equally universal. Ideally, the whole world, the *oikoumene*, lay within his frontiers and was the limit of his dominion. He alone had the right and title, as a kind of Cosmocrator, to be Overlord of the Universe. Disregarding historical actualities, steadfast adherence was given to the theory that other Christian princes could only be, as it were, deputies of the Christ-loving Emperor, and that territories which had formerly belonged to the Empire but which were now, as a trial imposed on them by God, in the power of unbelievers, would one day be returned to their rightful sovereign, the defender and propagator of the Christian Faith. The concept at least of an ideal supremacy was thus constantly stressed. To the Byzantines, then, there was only one Emperor in the world, their Autocrator. This idea found expression in the refusal to grant the title of Basileus to the German Emperors which was almost fanatically maintained: Isaac Angelus, the Emperor of the 'Romaioi', could call even a Frederick Barbarossa simply 'king of Alamannia', a fact which clearly demonstrates the persistence of this theory of a single *imperium*, uniquely protected by God and represented by the Byzantine Emperor. In illustration of this claim to an ideal super-eminence, it may be mentioned that the system of a fictitious organisation of world government was given expression in Byzantium by the official grading of all princes in a hierarchy, their places being determined by invented degrees of affinity to the Emperor.[2] The same fiction was further supported by the bestowal of Byzantine court offices on foreign princes, who thus appeared to be subordinate to the supremacy of the Autocrator.

Within his own Empire, the powers of the Emperor were not laid down in any written constitution, and were thus unrestricted, at least in theory. Everything, wrote Leo VI, is subjected solely to the providential care and governance of the Emperor, and his Empire is

---

[1] *De cerim.* I, 2, p. 36, 23–5; p. 37, 2–4.

[2] *De cerim.* II, 48, pp. 686 ff. F. Dölger, 'Die "Familie der Könige" im Mittelalter', *Byzanz und die europäische Staatenwelt* (Ettal, 1953), pp. 34 ff. G. Ostrogorsky, 'Die byzantinische Staatenhierarchie', *Sem. Kond.* VIII (1936), 41 ff.; 'The Byzantine Emperor and the Hierarchical World Order', *SEER*, XXXV (1956), 1–14.

a monarchy.[1] Everything is subject to the imperial majesty, and all his subjects, from the highest to the lowest, style themselves his δοῦλοι, his bondmen, even his slaves. As in earlier times, the Auto-crator was commander-in-chief of the army, and could decide on peace or war without being bound to take the advice of his counsellors. This right was exercised by a long line of able soldiers, right down to Constantine XI, who fell in the struggle for his capital city. Furthermore, the Emperor was the sole and unfettered law-giver. In this capacity he organised and supervised the administration. He appointed the officials as he did the officers, designated their functions and decided their rank. The financial administration claimed special attention, since the whole welfare of the state depended on its successful conduct. The ruler decided what taxes should be raised and for what purposes the revenue they brought should be used; and he alone controlled all access to the imperial treasury. The Emperor was also the supreme judge; for his interpretation of the law was final. His authority extended also over morals, which he supervised and tried to regulate, at least in externals, as for example by sumptuary laws.

A particular obligation of the Emperor was to care for the well-being of the Christian Church, for it was in the harmonious co-operation of the Church that the Empire would find a firm civilising bond to hold it together. This principle, handed down from the time of Constantine the Great, was always one of the chief objects of imperial policy. Organising the Church so as to make it a prop of the state was thus not only an essential task, but also a traditional right which devolved on the Emperor. The Church became a state Church; it was within the state and remained a part of the organisation of the state. The Church of the eastern half of the Empire did not lose sight of the fact that the victory of the Church was achieved with the help of the Emperor, and it was always prepared to acknowledge his authority. And just as in ancient Rome binding constitutional standards had been set by the accidents of precedent, so was this also the case in the Empire of the 'Romaioi'. It is highly significant that the *Codex Justinianus* itself, the codification of imperial law in the name of Jesus Christ, which begins with a section devoted to the illustrious Trinity and the Catholic faith, should in that very same first book couple the laws concerning the organisation of the Church, its privileges and its defence against its enemies with the laws concerning the rights and obligations of officials. The Emperor also made his contribution to the formulation of canon law. This recognition of

---

[1] *Novels* 46 and 78 (ed. P. Noailles and A. Dain, p. 185 and p. 271). Cf. E. Barker, *op. cit.* pp. 99–100.

canon law by the ruler (who even acknowledged that in some cases it had a higher authority than the civil law) could, moreover, lead to the situation in which a Leo VI might revoke a number of laws as contradictory to the canons and introduce into his novels decisions which Councils had imposed on the clergy and laity; though admittedly he might on occasion do the opposite and impose the civil law on the Church with the excuse that it would be better than the ecclesiastical rule.[1] Another path led in the same direction. Following the example of Constantine the Great, the Emperor summoned General Councils and presided at their sessions, either in person or through an authorised deputy. He confirmed their canons, gave them the force of law by their publication, and took steps to see that they were enforced. Opposition to the decisions of the Councils counted not only as heresy but also as insubordination to the authority of the state, which was embodied in the person and will of the Emperor. In view of the sanctity ascribed to him, such opposition could thus be considered both treason and sacrilege. If in addition the Emperor appointed bishops and even Patriarchs, and in certain cases deposed the unruly, he could always regard such intervention as being part of his duty of preserving good order in the Church, provided that certain traditional forms of election and deposition were observed. The *Book of Ceremonies* discusses the appointment of the Patriarch in some detail.[2] The metropolitans had to propose three candidates for the vacant patriarchal throne, and after a free vote had been taken three names were forwarded in writing to the Emperor. If the Emperor was agreeable to the election of one of those named, he appointed him forthwith and confirmed his election. If none of the candidates found favour with the Emperor, he designated his own candidate, and told the metropolitans that this was whom he wished. In accordance with law and custom the metropolitans then acquiesced in the choice, so long as the candidate was worthy of it, and with magnificent ceremonial the Emperor instituted the Patriarch with the words: 'by the grace of God and by our imperial power which proceeds from God's grace this man is appointed Patriarch of Constantinople'. This model was still being followed in the fourteenth century, and the greater reliance which the Emperor then seemed to place on the proposals of the metropolitans is more apparent than real.[3]

If the state was careful for the discipline of the Church, it also watched over the preservation of good doctrine. It is thus not sur-

[1] *Novels* 16 and 18 (ed. Noailles and Dain, p. 63 and pp. 71–2).
[2] *De cerim.* II, 14, p. 564, 4ff.
[3] Ps.-Codinus, *De off.* XX, p. 101, 15ff.; Symeon Thessalon., *De sacris ordinibus* c. 224ff., *MPG*, CLV, 437ff.

prising that Emperors who were interested in theological questions also sought to exert a personal influence over the formulation of dogma. Justinian I may be cited as an example of just such an Emperor. Imperial claims to decide ecclesiastical questions by the authority of the state, that is by the personal intervention of the Emperor, were particularly prominent during the iconoclastic controversy. Manuel I Comnenus, with his truly Byzantine passion for theological discussion, may also be mentioned in this connection.[1]

This autocracy, which expressed itself in both lay and ecclesiastical matters, has been described as a Christian Caliphate[2] or as the rule of priest-kings.[3] It is still more frequently known under the designation 'caesaropapism'. But the approximation of this 'autocracy by the will of God' to a theocracy has been exaggerated. It is true that from an early period in the history of Byzantium the Emperor was described as 'priest and king' ($\epsilon\epsilon\rho\epsilon\upsilon\varsigma$ $\kappa\alpha\epsilon$ $\beta\alpha\sigma\iota\lambda\epsilon\upsilon\varsigma$), and Marcian was even acclaimed as $\dot{\alpha}\rho\chi\iota\epsilon\rho\epsilon\upsilon\varsigma$.[4] But Justinian, in his Sixth Novel, made a clear distinction between the *sacerdotium* and the *imperium* as two separate gifts of God's grace to mankind, an idea which was later again given expression by John I Tzimisces.[5] But it would not on this account be justifiable to speak of a separation of the two institutions in Byzantium. It is true that such ideas are to be found in the *Epanagoge* (II, 1–3), the legal textbook commissioned by Basil I but which never received his *imprimatur*; but these passages merely represent an attempt by the Patriarch Photius to imitate the relationship prevailing in the West.[6] Moreover, although Justinian, in the Novel already mentioned, claimed that it was the right of the Emperor to supervise the affairs of the *sacerdotium*, he did not do so by reason of any ecclesiastical authority. It is true that the imperial dignity was so highly valued in Byzantium that the Emperor was invested with attributes which could be described as liturgical in the ecclesiastical sense; yet not even the admission of the sacred person of the Emperor to the sanctuary, a privilege otherwise reserved to the clergy, could make of him a priest. The later admission of the Emperor to the lower ranks of the clergy, which gave him clerical privileges, would make little difference in this connection. For even without such privileges the Autocrator, in the eyes of the people, was second only to God and was expected to defend the Church and the Orthodox

---

[1] Nic. Chon. VIII, 5, pp. 274–5 (*CSHB*).

[2] J. B. Bury, *The Constitution of the Later Roman Empire*, p. 33.

[3] O. Treitinger, *op. cit.* 124 ff.

[4] Cf. L. Bréhier, '᾽Ιερεὺς καὶ βασιλεύς', *Mémorial L. Petit* (*AOC*, I, 1948), 41 ff.

[5] Leo Diaconus, VI, 6, p. 101 (*CSHB*) (=*MPG*, CXVII, 804 ff.); cf. E. Barker, *op. cit.* pp. 75–6.

[6] F. Dölger, *BZ*, XLIII (1950), 146 ff.

Faith. The Patriarch Menas in the time of Justinian could indeed express the ordering of the Church within the state—or indeed the subordination of the Church to the state—by saying that nothing should be done within Holy Church which was contrary to the mind and will of the Emperor.[1] But this would not and should not imply that the Emperor was as infallible in the spiritual sphere as he claimed to be in the secular. For although Justinian had most vigorously enforced his will even on dogmatic questions, he had nevertheless observed the rules of the state Church, which required either the concurrence of the Patriarchs through subscription or else a conciliar decision. And if, in the heat of the iconoclastic struggle, Leo III described himself as Emperor and Priest,[2] such claims were counterbalanced by equally vigorous statements made by the champions of the independence of the Church (for example, John of Damascus or Theodore the Studite) concerning the lay character of imperial power.[3] In the succeeding period opinions continued to fluctuate between these extremes: for example, Nicetas Choniates, in his description of the work of Manuel I, could say that the Byzantine Emperor regarded himself as an infallible judge in matters human and divine,[4] while Theodore II Lascaris, in his dispute with the Pope, advanced the claim to be supreme judge in ecclesiastical affairs. But it was precisely over the pursuit of this policy of reunion with Rome that the Church, supported by the majority of the faithful, showed itself finally victorious against the claims of the monarch to decide on questions of doctrine. And is it really possible to speak of caesaropapism when, even at times when the Church was prepared to allow the Basileus the right of supreme direction, the Patriarch, as the guardian of church discipline, was able to excommunicate an Emperor, as Ignatius did Bardas, the all-powerful director of affairs of state, or as Nicholas Mysticus did Leo VI? It is right and important to notice that such measures were directed only against the person of the monarch and not against the institution of the monarchy. It remained exceptional for a Patriarch, such as Michael Cerularius, to toy with the idea of exalting the spiritual above the secular power. Nevertheless this much is clear, that as soon as the Emperor, the acknowledged protector of the Church, seemed to offend against the precepts of religion, he found himself confronted by the unmistakable opposition of the Church. And therein lies the sign that this unrestricted despotism nevertheless found somewhere its limit.

[1] E. Schwartz, *Acta concil. oecum.* III, p. 181, 33 ff.; *Zur Kirchenpolitik Justinians* (*SBAW*, 1940, II), 43 f.

[2] Jaffé-Ewald, *Regesta pontificum*, 2182.

[3] John of Damascus, *De imaginibus or.* II, 12 (*MPG*, XCIV, 1296); George the Monk, II, p. 779 f. (ed. C. de Boor).   [4] Nic. Chon. VII, 5, p. 274 (*CSHB*).

There were similar limitations to restrict the Byzantine Emperor from another quarter, although the very existence of the autocracy depended on the fact that there was no other existing institution with equal authority which could rightly and lawfully oppose it. Thus the Emperor was expected to observe the laws although he himself was the unique lawgiver and although God had even set the law beneath him, since He had sent him to mankind as the living law (νόμος ἔμψυχος), to use a phrase of Justinian's which links up with Hellenistic political thought.[1] In the last quarter of the eleventh century this idea found expression in the phrase 'the Emperor is below no law but is himself the Law'.[2] This is an extension of a conception and claim coming down from the Roman Empire, the idea of the 'princeps legibus solutus'.[3] And under the last of the Comneni, the famous canonist Theodore Balsamon could carry this principle one stage further and say that the Emperor was beneath neither the laws nor the canons.[4] Again, Andronicus II emphasises that as ruler he is above all laws.[5] And in a Novel of Michael VIII of 1270, the imperial dominion, the βασιλεία, is still found linked to the older idea by being described as the living law.[6] Yet it was once again Justinian who, by accepting a Constitution of Valentinian III in which the sovereign is described as bound to the laws (*legibus adligatus*), had shown himself open to another idea, which is summed up in the words: 'for our authority depends on the authority of the law, and indeed the subordination of sovereignty under the law is a greater thing than the imperial power itself'.[7] This principle is also acknowledged in the *Basilica*,[8] and thus one can speak of 'an authority bound by the law' (ἔννομος ἐπιστασία).[9]

The law naturally included enactments concerning the administration, and in the course of a long and troubled history it is understandable that there were many changes in this department. Nevertheless a certain conservatism can be detected—and the word conservatism

---

[1] *Novel*, 105, 2, 4; A. Steinwenter, 'ΝΟΜΟΣ ΕΜΨΥΧΟΣ. Zur Geschichte einer politischen Theorie', *Anzeiger Akad. der Wissenschaften Wien, phil.-hist. Kl.*, LXXXIII (1936), 250 ff.

[2] Cf. λόγος νουθετητικὸς πρὸς βασιλέα in *Cecaumeni strategicon et incerti scriptoris de officiis regiis libellus*, ed. B. Wassiliewsky and V. Jernstedt (St Petersburg, 1896), p. 93; O. Treitinger, *op. cit.* p. 215, note 15.

[3] Ulpian, *Dig.* I, 3, 31; cf. I, 4, 1 pr. (= *Institut.* I, 2, 6; *Basilica*, II, 6, 1).

[4] *RP*, III, p. 349, 31 ff.

[5] *Jus graeco-romanum*, I, *nov.* 38, p. 560 (Zepos); V, p. 28 (Zachariae von Lingenthal).

[6] *DR*, 1972.

[7] *Cod. Just.* I, 14, 4.

[8] II, 6, 9.

[9] *MPG*, CXIII, 460; cf. *Epanagoge*, I, 6 f.; M. Dendias, 'Etudes sur le gouvernement et l'administration à Byzance', *Atti del V Congresso Intern. di Studi Bizantini*, I = *SBN*, VI (1939), 126 f.

does not necessarily in this context mean petrifaction—and for this the credit must go to the binding power of legal tradition. There must indeed have been many Byzantine officials who would have sympathised with the opinion expressed on one occasion by the Quaestor Proculus in opposition to his Emperor Justin I when he said: 'I am not accustomed to taking up with novelties; for I know only too well that security cannot be rightly preserved in the face of innovation.'[1] Then the senate, although it lacked any established constitutional right, could also make its influence felt in this way and could impose its will, particularly on weak Emperors; in fact the senate now consisted only of the highest dignitaries and could act in its own capacity as council of state.[2] It must also be remembered that until the ninth century the populace of Constantinople was organised politically in demes[3]—usually known as the Circus parties—and that they not infrequently forced the Emperor to negotiate with them; moreover even after the demes had lost their political significance, surviving only to play a decorative role in the various ceremonies, the displeasure of the people still made itself felt on occasion in unrest and uproar, not infrequently under the leadership of fanatical monks.

A remarkable example of the self-restriction of the Emperor is provided by the obligations which a newly elected Emperor took on himself with regard to his electors; the first Emperor to do this was Anastasius I.[4] Hence there arose a kind of pledge on election, which, if not legally, was at least morally binding on the Emperor. From this was finally developed—though precisely when is unknown—the institution of the regular coronation oath. In this oath the ruler affirmed his orthodoxy, promised to maintain inviolate the decisions of recognised Councils and the privileges of the Church, and in addition bound himself to be a merciful and just sovereign to his people and to refrain as far as possible from imposing the penalties of death and mutilation.[5] The later wording of the coronation oath indicates what his subjects expected from their Sovereign. Here again the theme is the obligations of the ruler. There is no concern with the

---

[1] Procopius, *Bell. Pers.* I, 11, 13.

[2] Ch. Diehl, 'Le sénat et le peuple byzantin au VIIe et VIIIe siècles', *B*, I (1924), 201 ff.; Aikaterine A. Christophilopoulou, Ἡ Σύγκλητος εἰς τὸ Βυζαντινὸν Κράτος (Athens, 1949), p. 92 f.; M. Dendias, *op. cit.* pp. 124 ff.

[3] A. Maricq, 'La durée du régime des partis populaires à Constantinople', and 'Factions de cirque et partis populaires', *Bulletin Acad. R. Belgique, Cl. d. Lettres*, v, 35 (1949), 119 ff. and 36 (1950), 396 ff.

[4] *De cerim.* I, 92, p. 422, 17 ff.; Theodorus Lector, II, 6, p. 135 (*CSHB*); Evagrius, *Hist. eccl.* III, 32, p. 130, 2 ff. (ed. Bidez–Parmentier); Theophanes, p. 136, 5 ff. (ed. C. de Boor).

[5] Ps.-Codinus, *De off.* XVII, p. 86, 18 ff.; cf. Constantine Porphyrogenitus, *DAI*, I, pp. 67 ff.

cares and burden of work imposed on an Emperor zealous in the cause of duty, which was already laid on him by his daily routine, but rather with the underlying spirit which animates his every action. Here is once more the echo of an older tradition, which was to become a means of limiting the autocracy. It is an echo which comes once again from the time of Constantine; for it was Eusebius, in his Panegyric on Constantine, who had introduced into the sphere of the Christian Empire the idea of charity towards mankind, φιλανθρωπία, a trait which the Hellenistic philosophers had already incorporated into their portrait of the ideal ruler.[1] Justinian I stressed the idea that all the obligations of the imperial office derived from φιλανθρωπία by making this the foundation of his work as legislator; he justified his imposition of the death penalty in a certain case by the argument that it was not inhumanity (ἀπανθρωπία) but, on the contrary, the highest degree of humane conduct (φιλανθρωπία) to afford protection to so many by the punishment of a few.[2] From first to last, the idea remained alive in Byzantium that an Emperor who desired to fulfil his mission justly and to the safeguarding of his subjects should be guided by *philanthropia*.[3] Admittedly, reality did not always correspond to the ideal. But, once accepted, the ideal was nevertheless always there as a deterrent, particularly since certain restrictions were imposed on the Emperor's actions by public opinion. It must not, of course, be imagined that such considerations created a genuine constitutional obligation, nor should anything of the kind be read into the alleged guidance of the moral law. The same caution must be observed in considering those Emperors, and they were the ablest, whose sense of responsibility was heightened by the idea, in harmony with the religious feeling dominant at the time, that their imperial authority was a gift of God.

How closely the Basileus was bound by tradition is revealed particularly by the ceremonial formalities, superficial though they may appear to be at first glance. The constant and restraining influence of court ceremonial, with its well-defined custom, was not to be lightly cast off to suit the capricious whim of the Autocrator. On the contrary, it was indeed most obvious that it was precisely in these ceremonies that the majesty of the Emperor found fullest expression in all its inaccessibility and super-eminence. The rigid rules of a quasi-liturgical ceremonial held an Emperor in their grip from the moment of his accession, and an imperial prince was compassed about

---

[1] N. H. Baynes, 'Eusebius and the Christian Empire', *loc. cit.*

[2] *Nov. Just.* 30, 11; cf. *Nov.* 129, pr.; *Nov.* 159, pr.; *Nov. Justini II*, 163, pr.

[3] H. Monnier, *Les Novelles de Léon le Sage* (Bordeaux, 1923), p. 43. Ps.-Codinus, *De off.* XVII, p. 87, 17 ff.

by them from the cradle to the grave; there were prescribed ceremonies for christenings, birthdays and marriage, as well as for funerals and court mourning. Constantine Porphyrogenitus, who himself compiled a *Book of Ceremonies* for the enlightenment and edification of his successors, counted his work as a necessary duty and explained its purpose: by following such a commendable order the imperial power would show itself in a better aspect and become raised to a higher dignity, thus filling foreigners and subjects alike with admiration.[1] The author does not even shrink from describing his own concern for achieving a well-conducted ceremonial as a reflection of the exertions of the Creator in bringing order into the world.[2] The *Book of Ceremonies* can rightly be described as the codification of court ceremonial and as portraying an essential feature of Byzantine state-craft, which, in many devious ways, is still at work today, using just such apparently superficial means of expression. The reader can follow, through a long catalogue, the details of the ceremonies prescribed for all possible occasions and thus share in the life and activity of the Emperor and his court. We hear not only of the celebration of the great feasts of the Church, with their processions and services, but also of the ceremonial forms which attended the festivals of the imperial house, the coronation of an Emperor, an Augusta or a co-Emperor, and of the part played by the court in the traditional folk festivals. Other matters are also dealt with, but whatever the subject discussed—his Majesty's departure for an expedition, the investiture of a high office-holder or the conduct of the royal table on special occasions—the arrangements for everything are laid down in advance even to the smallest detail, with particulars as to place and time, the people who should take part, their clothing, their arrival, and the acclamations which should greet them. The existence of a considerable imperial household, with numerous functionaries, servants, palace guards and representatives of the people, combined with the carefully observed order of precedence, increased the effect of conservatism. The importance of this organisation also emerges in reading the *Cletorologion* of the *atriclines* Philotheus, who was a kind of master of ceremonies; his work was composed in 899 and describes the rules of precedence observed at court banquets.[3] Moreover, it must be remembered that the ceremonial required the cooperation of the clergy, which thus rightly gave a liturgical complexion to the whole, as has already been explained. It is noteworthy that

[1] *De cerim.* I, pr., p. 3, 4 ff.

[2] *Ibid.* p. 5, 6 ff.

[3] J. B. Bury, *The Imperial Administrative System in the Ninth Century*, with a revised text of the Kletorologion of Philotheos (British Academy Supplemental Papers, I, London, 1911), pp. 11 ff. and 131 ff.

even on purely secular occasions the company was dismissed after a word to the Palace steward (the *papias*) derived from the liturgy of the Mass.[1] Even in the fourteenth century, when the glory of the Empire was already in eclipse, a book could be written on the *Officia* (wrongly ascribed to George Codinus) which still had the ceremonies and their proper conduct as its theme, thus testifying to the permanence of tradition down the centuries. A manuscript from Athos of 1433 even contains the traditional acclamations in honour of the Emperor John VIII.[2] The Emperor still continued to be at the heart of things. There was nothing apart from him; his presence was necessary to the ritual and, indeed, gave the whole ceremonial its meaning. But the ceremonies themselves bound the Emperor by inviolable rules and thus made an essential contribution to preserving the conservative character of the Byzantine Empire.

In view of all these considerations, it becomes difficult—in fact it is impossible—to apply any of the labels familiar to modern constitutional theory to the Byzantine autocracy. The Byzantines themselves accepted the Empire as *sui generis*, because it was sent from God, and any idea of theorising about it never entered their minds. It was also regarded as being unique, and there was thus nothing to be gained by comparing it with other forms of government. Nevertheless, apart from a few and almost Utopian attempts at innovation in the period of its decline (for example, by Theodore Metochites or George Gemistus (Plethon)), as an institution the autocracy was never challenged, a fact which serves to prove how well it was adapted, with all its peculiar characteristics, to the conditions of the times it served.

II

The exalted person of the autocratic Emperor was the heart and driving force of the administration, whose highest authority was concentrated in the palace. It is thus not surprising that the palace officials, who were in such close contact with the person of the Emperor, should have permanent and conspicuous importance, and that all the other officials, who were included in the court order of precedence by the title of their rank, should also in some way be brought into a close relationship with the person of the ruler. The officials, indeed, exercised their power only in virtue of the authority radiating from the Emperor, who was under the favour of divine grace. The

---

[1] ἄπελθε, ποίησον μίνσας, *De cerim.* ΙΙ, 1, p. 521, 4; cf. Ι, 14, p. 95, 1 and Liutprand of Cremona, *Antapodosis*, v, 21, p. 142, 5: 'emissis omnibus dato signo, quod est mis'.

[2] Codex Athous Pantocrator 214, ed. H. J. W. Tillyard, 'The Acclamation of Emperors in Byzantine Ritual', *Annual BSA*, xviii (1911–12), 239–60; cf. E. Wellesz, *History of Byzantine Music*, pp. 99 ff.

organisation developed in the early Byzantine period was thus retained, so that the chief offices of the court were identical with the
highest positions in the state, although the establishment of the theme
administration had so much altered the earlier structure of government that there is a fundamental difference between the fifth-century
political handbook, the *Notitia Dignitatum,* and the lists of officials
of the ninth and tenth centuries.

The separation which existed in principle between the civil and
military power before the time of Justinian was abandoned by him
in the reconquered lands of the West and in a few of the eastern
provinces. The reunification of the two powers was continued as a
consequence of the reforms initiated by Heraclius and furthered by
the Emperors of his dynasty until it reached its permanent expression
in the theme organisation of the ninth and tenth centuries. Neither
this process nor the transformation of the central organs of government seems to have followed any unified plan or to have been the
result of a single decision. The former high offices of the central
administration underwent a gradual transformation as their functions
became divided. As the number of such functionaries increased their
competence diminished, while their dependence on the Emperor grew
greater. The far-reaching decentralisation of the earlier imperial administration, which had resulted in the independence of the higher
offices, was gradually replaced by subjection to a stricter central
control. This process was assisted by the diminution of imperial
territories in both West and East. Nevertheless, the titles of important offices which no longer had any significance in practice still
survived, though only as titles of rank. Latin, which had otherwise
long since disappeared from the Greek world of the Byzantine Empire, still lingered on in a few of these titles, while the designation of
actual officials had become almost exclusively Greek. In the Byzantine state there was a rigid order of precedence which was founded on
court titles of rank and which also included the actual officers of
state, who, indeed, bore court titles according to the importance of
their office. The holder of a 'dignity' (ἀξία) was someone who possessed not only a title of rank but also the office distinguished by the
title. Philotheus, who described himself as imperial *Protospatharius*
and *Atriclines,* thus occupied a court office (that of *Atriclines*), which
made him responsible for the ceremonial conduct of banquets in the
palace, with the duty of inviting guests of the proper rank, receiving
them and placing them at table, and in addition had also the honorary
title of *Protospatharius.* In his *Cletorologion,* which was a list to aid
in the fulfilment of his tasks, Philotheus distinguishes between two
classes of dignities (ἀξίαι): one kind was purely honorary and was

granted by the Emperor by means of a diploma or by investiture with the insignia (διὰ βραβείων); the other sort, which were the real offices, were granted by edict, that is by the edict of the imperial cabinet (διὰ λόγου). Apart from the titles of rank reserved for members of the imperial house and for eunuchs (which will be dealt with below), Philotheus, writing at the turn of the ninth century, knew of fourteen ranks in the hierarchy. It was possible to rise from the lower to the higher ranks; the last honorary title attained was held for life. The highest rank was that of a *Magister*,[1] reminiscent of the once influential *Magister officiorum*. Up to the mid-eighth century there was only one *Magister*, who, in his capacity as leading senator, could deputise in the absence of the Emperor, but later the number rapidly increased, so that Liutprand of Cremona, writing of the year 946, could already give an account of twenty-four *Magistri*.[2] After them came the *Anthypatoi*, which was the Greek form of the title of Proconsul, and then the Patricians. The *Dishypatus* ranked between the next two offices in the hierarchy, both of them military in origin, the *Protospatharius* and the *Spatharocandidatus*, while between the *Spatharius* and the *Strator* came the *Hypatus*, which kept alive the Greek form of the honorary consulship; after the candidates and mandatories came the *Vestitores* and *Silentiarii*, who bore titles originally connected with court offices in the imperial wardrobe and audience-chamber (*silentium*). The *Stratelatai* and Apo-eparchs, formerly the *Magistri militum* and the praetorian prefects, were in the lowest ranks, which shows how much the more eminent positions of the early Byzantine period had diminished in value. There was only one court dignity reserved for women, the *Zoste Patricia*, which ranked above the *Magistri* and was usually reserved for members of the imperial family; above it there were only three higher grades, those of *Curopalates*, *Nobilissimus* and Caesar.[3] The privileged position of those officials who served directly in the household or the court gave eunuchs precedence above all others of the same rank. Eight honorary titles were reserved for eunuchs; the highest of these grades was also *Patricius*, and the next after it *Protospatharius*, while the others had their own special designations, in the following order: *Praepositus*, *Primicerius*, *Ostiarius*, *Spatharocubicularius*, and *Nipsistiarius*. These last two were originally servants in the bedchamber and baths. Eunuchs played an important role in Byzantium. A number of court offices were generally reserved for them, though not exclusively, and

---

[1] A. E. R. Boak, *The Master of the Offices in the Later Roman and Byzantine Empires* (New York, 1919), pp. 117 ff.

[2] *Antapodosis*, VI, 10, p. 158, 11.

[3] R. Guilland, 'Etudes sur l'histoire administrative de l'empire byzantin: le césarat', *OCP*, XIII (1947), 168 ff.

they were eligible for almost all positions in Church and state.[1] All these titles of rank were conferred by the Emperor in person in ceremonial audience by the gift of a diploma or insignia. Thus the *Magister* received a white tunic interwoven with gold thread, a cloak embroidered with gold, and a belt set with precious stones. The *Patricius* received his diploma in an ivory diptych, the *Protospatharius* had a golden neck-chain set with precious stones, the *Spatharius* a sword with a golden handle, the *Strator* a golden and bejewelled whip, and so on. Those who were invested with honorary titles had to pay a considerable fee in gold to certain court officials. Philotheus also makes a distinction between senatorial (εἰς συγκλητικούς) and imperial (βασιλικαί or προελευσιμαῖοι) honours. The senatorial dignities included the grades from *Stratelates* to *Vestitor*, the *Hypatus* and the *Dishypatus*; imperial dignities were those which entailed participation in imperial ceremonies and were probably military in origin and were part of the immediate retinue of the Emperor. At the beginning of the scale, therefore, two ways of advancement lay open, one civil and the other military, both leading to the Patriciate, after which the two paths were joined.

As already mentioned, the offices which were not sinecures were conferred by imperial edict. It was the Emperor alone who decided on the grading, appointments, salaries and dismissals. The prospect of advancement, and with it a rise in rank and salary, was the chief means of stimulating the ambition of officials. The personal dependence of the higher officials on the Emperor was perhaps most strikingly demonstrated in the scene which took place in the week before Palm Sunday when, in one of the audience-rooms of the palace, the Emperor himself paid out their salaries, a proceeding which did not fail to make its impression on Liutprand of Cremona, the ambassador of Otto the Great.[2]

Even when the structure of officialdom had reached its highest development, there was still a considerable number of positions connected exclusively with service at court, and these, as already mentioned, were mostly filled by eunuchs. They were in the direct service of the Emperor and administered his household. The most important of these was the Grand Chamberlain, now styled *Parakoimomenos*, that is, one who slept next to the imperial bedchamber, and who therefore held a position of great trust which often brought with it great influence as well; for example, Basil, who played an important part under Constantine VII, became chief minister and all-powerful

---

[1] R. Guilland, 'Les eunuques dans l'empire byzantin. Etudes de titulature et de prosopographie byzantines', *REB*, I (1943), 197ff.; 'Fonctions et dignités des eunuques', *ibid.* II (1944), 185ff.; see also below: Bibliography, pp. 405–6.

[2] *Antapodosis*, VI, 10, p. 157, 28ff.

under John Tzimisces and his successors, and abused his position to acquire an enormous fortune. The possibility of such abuse was never overlooked and was not treated lightly, but this was outweighed by the realisation that eunuchs were in any case excluded from the throne and could thus never become usurpers. *Praepositus*, once a position of pre-eminence, was now the name given to one of the titles of rank reserved for the eunuchs, but it still also survived as an office, though the duties attached to it were the more modest ones of Master of Ceremonies. The *Protovestiarius*, who was in the second rank of the effective offices reserved for eunuchs, controlled the royal wardrobe and the treasury attached to it;[1] this office survived until the fall of the Empire, growing in importance all the time, and in the later period was far from being a prerogative of eunuchs. There were also the functionaries of the imperial tables, both for the Emperor and the Augusta ($\acute{o}$ $\grave{\epsilon}\pi\grave{\iota}$ $\tau\hat{\eta}s$ $\tau\rho\alpha\pi\acute{\epsilon}\zeta\eta s$), and the Butlers. Each palace was in charge of a castellan, a *Papias*, who had under him a large staff (as did the other functionaries named above) and the assistance of a *Domesticus*.

As already mentioned, the course of time wrought many changes, both in the titles of rank and in the importance of the court offices. For example, the new rank of *Proedrus* was created for the all-powerful *Parakoimomenos* Basil. The holder of this dignity was not in fact the President of the Senate, but was the highest in rank of the senatorial dignitaries. When it came about that the number of people holding this rank multiplied, about the middle of the eleventh century, an attempt was made to meet this difficulty by creating the rank of *Protoproedrus*. Both titles survived into the twelfth century, with gradually diminishing importance. A similar process can be seen at work in the case of the *Magistri* in the eighth century, when a *Protomagister* was created. This title also had a long life, until the fourteenth century, although its value admittedly depreciated. Other designations of rank, such as *Spatharocandidatus*, *Protospatharius* and even *Patricius*, also eventually disappeared, a consequence of the general depreciation in titles which arose from their being frequently conferred on subordinate officials. When compared with other sources of the period, the anonymous Catalogue of Ranks dating from the fourteenth century, which still gives all the old titles of rank, is clearly not to be taken seriously: this information can only be in the nature of historical reminiscence.[2] Moreover, even the title of

[1] J. Ebersolt, 'Sur les fonctions et les dignités du Vestiarium byzantin', *Mélanges Charles Diehl*, I (Paris, 1930), 84 ff.

[2] Ps.-Codinus, p. 217, 99 ff. (*CSHB*); E. Stein, 'Untersuchungen zur spätbyzantinischen Verfassungs- und Wirtschaftsgeschichte', *Mitteilungen zur osmanischen Geschichte*, II (1925; reprinted separately, Amsterdam, 1962), 30.

Nobilissimus, which was used originally only for members of the imperial house, had another title set above it, that of *Protonobilissimus*, which was still an office of much consequence in the twelfth century, until it too began to depreciate. This led to the creation of the *Protonobilissimohypertatus*, which, in turn, under the Palaeologi, finally degenerated into the designation of a provincial official.[1] From the time of Alexius Comnenus many innovations were in fact made in the higher grades of the court titles. Thus, there was the *Sebastocrator*, ranking above Caesar, and the *Panhypersebastus* and *Protosebastus*, who came between the Caesar and the *Curopalates*, while between the *Curopalates* and *Nobilissimus* were now introduced the *Sebastus* and *Protonobilissimus*. The dignity of *Despotes* was certainly created as early as the time of Manuel I Comnenus; it was conferred only rarely in the thirteenth century, though afterwards it became more frequent, and ranked before *Sebastocrator*. Like Caesar, *Despotes* and *Sebastocrator* were peculiar to the royal family, and all three dignities carried the privilege of being addressed as 'Imperial Majesty' ($\beta\alpha\sigma\iota\lambda\epsilon\acute{\iota}\alpha$)[2]. The other new titles mentioned above were usually created for individuals, with the exception of the title of *Sebastus*, which was ultimately borne by the majority of the *Duces* of the themes, who had formerly held the rank of *Patricius*.[3]

The imperial administration centred in Constantinople comprised only the civil offices. The generals stationed there and the admirals of the home fleet had nothing to do with the administration, not even later, when the Grand Domestic ($\mu\acute{\epsilon}\gamma\alpha\varsigma$ $\delta o\mu\acute{\epsilon}\sigma\tau\iota\kappa o\varsigma$) had become commander-in-chief of the army, deputising for the Emperor, or acting as his chief-of-staff on campaign, and the Grand Drungarius was High Admiral. Philotheus, speaking of the administration, makes a distinction between $\kappa\rho\iota\tau\alpha\acute{\iota}$, judicial offices, and $\sigma\epsilon\kappa\rho\epsilon\tau\iota\kappa o\acute{\iota}$, primarily financial offices; but this distinction never became absolute, especially since, with the course of time, there was a marked tendency for some departments to widen their sphere of activity at the expense of others. The highest position among the *Kritai* was filled by the Eparch, the City Prefect, who retained the old title and with it most of its former duties. 'Father of the city', as he was called by Constantine VII Porphyrogenitus,[4] he ranked first among the civil officials and was a person of the highest importance. This is illustrated by a remark of

---

[1] E. Stein, *op. cit.* pp. 30 f. F. Dölger, 'Der Kodikellos des Christodulos in Palermo', *Archiv für Urkundenforschung*, II (1929), pp. 24 ff. (reprinted in *Byzantinische Diplomatik* (Ettal, 1956), pp. 10 ff.). V. Laurent, 'Notes de titulature, II. Le protonobélissimat à l'époque des Paléologues', *EO*, XXXVIII (1939), 362 ff.

[2] Ps.-Codinus, *De off.* III, p. 16, 6 ff.

[3] E. Stein, *op. cit.* p. 31.

[4] *De cerim.* I, 52, p. 264, 12; II, 3, pp. 528 ff.

Psellus describing the office as an imperial dignity, lacking only the purple.[1] No eunuch was allowed to be Eparch. In his judicial activities the Eparch was assisted by the Logothete of the Praetorium, and in the city administration by the *Symponus* or *Legatarius*, and also by a numerous staff. The *Book of the Eparch*, a collection of rules chiefly relating to the regulation of trade and commerce in Constantinople, made in the time of Leo VI with some later additions, gives detailed information covering the range of his duties.[2] He had charge of the guilds and their activities, including the supply of provisions to the capital. Under his command were the police who guarded streets and buildings and also the fire-brigade. He saw that Sunday was observed as a day of rest and kept foreigners who came to the city to trade under surveillance. In addition, until the time of Michael VII, he acted as president by proxy in the imperial court of justice. In later times his most important functions passed to other high officials, and under the Palaeologi the name Eparch survived only as a court title.[3] But his department was then combined with those of the *Quaesitor*, an office created by Justinian I, and of the city *Praetor*. He was the head of a court of appeal and decided in the first instance marital disputes and questions of wills and guardianship. Secretaries who had formerly been in the immediate service of the Emperor were now transferred to his department. The only department to continue independently was the office of petitions ($\epsilon\pi\iota$ $\tau\hat{\omega}\nu$ $\delta\epsilon\dot{\eta}\sigma\epsilon\omega\nu$) under the direction of the successor of the former *Magister memoriae*.[4] Under the Palaeologi this official still received petitions addressed to the Emperor handed in when the ruler went out in cavalcade.[5] The earlier office of *Quaestor* must have survived until the Latin conquest, but later became only a title of rank.[6]

The *Secretici*, so named after their offices, the *Secreta*, were mostly financial officials. Those of higher rank were usually called Logothetes (literally accountants); the others were named *Chartularii* (actuaries), with the name of their particular department added. These were the separate departments which had developed out of the financial office of the Praetorian Prefect, which had itself become enlarged at the expense of other financial offices. The new departments also found it possible to widen their field of activity at the

[1] x, 3 (I, p. 30, ed. Renauld): βασίλειος δὲ αὕτη ἀρχή, εἰ μὴ ὅσον ἀπόρφυρος.

[2] J. Nicole, Λέοντος τοῦ Σοφοῦ Ἐπαρχικὸν βιβλίον (Geneva, 1893); A. Stöckle, *Spätrömische und byzantinische Zünfte, Klio*, Beiheft IX (Leipzig, 1911); Eng. trans. E. Freshfield, *Roman Law in the Later Roman Empire* (Cambridge, 1938). See below: chapter XXI, p. 68.

[3] Ps.-Codinus, *De off.* v, p. 35, 22; E. Stein, *op. cit.* p. 38.

[4] J. B. Bury, *op. cit.* pp. 73 ff., 77 ff.

[5] Ps.-Codinus, *De off.* v, p. 39, 22 ff.

[6] *Ibid.* p. 40, 1 ff.; E. Stein, *op. cit.* pp. 41 and 39.

expense of other former special offices.[1] The Logothete τοῦ γενικοῦ, for example, who was responsible for the land-tax, and was thus a particularly important official, also supervised the maintenance of aqueducts and the revenue from mines. He had under him a number of separate departments for the assessment and collection of taxes. But although we still come across a Logothete τοῦ γενικοῦ in the first quarter of the fourteenth century in the person of Theodore Metochites under Andronicus II, in the Pseudo-Codinus (p. 34, 16) it is given only as a title and the functions of the office are no longer known.[2] The Logothete τοῦ στρατιωτικοῦ controlled the pay and commissariat of the army and was thus a kind of Quartermaster-General and Paymaster-in-Chief. He kept a record of the officers and troops. But as an effective finance officer he disappears from view from the twelfth century.[3] The official named ἐπὶ τοῦ εἰδικοῦ was in charge of a special branch which supplied equipment for the troops and for this purpose exercised control over state factories.[4] The *Chartularius* τοῦ βεστιαρίου, with his related duties, some of them inherited from the former *Comes sacrarum largitionum*, may fitly be mentioned next. He had under his control the *Vestiarium*, literally the state wardrobe, that is to say the place where various products were kept, whether as raw material or in manufactured form.[5] A special department which had once been under the *Comes rerum privatarum* was now controlled by the Logothete τῶν ἀγελῶν; he supervised the stud-farms of Asia Minor, where horses were bred for the army; in time of war he had to assemble horses for the use of the Emperor. For these reasons he is classed by Philotheus as an army official (στρατάρχης). The office seems to have survived only until the eleventh century, although it is mentioned as a title in the Pseudo-Codinus.[6]

The chief financial officer was the *Sacellarius* (σακελλάριος), who supervised all the offices having financial duties, that is to say, all the *Secreta*. There was a *notarius* representing the *Sacellarius* in each of the separate departments. For a time the *Sacellarius* seems to have been called *Megas Sacellarius*, in keeping with the titles of the heads of the other central offices. At the end of the eleventh century this title was superseded by that of *Megas Logariastes*, or Chief Accountant. In the last two decades of the twelfth century there was once

---

[1] E. Stein, *Studien zur Geschichte des byzantinischen Reiches* (Stuttgart, 1919), pp. 148ff., 159ff.

[2] J. B. Bury, *op. cit.* pp. 86ff.; F. Dölger, *Beiträge zur Geschichte der byzantinischen Finanzverwaltung* (Leipzig–Berlin, 1927), pp. 19f.

[3] F. Dölger, *op. cit.* p. 21.

[4] J. B. Bury, *op. cit.* pp. 98f.

[5] F. Dölger, *op. cit.* p. 24; J. B. Bury, *op. cit.* pp. 95ff.

[6] Ps.-Codinus, *De off.* v, p. 40, 8; J. B. Bury, *op. cit.* p. 111; F. Dölger, *op. cit.* p. 24.

again, in addition to the *Megas Logariastes*, a *Megas Sacellarius*, who was at that date apparently head of the *Vestiarium*. The title of *Megas Logariastes* survived into the time of the Palaeologi, although his office had disappeared.[1] While the *Sacellarius* was still in control of his own department he had as his chief subordinate the *Chartularius* of the *Sacellium*; but once the *Sacellarius* had risen to be general controller of all the offices, the *Chartularius* achieved independence as the head of the state gold-reserve.[2]

The *Protoasecretis*, the head of the imperial chancery, who by reason of his close relationship to the sovereign was among the most important of all the officials, is also classified by Philotheus among the *Secretici*. In time this position came to be filled mostly by judicial officials; in the mid-eleventh century the *Protoasecretis* acquired a subordinate in the ἐπὶ τῶν δεήσεων.[3] In this connection may be mentioned the ἐπὶ τοῦ κανικλείου, or Custodian of the Imperial Inkstand, who was responsible for holding in readiness the imperial quill-pen and the red ink required for the signature. However, judging by the importance of its holders, this office seems to have been by no means a court sinecure, and these officials must have played an important role in matters of record.[4] The two last mentioned offices were often combined with that of *Mysticus*, that is, the secretary who wrote the confidential and private letters of the Emperor.[5] Among those who administered the imperial property, the *Orphanotrophus* occupied a position apart; he was the director of a large orphanage in Constantinople, richly endowed by the Emperor, and was usually a priest. In the ninth century he belonged to the Patriciate. Institutions concerned with social welfare, such as hostels, poor-houses and hospitals, were in the main left to the care of the Church, although the Emperors often gave them considerable endowments from domain land. On this account they remained under the financial control of the state and were to a large extent supervised by an office dealing with state domains. The office of *Orphanotrophus* shared the fate of the other offices and ended by degenerating into a mere title.[6]

The Postmaster-General also had the title of Logothete as Logothete τοῦ δρόμου and was counted among the *Secretici*, although he was not, properly speaking, part of the financial administration. Apart from making payments for the upkeep of the postal service and

---

[1] Ps.-Codinus, *De off.* IV, p. 24, 7 and V, p. 39, 7; F. Dölger, *op. cit.* pp. 16 ff.

[2] F. Dölger, *op. cit.* pp. 24 ff.

[3] F. Dölger, 'Der Kodikellos des Christodulos', *op. cit.* pp. 55 ff.

[4] *Ibid.* pp. 44 f.

[5] *Ibid.* p. 56.

[6] Ps.-Codinus, *De off.* V, p. 41, 4; F. Dölger, *Finanzverwaltung*, p. 43; J. B. Bury, *op. cit.* pp. 103 f.

for gifts to foreign embassies, a considerable part of his duty must have been taken up with supervising the services exacted from subjects in connection with the public postal and transport arrangements. In the course of time this official contrived to extend his activities in the same way as his predecessor, the *Magister officiorum*. Like him, he became a kind of Foreign Minister, for which purpose he was given a staff of interpreters. He was accepted first and foremost as the chief adviser of the Emperor in foreign affairs, and was received by him daily in audience. He had in addition certain powers in maintaining security in the provinces and a special jurisdiction over privileged foreign visitors, and thus acquired a particular control over the privileged Venetian merchants. He combined with all this duties which could more properly be ascribed to a Minister for Home Affairs, such as the institution in office of high officials and functionaries who had received promotion. After the Latin conquest the office of this Logothete also disappeared and it degenerated into a mere title of rank.[1] Philotheus describes certain positions as 'special offices' (εἰδικαὶ ἀρχαί); mention has already been made of one of these, the *Chartularius* ἐπὶ τοῦ κανικλείου, and another, the *Syncellus*, may be referred to here. He was a high cleric, who often proceeded later to the patriarchate; he was appointed by the Emperor in agreement with the Patriarch, and was instituted with much pomp at a ceremony held in the palace. He took precedence over all the ordinary officials and acted as a kind of liaison officer between the Emperor and the Patriarch.[2] The *Protostrator* also belongs to the category of special offices: as Chief of the Grooms (στράτορες), the *Protostrator*, together with the κόμης τοῦ σταύλου, later rose from these small beginnings to a position of great and general importance.[3] In the same way, the master of the horse was later transformed into the *Contostaulus* or *Megas Contostaulus*, fashioned on the model of the Norman *Comes stabuli*, and also acquired a high general standing.[4]

The provincial administration was carried out by the Theme organisation which had meanwhile come into being. At the beginning of the ninth century there were only ten, but by the time of Philotheus the number had already increased to twenty-six. They ranked in the following order, according to the standing of their Governor: on the Asian side, Anatolikon, Armeniakon, Thracesion, Opsikion,

[1] *De cerim.* II, 1, p. 520, 6ff.; II, 3, p. 525, 20ff.; *DR*, 781; Ps.-Codinus, *De off.* v, p. 36, 8; J. B. Bury, *op. cit.* pp. 91ff.; F. Dölger, *Finanzverwaltung*, pp. 22ff.

[2] *De cerim.* II, 5, pp. 530ff.; J. B. Bury, *op. cit.* pp. 116f.

[3] R. Guilland, 'Etudes de titulature et de prosopographie byzantines: Le protostrator', *REB*, VII (1950), 156ff.

[4] R. Guilland, 'Etudes sur l'histoire administrative de Byzance: le grand connétable', *B*, XIX (1949), 99ff.

Bucellarion, Cappadocia, Charsianon, Colonea, Paphlagonia, Chaldia; on the European side, and of equal rank with these Asian themes, were Thrace and Macedonia. The remaining western and the three maritime themes ranked below the others: Peloponnese, Nicopolis, Hellas, Sicily, Strymon, Cephalonia, Thessalonica, Dyrrachium, Dalmatia and the remote Cherson. In addition there were the maritime themes of the Cibyrraeots (which ranked after Nicopolis) and Samos and the Aegean Sea, which came between Dyrrachium and Dalmatia. In making up his list, Philotheus seems to have overlooked Longobardia. Still more themes were created later, particularly as the frontiers of the Empire expanded. Thus, the *Book of the Themes* of Constantine VII Porphyrogenitus mentions the themes of Mesopotamia, Lycandus, Sebastea, Seleucia and Cyprus. Cyprus, which was made into a theme by Basil I, soon afterwards once again fell under Arab rule. Although there were further losses of territory, the number of themes continued to grow, until by the end of the twelfth century it was double what it had been in the time of the Macedonian dynasty.[1] Even before this, the desire to limit the expansion of these largely independent administrative districts had led to themes being split up, for in troubled times many a governor had succumbed to the temptation of playing off his own power against that of the Emperor; but it was still necessary to guard against the formation of a property-owning military aristocracy, and conversely, the ruling class had in their own interests seen to it that the machinery of administration remained intact despite the losses of territory.[2] Almost all the governors of the themes were called *Strategus*, or general, and their title thus reflected the military origin of their office; the only exceptions were the governors of the theme Opsikion, who was *Comes*, and of the Optimaton, who was *Domesticus*.[3] The theme governors were directly subordinate to the Emperor. The themes seem to have been divided into two groups, according to their evolution: the eastern group, consisting of those of Asia Minor, also included Thrace and Macedonia, but not the maritime themes, which, with the rest of the Balkans, Italy and Cherson in the Crimea, formed the western group. The eastern *Strategi* had a higher standing. According to Philotheus, they ranked directly below the *Syncellus* and before the City Prefect. It was this especially privileged position accorded to officials who were in origin military which gave the Byzantine Empire the special stamp characteristic of so large a part of its history. The

---

[1] See the list in the Chrysobull of Alexius III Angelus (1198), *DR*, 1647.

[2] E. Stein, 'Untersuchungen zur spätbyzantinischen Verfassungs- und Wirtschaftsgeschichte', *op. cit.* pp. 19 ff.

[3] On the decline in his rank and status, cf. Constantine Porphyrogenitus, *De Thematibus* (ed. A. Pertusi), p. 132.

Strategi of the eastern and maritime themes drew their salaries from the central treasury, while the others were dependent on the revenues from their provinces. In addition to their military staff, the governors had at their disposal a considerable body of civil officials to deal with the combination of military, civil, judicial and financial duties which made up their command. But attempts were also made by the central government to take a hand in the administration. For example, the *Chartularius* of the theme, who amongst other duties supervised payments to the soldiers, was also answerable to the Logothete τοῦ στρατιωτικοῦ. Moreover, the Judge of the Theme in civil actions, the *Praetor*, and the *Protonotarius* (who was among the subordinates of the *Chartularius* of the Sacellium) were also subordinate to the *Strategus*, at least from the tenth century. But this arrangement was always subject to certain reservations, as may be illustrated from a passage in the so-called *Tactica* of Leo which refers to the three offices just mentioned: 'they should, admittedly, in some matters submit to the orders of the *Strategi*, but on the other hand the Emperor thinks it safer that they should present their accounts to the imperial central administration so that the Emperor may have exact knowledge of the state of his civil and military government.'[1] It is still not known in detail how the obligations of these officials were regulated; but it is clear that the central government reserved to itself a certain right of supervision in order to control and check the *Strategi*. In addition, the bishops were now required to keep watch over the conduct of the administration in their dioceses, and subjects were encouraged to seek legal redress against oppression.

It was possible to appeal from the provincial courts. The Emperor in his imperial court (the βασιλικὸν κριτήριον), which was composed of high-ranking dignitaries, remained the supreme court of appeal, and jurisdiction over the highest officials was reserved to him. There were two other high judicial authorities almost level with the Emperor: the City Prefect (who acted as President of the imperial court in the absence of the Emperor,[2] just as the *Drungarius* τῆς βίγλης was to do later) and the *Quaestor*. Although several of the earlier Emperors liked to hear appeals in person, a reform of Manuel I in 1166 restricted the possibilities of appeal and laid down the procedure to be followed in the four imperial courts of justice in Constantinople.[3] After the reconquest of the city, Michael VIII reinstated the Emperor's court, but only as a single βασιλικὸν σέκρετον, or a simple σέκρετον. His successor, in 1296, reduced the number of judges to

---

[1] Leo, *Tact.* IV, 33, 62 (ed. R. Vári); J. B. Bury, *op. cit.* p. 44; F. Dölger, *Finanzverwaltung*, pp. 68 ff.

[2] *DR*, 1467.   [3] *DR*, 1465.

twelve and created a court composed of highly placed clerics and laymen which could give final judgement in the absence of the Emperor. This institution soon became discredited, and Andronicus III, in 1329, gave the *sekreton* only four 'General Judges of the Romans' (καθολικοὶ τῶν 'Ρωμαίων κριταί), two clerics and two laymen. Although three of these judges had been found guilty of venality after the lapse of only eight years, the institution survived to the end of the Empire, though with many alterations dictated by experience. The growing influence of the Church is reflected in the increase of competition between the court of the Emperor and that of the Patriarch. From the very beginning, indeed, there had always been at Byzantium an ecclesiastical jurisdiction to rival the civil, though in varying degrees. The ecclesiastical courts had competence when the accused was a cleric and also in civil causes if both parties were clerics. From the eleventh century certain cases, such as those involving marriage and charitable foundations, were reserved to the Church.[1] After the interlude of the Latin Empire, the line between the civil and ecclesiastical jurisdictions became increasingly indistinct, as a consequence of the growing power of the Church. Roman law, which continued to exert its influence through the great compilation of the *Basilica*, still played a role of outstanding importance in the administration and formulation of law, although its influence was considerably modified by the penetration of Christian ideas. The intermingling of civil and church law, of the *nomoi* and the *canones*, gave rise to a new species of law: this '*Nomocanon*', as it was called, extended its influence into the Balkans and was not only of fundamental importance for the still remaining Greek parts of the world, but also of considerable effect in the development of Roman canon law.[2]

At first glance, Byzantine criminal law seems to show little trace of ameliorative Christian influence. It is true that the *Ecloga* of Leo III restricts capital punishment to the crimes of murder, high treason, desertion from the armed forces and unnatural sexual practices, but it also provides for a whole range of punishments by mutilation, which were unknown to the law of Justinian, and which appear to be identical with the list given by the customary laws developed in the seventh century. Admittedly penalties of mutilation (such as blinding, or cutting off the hands, tongue or nose) are in many cases now substituted for the death penalty, but they are also now imposed

---

[1] E.g. *DR*, 1127. Cf. A. P. Christophilopoulos, ''Η δικαιοδοσία τῶν ἐκκλησιαστικῶν δικαστηρίων κατὰ τὴν Βυζαντινὴν περίοδον', *EEBS*, XVIII (1948), 192 ff.

[2] St G. Berechet, 'Influssi del diritto canonico bizantino dopo la caduta di Costantinopoli sul diritto canonico romano', *Atti del V Congresso Intern. di Studi Bizantini*, I = *SBN*, VI (1939), 586 ff. See below: chapter XXI, pp. 61 ff.

in others where Justinian would have merely exacted a fine. But to a sterner generation than ours the replacement of the death penalty by mutilation may even have appeared in the guise of a mitigation of severity, and mutilation itself might be justified by the words of St Matthew (xviii. 8, 9): 'if thy hand or thy foot offend thee, cut them off...and if thine eye offend thee, pluck it out', and by the fact that the offender was thus given opportunity to repent of his misdeeds. Moreover, it may be recalled that at a later date the Emperor in his coronation oath bound himself to be merciful and humane towards his subjects, to refrain from capital punishment and mutilation, so far as this was possible in the interests of justice and propriety; he also avowed that he would pursue righteousness and truth.[1] John II Comnenus, indeed, enjoyed the unique reputation of never having imposed any corporal punishment. There were also the punishments of confiscation of property and fines. Persons accused of an offence were always kept in prison until their trial, although imprisonment as a punishment was at first unknown in Byzantine law. From the twelfth century onward, however, many political offenders were imprisoned, until death released them from their cruel fate; their prison was the Anemas tower in Blachernae, which took its name from a rebel held there in the time of Alexius I. Banishment to a monastery, on the other hand, was always quite a common punishment and one which clearly shows the influence of the Church on the penal system. Justice was not infrequently tempered with mercy by the exercise of the imperial prerogative of pardon. In addition, Nicephorus III Botaneiates revived an old rule going back to Theodosius I by which thirty days should be allowed to lapse between the pronouncement of a sentence, whether of death or mutilation, and its execution.[2] The right of asylum, always energetically defended by the Church courts against infringement by the state, further mitigated the stringency of the penal laws. Few offenders were excluded from its efficacy.[3] The Church took in hand the punishment and rehabilitation of offenders who claimed the right by confining them in a monastery. Constantine VII Porphyrogenitus tried to deprive convicted murderers of the right of asylum, but later, undoubtedly as the result of ecclesiastical pressure, modified his ruling, which now insisted that the offender, after accepting punishment by the Church, should be permanently exiled, and which also made regulations concerning his property.[4] Manuel I, in 1166, sought to remove the disadvantages arising from this ordinance, which showed themselves all the more clearly the longer it was in force.[5] He ordered that murderers were to be ener-

---

[1] Ps.-Codinus, *De off.* XVII, p. 87, 8 ff.   [2] *DR*, 1047.
[3] *Ecloga*, 105 ff.   [4] *DR*, 676.   [5] *DR*, 1467.

getically pursued; if nevertheless a murderer achieved the asylum of
St Sophia, after accepting punishment from the Church he was to be
exiled to a distant province of the Empire, there to live out his days
in a monastery; in cases of wilful murder, the offender was to be
actually incarcerated for life, without taking monastic vows. This
regulation continued in force. It is noteworthy that in this autocracy
of orthodoxy the right of asylum was denied to traitors, and also—a
sign of the thorough penetration of the financial machine—to default-
ing taxpayers and fraudulent taxation officials.

The complicated and extensive machinery of government continued to function even after numerous disasters had fallen on the
Empire from without; in fact, titles of rank continued to proliferate.
Then, as formerly, the hierarchy of officials played their part in preserving the traditionally conservative attitude, although they were
forced to accept many changes, largely as a result of the increasing
poverty of the state. The Seljuq invasion of Asia Minor made it
necessary to reorganise the provincial administration and the themes.
From the late eleventh century, the *Strategi* were transformed into
Duces, a title which had formerly belonged to the governors of smaller
districts, who had been only loosely connected with the *Strategi*;[1]
Strategus occurs in the later period only under John III Vatatzes in
connection with the new district made out of the territory once forming the theme of Thessalonica.[2] Although at the same period there
seems to have been an increase in the powers of a few high administrative officers in the central government, against this must be set a
probable diminution of their spheres of influence. But we still lack a
clear over-all picture of the machinery of government in the late
Byzantine period, although a few detailed studies do exist. The *Book
of Offices* (wrongly ascribed to the *Curopalates* George Codinus) is
admittedly a source from the fourteenth century, but the picture it
gives is of what the outward appearance of the Empire still contrived
to present rather than of the melancholy reality within. As has
already been remarked more than once, a considerable number of the
former offices were now only titles of rank, and in many cases people
no longer knew what these offices had once meant. In addition to the
Patriarch, who had acquired a far-reaching influence over the civil
administration, the Grand Logothete (who seems to have ousted both
the Logothete τοῦ δρόμου and the Logothete τῶν σεκρέτων, in his time
a very influential official)[3] and the high-ranking military officers between them conducted the business of a state which had now shrunk

[1] E. Stein, *op. cit.* pp. 20ff.

[2] O. Tafrali, *Thessalonique des origines au XIVe siècle* (Paris, 1919), pp. 234ff.

[3] E. Stein, *op. cit.* pp. 34ff.

to very small dimensions. For it must be remembered that the Balkan territories restored to the Empire from alien rule were withdrawn from the central administration as more or less independent domains.

A particular merit of the Byzantine bureaucracy was the sound education of its members. The officials shared in the high general level of education of their class of society. The fact that Constantine VII Porphyrogenitus made grants to the students in his university shows the importance attached by the state to maintaining a well-educated bureaucracy.[1] When compared with the standard laid down by Justinian, it must be admitted that legal education declined with the course of time and became a narrowly limited professional training, until Constantine IX Monomachus revived the old school of law at Constantinople in 1045.[2] The School was directed by the 'Guardian of the law', the *Nomophylax*; a certificate from the *Nomophylax* was required from all notaries and advocates before they could practise, and particular attention was to be directed to graduates of the School in filling vacancies in the imperial service. In theory admission to the influential and lucrative official positions was open to everybody. But in course of time an official aristocracy had been formed, which did not make promotion easy for newcomers. At the same time a provincial aristocracy of landowners had been developed, particularly in Asia Minor. The result was an alliance between the Emperor and the highly trained officials against this growing menace, which produced an ominous rivalry between the civil bureaucracy and the military commanders who were recruited from the landed aristocracy and who were always striving for power. It must be admitted that this hostility led finally to a serious neglect of the army and was not without its contribution to the collapse of the Empire's system of defence. Even so, when the Comneni came to adopt their more powerful policy there was a reaction against the predominance of the civilians and a prolonged revival of the supremacy of the military aristocracy. This, together with the extension of the system of the *pronoia*, which ended by being directed chiefly to military purposes (see below, p. 41), gave rise to a feudal organisation and created an administrative situation which the Latin conquerors must have found not unlike their own feudalism; contact with the West further intensified and accelerated this process. Yet despite the partial and momentary collapse of the bureaucracy at this period, the machinery survived sufficiently intact for the Palaeologi to rebuild on the old foundations, so that the civil service once again became a buttress to the state in its long struggle for existence.

[1] F. Fuchs, *Die höheren Schulen von Konstantinopel im Mittelalter* (Leipzig, 1926), pp. 22 f.   [2] *DR*, 863.

The governmental machinery of the Byzantine Empire may appear unwieldy and bureaucratic, but it conformed to its own standards and had remarkable powers of resilience. It was undoubtedly partly responsible for the conservative complexion of the Empire, but it was also flexible enough to carry out its tasks despite the fluctuating fortunes of the state. It is undeniable that this extensive administrative apparatus was in itself a heavy burden on the state finances, and this alone, even without the not infrequent additional evils, would be enough to account for complaints of the intolerable weight of taxation. The courts, for example, were filled with cases arising from the greed and corruption of officials, evils which the Emperors perpetually combated (cf. Leo III's preface to the *Ecloga*) but could never eradicate. Scarcely less important was the system of dues, which the officials were always working to develop and increase to their own advantage,[1] and also the sale of offices, which was more or less clandestine.[2] Even a relentless campaign like that conducted by Andronicus I Comnenus against corruption and well-nigh ineradicable malpractices needed a reign of terror to achieve even a temporary success. And just because the bureaucracy was, or should have been, the principal instrument in the fulfilment of the Emperor's will, it was by no means easy for the Emperor to carry a point against it. Indeed, it was not unusual for the higher officials to impose their own will on the Emperor. But with all its failings, the bureaucracy seems to have been deeply conscious of its role as servant of the state. The officials were regarded as forming a link between the ruler and his subjects, as indeed they did, and in the last resort they were the custodians of law and justice. Together with the Church, these officials, with their activity which, like that of the Church, extended over the whole Empire, and with their official language of Greek, contributed to the Hellenisation of the numerous foreign elements within the Empire, or as they themselves would have put it, towards their Romanisation. The bureaucracy thus had a share in promoting the unity of the Empire. All in all, this was a costly and at times unwieldy bureaucracy, but it was also an instrument with a great capacity for resilience which helped the state to surmount many crises and assured its long survival. It was the bureaucracy which through the centuries gave the Byzantine state its special character, for the bureaucracy was an intrinsic part of its existence.

---

[1] F. Dölger, 'Zum Gebührenwesen der Byzantiner', *Etudes dédiées à la mémoire d'A. Andréadès* (Athens, 1939), pp. 35ff.

[2] G. Kolias, *Ämter- und Würdenkauf im früh- und mittelbyzantinischen Reich* (*Texte u. Forsch. zur byzantin. u. neugriech. Philologie*, xxxv, Athens, 1939).

III

For long stretches at a time the history of the Byzantine Empire is a history of wars. It is thus not surprising that the army played an important role, nor that the government of the Empire itself was increasingly determined by its military organisation and subordinated to military necessities, as has already been shown. Emperors who concerned themselves seriously with their Empire, taking the field in person in the interests of its defence or profit, had a clear understanding of the importance of the army and a watchful eye for its wellbeing, including the personal welfare of the soldiers. Even the distinctly unmilitaristic Constantine VII Porphyrogenitus could say 'The army is to the state as the head is to the body; neglect it, and the state is in danger'.[1] So long as the army was kept up to strength and in a high state of preparedness, ready on the instant to obey the Emperor and do its duty, the state had at its disposal a keen-edged weapon of defence. Conversely, when signs of decay became apparent in the army, general weakness also set in.

The organisation of the army obtaining in the early Byzantine period was not completely abandoned even after the institution of the themes by Heraclius and their further development by his successors.[2] It was not merely that the names of earlier corps and special formations were retained for the great military districts of Asia Minor. Even the unification of military and civil power, which was now brought to completion, had been adumbrated under Justinian, and there was further precedent for it in the Exarchates fully developed in the West under Maurice and in some provinces of the East.[3] Maurice, under the stress of necessity, recruited his army largely from the subjects of the Empire, particularly from the inhabitants of the newly conquered Armenian regions.[4] From the *Strategicon*, a manual attributed to Maurice, we learn that all subjects under forty had an obligation to serve in the army. A distinction is made between the *élite* corps, made up from a carefully-chosen minor-

---

[1] Zachariae von Lingenthal, *Jus graeco-romanum*, III, 261.

[2] For a different view, cf. N. H. Baynes, 'The Emperor Heraclius and the Military Theme System', *EHR*, LXVII (1952), 380 ff.; A. Pertusi, *Costantino Porfirogenito De Thematibus* (Vatican, 1952), p. 110. For the opposite opinion, cf. F. Dölger, *BZ*, XLV (1952), 391; W. Ensslin, 'Der Kaiser Herakleios und die Themenverfassung', *BZ*, XLVI (1953), 362 ff.; G. Ostrogorsky, 'Sur la date de la composition du Livre des Thèmes et sur l'époque de la constitution des premiers thèmes d'Asie Mineure', *B*, XXIII (1954), 31 ff.

[3] E. Stein, *Studien*, p. 161; *id.*, *Histoire du Bas-Empire*, II (1949), 802 and 466 f., 473 ff., 749. Ch. Diehl, *Études sur l'administration byzantine dans l'exarchat de Ravenne* (Paris, 1888), pp. 3 f.; *id.*, *L'Afrique byzantine* (Paris, 1896), pp. 303 f.

[4] *DR*, 104, 108, 137.

ity, the *epilekta*, and the weaker and less important contingents which composed the ἀσθενῆ or ὑποδεέστερα. The crack troops included the *Buccellarii*, the *Foederati* and the *Optimates*. The *Buccellarii* were the household troops attached to officers of the rank of general; the *Foederati* were no longer recruited chiefly from foreigners but from the most warlike contingents raised within the Empire, for example those of the Balkans and Isauria; the *Optimates* were selected from the best of the other corps. It will be seen that the names of these troops were all Latin, and Latin was still used for giving them their orders.[1]

It was with these and other picked troops that Heraclius won his victories against the Persians. An important element in this success was undoubtedly the fact that the Emperor promised to settle his troops in the provinces of Asia Minor which were most threatened by the enemy (and which were also highly developed), and thus heightened considerably the will to victory among his soldiers.[2] Unfortunately it is not possible to discover from the sources the full extent of Heraclius' original plan of reorganisation, and we thus cannot judge of his success. In any case, the new order at first was only allowed to establish itself in Asia Minor, on account of the victorious inroads of the Arabs, whose military education was at least partly due to their former allies, the Romans and the Persians.[3] In Asia Minor, there were the following themes or army corps: *Anatolikon*, the successor of the former army of the Orient; *Opsikion* (*Obsequium*, the troops formerly attached to the *Magistri militum praesentales*); and *Armeniakon*, formerly under the command of the Armenian army chief. Their governors were known as *Strategi* (*Comes* in the case of the *Opsikion*), and may therefore be regarded as the successors of the *Magistri militum*. The picked regiments, however, the *epilekta*, were at first established in special districts of the larger themes in their own right. Thus the *Buccellarii* and the *Optimates* were separated from the *Opsikion*, while *Thracesion* (a division taken from Europe to Asia Minor in the army of the East) was separated from *Anatolikon*; the *Foederati*, however, although they were also settled together in one place, were always part of *Anatolikon*. The exact date of the foundation of the first maritime theme, that of *Carabisiani* on the coast of Asia Minor, is unknown, but it must have been towards the middle of the seventh century.[4] The themes of

---

[1] F. Aussaresses, *L'armée byzantine à la fin du VIe siècle d'après le Stratégicon de l'empereur Maurice* (Paris, 1909), p. 10, 12 ff.; E. Stein, *Studien*, pp. 123 ff., 127, 132.

[2] E. Stein, *ibid.* pp. 132 ff.

[3] W. Ensslin, 'Die weltgeschichtliche Bedeutung der Kämpfe zwischen Rom und Persien', *Neue Jahrbücher*, IV (1928), 412 ff.

[4] A. Pertusi, *op. cit.* p. 149.

Thrace and Macedonia must have been created earlier than the other western themes, since Philotheus ranks them with the eastern group; there may originally have been one large theme of Thrace, Macedonia being separated from it at the end of the eighth century. The next themes to be founded were those of Hellas and Sicily, under Justinian II.[1] Even when the development of the system had been carried much further, the eastern themes still retained their initial precedence, at first no doubt because of their earlier foundation and later because of their brilliant achievements in the defensive wars against the Arabs. Themes created later were given geographical names (see above, p. 28).

The distribution of the military forces of the Empire was based on the theme organisation, which, as already mentioned, developed under their *strategi* into units of administration for both civil and military affairs. Each of these units, or provinces, supplied one *thema* (or army corps, to use a modern expression). The *thema* was divided, according to its size, into two or three *turmai*, each under a turmarch, who was both divisional commander and administrator of his section of the province. The further subdivision of the army is difficult to describe, since there were constant changes and the themes varied so much in size. But the divisions mentioned in the *Strategicon* (late sixth and early seventh centuries) seem to have survived, since the later *turmai*, *moirai* and *banda* correspond to the *mere* (divisions), *moirai* (brigades) and *tagmata* (regiments) of the earlier source. The *bandon* took its name from the Germanic word for banner. According to the *Cletorologion* of Philotheus the *Strategus* had under him the *turmarchai* and the *merarches*; it thus seems that the theme was at that time divided geographically into two *turmai*, but militarily into three divisions, and that the commander of this third division, which was not a separate administrative district, had the old title of *merarches*.[2] After the *turmarchai* and the *merarches* came the *drungarii* (the commanders of the *moirai*), and the *kometes* (*comites*), the leaders of the *banda*. The disposition is described somewhat differently in an Arabian source, dating from about 840 to 845.[3] Ibn Khordādbah, the author, generalising from his experience of a single theme, gives the following picture. The *Strategus* commanded 10,000 men divided

[1] Pertusi, *op. cit.* pp. 156, 162, 170, 178; W. Ensslin, 'Zur Verwaltung Siziliens vom Ende des weströmischen Reiches bis zum Beginn der Themenverfassung', *Atti dell' VIII Congresso di Studi Bizantini*, I = *SBN*, VIII (1953), 364.

[2] J. B. Bury, *The Imperial Administrative System*, p. 42.

[3] C. Barbier de Meynard, 'Le livre des routes et des provinces', *JA*, sér. VI, t. V (1865), 480 ff.; *Kitâb al Masâlik wa'l Mamâlik*, ed. M. J. de Goeje, *Bibliotheca Geographorum Arabicorum*, VI (Leyden, 1889), 84; H. Gelzer, 'Die Genesis der byzantinischen Themenverfassung', *Abhandl. der Kgl. Sächs. Gesellschaft d. Wissenschaften* (1899), p. 114.

into two *turmai* of 5000, each under a turmarch. The *turmai* were divided into five *banda* of 1000, each under a *drungarius*. Each *drungarius* commanded five pentarchies, each led by a *comes*. The pentarchies were composed of five pentecontarchies, each containing forty men, though the name suggests that they must originally have had fifty; the smallest unit was the decarchy of ten men led by a decarch. Of the officials composing the staff and secretariat of the *Strategus* mention may be made of the *Domesticus* of the theme, who had the rank of a *Strator*, and the *Chartularius*, who had to keep the muster-roll up to date and who was responsible for paying the men, although, as already mentioned (cf. above, p. 29), he had to render account for this money to an organ of the central government.[1]

The consolidation of the themes was further assisted by the foundation of small military frontier districts, the *kleisurai*,[2] commanded by Kleisurarchs. The word literally means 'frontier-passes', and the *kleisurai* were first founded to protect and defend the mountain invasion routes at the time of the renewal of the conflict with the Arabs; they also featured in the wars with the Bulgars. As such districts grew in importance they became the basis of new themes.[3] The *akritai*, who were the successors of the former *limitanei*, or frontier defenders, were independent of the troops forming the standing army of the theme, though they were on occasion subordinated to the theme *Strategus*. Led by their officers, who might be described as a kind of margrave, the *akritai* were continually engaged in petty warfare in defence of the actual military frontiers. They were stationed in strongholds and forts along the length of the threatened frontiers and provided with a system of signalling enabling them to make contact with each other; their tasks were to make reconnaissance of the enemy's intentions, to hold off attacks by taking swift counter-action or to create havoc in enemy territory by their own forays. Such frequent and adventurous affrays with infidels and brigands (*apelatai*, or cattle thieves) form the basis of the Akritic sagas, seen at their most characteristic in the Byzantine folk epic of Digenis Akritas, which reflect the conditions of the tenth century and furnish into the bargain much rich historical material concerning the wars between the Byzantines and the Arabs.[4]

Besides the theme armies of the provinces, the *thematikoi*, there were also troops stationed in Constantinople and its environs; these were known by the old name of *tagmata* (the *tagmatikoi*). They in-

---

[1] J. B. Bury, *op. cit.* pp. 43 ff.

[2] Cf. Suda (Suidas), s.v. κλεισοῦραι.

[3] Cf. A. Pertusi, *op. cit.* pp. 147, 166.

[4] H. Grégoire, Ὁ Διγενὴς Ἀκρίτας. Ἡ Βυζαντινὴ ἐποποιία στὴν ἱστορία καὶ στὴν ποίηση (New York, 1942).

cluded the mounted formations of the *scholarii*, the *excubiti* and the *hikanatoi* (each under a *Domesticus*) and the *Arithmos* of the *bigla* (*vigiliae*), whose special duty it was to guard the palace or, on campaign, the imperial headquarters: they were commanded by a *drungarius*. In addition there was a regiment of infantry, the *numeri*, under a *Domesticus*, and furthermore the troop under the *Comes* of the Walls (τῶν τειχῶν), a title which probably referred to the long walls built about forty miles to the west of Constantinople by Anastasius I. This troop remained behind as a garrison even when the other *tagmata* went into battle as a kind of bodyguard for the Emperor or for his deputy as commander.[1] But his real bodyguard was the *hetaireia* (literally 'the retinue'), composed mainly of foreign mercenaries and commanded by the *Hetaireiarches*.[2] The *Domesticus* of the *scholarii* ranked directly below the *Strategus* of Anatolikon, which was the highest ranking of the themes. In the tenth century this *Domesticus* took over the supreme command of the army on occasions when the Emperor himself was not present in the field. Basil II, perhaps in an effort to undermine the overweening predominance of this command, halved it, making one *Domesticus* for the East and another for the West; these officers later came to be known (though at first unofficially) as Grand Domestics.[3] The estimates of the strengths of the individual *tagmata* vary greatly, ranging between 4000 and 1500.[4] Ibn Khordādbah assesses the total strength of the army in the ninth century at 120,000, while Kodāma estimates the army of the East alone at 70,000.[5] These high figures, compared with the 150,000 estimated to have represented the total strength of the much larger Empire of the time of Justinian, show how greatly the military needs of the Empire had increased. Moreover, between the tenth and the twelfth centuries, the actual military levy available for campaigning rarely exceeded 30,000 men, and was much more often less.

The cash pay of the soldiers was relatively small, but their chief subsistence came from the hereditary military landholdings (στρατιωτικὰ κτήματα) granted in return for military obligations. These military holdings, the backbone of the whole military system, were middle-sized peasant estates and provided the holder with enough to live on and to equip himself for his military duties. In addition, a theme soldier in the first year of service received one *solidus* in cash; this was increased by one *solidus* annually until the twelfth year when the

---

[1] J. B. Bury, *op. cit.* pp. 47–68.
[2] *Ibid.* pp. 106f.
[3] R. Guilland, 'Le grand domesticat à Byzance', *EO*, xxxvii (1938), 53ff.; cf. V. Laurent, 'Notes complémentaires', *ibid.* pp. 65ff.
[4] J. B. Bury, *op. cit.* pp. 53f.
[5] J. B. Bury, *History of the Eastern Roman Empire* (London, 1912), p. 226.

maximum of twelve *solidi* was reached. The maximum of the soldiers of the *tagmata* and of the subordinate officers was probably sixteen *solidi*.[1] The salaries of the officers were considerably higher. According to Ibn Khordādbah, the salary of the *strategi* of the eastern themes ranged between forty and twenty-four gold pounds, according to the importance of the theme. The turmarch received twelve pounds, the *drungarius* six, the *comes* three, the pentecontarch two and the decarch one. Under Leo VI there was a revision of the salaries of the *strategi*, occasioned by the increase in the number of themes. There were now to be five salary grades: for *strategi*, four grades of forty, thirty, twenty and ten pounds, and for the kleisurarchs one grade of five pounds. Except in the highest rank, therefore, salaries were cut, and this perhaps also applied to the other officers.[2] There are instances of higher rates of pay in special cases (as for example in the campaigns against Crete of 902 and 949); this may have been because pay had been in arrears, or it may have represented a special extra allowance for service overseas.[3] The bodyguards of the *hetaireia* were exceptionally well-paid and on this account aspirants to the corps paid a considerable entry fee.[4] It must also be remembered that the soldiery shared in the profits of loot.

So long as the system of combining a military holding with the obligation to provide a heavily armed horseman remained a reality there was little difficulty in finding native recruits. It is not surprising that the Emperors were at pains to preserve this arrangement and endeavoured to protect military peasant holdings from pressure to sell to great landowners and from fragmentation, as may be seen from the *Novels* of Romanus I of 922 and 934 and later edicts of Constantine VII.[5] Even Nicephorus II Phocas, in other respects conciliatory towards the magnates, sought to stabilise the holdings of the *stratiotai* by raising from four to twelve gold pounds the value of property encumbered with the obligation of providing a heavily armed soldier.[6] His predecessor and namesake Nicephorus I, on the other hand, had conscripted even the poorer peasants for military service by making the village community liable for their equipment, at the rate of eighteen and a half *solidi* annually.[7] In the end these protective measures failed, since the aristocracy of Constantinople were always on the look-out for land as a capital investment. Moreover, the growing hostility of the civil officials of the central government had as one of its effects the neglect of the army, which in the

---

[1] J. B. Bury, *History of the Eastern Roman Empire*, p. 236; E. Stein, *Studien*, p. 143.
[2] *De cerim.* II, 50, pp. 696f.; J. B. Bury, *op. cit.* p. 225; H. Gelzer, *op. cit.* pp. 116–21.
[3] *De cerim.* II, 44f.; J. B. Bury, *op. cit.* p. 227, note 1.
[4] *De cerim.* II, 49, pp. 692f.   [5] *DR*, 595, 628, 673.
[6] *DR*, 721.   [7] Theophanes, p. 486, 24f.

course of the twelfth century led to the decline of the Empire's defensive strength. The defeat at Manzikert in 1071 and the permanent establishment of the Seljuq Turks in Asia Minor meant the actual destruction of the theme organisation in that area, no matter what a Manuel I Comnenus might hope to achieve by reviving the old regulations against the alienation of military holdings.[1]

The way had been paved for this decline by the practice which had already begun to reappear in the tenth century of employing foreign mercenaries. Moreover, in the western themes at least, it was already possible to evade military service by making a money payment,[2] and permission was ultimately given to the tenants of the remaining military holdings to take the same course.[3] Foreigners had always played a prominent role in the *hetaireia*. Over the centuries the imperial army came to be served by a medley of Khazars, Pechenegs, Russians, Scandinavians, Georgians, Slavs, Arabs, Turks and later on 'Latins' of every kind. A new bodyguard, the Varangian guard, achieved outstanding importance. The Varangian guard was originally an emergency troop of Russian-Scandinavian mercenaries, but in the first half of the eleventh century they developed into an actual bodyguard, ousting the old guard supplied by the *tagmata*, who, with the exception of the *hikanatoi*, finally disappear in the course of this century. The Varangians were at first chiefly Icelandic, Danish and Norwegian warriors seeking their fortune in 'Miklagard', the name used in the sagas for Constantinople, but by the time of Alexius I Comnenus the guard was composed chiefly of Anglo-Saxons.[4]

Alexius, however, sought to re-enlist his own subjects in the imperial army. But if we find mention of 'military holdings' in this later period, the expression can hardly be understood in the sense it had had in the heyday of the theme organisation. The holders of such land were now the so-called pronoiars (προνοιάριοι), that is to say 'recipients of *pronoiai*'. This meant that property was granted for a term of years, with full right to enjoyment of the income, against the obligation to perform certain services, which now in fact meant that military service was included. Thus the holder could be described simply as a warrior (στρατιώτης). He was obliged to serve in person as a horseman and to provide a number of men, according to the size of his *pronoia*. The state retained the proprietary rights of these

---

[1] *DR*, 1535.

[2] Const. Porph., *DAI*, I, c. 51, p. 256.

[3] Scylitzes-Cedrenus, II, p. 608.

[4] A. A. Vasiliev, 'The Anglo-Saxon Immigration to Byzantium in the Eleventh Century', *Annales de l'Inst. Kondakov*, IX (1937), 39 ff.; cf. F. Dölger, *BZ*, XXXVIII (1938), 235 ff.; R. M. Dawkins, 'The later history of the Varangian Guard', *JRS*, XXXVII (1947), 19 ff.

holdings, which could neither be sold nor inherited, and if the holder did not fulfil his obligations the property could be confiscated. This system soon led to a feudal arrangement having certain similarities to that of the West. Moreover, other types of properties were now also encumbered with the duty of providing soldiers, in this case light infantry. It was one of the Palaeologi, Michael VIII, who first made *pronoia* land hereditary: as Pachymeres said, the *pronoia* held for life now became immortal.[1] However, *pronoia* property still remained inalienable and burdened with the obligation of military service.[2]

Attempts were made to check the depopulation of many frontier districts, caused by the raids of the Seljuqs, Serbs and Hungarians, by the settlement there of prisoners of war, pressed into service to guard the frontiers. This was not always to the advantage of the territories concerned. But from the time of the Comneni the need to employ foreign mercenaries became increasingly obvious. So long as such troops remained under Byzantine command and were well-disciplined they could be regarded as a valuable addition to the defences of the Empire and thus to the power of the central government. But the situation was greatly altered when leading mercenaries themselves acquired higher commands and could thus, in the manner of condottieri, exploit their position to set their own interests above those of the state. The hatred felt by the population for the 'barbarians' could even lead to open conflict. The sudden collapse of the Empire under the Angeli was in large part due to the absence of any will to resist in the army, which now contained nothing but mercenaries. In the period of reconstruction under the Lascarids and the Palaeologi serious attempts were made to restore the striking power of the army; there was no longer, however, any question of a unified military organisation, but rather of a series of makeshifts. Ultimately the army once again became largely an army of mercenaries, whose effective strength and morale in battle was a reflection on the poverty of the imperial exchequer.

The army's most important weapon was always the cavalry, the *caballarii*. The heavy cavalry, the successors of the late Roman cataphracts, wore steel helmets and either ring or chain mail, and carried swords, daggers, a lance or battle-axe, and bows. Their warhorses were protected by breast and frontal plates. These were the squadrons used to attack in mass formation. The light horse, the *trapezitai* or *monozonoi*, were used for rapid assaults, reconnaissance, and to cover the movements of other troops. Their chief weapon was

---

[1] Pachymeres, i, p. 67 (*CSHB*).

[2] On the whole question of *pronoia*, cf. G. Ostrogorsky, *Pour l'histoire de la féodalité byzantine* (Brussels, 1954) and P. Lemerle, *RH*, ccxix (1958) and ccxx (1958).

the bow. The heavy and light infantry still played a not unimportant subsidiary role. They were also armed with the bow, though some divisions had javelins as well. The mail-clad heavy infantry carried spears, and swords or battle-axes. Each *bandon* had its own baggage-train, which often included a large number of non-combatants. The heavy baggage (the *tuldon*) also contained material for building bridges. The Byzantine army also possessed mobile field artillery, catapult engines mounted on carts for the projection of stone missiles (μαγγανικὰ ἀλακάτια) or arrows (τοξοβάλλιστρα);[1] these were in charge of gunners. During prosperous periods the arsenal at Constantinople (the Mangana, in the First Region of the city at the foot of the Acropolis) contained a large store of war-engines of every description.[2] Military engineering had reached a high level of development. Nor did this very well-organised army lack medical services; there were the mounted *deputati* whose task it was to evacuate the wounded, and who received a special reward for each man whose rescue they thus procured.

We are fortunate in having a whole series of military handbooks, ranging in date from the introduction of the theme organisation down to the so-called *Strategicon* of Cecaumenus in the eleventh century, which afford us an insight into the development of the art of war at Byzantium, and which show us that it was practised as an applied science. Nothing was left to chance, if forethought could prevent it. The characteristics of the enemy of the moment were always carefully considered when troops were being trained and armed, and the same care was given to the preparation and execution of a plan of campaign, which might employ a variety of tactics and which never neglected defensive requirements. Defence, indeed, had always first priority, since a sound defensive system was necessary if the none too numerous troops were to be husbanded and kept in good fettle. Offensive tactics are most fully displayed in the regulations for the conduct of a siege. The defence of the frontiers was still modelled on the late Roman *limes* system, with fortified posts, small forts, and a guard on the passes and roads by which an enemy might approach. Towns in the interior were walled. A system of optical signals warned of the approach of the enemy. If the frontier forces were unable to ward off the attack, the infantry were called in to block the enemy's way of retreat while light cavalry harassed him, hindering his advance until the *strategus* could mobilise the main body of troops to repel the attack, having also sent the news to the neigh-

---

[1] Leo, *Tact.* 5, 7; 6, 27; 14, 83; 15, 27.
[2] R. Demangel and E. Mamboury, *Le Quartier des Manganes* (Paris, 1939), pp. 7 ff.

bouring themes. There is no lack of detailed instructions for conduct in the line of battle; nevertheless, an able general was expected to act independently and have his own ideas. The ruling principle was to avoid the risk of battle if there was any possibility of achieving success by other means. There were orders for troop movements and their protection, planned combinations of separate corps to be achieved in battle, and the observation of the enemy, including espionage; negotiations with the enemy as a delaying tactic and every kind of stratagem, such as feigned flight and ambush, were also discussed. If subtlety and deception could win the day, they were to be preferred to a show of strength. We are given an interesting glimpse of the petty frontier warfare against the Arabs in the instructions compiled by an officer in the entourage of Nicephorus II Phocas.[1] Thorough-going and individual training (not infrequently directed by the Emperor in person), strong discipline and battle experience all combined, in good periods, to make this army an effective weapon in the hands of its leaders.

The fighting spirit of the troops was raised and fired by the acknowledgment and reward of special services and by continual references to the high importance of their task. In addition to the exhortations of their superior officers, the troops had the benefit of the services of orators who formed, as it were, a body of lay preachers, the *cantatores*: these inspired the men by speaking of their duty to the Emperor and the Empire, towards God and the Christian religion, with emphasis on the rewards of valour in this world and the next. If this seems to betray a religious leitmotiv, the impression is reinforced when it is realised that each day began and ended with prayer and the singing of the *Trisagion*. Clergy accompanied the army and solemn services were even held on the field of battle. Even the pass-word (*signon, signum*), issued afresh each evening, usually had a religious content.[2] The Greek battle-cry 'the Cross has conquered', like the earlier Latin one 'God with us', is further evidence that the religious spirit had penetrated the army. In this connection may also be mentioned the important part played by the veneration of military patron saints in the imperial army, saints such as the Archangel Michael, '*Archistrategus*' of the Heavenly Hosts, and the knightly martyrs, such as St George, St Demetrius and others. The wars with the Arabs at times suggest crusading ideas.[3] Indeed,

---

[1] Pseudo-Nicephorus Phocas, Περὶ παραδρομῆς πολέμου (ed. C. B. Hase, *CSHB*); *MPG*, cxvii. Cf. Y. A. Kulakovsky, 'Στρατηγικὴ ἔκθεσις καὶ σύνταξις', *Mém. Acad. Imp. de Pétersbourg*, 8 ser., viii (1908).

[2] *De cerim.* i, App. p. 481, 11 ff.

[3] But see V. Laurent, 'L'idée de guerre sainte et la tradition byzantine', *RHSE*, xxiii (1946), 71 ff.

Nicephorus II Phocas held the opinion that death in battle with the infidel counted as an actual martyrdom, though he could not get the Church to agree with him.[1] Byzantine battle songs from the best periods of the army are really hymns, breathing a proud fighting spirit in which trust in God is combined with sublime self-confidence. In the Epic of Digenis Akritas (cf. above, p. 38) in which the ideals of this heroic age are nostalgically recalled, the fighting spirit of the Byzantine army finds its continuing expression. Yet here, too, is re-echoed the indomitable self-assurance of the military aristocracy which helped to discredit the old military organisation in the eyes of the government and the civil bureaucracy. And yet, and despite all the fluctuations of strength and weakness which occurred over the centuries, the Byzantine army must have the credit of having been the chief bulwark of Europe against the Arab flood. Even in the later periods of decline, to which the West made its own contribution by striking the Empire in the rear, this army could still soften the impact of the Turkish invasion, although it could not for ever stave off its onward progress.

IV

The fleet shares with the army the renown of having averted the peril of Arab attack. The creation of a battle fleet, indeed, is one of the titles to fame of the Byzantine rulers. To the Romans, the Mediterranean was in truth 'Mare Nostrum', and until the Vandal invasion the Roman fleet was engaged more in police duties than in warlike activities. The skill of the Vandals at sea forced the Empire to take counter-measures for a time, although sea-power was still to play only a subordinate part in the wars of Justinian; however, when sea-battles did occur, as in the war with the Ostrogoths, the seamen of the coasts of the eastern Mediterranean finally showed their superiority. The modest fleet of Heraclius was able to prevent the Persians from crossing the Bosphorus and thus destroyed their plan of a joint attack with the Avars on Constantinople. Later, when the Arabs were forcing the Empire to fight for existence, the importance of a fleet was again fully recognised, particularly when Mu'āwiya, as governor of Syria, with a newly assembled Phoenician and Egyptian fleet, took first Cyprus, then Rhodes and Cos, and finally defeated the Emperor Constans II in a sea-battle off the coast of Lycia. It was not only Greek fire which checked the powerful and tenacious assault of the Caliph Mu'āwiya's Arab seamen on Constantinople, but also the counter-operations of the fleet, which had been created as part of the system of themes within the framework of the military reinforcement

[1] Zonaras, 16, 25, III, p. 506 (*CSHB*).

of the Empire. In 687 the maritime theme of the Carabisiani was in existence;[1] the name is derived from *carabos*, a kind of ship. The fleet and manpower was supplied by the coastal districts of Asia Minor and the Aegean islands. Command was vested in the *strategus* of the Carabisiani, or the τῶν πλοϊζομένων, whose headquarters were at Samos; under him were two admirals, or *drungarii*. From the beginning an important part was also played by the Cibyrraeots (named after the town of Cibyra in Pamphylia), under their *drungarii*. The decisive role of the fleet in insurrections at the end of the seventh and in the early eighth centuries, combined perhaps with the partiality of the seamen towards the icons, led to a division of the unified command of the fleet and to a temporary reduction of strength; but this also coincided with an abatement in the Arab counter-attacks. Under Leo III the theme of the Carabisiani was replaced by two naval units; one was that of the Cibyrraeots, in south and south-east Asia Minor, under a *strategus*, and the other that of the Dodecanese or the Aegean Sea, under a *drungarius*.[2] It was only in the ninth century, when the Andalusian Arabs took Crete, and under the leadership of the Aghlabids of Tunis established themselves in Sicily, using this stronghold as a base from which to ravage the coasts of the Empire, without meeting at first any noticeable rebuff, that strenuous efforts were made to atone for the former neglect of the fleet. Michael III and his successor Basil took the work of reconstruction in hand. Before the end of the ninth century the two existing maritime themes (now both under *strategi*) were joined by a third, the theme of Samos. The *strategi* of the fleet ranked with those of the western themes but drew their salaries from the central exchequer: since this was only ten gold pounds they clearly ranked in the lowest salary scale of the *strategi*.[3] The European coastal themes were also drawn into the naval service, in particular Peloponnese, Cephalonia and Nicopolis.[4]

There was also the imperial fleet (βασιλικοπλόϊμον), stationed at Constantinople and independent of the theme fleets (θεματικοὶ στόλοι); this was commanded by the *drungarius τοῦ πλοΐμου*, who in the first half of the ninth century (according to the *Tacticon* of Uspensky) ranked after the *domestici* and *chartularii*. The reorganisation of the fleet already mentioned brought promotion to this officer:

---

[1] Mansi, IX, 737; A. Pertusi, *op. cit.* p. 149.

[2] *Ibid.* p. 150.

[3] *De cerim.* II, 50, p. 697, 8 ff.; J. B. Bury, *The Imperial Administrative System*, p. 40.

[4] J. B. Bury, 'The Naval Policy of the Roman Empire in relation to the Western Provinces from the 7th to the 9th century', *Centenario di Michele Amari*, II (Palermo, 1910), 21 ff.; L. Bréhier, 'La marine du Byzance du VIIIe au IXe siècle', *B*, XIX (1949), 1 ff.

according to Philotheus he ranked thirty-eighth, after the Logothete
τοῦ δρόμου, or possibly before him. This *drungarius* was counted
among the stratarchs.[1] When the whole fleet combined in action he
could assume the supreme command. It is clear that the enemies of
the Empire were forced to reckon with its naval strength. If Constantine VII Porphyrogenitus boasted of a naval supremacy reaching
to the Pillars of Hercules it must be assumed that his historical
reminiscing had got the better of his appreciation of actual fact.[2]
But Nicephorus II Phocas, the conqueror of Crete, had much more
justification in declaring to the envoy of Otto the Great (Liutprand
of Cremona) that he was the sole possessor of sea-power.[3] The
De officiis regiis libellus, written in the eleventh century, also
claims the fleet as the chief title to fame of the Roman Empire
although it was already in fact falling into decay.[4] Even in the days
of its glory the fleet had taken only second place in the defence of the
Empire; once tension had relaxed with the slackening of external
pressure, the fleet suffered perhaps even more than the army from
the anti-militaristic attitude of the government. The invasion of the
Seljuqs, which disrupted the organisation of the provincial fleet of
Asia Minor, contributed heavily to a further decline. It is true that
Alexius I Comnenus later tried to repair the damage; he united what
remained of the theme navies with the imperial fleet (βασιλικὸς
στόλος) under a Grand Admiral, the *Megas Dux*,[5] who had as his chief
subordinate a Vice-Admiral, the *Megas Drungarius*, and these two
commands survived to the end.[6] But the great influx of mercenaries
into the fleet and the enlistment of aid from Venice and Genoa (at
first only occasionally but later as a matter of course), in return for
trading concessions, shows that this was a period of growing weakness. The fleet continued to fall rapidly and obviously into decay. The
Doge Dandolo knew only too well the weakness of the former master
of Venice when he launched the successful attack on Constantinople
in the Fourth Crusade. The period of reconstruction gave the Emperors at Nicaea further opportunity to recognise the importance of
the fleet, and Michael VIII Palaeologus built his fleet with an eye to
its use as a serviceable weapon. But it was always too weak to gain
anything but isolated victories, and could take no effective part in

[1] *De cerim.* II, 44, p. 651, 18; J. B. Bury, *The Imperial Administrative System*,
pp. 137, 14; 140, 25; 147, 14 and 149, 12; cf. 138, 29.
[2] *De thematibus*, 10, 5ff., p. 94 (ed. A. Pertusi).
[3] Liutprand, *Legatio*, 11, p. 182, 11 (ed. J. Becker): 'navigantium fortitudo mihi
soli inest.'
[4] P. 101 (ed. B. Wassiliewsky and V. Jernstedt, with Cecaumenus' *Strategicon*):
ὁ στόλος ἐστὶν ἡ δόξα τῆς Ῥωμανίας.
[5] Anna Comnena, VII, 8; IX, 1 (II, p. 115 and p. 158, ed. B. Leib).
[6] Ps.-Codinus, *De off.* V, p. 28, 12ff. and p. 36, 20ff.

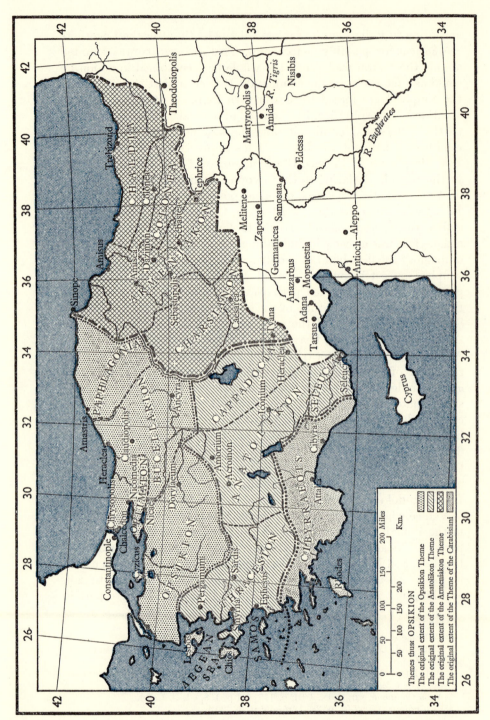

Map 1. Byzantine themes from the seventh to the ninth century.

Themes thus: OPSIKION
⬚⬚⬚ The original extent of the Opsikion Theme
▨▨▨ The original extent of the Anatolikon Theme
▩▩▩ The original extent of the Armeniakon Theme
▦▦▦ The original extent of the Theme of the Carabisiani

THRAKESION
ANATOLIKON
OPSIKION
OPTIMATON
BUCELLARION
PAPHLAGONIA
ARMENIAKON
CHALDIA
CHARSIANON
COLONEA
CAPPADOCIA
SELEUCIA
CIBYRRAEOTS

Constantinople
Chalcedon
Cyzicus
Nicaea
Nicomedi
Chrysopolis
Heraclea
Amastris
Claudiopolis
Dorylaeum
Ancyra
Pergamum
Sardis
Smyrna
Ephesus
Samos
Chios
Lesbos
AEGEAN SEA
Rhodes
Amorium
Acroinon
Iconium
Heraclea
Tyana
Caesarea
Sebastopolis
Amasea
Dazimon
Sinope
Amisus
Trebizond
Coloneat
Sebastea
Tephrice
Theodosiopolis
Melitene
Zapetra
Samosata
Germanicea
Anazarbus
Mopsuestia
Adana
Tarsus
Seleucia
Cyprus
Antioch
Aleppo
Edessa
Amida
Nisibis
Martyropolis
R. Tigris
R. Euphrates

Km.
0   50   100   150   200
0   50   100   150   200 Miles

the competition between the Italian sea-powers for the mastery of the Mediterranean.

Byzantine warships in general were known as dromons (δρόμονες). But the actual dromons were the real battleships, boats of varying size with two banks of oars and occasionally also with sails to aid in swiftness, and having a complement of from a hundred to three hundred men, according to the size of the vessel. According to the *Tacticon* of Leo a dromon of medium size would have a crew of 130, 100 of whom were oarsmen.[1] Ships of a special construction, also with two banks of oars, were called *pamphyli*. They had greater speed and could be easily manœuvred, but despite these features, more characteristic of a cruiser, they were also used in set battles. In the tenth century the flagship of the admiral was a particularly large *pamphylus* with an equally superior turn of speed, and a hand-picked crew.[2] In addition there were despatch boats with only one bank of oars used for small expeditions and observation; these were called *galaiai* and *moneria*.[3] They were manned by the holders of sailors' estates in the maritime themes and also by Mardaites from Amarus, who were settled in the coastal provinces; at a later date aliens were also used. In the tenth century the strength of the imperial fleet exceeded that of the theme fleets: for the expedition against Crete of 902 the fleet based on Constantinople sent 60 dromons and 40 *pamphyli*, while the maritime themes together sent only 35 of each category, though there were a further 10 dromons from Hellas.[4] It is impossible to determine from the sources the average total strength of the fleet; moreover, trading vessels were on occasion pressed into service in time of war, and worn-out ships were also recommissioned. A particularly useful weapon was the ramming spur, since Byzantine men-of-war could be manœuvred with such ease.

But the real superiority of the East Roman fleet was chiefly due to the weapon of Greek fire, an invention of the Syrian Greek Callinicus of Heliopolis (Baalbek); though it might be more accurate to describe it as the rediscovery of an older invention, since it is known that under Anastasius I Constantinople was defended by the use of some inextinguishable burning substance produced by a certain Athenian named Proclus.[5] The manufacture of this Greek fire, which had been improved in the course of time, was a strongly guarded state secret.[6]

---

[1] Leo, *Tact.* 19, 4. Cf. P. Serre's reconstruction, in *Les marines de guerre de l'antiquité et du moyen âge* (Paris, 1885), pp. 89 ff.

[2] Leo, *Tact.* 19, 37. [3] *Ibid.* 19, 10.

[4] *De cerim.* II, 44, p. 652, 9 ff.

[5] Theophanes, p. 354, 14 ff.; Const. Porph., *DAI*, I, c. 48, 29, p. 226; Malalas, p. 403, 14 ff. (*CSHB*); John of Nikiu, p. 89, 78 ff. (ed. R. H. Charles).

[6] Const. Porph., *DAI*, I, c. 13, pp. 73 ff.

A ninth-century treatise, which has survived only in a Latin translation, gives a few vague hints indicating that it was compounded of
sulphur, saltpetre and naphtha.[1] Catapults hurled the burning substance on to the enemy ships. In addition, the ships' bows were
fitted with tubes (σίφωνες) from which projectiles could be fired,
probably by a kind of gun-powder; these would explode on hitting
anything, as did the hand-grenades, which were provided with a fuse.
Despite this great superiority of armament, there was even greater
caution over sending the fleet into action than in the case of the
army, as we know from the instructions laid down by Leo VI. The
admirals were allowed to offer set battle only if they possessed
numerical superiority and if the engagement was unavoidable in the
interests of defence. Great emphasis was laid on the training and
drilling of ships' companies and on acquiring sound knowledge of
navigable waters and coastal topography. Orders were given by
means of a signalling system involving flags and lights. All in all,
however, despite several important technical achievements and good
direction, the impression remains that the science of seamanship did
not achieve the development which might have been expected in
Byzantium, when one considers the importance of the fleet for the
defence of the Empire. Moreover, despite the achievements of the
navy, which were at times considerable, it never gained the prestige of
the army and had to be content with a secondary rank. A Michael VIII
could rightly comprehend that only supremacy at sea could bring real
security to Constantinople:[2] but he lacked the means and opportunity
of putting his ideas into practice. The handful of ships, most of them
foreigners, with which Constantine XI met the Turks in his last
battle, achieved one last fleeting success before the destiny of the
Empire was sealed:[3] thus, even in demise, there was remembrance
of better times past.

V

For the Byzantine Empire, as for any state, war was merely a
continuation of foreign policy by another means. Yet despite the
numerous wars which fill its annals, it cannot really be said that the
Byzantine state was warlike by nature. On the contrary, there was a
preference for the use of diplomacy as a means of advocating and
protecting the country's interests. Even bellicose Emperors thought
it was advantageous to reach their aims by the diplomatic arts rather

---

[1] M. Berthelot, *La chimie au moyen âge*, I (Paris, 1893), 100f.
[2] Pachymeres, IV, 26 (I, pp. 309–10, *CSHB*).
[3] Ducas, c. 38 (*MPG*, CLVII, 1077); Phrantzes, *Chron. maj.* III, 3 (*MPG*, CLVI, 836);
Critobulus, I, 40–41 (*FHG*, V, pp. 84–6).

than by the sword. At all periods there was thus a highly subtle diplomacy at work. We must not, however, measure its achievement by the standard of modern diplomatic services. There was no permanent diplomatic representation abroad, with the late exception of that at the Turkish court.[1] Nevertheless, Byzantine history is made up of a long and unbroken succession of diplomatic negotiations.

Admittedly, there was no central administrative office concerned exclusively with foreign policy. It is true that the Logothete τοῦ δρόμου can in a sense be described as a kind of Foreign Minister; but it must not be forgotten that he had a number of other duties and that he was concerned largely with the formal apparatus of foreign relations. Despite the close relations between the Logothete τοῦ δρόμου and the Emperor, it was the Emperor who had the last word. And even he was bound by the formalities of protocol to a tradition which long experience had perfectly adapted to different states and peoples, adding an essential element to the prestige of the Emperor and the Empire *vis-à-vis* the outside world. The claim of the Byzantine rulers to a position of overriding supremacy remained indefeasible to the end: witness its expression in the artificial system of relationships known as the 'family of the kings', a concept which was at once secular and political and spiritual and mystical.[2] Admittedly, in practice the historical situation not infrequently led to certain concessions and modifications, but these were always regarded as merely temporary arrangements.

The reception accorded to foreign guests and embassies was hedged about with a precisely regulated and ceremonious etiquette from the moment of their arrival at Constantinople. The aim was to impress foreigners by the splendour of the capital and the pomp of the court and its ceremonial. The formalities and rank prescribed for an ambassador were determined by the importance of the country he represented. Liutprand of Cremona, the envoy of Otto the Great, remarked with some distaste that the Bulgarian envoy was ranked before him: this was because the Bulgars, as representatives of a ruler closely linked with the imperial house, had since 927 been given precedence over all other foreigners.[3] An envoy's first impression of his reception by the Emperor must usually have been overwhelming. The foreigner was led into the Audience Hall of the palace through rows of imperial bodyguards with glittering arms and past the assembled throng of high dignitaries in rich vesture. One final curtain was drawn aside to expose the Emperor clad in his robes of state and

---

[1] Phrantzes, *Chron. minus, MPG,* CLVI, 1028.
[2] See above: p. 9, n. 2.
[3] Liutprand, *Legatio,* c. 19, p. 186 (ed. J. Becker).

seated on his throne. Golden roaring lions watched about the imperial throne and mechanical golden birds sang in a gilded tree. And while the envoy made the three prescribed prostrations, the throne was raised aloft to mark the unapproachability of the now yet more richly bedecked monarch. During this first audience the Emperor remained motionless and silent, like the image of a saint; only the Logothete spoke to the visitor, and even his words were determined by protocol, as was the salutation pronounced by the envoy. If Liutprand was prone on occasion to boast that he had felt no particular amazement at this reception when he first went to Constantinople, this must be accounted an exaggeration, even though he had previously made detailed inquiries about what was likely to take place.[1] The envoy might later be invited to the imperial table and received in special audience. For the rest, ambassadors were very closely watched during their stay in the Empire and in Constantinople. And just because the Emperor expected information from his own ambassadors based on their observations made during their travels and sojourns in foreign lands, care was taken to ensure that foreigners at Byzantium did not see or hear more than the imperial government desired they should. In general ambassadors were admittedly afforded the protection of international law, but in matters of ceremonial they were entirely subordinate to the imperial will and in some cases even had to atone for any lack of respect towards the Autocrator on the part of their own masters by suffering imprisonment.[2]

Anyone who went abroad—missionaries, for example, or merchants, as well as the officially commissioned ambassadors—was expected to bring back information for the assistance of the imperial government. For example, such people could give advice on persons who might possibly be given presents and thus persuaded to use their influence to further the aims of the Empire, and on the kind of presents which would be acceptable. Much of the advice given by Constantine VII Porphyrogenitus in his book *De Administrando Imperio*, written to instruct his son in the practice of affairs, was probably built up on the basis of such intelligence.[3] In time a carefully balanced scale of present-giving seems to have been evolved.[4]

Such was the part played in diplomacy by the central government. Local officials in frontier districts must also have had special authority to keep a watch on neighbouring states and peoples and power to enter into diplomatic relations with them. Such powers were enjoyed

---

[1] Liutprand, *Antapodosis*, vi, 5, p. 154, 5ff; *De cerim.* ii, 15, p. 566, 15ff.; ii, 47, p. 680, 1ff.

[2] E.g. the legates of Pope John XIII: Liutprand, *Legatio*, c. 47 and c. 49, pp. 200–1.

[3] J. B. Bury, *BZ*, xv (1906), 538f.

[4] *De cerim.* ii, 44, p. 661.

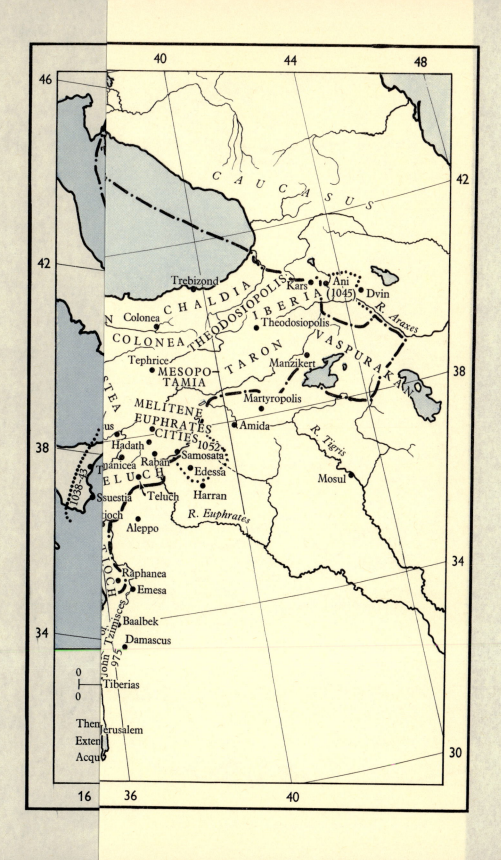

CAUCASUS

Trebizond

CHALDIA

Colonea

COLONEA

Tephrice

MESOPO-
TAMIA

MELITENE

EUPHRATES
CITIES

Hadath

1038-43

Tananicea

Raban

Teluch

Ssuestia

tioch

Aleppo

Raphanea

Emesa

Baalbek

Damascus

John Tzimisces

975

Tiberias

Then
Exten
Acqu

Jerusalem

THEODOSIOPOLIS

Kars

Ani
(1045)

Dvin

IBERIA

Theodosiopolis

R. Araxes

TARON

Manzikert

VASPURAKAN

Martyropolis

Amida

R. Tigris

1052

Samosata

Edessa

Mosul

Harran

R. Euphrates

16   36   40

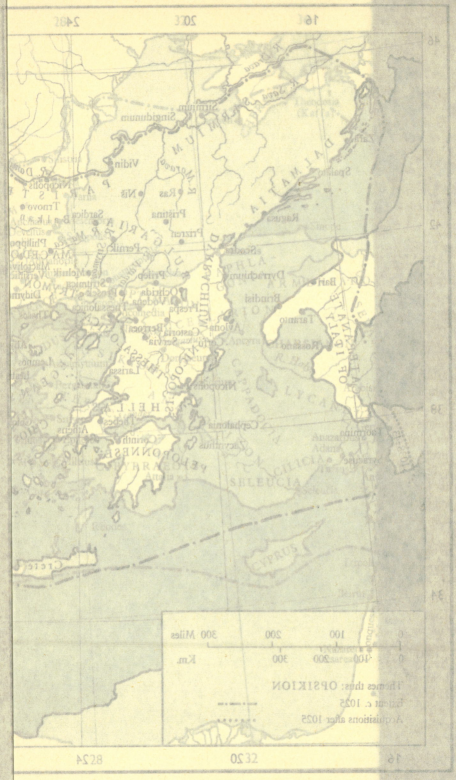

Map 2. The Byzantine empire, c. 1025.

by the *strategi* in Italy (later catepans): in this they resembled their predecessors the exarchs, enjoying at times great independence and treating not only with the Arabs but also, on occasion, with the Pope. The *strategus* of Cherson also had an important part to play in the dealings of the Empire with the peoples of the steppes, the Khazars, and, at a later date, the Pechenegs.

Byzantine diplomacy has already appeared as a costly undertaking, with its impressive outlay of expenditure on behalf of individual embassies, together with the numerous and expensive presents which were offered; this cost was further increased by the fact that it was not considered derogatory to the prestige of the Empire to make regular payments to foreign princes in the interests of peace, as occasion demanded. To those who received it, this ready flow of money appeared as tribute; but to the Emperor it represented a wise principle of government and a diplomatic victory. Money might also be paid out as a subsidy for help in time of war. The Byzantine government usually observed its treaty obligations; nevertheless it was not regarded as wrong to incite a third party to enmity towards a country presently allied to and at peace with the Empire. Much of the advice given by Constantine VII to his son Romanus, which is contained in the *De Administrando Imperio*, deals with such possibilities and the advantages likely to accrue to the Empire as a result. In any case the prospect of handicapping an actual or potential antagonist in good time was always regarded as a reasonable and profitable ground for action. For this reason pretenders and political refugees were always welcomed in Constantinople as possible tools to be used in the government's scheme of foreign policy; in short, by its reception of such people, the Byzantine government was able to exert a certain amount of pressure on foreign powers.

Political marriages also played an increasingly important part in Byzantine diplomacy. It is true that Constantine Porphyrogenitus thought it incongruous and wholly preposterous for an imperial prince or princess to marry a foreigner, and particularly a northerner.[1] But there had already been Khazar princesses who had married Emperors, the wives of Justinian II and Constantine V, and before the tenth century had run its course the purple-born Anna, granddaughter of Constantine VII, had become the wife of Vladimir of Kiev, though this was an exceptional case, the result of special external pressure. It was only later, and particularly under the Nicaean Emperors and the Palaeologi, that marriages between imperial princesses and foreigners, Slav rulers in particular, became relatively frequent. A number of the Empresses of the Palaeologi were

---

[1] *DAI*, c. 13 (I, pp. 104 ff.).

westerners. These marriage alliances often failed to produce the results expected of them, chiefly because Byzantine pride was such that foreign Empresses were never allowed to become popular.

The work of the Christian missionaries was at times also of considerable diplomatic effect; in fact the successful conversion of neighbouring heathen peoples can to some extent be accounted as a triumph of imperial diplomacy. However, such peoples were by no means permanently freed from a frankly non-Christian cupidity which they tried to satisfy at the expense of the Empire and which could not always be curbed by diplomatic means. Still less successful—on the long view in fact it was a distinct failure—was the attempted union with the Western Church (to be achieved only by making concessions in dogma and submitting to the papal supremacy) in the hope of gaining western support. Such attempts always foundered on the alert watchfulness of the Emperor's own subjects, who were prepared to meet them with an increasingly ready resistance.

All things considered, Byzantine diplomacy in all its forms was a very expensive business, and depended ultimately for its success on the financial reserves and potentialities of the state. And yet, apart from this, it must be allowed that the Byzantines, who have often been wrongly accused of clumsiness and rigidity, in their employment of diplomacy always showed, even in the worst periods, a remarkable flexibility and power of adaptation to the demands of the moment. It is true that they did not shrink from objectionable methods even in diplomacy, but history would be hard put to it to find any other state less guilty. And over the centuries these very capacities and the accumulated experience of the Byzantine government in the field of diplomacy were a constant source of the Empire's superiority and were often used to excellent effect.

CHAPTER XXI

BYZANTINE LAW

In November 534 Justinian issued the revised edition of the *Codex* and in doing so completed the Justinianian codification, which comprised three books of law, the *Digest* (or *Pandects*), the *Codex* and the *Institutes*. During the rest of his long reign the Emperor made amendments and additions to this codification in constitutions which were called *Novels* (*Novellae post Codicem constitutiones*, νεαραὶ μετὰ τὸν κώδικα διατάξεις), and were not incorporated in the body of the codification.[1] This codification exerted such a powerful influence on later legal development and is so much a final summing-up of Roman law that it is usual to regard it as the beginning of a new era of legal history, that is, the Byzantine period. So great was the influence of this codification—this mighty edifice, constructed out of the material of classical jurisprudence—that it dominated the Greek East until the fall of Constantinople and even later, while in the course of the middle ages it also conquered the whole of western Europe as the result of the remarkable phenomenon that has been called the reception of Roman law. The dominating influence of Justinianian law gives an appearance of immutability to Byzantine law; on the surface Byzantine legal development seems to reflect the predominance of now one, now another, aspect of the Justinianian system. Yet this rigidity is often more apparent than real; the Justinianian texts which were translated into Greek are often of academic rather than practical significance and the original sources have acquired an entirely new meaning because of revised interpretations.

One cannot but assume that the Justinianian codification was preceded by a period in which legal scholarship attained a fairly high level; the codification itself and the wealth of juristic literature associated with it are inconceivable without a long and thorough preparation. The few available sources suggest that this high standard was especially connected with the law school at Beirut, which was of great importance, even after 534, until a devastating earthquake put an end to its existence in 551. But while there is fairly adequate information concerning the teaching at this law school, based on references to the curriculum in the introductory constitutions to the Justinianian codification, there is comparatively little

---

[1] By the term 'Justinianian codification' the Corpus of *Institutes*, *Codex* and *Digest* (or *Pandects*) as a single whole is understood. When the *Novels* as well are referred to, the term 'Justinianian legislation' is used.

evidence for the scholarly activities before the codification. The few fragments of legal literature of that period point to an exegesis of the classical Latin sources possibly given in lectures to students.[1]

Leading lawyers of the Empire served on the commissions entrusted with the codification, and originally the greater part of the research necessitated by the new legislation was done by these committee members. They set themselves the task of making the elaborate and difficult system of legislation accessible for practical use. The first thing required for that purpose was that it should be translated into Greek. When Justinian decided to issue his codification mainly in Latin he must have done so for a variety of reasons: his own personal preference, the fact that Latin sources of law had been used in the past, the presence of an important if not numerous Latin-speaking minority still living in his Empire, and his hope of re-establishing his power in the West and thereby the Roman domains to their original extent. But this ideal was only partially realised, while in the preceding centuries the importance of these western regions had diminished in comparison to that of the East, where knowledge of Latin was rapidly declining. It was therefore essential to make the legislation accessible to those to whom it was unintelligible by reason of its language. This was first done at the two universities, Constantinople and Beirut. In Justinian's day, education at these centres was entirely dominated by linguistic difficulties connected with the legal sources. From 535 onwards there were two faculties of law in the Roman empire. The older and more famous centre, attracting students from far and wide, was at Beirut; the second formed part of the university of Constantinople. Each faculty contained a very limited number of professors, probably four, who received government remuneration and were entitled to make use of public classrooms. Apart from these, there were probably teachers who taught in their own homes and whose stipend consisted of their students' tuition fees. Each professor's instruction covered the whole field of jurisprudence; a pupil had only one professor who, in the course of four (and after 534, five) years, initiated him in every aspect of the law.

The curriculum is known in all its detail. After 534 it included the three branches of the Justinianian codification (*Institutes*, *Digest* and *Codex*). Out of the 50 *Digests* only 26 were dealt with at the lectures (βιβλία πραττόμενα); pupils were supposed to study the other books on their own (*per semet ipsos*). It is probable that in about 555 a sixth year was added to the course for the purpose of studying the

[1] In Justinian's days the legal sources were always used in the original language, that is, chiefly in Latin.

ever-increasing number of novels. The very extensive law literature of those days largely emanated from lecture courses and consisted of lecture notes, sometimes written up in considerable detail. Only two of these edited notebooks have been handed down complete: the *Paraphrase of Institutes* by Theophilus and the *Epitome Novellarum* by Julian. Of the remainder, numerous fragments have survived. These are taken from commentaries on the *Digest* by Theophilus, Stephanus, Isidore and Cobidas, and on the *Codex* by Thalelaeus and Isidore. These writings clearly reveal the educational system of the *antecessores* (ἀντικήνσορες), as the professors of law were called. The legal sources were dealt with twice, passage by passage. First the professor would dictate a continuous paraphrase or translation, called the Index, and during the second lecture he would make general observations on the same passage (παραγραφαί). This second lecture would take the form of an interrogation and the *antecessor* would answer questions put to him by the students (ἀπορίαι καὶ λύσεις, ἐρωταποκρίσεις). This system of double lectures was a direct result of the language problem that most of the students had to contend with. The codification was almost entirely compiled in Latin but the majority of the pupils were Greek-speaking, so that they had some difficulty in reading the Latin sources. The Index served to familiarise them with the general contents. The Latin text (τὸ ῥητόν) was dealt with during the second lecture. Prior to their studies in law young men would often attend instruction in rhetoric during which they would acquire some familiarity with Latin. While Agathias was taking this preparatory course at Beirut the town was completely destroyed by the earthquake of 551, so that he had to continue his studies in rhetoric at Alexandria.

There were of course Latin-speaking students who attended lectures held in Latin. As long as the codification alone was concerned they had no need of the Index, but the situation was reversed when in about 555 the curriculum was expanded to include the novels, which were issued mainly in Greek. Here it was the Latin-speaking students who were in need of an index, and so the only surviving Index of the novels, that of Julian, is in Latin. These various linguistic difficulties gave rise to another remarkable expedient: the *interpretatio κατὰ πόδας*. The many surviving fragments of the *Kata Podas* of the *Codex* show a completely literal translation which for this reason alone would often be unintelligible, quite apart from having been handed down in an extremely corrupt version. From the nature of the corruptions it can be deduced that these translations were originally written above the lines of a Latin manuscript of the *Codex*. Thalelaeus made use of such versions in his lectures. The Latin of the *constitu-*

tiones which were included in the *Codex* was so difficult that the Greek student, even with the help of an index, obviously could not make sense of it. That is why Thalelaeus, in his παραγραφαί lectures, provided a Latin *Codex* text (ῥητόν) which contained an *interpretatio* κατὰ πόδας. Other professors seized on different expedients; Isidore for instance added to the index of every *constitutio* in the *Codex* a small glossary of difficult Latin words and their Greek translations. For Latin students, who had similar difficulties with the Greek novels, there was a Latin *Kata Podas*, which has survived under the name of the *Authenticum*. At about the time of Justinian's death (565) there were apparently certain significant changes in the system of education. Latin texts seem to have been abandoned, so that the notes on the *Digest* which derived from the so-called Anonymus II, otherwise known as Enantiophanes, do not elucidate the Latin original, but a Greek abstract, the *Summa Anonymi I*. Theodore of Hermopolis' interpretation of the *Codex* is also based on a Greek synopsis. There was now no distinction made between the books of the *Digest* which were dealt with in lectures and those which were not (βιβλία πραττόμενα and ἐξτραόρδινα); as a result citing from the *Digest* according to *partes* fell into disuse. Finally the *antecessores* themselves were no longer mentioned; of the three jurists of this later period whose works have been entirely or partially preserved (Theodore, Athanasius, Enantiophanes), two were barristers (σχολαστικός), while nothing is known about the third. All this seems to suggest that the faculty of law at Constantinople came to an end about the time of Justinian's death (the law faculty at Beirut had ceased to function in 551) and that barristers were now in charge of legal education.

A great deal of written material has come down to us from the teaching by the *antecessores*. This chiefly consists of lecture notes which have been written up, sometimes extensively so (possibly by the pupils). Only two of these reports have survived in their entirety. The first is the *Paraphrasis Institutionum* of Theophilus, in which the writer combined the Index and the παραγραφαί. The *Paraphrasis* is based on a lecture on the *Institutes* given during the academic year 533–4, as is evident from the fact that there is a reference to the first *Codex* of 529. The beginning is missing, possibly because the *Institutes* were not published until some time in November, whereas the lectures began in October. The Latin Index of Novels compiled by the *antecessor* Julian, as well as a small section of his παραγραφαί, have also been preserved complete. It is not known whether it was Julian or some unknown *antecessor* who used the surviving *Authenticum*. Apart from these, there are several longer and shorter fragments of the Index of the *Digest* and the *Paragraphai* on the *Digest* of

Stephanus[1] and of the Index and *Paragraphai* on the *Codex* of Thalelaeus, as well as of the *Kata Podas* used by him. Little remains of the other lectures given by Isidore, Cobidas and Anastasius.

Apart from these lecture-notes, the *antecessores* have left a number of writings which were published at the time in book form. None of these exists in its entirety, but many fragments have survived, notably from the *Digest* summaries of Cyril and Anonymus I, the *Digest* translation of Dorotheus, and the *Codex* summary of Anatolius.

In view of this wealth of literature it is hard to see the purpose of Justinian's ban on the commentaries. In the *Constitutio Deo auctore*, cap. 2, and in the *Constitutio Tanta* (Δέδωκεν) the Emperor prohibited the linking (*adnectere*) of the *Digest* to the commentaries; all he allowed were *Indices* (mentioned only in the *Constitutio Deo auctore*), *Paratitla* ('admonere per titulorum suptilitatem') and *Interpretatio* κατὰ πόδας. The reason for the ban was fear of confusion, which according to the Emperor had once occurred when the Praetoric edict was furnished with commentaries. But although the ban was accompanied by heavy penalties, there is nothing to show that it was at all effective. Possibly the Emperor wished to prevent the *Digest* from being glossed, since this could so easily cause corruption of the text. If the ban was intended to prevent interpretation by lawyers— and the wording could be understood in precisely this sense—then the Emperor failed to achieve his purpose. From the very outset there was divergence of opinion about the meaning of parts of the *Digest*; in fact two schools are mentioned, the Κωριδιανοί and the Θυλακιανοί, which might be compared with the Sabians and the Proculians.[2]

The period of the *antecessores*, which ends about 565, was the golden age of Byzantine law. Under Justinian's successors, Justin, Tiberius and Maurice, two more collections of excerpts from Justinianian novels were made, one by Theodore of Hermopolis, and one by Athanasius of Emesa, who were both barristers (σχολαστικοί). Another writer, working under Justinian's successors, is known as the Anonymus II, sometimes called Enantiophanes (ὁ Ἐναντιοφάνης) or Enantius (ὁ Ἐναντίος). This unidentified writer annotated the *Digest* summary of Anonymus I; his notes consist mainly of references to parallels (παραπομπαί). Furthermore he composed the treatise on legacies and *donationes mortis causa*, a work περὶ ἐναντιοφανείων and a nomocanon in XIV titles. Understandably attempts have been made to prove that the two Anonymi were one and the

---

[1] Heimbach places Stephanus, Cyril, Anonymus I and Cobidas too late; they were working between 540 and 550.

[2] Cf. the *scholion* in Ferrini, *Opere*, I, p. 172.

same person, but there is no justification for assuming this. The cross-references of the Anonymus II can serve as an accurate and reliable guide to the whole of the Justinianian legislation. The work περὶ ἐναντιοφανείων—from which later Byzantines made up the proper name Ἐναντιοφάνης or Ἐναντίος—consisted of similar references; it is by no means restricted to the real or imagined inconsistencies of Justinianian legislation (as the title seems to suggest), and the παραπομπαί that go under the name of Enantiophanes are often practically the same as those which are found under the name of the Anonymus. It is therefore not clear what purpose the work περὶ ἐναντιοφανείων was intended to serve since there was already the annotated *Digest* index. Of the little work on legacies nothing is known except the title. The *Nomocanon XIV titulorum* will be considered below.

The legal literature before Heraclius has been discussed in some detail, because this older Byzantine jurisprudence was the basis of practically all later Byzantine law. As already emphasised, this literature did in fact replace the original text (τὸ ῥητόν) of the Justinianian codification. It is impossible to tell exactly how long manuscripts of the original text remained in circulation; it seems that about 1050 the Latin *Codex* could still be read in the manuscripts of Thalelaeus (*Tract. de Peculiis*, 7). But by then these texts were seldom used owing to the general inability to read Latin. It is obvious that this development endangered the stability of legal foundations, since a single codification had now been displaced by a series of Greek versions. However much the editors had aimed at faithfully reproducing the contents of the Latin original, discrepancies must inevitably have appeared, as can be seen for instance in the differences between Cyril's index and that of Stephanus.

Whereas the Justinianian codification forms an unchanging element in Byzantine legal history, alterations in the law were mainly introduced by imperial constitutions or novels. Justinian himself had already issued important legislation after his codification; one need only think of the great Novels 118 and 125, which inaugurated a whole new system of intestate succession. These novels were never compiled into an official collection; various private compilations were, however, in circulation. After the Anonymus II, who used another collection now lost, the collection of 168 novels, composed about 580, came into general use. This collection of 168 novels has been adopted for instance in the edition of Schoell-Kroll. Besides novels of Justinian it contains some constitutions of Justin II and Tiberius II as well as some edicts of the Praefectus Praetorio.

The contents of the Justinianian novels cannot be discussed here, and in any case it is still usual for them to be incorporated in summaries of Roman law, for it is customary to consider them as supplements to the codification. In Byzantium, too, Justinian's novels shared the fortunes of the codification; thus, for instance, they formed part of Leo VI's *Basilica*.

The later Emperors also issued novels, but these laws lacked the prestige that the name of the great Justinian had conferred. In the time of Leo VI (886–912) these later constitutions had almost entirely gone out of use; consequently they have with a few exceptions all been lost. Of Justin II only three constitutions have been preserved apart from the ones that occur in the *collectio 168 novellarum*; of Tiberius II only two; of Maurice there is only a fragment of a constitution; of Phocas nothing. Four novels of Heraclius obviously owe their preservation to the circumstance that they deal with ecclesiastical matters. In this connection the novel of Justin II should be noted which abrogated the relevant clause of Novel 117 of Justinian and provided that marriages could be dissolved at the mere option of both parties; evidently the influence of canon law on the civil law at that time was not very great.

New law could come into existence not only by means of constitutions, but also by so-called custom, which, curiously enough, Justinian allowed to remain as valid law and for which he even made elaborate regulations (*Dig.* I, 3; *Cod.* VIII, 52). Knowledge of this customary law is extremely limited. On the other hand, in some frontier provinces the official law was ignored in important points and replaced by the law of neighbouring tribes living beyond the frontiers (*Nov. Justiniani* 154; *Nov. Justini II*, Coll. I, Nov. 3).

Before discussing the next period, Heraclius I to Basil I (610–867), a special kind of collection, the *nomocanones*, should be noted. In the Byzantine Empire, as elsewhere, two sovereign powers existed side by side: State and Church. Both issued legal rulings; by the side of the secular laws (νόμοι πολιτικοί) stood the ecclesiastical canons (κανόνες). The respective spheres of jurisdiction of these two legal systems were not clearly delimited; the Emperor often considered himself entitled to issue novels about purely dogmatic subjects, while the Church often tried to enforce the observance of its canons in the secular world. Contradictions were bound to lead to clashes between Church and State, and it is owing to the forbearance usually shown on both sides that such conflicts did not occur more often. Yet clashes could not be avoided; a well-known instance is that between the Patriarch Nicholas Mysticus and Leo VI on account of the Emperor's fourth marriage. In such conflicts the political situation was often the deciding factor. There was, however, a group of writings in which secular and ecclesiastical law was compared, usually by simply putting the relevant rulings side by side. These writings are called *nomocanones*. Some *nomocanones* are known which date as far back as Justinian's days, and in which secular and ecclesiastical law are still kept apart to the extent that canon law is given first, without interruption, and is then followed by secular law. But later the νόμοι and the *canones* were welded together into greater unity, and the writer of one of these *nomocanones*—the so-called *Nomocanon XIV titulorum* —is the Anonymus II who has already been mentioned under the name of Enantiophanes.

The vicissitudes of the teaching of law after Justinian are not clear. Vague and obscure reports hint at a decline under Phocas, and at restoration under Heraclius, but it can safely be assumed that at the time when the output of juristic writings was interrupted, that is, about 600, teaching had also fallen off. In the preface to the *Ecloga Isaurorum* (741) we look in vain for a professor among the members of the commission appointed. Consequently extant writings dating from the two and a half centuries between Heraclius (610–41) and Basil I (867–86) have an entirely different character and are much more primitive than those of the previous period. Very little indeed has come down to us from this later period: three novels, one of Leo IV and two of Irene, one official digest called the *Ecloga Isaurorum*, as well as two private codes, the so-called *lex Rhodia* and the so-called *leges rusticae*, both of which most probably belong to this period.

The *Ecloga* was presumably issued in 741[1] by the so-called Isaurian Emperors Leo III and Constantine V. It presents a short summary of the law then current, devoting in particular much space to family law. It seems that the *Ecloga* used as its sources not only the Justinianian legislation, but also the now lost novels of later Emperors, including those of Leo III and Constantine V themselves (*Prooem.* 2); these are the novels presumably referred to by that part of the title which indicates that Justinianian law had been altered in a more humane sense. It is not however likely that new law was introduced by the *Ecloga*. Accordingly the legislation which the *Ecloga* was intended to summarise was by no means abolished; the Justinianian legislation in particular remained in force though subject to derogation by means of later novels. The preface states that the law was dispersed in many books and that these books were too complicated, especially for the provincials; therefore, the Emperors had appointed a committee of three lawyers to make a comprehensive examination

[1] For a different dating see G. Ostrogorsky, *History of the Byzantine State* (Oxford, 1956), p. 134, and also above: pt. I, chapter III, p. 65.

of these books (the reference is probably to the Greek commentaries of the sixth and seventh centuries) and to extract from them the legal rulings in most frequent use. This committee consisted of the *quaestor sacri palatii* and two *magistri scriniorum*.

In the *Ecloga* the law is summarised in eighteen titles, some of which are very short, for example, those on *emptio-venditio* and on *depositum*. Important contracts, such as the *locatio-conductio operis faciendi*, are not treated at all. From this it appears at once that the *Ecloga* cannot possibly have settled the legal relationships of a great commercial city; it has in mind rather the needs of the provinces. There are moreover notable deviations from Justinianian law: no distinction is made, for instance, between *tutela* and *cura*; similarly other deviations can be observed in the law of succession. The system of punishments, often consisting of mutilation, also differs from Justinian's. Another striking feature is that for a contract of marriage the permission of both parties, bride as well as bridegroom, is required, that the marriageable age is fifteen for men and thirteen for women, that the marriage might be contracted by a deed by which the material effects were settled (apparently a new arrangement of the Isaurian Emperors, which did away with the above-mentioned novel of Justin II), and lastly that the *patria potestas* over children after they had attained their majority seems to have disappeared.

The Isaurian Emperors have wrongly been regarded as great legal reformers; only in a few odd cases can it be established that the deviations of the *Ecloga* from Justinianian legislation were introduced by Leo III and his son; most of these innovations probably derive from constitutions of their predecessors. Innovations have also been surmised where in reality Justinianian law was still followed; the law of dowry as it appears in the *Ecloga*, which is no more than a systematic résumé of the rulings of Justinian, has incorrectly been thought to introduce an entirely new system, even hinting at common ownership of property between husband and wife.

Basil I and his son Leo VI, who for religious reasons were very hostile to their Isaurian predecessors, formally abrogated the *Ecloga*; they considered it 'not a summary but a perversion of the law'. Nevertheless the *Ecloga Isaurorum* remained in use for a long time, especially in the provinces; centuries later traces of it are still found in South Italy and in Serbia, and even legal scholarship and legislation in the capital could not escape its influence.

It is unknown when the so-called *lex Rhodia* (the Rhodian Sea Law), a private collection of legal rulings bearing on shipping and maritime commerce, came into being. Of the three parts of which this work is composed, the first is a very confused preface, to which in its present form no reasonable meaning can be attributed. Yet it is possible that the oldest core of the work is to be found in this very preface. For in the well-known *Digest* fragment XIV, 2, 9 (*Volusius Maecianus e lege Rhodia*) there are some passages that also occur in this preface. Now opinions may differ as to whether the *Digest* borrowed these passages from the preface or whether the author of the preface later incorporated them into his writing to give it a more authentic appearance. The former supposition seems the more probable, for in the *Digest* fragment an existing *lex Rhodia* is confirmed and it is surely plausible to argue that our preface consists of the mangled remains of this maritime law. The second part of the *lex Rhodia* also possibly contains earlier elements; it consists of 19 excerpts, at least two of which, 17 and 18, were made from a text that was called ὁ Ῥόδιος νόμος. The third part does not however provide a single clue as to the date of its origin, but it can hardly be older than the seventh century. Nothing however can be maintained with certainty about the dating of the *lex Rhodia* in its present form except that it must be older than the tenth century, the period to which the manuscript tradition dates back.

The so-called *leges rusticae* (or Farmer's Law), likewise a private code for provincial use, also appear to date from the end of the seventh or from the beginning of the eighth century. The manuscripts wrongly attribute this codex to Justinian I whose codification unmistakably influenced its contents. The *leges rusticae* have especially attracted attention because they contain data about conditions in the country; their importance is, however, diminished by the fact that nothing whatever is known about their date and place of origin. The rural population to which they refer seems to have consisted of tenants who were not attached to the land and of small landowners. The absence of dependent peasants (πάροικοι) from the *leges rusticae* is no proof at all that this class did not then exist in the Byzantine Empire; it is very possible that these laws were written only for a certain district.

Only two[1] complete novels have been preserved from the period between Heraclius and Basil I. One of them is the Empress Irene's novel in which, from religious motives, she abolished legal oaths and also the oaths required in *Nov. Just.* 73 for the confirmation of a deed. She also laid it down that all contracts—both written and oral—should be made in the presence of five or seven witnesses. The contractual deeds were in some cases to be drawn up by public notaries; in most cases the parties could do it themselves. Does this mean that

---

[1] To these two Greek *constitutiones* should be added the Latin bull of the year 727, edited by E. Besta, *Studi Fadda*, I (Naples, 1906), 289 ff.

every *nudum pactum*, provided these regulations were observed when it was made, acquired complete legal validity, or is a *stipulatio* still required? In other words, does this novel of Irene put an end to the closed system of contracts of Roman law? This is unlikely; moreover it is known that as a result of a series of legal suppositions the *stipulatio* had already degenerated into a fixed formula in the deeds.

The reign of the Macedonian Basil I (867–86) brought about a renaissance of Justinianian law; under him and his son Leo VI the Justinianian legislation was stripped as much as possible of later additions so that the constitutions of the Emperors of the three intermediate centuries seem to have become dead letters. The immediate cause of this renaissance seems partly to have been the legal confusion already hinted at in the preface to the Isaurian *Ecloga*. On the other hand the powerful influence of the Patriarch Photius must be borne in mind. The sources provide very little information about this renaissance, the results of which (*Prochiron, Epanagoge, Basilica*) have for the greater part been preserved. Like the Isaurian *Ecloga* these books do not aim at creating new law, but only at making the existing law accessible; in this case the existing law was the Justinianian legislation. It was therefore still permissible after the promulgation of the Macedonian books of law, especially the *Basilica*, to appeal directly to the Justinianian legislation, and this was, in fact, sometimes done. The *Epitome legum*—a private collection of rules of law from the year 920—gathers most of its material directly from the sixth- and seventh-century commentaries, passing over the *Basilica*. The anonymous writer of the *Meditatio de nudis pactis* (about 1050) advises his friend to continue to use the *Digest* (that is, Stephanus' index) rather than the *Basilica*, because it contained more than the *Basilica* (*Meditatio de nudis pactis*, VI, 26).

Until well into the twelfth century the original Justinianian sources were still referred to rather than the *Basilica*, and it was not until 1169 that the imperial Court of Justice made a sensational decision in which the older legal sources were overruled by the *Basilica*, which thus gained the status of *legis auctoritas*. The occasion was as follows. In 1169 the episcopal see of Amisus had been vacant for a year. It was the duty of the metropolitan of Amasea to appoint a new bishop but for some reason or other he failed to do so. The patriarch of Constantinople had pressed him in vain and in the end the patriarch himself proceeded to make the appointment of the new bishop. In support of his action he could invoke a Justinianian law, but this had not however been included in the *Basilica* and the question arose as to whether this meant that the law had lost its *legis vigor*. According to the patriarch this was not so; but the

metropolitan maintained the contrary. It is clear from this that the
Justinianian law—or at any rate part of Novel 123—could not have
lost its *legis auctoritas* in about 900, for if so, then it is inconceivable
that this question would have been disputed as much as a century
and a half later. By that time to all intents and purposes the
Basilica had become the only form in which the Justinianian law
was known, and that is presumably why the imperial court of justice
gave judgement in favour of the metropolitan, ruling that a law
which was not included in the *Basilica* was invalid. At the time,
those concerned with legal matters were well aware of the crucial
significance of this verdict, and the patriarch commissioned the
learned monk Balsamon—who left this full account of the problem—
to investigate what other Justinianian laws were affected by this
ruling. Balsamon acquitted himself of his task by writing a commentary on the *Nomocanon XIV titulorum*.

Basil I, then, conceived a plan of making the Justinianian legislation more accessible by removing from it the clauses that had fallen
into disuse, by selecting for each law one of the current Greek versions,
and by arranging the fragments thus gathered in a new order so that
Digest, Codex, Institutes and novels would be amalgamated into one
system. Also he had the Latin technical terms replaced by the Greek
equivalents (ἐξελληνισμός), and he described these activities as the
ἀνακάθαρσις (*repurgatio*). Whether Basil I lived to see the completion
of this work the ambiguous sources do not reveal; his plans seem to
have fluctuated with regard to the scope and the arrangement of the
repurgatio; to this fact we may owe the preservation of two shorter
summaries of the law, the *Prochiron* and the *Epanagoge*, each of
which seems to have fitted in with a different project of the larger
work. The *Prochiron* (Πρόχειρος νόμος) is composed of forty titles the
contents of which have for the greater part been derived from the
Justinianian legislation; only a few clauses were taken from the
Ecloga and possibly from the constitutions of Basil himself. The
Epanagoge ('Επαναγωγή), likewise consisting of forty titles, is little
more than a new improved edition of the *Prochiron*.

Even if it is not clear whether Basil actually saw the promulgation
of his *repurgatio* or whether, as the sources might perhaps suggest,
two different editions appeared during his lifetime, the *repurgatio*
issued by his son Leo VI (886–912) and generally called by the name
of *Basilica*, has for the greater part been preserved until the present
day. In this great enterprise, consisting of sixty books, the *Digest*,
the *Codex* and the novels have been amalgamated into one work;
only very little was derived from the *Institutes*. For the *Digest* the
Summa Anonymi was as a rule used, for the *Codex* the translation

attached to the commentary by Thalelaeus and for the novels the original Greek text or the summary either by Theodore or by Athanasius. Hardly any alterations were made in these texts apart from the ἐξελληνισμοί. Thus many offices were mentioned and regulated in the *Basilica* that no longer existed in Leo VI's time.

The *Basilica* soon ousted the sixth- and seventh-century commentaries; only Theophilus' paraphrase of the *Institutes* could hold its own.[1] The old commentaries could be dispensed with all the more easily after their contents had been added to the *Basilica* in the form of scholia. A number of *Basilica* manuscripts present this apparatus of scholia more or less complete; to the text, which is usually that of the Anonymus, scholia were added giving versions by Cyril, Dorotheus and Stephanus, as well as exegetic annotations under the names of Stephanus, Anonymus and Enantiophanes.

It is obvious that legislation which was four centuries old could not be applied without alteration; in a collection of 113 novels Leo VI intended to provide the necessary corrections and reforms. A detailed survey of the contents of these novels is impossible here, and moreover some of them are not of great importance, either because they applied only to very rare cases, or because they were never applied at all. Special attention was paid by the Emperor to the laws of marriage and succession. We see how the bond created by a betrothal, if blessed by the Church, becomes almost as binding as the marriage bond itself (*Nov. Leon.* 74). Later—in 1084 and 1092—two constitutions of Alexius Comnenus went even further in this direction.[2] The impediments to marriage were extended according to the tendency of the age (*Nov. Leon.* 3, 24, 98). The blessing of the marriage by the Church was made compulsory (*Nov. Leon.* 39); the justified reasons for divorce were defined in greater detail (*Nov. Leon.* 30, 31, 32, 111, 112). In the field of the law of succession we need only mention the stipulation that on giving a daughter in marriage the father could make a valid testamentary disposition by contract (*Nov. Leon.* 19). Although the Emperor took less interest in the laws of commerce and of contract, there is one novel which, though of little practical interest, has some importance for the theory of the law of contract from the point of view of principle. For the closed system of contracts still existed, which meant that not every agreement was given legal effect, but only a limited number, which had, however, greatly increased since the late Roman period. Moreover, contracts that had

---

[1] From the *Tractatus de Peculiis* (about 1050) it appears that the author could still consult Thalelaeus' *Codex* commentary with the Latin text added to it. The *Meditatio de nudis pactis* has been mentioned above, p. 65.

[2] *DR*, 1116, 1167.

not been recognised—the so-called *pacta nuda*—could be given indirect legal effect by having a *stipulatio poenae* added to them. But a number of contracts not enjoying legal protection, that is, *pacta nuda*, still remained and were not joined on to a *stipulatio poenae*. Leo VI now stipulated in his 72nd Novel that these *pacta* should also have legal validity on condition that the document in which they had been laid down was provided with the sign of the cross or an invocation to the Holy Trinity. From this it may be concluded that if this sign is lacking and there is no evidence of any other recognised form of contract, the *nudum pactum* cannot give rise to legal action. The use of this procedure does not mean that the novel affected the principle of the closed system of contracts, as has sometimes been argued. Leo did however add a new group to the recognised contracts already known; to use a technical term, he created a new *causa civilis obligandi*. It may be questioned whether Leo was conscious of the importance of the principle involved, for in the *Prooemium* he shows a serious misapprehension of the essential character of the *pacta nuda*, a misapprehension which later was still widespread and which the author of the *Meditatio de nudis pactis* tried to remove about the middle of the eleventh century. It seems that Leo VI's 72nd Novel did not find acceptance at first; it was not until the fourteenth century that it penetrated into legal theory.

Leo VI's novels were the last outstanding reform of civil law and after this there were no great changes. Yet he was a fertile, rather than a great, legislator. The framework of the *Basilica* had originated with Basil I; and Leo's laws testify to a compiler's assiduity rather than to original thought. The same thing can be said of the *Lex Militaris*, also due to Leo VI, a collection of rules intended for military circles, drawn partly from the *Codex* and *Digest*, and partly from the now lost work of a certain Rufus. In his novels Leo had an opportunity of showing originality, but from these novels it appears only too often that he could not distinguish between essentials and non-essentials and that he was not infrequently on bad terms with the theory of law. The most successful instance of his legislation is the so-called *Eparchicon Leonis*. An *Eparchicon* is an imperial instruction to a praefectus (ἔπαρχος); the *Eparchicon* in question is addressed to the City Prefect and is concerned with the system of guilds in Constantinople, which was under the supervision of this official. The guilds (*collegia, corpora,* σωματεῖα, συστήματα, τέχναι) were already in existence in early imperial times. They were gradually incorporated into the organisation of the state; on the one hand they obtained legal monopolies, on the other hand certain public duties (*munera,* λειτουργίαι) were imposed on them. It was the duty of the soap-boilers, for example, to wash the clothes of the imperial court, that of the college of navigators had always been the transport of the *annona* to the capital. In the *Codices Theodosianus* and *Justinianus* these bodies were frequently mentioned, and from the *Eparchicon Leonis* it appears that in the tenth century they still found themselves in practically the same position. Notaries, jewellers, silk merchants of various kinds, linen merchants, druggists, candle-makers, soap-boilers, grocers, leather-dressers, butchers and many others were subject to strict rules.

The manuscript in which Nicole discovered the *Eparchicon* (Ἐπαρχικὸν Βιβλίον) in 1892 also contains the *Leges* (Νόμοι) of Julian of Ascalon, a collection of rules concerning the use and the building-up of real estate. These rules, divided into four groups according to the four elements (fire, air, earth, water) were originally intended for Ascalon in Palestine and were only later current in the Empire as a whole. Julian presupposes a type of law different from Byzantine law; for instance he knows the regulations governing ownership of the floors of a house. The work concludes with a number of excerpts from imperial novels, some perhaps of the usurper Basiliscus (476). It is unknown when Julian lived; from the circumstance that the *Leges* have been handed down together with the *Eparchicon* it may be conjectured that he lived under Leo VI.

Macedonian collections, with or without the Isaurian *Ecloga*, supplied the material for a great number of excerpts, sometimes arranged systematically, sometimes alphabetically. They are known by names such as *Ecloga ad Prochiron mutata*, *Prochiron auctum*, *Prochiron legum*, *Epanagoge aucta*, *Synopsis maior* and *minor*; the *Ponema iuris* of Michael Attaleiates, issued in 1073 or 1074, can also be classed with this group. Although such texts are important for a detailed study of the sources, an elaborate description of these rather colourless documents need not be given here; suffice it to say that in course of time they often superseded the over-elaborate Macedonian collections. This series of legal collections was continued after 1261 as if there had been no Latin domination. It finds its conclusion in the so-called *Hexabiblus* of Constantine Harmenopulus, issued about 1345, a work consisting of several older and similar documents, chiefly from the *Prochiron*. Although the *Hexabiblus* does not excel in depth and originality, it enjoyed a widespread and lasting currency; long after the end of the Turkish domination it held good in the kingdom of Greece as a source of law. In the preface Harmenopulus describes how he procured the *Prochiron* and expected to find in it the necessary and handy rules of law. Being disappointed by the contents, however, he decided to revise the work with the aid of the *Synopsis maior*—Harmenopulus says 'the *Basilica*'—the *Peira*, the *Leges* of Julian of Ascalon, novels and other sources.

When Basil I assumed the government the state appeared to be doing nothing at all for the teaching of law; the training of lawyers was in the hands of the guilds, notably that of the *tabularii*. According to the *Eparchicon Leonis*, one who wished to become a member of the guild had to know the law, write an excellent hand and possess a good style of writing and speaking. One had to know the *Prochiron* by heart and to have studied the *Basilica*. It was not until 1045 that the state revived legal instruction. In that year Constantine IX Monomachus provided quarters near the church of St George and appointed a *nomophylax* as the head of the law school to be established there as part of the reorganised university; the *nomophylax* became an ex-officio member of the senate and received a salary of four pounds as well as official robes and disbursements.[1] The *nomophylax*, it was specially stated, was required to have command of the Greek and Latin languages; he also became head of the library and was assisted in his duties by *tabelliones* and barristers.

The choice of the first *nomophylax* was a happy one; the Emperor selected for this office John Xiphilinus (the later Patriarch and the grandfather of the well-known epitomiser of Dio Cassius), who was no less capable as a jurist than as a theologian. He succeeded in making the law-school the centre of legal scholarship and encouraged research; he himself wrote many scholia on the *Basilica* which go under the name of John Nomophylax. Perhaps he also wrote the *Meditatio de nudis pactis* mentioned above. From this time, too, there has come down to us the precious collection of decisions of the judge Eustathius, collected by an unknown jurist. In this *Peira* can be found the practice of Byzantine jurisdiction of the eleventh century. The pleasure derived from the reading of these decisions is diminished only by the corrupt state in which they have been handed down to us. Another work that was often used was the (now lost) treatise on actions by Garidas, in which several actions were treated in alphabetical order. About this time or a little later lived Calocyrus Sextus, Constantine of Nicaea and Gregory Doxapater, a native of the same town, who all left many scholia on the *Basilica*. And in the Comnenian period an index to the *Basilica* was compiled which was given the name of *Tipoukeitos* (from τί ποῦ κεῖται). For the sake of curiosity mention may be made of the verse summary of the law by the scholar Michael Psellus, whose aim was not, however, to create immortal poetry but rather to present his pupil, afterwards the Emperor Michael VII Ducas (1071–8), with a textbook that was easy

[1] *DR*, 863.

to memorise. A little later Hagiotheodorita wrote his scholia on the *Basilica*. Further there has come down part of an anonymous, very lengthy but lucid, commentary on selected passages of the *Basilica*, the so-called *Ecloga librorum I–X Basilicorum*, published in 1142. It was the law-school, too, that produced the innumerable short anonymous notes written between the lines in nearly all the *Basilica* manuscripts.

Throughout the ages the theory of law has tended to be far removed from its practice, and in this respect the Byzantine Empire was no exception. It is by no means easy, for instance, to get a clear picture of how legislation was being applied in Justinian's time. The Justinianian novels often reflect a legal situation that in no way corresponds with the codes of law, as when the Emperor holds that the *stipulator* can institute proceedings (*actio ex stipulatu*) not only against the *promissor* but also against the third party who has obtained the promised matter (Nov. 162, cap. 1). The imperial chancery did not, it seems, make any distinction between *actiones in rem* and *in personam*, a distinction which was one of the corner-stones of Roman law. And again, the Emperor assumes that what is purchased with borrowed money becomes the property of the money-lender (Nov. 136, cap. 3); he confuses a tacit mortgage with the obligation to draw up a mortgage (Nov. 22, cap. 44 2); he describes every plea of the defendant with the word παραγραφή (*exceptio*: Nov. 90, cap. 4). It may be concluded from this that the codification compiled by the *antecessores* was to a large extent purely academic.

The fact that the rules of the codification are copied again and again in all subsequent legal collections—the *Basilica*, the *Prochiron* and the many private manuals, of which Harmenopulus' is the latest— tells us very little about the practice of law. Only very rarely can any conclusion be drawn about the practical application of a rule of law from the fact that it is, or is not, mentioned in a particular work. It is well known that many of the texts contained in the *Basilica* had long been obsolete. For instance, many of the offices mentioned in the sixth book of the *Basilica*, among others those of the *consules, proconsules, moderator Arabiae, proconsul Palestinae*, had fallen out of use long before 900.

As to the practice of law and how it compares with the literature there is only scant evidence; the most important data come from the excerpt, mentioned earlier, of the protocols of the metropolitan judge Eustathius, the so-called *Peira*, compiled shortly before 1050. It is surprising that such an important work has received so little attention from scholars in the past. The excerpt consists of reports on disputes which are often hard to fathom. Eustathius likes to account

for his decisions by referring to the *Basilica* or to the older commentators; one gets the impression, however, that the quoted texts
are often extraneous. In many cases his verdicts lack any support
from legal arguments. This material, which exists in abundance
from the tenth century onwards, only very rarely alludes to the
Basilica or at the extant academic writings.

In the Roman Empire republican institutions had been preserved,
and long remained in existence although their real importance had
often dwindled to a mere shadow. A senate, for example, still existed
under Justinian I although its competence was no more than ad-
visory (*Cod.* I, 16). The consulate likewise held its own, but under
Justinian lost its eponymous character and degenerated into an
honorary title of the Emperor. The earlier autonomy of the provincial
towns under their *curiae, duumviri* and *quattuorviri* left traces far
into the Byzantine period. It was Leo VI who ultimately abolished
these for the most part merely theoretical encroachments on his
absolute rule. He deprived the senate and the *curiae* of their remaining authority (*Nov. Leon.* 78, 46 and 47) and abrogated the *Nov. Just.*
105 (*Nov. Leon.* 94), thereby indicating that the consulate was no
longer open to anyone but the Emperor. These novels merely confirmed a state of affairs that had been a fact for centuries, and were
the result of the Emperor's childlike pleasure in enacting laws rather
than of any necessity; yet it may be said that Leo VI established
absolute monarchy in theory as well as in practice.

As early as the Macedonian period we find the seeds of the political
development which in the course of the following centuries was to
undermine the imperial authority. And during the last five centuries
of its existence the structure of the Byzantine state, and consequently of its public law, underwent radical changes. But the
Byzantines never brought themselves to work out a theoretical assimilation of these new rules of public law; the numerous manuals of
the tenth to the fourteenth centuries are entirely devoid of anything
of this kind.

After the first half of the eleventh century only public law showed
any further development; private law did not undergo any important
change. It is true that in the eleventh and twelfth centuries numerous
novels about subjects pertaining to private law were issued, but they
are all additions to and corrections of minor points of the existing
system. The only important work was the novel of Constantine VII
Porphyrogenitus which stipulates that one-third of intestate estate
shall in the absence of children fall to God, that is to the Church,
a clause that promoted the fatal accumulation of property in
mortmain. Another striking novel is that of Alexius I Comnenus

(1092) which, in conclusion of a long development, allowed the dissolution of a betrothal that had received the blessing of the Church only for the same restricted reasons as those for which a divorce could be claimed.[1]

The first traces of later centrifugal developments are found at a very early date in the field of taxation, that dominating factor of the social life of the late Roman and Byzantine periods. Since the third century of our era the system of taxation had been that of the *iugatio-capitatio*, and, with many alterations, it remained in force during the whole of the Byzantine period. As the name indicates, this system established on the one hand a taxation according to the yield of the soil, on the other a capitation fee per head of the labouring population. It was complicated by the fact that part of the *iugatio* was not assessed in money but in kind (*annona*, σιταρκία);[2] later it was often made possible, however, to commute the *annona* into the payment of a fixed price in money. One of the difficulties of the study of this fiscal system is the multiplicity and the continual change of appellation; καπνικόν, for example, which occurs from the ninth century onwards, seems to be identical with the later κεφαλητίων and to indicate the *capitatio*.

It was not so much these taxes in themselves as the settlement of the liability with respect to taxes due and their collection that exercised great influence on the law. At an early date great landowners were charged with the collection of taxes from their *coloni*, and were accordingly provided with public means of power (e.g. *Cod. Theod.* XI, 1, 14). Another old tradition of great importance for the development of the law was the continually changing system of collective liabilities. For the middle of the tenth century considerable insight into the prevailing fiscal system is afforded by a theoretical treatise that calls itself *Didascalia*.[3] This *Didascalia* seems to be an introduction intended for land registry officials and must have been written shortly after the death of Leo VI. It shows that a village (χωρίον) usually also formed one tax unit and was collectively assessed at a certain amount. This liability for each other's taxes (ἀλληλέγγυον) results in rules of law which are incompatible with the law of the *Pandects*. The *leges rusticae*, for example, already state that if an owner leaves without having paid his taxes, the crop is due to the person who has appropriated the land and paid the taxes; if, however, one tills someone else's land without paying taxes, then one has to

---

[1] *DR*, 1167.

[2] This *annona* = σιταρκία should not be confused with the compulsory selling of corn to the State (*annona* = συνωνή).

[3] Often indicated as *Tractatus Ashburneri* after the first editor.

compensate the owner for twice the value of the crops as a punishment. A similar infringement of civil law by fiscal interests may be observed in the system of the *adiectio sterilium* (ἐπιβολή); for if a field had been left and by lying fallow (γῆ κλασματική) threatened to become worthless for taxation, a compulsory assignment of this land took place to people who thereby also became liable for its taxes. Thus it appears that from fiscal motives a system of loss and acquisition is here created that is unknown to the civil law of the *Pandects*.

The liability for each other's taxes entails a certain participation in the disposal of real property, for the peasants of the village will enter into a community of liabilities (ὁμάς) with a possible new owner (or long leaseholder). Consequently these potentially responsible persons are given the right of pre-emption (προτίμησις), the first traces of which are found as far back as the age of Constantine the Great. The first elaborate regulation known is laid down in a famous novel of Romanus I Lecapenus of the year 922. In the case of alienation of land five categories of people had the right of pre-emption; they are probably the same persons who were in danger of a possible *adiectio sterilium*. The importance of this right of pre-emption was lessened by the fact that the person in possession of it had to pay a purchase price within the short term of 30 days; this regulation meant that it was mainly those who had a considerable fortune and therefore had liquid funds at their disposal at any given moment who could make use of the right. Now to this well-to-do class belonged in the first place the so-called 'powerful' (*potentiores*, δυνατοί), the class of the noble landlords who were a menace to the central government. In order to prevent the *potentiores* from extending their *de facto* power and from infiltrating into the village communities of the *humiliores* by making use of the right of pre-emption, Romanus stipulated that a *potentior* was not allowed to acquire land from a *humilior*, either by the right of pre-emption or in any other way. By *potentiores* he meant, according to a novel of 934, *magistri*, *patricii*, *strategi*, civil and military officials, senators, metropolitan bishops, archbishops, abbots and procurators of the imperial estates.

This introduces a series of measures by means of which the Emperors tried to prevent further expansion of the power of the *potentiores*, who were a menace to the central government not only because of their wealth but because they had acquired authority in the sense of the public law over their dependent tenants (πάροικοι). It would seem that in the tenth century the peasantry had become so weak that there was a danger that they might not be able to withstand the pressure of the *potentiores*. Consequently, when the famine of the year 927 had dealt another blow to the peasants and many of them had got into the *potentiores'* debt and were in danger of sinking to the condition of dependants, the Emperor stipulated, in 934, that all alienations executed by *humiliores* in favour of *potentiores* would be null and void and that this act would have retrospective effect from the year 927. Land that had been alienated was to be returned to the *humiliores*, if possible against an indemnification. Constantine VII Porphyrogenitus made this regulation even more stringent in 947; he drew up a number of stipulations for the payment of compensation and even laid down that a peasant possessing less than 50 gold pieces need not make any reimbursement. There is a remarkable stipulation of Nicephorus Phocas (967) which prevents not only acquisition from *humiliores* by *potentiores*, but conversely the acquisition from *potentiores* by *humiliores*. After that the land in the Empire was divided into two sharply marked categories, comparable to the French *fiefs nobles* and *fiefs roturiers*. There can be hardly any reason for such a stipulation but that the landownership of the *potentiores*, ἀρχοντικὰ κτήματα, was considered unsuitable for the *humiliores* on account of the public rights attached to it.

From this it is clear that the Emperor could govern in one of two ways, either through the medium of his civil service or by granting *beneficia* or special privileges. The civil servant represents the head of state, the beneficiary takes over a limited part of the imperial authority. The benefices probably date from the time of the Roman Empire; there is, however, no clear information about them until the eleventh century. It was Constantine IX Monomachus (1042–55) who was the first to bestow a *pronoia*, that is, a life-benefice under which the beneficiary was allowed the yield of taxation from a certain region and was given part of the jurisdiction over it.[1] The beneficiary, called a *pronoetes*, or pronoiar (προνοιάριος), generally accepts certain obligations, for example, the maintenance of a fortress, the supply of soldiers or in some cases also the payment of tribute. Thus the pronoiar has public authority; the region 'bestowed' on him does not become his own nor are the inhabitants of that region (πάροικοι) his slaves in terms of civil law. It is as well to emphasise this, for the wording of the Byzantine sources, like the western sources, in this respect, is remarkably deceptive. For example, matters relating to public law are described in terms borrowed from civil law. The *pronoia* is constantly referred to as δεσποτεία, 'property'. The πάροικοι are called δοῦλοι, 'slaves'; here the real meaning of δοῦλος is 'sub-

---

[1] Nicetas Choniates, p. 272 (*CSHB*). On the controversial subject of grants in *pronoia* and military service see G. Ostrogorsky, *La féodalité byzantine*, and P. Lemerle, 'Esquisse pour une histoire agraire de Byzance', *RH*, cxix (1958) and cxx (1958), and 'Recherches sur le régime agraire à Byzance: la terre militaire à l'époque des Comnènes', *Cahiers de Civilisation Médiévale*, ii (1959). [See Gen. Bibl. v.]

ordinate'. That is why they have the *ius connubii* and the *testamenti factio activa*. Only those who are directly under the imperial officials are ἐλεύθεροι, freemen within the meaning of public law. The granting of the benefice is consistently called δωρεά, 'gift'. But it would be wrong to infer from this that the pronoiar did not accept any obligations. Every imperial reward was a gift, since the Emperor could have no obligations by virtue of the axiom *princeps legibus solutus est*.

The tax which the πάροικος paid annually to the pronoiar is described as μίσθωμα or πάκτον (the German word *Pacht*), terms once again borrowed from civil law. This extension of the terminology of civil law has caused a good deal of misunderstanding. The 'gifts' of the *pronoiai* are often interpreted as marks of favour and the 'bondage' of the πάροικοι is often dramatised. In fact the πρόνοιαι and the χαριστίκια (rights over monastic property granted to individuals) were a form of administration which had certain advantages over administration by civil servants. Nevertheless it is clear that the lavish dispensation of privileges of this kind caused a weakening of central authority; that is why certain emperors opposed this policy.

But while the granting of πρόνοιαι and χαριστίκια concerned public law, the distribution of land to soldiers was essentially a civil matter. Even in the early Roman days the defence of the frontiers was sometimes entrusted to the peasant population living near the frontier; sometimes a frontier peasantry was created by the allotment of land, especially to barbarian immigrants. This idea of strengthening the frontiers through so-called 'frontier peasants', or *limitanei*, was still alive in the tenth century, but the causes that threatened the free peasants in general also necessitated the protection of the frontier peasantry. In this way the Emperor made the *limitaneus* the owner of a farm, and in return the *limitaneus* had the obligation of performing military service. Although alienation of farms was impossible in principle, it appears that in times of bad harvests speculators did buy these up. Not only was there a danger here of several farms falling into the ownership of one man with a consequent reduction in the number of *limitanei*, but also, by some obscure means, the new owners managed to assume the authority of public law over the occupant (who now had the status of tenant), thereby considering themselves qualified to grant exemption from military obligations. It was again Romanus I Lecapenus who tried to prevent this by his novel of 922 and by others of a later date. He prohibited alienation of soldiers' farms (στρατιωτικὰ κτήματα) and gave this prohibition retrospective effect for a period of thirty years. This prohibition of alienation was repeated and elaborated by Constantius VII Porphyrogenitus, Romanus II and Nicephorus II Phocas.

These laws could only very temporarily check the development of the great magnates, and they were for the most part ineffective. The laws against the *potentiores* must always have been difficult to enforce; by the time of Harmenopulus (about 1350) they 'had long been in abeyance'. Thus the *potentior* developed more and more into a sovereign ruler within his own jurisdiction; he collected the taxes and paid in the general assessment (ῥίζα) of his territory to the λογο-θέσιον, and he might be obliged to supply a certain number of soldiers from his territory. When the Palaeologian Emperors could no longer exercise sufficient authority over these magnates from the capital, they put several districts of the already very shrunken Empire under the direct supervision of relatives. The extent to which these δεσπόται, too, considered themselves sovereign in their despotates is evident from the case of Andronicus Palaeologus who sold the despotate granted to him to Venice for 50,000 gold pieces.[1] Monasteries also acquired extensive possessions over which they exercised authority; the numerous *pittakia* from the monastic archives show how the monastic lands were developing into small states under theocratic rule. In the case of the monasteries of Mt Athos this development very nearly reached completion, and during the Turkish as well as the late Byzantine period, Athos was in practice almost an independent republic.

Thus Byzantine administrative and legal development was characterised by increasing delegation of authority by the central government to others, either to such as naturally possessed legal personality or to corporate bodies to which it had been granted, such as monasteries, churches or municipalities, the last-mentioned in that case being regarded not as an administrative unit of the central government but as a territorially defined community bound together by self-interest. These persons or bodies entrusted with public authority often enjoyed immunity within the domains under their jurisdiction; they could execute their power without supervision by the central government. In their turn they could perform similar delegations, and the graded government that resulted from this shows some resemblance to western feudalism.

---

[1] (S)phrantzes, p. 69 (ed. J. B. Papadopulos, Leipzig, 1935). On developments of the Palaeologian period see also pt. I, chapter VIII, pp. 378 ff., and for judicial arrangements in general see above, chapter XX, pp. 29 ff.

CHAPTER XXII

SOCIAL LIFE IN
THE BYZANTINE EMPIRE

To attempt a sketch of social life in the Byzantine Empire during the centuries of its glory and decline would be a formidable undertaking, even if the space allotted to it were without limit. The collection of materials for such a study might occupy many volumes. Nor is the student presented, as is often assumed, with a uniform and static picture of those times, even though many important elements may persist during each phase. In truth, the changes and developments are not less remarkable than the conservatism. The theoretical principle of Byzantine society, in the fourteenth as in the eighth century, was that of a unified autocracy in which every part of the political, military and economic machine was mortised and adjoined to the crown; and the crown itself was the material reflection of that unique heavenly sovereignty which gave it form and significance. The internal history of Byzantium is the story of a struggle which brought with it profound changes in the practical life and opinions of almost every class of society. The political outlook of the free peasant-soldier of the tenth century, dependent on and the servant of his Emperor, was altogether different from that of his grandson in the eleventh, who lived as a serf on the estate of some military or civil magnate. The political outlook of a citizen of Constantinople whose cheap food and charitable relief were guaranteed by State and Church in the eleventh century, was different from that of his grandson whose bread was at the mercy of an agricultural economy of large landowners and foreign entrepreneurs, with which the imperial bureaucracy could no longer interfere without endangering the very existence of the urban population. The cultural influence of ancient Greek letters upon the Byzantine civilisation was, as is well known, profound; yet that influence can by no means be considered as a stable phenomenon, of equal potency in the reigns of Constantine V and Constantine VII, of Basil II and John VI. Social life is affected only in a limited degree by political theory. If therefore in this essay we turn our eyes principally to the state of society during those centuries when political theory came nearest to being realised in the facts of military, social and economic life, that is, during the ninth to twelfth centuries, it is for the reason that after this period the fundamental props of Byzantine civilisation were one by one loosed and uprooted, with the decay of imperial authority, the loss of imperial provinces, the growth of independent territorial power and of a free mercantile economy, and the penetration of western ideas, customs and populations.

Any study of Byzantine life must begin with the capital. She had, since her foundation, stood pre-eminent in the Empire. But the events of the seventh century, which had removed from her the rivalry of Alexandria, Antioch and Jerusalem, and the events of the eighth century, which had sundered her from contact and sympathy with Rome, had left her in solitary splendour, the undisputed head of Orthodox Christianity, the city guarded of God, the peculiar care of the Blessed Virgin, and the queen of all cities. She was the home of Christ's vicegerent, the seat of all administration, the entrepôt into which flowed all the commerce and all the wealth allured by her market or amassed by her taxation. To possess her was to possess the Empire. She might, and often did, stand alone and self-sufficing when all else was lost. The ancient splendour of her buildings, the beauty of her monuments, the magic and phantasy of her appointments, the profound religious awe inspired by her three hundred churches, her sacred palace and her inexhaustible catalogue of holy relics, amazed the eyes of all who visited her; and to this unfeigned reverence and astonishment she owed no small part of her political authority. Byzantium, like her predecessor Rome, has given her name to a whole civilisation.[1]

The population of Byzantium has been the subject of much discussion: for although the texts relating to her life are innumerable, very few afford any reliable indication as to statistics. It is probable that, despite the very high rate of mortality, the number of her inhabitants remained fairly constant between the eighth century and the Fourth Crusade, after which it very substantially declined. Although the area comprehended within the vast triangle of land and sea walls was at no time uniformly populous, it may be said with some certainty that not less than half a million persons dwelt within it, and perhaps as many as eight hundred thousand. Thessalonica came next to the capital, though at a very great distance; and the population of Thessalonica in the tenth century was not less than two hundred thousand. The number of destitute persons in Constantinople during the same prosperous century was at least thirty thousand, and the number of thieves and other criminals may not have been very much less. It is hard to think that in a city where the police were exceptionally active and where a most accurate municipal

---

[1] S. Runciman, *Byzantine Civilisation*, pp. 179–206; L. Bréhier, *Le monde byzantin*, III, pp. 594–5 (bibliography). [See Gen. Bibl. v.]

organisation supervised ingress and regulated employment, these elements can have exceeded five per cent of the total population, even though the 'poor' were an officially recognised and socially important part of its composition.[1]

This great mass of persons consisted in the main of three classes: the governing class, that is to say, the palace officials and the departments of civil administration, with their enormous bureaux; the commercial and trading class, of merchants, artisans and shopkeepers; and the lowest class, of labourers, of slaves and of the 'poor'. The first class, consisting of the civil service, was peculiar to the capital, and amounted to many thousands. Though it was productive of no real wealth, and indeed consumed a vast amount of the substance of the Empire, the state could not have existed without it; and it also performed the supremely important task of fostering secular education. Since the revival of Greek letters in the ninth century, a thorough and Hellenistic education had been the passport to advancement in the civil service. Hence erudition became economically as well as intellectually desirable, and any clever youth might aspire to a distinguished academic career, followed by a clerkship or secretaryship in some government department. It was this bureaucratic aristocracy, constantly recruited from the best brains of the middle and even the servile class, which formed the dominant element in the capital, and was at bitter and disastrous feud with the landed interest of the great military magnates. But, apart from its administrative and educative functions, this class also fostered a tendency which was of great historical importance. Its whole outlook was Greek, and what would in a later age have been called national. In theory the Empire was oecumenical, and recognised no separate nationalities within its borders. Subscription to the authority of Emperor and Orthodoxy made of the Slav and the Turk as good a Byzantine as the heirs of Old Rome, versed in all the culture of classical antiquity. But in practice this could not be so. The educated class of the capital despised and slighted the foreigner and the boor, even though he had risen to the summit of earthly power or gained the most brilliant victories in the field. Among the great Emperors of the Macedonian dynasty only Basil II, whose statesmanship was not inferior to his military genius, seems to have realised the danger of this intellectual pharisaism in an Empire compounded of so many racial traditions. The educated bureaucrat became in the mind of the outside world the typical Byzantine, Orthodox, proud and intensely exclusive. He hated the round visage of the Slav. He hated the heresy of the bold

[1] P. Charanis, 'On the Social Structure of the Later Roman Empire', *B*, XVII (1944–5), 50; and in *The Joshua Starr Memorial Volume* (New York, 1953), pp. 137–41.

Armenian. But above all he hated a Frank. 'Between us and the Franks', wrote the twelfth-century historian Nicetas Choniates, 'is set the widest gulf. We are poles apart. We have not a single thought in common. They are stiff-necked, with a proud affection of an upright carriage, and love to sneer at the smoothness and modesty of our manners. But we look on their arrogance, and boasting, and pride, as a flux of the snivel which keeps their noses in the air; and we tread them down by the might of Christ, who giveth unto us the power to trample upon the adder and upon the scorpion.'[1]

These expressions are such as might have been used by a Greek at the time when the Orontes was polluting the Tiber. And the state of mind which they illustrate is one of the most permanent legacies of Byzantine civilisation to the later history of the eastern Mediterranean.

The dominant characteristic of this class, as already emphasised, was its devotion to secular education: and education meant erudition in the Greek classics and an ability to compose according to the rules and with the embellishments of ancient rhetoric. The military class, who devoted their lives to arms and agriculture, regarded these acquirements with real or assumed contempt. The most prominent of the military aristocracy were often unable to write a sentence in the simplest Greek without some grammatical or orthographical blunder. The conservative wing of the Church looked on the 'foreign' or 'pagan' learning with undisguised suspicion. The poorer classes, owing to shortage of books no less than to shortage of means, were mainly excluded from it. The class of the Hellenist scholars, therefore, though they have left the imprint of their culture on almost every page that survives from Byzantium, and though our own debt to them is incalculable, was at no time large in proportion to the total population even of the capital itself.[2]

None the less, the tradition which assigned to ancient Greek letters the chief place in the education of a civilian remained constant; and the support given to instruction in this field by the government, if not, even after the ninth century, absolutely continuous, was generous and recurrent. The youth who had talent and means was put early to the grammarian, and by the age of fourteen was thoroughly grounded in the niceties of ancient grammar and the masterpieces of ancient literature. He moved thence to the rhetorician; and from him to the professors of philosophy, mathematics or physic. The substance of all this instruction derived from the ancient world; and the

---

[1] Nicetas Choniates, pp. 391–2 (*CSHB*).
[2] Cf. Psellus, *Chronographia*, ed. E. Renauld, I (Paris, 1926), pp. 18–19; L. Bréhier, *op. cit.* p. 604 (bibliography); H.-G. Beck, *Theodoros Metochites* (Munich, 1952), p. 90.

graduates of this discipline were accomplished, if not brilliant or original, classical scholars.

It may well be asked why, with such resources at their disposal, Byzantine scholars remained content, century after century, to memorise Homer, to annotate Pindar or to mimic Lucian. They were surrounded by the books and statues of antiquity; yet there was numbered among them no Dante, no Petrarch and no Leonardo. The western revival of letters led to, or assisted, the escape of the human spirit from the prison of dogma; and it was thus able to increase a thousand fold the slender capital which had survived from destruction by iconoclast, crusader or Turk. Like the Sibylline Books of old, the classical heritage proved most valuable when it was most diminished. The Greek libraries of Photius and Arethas were indeed not so copious as those of Cicero and Quintilian, but many times more ample than those of Politian and Erasmus. But the crop reaped from this plentiful seed was, by comparison with the bounteous harvests of the West, meagre in the extreme. And the classical achievement of Byzantium may only too justly be likened to the achievement of the unprofitable servant who hid his talent in a napkin. There were many causes for this: and two of the chief were the jealousy with which Orthodoxy regarded the teachings of paganism, and the circumstance that the Greek of the medieval Empire was still recognisably the same language as that in which the classical authors had written. The first of these impediments meant that any study of the old philosophers which was not limited to pure scholarship was highly dangerous; and even scholarship itself, if too brilliant and profound, gave rise to suspicion of heterodoxy, as Photius and Psellus found good reason to confirm. On the other hand, the vast prestige of the classical authors and stylists imposed on their medieval students the obligation to correct their own idiom into what was almost a foreign tongue; and in their bondage to the letter, they tended to lose sight of the spirit of their originals.

The study of the poets and thinkers of antiquity thus served at Byzantium to instruct rather than to inspire. They were the food of the grammarian, the scholiast and the antiquary. But in at least one branch of creative literature the classical revival early showed and long maintained its fertilising influence. Historiography in the dark age of Byzantium, from the seventh to the ninth centuries, where it was practised at all, scarcely rose above the humble level of chronicles or annals. The humanism which had distinguished Plutarch, the integrity which had raised the masterpiece of Polybius to supremacy even among the historians of Greece, had been largely abandoned. And their place had been supplied by a simple record of action, judged according to a harsh and inflexible criterion of theological prejudice. The recovery of the texts of the ancient historians effected a speedy and spectacular reform in this department. Individual character was again sifted and appraised. Good was again discerned in the villain, and evil in the hero. It is hard to determine whether the study of classical models was a cause, or merely a suitable concomitant, of the revival of humanism in the late ninth and tenth centuries. But both humanism and humanity are unmistakable not only in the letters but in the practice of that epoch. The legislation of Leo VI is constantly revising the harsher statutes hitherto in force, in favour of a more humane regimen. In 797 Constantine VI was blinded; and in 867 Michael III was brutally murdered. In 920 Constantine VII was merely retired to his library. In 913 the harsh reprisals ordered by the regents were restrained by the judicial bench, who asked how they could commit such cruelties in the name of an innocent child? But if we consider the influence which the rediscovery of Hellenistic art-forms exerted on the development of tenth-century art; and if we contrast the treatment meted out by Theophanes to Constantine V with the treatment which the Continuator of Theophanes, well versed in Plutarch and Polybius, accords to the equally heretical Theophilus; we shall not be tempted to underestimate the contribution made by classical studies towards a reform of educated opinion. It would be unjust not to point to the great influence of Plutarch in this, as in the later western, revival. His acute discernment of individual character and his luminous style were the inspiration of the first great historical work which survives to us from the tenth century. John Mauropous wished him in heaven, in words which recall the tender grief of Dante at beholding the great men of old in limbo. And the perverse and prolix John Tzetzes, when reduced by poverty to selling his books, kept by him the works of a single author, Plutarch.[1]

It would, however, be incorrect to assume that such enlightenment as a few scholars and civilians obtained from the ancient classics was at all effective in scattering the shades of superstition, which governed the minds and thoughts of men to a degree which in our age we can scarcely imagine. Even during that century of classical Greece which Bury called the Age of Illumination, the most casual reading of Thucydides or Aristophanes betrays the prevalence of every kind of obscurantism. And in the medieval world the Byzantine was daily and hourly encompassed by the supernatural, by the ominous or the

---

[1] *Les Novelles de Léon VI le Sage*, ed. Noailles-Dain (Paris, 1944), pp. 129, 229–36, 237, 245, etc.; J. M. Hussey, *Church and Learning in the Byzantine Empire* (Oxford, 1937), pp. 22 ff.; R. J. H. Jenkins, 'The Classical Background of the *Scriptores Post Theophanem*', *DOP*, VIII (1954), 13–30.

miraculous, by the beneficence of saints or the maleficence of demons. Men of culture, such as the Continuator of Theophanes, or the author of the Lucianic *Philopatris*, or Nicetas Choniates, might condemn, or affect to condemn, belief in omens or resort to astrological prediction. But such belief and such resort were well-nigh universal among the laity, and were not altogether unknown among churchmen. The vital effect of such beliefs on the whole outlook of mankind forms a subject so vast and various that we cannot now seek to develop it. But we may point, by way of example, to one single aspect of it which is, obviously, of deep significance for both religious and secular history: that is, the power of the illusionists. These practitioners, who cultivated an influence over simple and rude intelligence, the secret of which has long been lost in Europe, were able to create pleasing or hurtful images which their victims received with entire conviction, and often retained without any suspicion that they had been imposed upon. Many of these illusions were harmless, and provided merely as entertainment. Others were recognised as the practice of conjurors. But who shall say how many strange sights, how many miraculous feats, that have passed into chronicle or hagiography, may not owe their origin to this mysterious power of hypnotic persuasion? We have a very clear account of one such practitioner, Michael Sikiditis, in the reign of Manuel Comnenus. Another may well have been that Theodore of Santabaris whose malign influence disturbed and perhaps deranged the overwrought faculties of Basil the Macedonian.[1]

Below the administrative class came those who earned their bread by some profession or trade. The position of the mercantile class altered very substantially with the relaxation of state control and monopoly and the influx of foreign traders during the Comnenian age. In the tenth and eleventh centuries the oppressive and meticulous supervision by the state bureaucracy over all merchandise and trading hampered initiative and discouraged the venturing of capital. This policy delayed the growth of a strong native bourgeoisie; with the result that when the arm of the government grew weak, the commerce of the Empire fell into the hands, not of the Byzantine, but of the foreign merchant. It is not possible to discern any group of persons who could accurately be called a bourgeoisie before the twelfth century. This suppression of commercial enterprise, which operated through a system of controlled guilds and a rigorous limita-

---

[1] Nicetas Choniates, pp. 192–4; Georg. Mon. Cont., p. 693; cf. N. H. Baynes, *Byzantine Studies and Other Essays* (London, 1955), pp. 6–7, who points out the liberation which Christianity brought to that demon-haunted world of the Hellenistic age which continued into Byzantine times.

tion of profits, was no doubt a necessary concomitant of the unified state administration. But the consequences were harmful: not least, in that the bourgeoisie, when at last it arose, tended inevitably to throw in its lot with the forces which were working against the solidarity of the Empire. The one means, apart from the army, whereby a youth of the 'middle' sort could aspire to wealth and dignity was to rise into the ranks of the civil service. And though the failures were, as the satirist Prodromus discovered, more numerous than the successes, an ambitious parent of a clever son was willing to further him along this road, even if it meant that son's resigning the hope of posterity and becoming a eunuch. The career of Michael Psellus, who however was not subjected to this last indignity, provides a striking but not exceptional instance. His father, though of good family, was a merchant of moderate means; his mother, though a lady of quite extraordinary ability and force of character, was of humble stock. The son was to have followed the father in trade, where his talents would have been wasted. Instead, he followed learning, and by his wits and application rose to be the servant and chief counsellor of successive Emperors.[1]

Efforts have been made, on some fragmentary but plausible evidence, to establish the existence of a 'class' rivalry between the city aristocracy and the commercial interest, which is thought to have manifested itself, until the seventh century, in the strife between the Blue and Green factions of the Circus. But the vigorous measures taken by the Heraclian house to extend state control, and the final settlement, in the ninth century, of the iconoclast struggle, which had undoubtedly caused a deep social cleavage, render it difficult to discern any such rivalry in the Byzantium of later centuries. Under the Macedonian sovereigns, at any rate, the city populace as a whole appears to have supported the imperial house in its struggle with the military aristocracy, whose strength lay, not in the city, but in their provincial estates.[2]

[1] Μιχαὴλ Ψελλοῦ Ἐγκώμιον εἰς τὴν μητέρα αὐτοῦ, ed. K. N. Sathas, Μεσαιωνικὴ Βιβλιοθήκη v (Paris, 1876), pp. 12–13; *Poèmes Prodromiques en grec vulgaire*, ed. D. C. Hesseling and H. Pernot (Amsterdam, 1910), pp. 72–83; P. Charanis, 'On the Social and Economic Structure of the Byzantine Empire in the Thirteenth Century and Later', *BS*, xii (1951), 148–50; Ph. Kukules, Βυζαντινῶν Βίος καὶ Πολιτισμός, ii, 1 (Athens, 1948), pp. 179–258. [See Gen. Bibl. v.]

[2] A. P. Djakonov, 'Vizantijskie dimy i fakcii v V–VII vv.', *VS*, i (1945), 144–227; cf. M. Paulova's review of this, *BS*, x (1949), 81–7. For the more persistent rivalry of *religious* factions which may have continued the social-political rivalry of the Circus, see F. Dvornik, 'The Circus Parties in Byzantium', *BM*, i (1947), 119–33, and *id.*, 'The Patriarch Photius in the light of recent research', *Berichte zum XI. Internationalen Byzantinisten-Kongress* (Munich, 1958), p. 10, note 45; for the political activities of the commercial guilds, see S. Vryonis, 'Byzantine δημοκρατία and the Guilds in the Eleventh Century', *DOP*, xvii (1963).

The commercial body was supplemented by a large number of petty traders, shopkeepers, tavern-keepers and the like. And below them was the floating population of day-labourers and those who were scarcely worse off than labourers, the beggars, the thieves and the whores. A reasonably clear picture of the conditions of life of this lowest class may be gained from scattered references in the chronicles and in the lives of popular saints.[1] In reviewing the supplies of foodstuffs, which during the tenth and eleventh centuries were cheap and plentiful in the capital, we must remember that the capital enjoyed a privileged position. It was of vital importance for the government to preserve the loyalty of the populace, and to keep them in mind that their relatively favourable conditions of life depended on the personal care and favour of the Emperor. This policy succeeded so long as the government was strong enough to control the rural economy, at least in the neighbouring provinces; and the efforts of Emperors such as Theophilus or Basil I or Romanus II to maintain prices, even in times of famine, at an artificially low level in the city were repaid handsomely by the adherence of the populace to the legitimate house in times of political unrest. As soon as government control in the provinces was relaxed, and large stores of grain could no longer be purchased at fixed prices and hoarded in the vast granaries of the city, the traditional loyalty of the populace at once declined. The citizens who rose to defend Leo VI in 886 and Constantine VII in 944, and who rose again to defend the latter's great granddaughter in 1042, had by 1182 become the inconstant rabble who were 'by nature indifferent to the person of the Emperor, and would tear in pieces tomorrow the prince whom they had crowned today'.[2]

The price of bread was, as usual, the cardinal factor in the city's economy. The loss of Egypt in the seventh century had put an end to the wholesale distribution of free bread which had been a conspicuous feature of life in ancient Rome and the earlier days of Byzantium. None the less, successive Emperors contrived to keep the price of wheat in the city stabilised at about four shillings the bushel, and of barley at about two-thirds of that sum. This implied the sale of a loaf of bread at about two half-pence. A daily ration of dried peas or beans cost no more than a half-penny, and of green vegetables the same. Wine sold at about sixpence the quart, and oil for about twice that sum. Fish, both fresh and dried, was cheap. It

[1] See especially A. P. Rudakov, *Očerki vizantijskoj kul'tury po dannym grečeskoj agiografii* (Moscow, 1917), pp. 110–37.

[2] Nicetas Choniates, p. 305 (*CSHB*); cf. G. I. Bratianu, *Etudes byzantines d'histoire économique et sociale* (Paris, 1938), pp. 137–41; J. L. Teall, 'The Grain Supply of the Byzantine Empire, 330–1025', *DOP*, XIII (1959), 89–139.

was therefore possible to support life on as little as six or eight half-pence a day; and to secure a satisfactory, if not a varied or appetising, diet for twelve or fifteen. The average remuneration of the lowest paid free worker was probably fifteen or sixteen half-pence a day; and that this meagre sum was regarded, during the tenth century, as a minimum on which life could be supported is suggested by the fact that Romanus I gave to the city prostitutes a weekly dole of four shillings, for the purpose, we must conclude, of providing them with at least a possible alternative to the sale of their bodies. But many even among the beggars earned more than this: for the daily revenue from a favourable pitch might amount to as much as thirty half-pence.[1]

The other prime necessaries of life, clothing and lodging, were by comparison much dearer. The silks and brocades in which the wealthier sort walked or rode, and the immense supplies of which dazzled the eyes of Benjamin of Tudela, were sold at great prices. But even coarse woollens and sackcloth were not cheap. A rough blanket cost three shillings; and the single garment of St Andrew the Fool, which, if not tattered, must have been indescribably filthy, could sell for a shilling and the proceeds be divided among twelve whores at two half-pence a head. It was no uncommon sight to see the poor shivering in a makeshift covering of straw.

The misery of inadequate clothing was enhanced by the inadequacy of shelter. Away from the palaces of the great and the respectable two-storied houses of the well-to-do were large areas of tenements or huts, intersected by dark and filthy alley-ways where, except for the city watch, none but the most abject ever set foot. Yet even these overcrowded and insanitary areas were quite insufficient to shelter the crowds of beggars, of broken soldiers, of runaway peasants, or of poor folk who flocked to the capital for redress of their grievances. Large numbers slept out of doors, in the arcades which lined the main thoroughfares, in the Hippodrome, or in the church porches; or crowded for warmth round a glass-house or even on a dung-hill.[2]

The lot of these unfortunates, and not of them only but of the whole populace, was embittered by endemic and epidemic pestilences,

---

[1] *Vita S. Andreae Sali*, *MPG*, cxi, 656; Theophanes Continuatus, p. 430; cf. G. Ostrogorsky, 'Löhne und Preise in Byzanz', *BZ*, xxxii (1932), 298–9, 320–3; Bratianu, *op. cit.* p. 147. For the Byzantine *nomisma*, *miliaresion*, *keration* and *follis* I follow the practice of J. B. Bury and use the English denominations sovereign, shilling, sixpence and half-penny. The usage appears to be justified in a survey which is not specifically economic. The Byzantine money had nothing like the purchasing power that has sometimes been claimed for it: see Ostrogorsky, *op. cit.* pp. 327–8.

[2] *Vita S. Andreae*, 653; cf. Kukules, *op. cit.* ii, 1, pp. 94–5.

such as were bred by absence of sanitation and, even in the highest ranks, were scarcely alleviated by medical skill. In the eleventh century, an age to which all the resources of ancient medicine were open, the best advice which the sage Cecaumenus could give to a patient was to steer clear of the Faculty, and entrust his recovery to repose and Providence; nor was his advice at all cynical. Epidemics such as that of the bubonic plague in 745, or of the Black Death in 1349, during which the living were insufficient to bury the dead, were rare. But it seems clear that enteric fever and smallpox were at all times endemic, and were a severe check on the increase and even the maintenance of the city population. It is not surprising to learn, on the highest authority, that the expectation of life, at least in cities, was short. The Emperor Alexius I tells us that few lived to the age of sixty. Instances of longevity were indeed not wanting; but they are chiefly recorded of churchmen, whose sober regimen, recluse life and spartan habits sometimes preserved them into the eighties and nineties. A most striking example of the ravages caused by disease and infantile mortality in the city is to be found in the history of the imperial family of Basil the Macedonian. Basil, himself one of a large country-bred family, had at least five sons and four daughters; but, in the male line, he had but one surviving grandson, one great-grandson and two great-great-grandsons, and after his three great-great-great-granddaughters his direct posterity became extinct. Of his sons one died an infant, one was made a eunuch and two died without issue. The remaining son, Leo VI, had three wives who predeceased him, though he himself died at the early age of forty-five; and of his sons one scarcely survived his christening and the other was a lifelong invalid. If such was the fate of the highest family in the Empire, which sprang from a splendidly healthy stock, lived in seclusion and luxury, and enjoyed all that wealth and skill could provide, a simple calculation *a fortiori* will suggest the extent of premature mortality among the ordinary citizens. Psellus was the third of a family of three; his elder sister died, perhaps of cancer, as a very young wife; and his only child, a daughter, was taken off by smallpox at the age of fourteen.[1]

In all ranks of society harlotry was rife, and was certainly encouraged by the rigorous seclusion of women in polite society. No respectable woman ever appeared in the streets unveiled; and even in her house she never dined with a stranger, or entered his presence

---

[1] *Cecaumeni Strategicon*, ed. B. Wassiliewsky and J. Jernstedt (St Petersburg, 1896), p. 53; *Alexii Carmina*, ed. P. Maas, *BZ*, xxii (1913), 354; Psellus, Εἰς τὴν θυγατέρα Στυλιανήν, ed. K. N. Sathas, Μεσαιωνικὴ Βιβλιοθήκη, v, pp. 77–9. The best doctors, in the East as in the West, were Jews.

except silently and with downcast eyes. This seclusion tended, as usual, to promote associations of a criminal character between the sexes. Though the slender licence granted to prostitution by Constantine the Great was repeatedly revoked, and though severe penalties were pronounced against keepers of disorderly houses, the evil was never checked. Inn-keepers, tavern-keepers and bath-keepers regularly augmented their gains by maintaining whores, of whom penury and the deceitful promises of itinerant pimps procured an inexhaustible supply. The large majority of these wretched creatures lived in the most abject squalor, providing their services for a few half-pence and widely disseminating the filth and diseases incident to their profession. They were commonly at the centre of drunkenness, riot and disorder. Their number cannot be computed with any accuracy; but we shall not err in putting it at many thousands.[1]

The depressed state of the free manual worker was due in large measure to the institution of slavery: for the slave could do that for which the free workman must be paid. The conditions of the slaves themselves varied very greatly according to the circumstances and temper of their masters. The darling of a wealthy citizen might be in a better plight, and entrusted with greater authority, than many free men. He might be the bosom friend of the children of aristocrats. He might go perfumed and in silk. But he had few or no rights at law. And the servile labourer on an estate, or the wretched chattel of some inhumane and immoral tyrant, might live a life so deeply prostituted and degraded that death, even when it came, as it often did, in cruel torments, could not be regarded as anything but a merciful release. The frequency and vigour with which churchmen at all times inveighed against the ill-treatment of slaves makes it only too certain that such ill-treatment was common enough; and we are justified in believing that during the centuries when slaves were cheap, that is, during the ninth to eleventh centuries, their general lot was far less enviable than that of the most penurious among the free population. The Church took up an honourable position against slavery, basing itself upon that Scripture which recognises neither bond nor free among those who are baptised into Christ. But Christian precept, even when reinforced by the growing humanity which is such a striking feature of tenth-century legislation, was not strong enough to abolish the servile condition. The great victories of Romanus I, of Nicephorus II and of John I flooded the market with cheap human merchandise. It was not until the hard facts of military defeat, closed markets and declining wealth had stopped the sources that slavery, in the twelfth century, began to die out, and give to the

[1] Kukules, *op. cit.* II, 2, pp. 117–62.

free worker the economic power which national prosperity had hitherto denied him.[1]

The state of the city at night hardly differed from that of any large city in Europe until the nineteenth century. Only the larger houses and factories in the main thoroughfares were illuminated. When darkness fell, the homeless sank down in such corners as they could find; while a crowd of footpads and house-breakers swarmed to their prey from the alleys and hovels. The streets were patrolled by the mayor's watch, accompanied by a strong force of the imperial guard, who announced their approach by loud cries. A curfew was imposed at an early hour; and a severe flogging, summarily inflicted, was the lot of any who were thereafter found wandering abroad without good reason. But stringent penalties could not repress the marauder. Houses were entered by skeleton keys, or by main force, and the goods purloined; while the petty thief roamed the streets and pilfered the miserable belongings of those who slept out of doors.

From much of this squalor and disease and misery the wealthier inhabitants were of course protected. But from one nuisance even the fortress-palace of the Emperor was not exempt. In the reeking alley-ways of the poor, the ordures lay in heaps. The stenches which arose polluted the air; and were combated in the mansions of the great by liberal sprinklings of rose-water and by the smoke of aromatic herbs burning in cauldrons. By a revealing edict the manufacturers and vendors of perfumes plied their trade at the palace gate; and among the most grateful gifts afforded to mankind by the corpse of a saint was a delicate effluvium, which gave promise of the sweet and balmy odours of Paradise.[2]

We should, however, be far from obtaining an accurate picture of life in the city if we dwelt solely upon its harsher aspects, and omitted to record the gentler. In the large majority of households the domestic and Christian virtues were cultivated. The seclusion of women did not cut them off from family happiness: indeed, it tightened the bonds of love between father and daughter, brother and sister, mother and son. The celebrated encomium of Michael Psellus on his mother gives us a unique and charming picture of family life in the middle class. The mother was a woman of strong principle, high-minded and unremittingly laborious, who governed her house, her parents, her children and her husband with relentless, if kindly, exactitude. But she lulled her children to sleep with tales of the childhood of Isaac and Jacob, and of Mary and the infant Jesus,

---

[1] Ostrogorsky, *op. cit. BZ*, xxxii (1931), 300; A. Hadjinicolaou-Marava, *Recherches sur la vie des esclaves dans le monde byzantin* (Athens, 1950), pp. 54–7, 89.

[2] Rudakov, *op. cit.*, p. 119; Kukules, *op. cit.* iii, 209–14; *Vita S. Andreae*, 709.

refusing to allow them to be terrified by stories of demons and hob-goblins with which servants in all ages love to appal their charges. Though averse to displays of affection, she would kiss them tenderly when she thought them asleep. The son's true and lasting affection for his mother, his sister and his daughter is strong proof of the sanity and kindliness of his own upbringing. Something of the same domestic happiness may be seen in the families of the Emperor Constantine VII and of the Emperor Alexius I.[1]

But perhaps the most striking feature of life at Byzantium was the universal spread of Christian charity. This was indeed the cardinal benefit bestowed on mankind by the humane and unambiguous precepts of the Gospel, and especially of that Scripture which promises salvation to them who have given meat and drink to the hungry and thirsty, entertained the stranger, clad the naked, and visited the sick and the prisoner. By many this charity was bestowed out of pure love; but in many other instances the menace of an unspeakably fearful retribution for neglecting it was productive of the same practical results. The spiritual benefits of conferring charity naturally depended on the existence of a class on whom that charity might be conferred. The 'poor' were thus an integral part of society. Our Lord had stated that they were 'always with us'; and they knew their value. 'Paradise knocks on your doors', cried the beggars as they called for alms; and alms were freely bestowed. Begging was a recognised profession, from which, as from other professions, intruders were expelled. The more valuable pitches were jealously preserved. Every church porch was besieged by mendicants, whose importunity was certain to provide them with a liberal supply of their daily bread. But organised charity far transcended the limits of casual relief. The city was justly famous for its hospitals, its orphanages and its hostels for the aged and destitute. The imperial family took the lead in establishing these institutions. Many of its female members actively employed themselves in ministering to the sick, and even made a practice of visiting the darkest and foulest recesses of human misery, the Byzantine prisons. But the Church was the chief trustee and almoner. Huge sums, arising from bequests, donations or endowments, flowed annually into her coffers for distribution to the needy; and this distribution was carried out with an honourable fairness and punctuality. A special crisis might call for a special exercise of charity. In the cold winter of 927–8 the Emperor disbursed among the poor, whom he had housed in churches and temporary shelters, the large sum of twelve thousand shillings monthly.

---

[1] Psellus, *Encomium*, ed. K. N. Sathas, Μεσ. Βιβλ. v, p. 17; Runciman, *Byzantine Civilisation*, p. 202; Bréhier, *Civilisation byzantine*, pp. 10–24, 592–4 (bibliography).

The same Emperor in his will provided for the free distribution of thirty thousand loaves daily during the days of his funeral; and made besides many charitable bequests amounting in sum to several thousand pieces of gold.[1]

Religion and religious impulses were however not responsible for all of the existing charities. Vestiges still remained of those public largesses which originated in ancient Rome. At the games which commemorated the foundation of Constantinople, loaves and vegetables were piled high in the Hippodrome; and a large fishing-smack, mounted on wheels and filled to overflowing with fresh fish, was drawn along and the contents scattered among the people. It is reasonable to conclude from all this that, at least in the capital, Church and State provided what would now be called 'social services' far in advance of anything to be found elsewhere in Europe.[2]

While so much was lavished on the bodily and spiritual welfare of the citizen, his passion for amusement was not less fully satisfied. The city was enlivened by a multitude of spectacles. Many of these, as was to be expected, were cruel and degrading; crowds gathered to see the parade or immolation of some horribly defaced and mutilated traitor or criminal; and the atrocious executions ordained by Andronicus I were the natural prelude to his own lingering and terrible end, which however he bore with characteristic fortitude. But not all spectacles were so tainted. A triumphal procession might recall the dignity and beauty of Empire, when the route, bedecked with flowers and paved with rich tapestries, was trodden by magistrates, soldiers and prisoners, and by white horses shod with gold. But the Hippodrome, with its endless succession of displays, was the secular meeting-place of rich and poor. Here, encircled by tiers and galleries adorned with the masterpieces of antique statuary, the horse-race and the foot-race ran their course; hares and hounds traversed the mazes of the hunt; the elephant and the giraffe, the bear and the tiger, were paraded; the circus-rider stood on the backs of his galloping steeds; and the ever popular acrobat walked or danced upon his rope a hundred feet above the arena.[3]

These displays united with many other curious scenes and devices to endow Byzantium with her universal reputation as the Mother of Wonders. On her walls trumpets blown by no human breath marshalled her ships to war. In her palaces golden lions roared, and golden birds twittered in golden branches. Time-pieces of curious design

---

[1] Kukules, *op. cit.* II, 1, pp. 64–178; Kukules in *Mémorial Louis Petit* (Bucarest, 1948), pp. 254–71; Theophanes Continuatus, pp. 417–18, 430.

[2] *De Cerimoniis Aulae Byzantinae*, pp. 343, 345 (*CSHB*).

[3] Kukules, *op. cit.* III, 73–80; Bréhier, *op. cit.* pp. 93–107.

marked the passage of the hours. Horses of supernatural prescience gave tidings of victory or defeat. Monuments, often surviving from remote antiquity, were invested with magical and sympathetic power. For her Emperor, as for the priest-kings in the dawn of history, the clouds might gather, and the earth be deluged by life-giving rains. All these marvels, compounded of the relics of ancient science and of the rooted superstitions of a hybrid and credulous populace, spread in magnified and transmuted report through the nations of the East and West, and reappeared in the now wholly miraculous dress of medieval romance, in the golden birds which sang on the linden-tree to Wolfdietrich, or in the thunderous showers which accompanied a libation from the secret spring of Broceliande.[1]

While much of the outward splendour of the capital derived from its native industries and its foreign trade, its economic strength lay chiefly in the produce and taxation of its provinces, which provided it with cheap food and the means with which to defray the enormous cost of imperial administration. The theory of rural organisation since the seventh century had been that the land was divided into smallholdings, which were the freehold of the head of the family. These holdings in turn were grouped in communes or villages, and these villages formed separate units of taxation: that is to say, each village was assessed at an annual sum which all the proprietors within its circumscription were jointly held liable for subscribing. The small-holdings served a military purpose also, since the more valuable of them were the property of peasant-soldiers, who, from the seventh until the eleventh century, formed the backbone of the imperial armies. In examining the social life of the provinces, therefore, it is necessary to begin, not as in the capital with the highest social class, but with the peasant proprietor and his village. For although it would be untrue to say that the smallholding system, even in the days of its comparative prosperity, ever superseded the older system of large landed estates, yet it was the chosen instrument of imperial policy, and with it the Byzantine economy stood or fell.[2]

The nucleus of a commune was a group of mud-brick houses, thatched or occasionally tiled, and surrounded by walled courtyards, in which the well was sunk and over which strayed the more domestic animals. In among this group of houses were set the vegetable

[1] Cf. Ch. Diehl, 'Quelques croyances byzantines sur la fin de Constantinople', *BZ*, xxx (1929–30), 192–6; Kukules, *op. cit.* I, 2, p. 238; P. Riant, *Les Scandinaves en terre sainte* (Paris, 1865), p. 200; C. B. Lewis, *Classical Mythology and Arthurian Romance* (Oxford, 1932), pp. 78, 215.

[2] G. Ostrogorsky, *Cambridge Economic History of Europe*, I (Cambridge, 1941), 194–223, 579–83 (bibliography); P. Lemerle, 'Esquisse pour une histoire agraire de Byzance' [See Gen. Bibl. v]; P. Charanis, *op. cit., B*, xvii (1944–5), 42–57.

gardens. Beyond the immediate area of habitation stretched the
territory appertaining to it, which consisted of strips of arable land
and walled vineyards or olive-yards—all of which were the freeholds
of individual proprietors—and of an area of common pasturage for
sheep and oxen and goats. On the periphery were the copses of oak
or chestnut in which the peasant cut his wood, and the swineherd
pastured his hogs. The methods and instruments by which these lands
were cultivated showed little if any advance on those of ancient times.
The mattock and the spade, the sickle and the pruning-knife were
indeed not susceptible of any revolutionary improvements. But the
primitive method of ploughing, and of all animal traction, militated
against a proper exploitation of the soil and contributed to the impoverishment of the cultivator. The light plough was drawn through
the shallow furrow by a pair of lank oxen; and, light as it was, they
could have drawn no heavier burden. The antique principle of forward
yoke and choking neck-band was until the twelfth century universal;
and it has been calculated that a pair of horses, harnessed in this
manner, could not, without danger of asphyxiation, draw in a wheeled
vehicle a load of more than about ten hundredweights, or many times
less than what the same animals, harnessed with shoulder-halters, can
now draw with ease. This wastage of animal power combined with the
high price of the draught-animals themselves to keep alive the practice of porterage on human backs; and gave an advantage to the
large landowner who could afford to maintain gangs of slave porters.
The grain was still trodden out by oxen; and much of it was ground
by the primitive hand-mill. The fields were not systematically
manured, although after harvest-tide the cattle were permitted to
browse amidst the stubble.[1]

The population of the villages must at all times have varied greatly,
according to the quality and fertility of the soil. In the post-
crusading epoch, for which alone some significant figures can be
obtained, we hear of villages of between fifty and five hundred inhabitants. Yet there is some reason to think that, in earlier centuries,
many were larger than this. The rudimentary accounts which we
possess of the village in the tenth century give the impression of an
expanding unit, which regularly felled or burnt its peripheral woods
to provide additional lands for an expanding population. The rural
population of this period cannot be measured by comparison with the
strikingly low figures of reproduction, however these are to be ex-

---

[1] Cf. A. P. Každan, *Agrarnie Otnošenija v Vizantii XIII–XIV vv.* (Moscow, 1952),
p. 43; Lefebre de Noëttes, 'Le système d'attelage du cheval et du bœuf à Byzance et
les conséquences de son emploi', *Mélanges Charles Diehl*, I (Paris, 1930), 183–90;
E. E. Lipšić, *VS*, II (1946), 105–16.

plained, which are extant for a group of villages at the beginning of the fourteenth century.[1]

It is probable that, until rural life was disrupted by internal and external causes during the twelfth and thirteenth centuries, the lot of the poorest peasant was, from the viewpoint of bare sustenance and survival, preferable to that of the lowest class in the city. His daily wage was but twelve half-pence. His dress was a single black smock and a pair of knee-boots. His diet was meagre: for the staple was barley bread, baked on cinders, and pulse, eked out, as local circumstances permitted, with fish or olives or honey. But his food was clean and his water untainted. His life was healthy, and relatively free from infectious disease. The histories of the rural saints provide abundant evidence that life could be supported in full vigour to a great age on a diet so spare as, by modern standards, would be judged barely sufficient to preserve the frame from dissolution. The wealthier peasants fared much better, being supplied with mutton, bacon, poultry and wine of their own breeding and cultivation.

Education and even learning were not wholly beyond the reach of the poor country child, though such learning was of an exclusively ecclesiastical character. Much might depend on the position of his village, and the proximity of a monastery with books and monks who could read them. The seminaries provided for 'children of the world' in city monasteries had their counterparts throughout the countryside; and to them would repair such children as had ambitious parents, rising long before dawn and toiling all day at their alphabets and their edifying texts. The monastic preceptors demanded no large fee for dispensing such knowledge as they possessed. The exceptionally gifted, laborious and pious could thus pass the gates of learning, and become mighty in the Scriptures. Such was in fact the commencement of the career of many of the rural saints, and of some few who, after long years of holy seclusion and asceticism, attained to high ecclesiastical preferment. Moreover, the clever child who could purchase and profit by his schooling might hand it on to his poorer, less fortunate playmates. One of the most endearing characteristics of the Hellenistic civilisation in every age has been a respect and indeed a passion for letters. And a celebrated folk song, still in general use, tells how St Basil of Caesarea, when still a child, laid by his staff and traced out the alphabet for the benefit of some roadside urchins.

The life of the peasant cultivator was, as always, harsh and labori-

---

[1] G. Ostrogorsky, *Pour l'histoire de la féodalité byzantine* (Brussels, 1954), p. 269; F. Dölger, *Aus den Schatzkammern des Heiligen Berges* (Munich, 1948), p. 189; A. P. Každan, *op. cit.* pp. 41–2.

ous. But diversions, though rare and simple, were not altogether
lacking. The great festivals of the Church gave occasion for relaxation
and merry-making. And, beside these, there were few even among
the most distant villages that were not visited from time to time by
entertainers of a more secular description. The rustics flocked to stare
at a performing ape, a tame serpent, a dancing bear or a sagacious
dog; and the itinerant keepers of these animals, who were mostly
gipsies, were assured of a living by their exhibition. Monsters of the
human species, giants, dwarfs or pairs of Siamese twins, were equally
attractive, and were invested by superstition with the additional
prestige of prodigies. A whole tribe of contortionists and jugglers,
acrobats and tight-rope walkers, conjurors and thimble-riggers
travelled from village to village. Lastly, the illusionists, a class of
entertainers extinct in western Europe since the Renaissance, could
entrance an audience of holiday-makers or wedding guests from dawn
to dusk with visions of wonder and enchantment.

The chief occasions upon which these, and many other, delights were
offered, were the Fairs. These gatherings ranged in magnitude from
the annual and internationally famous Fairs of Thessalonica or
Ephesus or Trebizond down to the small markets which each district
held many times a year in its local market town. The smaller markets
were an indispensable feature of the rural economy. It was there that
beasts, oil, wine, grain or vegetables, together with simple household
utensils, were purchased or exchanged. It was there also that such
entertainments as we have described could most profitably be ex-
hibited. It was there that were practised the rustic sports of dancing,
running, wrestling, single-stick and archery. The Church, although
its own calendar often gave the occasion for such meetings, viewed
these and other less edifying amusements with some disapproval.
But the State recognised their social value, and, as was its habit,
turned the Fairs to account by exacting a heavy toll of market-dues.[1]

Such in brief outline was the apparently reasonable system of rural
society during the centuries under review. Yet, even during the
period when the central government was strongest, that system was
assailed by disease on every hand. Political, economic and natural
causes combined to overthrow it; and when these are listed, it is
indeed surprising that the system endured even as long as it did. The
small, freehold properties were never, at the best of times, far removed
from insolvency. The smallholder depends for his survival chiefly on
two factors: a peaceful countryside and an equable climate. He lives
upon what he grows and can market from year to year. He has few
reserves, and little or no hoarded capital. A bad harvest, still more

<hr/>

[1] Kukules, *op. cit.* III, 247–83.

a succession of bad harvests, must ruin the most industrious, and drive him to the money-lender, to sale of his property and his freedom, or to flight from his debtors. Two recurrent scourges which were as fatal as the Saracen or the Bulgar to the rural economy were drought and locusts. The lives of the saints record instance after instance of the disaster and misery brought on by these natural pestilences.[1]

Once the small proprietor, through a failed crop or the death of his working cattle, was unable to pay his way, he had little hope, save in the charity of his neighbours, of avoiding complete insolvency. And to be insolvent was no light matter. He had to face the annual invasion of a cruel and rapacious body of tax-collectors, accompanied by a posse of soldiers, whom no pleas of misfortune or act of God could move from exacting the uttermost farthing of their dues, and very frequently more than their dues. The peasant was at all times overburdened by taxation; and the huge cost of imperial government, especially during the long and almost uninterrupted periods of hostilities, rendered such taxation a melancholy necessity. The vital importance of collecting the full measure of taxes, even at the time when the collectors were still government servants and not private contractors, must account for the savage penalties inflicted on the insolvent. Defaulters were summarily flogged, and their goods distrained. Often the punishments were more dreadful still. At the beginning of the twelfth century the wretches who were deputed to collect the taxes in the island of Cyprus resolved, in addition to flogging the defaulters, to set hungry dogs upon them to tear their flesh. It would be pleasant to suppose that this fearful instance of barbarity was exceptional, occurring in a remote quarter of the Empire at a time of disorder and weakness. But the supposition would be unjustified. In the tenth century, at a time of prosperity and good order, debtors were removed in batches to the local gaol, where it appears that they were not only beaten but tortured as well. It is not surprising that many proprietors absconded, either to swell the city mob, or to join a gang of brigands, or to escape beyond the frontiers. For their debts, their brethren, by virtue of the law of 'common responsibility', became at once liable. And even though, where districts had been thoroughly devastated by foreign invasion, the government was occasionally forced to relax this vicious principle, the fate of the tax-payers of Cyprus is a grim reminder of the persistence and cruelty with which it was enforced.[2]

[1] A. P. Každan, *op. cit.* p. 48.

[2] Cf. F. Dölger, 'Zu dem Abdankungsgedicht des Nikolaus Muzalon', *BZ*, xxxv (1935), 13–14; *Vita S. Mariae Junioris* (*AASS*, Nov. iv), 693 d; G. Rouillard, *La vie rurale dans l'empire byzantin* (Paris, 1953), pp. 100–7, 136; A. A. Vasiliev, *History of the Byzantine Empire* (Oxford, 1952), p. 480.

If to these natural and political causes of decline are added the almost annual invasions from the East and the long periods of occupation and pillage by western hordes, it will not seem strange that the peasant proprietor, in theory a vital prop of the state's organisation, was a prop which could never have continued to sustain the burden imposed upon it. The communities of free proprietors would inevitably have disappeared far sooner than they did had it not been for a factor whose importance, both in peace and war, was fully appreciated by the central government: that is, the solidarity existing between the members of each particular group. Inter-marriage among the families was naturally frequent, and was productive of a corporate spirit not less valuable to the village society than to the fiscal system. Neighbours were almost always good neighbours, and for the best and strongest of reasons.[1]

None the less, the maladroit policy of the government, guided as it always was by the theory rather than by the practical experience of administration, could only end in bringing about the very state of affairs most fatal to it. The impoverishment of the peasantry fundamentally affected the prosperity of the Empire, both political, economic and military. Despite a series of well-conceived legal prohibitions, the ruined smallholder was forced by sheer necessity to resign his land and liberty, in sale or in mortgage, to the large proprietor. At first in single plots, at length in whole districts, the peasants' freehold fell into the circumscription of the estates of the 'powerful'. These acquisitors, whose estates have, inaccurately but not altogether absurdly, been denominated 'feudal', were chiefly responsible for the breakdown of the state control over provincial finance. Imperial edicts might denounce them as tyrants and wolves. But to the peasants who became their tenants and serfs they at first appeared in the guise of saviours, who, while exploiting their labour, could at least preserve them from maltreatment and starvation. It is a highly significant circumstance that when in 932 a peasant revolt ensued upon a succession of disastrous harvests, the leader of the rebels won their fidelity by pretending to be that Constantine Ducas, scion of one of the chief aristocratic houses of Cappadocia, who had nineteen years earlier lost his life in a criminal attempt on the palace and the crown.[2]

Equally disastrous was the effect which imperial tyranny exerted on the minds of the peasant soldiers. The armed forces of Byzantium, both military and naval, were far superior to those of their antagonists in every department except the most vital of all, that of morale.

---

[1] *Imp. Leonis Tactica, MPG*, cvii, 708; *AB*, xiii (1894), 83.
[2] Theophanes Continuatus, p. 421.

They were furnished with the most effective devices and the most perfect equipment. They were stiffened by brigades of highly paid mercenaries. But the main body consisted of soldier-civilians, who served their campaigns and returned to the plough. It was not to be expected that there should be found in their ranks that rooted and habitual discipline which is proof against all the accidents of surprise, of ineffectual leadership or of political circumstance. Nor was there present that homogeneity of national sentiment which has often supplied the deficiencies of training and experience: that sentiment which upheld republican Rome in all the trials of her struggle against Carthage. The ranks were recruited from a mixed population, many of whom were but recently settled in the Empire and but recently converted to Christianity. It was required of the officers that they should have command of more than one foreign vernacular. The idea that the Empire's wars were crusades for Orthodox Christianity, though present in the minds of the government and of some senior officers, could hardly be adopted by the rank and file. And the idea that the soldier was fighting for Emperor and fatherland was too often stultified by the inhuman conduct of the Emperor's own tax-collectors. The result was that military success depended, to an extent far greater than was expedient for internal security, on the personality of the individual commander. The most successful generals of the tenth century, with a single important exception, were all military aristocrats for whom leadership in war was an hereditary profession. The two greatest were, by an inevitable consequence, able to seize the crown, and several others came within measurable distance of doing so. The Emperor Constantine VII claimed that his soldiers were his spiritual children, who fought for their Emperor as the Christians fought for Christ. But the soldiers themselves proclaimed that they fought and died for love of his marshal, Nicephorus Phocas.[1]

The military aristocracy, therefore, until with the Comnenian dynasty they at length made good their claim to imperial power, were an object of continual suspicion and hatred to the central government, who were at their wits' end for means to repress or cajole them. The very existence of an aristocracy of birth was anomalous; yet in practice the words 'well-born', 'of well-born parents' were powerful at all times in Church and State. From at least the earlier part of the ninth century a recognised nobility is found among the great

[1] *Imp. Leonis Tactica*, 700, 709, 828; Zonaras, ed. L. Dindorf, IV (Leipzig, 1871), p. 82; R. Vári, 'Zum historischen Exzerptenwerke des Konstantinos Porphyrogennetos', *BZ*, XVII (1908), 79; *De Velitatione Bellica*, in Leo Diaconus, pp. 238–41 (*CSHB*); Theophanes Continuatus, p. 478.

clans of eastern Anatolia, whose influence was felt both in military
and in civil life. St Irene, a noble lady of Cappadocia, who in the
middle of that century resigned a splendid career in the world to
embrace the monastic life, was made abbess of the monastery of
Chrysovalantion when hardly more than twenty years of age. It is
not probable that mere piety can have brought her this early promotion. The immense influence in state affairs during the Macedonian
epoch of such families as Phocas, Ducas and Argyrus is apparent in
every page of its history. And the danger which they constituted to
the crown is equally unmistakable. Their country palaces were courts
in miniature. Their domains and revenues were constantly increasing.
Every resource was invoked to check the increase. They were perpetually spied upon by the Emperor's agents, so that timely warning
might be received of revolt or conspiracy; the city populace was
incited against them; and the imperial navy, the only branch of the
native forces which could be trusted to remain loyal to the crown, was
held in readiness to forestall a crossing of the Bosphorus and an
assault on the capital. All these measures proved at last ineffectual;
and served only to widen the gulf between government and bureaucracy on the one hand, and the military might of the provinces on
the other.[1]

An interesting account of social conditions prevailing among the
rural gentry during the eleventh century is to be found in the precepts
and anecdotes of Cecaumenus, the descendant of a military family
which hailed from Thessaly. The sum of his counsel to the landed
gentleman in peace-time is to stay quietly on his estate, to eat his
own bread in the sweat of his brow, and to avoid the money-lender
like the plague. Office under government should indeed not be declined if it comes unsought, since all power is from God; but it must
never be canvassed or bought. To underwrite a government contract
is foolish if not wicked; nor is it wise to lend money to another to
help him to undertake such a contract, still less to finance him in a
commercial enterprise. The sermon preached by Cecaumenus on the
Isocratean text, that a man should be prudent in his converse, presents us with a dismal picture of scheming, spying and treachery in
provincial society. Anybody who seeks support in voicing a public
grievance is, as likely as not, an agent provocateur. Not even a
private dinner to friends is free of the spy. The lightest word, the
most innocent action, will be reported in mangled form to the

---

[1] Cf. G. Ostrogorsky, *History of the Byzantine State* (Oxford, 1956), pp. 253–5;
A. P. Každan, 'Krestjanskie Dviženija v Vizantii v X v. i Agrarnaja Politika
Imperatorov Makedonskoj Dinastii,' *VV*, v (1952), 83; R. Guilland, 'La noblesse de
race à Byzance', *BS*, ix (1948), 307–14.

governor. The state of private morals is so low that friendship, or what passes for such, is a positive evil: for the friend, even if not a spy, is certainly a potential destroyer of domestic happiness. The safest course, where all courses are perilous, is that of unswerving loyalty to the Emperor, of quietism and of isolation. We might be tempted to suppose that this advice comes from a disappointed and cynical curmudgeon, were it not also clear from his treatise that he is a man of wide experience, sound common sense and sterling rectitude. His prejudice against the bureaucracy and the secular clergy is indeed that of his class. But it is a melancholy reflection that even the most harmless and circumspect life among the upper ranks of rural society could be productive of so little domestic security and content.[1]

In an Empire which, despite its noble theory of internal unity, was rent by so many and deep-seated contradictions, it would be reasonable to look to the impulses of Orthodox Christianity, as disseminated by its splendid ecclesiastical organisation, as the one link which could bind throne and bureaucrat, magnate, soldier and peasant into one whole, and almost into one nation: the more so, since it is well known that, during the centuries of Turkish domination, that Church was the chief agency which preserved and fostered national feeling in the Greek-speaking portions of the Turkish Empire. It is true that in the Byzantine Empire also the force of religious feeling must not be underestimated. In the capital all classes were fervently and even fanatically Orthodox. Even in the provinces the upper ranks of society were sincerely religious, and well versed in biblical and hagiographical lore. If Christianity had been equally potent among the peasantry, and thus among the common soldiery as well, it would have bred in them that vital sense of Orthodox solidarity which could by itself have preserved their Empire. But there is reason to think that this thorough permeation was never achieved. The Christian faith, with its austere morality and its doctrinal subtlety, could make little impression on illiterate and brutish rustics, drawn from many lands and many racial traditions. The most it could hope to do was to outmatch the superstitions of the countryside by the power of its own magic. The Saviour himself, in a far more cultivated society, had been forced to appeal to popular imagination by arresting displays of supernatural power. The popular saints of Byzantium, noble and pure as they most often were, had likewise to approach their fellows through the paths of miraculous healing, rain-making or inspired prediction. Moreover, the saints themselves affected the solitary, and undertook no systematic teaching; and in this they differed

[1] *Cecaumeni Strategicon*, pp. 36 ff.

very markedly from the western orders of preaching friars. The parish
priest was often as ignorant as his flock, and was indeed in later times
transferred as a serf among serfs from one great estate to another.[1]
It is highly probable that the work of the iconoclasts retarded to an
enormous extent the establishment of sound doctrine among the
peasantry, by closing the visual channels to knowledge for those to
whom the written could never be open; and the seven spirits of pagan
superstition poured into the chamber which had been swept and
garnished of the single uncleanness of icon-worship.[2]

It is further to be noted that the popular saints, humble and
ascetic though their lives might be, were themselves hardly ever of
the humblest origin, and often of origins very far from humble. They
were all literate, and indeed capable of some degree of scholarship.
There appear to have been few whose parents were below the rank of
prosperous farmers, such as were those of St Luke the Younger and
St Luke the Stylite. Even the crazed St Andrew, whose life was
passed in the extreme of misery and torment which could be suffered
by the most indigent among the city population, had once been the
confidential servant of a high functionary, by whom he had been
educated and at whose instance he had made a profound study of
Scripture; nor, even in the days of his bitterest privation, was he
thought an unfit companion and preceptor of one who afterwards
ascended the patriarchal throne.

The pride and pomp of religion, which filled the capital and the
large towns, and which was more spiritually interpreted in a thousand
seminaries, awoke only a feeble echo in the remote hamlets of Anatolia and Hellas, where the bear-leader peddled his tufts of prophylactic fur, the venerable 'centurion' assumed a divine wisdom
and almost a divine status, the magician foretold from the shapes of
the sunset clouds the future of those who resorted to his skill, and the
very monks themselves, dedicated to the worship of a higher creed,
were not ashamed to invite old witches to prophesy according to the
patterns formed by barley-grains. All these impostors were denounced by the Church; but the very fact that such denunciations
were repeated century after century is striking proof of their in-
efficacy. Paganism, with its roots securely planted in the periodicity
and aberrations of Nature, met the needs of those whose lives began
and ended with the soil and its tillage. As late at least as the twelfth
century and probably much later, the peasants who poured the fresh

---

[1] A. P. Rudakov, *op. cit.* p. 179.

[2] On the role of the Church and monasticism see chapters XXIII–XXVI and on the
power of the saint in particular see N. H. Baynes and E. Dawes, *Three Byzantine
Saints* (Oxford, 1948).

must into the vats burst into guffaws of simulated intoxication to humour a wine-god whose name and worship had been officially extinct during thirty generations. It has often been remarked that the content of modern Greek folk-lore is decidedly pagan, and that much of it derives, directly or indirectly, from the pre-Christian age. At first sight the phenomenon is surprising, when we consider by how many centuries of spiritual, doctrinal and national Christianity the ancient world is divided from our own. But the explanation is simple: the Byzantine peasantry was multifarious in origin, and its composition was constantly changing. There was no settled stock upon which true Christianity could be grafted from generation to generation. A tincture could be imparted, but it was soon contaminated, and fused but too readily with older beliefs evolved in a more humanistic age, which, primitive and superstitious as they were, yet bore a more immediate relation to the daily life and needs of the countryman.[1]

The Byzantine state, as we said at the beginning, is often regarded as a monument of conservatism. Conservatism was in fact the characteristic feature of its spiritual and imperial faith, and, in so far as its Emperors were able to maintain it, of its practice also. Yet, after all, its long story is one of movement, of that movement which one of the old philosophers picturesquely describes as the periodical encroachment of strife and division upon the kingdom of unity and love. Still, amid all change, may be discerned a solid and ever hardening core which survived the decay of the husk; and the seeds of this core are Orthodoxy and Hellenism, and the nation which these two factors united to create and sustain. It was, as we saw, among the educated class of the capital that these forces worked most strongly; and it is the pride and glory of this class that with all its narrow puritanism it could discern in Homer and Aristotle and Menander treasures no less worthy of preservation than those of Holy Scripture. We end, as we began, at Byzantium.

[1] Σύνταγμα τῶν θείων καὶ ἱερῶν κανόνων, ed. G. A. Rhalles and M. Potles, II (Athens, 1852), pp. 440–52; N. B. Tomadakis, Ὁ Ἰωσὴφ Βρυέννιος καὶ ἡ Κρήτη κατὰ τὸ 1400 (Athens, 1947), pp. 112–21; L. Oeconomos, 'L'état intellectuel et moral des Byzantins vers le milieu du XIVe siècle d'après une page de Joseph Bryennios', *Mélanges Ch. Diehl*, I, 225–33; Rouillard, *Vie rurale*, pp. 197–202; Rudakov, *op. cit.* p. 176.

CHAPTER XXIII

THE SECULAR CHURCH

The peace of Constantine inaugurated a complete transformation in the standing of the Church. For three long difficult centuries it had struggled for its very existence against the opposition of the Roman state. That state had now come to its support, and lent power and authority to its ministers. Christians could face the future with confidence and joy. The vital problems implicit in the new situation emerged only gradually. Most important of all was the changed relationship of the Church with the Emperor and the state. The Roman conception of Empire remained unaltered: the task of Rome would always be to rule the world, but its responsibilities now included the transmission of peace and truth to all peoples in the name of Jesus Christ.

I. CHURCH AND EMPEROR

There was a fundamental change in the conception of the status of the Emperor. Christians could not regard him as divine, or even of divine descent. But—and here the way had been prepared by the syncretism of later Roman religion and by neoplatonic philosophy— they now thought of him as the chosen instrument of God, a man selected by Providence to become the divine representative on earth. This lifted his position so high above that of other mortals that many rites and ceremonies formerly belonging to the cult of the Emperor could be adapted to meet the new situation. Such terms as the *sacrum palatium* of the Emperor, the *sacratissimae institutiones* and the *divinae subscriptiones* could continue to be used. The ruler was hedged in by a solemn ritual, which scholars have called 'the imperial liturgy', strongly reminiscent of the liturgy of the Church. But whereas in pagan society the state had organised ceremonial worship with the Emperor at its head as Summus Pontifex, the Founder of Christianity had established an independent Church with a hierarchy deriving its authority from Him. After some hesitation Constantine himself pointed the way towards a new development; he incorporated the Church within the framework of the state. This meant that it was to become a 'state Church' which was not only under the special protection of the state, but also subject to its direction; a development facilitated by the fact that the aims of both were identical. Both had to win the world for Christ.

The Emperor was now raised above the Church, a position which gave him a number of prerogatives. For instance, he summoned councils, presided over them in person or through his officials, sanctioned decisions and published them in the form of decrees. He gave his own judgement on matters of discipline or liturgy and had a predominating influence in the election of Patriarchs. He founded new episcopal sees and raised the rank and status of the already existing metropolitan sees, archbishoprics and bishoprics. In due course many Emperors even tried to overrule the Church in matters of faith, but the results of such imperial intervention were generally short-lived.

In view of their far-reaching interference in church affairs the Emperors have been accused of 'caesaropapism', although some scholars, particularly in recent years, have rejected this term.[1] It must, however, be admitted not only that the Emperors frequently encroached upon ecclesiastical territory in such a way as to suggest 'caesaropapism', but that the competence of the Church was so ill-defined as often to make difficult the assertion of its freedom of action. All the same it is scarcely correct to define the normal relationship between Church and state in Byzantium by such a term. The Emperor was by no means the ruler or the head of the Church; he merely had a right of supervision. This was quite clearly stated in Justinian's Novel, no. 6, pr.: 'Maxima quidem in hominibus sunt dona dei a superna collata clementia sacerdotium et imperium, illud quidem divinis ministrans, hoc autem humanis praesidens ac diligentiam exhibens; ex uno eodemque principio utraque procedentia humanam exornant vitam. Ideoque nihil sic erit studiosum imperatoribus, sicut sacerdotum honestas, cum utique et pro illis ipsis semper deo supplicent.' Here the Emperor's task was to watch over the priesthood, and nothing more. In the last centuries of the Empire both official synodal communications and the canonists must have had something similar in mind when they referred to the ecclesiastical role of the Emperor, for they used in this connection the term '$\epsilon\pi\iota\sigma\tau\eta\mu o\nu\acute{\alpha}\rho\chi\eta\varsigma$ of the Church'.[2]

---

[1] See also pt. I, chapter IV, pp. 133ff. and above, chapter XX, pp. 12ff.; *Byzantium*, ed. N. H. Baynes and H. St L. B. Moss (s.v. 'Church and State' in the index). See also G. Ostrogorsky, 'Otnošenie cerkvi i gosudarstva v Vizantii', *Sem. Kond.* IV (1933), 121–34 (with German summary), and the review by F. Dölger, *BZ*, XXXI (1931), 449; J. M. Hussey, *Church and Learning in the Byzantine Empire*, pp. 125, 132–57 and *passim*. On Justinian, L. Wenger, *Canon* (Vienna, 1942) (v. Cäsaropapismus) is of fundamental importance. On the significance of the *Epanagoge* in this connection see G. Ostrogorsky, *History of the Byzantine State*, pp. 213ff.

[2] Cf. the synod of 1147 which deposed the Patriarch Cosmas II, *RP*, v, p. 309. *GR* does not mention this synod, but see Grumel's note, *GR* 920 (crit. 2). On the canonists see Theodore Balsamon, *In can. 12 Ant.*, *MPG*, CXXXVII, 1312, and

Hence the clear distinction made throughout between ecclesiastical canons and secular laws, even though the latter might affect the Church. The most important corpus of ecclesiastical rulings, the *Nomocanon in 14 Titles*, clearly distinguishes between canons, which are always mentioned first in every chapter, and the secular laws which follow under the heading 'the law' and are merely summarised. Even a canonist like Theodore Balsamon at the end of the twelfth century, who was extremely devoted to the Emperor, considered that laws should give place to canons.[1] One must also remember that many secular laws affecting the Church may have been passed on the initiative of the Church itself because the state had the means to enforce them while the Church had not.

It is certain that the Emperor did not possess priestly power, but was dependent on the priesthood for the performance of religious rites. His only liturgical prerogatives were entry into the sanctuary and reception of the Holy Communion according to the rites prescribed for priests and deacons. It is undeniable that Emperors often recognised little limitation of their authority, but there is not sufficient evidence to justify the use of the term 'caesaropapism' for the recognised and normal relationship between Church and state.

II. THE 'OECUMENICAL' PATRIARCH

When peace was made between the Roman state and the Church, the majority of Christians were Roman subjects, but there were some Christian communities outside the Empire in neighbouring lands, in Armenia, Georgia, Mesopotamia—at that time the centre of the Persian Empire—and later in Ethiopia. Within the Empire the organisation of the Church had been largely adapted to the existing political structure. Diocletian had introduced a new division of the provinces for administrative purposes, and the Church followed his example by creating ecclesiastical provinces under the direction of a metropolitan, who resided in the capital of the province. This system was accepted and imposed by the Council of Nicaea (325), where for the first time representatives of the whole Church within the Empire were gathered together. But even as early as this, the beginning of a more complex organisation can be perceived; the

Demetrius Chomatianus, *Ad Const. Cabasilam, quaest. 4*, ed. J. B. Pitra, *Analecta sacra et classica Spicilegio Solesmensi parata*, VI (Rome, 1891), p. 631. This term is also used by the Emperors, e.g. Isaac II, ed. J. Zepos, *Jus graeco-romanum*, I, p. 430; Michael VIII, in a letter to the Patriarch Joseph, *MM*, V, p. 247. *Epistemonarches* was the name of the person responsible for order and discipline in schools and also monasteries. See Ducange, *Gloss. Graeci* on the Studites; cf. *MPG*, XCI, 1709, 1781.

[1] Theodore Balsamon, *In tit. I*, cap. II, *Nomocan.*, *MPG*, CIV, 981.

Bishop of Rome could exercise jurisdictional rights over the whole of Italy, likewise the Bishop of Alexandria over Egypt, Libya and the Pentapolis, and to a lesser extent the Bishop of Antioch over the oriental dioceses (I Nicaea, can. 6). In the course of the fourth and fifth centuries the Bishoprics of Constantinople and Jerusalem were added to these 'arch-metropolitan' sees, as they have been called. Justinian confirmed this in his novels and recognised the organisation of the Church into five Patriarchates (this term was by then in use) with the Pope of Rome at their head. This development had not been achieved, however, without bitter strife. When Constantine moved his residence from Rome to Byzantium on the Bosphorus (330), this city was the seat of an ordinary suffragan of the Bishop of Heraclea, whose see cannot be shown with certainty to have existed before the beginning of the third century. It is a controversial point whether the Bishop of the new capital was freed from the jurisdiction of the Bishop of Heraclea in Constantine's day, but as he inevitably became the Emperor's adviser in ecclesiastical matters, he came naturally to occupy an exceptional position. The First Council of Constantinople (381), which finally destroyed Arianism, undoubtedly carried out the wishes of Theodosius when in its third canon it made the Bishop of Constantinople, the New Rome, second in rank only to the Bishop of Old Rome, and gave him the same prerogatives. The Bishops of Alexandria, hitherto the most important see of the East, did not suffer this humiliation in silence. Before the Council met, Peter of Alexandria had already tried to claim the Bishopric of Constantinople for his protégé Maximus. A series of famous quarrels ensued, Theophilus against John Chrysostom, Cyril of Alexandria against Nestorius, Flavian against Dioscorus, in conflict over principles, at times worthy and at times disreputable. The initial victory of the last-mentioned Bishop of Alexandria at the 'Robber Council' of Ephesus in 449 was turned into final defeat at the Council of Chalcedon in 451. Dioscorus was not only deposed, but at a special meeting held at the end of the Council, the third canon of Constantinople was solemnly confirmed and the metropolitans and bishops of the three smaller secular dioceses, Asia, Cappadocia and Thrace, were made subordinate to the Bishop of Constantinople. This meant that the holder of that office acquired the juridical position which he had tried to obtain ever since the Council of Constantinople (381). It can be argued that this decree, later known as the twenty-eighth canon of the Council of Chalcedon (451), was illegal, not only by reason of the circumstances in which it was passed, but also because of the protests of the Pope, which were so emphatic that the Emperor Marcian and the Patriarch

Anatolius himself finally gave in—a fact mentioned for the first time in the collected canons at the end of the following century.[1] But in actual fact in the Eastern Church the decree remained the foundation-stone of the special position of the Patriarch of Constantinople and is so regarded to this day.

In course of time the development of the Patriarchate of Constantinople was decisively influenced by the monophysite controversy which led to the religious secession of a very large number of the Christians in Egypt, Palestine and Syria, while the Arab conquests in the seventh century brought about their political separation. So in the East the Byzantine Patriarch, who had meanwhile assumed the title of 'Oecumenical' in spite of papal protests, was left without any rivals within the Empire. The West was overrun by barbarians, and the Popes could make their authority felt only in exceptional circumstances, for instance when disruptive heresies in Byzantium made the re-establishment of orthodoxy imperative. The links between Rome and central Italy and the Byzantine Empire grew weaker, and this growing alienation was increased by the papal alliance with the Franks and Germans, which led first to political and then to ecclesiastical severance (1054).

Before this stage was reached, the Patriarch of Constantinople had already increased his power. This was partly at the expense of the Roman Patriarchate, for the provinces of eastern Illyricum, Thessalonica and Greece and also southern Italy and Sicily, which had previously been under Roman jurisdiction, were transferred to the Patriarchate of Constantinople by the Emperor Leo III. In addition, imperial conquests in the East made it possible to add new provinces such as Isauria to the Patriarchate of Constantinople, while the conversion of peoples outside the Empire, especially in Russia in the late tenth century, meant that the metropolitans and bishops of these regions were subordinate to the Patriarch of Constantinople.

The position of the Patriarch was impressive not only as far as the outside world was concerned; within the Empire he was from the political point of view the most respected and influential person after the Emperor. From the accession of Anastasius I (491–518) it became customary for the Patriarch to receive the confession of faith of the newly elected Emperor. He also crowned him, thus giving the Emperor, at least in the eyes of the people, a religious consecration. Some Patriarchs even succeeded in forcing their will upon the Emperor. This happened with Nicholas I, at least during the early

---

[1] On Chalcedon and the rank of Constantinople see Etterman, 'Ausgestaltung des Konstantinopolitanischen Primats', *Das Konzil von Chalkedon*, ii, ed. A. Grillmeier and H. Bacht (Würzburg, 1953), 459–90.

minority of Constantine VII, in the case of Polyeuctus and John I Tzimisces, and of Michael Cerularius and Constantine IX Monomachus. But the Patriarch was first and foremost the head of the Byzantine Church and although the term 'dyarchy', in the sense of the joint rule of Emperor and Patriarch, has been applied to Byzantium, this overrates the power of the Patriarch. The fact is that in later times the Patriarchs overruled the Emperors only in matters of faith, particularly where reunion was in question, and here they had the great majority of the monks and of the whole people behind them.

It was the Emperor's prerogative to elect the Patriarch from among three names put forward by the synod, or if he did not approve of any of these, to appoint a different candidate. He could, at least in practice, force an uncongenial Patriarch to resign, or with the aid of the synod depose him. Out of the 122 Patriarchs elected between 379 and 1451, fifty-three were deposed or forced to resign, and of these at least thirty-six did so at the instigation of the Emperor. It is significant of ecclesiastical developments that from the fourth century up to the iconoclastic controversy Patriarchs were elected almost exclusively from the ranks of the secular clergy, especially the clergy connected with the Church of St Sophia, whereas from the iconoclastic controversy to the conquest of Constantinople by the Latins, apart from six or seven laymen, mostly monks were chosen. There was of course a striking contrast between the somewhat uncultured monks and the secular clergy with their humanist education. In the last two centuries of the Byzantine Empire the decisive question in the election was whether or not the candidate either favoured reunion with Rome or supported Palamism and the hesychasts.

As head of the Byzantine Church the Patriarch was responsible for seeing that it lived in accordance with the teachings of the Holy Scriptures and the precepts of canon law. He had to remonstrate when the Emperor himself infringed them. There are not many instances of Patriarchs expressing disapproval of the Emperor's behaviour, but they do occur. Up to the eleventh century the more intricate problems, particularly doctrinal controversies, were settled by the General Councils in the presence of delegates of the apostolic see and the oriental Patriarchs. After the schism with the West the function of these General Councils was taken over by synods of a particularly solemn character, at which not only the metropolitans and bishops were present, but also the Emperor, part of the senate, and ecclesiastical and certain secular officials. Matters concerning patriarchal administration were normally dealt with by the so-called σύνοδος ἐνδημοῦσα or resident synod, to which bishops living in the capital (ἐνδημοῦντες) were summoned. As early as the Council of

Chalcedon (451) some bishops had protested that these synods arrogated to themselves the right to interfere in other Patriarchates. This interference ceased later on, but from the beginning of the tenth century there was increasing centralisation within the Patriarchate of Constantinople. From that time onwards metropolitans and autocephalous archbishops, not ordinary bishops as hitherto, were invited to attend the synod. At the same time the election of metropolitans, which had so far been the prerogative of the bishops in each province, was transferred to the resident synod.

The Patriarch, together with the synod, enacted his laws and regulations. These concerned matters of faith, the liturgy, the institution of feast days, rites and ceremonies, and the elucidation and application of canons. Many rulings were concerned with the sacraments, especially that of marriage. In matrimonial and administrative disputes the synod acted as a court of justice. Patriarch and synod also wielded disciplinary authority; they could inflict on those who disobeyed the laws of the Church such ecclesiastical punishments as deposition and suspension in the case of clerics or excommunication in the case of laymen. Apart from his ecclesiastical authority, the Patriarch played an important part in political life. He advised the Emperor on countless matters, and during an imperial minority was a member, and sometimes president, of the council of regents.

III. RIGHTS AND DUTIES OF METROPOLITANS AND BISHOPS

The hierarchy below the rank of Patriarch was subdivided into metropolitans, autocephalous archbishops and bishops. According to custom dating from the early days of the Church there was a metropolitan as head of each ecclesiastical province, while bishops whose sees did not come under a metropolitan and did not include other bishoprics were called autocephalous archbishops. When a new bishop was to be elected the provincial synod proposed three candidates out of which the metropolitan chose one. Similarly in the election of a metropolitan; to begin with the Patriarch had the right to choose one of three nominees, a procedure which, as has already been pointed out, was changed at the beginning of the tenth century. Occasionally the Emperor tried to exert pressure in the sphere of episcopal elections. For instance, Nicephorus II Phocas passed a law (about 964) to the effect that the consecration of bishops required imperial sanction. But his successor repealed this anti-ecclesiastical enactment and on the whole the Church succeeded in retaining control over the election of its bishops. On the other hand, as already noted, Emperors from the tenth century onwards claimed the right to raise the status of a bishopric to that of an autocephalous arch-bishopric, or even of a metropolitan see. This had various unfortunate consequences; for instance, promotion might be made for purely personal reasons, and, since it proved impossible to create sufficient new provinces for the increased number of metropolitans, the original function of this office was lost. As early as the eleventh century the Patriarch tried to resist this development but Alexius I and his successors down to the end of the Empire stuck to their claim and exercised the right of creating new metropolitans or reducing the status of existing ones. In the tenth-century *diatyposis* of Leo VI fifty-one metropolitans were entered with an equal number of auto-cephalous archbishops, but the *Ekthesis* of Andronicus II in about 1300 mentioned 112 metropolitans and the somewhat later *Notitia* twenty-five archbishops. By the second half of the fifteenth century the number of metropolitans was reduced to seventy-two, that of the archbishops to eight.

The metropolitan presided over the provincial synod, which according to the fifth canon of the First Council of Nicaea and other legal sources was to be held twice a year to decide on matters of importance to the whole province, and at the same time to act as a court of appeal against sentences passed by the provincial bishops. Later on, a single annual convocation was considered sufficient but even in this mitigated form the regulation was not carried out. The metropolitan was charged with the supervision of the dioceses of the whole province and could if necessary inflict ecclesiastical punishment on a rebellious bishop. On the other hand he was not allowed to perform liturgical acts in any of the dioceses under him without permission of the local bishop. Itinerant visitation was apparently not customary in the Orthodox Church.

Justinian was the first to fix the minimum age for the consecration of a bishop at 35, afterwards 30 years. Candidates had to have sufficient education, that is, as the Second Council of Nicaea (787) laid down, they must know the whole psalter by heart; moreover they had to promise to study the canons, the Gospels, the Epistles, and indeed the whole Bible, thoroughly and not merely superficially, and to follow the precepts contained in them and instruct their flocks accordingly. If a candidate for a bishopric was married, he had to separate from his wife, and in order to ensure the proper carrying out of this regulation she had to enter a nunnery some distance from his cathedral city (*Concil. Trull.* can. 48). After the iconoclastic controversy it became usual for a bishop to assume the monastic habit before consecration. In the last decades of the Empire Symeon of

Thessalonica could praise monastic discipline and affirm that it ruled
the whole Church. It was by then rare for a layman to be elevated to
the rank of bishop, and in such cases the Church required that he
should take the monastic habit.[1]

According to the fourth and fifth canons of the First Council of
Nicaea, bishops were elected by the episcopal synod over which the
metropolitan presided. This did not mean that the people and the
clergy of the vacant diocese had no share in the procedure. Sometimes
one, sometimes another, of these three parties seems to have taken
the initiative. But an attempt was made to restrict the part played
by the people in order to reduce possible intrigues and uproars.
Justinian limited a share in the election to the *honoratiores*; in Novel
123, c. 1, he decreed that the clergy and the more substantial citizens of
the cathedral city, having sworn to cast their votes impartially, should
nominate three candidates, all of whom should have the qualifications
prescribed by secular and canon law. The consecrating metropolitan
should then on his own responsibility choose the most worthy of the
three. Later on the right of nomination was confined to the other
bishops of the province while the metropolitan elected one of the
three candidates proposed by them. Even then the clergy and the
people had a share in the procedure by means of acclamation, or some
such form of approval.

The bishop had complete control over the diocese in ecclesiastical
affairs; clergy and monasteries were normally subordinate to him.
Above all he was responsible for preaching the revealed truth to the
faithful committed to his care and for ensuring that no false doctrine
led his flock astray. It was his right and his duty to inflict heavy
penalties, even excommunication, whenever either divine commands
or the rulings of the Church were disobeyed. He could also administer
justice, whether acting as arbitrator in a case between laymen, or as
judge when the clergy were involved.

The bishop was responsible for the management of estates or other
property belonging to the diocese, although he naturally left their
actual administration to stewards (*oeconomi*). Such matters were also
discussed in the synods, for whatever the bishop acquired after his
ordination belonged to the diocese, with the exception of gifts from
near relatives. Again and again canons and laws urged the necessity
of episcopal residence in the see, and made it compulsory to obtain
permission from the Patriarch before visiting the capital. From the
eleventh century onwards this rule had to be relaxed because many
bishops were driven out of their sees in Asia Minor and Syria by the
Turks and forced to come to Constantinople for help.

---

[1] Symeon of Thessalonica, *De sacerdotio*, *MPG*, CLV, 964.

IV. THE DIGNITARIES OF THE CATHEDRAL CHURCHES

In the early Church bishops were assisted in their sacred office by priests, and helped in their pastoral work, in the management of Church property, and in works of charity, by deacons. Soon one of the latter came to occupy a special position as the bishop's 'ear and mouth, heart and soul'.[1] In the fifth century he became, as archdeacon, the chief assistant of the bishop in his rule over the diocese. Although only a deacon he surpassed all other members of the clergy in prestige and authority. When the Patriarch Anatolius wished to get rid of an archdeacon he disliked named Aetius he made him a priest, and by so doing actually reduced his power whilst appearing to promote him. It was only because Leo I took a firm stand that Anatolius was finally obliged to reinstate him.

First in rank among the priests was the archpresbyter whose authority was however less than that of the archdeacon. In the fourth and fifth centuries the *oeconomus* appeared as the administrator of Church property, together with notaries and other officials of the kind. Increasing differentiation and multiplication of ecclesiastical offices brought a corresponding increase in the numbers of the clergy. Justinian wished to curb this development and in 535 decreed that the number of the clergy attached to the Great Church, that is, St Sophia, and the three subsidiary churches which were dependent on it, should be limited to 60 priests, 100 deacons, 40 deaconesses, 90 subdeacons, 110 readers, 25 cantors, and 100 door-keepers, in all 525 persons.[2] Some years later, in 612, Heraclius had to confirm a regulation made by the Patriarch Sergius in an attempt to reduce the number of clergy in St Sophia, which had again grown excessive. This time the number was limited to 80 priests, 150 deacons, 40 deaconesses, 70 subdeacons, 160 readers, 25 cantors and 100 door-keepers. Besides these it had been possible to add without infringement of canon law such deserving persons as had made some special benefaction to St Sophia. But since the number of these 'supernumeraries' had also increased they too had to be restricted and were limited to 2 *syncelli*, 12 *cancellarii*, 10 *ecdici*, 12 *referendarii*, 40 *notarii*, 4 priests, 6 deacons, and 2 readers.[3] All these offices cannot be discussed in detail but it is essential to say something about the *syncellus*. Originally he was not an official or a dignitary, but a confidant, a 'familiaris' of the Patriarch whose 'cell' or residence he shared. It was natural that the Patriarch should consult him on

---

[1] *Didascalia et constitutiones apostolorum*, II, 44, ed. F. X. Funk (Paderborn, 1906), p. 130.

[2] *Nov. Just.* 3, 1. [3] *DR*, 165.

matters of importance, and he thus became increasingly influential, so much so that in the ninth and tenth centuries he occupied the highest position after the Patriarch. From the sixth century onwards he frequently succeeded to the higher office. Stephen, the son of the Emperor Basil I, and Theophylact, the son of Romanus I Lecapenus, were both *syncelli* before being elevated to the patriarchal throne in 886 and 933 respectively. In court ceremonial the *syncellus* took precedence over the metropolitans and was entitled to membership of the senate. He had episcopal prerogatives, even though he might be ordained only as a priest or deacon. It was not until after the middle of the tenth century that metropolitans occasionally succeeded in securing the office. Then several *syncelli* were appointed at the same time. But the demand of the new metropolitan-*syncelli* to take precedence over other metropolitans because they were senators led to impassioned scenes. Constantine X finally rejected this claim as unwarranted (1065).

As titles in Byzantium began to lose their value, the ambition of the metropolitans was no longer satisfied with that of *syncellus*; under Constantine IX Monomachus (1042–55) the first mention of a *proto-syncellus* is found; in course of time the titles of πρόεδρος τῶν πρωτοσυγκέλλων and πρωτοπρόεδρος τῶν πρωτοσυγκέλλων were created. But whereas such titles were merely honorary, the *syncellus* or *proto-syncellus* continued to act as the spiritual father of the Patriarch. After the conquest of Constantinople by the Latins he was called μέγας πρωτοσύγκελλος. The *syncellus* was nominated by the Emperor and was the spiritual father of the Patriarch and of the Emperor himself.

The *syncelli*, who actually lived with the Patriarch, were distinguished from those officials who resided elsewhere. The most important of these were known from the eleventh century onwards as *exokatakoiloi* (ἐξωκατάκοιλοι).[1] They formed a group of five (πεντάς) which later became the first *pentas* of the nine *pentades* amongst which the patriarchal clergy was distributed.[2] These original five were the μέγας οἰκονόμος, the μέγας σακελλάριος, the μέγας σκευοφύλαξ, the μέγας χαρτοφύλαξ and ὁ σακελλίου. A novel of the Emperor Alexius I confirmed the right of the *exokatakoiloi* to have their own *secreton*. This meant that they formed a kind of ecclesiastical ministry for dealing with important affairs of the Church.

The Great Oeconomus was responsible for the management of the property of St Sophia, the Great Church, and of the Patriarchate. Until 1057 he had always been nominated by the Emperor, who had

---

[1] Cf. Chrys. Demetriou, Οἱ ἐξωκατάκοιλοι ἄρχοντες τῆς ἐν Κωνσταντινουπόλει Μεγάλης τοῦ Χριστοῦ Ἐκκλησίας (Athens, 1927), pp. 27–50, for discussion of this obscure term.

[2] Ps.-Codinus, *De officiis*, I, pp. 116ff. (*CSHB*); *MPG*, CLVII, 133ff.

thus some measure of control over this property. In that year, however, the newly installed Emperor Isaac Comnenus handed over to the Patriarch the right of choosing not only the Great Oeconomus himself but also his officials, as a token of gratitude towards Michael Cerularius, to whom he owed his accession.

The task of the Great Sacellarius was to supervise the monasteries and be responsible for their discipline and similar matters. The Great Skeuophylax was in charge of church vessels and equipment. His duties actually embraced everything pertaining to the solemn and proper performance of divine service, such as the provision of vestments and the illumination and decoration of the church, while he was also responsible for the ecclesiastical treasures, precious objects and liturgical books. The Great Chartophylax was originally in charge of the library and archives of the Patriarch. Gradually, however, his office became the most important in the patriarchal administration. In the eleventh century he even took precedence over metropolitans and bishops because, as Alexius I explicitly stated in a novel, the Chartophylax was to the Patriarch what at one time Aaron had been to Moses, that is, a kind of Vicar-General. In addition to the duties originally entrusted to him he was charged with the supervision of the clergy: all clerical ordinations required his sanction. He conducted the election of the bishops, and in the capital all marriages had to be brought to his notice and could be solemnised only with his permission. He exercised disciplinary power over the clergy and could inflict appropriate penalties. His position gave him authority to take juridical decisions in doubtful cases, and we still possess published rulings which had the validity of authentic definitions. Finally, he was also the head of the patriarchal chancery and in this capacity he signed the written notices issued by the Patriarch himself.

The official in charge of the *sakellion*, the last of the *exokatakoiloi*, supervised and took care of the 'catholic' churches (καθολικαί), that is, parish churches. Towards the end of the twelfth century the Patriarch George Xiphilinus moved the *protecdicus* into the group of the first five. He later took the place of the official of the *sakellion* and formed a tribunal to deal with offences of the clergy. Moreover, it was part of his function as 'first defender' to assist those who appealed to the Church for protection; for example, peasants who were in danger of being enslaved by the great landowners. Hence his competence to judge in matters concerning the right of sanctuary.

These different offices are found existing to the very end of the Empire and after. In later times, however, the distinctions between their various functions could often be no longer observed through lack of personnel.

Both the metropolitan and the episcopal curias had the same or similar officials as those of the Patriarch, according to the importance of the respective churches.

V. THE LOWER CLERGY

It has already been indicated that the position of members of the clergy within the hierarchy did not always depend on the rank to which they had been ordained. The highest offices after that of bishop were usually held by deacons. There was a distinction between ordinations performed at the altar ($\chi\epsilon\iota\rho\sigma\tau\sigma\nu\iota\alpha$) and those performed away from the altar ($\chi\epsilon\iota\rho\sigma\theta\epsilon\sigma\iota\alpha$). The former were intended for priests and deacons, the latter for subdeacons and readers. In contrast with the western Church all members of the clergy, with the exception of bishops, were allowed to remain married if they had entered into a legal union before being ordained as subdeacon. After that it became impossible to marry legally. It is, however, true that this rule was not always fully observed. Whoever contracted a second marriage, even if it was a legal one, could not be ordained. A reader who had contracted a second marriage could not be promoted to a higher rank of the clergy. In fact a second marriage was considered as grave an obstacle to ordination as having as wife a widow, a divorced woman, a harlot or an actress. Candidates had also to have lived a blameless life in other respects; they must not have shed blood, even in self-defence. The positive requirements for ordination were an elementary education and a knowledge of the articles of faith (*Nov. Just.* 123, 12). The lower age-limit for priests was fixed at 30, for deacons at 25, for subdeacons at 20 years (*Concil. Trull.* can. 15).

The numerous instructions given for the professional activities of the clergy reveal on the one hand a concern for the edification of the flock and on the other a desire to avoid any scandal. In the early period the clergy were allowed to trade, but from the seventh century onward this was gradually stopped. Moreover the sources emphasise again and again that 'worldly activities' were forbidden; a priest was not allowed to be a leaseholder of a large estate, a revenue officer, a majordomo in a noble household, proxy in a lawsuit or a civil servant. In addition, other prohibitions occur which show that the clergy were not exactly fastidious in their efforts to earn a living. The canons prohibit usury, the keeping of public houses or brothels, money-changing or banking, the manufacture of ointment and the running of bath-houses. On the other hand it was apparently permissible to do manual work and to carry on such trades as cobbling or metal-working. The same holds good for agricultural labour which was the chief means of support for the majority of the clergy.

Priests were distinguished from laymen by their clothing and their tonsure, which, however, did not remove all the hair, as in the case of monks, but left the crown. Although they held certain privileges which relieved them of some of their burdens, nevertheless the status of the clergy was low. Justinian decreed that slaves could be ordained only with their master's knowledge and tacit consent, in which case they would gain freedom through their ordination (*Nov. Just.* 123, 17). An *ascripticius* on the other hand could be ordained even against the will of his master, but only on the estate to which he belonged, and on condition that he continued his agricultural labour. Leo VI, however, in his Novels 9, 10 and 11 again required the consent of the master where the person was to be ordained priest, monk or bishop. If this consent were withheld, the person in question, even if he were a bishop, was to be handed back to his master. In later times we find that among the *paroikoi* (that is, peasants who had obtained their personal liberty but were bound to live on the estate for a period of thirty years) priests and their families were frequently sold together with their property. Legally they were on the same footing as their fellow-villagers.

The organisation of pastoral work took shape only very gradually. In the letters of St Ignatius of Antioch, the bishop was still the only pastor of his flock, which gathered round him in the church while with the aid of priests and deacons he performed the holy liturgy. The first clear indication of a division of labour in towns is found in Alexandria. By the beginning of the fourth century the various churches had already been allocated to individual priests who celebrated the *synaxis* (probably the liturgy in the sense of the mass) and preached. In the country *chorepiscopi* ('rural' bishops) looked after the faithful. Here we can see a development similar to that in the ancient world, where the *polis* regarded the country merely as its domain. In the fourth century a conflict arose between the town bishops and their rural colleagues and lasted until the latter were either reduced to the rank of ordinary priests or replaced by members of the lower clergy.

As Christianity expanded new churches were founded in the towns side by side with those of the bishops and also on the estates of the big landowners. By Justinian's time a clear distinction could be made between two main groups: the churches which were immediately dependent on the bishop and were soon called καθολικαὶ ἐκκλησίαι and the 'chapels', the εὐκτήριοι οἶκοι which belonged to monasteries and charitable institutions, but could also be owned by private persons. This remained a fundamental distinction throughout Byzantine

history. In the 'catholic' churches[1] the bishop nominated the priests
and other members of the clergy who served them. Services were open
to all the faithful, as in the parish churches in the West. These
churches reserved the most important sacraments to themselves;
other churches and chapels were allowed only to celebrate the holy
eucharist and perform the baptism and the marriage services with
the bishop's consent. Actually it would appear from our very scanty
sources that these prerogatives were contested long and bitterly and
that the 'catholic' churches, in spite of the support given by higher
church officials, were on the whole the losers. It would in fact have
been impossible to provide for the spiritual needs of the faithful without the aid of private churches. And so chapels were built, not only
by the great landowners for their tenants, but also by humbler people
out of religious zeal. The chapels remained the property of the founders and they could give them away, sell or lease them and could appoint their priests, although the bishop had to sanction the appointment. Apart from these churches there were also the chapels of the
monasteries and nunneries. This explains why the number of 'catholic'
churches appears to be comparatively small. It has been calculated
that at the beginning of the tenth century Thessalonica, the second
most important town in the Empire, had four 'catholic' churches; in
1437 Constantinople had only eight in contrast to its two hundred
monasteries.

VI. ECCLESIASTICAL PROPERTY

The Church had owned property during the first three centuries of
the Christian era, but the legal form of that ownership is indeed still
debated. With the recognition of the Church by Constantine its whole
material situation was put on a new basis. The state not only acknowledged the Church's right to hold property, but the Emperors became
its greatest benefactors. Constantine himself granted to the clergy
and to nuns who had taken the veil the *annona*, a free gift of corn, and
made rich donations to churches. More important, he allowed
churches to accept legacies and even in certain cases gave them the
right to inherit *ab intestato*. Later the Emperors Theodosius II and
Valentinian III granted this right in the case of members of the
clergy who did not leave such relatives as were entitled to inherit
(434). The faithful made ample use of this privilege to remember
the Church in their wills, and the final provision for the welfare of the
soul formed a normal part of their bequests. A novel of the Emperor
Constantine VII Porphyrogenitus issued between 945 and 959 decreed
that if a person died intestate and childless one third of his inherit-

---

[1] To be distinguished from the *catholicon* or main church of a monastery.

ance was to be used for devout purposes. The usual donations such as gifts in money or produce, collections, first-fruits and the like, continued to be offered as before, but Justinian wished them to keep their voluntary character and threatened the bishop and the clergy with severe penalties if they did not conform to his ruling. The real estate of the Church, the *praedia urbana et rustica*, continually increased; gardens, woodlands, vineyards, religious buildings and commercial offices began to form the principal part of its property. For instance a remarkable donation of 1100 shops and workshops in the best part of the city was made by the Emperor to the Church of Constantinople, on condition that the returns were used to provide for burial of the dead free of charge. In addition to the real estate there were the capital funds in money and precious objects, the rent of plots of land and houses, the *coloni* and slaves used for agriculture. On the strength of imperial decrees the Church also obtained property belonging to pagan temples and to heretics. Fines formed another source of income, and according to the legislation of Justinian, these could be frequently imposed. Officials were fined for unlawful acts against the bishops or clergy, but these ecclesiastics could themselves be similarly punished, not only in cases of simony, which was very strictly forbidden, but also for other misdemeanours such as marriage after ordination, absence from obligatory residence, or a breach of the laws protecting Church property.

The enormous increase in the property of the Church naturally brought with it corresponding administrative developments. Originally the estates within the diocese of a bishop formed a unit, and on the advice of his *presbyterium* the bishop delegated their management to his officials, who distributed the produce. With the vast increase in property this ceased to be practicable. To begin with, an estate could no longer be managed as a single unit, and subordinate officials (that is, the rector of a church or the *oeconomus* of a charitable institution) had to decide of their own accord what to do with the produce as it came in. Then unity of property gave way to the distribution of items among various bodies, as for instance, when gifts were made which the donors specifically intended for the churches and charitable institutions which they had founded and not for the diocese. The legislation of Justinian made it very clear that gifts from the faithful became the property of a particular church or institution, not of the Church in general or the saint in whose honour they were bestowed. And so a new legal concept grew up by which an institution could be regarded as a person in a juridical sense and as distinct from a corporation, because it was not its members—even collectively—who had the right of ownership but the institution as such. The administration of the property of such foundations as churches and charitable institutions was entrusted either to the priests, who according to the deed of foundation were responsible for the church services, or to the *oeconomus* of the institution, whom the bishop appointed. The bishop supervised the administration of the various charitable institutions, as for instance almshouses, hospitals and pilgrims' hostels, but he could not undertake their management himself.

The most important ecclesiastical source of revenue for religious institutions was landed property. Where the management of an estate was handed over to others it was usual to grant *emphyteusis*. This was the right to hold an estate in usufruct; it could be inherited or sold, but it was given only on condition that the land did not deteriorate and that a *canon* or form of rent was paid yearly. This meant in practice that the Church lost quite a number of estates, and Justinian's legislation, to which later Emperors referred, decreed that an *emphyteusis* should be drawn up in writing and should not be in perpetuity but only for the lives of the recipient himself and two of his heirs in the direct line. It would appear, however, that these regulations were not always adhered to. Apart from *emphyteusis*, it was customary to grant long leases, which were limited by law to 30 years (sometimes 27 or 29). It is obvious that with this type of lease ecclesiastical property in the hands of dishonest or reckless managers might seriously diminish in value.

This was against the ruling of the Church, especially as the law of the inalienability of church property was generally accepted. Councils (*Concil. Trull.* can. 49 and *II Nicaea*, can. 12) as well as Emperors (for example, *Cod. Just.* I. 2, 21; *Nov.* 7; 46; 66; 67; 120) stated that the only exceptions to the rule were to provide funds for the liberation of slaves, assistance to the poor, and in cases of emergency such as inevitable expenditure or the opportunity to exchange barren ground or useless possessions.

The Church itself also had to defend this basic law of the inalienability of ecclesiastical property against imperial encroachment. It protested vigorously when Emperors, even in particularly difficult circumstances, had recourse to the expedient of selling church property. Such was the case with Isaac Comnenus, who desperately needed to fill a treasury depleted through mismanagement for pressing military needs. A feud developed between Isaac and the powerful Patriarch Michael Cerularius, which led to the latter's dismissal. Alexius I Comnenus, who had disposed of church treasures with the consent of the synod, nevertheless considered it necessary to do public penance for this. Such instances show the strength of general opinion that ecclesiastical property ought not to be diverted to secular uses.

VII. THE MAINTENANCE OF THE CLERGY

We have already seen that one of the main claims on church property was the necessity to provide for the livelihood of the clergy, who were not allowed to impose taxes or claim fees for religious ministrations. First of all there was the bishop, who defrayed his living expenses out of the revenue of the diocese. Here an important change was made during the eleventh century when we hear of revenues which went to the bishop directly and were intended for his maintenance, and in this development ecclesiastical usage was following the example of secular administration. The long struggle against the prevailing custom of claiming fees and gratuities had reached a point where the legislator decided on a compromise in order that at least some restriction might be placed on these exactions.

The first *canonicon* or ecclesiastical tax levied on the country was immediately assigned to the bishop. It is significant that the first mention of this is found in imperial legislation. Isaac Comnenus (1057–9) and later Alexius I Comnenus (1081–1118) made the usual, but hitherto voluntary, offering of the first-fruits compulsory. The amount was precisely defined: from a village consisting of 30 families the bishop was to receive yearly 1 gold coin, 2 silver coins, 1 goat, 9 bushels of wheat, 6 measures of wine, 9 bushels of barley and 30 fowls; from smaller villages proportionately less. Both free peasants and bondsmen were apparently liable to pay taxes, though there were certain exceptions. This form of taxation seems to have persisted in later times, as patriarchal rulings show, although what was strictly due could not always be collected. At any rate Balsamon declared that famine and hard times caused this tax to be forgotten, and that bishops received only a fraction of their due and were content with what people gave from custom or in goodwill.[1]

The decree forbidding bishops to claim special gifts from the clergy was often repeated, until it appears for the last time when Sisinnius was Patriarch (996–8). The practice was so deeply rooted that a few decades later the Patriarch Alexius the Studite had to find a compromise. Only priests were obliged to pay the bishop a *nomisma* each year as their *canonicon*.[2] Later sources prove that this applied both to parish priests and those who served private chapels. Eventually the bishop also obtained the *canonicon* from the monasteries. Once again Sisinnius declared that this was illegal, but without success. This tax imposed on the monasteries was never again called into

---

[1] Theodore Balsamon, *Resp. ad Marcum patr. Alex.* 59, *RP*, IV, p. 492 (= *MPG*, CXXXVIII, 1005, *Resp.* 57).

[2] See *GR*, 851.

question during the following centuries; the bishops protested only because the patriarchal stavropegial monasteries did not pay their *canonicon* to the local bishop but to the Patriarch direct. An agreement was reached in the end whereby only those churches and monasteries which had been actually founded with the *stauropegion* of the Patriarch were to pay him. Chapels and other buildings which had been added to these, or had been constructed within their territory, had to recognise the episcopal claim and pay the bishop the *canonicon*.[1]

In addition to this *canonicon*, which people of all classes in the diocese owed to the bishop as their spiritual head, there were other exactions which should be mentioned, especially the duty on ordination. Now the Church had always strongly condemned simony, the purchase of a spiritual office or of ecclesiastical ordination. It was prohibited by both secular and canon law, not that this prevented it from occurring from time to time. The Church might have permitted the payment of a modest fixed sum, not for the ordination itself, but on the occasion when it took place—as happened in the case of other sacraments—if it had not feared that this might open the door to worse abuses. Justinian allowed only the newly installed Patriarch to bestow gifts on bishops and clergy according to time-honoured custom. The gifts which the metropolitan could confer on whoever ordained him, whether his own synod or the Patriarch, were also prescribed, while the same held good for the bishops, ordained by the Patriarch or the metropolitan, down to the clergy and their colleagues who assisted at their ordination (*Nov.* 123, can. 3; 16). This decree remained valid for the next four centuries. It was again the eleventh-century Patriarch Alexius the Studite who went beyond it. He stated in a decree, which was later confirmed by the Emperor Isaac Comnenus, that for his maintenance a bishop should receive from a reader he had ordained one *nomisma*, from a deacon or priest three, making a total of seven for all the orders, including priesthood.[2] Andronicus II was the first to attack the customary practice of bishops who rewarded those consecrating them as well as the officiating clergy; the reason for this was not however zeal for ecclesiastical reform but, if the historian Pachymeres is to be believed, annoyance with the bishops who had refused his request that they should threaten with anathema those daring to oppose the coronation of his son as co-Emperor.[3]

All the various kinds of *kaniskia* and other perquisites cannot be discussed here, but mention may be made of marriage fees because

[1] *GR*, 1179, 1180, 1185.　　　　　　[2] *Ibid.* 851.
[3] Pachymeres, II, pp. 197–200 (*CSHB*).

these have survived to this day. A decree of the Emperor Constantine IX Monomachus, confirmed by Alexius I, states that bridegrooms should give one gold coin and brides 12 yards of cloth to the bishop on the occasion of their wedding.[1] We also know from other documents that the bishop's sanction was required for all marriages. In Constantinople itself the Chartophylax dealt with requests for marriage licences and the priests needed his 'bulla' for the benediction. In the poverty-stricken days towards the end of the Empire the Patriarch Matthew gave instructions that bishops should be content with whatever the betrothed gave.

Cathedral clergy were generally provided for by the bishop. In his sixth novel Justinian distinguishes between unendowed and endowed churches. The bishop's church was responsible for the clergy of the former, as well as for its own; while the founder of an endowed church was obliged to settle the amount needed for the maintenance of its clergy in the deed of foundation. The old system of undivided property and administration was therefore maintained as far as the unendowed churches were concerned, and in the following centuries it remained valid on the whole for the cathedral clergy as well. In other words, we do not find the distribution of property which prevailed in the West, and which guaranteed to bishops and canons separate prebends; we find instead that bishops used the revenues of the cathedral to provide grants and stipends for the maintenance of their clergy. It did sometimes happen that salaries were paid from other sources. This is shown by the notebook of a church official in Thessalonica.[2] This priest, who belonged to the metropolitan church, received as salary for himself and his colleagues certain sums of money coming partly from the revenues of other important churches in the capital and partly from the proceeds of the feasts of patron saints, the lease of fishponds or a ship, or the rent of workshops. This money was distributed yearly or half yearly.

The maintenance of the clerics of the 'catholic' or parish churches differed from that of the other clergy. There can be no doubt that they also received a salary or the equivalent in provisions. But here we find an arrangement which resembled, if remotely, the Latin *beneficium*. The main churches in Constantinople and in the provinces had certain property set aside for the provision of the officiating clergy, the so-called *klerikaton*. These *klerikata* were usually church estates put out to lease, often for life, in return for church services which the lessee had to perform. Sometimes, it would appear, the

---

[1] J. and P. Zepos, *Jus graeco-romanum*, I, p. 312.

[2] S. Kugeas, 'Notizbuch eines Beamten der Metropolis in Thessalonike aus dem Anfang des XV. Jahrhunderts', *BZ*, XXIII (1914–19), 143–63.

property concerned was a peasant farm, elsewhere it formed part of a large estate, perhaps fields, vineyards or olive groves. The lessee had only the usufruct, the Church remained the owner. Sometimes the lessee had to pay in addition a low rent, intended as an acknowledgment of church ownership, not as the full equivalent of the value of the lease. The lessee was not allowed to dispose of the property, nor to give it away as a dowry or as a legacy. When however his sons were members of the clergy and were prepared to perform church services it did apparently quite often happen that the *klerikaton* passed from father to son. Actually these rules were frequently broken. Bishops and others repeatedly complained that the heirs of deceased members of the clergy were not prepared to hand over the *klerikata* to the ecclesiastical authorities and actually brought pressure to bear upon the bishops to get themselves appointed instead of more deserving persons. And this even occurred when they were laymen and had to get others to take the church services. In some cases they refused to pay the fixed rent or only produced a fraction of it. In all such instances the Church stood in danger of ultimately losing the property.

The sources for the existence of *klerikata* all belong to the last three centuries of Byzantium. It is uncertain whether, or to what extent, they are found earlier. Previously we hear more about the *diaria*, emoluments which were probably paid not only in money but in produce. These are also frequently mentioned in later centuries.

The clergy of the parish churches, then, obtained their livelihood either from the bishop or through property belonging to the diocese or to individual churches. According to Justinian's legislation it was the duty of the founders of private churches not only to be responsible for the provision of church services and lighting but also to provide for the maintenance of the clergy in their foundation charter. The founder thereby acquired the right of appointing his priests, on condition that the bishop's sanction was obtained. These private churches, which remained the property of the owner, became very numerous. In addition to the time-honoured practice of providing for the services, a different arrangement also grew up by which owner and priest made an agreement, valid for an agreed time, about the latter's salary. The priest would undertake to sing vespers and matins (*orthros*) and to hold commemoration services and those on Sundays and feast days. Not infrequently the church collections were considered to be the priest's salary, though sometimes, as for instance when the chapel owned a famous image of the Mother of God, the owner and priest would share them. As in the West, there were instances of priests owning the church which they served, and there existed hereditary churches, belonging to priests and for several generations passing from father to son.

Finally there were many priests and clergy who lived, like other tithe-paying farmers, as *paroikoi* on the estate of a big landowner or a rich monastery. Economically they were in the same position as the other *paroikoi*, that is, they lived with their families, as far as possible on the produce of agriculture and stockfarming on a small scale, and had to pay the same taxes. In the extant *praktika*, lists drawn up for purposes of taxation, we usually find a number of priests and clergy mentioned who are not distinguished from their fellow *paroikoi*. When Manuel I Comnenus in 1144 relieved the priest-*paroikos* from at least certain taxes, so many people in the country-side became priests that it was no longer necessary for one priest to serve two churches, as had previously often been the case. In their professional capacity these *paroikoi*-priests received the same presents as other groups of priests already discussed. They received oblations, voluntary gifts in the form of money or produce, and later the so-called stole-fees, given on the occasion of religious services, administration of the sacraments and so on. These probably always existed in one form or another, but there is little information on the subject. The Church Fathers, the Councils, and also secular legislation, mentioned them with disapproval, for there was always the danger of simony, which the Church condemned. Later an attempt was made to maintain at any rate their voluntary character. Balsamon, for instance, stated in reply to the 31st question of the Patriarch Mark of Alexandria that he would permit a modest and voluntary gift on the occasion of a baptism, holy communion or ordination, but that if a priest should ask for more than what tradition had fixed or the recipient could afford then he should be deposed.[1]

VIII. ECCLESIASTICAL JURISDICTION

In the age of the persecutions Christians naturally appealed in cases of dispute to the bishops as the leaders of the Church. In this they were following the instructions of St Paul (I Cor. vi. 1). When the state became Christian this changed. It is true that the Emperors, following the example of Constantine, allowed contesting parties to bring their disputes before the tribunal of the bishops (*episcopalis audientia*),[2] and since this tribunal assured a more impartial judge-

---

[1] Theodore Balsamon, *Resp. ad Marcum patr. Alex.* 31, *RP*, iv, p. 471 (= *MPG*, cxxxviii, 980, *Resp.* 28).

[2] There is considerable literature on the debated question of the *episcopalis audientia*. It is controversial whether the Sirmond Constitution *ad Ablabium* (333) of Constantine the Great (so called after the name of the first editor) is genuine or not.

ment than did a secular court it was often besieged by suitors.
Nevertheless the majority of lawsuits were probably tried by secular
judges. There were, however, certain groups of persons to whom the
Church stood in a particular relationship, and for this reason it was
unwilling to relinquish the right to judge them. The principal group
of this kind was, of course, the clergy.

The earlier Councils not only took for granted the trial of clerics
in ecclesiastical courts in all matters which were the concern of the
Church, but they explicitly stated that clergy could sue each other
only in such courts. This is laid down for instance in the 9th Canon
of the Council of Chalcedon, where the procedure for appeal was also
fixed, although nothing was said here about proceedings taken by
laymen against the clergy. Justinian however allowed laymen to
bring before the bishop their complaints against clerics, monks,
deaconesses, nuns and female ascetics. If the parties were satisfied
with the sentence, the governor of the province had to carry it out,
otherwise he had to pronounce his own sentence, against which however it was possible to appeal. If a member of the clergy had been
found guilty of crime, the bishop had first to declare him to be deposed, after which the secular judge could inflict the penalty. If the
charge was first made before a secular judge, deposition by the bishop
was to follow the sentence. If however the bishop disagreed with
the sentence, both he and the judge were to appeal to the Emperor
for a decision.

These rules, however, did not satisfy the Church, especially since
secular judges were given to arresting members of the clergy, hauling
them into court and sentencing them in the most arbitrary fashion.
Heraclius therefore passed a new law (629)[1] which safeguarded the
position of the clergy in the courts. All civil suits brought against
bishops, clergy and monks who belonged to the Church of Constantinople or lived in the capital, were to be brought before the Patriarch, or a judge delegated by him. Those who came from outside
Constantinople could also appeal to the Patriarch, unless they preferred to go to a secular court. The same held good for the provinces,

There are different opinions as to the nature of episcopal juridical powers, particularly
as to whether the bishop held only the restricted authority of a judge or whether he
also acted as arbiter and mediator. Some scholars particularly emphasise the significance of the *episcopalis audientia*, as F. Bossowski, 'Quo modo usu forensi audientiae
episcopalis suadente non nulla praecepta ad instar iuris graeci aut hebraici etc. in iure
Romano recepta sint exponitur', *Acta Congr. Iur. Internat.* (Rome, 1935), I, 361–410;
also G. Vismara, *Episcopalis audientia* (Milan, 1937). Others, however, are more
cautious, for example, A. Steinwenter, 'Zur Lehre von der episcopalis audientia', *BZ*,
XXX (1929–30), 660–8, and Vratislav Buček, 'Episcopalis audientia eine Friedens- und
Schiedsgerichtbarkeit', *ZSR*, Kan. Abt. I, 28 (1930), 453–92.

[1] *DR*, 199.

where bishops and metropolitans were competent to judge the clergy and the monks who were their subordinates. Secular and military officials were explicitly forbidden to interfere. It was also important that the ecclesiastical judge was responsible for the execution of the sentence.

Certain new decrees were also passed at the same time to deal with criminal cases. In Constantinople the Patriarch or his delegate, in the provinces the bishops or metropolitans, were to pass judgement on criminal charges against the clergy and to punish the guilty according to canon law. If in the opinion of the ecclesiastical judges the accused were involved in a serious crime and were to be sentenced accordingly, he was first to be unfrocked and then handed over to a secular court.

Although the novel of Heraclius was not incorporated in the *Basilica*, it remained the basic law for ecclesiastical jurisdiction even in the later period. On various occasions Emperors confirmed this jurisdiction of the Church and tried to safeguard it against infringement by secular officials. In this connection a novel of Alexius I[1] re-established the rule which had remained valid in Byzantium, that the plaintiff must appeal to the court which had jurisdiction over the defendant. This meant that the rules for the trial of the clergy by an ecclesiastical court only applied when a cleric was not the accuser but the defendant. Balsamon complained bitterly that the special juridical position of the clergy was often infringed, not only through the fault of the secular officials but of the clergy themselves. Bishops, priests and monks were forced to appear in secular courts without imperial mandate and protests denying the competency of these courts were ignored. According to the canons, clerics who refused to appear before an ecclesiastical court were to lose their rank; in civil lawsuits they had to waive their claims—even if they had won their case—if they desired to keep their rank. In fact such punishments were apparently rarely inflicted.

In cases of appeal, the bishop pronounced the first judgement on complaints against the clergy, the metropolitan the second, and the Patriarch the final judgement. If a bishop had to appear in court, the case was tried by the metropolitan who, together with the other bishops in the province, passed sentence. A metropolitan was tried by the Patriarch. According to Justinian there could be no appeal from the verdict of the Patriarch, which was final (his jurisdiction was thus modelled on that of the *praefectus praetorio*, who had the same privilege). It was, furthermore, possible to appeal to the Apostolic See, as Gregory Asbestas did in the ninth century by appealing against the decree of deposition issued by the Patriarch Ignatius.

[1] *DR*, 1071 (July 1087).

When a General Council had been convened in order to decide on matters of faith, it also passed judgement on bishops accused of heresy and other offences. On other occasions the judgements of metropolitans and Patriarchs were usually passed in synod, that is with the assistance of the provincial bishops or the resident synod (*synodos endemousa*). In accordance with the canons of Carthage (418), especially Canon 12, the presence of twelve bishops, apart from the metropolitan or the Patriarch, was required in dealing with criminal charges against a bishop, six if the accused was a priest, and three if he was a deacon. In the opinion of Balsamon the same number was required for civil lawsuits, such as theft, which brought the accused into disrepute.[1]

Justinian had already granted ecclesiastical judges the sole right of dealing with purely Church matters. It was however different when questions arose which were generally held to be the concern of both ecclesiastical and secular authorities. This was especially the case with marriage, where the attitude of the state was based on pagan tradition and opposed to the teaching of the Church. Matrimonial cases were therefore not left to the ecclesiastical courts. It must be remembered that a civil marriage could be dissolved simply on the strength of a request by both parties, while according to the Church it was indissoluble, except (at least in the East) in cases of adultery. In course of time, however, this conflict died down and a novel of Alexius I Comnenus supported the claims of the Church by granting it sole right to judge in matrimonial cases (1084).[2] (In the same novel the *psychika*—that is, all gifts for the welfare of the souls of the deceased, such as pious foundations—were brought under the jurisdiction and executive power of the Church.) But although we possess a number of ecclesiastical rulings on matrimonial disputes dating before and after this novel, secular judges continued to concern themselves with such cases.

In the procedure of actual lawsuits the Church took over a number of rules from Roman law, but these were more a matter of custom than the explicit canonisation of secular laws. Generally speaking, however, ecclesiastical procedure was less strict: the provision of sureties, required by civil law, was not needed. By way of exception the 6th Canon of the First Council of Constantinople (381) took over the threat of retaliation when a charge was brought against a bishop. This meant that the plaintiff had to declare that if he lost his suit he was prepared to undergo the punishment the bishop would have incurred if sentenced. This rule arose out of the circumstances of the

[1] Theodore Balsamon, *MPG*, cxxxviii, 57 ff.
[2] *DR*, 1116.

time, and the abuse of such charges against bishops. Normally religious sanctions took the place of securities. The testimony of witnesses was reckoned as the most important legal evidence (as in the Bible); after it came documentary proof and the oath of purgation, which did not come from Roman law. The Church however rejected torture. Contempt of court was considered a serious offence in ecclesiastical courts.

IX. THE CHURCH AND THE PIETY OF THE FAITHFUL

So far only the external organisation of the Byzantine Church has been considered. It was within this framework that its motivating principle, its spiritual life, was lived. This Church considered itself a part of the Church which Christ had founded and believed its task to be the leading of the faithful towards him. In so doing it was helped by the organisation already described, but it also had ways of influencing more directly the souls entrusted to it. The Byzantine Church considered itself to be above all a living fellowship of Christians. It is significant that its first requirement was orthodoxy, the acceptance of the established truth. The Greeks undoubtedly had a particular gift for speculative thought and dialectic, and this may explain why—to a greater extent than in the West—the great Christological and Trinitarian mysteries formed the main subject of discussion and religious controversy. But behind this there existed the firm conviction that only the true faith could be the real foundation of the Christian life. The preservation of this faith was therefore jealously guarded. In the late fifth century for example the Emperor Anastasius I (491–518) had to prove his orthodoxy by a declaration of faith made to the Patriarch on his accession to the throne.[1] Nevertheless there was certainly no lack of heresies in the Byzantine Empire. If the periods when the monophysite, monothelete and iconoclastic heresies held sway in Byzantium are taken together, they amount to several centuries, and often the intervention of the Roman See and the attitude which it took played an important part in the restoration of orthodoxy. The success of heretical movements largely depended on general political considerations or on the influence of the Eastern provinces of the Empire, whose religious attitude often differed considerably from that of the capital. After the ninth century however orthodoxy remained the watchword of Byzantium. This was the reason why the schism of the eleventh century became an unbridgeable cleavage; the Byzantines were not prepared to give up

[1] A recognised coronation oath as such is first known in the ninth century; see above: chapter xx, pp. 3 and 15.

orthodoxy as they understood it for the sake of political advantages. The failure of the numerous attempts at reunion can largely be ascribed to the fact that the West did not sufficiently realise this, while the same attitude towards orthodoxy also explains why the Byzantine Church attached such immense importance to the General Councils. They were the protectors of the true faith against Arius and Macedonius, Nestorius and Eutyches, against monotheletes and iconoclasts. This is the reason why the Orthodox Church is called even now 'the Church of the seven General Councils'.

One result of this fervour for the orthodox cause was the very high esteem in which the sources of revelation were held. The faithful were made acquainted with the Holy Scriptures, Old and New Testaments, in the liturgy and even more in sermons. In the opinion of an expert[1] on the literature of Byzantine sermons the Orthodox Church has been more prolific in the field of religious oratory than in any other branch of theology. The importance of the sermon, which was in the first centuries of Christianity a fixed part of the service, was later reduced, but there was nevertheless always a considerable amount of preaching in Byzantium. Above all this was compulsory for the bishops. The 19th Canon of the Council in Trullo (691) decreed for a bishop the task of instructing the clergy and the people daily or at least every Sunday. He had on these occasions to explain to his audience the thoughts and judgements contained in the Bible according to the interpretation which the Holy Fathers had given to the texts in question. Even if this rule was not always adhered to it shows how much was expected of the bishop in the matter of preaching.

Alexius I Comnenus appointed his own *didaskaloi* in the Church of Constantinople, whose task it was to preach in place of the Patriarch. The Emperor gave them a fixed salary in order to demonstrate how much importance he attached to their work and decided that on their promotion they should take precedence of high dignitaries. Alexius also exhorted provincial bishops to follow the apostolic example in 'feeding their flocks' and to appoint parish priests able to instruct their people in moral and doctrinal truths. Even the Emperors did not consider it beneath their dignity to compose sermons, and some of them, Leo VI for instance, delivered such sermons before their own court. Most of the sermons which have been preserved naturally deal with religious festivals and their symbolism, others are panegyrics upon the saints; another form is that of the homily based on a sacred text intended to open up for the people the meaning and mystery of the Gospel.

---

[1] A. Ehrhard in Karl Krumbacher, *Geschichte der byzantinischen Litteratur* (2nd ed. Munich, 1897), pp. 160–76.

Listening to sermons would not however give the Byzantines their first introduction to the Holy Scriptures. Throughout their childhood elementary teaching was usually given with reference to them. A number of stories from the lives of saints and other sources show that the clergy participated to a great extent in the education of the young. The Second Council of Nicaea (787) prohibited the clergy from following professions unsuitable to their station, but it urged them to instruct children and slaves by interpreting the Bible. Balsamon, when explaining another canon, mentions that members of the clergy were forbidden to beat anybody on pain of suspension, with however the definite exception of those who as teachers had to cope with unruly pupils.[1] We learn from other sources that the clergy were often in charge of schools and that monasteries frequently ran schools which were not intended only for prospective monks. It is known for instance that the later Emperor Isaac Comnenus and his brother John were sent by the Emperor Basil II, who had adopted them, to the Studite monastery in Constantinople for their education. It is clear and can often be proved that, in such schools and in all teaching done by priests, the Scriptures must have played an important part. Of all the sacred books the psalms usually took first place, probably because of their high personal and emotional religious content. Amongst others, the patristic writers especially recommended Proverbs, Ecclesiasticus, the Song of Songs and Genesis.

The Holy Scriptures and sermons were thus a formative influence in determining the piety of Byzantine Christians. But they were not exclusively important. Although sacramental theology was only developed towards the end of the Byzantine Empire, it was the *mysteria*, the sacraments, on which the Christian life was grounded. These brought individuals into the unity of the whole Church. This was especially true of baptism, the sacrament in which man is buried with Christ unto death and by which he may walk with him in newness of life. In the rites of the Byzantine Church, the sacrament of the Holy Ghost, confirmation, was closely connected with baptism, if this was performed by a priest. But the central act of the liturgy was the Holy Sacrifice, the *tremenda mysteria*.

It has often been said that the splendour of the Byzantine service, the sumptuous vestments, the singing, the illumination, the venerable icons, exalt the mood of strangers and believers alike. This is certainly true, but it must not be forgotten that such splendour and radiance were possible only in the cathedrals and in churches belonging to rich monasteries. Still, places of worship in poor villages could also bring peace and joy to the hearts of the faithful, and the reason for this

[1] Theodore Balsamon, *In can. 9, Concil. I et II, MPG,* cxxxvii, 1049.

rested primarily on a firm belief in the sacramental power of the Holy Sacrifice. Moreover the solemn ceremony and the lively antiphonal singing between the priest and the people were wonderfully suited to the expression of their religious experience. We can see how deep was this conviction of their faith—even if at times it produced strange flowering—from the stories of the *Pratum Spirituale* of John Moschus and similar writings. The *Pratum Spirituale* also shows that the custom of taking home the Blessed Sacrament in order to partake of it during the week was still widely practised in the sixth and seventh centuries. Later on reception of Holy Communion, even by devout Christians, was far less frequent. Nevertheless it may be assumed that, if Holy Communion was received in the monasteries on Sundays and often on other occasions until the thirteenth century, zealous laymen may well have done the same even if less regularly. Moreover Balsamon stated in one of his synodal answers to the Patriarch Mark of Alexandria that in his opinion all people without exception, whether clergy, monks or laymen, might be allowed Holy Communion daily, provided that they had prepared themselves for it by leading holy lives.[1]

The history of the sacrament of penance in the Byzantine Church is far more obscure than that of the eucharist. The abolition of the penitential priest by the Patriarch Nectarius at the end of the fourth century made it a matter for the individual conscience whether or not to approach this sacrament. Gradually public penance became obsolete except in the case of very serious crimes; there the practice was upheld until the end of the Empire. For other transgressions private penance took its place. It is uncertain how far the example of the monasteries with their habitual confession of sin influenced this private penitence. It must have been firmly established towards the end of the ninth century: the penitential *nomocanon*, which has been wrongly ascribed to St John the Faster, Patriarch of Constantinople (582–95), apparently dates from the ninth or tenth century, although it contains some earlier material. Long penance of many years' duration was mitigated, and instead of public penances to be performed before the eyes of the world, other punishments were imposed such as exclusion from Holy Communion, fasts during certain days of the week or at special times, daily prayers or a number of genuflexions, also to be performed daily. In contrast with the West, a penitent could choose his confessor but had to adhere to his choice and could not be released without his confessor's consent. It is clear that for most people confession was an important event which did not occur

---

[1] Theodore Balsamon, *Resp. ad Marc. patr. Alex.* 17, *RP*, IV, p. 460 (= *MPG*, CXXXVIII, 968, *Resp.* 16).

very often. Emperors and influential people had confessors just like the other devout Christians. These were preferably chosen from the monasteries. The question whether monks who had not been ordained priest could absolve from sin agitated the minds of men in Byzantium for several centuries. It is difficult to decide whether the confessions which in the monasteries were made to the abbot were followed by a sacramental absolution if the abbot was a priest, in other words whether there existed a kind of 'devotional confession'. In any case it must be realised that the *hegumeni* were by no means all priests.

Apart from baptism, confirmation, the eucharist and penance there were other rites for the sanctification of life and for the creation of a closer bond between the Christian and his Lord. There were for instance the blessing of betrothal and marriage, extreme unction, the different benedictions given on the occasion of various events in life. They were all intended to lift the life of a Christian above its earthly limitations and make it part of what the Fathers called the divine existence. The finest example of this 'sacramental mysticism' of Byzantium is the fourteenth-century work by Nicholas Cabasilas called *On Life in Christ*.

There were also other means by which the Church prepared the faithful for the life to come—the prayers of the liturgical hours, the veneration of the saints, for instance in the icons, the ecclesiastical feasts and fasts and times of penance, the pilgrimages to holy places and the guidance given for leading a morally pure life—but this is not the place to enlarge upon these.

The Byzantine Church, for all its human shortcomings, ultimately had a profound significance for Byzantine Christians. Like the State with which it formed a single entity it incorporated the great past, the great tradition, the great task of East Rome. Unlike the State, it pinned its hope on the future, especially when political disintegration set in. To this day the Orthodox credit the Church with having given them that faith and piety which has enabled them to survive for centuries under the burden of alien rule without ever renouncing their allegiance to Christ.

CHAPTER XXIV

BYZANTINE MUSIC AND LITURGY

I. MUSIC IN COURT CEREMONY

The writings of Byzantine historians show the important part which music, both secular and sacred, played in daily life in the Eastern Empire. But while manuscripts of ecclesiastical music have come down to us from the tenth century onwards in such numbers that we can get a clear picture of its state and development from the Macedonian renaissance to the fall of Constantinople, no trace of secular music has been found. The lack of any document of secular music can however easily be explained. Music needs a special system of signs to fix it in writing. Greek musical notation was no longer used. The system of Byzantine neumes, which first appears in surviving hymn-books of the late ninth century, was used exclusively for writing music of the Church on parchment. Secular music was not considered important enough to justify the use of this precious material. There is therefore no trace of the music for the comic, satyric or tragic masques which were so popular, though they were condemned by ecclesiastical writers as 'the pomps of the devil'[1] and prohibited by the Council in Trullo,[2] nor has the music for mimic dances or for folk-songs and folk-dances survived. It is significant that even in the case of the numerous Acclamations, that is, the chants used in court ceremonies, not a single example has come down to us in musical notation, with the exception of a few Polychronia with which the imperial family were greeted when they visited a monastery.[3] One of these Polychronia dating from about 1433, in honour of the Emperor John VIII Palaeologus (1425–48), the Empress Mary and the Patriarch Joseph II (1416–39), is closely related to a plain-chant melody of the tenth century, the Kyrie 'Jesu Redemptor'.[4] It may therefore be assumed that the Acclamations sung in church to greet the Emperor, or an ecclesiastical dignitary, belonged to the standing repertory of liturgical chants. This view is confirmed by the fact that in the texts of the other surviving Poly-

---

[1] E. Wellesz, *A History of Byzantine Music and Hymnography*, 2nd ed. (Oxford, 1961), pp. 94–5.

[2] Canon 62 (Mansi, XI, 971).

[3] Cf. H. J. W. Tillyard, 'The Acclamation of Emperors in Byzantine Ritual', *Annual of the British School at Athens*, XVIII (1911–12), 239–60.

[4] Cf. *Revue Grégorienne*, XXX (1951), 36. The Polychronion is preserved in Codex 214 of the Pantocrator monastery on Mt Athos.

chronia no names of Emperors and Empresses appear; the names of those reigning at the time had to be supplied, and sung to typical psalmodic formulas, similar to those of the western Laudes Regiae.[1] Though the music of the Acclamations in court ceremonies is lost, there is no reason to believe that they were different in style from those performed on festal days of the Church, since the daily life of the Emperor was ordered by a sequence of ecclesiastical and public functions.

The *Book of Ceremonies* by Constantine VII Porphyrogenitus (913–59) is the best source for the study of the texts of the Acclamations and gives the occasions and methods of performance. The cheering of the Emperors and Empresses is always given with the standing formula: 'Many years to you, so-and-so and so-and-so (ὁ δεῖνα καὶ ὁ δεῖνα), Autocrators of the Romans',[2] which shows that these chants belonged to the ceremonial repertory. We also often find the Mode (ἦχος α′, ἦχος β′ and so on) in which these Acclamations were sung. Acclamations in ecclesiastical ceremonies were sung by the two choirs of Psaltae who were members of the clergy and had taken holy orders, those in secular ceremonies by the two choirs of Kractae who were court officials and laymen. When the Emperor took part in a procession, or went to church, both groups of singers, the Kractae and Psaltae, sang the Acclamations together, the responses being made by the crowd.

The different names for the chants sung during processions occur in the *De cerimoniis*: Apelatika, for the chants sung on Easter Monday when the Emperor went to church in a solemn procession; Dromika, when he returned to the palace after the service, followed by his courtiers and his guard, all on horseback. It has been pointed out that the Apelatikon was a kind of 'conductus' or slow processional song, the Dromikon a quick and gay secular one.[3] It was customary to sing the Dromikon; but when the Emperor wished, he could order the slow Apelatikon to be sung. It may be assumed that on his way to church the Emperor walked on foot in the procession, but on the way back he and his retinue went on horseback and the singers followed in carriages, as was done in the Trionfi of the Renaissance, which were obviously modelled on the Byzantine ceremonies.

Information about the use of instruments in court ceremonies is scarce. It is not easy to find out whether the term *organon* stands for organ, or instrument in general. The portable pneumatic organ, which

---

[1] Cf. E. H. Kantorowicz and M. Bukofzer, *Laudes Regiae* (Univ. of Calif. Press, 1946), p. 202.

[2] Cf. *De cerimoniis*, ed. A. Vogt (Paris, 1939), II (1), p. 88 (=I, p. 278, *CSHB*).

[3] J. Handschin, *Das Zeremonienwerk Kaiser Konstantins und die sangbare Dichtung* (Basle, 1942), pp. 16–17.

in the fourth century had replaced the hydraulic organ, is known to us from a relief on the obelisk of Theodosius I (379–95) in Constantinople. Portable organs, covered with gold and silver, were used in the Hippodrome, in processions, and during banquets and receptions in the imperial palace; their use in church is never mentioned in Byzantine sources. The only occasion on which instrumental music was admitted was on Christmas Eve, when the imperial band, consisting of trumpeters, horn players, pipers and cymbal players accompanied the singers when they intoned the Polychronia for the occasion, and played between the hymns, and also when the court officials left the church.[1]

Constantine VII's *De cerimoniis* (i, c. 1) also contains a list of liturgical Acclamations in Latin which were sung at Christmas, Epiphany, Easter, Pentecost and the Transfiguration by the *cancellarii quaestoris* when the Emperor went to St Sophia; for example: Δὲ Μαρίε Βέργηνε νάτους ἐτ Μάγια δ'ωριέντε κοὺμ μούνερα ἀδοράντες ('De Maria Virgine natus et Magi de Oriente cum muneribus adorantes').[2] Another group of Latin Acclamations, sung to greet the Emperor when he dined in the 'Great Triclinus', is given in chapter 84 (75).[3]

Music in ceremonies was not confined to Acclamations and hymns of praise; it included instrumental performances, dances and even a kind of ballet, the 'Gothic pageant', performed on the ninth day between Christmas and Epiphany by four dancers dressed as Goths, two from the faction of the Blues, two from that of the Greens.[4] Music and dance accompanied the festivals which took place every year. Some of them were of pagan origin, like the Calendae, which seem to have been taken over directly from Rome, the Vota, celebrated on 1 January in honour of Pan, and the Brumalia, a late autumn festival, offered by the Emperor to certain classes of the population. These festivities had been forbidden 'once and for all' by Canon 62 of the Council in Trullo (691); but they were rooted so deeply in Byzantine life that the prohibition had no effect. The Orthodox clergy themselves tolerated and supported them[5] in their christianised form, together with other celebrations of the season, such as the Orgies of the Maioumas which survived in the 'Hippodrome of Vegetables'. This was the usual name for the races on 11 May, the national festival of Byzantium, the day of the inauguration of New Rome by Constantine in A.D. 330. The festival was celebrated in the presence of the Emperor and the Patriarch of

[1] Pseudo-Codinus, *De officiis*, p. 53 (*CSHB*).
[2] *De cerimoniis*, ii (1), p. 169 (=i, p. 369, *CSHB*).
[3] *Ibid.* pp. 171–2 (=i, pp. 370–1, *CSHB*).
[4] *Ibid.* pp. 182–5 (=i, pp. 381–6, *CSHB*).
[5] V. Cottas, *Le théâtre à Byzance* (Paris, 1931), pp. 20 ff.

Constantinople with music and dances by the crowd, who at a sign given by the Emperor were feasted with vegetables, fish and sweets in the arena. The Acclamations on that occasion were divided between the herald of the Palace (φωνοβόλος), the precentors of the Blues and Greens, and the people.[1] The festival on which the carnival races were held, the 'Hippodrome of Meat' (ἱπποδρόμιον μακελλαρικόν), replaced the pagan Lupercalia, which name is preserved in the manuscript of the *De cerimoniis* in abbreviation (τοῦ λεγομένου Λουπερκ΄).[2] It marks the last day on which it is permitted to eat meat before Lent and at the same time, as did the Lupercalia, heralds the beginning of spring. The memory of this old pagan celebration survived in a spring-hymn, sung by the alternating choirs of two groups of the city administration, the Blues and Greens. One group began: 'See spring has come again, lovely spring'; the other group continued: 'bringing health and joy and happiness'.[3] The term *choreutikon*, given to the spring-song, indicates that the choral singing was accompanied by dances.

Even from this short survey the great variety of the music in the ceremonies is apparent, and also the tendency, which shows itself throughout the whole course of Byzantine civilisation, to keep all court ceremonies, public entertainments and festivals within a framework of carefully prearranged chants, songs and dances. In ecclesiastical ceremonies music played an even more important part, and that on a higher level, since the *anni publici circulus* was only a reflection of the *anni ecclesiastici circulus*, and both had as their centre on earth the Emperor in his dual function as Autocrator and Christ's vicegerent.

II. THE ORIGINS OF BYZANTINE
ECCLESIASTICAL CHANT

Byzantine chant was an integral part of Byzantine liturgy. Like that of the music of the other Christian rites, both Eastern and Western, its function was to heighten the solemnity of the service. Its development and, finally, its abundant use in the last centuries of the Empire were closely connected with the expansion of the liturgy, as were its origins. Byzantine chant derived from the same source as Byzantine liturgy, from Early Christian worship, and particularly from that element in it which the Christianity of the Apostolic age had taken

---

[1] *De cerimoniis*, ii (1), pp. 143 ff. (= i, pp. 340–9, *CSHB*); see also A. Vogt's Commentary, ii (2), pp. 155 ff.

[2] *Ibid.* ii (2), pp. 172 ff. (Commentary).

[3] *Ibid.* ii (1), pp. 164–8 (= i, pp. 364–9, *CSHB*). Metrical reconstructions of this and other songs transmitted in *De cerimoniis* have been given by P. Maas, 'Metrische Akklamationen der Byzantiner', *BZ*, xxi (1912), 37 ff.

over from the Jewish service of the Temple and the Synagogue on Saturday morning: the congregational praise of the Lord 'in psalms, hymns and spiritual songs' which is referred to in the Epistle to the Ephesians (v. 19). From the context it is clear that this indicates a liturgical usage with which the readers of the Epistle were well acquainted, because at that time the newly-baptised Christians still regarded themselves as members of the Jewish religious community and continued 'daily with one accord in the Temple' (Acts ii. 46).

Though no musical manuscript from these early days of Christianity has survived, it is possible to form some idea about the different types of chant to which the Epistle to the Ephesians refers. Psalmody means the cantillation of the psalms and canticles, and, at a later date, of doxologies modelled on them. Hymns were songs of praise of a syllabic type. Spiritual songs comprised a large number of richly ornamented chants of a jubilant or ecstatic character, for example the Alleluias. With the expansion of Christianity beyond Jerusalem and the conversion of Gentiles, above all in the region of Antioch, there arose the necessity of holding meetings for prayer together with Supper-celebrations in private houses, where the Jewish type of worship consisting of Scripture, Homily and Prayer was concluded with the commemoration of the Lord's Supper. For this type of worship the Christian communities took over the chants of the Synagogue even before the destruction of the Temple. The precentor chanted a psalm, or a song improvised on the pattern of a psalm or of one of the canticles, and the congregation answered with a doxological formula or simply with 'Amen' (I Cor. xiv. 16).

In this earliest period of Christianity, when worship was enthusiastic up to the point of *glossolalia*, 'speaking with tongues', when St Paul reminds the Corinthians that at their gatherings everyone has 'a psalm, a doctrine, a tongue, a revelation, an interpretation' (I Cor. xiv. 26), the formative element of the new liturgy consisted in maintaining the order of prayers and chants of the Synagogue as a basis for the ritual. When the Christian communities increased, and bigger halls were required for their gatherings, antiphonal singing of psalms was introduced, with which the Jewish Christians were familiar from the Temple. In the Christian era antiphonal singing, that is, singing in two alternating choirs, is first mentioned by Philo in his book *On the Contemplative Life*.[1] Here he describes the alternating singing of the Therapeutae and Therapeutrides, men and women probably of a Jewish religious sect, said to exist near Alexandria. Philo's description has been included by Eusebius in his *Ecclesiastical*

---

[1] Cf. Philo Alexandr., ed. L. Cohn and S. Reiter, VI (Berlin, 1915), pp. 46–71.

History[1] and, following his authority, has been regarded as a description of the celebration of Pentecost by the earlier Christian Church of Alexandria.[2] Though this view has been proved to be wrong, Philo's description is valuable because reference is made to the Hymn of Victory in Exod. xv. 20-1 which in later Byzantine hymnography was to play such an important part as a model for the odes of the first mode ($\tilde{\eta}\chi o\varsigma\ a'$).

Antiphonal choirs were first used by the Syriac-speaking followers of Arius.[3] The challenge was met in the Orthodox Church by Flavianus, later bishop of Antioch, and Diodorus, later bishop of Tarsus; according to Theodoret's *Historia Ecclesiastica*, they were the first to divide the choir into two parts and to teach them antiphonal singing of the psalms. 'Introduced first at Antioch, the practice spread in all directions and penetrated to the ends of the world.'[4] Apart from the fact that antiphonal chant embellished the service and increased the variety of singing, it became a most important means for furthering the understanding of the psalms and canticles in countries which became christianised because of the practice of singing these chants bilingually. Theodoret's *Religiosa Historia*[5] tells of a monastery on the Euphrates where Publius, a famous ascetic, had founded a monastery for Greeks and Syrians. When the Greeks started to sing hymns in their own language, the Syrians wanted to imitate them by singing chants in the vernacular. Publius therefore built a church where Greeks and Syrians sang alternately in two choirs, each in their own language, and he writes that this custom was maintained during his lifetime. The same practice was exercised wherever the Church's missionaries introduced chants into another country with a different language. Ample evidence of this is found in Western liturgical manuscripts, particularly from Magna Graecia in Italy where a number of chants were sung first by one choir in Greek, then by the other in Latin to the same melody.[6] The use of two languages in the church services was not however confined to antiphonal singing; the nun Aetheria who travelled to Jerusalem in the fourth century heard the lessons during Mass first read in Greek, and then translated into Syriac for those who did not know Greek, and into Latin for the rest of the congregation who knew neither Greek nor Syriac.[7]

[1] *Hist. Eccles.* II, xvii, 6 f.

[2] F. C. Conybeare, *Philo about the Contemplative Life* (Oxford, 1895), p. v.

[3] Sozomen, *Hist. Eccl.* VIII, 8.

[4] Theodoret, *Hist. Eccl.*, ed. T. Gaisford (Oxford, 1854), p. 106.

[5] *Relig. Hist.* c. v.

[6] See E. Wellesz, *Eastern Elements in Western Chant*, chh. 3–5, and Dom L. Brou, 'Les chants en langue grecque dans les liturgies latines', *Sacres Erudiri*, I (1948), IV (1952).

[7] Aetheria, *Journal de Voyage*, ed. H. Pétré (Paris, 1948), pp. 260-2.

To the treasury of Jewish psalms and hymns which the Church took over from the Synagogue new hymns were added, modelled on the pattern of those familiar to the Jewish Christians. Later on, however, with the conversion of pagans, many of their hymns were used after they had been expurgated and adapted to the Christian faith. To converts from Greek paganism, the singing of hymns at certain fixed hours was not an alien custom; from inscriptions something is known about the daily ritual of the temple at Epidaurus, where morning and evening hymns were sung, incense was burnt and lamps were lit.[1] The main material, however, for the increasing repertory of antiphonal chants and hymns was provided by the Gnostics, who excelled in this genre. Bardesanes (died 222) wrote a psalter of 150 songs in Syriac; his son Harmonius was the author of lyrical songs which he set to music. These poems of Harmonius and their melodies so enchanted the Syrians that Ephraem, his great Orthodox opponent, considered the best way of combating them was by writing poems in the same metre to Harmonius' melodies. From that time onwards, so Sozomen reports, the Syrians sang the odes of Ephraem modelled on the metre of Harmonius.[2] A feature common to all Syriac ecclesiastical poetry was that all corresponding lines of the stanzas were isosyllabic; they had to have the same number of syllables since they were sung to the same melody. Further prominence was given to two, three or four stresses in a line, according to its length, a principle which was taken over by the Byzantine poet-musicians in their hymns.

III. BYZANTINE HYMNOGRAPHY

The artistic qualities of Byzantine hymns, both of the poetry and of the music, can only be appreciated in the right way if their function is considered in relation to the service of the Orthodox Church. The words cannot be separated from the music, nor should they be read in a continuous sequence of stanzas, as they are printed in the anthologies of Byzantine poetry. It is necessary to turn to the Greek service-books in order to learn how the stanzas of a long poem were interrupted by monostrophic poems and doxologies, and the rubrics in the lectionaries containing the lessons from the Prophets, Epistles and Gospels must be studied in order to get a true picture of the performance of the hymns. For instance, the rubrics in a Prophetologium of the eleventh century[3] show how the Song of Moses from

---

[1] Cf. M. P. Nilsson, 'Pagan Divine Service in Late Antiquity', *HTR*, XXXVIII (1945), 63–9.

[2] Sozomen, *Hist. Eccl.* III, 16.　　　　　[3] Bodl. Cod. Laud. gr. 36.

Exodus was sung on Good Friday. The canticle was intoned by a soloist, the people responded after each verse, or group of two verses, with a refrain taken from the first line of the canticle. The canticle is introduced by a chanter (ψάλτης) who goes up to the ambon and announces: 'The Song from Exodus.' The deacon chants: 'Attention', and the Psaltes immediately begins:

The precentor. Let us sing unto the Lord, for he has triumphed gloriously.
The people. Let us sing unto the Lord, for he has triumphed gloriously.
The precentor. The horse and the rider has he thrown into the sea.
The people. For he has triumphed gloriously.
The precentor. The Lord is my strength and my protector, and he is become my salvation.
  For he has triumphed gloriously.
The people. Let us sing unto the Lord, for he has triumphed gloriously.

In this way all the eighteen verses are sung and the 'Lesser Doxology' is appended to the last verse, followed by the refrain of the chanter, and the response of the congregation.

The breaking-up of the canticle into a kind of antiphonal chant, divided between the precentor and the people, shows the growing preponderance of the music over the words. This tendency has its cause in the elaboration of Byzantine worship which started in the reign of Justinian.

The development of Byzantine liturgy is closely connected with Justinian's ecclesiastical policy of establishing religious unity throughout the Empire. During his long reign (527–65) he pursued his goal by supporting the building of churches and the foundation of monasteries. His most sumptuous undertaking was the building of St Sophia in Constantinople as the visible religious centre of Eastern Christianity. The whole Empire made contributions and 1000 craftsmen were at work. The splendour of the services at St Sophia can be gathered from a decree (535) by which the number of its clergy and of the three churches annexed to it was not to exceed 60 priests, 100 deacons, 40 deaconesses, 90 subdeacons, 110 readers, and 25 cantors.[1]

Thus a stimulus was given for the embellishment of the liturgy by an ever-increasing number of hymns. The official liturgical language of the Orthodox Church in Justinian's Empire was Greek. Mass was celebrated according to the Cappadocian-Byzantine type, which was the liturgy of Constantinople, and was based on three texts, namely, the liturgy[2] of St Basil, the liturgy of St John Chrysostom and the liturgy of the Presanctified. The liturgy of St Basil had its roots in Caesarea, the metropolitan see of Cappadocia, and was used in Con-

---

[1] Nov. III, 1, ed. Zachariae von Lingenthal, *Jus graeco-romanum*, I, p. 71.
[2] *Leitourgia* is the Byzantine term for Mass.

stantinople together with the Mass-formulary ascribed to St John
Chrysostom. From there the two liturgies spread over the Empire
and its provinces in the second half of the seventh century.[1] The
Mass of the Presanctified (*sc.* gifts) was celebrated during Lent on those
days before Easter when the Host had been consecrated during a
regular Mass on the preceding day.

In the sixth century[2] the first part of Mass, the liturgy of the Cate-
chumens, opened with the singing of the Trisagion by the chanters
who entered the church. This is called the 'Little Entrance'. The
celebrating priest offered 'Peace' to the congregation, and lessons
from the Prophets, the Epistles and the Gospel were read. After the
preaching of the Homily those who were under instruction but not yet
baptised had to leave and the doors were closed. The second part, the
Mass of the Faithful, opened with prayers, followed by the 'Great
Entrance', the procession during which the eucharistic loaves were
brought into the sanctuary (τὸ βῆμα) from the sacristy (ἡ πρόθεσις).
This ceremony was followed by the Kiss of Peace, the Creed and the
reading of the diptychs of the dead and of the living. The central act
of Mass began with the Anaphora, the eucharistic sacrifice, which
comprises the Lord's Prayer, the Elevation, Communion and Thanksgiving. Mass ended with the Apolysis, the Dismissal. It was only at
a later date that the ceremonies of the Prothesis at the beginning of
Mass were introduced, during which the offerings of bread and wine
were prepared in the sacristy; this rite developed to such length that
it became a kind of preparatory Mass.[3]

According to an imperial order of 564 (Novel 137, 6) all prayers had
to be said in a loud voice; this means they had to be read in a kind of
cantillation which was also used for the solemn reading of the lessons.
In the Byzantine Church three lessons were read, one from the Old
Testament, two from the New Testament. For these three books were
required: the Prophetologium, containing the lessons from the Old
Testament, the Apostolus or Praxapostolus, containing those from the
Acts and Epistles, and the Evangelium, containing those from the
Gospels.

Mass was celebrated frequently, but not necessarily every day.[4]
The Office however was celebrated daily and the monks were under
obligation to take part in the prayers during the night, in the morning
and in the evening.[5] This obligation, however, an obligation binding
on those within reach of the monastery or the church as the place

[1] Cf. A. Baumstark, *Die Messe im Morgenland* (Munich, 1906), pp. 55–8.
[2] Cf. F. E. Brightman, *Liturgies Eastern and Western*, I (Oxford, 1896), 527–34.
[3] S. Salaville, *An Introduction to the Study of Eastern Liturgies* (London, 1938), p. 23.
[4] P. J. Pargoire, *L'Eglise byzantine de 527–847* (Paris, 1905), p. 103.
[5] *Cod. Just.* I, iii, 41, 10.

of daily communal worship, was not binding on the monk or the cleric if he happened to be away from the monastery or church at the hour of prayer.

The Divine Office, called the Ecclesiastical Order (ἡ ἐκκλησιαστικὴ Ἀκολουθία) or Law (κανών), consisted of seven 'canonical hours' beginning at midnight with the Mesonyktikon, followed by the daybreak service (Ὄρθρος) and Lauds (Αἶνοι), which together formed one canonical Hour. The *Officium diurnum* comprised Prime, Terce, Sext, None, Vespers and Compline (Ὥρα πρώτη, τρίτη, ἕκτη, ἐννάτη, τὸ Ἑσπερινὸν καὶ τὸ Ἀπόδειπνον).[1] It was primarily the Hours of the Morning and Evening Office which were embellished by hymns. (The term 'hymn' is used here to cover the whole range of liturgical poetry.)

Hymn-writing flourished in Syria in the fourth century and seems to have started in Greek in the middle of the fifth century with Anthimus, Theocles, Marcian, Auxentius and others. These early hymns were short poems, consisting of one, two or more stanzas (Troparia). But at the beginning of the sixth century a new poetical form arose, associated with the names of Anastasius, Cyriacus, and, above all, of St Romanus, who was praised by Germanus, the author of a hymn in his honour, as 'Earliest first-fruit of beautiful hymns'.[2]

In content, the Kontakion is a poetical homily. Like its predecessor, the sermon of the Early Church, it has its place after the lesson from the Gospel. It consists of from eighteen to thirty, or even more, stanzas, all sung to the same melody. The stanzas therefore have the same number of syllables in each corresponding line, and the main stress accents on the same places of the lines. The Kontakion is regularly preceded by a short Troparion, the Prooemium or Koukoulion, which is metrically and melodically independent of it but linked to it by the refrain, with which all stanzas end. Prooemium and Kontakion are always written in the same mode. The stanzas of the Kontakion are connected either alphabetically or by an acrostic containing the name of the hymn-writer.

Romanus, a Jew by birth, was born at Emesa on the Orontes; he became deacon at Berytus and went to Constantinople in the days of Anastasius I (491–518).[3] Romanus is rightly considered one of the greatest hymn-writers of all times. In his youth he must have been decisively influenced by the Syriac poet Ephraem and his pupil Basil of Seleucia.[4] 'He thought in Syriac and sang in Greek', writes

---

[1] A. Couturier, *Cours de liturgie grecque-melkite*, II (Paris, 1914), 3.

[2] J. B. Pitra, *Analecta Sacra*, I (Paris, 1876), p. xxvi.

[3] G. Cammelli, *Romano il Melode: Inni* (Florence, 1930), pp. 9–22; *Sancti Romani Melodi Cantica*, edd. P. Maas and C. A. T. Trypanis (Oxford, 1963), pp. xv–xvii.

[4] Cf. P. Maas, 'Das Kontakion', *BZ*, XIX (1910), 290–8.

Emereau,[1] though this is indeed only half the truth. It is Romanus' genius as a poet which makes him so outstanding a hymn-writer. In his Kontakia he glorifies the Life and Passion of Christ, the mystery of the relation of the two natures in Christ and, being the defender of Orthodoxy against heresy, he violently attacks Nestorius and Eutyches as well as inveighing against the spirit of ancient Greek philosophy and poetry. His most famous Kontakion however, the Nativity Hymn, is free from polemics and dogmatic arguments. Up to the twelfth century this hymn was sung every year at Christmas during dinner at the imperial palace. Its prooemium: Ἡ παρθένος σήμερον τὸν ὑπερούσιον τίκτει (The Virgin today bears the Super-essential) is one of the few remains of Kontakia in the present service of the Greek Church.

It is the greatness of his vision combined with a powerful element of dramatic diction which makes Romanus the outstanding figure in Byzantine hymnography. His use of similes and his handling of the metre are unparalleled in Christian hymnography and justify his praise by Germanus.

There is only one hymn of this earlier period which can equal the Kontakia of Romanus in poetical power; this is the Akathistos, whose authorship is uncertain.[2] The Akathistos is the only hymn which has been preserved complete in the *Menaia*[3] and it is still sung in its original form in the Office of Saturday of the fifth week of Lent. Before the hymn was given this place it was sung divided into four sections in the Offices from 20 March to 25 March, the feast of the Annunciation.[4] The name derives from the rule that the singers had

---

[1] *Saint Ephrem le Syrien* (Paris 1919), p. 104.

[2] It is ascribed in the *synaxaria*—the *Acta Sanctorum* of the Greek Orthodox Church—either to the Patriarch Sergius or to George Pisides; in the *synaxarion* to the Latin version the hymn is attributed to the Patriarch Germanus. Cf. Dom M. Huglo, 'L'ancienne version latine de l'hymne Acathiste', *Muséon*, LXIV (1951), 27–61. A. Papadopoulos-Kerameus has suggested the Patriarch Photius as author: Ὁ Ἀκάθιστος ὕμνος. Οἱ Ῥῶς καὶ ὁ πατριάρχης Φώτιος (Athens, 1905). This, as well as the connection of the Akathistos with the Russian attack on Constantinople, has been refuted by M. Thearvic in his article 'Photius et l'Acathiste' in *EO*, VII (1904), 293–300. According to Thearvic the *synaxaria* refer to the 'délivrance miraculeuse' of Constantinople in 626, 677 and 717, but the siege in 860 by the Russians is not mentioned. Thearvic's refutation of the hypothesis of Papadopoulos-Kerameus has been generally accepted. Cf. E. Wellesz, 'The "Akathistos": a study in Byzantine hymnography', *DOP*, IX–X (1956), 141–74.

[3] The *Menaia* are a kind of Proper of the Saints in twelve volumes, one for each month of the year.

[4] Editions of the Akathistos in W. Christ and M. Paranikas, *Anthologia Carminum Christianorum* (Leipzig, 1871), pp. 140–7; Pitra, *Analecta Sacra*, I, 250–62; De Meester, Ἀκολουθία τοῦ Ἀκαθίστου ὕμνου—*Officio del Inno Acatisto* (Rome, 1903), and *L'Inno Acatisto* (Rome, 1905); C. del Grande, *L'Inno Acatisto* (Florence, 1948). On the place of the Akathistos in the office see N. Borgia, 'Ὡρολόγιον, "Diurnio" delle chiese di rito bizantino', *OCP*, XVI, 2 (Rome, 1929), 202–5. See also E. Wellesz, cited below, p. 145, note 2.

to sing it standing, contrary to the usual practice which was that the Troparia inserted between the odes of the Canon, called Kathismata, were sung sitting. The Akathistos hymn consists of twenty-four stanzas, connected by an alphabetic acrostic. It is a hymn in praise of the Virgin; each stanza is followed by an invocation to the Virgin in which her virtues are enumerated in an endless number of epithets and allegories.

In the prooemium, τῇ ὑπερμάχῳ στρατηγῷ, there is a reference to the miraculous aid of the Virgin, by which her city,[1] Constantinople, was liberated from siege by the enemy. This event may have been the liberation of the city from the Avars on 27 July 626, and accordingly Sergius, Patriarch of Constantinople 610–38, has been suggested as author of the Akathistos in its present form.[2] P. Maas,[3] however, and other scholars following him, consider that nobody but Romanus was a great enough poet to have written the Akathistos. Convincing arguments in favour of Romanus' authorship are the striking similarities between passages in the Akathistos and in hymns to the Theotokos by Ephraem the Syrian and Basil of Seleucia, and in the dialogue between Mary and the archangel Gabriel by Proclus (died 447). Another argument in favour of Romanus has been brought forward by C. del Grande.[4] In the seventh stanza the poet praises the Virgin for having dispersed the webs of the Athenians: Χαῖρε τῶν Ἀθηναίων τὰς πλοκὰς διασπῶσα. The term 'Athenians' would appear to refer to the philosophers of the School of Athens which was closed in 529 by a decree of Justinian, in which case the allusion suggests that the poem was written before that date, that is, in the days of Romanus.

The most striking argument in favour of Romanus, however, is to be found in the title of his Kontakion on Joseph in Egypt, which bears the words: εἰς τὸ ἄγγελος πρω[τοστάτης]—'to be sung to the melody "An angel of first rank"'.[5] This instruction clearly suggests that Romanus knew the hymn; indeed, it looks as though he composed the Kontakion on Joseph in the same metre as the Akathistos hymn.[6] If this is so, the legend that the Akathistos was sung in the

---

[1] Cf. N. H. Baynes, 'The Supernatural Defenders of Constantinople', *AB*, LXVII (1949, *Mélanges P. Peeters*, I), 165–77 (reprinted in *Byzantine Studies and Other Essays* (London, 1955), pp. 248–60).

[2] For a discussion of this see E. Wellesz, *Byzantine Music and Hymnography*, 2nd ed., pp. 194 ff.

[3] Cf. P. Maas in *BZ*, XIV (1905), 643–7; but see also Maas and Trypanis, *op. cit.* p. xviii.

[4] C. del Grande, *L'Inno Acatisto*, p. 18.   [5] Pitra, *Analecta Sacra*, I, 68.

[6] In the Typicon of Constantinople, Codex Patmos 266 (ninth century), the Akathistos is referred to as the Kontakion (κονδάκιον). Cf. A. Dmitrievsky, *Opisanie liturgičeskich rukopisej I, Typika* (Kiev, 1895), p. 124.

church at Blachernae in the night after the liberation of Constantinople in 626 is based on historical fact only if it is assumed that the prooemium, τῇ ὑπερμάχῳ στρατηγῷ, which refers to the victory, was written for this occasion, and was substituted for an already existing prooemium, τὸ προσταχθέν, which henceforth had its place in the Akathistos office towards the end of Vespers. The prooemium was sung by the Protopsaltes and there is no difficulty in believing that the crowd which, according to the legend, had gathered in the church to celebrate the liberation of Constantinople in a thanksgiving office, joined in singing with the choir the alternating refrains 'Alleluia' and 'Hail bride unbrided' after each stanza.

At the end of the seventh century the Kontakion was replaced by another musico-poetical form, the Canon, and only a few prooemia and stanzas of the former genre were kept in the liturgy. It has sometimes been asked why the Kontakion, which was poetically superior to the Canon, was replaced by it. Such a question could only be asked by those who have concentrated too exclusively on the hymns as literature instead of considering the inseparable connection between music and words, and the function of both in the liturgy. The Church had two reasons for this important change. The first, concerning the content, was connected with the nineteenth decree of the Council in Trullo of 691 which ordered daily preaching; the second, concerning the form, was related to the tendency to embellish the service by an ever-increasing number of songs. The origins of the Canon can be traced back to the sixth century;[1] its development was closely connected with that of the biblical Odes or Canticles, which had their place in the morning Office. Originally, no fixed number was prescribed. The first ordered collection of Odes appears in the fifth-century Codex Alexandrinus; here fourteen Odes are appended to the Psalter. The same number, as H. Schneider has shown,[2] occurs in the liturgies of Jerusalem and Constantinople in the fifth century. These fourteen Odes were not sung all together; the first ten were recited during the night preceding a festival, whereas the last four were solemnly sung during the morning Office.

During the sixth century the Church of Jersualem reduced the number of Odes from fourteen to nine, and shortly afterwards Constantinople accepted the same number. At that time the Palestinian monasteries must already have introduced short stanzas (Troparia) between the verses of the Odes, as can be seen from the report of the visit of two Palestinian monks, John and Sophronius, to Nilus,

---

[1] Cf. H. Schneider, 'Die biblischen Oden seit dem sechsten Jahrhundert', *Biblica*, xxx (Rome, 1949), 260.
[2] *Ibid.* pp. 245–52.

abbot of the monastery on Mt Sinai.[1] When they went to Vespers on Saturday and the Service during the night they asked Nilus why he did not have the 'Mesodia' sung after the third and sixth Ode, nor the Troparia to the Odes and to the Magnificat, as was the prescribed custom in the Orthodox Church (διατί, ἀββᾶ, οὐ φυλάττετε τὴν τάξιν τῆς καθολικῆς καὶ ἀποστολικῆς ἐκκλησίας;). The report shows that by the end of the sixth century the Church of Jerusalem had introduced, at least on Sundays, the singing of nine Odes in three groups, with hymns after each group. The more austere attitude of the Egyptian monasteries towards the rise of hymn-singing cannot have lasted very long. The Rylands Papyrus 466 from the Fayum, dating from the seventh century, already contains hymns to the eighth and ninth Odes,[2] and these two sets of stanzas belong to the oldest layer of Byzantine hymnography. Those of the first group are Doxologies, sung at Matins after the eighth canticle; those of the second group are Megalynaria, Magnificat Troparia, attached to the ninth canticle. The Megalynaria are modelled, as the rubric indicates, on the Troparion 'Thou who art more honourable than the Cherubim'[3] which is still in use in the Morning Office; it is repeated after each verse of the Magnificat.[4] Thus the two hymns are not remnants of an early stage of Canon writing, as suggested, but they derive from that special kind of minor hymnography which developed in early Christian worship and has been preserved in Eastern liturgy to the present day.

During the course of the seventh century Troparia were composed to each of the nine biblical Odes, or canticles. The number of Troparia increased during the eighth century, and finally the name Ode was transferred from the canticles to the new form of hymn. The last step was the omission of the nine biblical Odes, whose place in the liturgy was between Psalm 50 and Psalms 148–150, during the greater part of the year. Their place was taken by the Canons which consisted of Odes one, and three to nine. The second Ode, based on 'Give ear, O ye heavens' (Deut. xxxii), was omitted during the same period because of its mournful character. All the stanzas of an Ode were modelled upon the first stanza, which was called the Hirmus (εἱρμός). The cantillation of the biblical Odes was restricted in Lent. During this time of penance the number of Odes from the Canons was reduced to three from Monday to Friday, and on Saturdays to four. Accord-

---

[1] Cf. Christ and Paranikas, *Anthologia gr. carm. christ.*, pp. xxx–xxxi.

[2] Cf. C. H. Roberts, *Catalogue of the Greek and Latin Papyri in the John Rylands Library, Manchester*, III (Manchester, 1938), 28–35.

[3] εἰς τὸ μεγ(αλύνει) τὴν τιμιωτέραν τῶν Χερουβίμ.

[4] Cf. P. F. Mercenier and F. Paris, *La prière des églises de rite byzantin*, I (d'Amay-sur-Meuse, 1937), 118–19.

ing to a table drawn up by H. Schneider from the eleventh-century Triodion the scheme was as follows:[1]

Day	Number of Odes	Biblical canticle referred to and selection of Odes
Monday	Triodion	I (Exod. xv), viii, ix.
Tuesday	Triodion	II (Deut. xxxii), viii, ix.
Wednesday	Triodion	III (I Kings ii), viii, ix.
Thursday	Triodion	IV (Hab. iii), viii, ix.
Friday	Triodion	V (Isa. xxvi, 9), viii, ix.
Saturday	Tetraodion	VI (Jonah ii), viii, ix.
	Tetraodion	VII (Dan. iii, 26), viii, ix.
Sunday	Nine Odes	I, III–IX.

With each Ode twelve to fourteen Troparia were sung, but as a rule the singing began after the first part of the canticle had been recited.

With the introduction of the Canon, music begins to play an increasing part in the service. Not only did each of the nine Odes have its own melody, but monostrophic hymns, Theotokia, Staurotheotokia and others, were inserted between the Odes, and the Stichera, which correspond to the Antiphons of the Western Church, were introduced into the service, and sung in various parts of the evening and morning Office. The melodies of the Odes are of the syllabic type, but those of the inserted Theotokia, Staurotheotokia, and particularly those of the Stichera, show a richer pattern, as can be seen by comparing examples I and II below (pp. 154 and 155).

Canons were at first written only for the most solemn festivals of the year: for Lent, Easter and Pentecost. Later they were written for all festal days, and finally composed for each day of the year. The invention of this new form is ascribed to Andrew of Crete, who owes much to Romanus;[2] he may have been the first hymnographer, writing in Greek, to make use of the fully developed new genre.[3] His main work, the 'Great Canon', consisting of 250 stanzas, is a penitential hymn. It is sung in the Mid-Lent week, and each Troparion is followed by three prostrations.[4]

The first school of Canon-writers flourished in the monastery of St Sabas in Palestine in the middle of the eighth century; its leaders were John of Damascus and his foster-brother Cosmas of Jerusalem. John of Damascus (c. 700–c. 760), one of the prominent defenders of Orthodoxy in the iconoclast controversy, was also a prolific hymno-

---

[1] Bibl. Vatic. cod. gr. 30, fol. 34–72; cf. H. Schneider, *op. cit.* p. 267. Schneider's four articles on the Odes in *Biblica*, xxx (1949) represent the most comprehensive study of the subject.

[2] Cf. K. Krumbacher, *Geschichte der byzantinischen Litteratur*, p. 667.

[3] S. Eustratiades develops the theory that John of Damascus was the first to write Canons, between 730 and 740 (cf. p. i of the preface to his edition of the *Heirmologion* (Chennevières-sur-Marne, 1932). But this theory has not been confirmed.

[4] J. M. Neale, *Hymns of the Eastern Church* (London, 1863), p. 23.

grapher. Orthodox tradition attributed to him the introduction of the *Octoechus*, or Book of the eight modes, a collection of hymns devoted to the Common of the Season, arranged for eight consecutive Sundays. On the first Sunday the hymns were all in the first mode, in the second week in the second, and so on. John of Damascus however was certainly not the author of the *Octoechus*, since Severus of Antioch had already composed a work of that kind in the sixth century. In a brilliant study E. Werner has shown that the conception of the system of eight modes dates back 'to the beginning of the first millennium B.C.', and that the principle of the *Octoechus* originated in cosmological and calendaric speculations.[1]

John of Damascus' fame as a hymn-writer is based on his Canons. His Easter Canon is called 'The Golden Canon' or 'The Queen of Canons'. It is well known in J. M. Neale's poetical translation, which begins with the words: ''Tis the Day of Resurrection: Earth! tell it out abroad!'

Cosmas of Jerusalem (*c.* 760), like John of Damascus, became a monk of St Sabas, but was consecrated bishop of Maiuma where he administered the diocese until his death. Next to John, he is considered the greatest Canon-writer; his finest work is the Canon for Christmas Day.[2] He is the most learned of the Greek hymnographers; his verses are full of theological and dogmatic allusions, yet his poetical language is impressive and vigorous.

At the beginning of the ninth century the Studite monastery at Constantinople became the centre of hymnography. Against the growing fury of iconoclasm Theodore the Studite (759–826) and his brother Joseph, and Theodore and Theophanes, another pair of brothers, branded for their faith, became indomitable defenders of Orthodoxy and wrote their Canons in praise of the saints. Many of these hymnographers were themselves later canonised by the Eastern Church.

With the end of the iconoclast struggle, marked by the solemn celebrations on 11 March 843, a new flowering of hymn-writing began which was even supported by two Emperors, by Leo VI (886–912), who wrote eleven *Eothina* or Morning Resurrection hymns,[3] and by Constantine VII Porphyrogenitus (913–59), who composed the *Exapostilaria*, hymns referring to the appearances of Christ after the Resurrection. One of the most fascinating figures among the hymnographers of this period is the nun Casia, author of some Canons and

[1] E. Werner, 'The Origin of the Eight Modes in Music', *Hebrew Union College Annual*, XXI (1948).

[2] H. J. W. Tillyard, 'The Hymns of the Octoechus', *Mon. Mus. Byz. Transcripta*, III (1940), V (1949).

[3] *Ibid.* V, 61–84.

Troparia, among which the most famous, a hymn for Wednesday in Holy Week, 'Lord, the woman fallen in many sins', is still sung today.[1]

In the eleventh century hymnography became more and more conventional. The reason for the decline of this kind of religious poetry, once so favoured, was undoubtedly the fact that so many Canons for church festivals were in existence and the clergy were opposed to the introduction of new ones. It needed as strong a personality as John Mauropous, metropolitan of Euchaita, to introduce new Canons into the services. He is said to have instituted the festival of the Three Fathers, St Basil, St Gregory and St Chrysostom, on 30 January and the Canons sung at the Office of Orthros on this day bear his name.[2] A large number of Canons ascribed to John Mauropous has been found, but few have as yet been published. They are characterised by their acrostics and usually bear the inscription 'John Mauropous, Archbishop of Euchaita'.[3]

While hymn-writing came to an end in the East in the course of the eleventh century it continued in the Greek monasteries in Sicily, southern Italy, and in the Basilian house of Grottaferrata near Rome, where the Byzantine tradition has remained practically unchanged up to the present day.

IV. MUSICAL NOTATION AND THE STRUCTURE OF THE MELODIES

Byzantine music has come down to us in manuscripts dating from the end of the ninth century to the beginning of the nineteenth, when Chrysanthus introduced a simplified notation which made the printing of hymn-books possible.[4] Studies in Byzantine music, however, are mainly concerned with the period before the end of the fifteenth century. Under the Turkish domination music became influenced by that of the ruling nation; it became richer in ornamentation and the old modal system had to give way to oriental scales. The most plausible explanation of this is that the Greek clergy had to earn their living by teaching music to the sons of the ruling classes and were therefore obliged to learn to sing in the Turkish manner. It is known that even Petrus Peloponnesius, a famous composer of Byzantine melodies of the eighteenth century, wrote Turkish secular songs.[5]

[1] H. J. W. Tillyard, 'A Musical Study of the Hymns of Casia', *BZ*, xx (1911), 420–85.

[2] Cf. J. M. Hussey, *Church and Learning in the Byzantine Empire (867–1185)* (Oxford 1937), pp. 39 ff., 234 ff.; 'The Canons of John Mauropous', *JRS*, xxxvii (1947), 70 f. [3] *Ibid.* p. 72.

[4] Chrysanthos, Θεωρητικὸν Μέγα (Trieste, 1832).

[5] Cf. H. J. W. Tillyard, 'Modes in Byzantine Music', *Annual of the British School at Athens*, xxii (1916–18), 148.

The fact that there are no musical manuscripts from the period of the iconoclast controversy may be due to one of two reasons, either that the music was transmitted orally, or that the codices perished during the conflict. The second is more probable, since the earliest extant examples of Byzantine musical notation show a musical semeiography sufficiently advanced to prove there must have been an earlier stage of which no instances appear to have survived.

Unlike ancient Greek musical notation which indicated the note that had to be produced by an instrument or by the voice, Byzantine musical semeiography was from the beginning an *aide-mémoire* for the singer who knew the melodies by heart. These musical signs gave directions as to the pitch of the chant and indicated ornaments, rhythm and dynamic stresses in connection with the words;[1] they were closely connected with an even earlier system of signs, the so-called ecphonetic notation, which was used as a guide for the readers who had to chant the lessons. The ecphonetic notation developed from the system of Greek prosodic signs; it consisted, in fact, of these signs together with certain combinations of them, and it remained practically unchanged from the sixth century to the end of the thirteenth, although it would seem that the reading of the lessons developed during this period from a cantillation into a kind of chanting. This is evident from a table in a Prophetologium of the eleventh or twelfth century, *Codex Sinaiticus* 8, which C. Höeg discovered and published in his *La Notation Ekphonétique*.[2] According to Höeg, this table dates from the end of the twelfth century, and it shows the usual ecphonetic signs in red ink and above them Byzantine neumes in black ink, instead of the usual brown ink. Whereas the red ecphonetic signs are set at the beginning and the end of a phrase, the musical signs in black indicate a rich flow of the melody. There is an obvious discrepancy between the two systems which can only be solved by assuming that in the twelfth century the original *lectio solemnis* was turned into a florid chanting.

This neumatic notation was used from the ninth or tenth century onwards for the singing of hymns and other liturgical chants and is generally divided into three main groups:[3]

(1) Early Byzantine notation (palaeobyzantine, stroke-dot or linear notation), ninth/tenth–twelfth centuries.

---

[1] Cf. E. Wellesz, 'Early Byzantine Neumes', *Mus. Quart.* xxxviii (1952), 68–79.

[2] Cf. *Mon. Mus. Byz.: Subsidia*, i, fasc. 2 (Copenhagen, 1935), p. 21 and plate iii.

[3] The transcription of melodies in the Middle Byzantine notation is now virtually free from difficulty. The later stages of the Early Byzantine notation (Coislin notation) can be read with the aid of MSS. in the Middle Byzantine notation. Cf. Tillyard, 'Byzantine Neumes: the Coislin Notation', *BZ*, xxxvii (1937), 345–58 and 'The Stages of Early Byzantine Musical Notation', *BZ*, xlv (1952), 29–42.

(2) Middle Byzantine notation (hagiopolitan, round), eleventh–fifteenth centuries.

(3) Late Byzantine notation (Koukouzelian, hagiopolitan-psaltic), fifteenth–nineteenth centuries.

The earliest musical manuscripts show two different kinds of notation, one closely related to the Greek accents and the ecphonetic signs, and another containing, in addition to these, a great number of complex signs. The former type of notation belonging to the earliest stage of the ninth-century notation is called by H. J. W. Tillyard the Esphigmenian; a slightly different and later one the Andreatic; that of the tenth to twelfth centuries the Coislin notation. With regard to the latter type, as early as 1912 Tillyard had drawn attention to an even older system of notation in Codex Laura 67 which 'strikes out on a line of its own', and had discovered that the few pages of the Chartres fragment, two of them published by A. Gastoué,[1] were 'a portion of this very manuscript'.[2] R. Palikarova-Verdeil has made a detailed study of the notation of the Chartres fragment in her book on Old Slavonic notation[3] and she calls this the Kontakarial notation, because it was the model for the Old Slavonic notation which is known by this name to Russian musicologists. The term is, however, not particularly apt, because the so-called Kontakarial notation is not confined to musical manuscripts containing Kontakia, but is also used in Hirmologia and Sticheraria.[4] This highly complex notation can be found in Old Slavonic manuscripts up to the thirteenth and fourteenth centuries, but it disappeared completely from Byzantine manuscripts in the tenth century. Hymn-books after that date use the Coislin notation which consists in the main of dots and strokes. This last stage of early Byzantine notation gives exact directions for the execution, but is still inexact as to the size of the intervals. A movement upwards can mean a leap of a third or fourth, or of a fourth or fifth. This lack of precision as to the intervals was overcome in the thirteenth century by the addition of more signs,

---

[1] Cf. A. Gastoué, *Introduction à la paléographie musicale byzantine* (Paris, 1907), p. 97 and plate III. The fragment consisting of fols. 61–6 of Cod. Chartres 1753–4 was destroyed in 1944. Plates VI and VII in Mme Palikarova-Verdeil's book (see n. 3 below) both belong to the Chartres fragment: they are fols. 61^r, 62^v and 63^r and were cut out of Cod. Laura 67, reproduced in plate V.

[2] 'Fragment of a Byzantine Musical Handbook in the Monastery of Laura on Mt Athos', *Annual of the British School at Athens*, XIX (1912–13), 95–113.

[3] R. Palikarova-Verdeil, 'La musique byzantine chez les Bulgares et les Russes', *Mon. Mus. Byz.: Subsidia*, III (Copenhagen, 1953).

[4] The Dumbarton Oaks Research Library and Collection in Washington, D.C., possesses photographs of a Hirmologium and a Sticherarium, both with Old Slavonic musical signs, dating from the twelfth century. These have been published in facsimile; cf. *Fragmenta Chilandarica palaeoslavica. A. Sticherarium; B. Hirmologium* (*Mon. Mus. Byz.* V, Copenhagen, 1957; preface by R. Jakobson).

each of which was used for a distinct interval. By an ingenious way of adding the rhythmical and dynamic signs to the interval-signs Byzantine musical notation represents a more perfect system than that of Western neumes.[1] Moreover, in the course of the thirteenth and fourteenth centuries a great number of red signs were added as guides for the execution of groups of notes and phrases. These signs were particularly necessary for the richly developed chants of the Koukouzelian period. But with the decline of Byzantine chant in the period after the fall of Constantinople and with the full impact of Turkish music, only a few singers understood these signs, so that practically the same thing happened as in the earliest stage of Byzantine notation: the musical manuscripts were used by the precentors, who knew the music by heart, as an *aide-mémoire*.

Thus the main sources for the study of Byzantine chant are the hymn-books and the books of liturgical chants from the beginning of the thirteenth to the end of the fourteenth centuries. The hymn-books contain either the model stanzas of the Odes, the Hirmi, or the mono-strophic Stichera. Accordingly the first are called Hirmologia, the second Sticheraria. The melodies of the Hirmi are of the simple syllabic type; sometimes two notes are set to a syllable, rarely three or more. The Stichera are longer; two notes are set to a syllable, and at the end of a phrase an ornamental group of notes is used for preference in order to mark the cadence. Byzantine music is written in one of the eight modes which were taken over from the Syrian chant;[2] the Byzantine mode (*ēchos*) is therefore different from the ancient Greek mode, though the fact has been obscured by the theorists.[3] The eight Byzantine modes,[4] four authentic (κύριοι) and four plagal (πλάγιοι), comprise eight groups of melodies, each of which consists of a number of musical formulas characteristic of the group. In the course of its development an extended melody may modulate into another mode, but it must return at the end of the piece to the mode in which it started. Each melody therefore has at its beginning

---

[1] For an introduction to this system see H. J. W. Tillyard, *Handbook of the Middle Byzantine Notation, Mon. Mus. Byz.: Subsidia*, I, fasc. 1 (1935); Dom L. Tardo, *L'Antica Melurgia bizantina*, pp. 64–89, 267 302; E. Wellesz, *A History of Byzantine Music and Hymnography*, pp. 226–54.

[2] Cf. A. Tearmin and B. Puyade, 'L'Octoëchos syrien', *Oriens Christ.* N.S. III (1913), 82–104, 277–98; E. Werner, 'The Origin of the Eight Modes of Music', *Hebrew Union College Annual*, XXI (1948), 211–55.

[3] Cf. E. Wellesz, 'The Survival of Greek Musical Theory', chapter 2 in *op. cit.* pp. 46–77.

[4] Cf. H. J. W. Tillyard, 'The Modes in Byzantine Music', *Annual of the British School at Athens*, XXII (1916–18), 133–56; 'The Byzantine Modes in the Twelfth Century', *ibid.* XLVIII (1954), 182–90; O. Strunk, 'The Tonal System of Byzantine Music', *Musical Quarterly*, XXVII (1942), 190–204; 'Intonations and Signatures of the Byzantine Modes', *ibid.* XXXI (1945), 339–55.

the number of the mode to which it belongs, for example, ἦχος α΄, ἦχος β΄, πλάγιος α΄, πλάγιος β΄ (mode I, mode II, plagal I, plagal II) and, where modulation occurs, a *Phthora*. There are eight signs or *Phthorai* indicating transition from one mode to another.

An initial formula characteristic of mode II is, for example, the following sequence of notes: *b a g ab b*, its final cadence *a gf e e*, or *a bg a gf e e*. These two formulas are to be found in the first Ode of the Resurrection Canon by John of Damascus, taken from the Hirmologium Grottaferrata Cod. E. γ. ii, fol. 31ᵛ, which may serve as an example of the style of the Hirmi:

EXAMPLE I

Mode II

The careful adaptation of the flow of the melody and the coincidence of the accentuation of the melody with that of the words is evident at first glance. The difficult task of the poet-musician was to write the rest of the stanzas of each Ode not only in the same metre as the model stanza but also with the words so arranged as to give the same perfect blending of words and music in each stanza of the Ode. Hymns in which words and music were written by the same melode were called *Idiomela*, those in which a poet adapted a new text to an already existing melody were called *Prosomoia*. In the latter case it may happen that music and words do not blend as perfectly as when both were composed by the same hymn-writer.

Another difficulty is that the hymn-writer has to build up each of the nine Odes on the subject of one of the nine canticles, whatever the festival may be for which the Canon is written. In the instance just cited (example I) the first canticle, the Song of Moses, had to be worked into the Ode and the first stanza is based on the first verse of the canticle. The art of the hymnographer therefore was twofold: as a poet he had to connect the context of the canticles with that of the festival for which he was writing his Canon. As a musician he had to choose the formulas which were best suited to the text, to link them together, and to make the stress of the most important words coincide with the highest notes of the melody, thus joining words and music into an indissoluble unity.

The same principle of blending words and music can be seen in the Stichera, but here the task of the musician is the more important one, as these are monostrophic hymns. The content of the Stichera ranges from the development of verses of a psalm and doxologies to sequences presenting in a semi-dramatic form the Nativity and Passion of our Lord. The following Sticheron is a variation of the *Gloria in excelsis*, from fol. 98ᵛ of the Sticherarium Cod. Vindob. theol. gr. 181 (N); it was sung on Christmas Day. The form is A-B-B₁-A₁; the melismas on the first syllable of Δόξα and on the last of Βηθλεέμ are typical of mode II.

EXAMPLE II

Liturgical chants proper, that is, Psalms, Alleluias, Koinonika (Communion chants), have survived only in a small number of manuscripts dating earlier than the fourteenth century, and most manuscripts are of a later date. These chants show a more florid style, as can be seen from the Alleluia of a Koinonikon (Communio) taken from Cod. Cryptoferr. Γ. γ. i, fol. 42ᵛ.

EXAMPLE III

The inserted vowels and syllables give a clear idea of the technique of performing these long melismas; the melodic phrases were divided up into small groups of notes, allowing the singer to take breath and to give intense expression to each group. It is not known definitely whether the rich melismatic texture of these chants dates only from the beginning of the work of the 'Embellishers', but there is some reason to assume that these liturgical chants were from the outset of a richly ornamented type. This assumption is strongly supported by a study of the melodic structure of the Akathistos. The music of this famous hymn is transmitted in several manuscripts of which Codex Ashburnham 64, written at Grottaferrata in the second quarter of the thirteenth century, is the most valuable because it contains the notation for all the stanzas of the hymn.[1] The Akathistos is written

---

[1] Cf. the facsimile edition of *Contacarium Ashburnhamense*, ed. C. Höeg (*Mon. Mus. Byz.*, IV, Copenhagen, 1956). A study of the Akathistos and a transcription are given in E. Wellesz, *The Akathistos Hymn* (*Mon. Mus. Byz.*, *Transcripta*, IX, Copenhagen, 1957).

in the richly ornamented style characteristic of the Koinonika; but here the melismas are sung to repeated vowels of the words of the text, not to inserted vowels and syllables, as in the Koinonika.

The richly ornamented melody of the Akathistos in the thirteenth-century Codex Ashburnham is not a new stylistic feature. A fragment from the beginning of the hymn, giving the words Ἄγγελος πρωτοστάτης with superimposed neumes, is scribbled at the foot of folio 262 of the twelfth-century Codex Coislin 220;[1] but the neumes must have been copied from a Kontakarion of the tenth or late ninth century, since there is one sign, the Katabasma, in a shape which is found only in the earliest manuscripts. The grouping of the neumes to the words shows already at that early date a rich ornamentation of the melody so that one is entitled to assume that Byzantine music had from its beginning a syllabic style for the Troparia, a slightly embellished style for the Stichera and a richly ornamented one for the Kontakia, the Koinonika, and the other chants of the liturgy.

The twenty-four stanzas of the Akathistos are written to the same melodic scheme and have the same melodic phrase for the beginning:

EXAMPLE IV

<hr />

[1] This marginal note was discovered by Professor O. Strunk of Princeton University, who kindly placed it at my disposal, for which I am most grateful. For the shape of the Katabasma, mentioned above, see J.-B. Thibaut, *Monuments de la notation ecphonétique et hagiopolite* (St Petersburg, 1913), table p. 61.

But in the later course of the melody, particularly in the twelve *Chairetismoi*, innumerable changes are introduced to avoid a feeling of repetition. The most striking feature of the melodic line is the occurrence of cadences which are different from those of the Odes and Stichera: they are more akin to the early Western sequences than to other Byzantine hymns.

The greatness of Byzantine hymnography, the skill of the Maistores in adapting the music to the poem, can best be illustrated by giving in full the musical setting of the famous Kontakion ψυχή μου by Romanus.[1] The form is: A-AI-B. The melody is written in the second plagal mode. In the Hirmologia and Sticheraria melodies in this mode usually begin and always end on *e*, whereas in the Kontakaria they often start and end on *d*. After the first phrase (A) of the melody there follows the Intonation-formula νεαν(ες) which leads into the slightly varied repetition of the same phrase (AI). The full cadences of all the melodic phrases are identical.

It was only with the foundation of the *Monumenta Musicae Byzantinae* in 1931 that transcription of Byzantine hymns started on a large scale, but it is already clear that Eastern hymnography is in no

---

[1] Cf. Christ and Paranikas, *Anthologia gr. carm. christ.*, p. 90. 'My soul, my soul arise; why sleepest thou? The end is coming, and thou wilt be confounded. Be sober, that Christ the Lord may spare thee; for He is everywhere and filleth all things' (translated by H. J. W. Tillyard). In the Kontakaria the stanza follows immediately or soon after the first stanza of the Akathistos. The melody here given is taken from Cod. Ashburnham 64, fol. 112ᵛ–113. In the last line ὁ πανταχοῦ [παρὼν καὶ] τὰ πάντα πληρῶν the words in brackets are omitted.

EXAMPLE V

Ψυ - χή . . . . μου· ψυ - χή . . . .

. . . . . . μου . . . , ἀν - ά . . . .

στα, τί καθ - εύ . . . . δεις; νε - ε

- α - ν [ες] . . . τὸ τέ - . . . . λος ἐγ - γί . . . . .

. . . . ζει . . καὶ μέλ - . . . .

. . . . . . λεις θο - ρυ - βεῖ - . . . .

. . . . . σθαι. Ἀν - ά - νη - ψον . . . οὖν

. . . . , ἵ - να φεί - - σε - - -

. . . . ταί σου Χρι - στὸς . . . . ; . . . . ὁ Θε - - - -

δς . . . . ὁ παν - τα - - χοῦ . . . .

τὰ πάν - - - - - - . . . . τα πλη - ρῶν . . . .

way inferior to the Western. The Byzantine conception of art is based on Platonic and neoplatonic thought, adapted to Orthodox theology. According to this conception, the work of art belongs to the world of appearances. It is a projection of the Reality which is audible and visible only to the higher ranks of the Celestial Hierarchy. But through them, ἀπήχημα,[1] the echo of Divine Beauty, is transmitted to the lower ranks, and from them to the Prophets, the saints and the inspired artists, who in a state of elation paint an icon or compose a hymn. Thus the artist could never attempt to follow his own imagination. If he was a hymnographer he had to imitate an already existing hymn which was the echo, made perceptible to human ears, of the hymns sung in heaven. The occurrence of the same formulas in many hymns of the same mode does not betray any lack of creative imagination in the hymn-writer; it is indeed the inevitable outcome of that complete integration of art and theology which found its supreme expression in the liturgy of the Orthodox Church.

[1] Ps.-Dionysius, *De caelesti hierarchia*, c. 2, 4, *MPG*, III, 144; ed. G. Heil (Sources chrétiennes, 58, Paris, 1958), p. 83.

CHAPTER XXV

BYZANTINE MONASTICISM[1]

It was in Egypt at the end of the third and beginning of the fourth
centuries that Christian monasticism took root. Here men and
women left their ordinary life in the world in order to perfect themselves that they might be able to imitate God and have knowledge of
him. This lifelong process of purification was carried on by means of
withdrawal into solitude where unceasing warfare was waged against
the sins of the flesh and the sins of the mind. The first Christian monks
appear to have been St Antony and his contemporaries. They fled to
the desert, and also set up some houses for the common life along the
Nile. St Antony withdrew indeed before Constantine had brought
peace to the Church, and withdrawal for ascetic—and other—purposes was no new feature either in the Christian Church or outside it.
But with the acceptance of Christianity and the ending of persecution,
the pre-Constantinian movement gathered impetus, and was perhaps
even regarded as a new form of martyrdom for Christ's sake. In the
course of the fourth century the Scetic desert and the districts round
Nitria to the west of the Nile, and particularly the wilderness further
south on both sides of the Nile, known as the Thebaid, were peopled
by hundreds of Christians seeking perfection. They were not dualist
in their attitude towards the body, nor did they in other ways condemn God's creation, as their attitude to the countryside and to
animals shows. 'My book', replied St Antony to an inquiring philosopher, 'is nature, so that whenever I wish, I can read the words of
God'.[2] As contemporary evidence bears witness, these Christians
sought to return to the state of man before the Fall, to purify themselves of sins of the flesh and of the spirit. They attempted to do this
by perpetual warfare, whose stages are set out in what was to become
the classical model for the saint's life, the biography of Antony by
Athanasius. Here Antony's resistance to temptation from within is
described, his resistance to assaults of the demons from without, and
finally his emergence to perfect bodily condition as one who was now
the friend of God blessed by the charismata which were signs of this
holy state.

This quest for sanctification and perfection, this *vita contemplativa*,

[1] Byzantine monasticism is rooted in practice and precept dating from its inception;
in this chapter it has therefore not been found practicable to exclude reference to the
centuries before 717 and the period has been treated as a whole.
[2] Socrates, *Ecclesiastical History*, IV, ch. 23.

was pursued in various ways. Many followed St Antony's eremitic life, though complete isolation was often neither possible nor desirable. Beginners would take an experienced ascete as their spiritual director, as St Antony had done, and only gradually learn to discipline themselves in isolation. Sometimes seasoned hermits would go round visiting new monks living alone in order to strengthen those attacked by demons in the shape of evil thoughts. Often solitaries lived in cells scattered round a church and a bakery where they met on Saturdays and Sundays. Here they might get spiritual guidance; they could worship together; and get their supply of bread for the week. This flexible arrangement was known as a *laura*, meaning an alley-way, presumably with cells opening on to it, and it can well be visualised in terms of caves or cells, such as opened on to tracks along the sides of the rocky Palestinian gorges where lavras are known to have existed from the fourth century onwards. This arrangement left the individual a large measure of responsibility for his own daily life whilst ensuring him opportunity for common worship and spiritual advice.

At the same time there were organised communities in which an ascetic life was lived in company with others under the direction of a superior. The name of Pachomius, a converted Egyptian soldier, is associated with the development of the 'common' life (*coenobium*). A contemporary of St Antony, he at first tried to live as an anchorite, but judged this to make demands beyond the powers of many who were attracted to monasticism. He therefore set up houses not in the distant desert, but near the Nile, and eventually presided over a congregation of nine, as well as two women's establishments. The mother-house was at Pabou, and the rest were dependent upon it; they were thus filial and not members of a confederation. Lives of the saint have survived, as well as something of his rule, revealing the essentials of daily life in his houses and showing also the many problems presented by such enormous and sometimes unruly communities (said to have numbered 3000 under Pachomius, who is also reported on one occasion to have turned away as many as a hundred as being unsuitable). A wall enclosed the great complex of buildings —assembly hall, refectory, offices, different houses each for a group of about forty monks. Obedience to the superior was the keynote of this coenobitic life. Under his direction the monks took part in their daily services and prayer, and ate their meals in the refectory, received instruction in the Scriptures, and did the manual work assigned to them. As yet the liturgical hours were unknown, and communions usually celebrated by neighbouring priests on Saturdays and Sundays. Pachomius himself shunned ordination.

Such was the impression made by the exuberant self-sacrifice of the Egyptian monks that it had an immediate and lasting effect on the Christian world. The anchorites, especially those in Nitria, were visited, perhaps after a preliminary visit to the Holy Places, by men from the East Mediterranean and elsewhere. A literature of the desert fathers grew up, embodying the memories of those who had listened to the spiritual teaching of the early monks, or had recorded stories handed down by their disciples. It was from such sources as these, the lives of the desert fathers, particularly as told in Palladius' *Lausiac History*, or in the *Historia Monachorum*, and the *Apophthegmata Patrum*, that later generations in the monastic world, whether of eastern or western tradition, constantly fed their own spirituality. Fired by the example of the early monks, their way of life was followed throughout the Christian world. It may even have developed independently, perhaps in Asia Minor whence Chariton is said to have come to Palestine, perhaps in the Judaean desert between Jerusalem and the Dead Sea, though there is no denying the debt owed to Egypt. Contemporaries set up every form of monastic establishment from the anchorite's cell to the coenobitic house. Fourth-century churchmen, particularly bishops, were not without their doubts and tried to bring the movement within the diocesan framework. In this respect they owed something to the work of St Basil the Great, bishop of Caesarea. He had visited Egypt and in his own Cappadocia he tried to infuse some order into coenobitic life, leaving a number of rulings on problems which might arise in a community. He pointed out that it was in a community that man could fulfil the divine commandment to love his neighbour, but he was also known to have founded hermit cells near his monasteries. He left no monastic rule in the strict sense of the term, but his advice and teaching were widely respected by later monastic leaders, including St Benedict of Nursia as well as St Theodore the Studite.

St Basil, like other churchmen, realised the dangers of the solitary life for the unwary or the unruly, but this form of monachism continued unabated side by side with the coenobitic house. It is perhaps a mistake to draw too sharp a division between the two, for in the East Roman Empire there was sufficient flexibility to allow of the passage from one to the other and back. Some measure of control was also provided by the lavra, a form of monasticism that early took firm root in Palestine and Syria. Here until the check imposed by the Arab invasions, conditions proved especially favourable to the growth of monasticism. The Holy Land was an obvious goal for the devout Christian. Jerusalem, a cosmopolitan centre, became filled with monks and nuns and the solitude of the surrounding desert and craggy ravines and gorges riddled with caves challenged the aspiring anchorite. In the Gaza region to the south, in the Judaean wilderness, there grew up innumerable cells, often grouped into a lavra. Hilarion, who settled near Gaza, had known St Antony according to St Jerome, and here in the south, links with Egypt were strong. Chariton, who is said to have come from Iconium in the fourth century, appears to have founded three lavras between Jerusalem and Jericho, and a wadi there is still called after him.[1] In the early fifth century Euthymius, a priest who had come from Melitene on the Euphrates, founded both lavra and *coenobium*, though he himself retreated when possible into anchorite solitude. It is noticeable that the *coenobium* which he founded was used as a training-ground for monks who could later pass on to the more rigorous life of the lavra, or of the isolated hermitage. Euthymius died in 473. It was he who had given direction to Judaean monasticism, the influence of which has not always been fully acknowledged; it was fitting that Byzantine hymnody should give him a high place amongst ascetics. His work was continued by St Sabas (439–532), who came from Cappadocia to found his famous lavra as well as three other lavras, six *coenobia*, and four hospices. St Sabas' life, like that of St Euthymius, was written by Cyril of Scythopolis. Judging from the information given by Cyril, it looks as though some of the houses were autonomous, but with some suggestion of confederation. St Sabas' rule, if he wrote one, has not survived, but the living practice of his foundations remained to exercise a widespread influence on Greek liturgy and hymnody and even under Arab domination could still produce a St John of Damascus or St Cosmas of Maiuma. In this early period, writers from the East Mediterranean are unsurpassed for monastic vigour and liveliness. To Cyril of Scythopolis' lives can be added the *Ladder to Paradise* by John Climacus, abbot of the house on Mt Sinai, a work later on widely used by Byzantines and Slavs alike, or the varied stories of John Moschus' *Spiritual Meadow* or the writings of the monastic circle south of Gaza where Barsanuphius corresponded with John of Beersheba and both gave their rulings on a wide variety of topics to an equally wide circle of inquirers.

Firmly rooted in the early monastic spirituality and practice of Egypt, Sinai and Palestine, almost from its inception monasticism had flourished in those imperial lands which were to form the heart of the Empire long after the eastern provinces had fallen away. In Asia Minor, in and around Constantinople, in Greece and the islands,

---

[1] I owe this information to the kindness of the Rev. Derwas Chitty and am greatly indebted to him for a preview of his Birkbeck lectures on Early Monasticism, particularly those on Judaean monasticism.

in South Italy and Sicily, and in the Balkans, monasteries and hermits multiplied. Conciliar rulings, saints' lives, monastic sermons of
instruction, foundation charters and imperial privileges, bear witness
to the vigour of this movement in the life of the Church. They
demonstrate, too, that the forms which it took continued to be as
varied as in the fourth century. By its very nature the coenobitic
foundation had a more defined place in the diocesan framework and
was easier to legislate for than the individual anchorite, though not
in practice necessarily easier to control. Even so, information about
the life of individual houses is somewhat scanty, particularly before
the Studite reform. The numbers of monasteries can sometimes be
estimated, for instance thirty-nine men's houses in the diocese of
Chalcedon in 536. Or from the saints' lives it can be deduced that in
the early iconoclast period within a coenobitic house the *hegumenus*
might be living almost the life of an anchorite, withdrawn in solitary
prayer in his cell, while the community were at office, leaving his
second-in-command to administer the house. This was for instance
found in some of the monastic settlements thronging the slopes of
Mt Olympus in Bithynia, and coenobitic life seemed to be regarded
here as a lower stage for the less advanced.

Something of a breach in continuity was created in and around
Constantinople by the iconoclasts, who sought to penalise the monks
opposing this movement. Amongst those who suffered was Theodore,
first living in the Saccudion house in Bithynia in Asia Minor, and then
centred in the monastery of Studius in south-west Constantinople.
Here in the early ninth century he defended the use of icons, and
when circumstances permitted he inaugurated a reform of monastic
life. He thought that the deterioration which he found could only be
arrested by a return to the teaching of the fathers, and by this he
meant the old monastic leaders, such as the Egyptian monks or
Basil of Cappadocia or Dorotheus of Gaza. He did indeed stress St
Basil's writings (including among these the so-called monastic
rules), but it has been pointed out that his vocabulary may have
owed more to the sixth-century Gaza circle, or at any rate to Palestinian monachism, where monastic administration had by then developed
further than in fourth-century Cappadocia. Theodore was both spiritual director and administrator, and his writings, particularly his
Catecheses, illustrate his gifts and his difficulties. Obedience, poverty,
manual work—these were the means whereby his monks were to
return to the traditions of the fathers and to recapture the coenobitic
spirit of a St Pachomius or a St Basil. Theodore regarded the community as a whole and considered that the abbot could not live
entirely withdrawn in holy solitude. As superior he was the active

head of the *coenobium* and responsible not only for spiritual instruction but for the hierarchy of officials who shared the administration of the house. The various departments—kitchen, gardens, library— were all carefully provided for. Slaves and female animals were banned, and manual work stressed; surplus produce, if any, was given to the poor. The individual was exhorted to work with zeal, to welcome holy poverty, and to eradicate the human failings and selfishness which might impel a brother to seek out a warm spot in the kitchen on a cold day or to recoil when given an ill-fitting verminous garment from the common stock at the weekly distribution. Theodore laid down careful direction for the daily life of all the houses under his care. No aspect of administration seemed to escape him. In his practical wisdom and imagination he realised that the copyists would be more accurate if exempt from saying the Psalms while they worked; he legislated too on such vital subjects as penance and fasting; and above all his inspired spiritual direction showed that he had in mind for his monks no less high a goal than that aimed at by the solitary anchorite or the early Egyptian fathers.

Theodore's stress on the corporate life of the community with its corporate liturgical obligations, its manual work and its holy poverty was in the tradition of Pachomius or Basil or Dorotheus of Gaza. He insisted on absolute obedience, but he also urged moderation in ascetic practice so that his ideal should be within the reach of all. In the Studite Constitution, which was based on Theodore's teaching, his rulings on monastic discipline were summarised and his influence acknowledged. It opens thus: 'There are many different rules which prevail in the holy monasteries...but our tradition is that which we have received from our great father and confessor, Theodore. We are not alone in this, for a large section of the approved monastic world also accepts this as the best and the most royal rule which indeed avoids both extravagance and inadequacy.'[1] The powerful Studite house was no innovator, but it exemplified the monastic ideal in a coenobitic framework and exercised a strong influence on foundations of this kind, as for instance Athanasius' monastery on Mt Athos, or the Pečersky house in Kiev. Symeon the New Theologian, himself of equal, if not greater, authority than Theodore in the monastic world, had begun his novitiate in the Studite house and though he had to leave it for St Mamas under something of a cloud, he later showed his familiarity with the teaching of its famous abbot, which in some respects his own clearly resembled.

Any acceptance of the Studite tradition as 'the best and most royal rule' does not imply what acceptance of any such rule as that

[1] *MPG*, xcix, 1703.

of St Benedict of Nursia came to mean in the West. The Eastern Church knew no monastic 'orders', but only a single 'order'. Some or all of the Studite rulings might be incorporated into the foundation charter (*typicon*) of a house, or adopted by a reforming abbot, but there was no Studite order, any more than there was a Basilian order. There was great variety of detail, but the monk, whether in a *coenobium* or lavra or a hermitage, was primarily dedicated to his quest for the *visio Dei* through the *vita contemplativa*. There were no teaching orders, or military orders, or missionary orders, as in the West; though in the East many services were performed for the laity, they were subordinate and not in any way the primary aim of the monks. This does not imply that East Roman monasticism was marked either by uniformity or by lack of regulation. Literary sources, particularly the lives of the saints or the catecheses of a St Theodore or a St Symeon, reveal the depth of Byzantine spirituality amidst the wealth of detail on everyday life and practice. The conciliar rulings, imperial legislation, the extant *typica*, the commentaries of canonists, illustrate the carefully regulated place of monachism in the polity.

In its very early days monasticism had threatened to develop outside diocesan control, but wise episcopal and imperial policy had brought it within the framework of the Church. This was done by means of decrees in the general councils, supplemented by local church councils and by patriarchal and episcopal rulings. Monastic discipline, like other branches of ecclesiastical life, was also the concern of imperial legislation. Thus diocesan authority was preserved and the life of the Church was greatly strengthened by the presence of this growing reservoir of Christian spirituality. Monastic influence had from its inception exercised a powerful influence on public opinion. During the christological controversies of the iconoclast struggle, unruly monks at church councils, or obstinate monastic strongholds, such as the Palestinian or the Studite houses, had shown their strength. While iconodules such as John of Damascus might be the legitimate champions of orthodoxy, it was obvious that uncontrolled monasticism would be open to serious abuse. Hence the bishop's responsibility in this respect was continually emphasised. The Council of Chalcedon (451) laid down that monks should devote themselves to prayer and fasting and not intervene in ecclesiastical or political affairs; they were moreover to observe some *stabilitas loci* and were under the authority of the bishop of the diocese, whose permission they had to obtain if they wished to undertake essential work outside their house. Monasteries and oratories were only built with episcopal consent, and once founded, they were not to be converted to secular uses, nor their endowments alienated (canons 4 and 24).

Control of monastic foundations remained for various reasons a pressing problem throughout the middle ages. It was desirable to ensure that the house was adequately endowed, but it might also be expedient to control what proved to be a continual flow of wealth into monastic hands. The iconoclasts were openly hostile to monasticism, and occasionally even a most devout and orthodox Emperor, such as Nicephorus II, would attempt to bring the movement under stricter control. But such was its hold on all classes that this proved impossible, short of actual confiscation. Sometimes over-eagerness to found new establishments was due to monastic insubordination. The Council of Nicaea II (787) ordered the diocesan to condemn monks leaving their monasteries in order to set up their own small houses which they were often unable to complete for lack of funds (canon 17). When the iconoclasts were decisively defeated in the ninth century, there was such a show of enthusiasm for monasticism that the Council of Constantinople in 861 had to censure bishops for unwisely diverting episcopal revenue to the foundation of monastic houses. The laity who had also been indulging in over-hasty foundations were forbidden either to secularise their gifts or to nominate the head of their monastic house without episcopal permission. Evidently they had been regarding the foundations as private property and even appointing themselves as abbot.

The tenth-century Emperor Nicephorus II Phocas went so far as to forbid in general new foundations or the further endowment of monasteries with land. He himself realised what the monastic ideal at its best might be, and he had at one time even intended to become an anchorite on Mt Athos with his friend and confessor St Athanasius. He stressed the poverty of the holy fathers of Egypt and bitingly condemned the luxury and wealth of the monasteries of his day. He urged that charitable intentions should be directed towards helping existing establishments which lay in ruins for lack of funds rather than in setting up new houses. But he added that the foundation of hermit cells and lavras was permissible and praiseworthy as long as these did not attempt to increase their land beyond their immediate enclosures. This remarkable novel of 964 was based on an understanding of the highest aims of monasticism; it was also due to the realisation that property donated to monasteries might remain unproductive, thus depriving the state of urgently needed revenue. But the power of the Church and the strength of monasticism were such that the novel had to be repealed. Later Emperors and churchmen were also occasionally critical of over-wealthy monastic foundations clustering in the cities. Manuel I Comnenus for instance tried in 1158 to direct founders to remote and more suitable country districts, and in the fourteenth century the government, harassed by poverty and pressing needs of defence, appears to have appropriated monastic property in order to grant it out in *pronoia* or to replenish its waning resources. Measures of this kind were however exceptional, and imply no diminution of the honour in which the monastic life was generally held.

Founders of monasteries were drawn from all ranks, lay or ecclesiastical, men or women. The *typica* of some of the foundations of wealthy and powerful patrons such as the twelfth-century Comneni, or the eleventh-century lawyer Attaleiates, have survived. But often the small and perhaps short-lived house, built in a country district with the help of villager, is known only by some chance reference in a saint's life. A house might have a number of patrons and benefactors, and the rights of the founder could be passed on by inheritance or agreement, by delegation or by sale. By canon law the house had to have at least three monks, but apart from this the founder might state his own wishes. The *typicon* consisted of three parts: the first contained special liturgical obligations, including commemoration of the founder and his family; the second specified other particular obligations of the community, such as the care of the aged or sick; the third section, called the *brevion* (from the Latin *breve*), was a cartulary containing an inventory of the house's endowments. The *typicon* was normally approved by the bishop, and in some cases he himself might have helped to draw it up, as John Mauropous, the eleventh-century archbishop of Euchaita, is known to have done. It was deposited in the episcopal archives. It might also be approved by the Emperor or Patriarch. The houses on Mt Athos, for instance, got imperial sanction for their *typica*. There were in fact various kinds of foundation. The normal house was eparchial, coming directly under the diocesan. Occasionally other more privileged foundations might be patriarchal, or in the case of an autocephalous church such as Cyprus would be under its highest ecclesiastical authority, the archbishop. As might be expected, some houses sought imperial protection or were founded by imperial bounty; these enjoyed exemption from all save imperial authority, and were sometimes described by their founder as 'the houses of my Empire'. *Autodespotai*, or completely independent, houses claimed to be withdrawn from all jurisdiction whether patriarchal, episcopal or imperial. A charter of this kind was approved by Nicephorus III Botaneiates in 1079 when the sister of Constantine Cabalurus founded the monastery of St John the Baptist on the island of Strobelus.[1] But such total immunity was regarded as an infringement of canon law and from time to time was

[1] *MM*, vi, pp. 19–21 = *DR*, 1045.

condemned, as by the canonist Balsamon, or by the patriarchal decree of 1395.

Apart from jurisdictional distinctions, various different kinds of monastic foundation were found. The κοινόβιον, the coenobitic house, was the most usual form of regulated life for both men and women. The *metochion* (μετόχιον) was a small monastic dependency set up as an outpost for the management of a distant estate, or perhaps for some legitimate trading purpose, and was entirely under the control of the mother house. Double houses were not unknown, but were frowned on and forbidden by Justinian (nov. 123) and in 787 by the Council of Nicaea II (canon 20). In the late middle ages, Nilus, Patriarch of Constantinople, abolished an institution of this kind set up by his predecessor Athanasius. The term *laura* of early Egyptian and Palestinian monasticism, denoting a collection of individual cells under the direction of a superior, later came to be sometimes applied to a *coenobium*, for example the Great Lavra of Mt Athos, and a loose association of hermit groups for two or three anchorites under the direction of one or more experienced monks was designated by the term *kellion* (κελλίον). A *scete* (σκήτη) consisted of a number of *kellia* or *calybae* grouped under the direction of a leader called a *dikaios* (δικαῖος). It was linked with some monastic house which would send monks to its cells and it recognised the authority of the *hegumenus* of this house, though accepting responsibility for its own daily administration. An individual solitary might be known as a hermit (*eremites*), or a recluse (*inclusus*), or a hesychast (*hesychastes*, that is, one living in holy quiet, and not to be confused with the hesychast of the later middle ages practising certain specific disciplines).

A new foundation normally took place with the consent of the diocesan bishop, whose authority was emphasised from Chalcedon onwards. Episcopal dedication and blessing were accompanied by the fixing of the cross, usually on the site where the high altar was to be, hence the term 'stavropegial', which later became the term to be applied only to houses under patriarchal control. This may have been as early as the eighth century; and there is certainly a reference to a patriarchal stavropegial house in the late ninth-century *Epanagoge*. Such patriarchal houses acquired their own special foundation ritual. Usually after a delay of three years there was a ceremonial procession and the announcement of the founder's arrangements set out in the *typicon*. This delay of three years had been introduced by Justinian; his novels also laid down certain general rulings, as the enclosure of all buildings within a single wall and the provision that no monk might live alone except for anchorites and recluses having their own special cells within the monastic precincts (nov. 5). As well as for new foundations, canon law also provided for various contingencies, such as the restoration of a house, the completion of a new foundation by the heirs of a deceased founder, and, later, the possibility of an altered regime, though change from coenobitic to idiorhythmic life was discouraged. The position of the bishop was recognised by his commemoration in the liturgy and by the tax (*canonicon*) paid him. He was ultimately responsible for the spiritual and material well-being of the house, delegating an official for this purpose. He confirmed the abbatial election and consecrated the abbot and he provided the monastery with a court of appeal in case of need. Suppression of a religious house could be undertaken only for the gravest reasons, and in such a case the property of the house could not be alienated from ecclesiastical use.

Entrance into monastic life was regulated. There were certain restrictions on the acceptance of slaves: it was forbidden to alienate these from their masters (Council of Chalcedon, 451, canon 4); in certain circumstances runaways could be reclaimed within a three-year period (Justinian, nov. 5), or even after this (Leo VI, nov. 10); they lost their freedom and were returned to their masters if they left the monastery. Marriage was no bar to the monastic vocation provided that certain provisions were observed. The consent of both parties had to be obtained in order to dissolve a marriage or betrothal, and care taken to see that no injury was done in pecuniary matters. The dowry or marriage settlement had to be repaid, and provision made for dependants such as parents or children. Rulings vary on the age at which virgins might be accepted. According to the canons attributed to Basil the Great, 16 or 17 was fixed as the age at which young men and women might reasonably be supposed to understand the meaning of the step which they were about to take. The Quinisextum Council (691) had lowered this to 10 years. Leo VI (nov. 6) laid down from 10 years to 16 or 17, with the proviso that property could not be disposed of until the latter age was reached. Theodore the Studite had favoured 16 years. Later on medieval custom on Mt Athos varied. Subject to the fulfilment of certain family obligations, the monastery had the right of legal inheritance and could accept gifts. The novice was expected to give a single child's portion to the monastery, though it was possible to evade this obligation. On the other hand the monastic authorities might abuse their position and bring pressure to bear. This evil was often denounced. Heads of houses, whether men or women, were forbidden to demand money from those presenting themselves for entry to monastic life. Offenders were to be removed from their houses and placed in a subordinate position, unless the abbot was a priest, and then he was deposed from his rank if he persisted in this practice (Council of Chalcedon, canon 2). But the portion which the monastery was authorised to receive, whether from adults or from parents on behalf of their children, remained in possession of the house, even if the individual concerned left the house (Council of Nicaea II, 787, canon 19). Exception might however be made if the departure was due to some justifiable complaint against the abbot. In the case of a monk from one house being received into another, his dowry remained with the original house (Justinian, nov. 5 and 123).

Change of house was not normally sanctioned, and the desirability of *stabilitas loci* was firmly recognised both by ecclesiastical authority and by founders. It was evidently a recurrent problem. Justinian rebuked bishops or archimandrites who permitted changes. The Council of Nicaea II (canon 21) forbad nuns and monks to leave their houses, and said that should this occur the offenders were not to be regarded as members of the community which they went to, but merely as visitors (though not necessarily housed in the guests' quarters). In the eleventh century Michael Attaleiates expressly stated in his *typicon* that monks from other houses were not to be accepted in his foundation. Subject to certain safeguards laid down by conciliar and patriarchal rulings, it appears to have been recognised that there were occasions when a monk might be transferred from one house to another. He had to have a specific reason, approved by the superiors of both houses and by the bishop of the diocese. The bishop himself could, if he thought desirable, transfer a monk from one house to another (Council of 861, canon 4). On Mt Athos the Great Lavra in the late tenth century permitted its monks to move to another abbot with the consent of their present *hegumenus*, should this be considered desirable for their spiritual development. Should unusual difficulties arise, for instance if an abbot were a heretic, or if he refused permission to leave to a monk who felt that he was suffering spiritual harm, then in such cases patriarchal rulings suggest that the monk was free to depart provided that he gave due warning of his intention.

Entry into a monastery was followed by a period of probation. Justinian (nov. 123) spoke of a three years' novitiate for slaves and those who were unknown, giving the abbot licence to reduce this length of time for men of proved virtue. This was confirmed by the Quinisextum Council (691, canon 40) but in 861 the Council of Constantinople (canon 5) extended the three-year novitiate to everyone, except those dangerously ill who might be admitted to the monastic status at once, or those of outstanding virtue for whom six months was sufficient. Later practice occasionally reduced the more usual three-year period: St Athanasius' tenth-century *typicon* for the Great

Lavra on Mt Athos prescribed only a one-year novitiate. After the period of probation the solemn frocking of the nun or monk took place. The liturgical ceremony is set out in the *Euchologium*. It is not known exactly when this was compiled, but rules for the great and little habit are found in early manuscripts of the eighth or ninth century.[1] The distinctive black habit (*schema*) was assumed by the postulant at this ceremony, hence the term *schematologium* which is used for the section of the *Euchologium* dealing with monastic ceremonial. If the superior were a priest, he professed and tonsured the novice, otherwise a hiero-monk performed the ceremony in the presence of the superior of the house into which the novice was being received. The ceremony began with an exhortation setting out the purpose and practice of monastic life, and was followed by a number of questions and answers which made clear the novice's profession of poverty, obedience and chastity as well as the pledge of stability. 'Will you for the rest of your life observe obedience towards your superior and all the brethren in Christ?' he was asked, and 'Will you persevere in the monastery and in the ascetic way of life until your last breath?' and the response came back, 'Yes, reverend father, with God's help I will'.[2] Then came a short address on the trials of monastic life with prayers for the candidate, and the tonsure and frocking followed. The distinction between the two frockings, the great and the little habit, still preserved today, was known as early as the eighth century and there are separate rites for these in the *Euchologium*. The novice received the little habit on his profession as a monk; the great habit was assumed by those far advanced in the spiritual life. Canonists and monastic writers regarded both as signifying genuine monastic status, but some did not approve of the distinction. Theodore the Studite in his *Testament* wrote: 'There is only one monastic status (*schema*), just as there is only one baptism',[3] and his views were shared by later writers such as the revered fourteenth-century St Gregory Palamas, archbishop of Thessalonica.

The monastic system was monarchical and the house under the control of a superior known by various titles, as abbot, *hegumenus*, *proestos*, or if he were a priest or deacon, *cathegumenus*. An eleventh-century source stated that he had to be at least thirty-three years old, a monk of the house, if possible a priest, and above all possessed of outstanding spiritual qualities and wisdom. Though the abbot

[1] Cf. P. de Meester, *De Monachico Statu iuxta disciplinam byzantinam* (Vatican, 1942), pp. 82 ff.

[2] *Great Euchologium* (Rome, 1873), p. 226; for translations of the ceremony see E. A. de Mendieta, *La presqu'île des caloyers: le Mont-Athos* (Bruges, 1955), pp. 324 ff., or N. F. Robinson, *Monasticism in the Orthodox Church* (London, 1916), pp. 71 ff.

[3] Theodore the Studite, *Ep. ad Nicolaum*, *MPG*, xcix, 941.

was often a priest, this was not obligatory. In the days of the desert fathers, a superior would nominate his successor, and this practice was sometimes followed. But there was great variation in methods of election. A superior might be nominated by the founder and details of subsequent elections carefully prescribed in his *typicon*. Michael Attaleiates exhorted the choice of a man distinguished above all for his humility, 'for I judge this to be the greatest of all virtues, without which whosoever liveth is counted dead'. Sometimes the community, or at least the *pars sanior*, might elect their superior, or he might be chosen by the bishop or the Patriarch. In any case the election had to be confirmed by the bishop of the diocese, or by the Patriarch in the case of a stavropegial monastery. Normally the superior was chosen from the brethren of the house, but if there was no one suitable, resort might be had to another house; this was specifically laid down by the Empress Irene in the *typicon* for her nunnery. The superior usually held office for life, though it was possible in certain circumstances for him to be deposed or to resign. He might be deposed for some grave offence or for incapacity due to illness or old age, or he might voluntarily resign, sometimes because he wished to lead an eremitic life. In 1079 Christodulus resigned from the monastery of Stylos on Mt Latros because of ill-health and the Turkish incursions, and then later in 1087 from his house on Patmos because he wished to become a solitary. Deposition might even happen at the very outset of his office were a superior for instance to be found too uneducated ($\dot{a}\mu a\theta\acute{\eta}s$), since it was essential that he should be capable of understanding and carrying out the canonical rulings.

The superior was assisted in general matters by a group of officials, including a deputy abbot ($\dot{o}$ $\delta\epsilon\acute{\upsilon}\tau\epsilon\rho os$), and he would also have the advice of the community and the more informal help of an inner circle. He might if necessary consult those outside his own *coenobium*. He did indeed carry a heavy burden of responsibility, being answerable for the spiritual well-being of his flock as well as the good administration of the sheepfold. In some cases he himself might act as spiritual director, but he would also appoint one or more older monks for this purpose, and would assign individuals to their care. The ordering of the Office was entrusted to a group of officials. The *excitator* saw that the brothers woke up in time; the *epistemonarches* kept an eye on their behaviour during the actual services; the *taxiarches* was in charge of the ceremonial; and others were responsible for leading the choirs or for the care of the liturgical books. A further group was deputed to look after the upkeep and cleaning of the main monastic church (*catholicon*), the oratories and the small churches (*parecclesia*). The *candelaptes* saw that bread and wine, incense and candles were provided, and the *skeuophylax* was the custodian of the treasure and relics and the ecclesiastical books.

The temporalities and internal economy of the house were administered by the *oeconomus*, subject to the *hegumenus* and the diocesan according to the rulings laid down in the *typicon* and in canon law, which were designed to guard against alienation or mismanagement. Second to the abbot, this was a key position and in order to ensure continuity was often held for a considerable period. Besides internal administration of the house, the responsibilities of the *oeconomus* included the monastery's financial obligations to the diocesan and the payment of secular taxes from which its property was not normally exempt. He was assisted by a deputy, the *paroeconomus*, and a number of officials appointed to look after the different departments falling within this sphere. There would be a treasurer (*tamias*), a wardrobe master (*dochiarius*), a cellarer (*cellarites*), and various assistants, such as the deputy cellarer (*paracellarites*), the cook (*magirus*), the refectory master (*triclinarius* or *trapezarius*), and the monks in charge of commodities such as bread, oil, fruit and wine. The archives were in the care of the *chartophylax* assisted by the *chartularius*, the *notarius* and the *scriptores*; the *bibliothecarius* looked after the library. There was special provision for the sick and the infirm and for almsgiving to the poor, and a hospice was provided for travellers. A house, particularly a large imperial foundation, often had special responsibilities laid down in its *typicon*, such as the care of an orphanage or hospital. A share in the daily work was assigned to all, and where the founder's wishes did not already provide sufficient occupation for the community, some specific duties would be arranged.

The monastic community in action can be seen in the writings of abbots such as Theodore the Studite or Symeon the New Theologian. Theodore's monks were occupied on the monastic estate and indoors in the workshops and the domestic buildings. Work in the library and *scriptorium* was an important part of his regime. Living in the age of the iconoclasts, Theodore, like John of Damascus, realised how useful a weapon intellectual understanding could be if rightly directed towards a study of the Bible and the fathers. 'Learning', he wrote, 'is but foliage compared to the fruits of a good life, and the tree that bears nothing but foliage must be cut down and burnt. But the finest result is when the fruit is set amongst its foliage.'[1] The reconstruction of daily routine in a house such as the ninth-century

---

[1] Theodore the Studite, *Magna Catechesis*, Bk. 2, ed. A. Papadopoulos-Kerameus, p. 634, cited by I. Hausherr, *S. Théodore Studite*, pp. 32–3 (Rome, 1926 = *Orientalia Christiana*, VI).

Studite monastery or Symeon's late tenth-century house of St Mamas, both in Constantinople, shows the carefully regulated meals with nine sitting at a Studite table, and the somewhat austerely planned community wardrobe, and also the petty failings to be eradicated, as gossip about an erring brother or scraps of food concealed beneath bedding. There were two meals a day, and what was left over from lunch was used in the evening. Food was adequate and Theodore deprecated over-strenuous fasts which might unfit monks for their daily chores; his houses abstained from cheese, oil and fish on Wednesdays and Fridays, and there were also special periods of fasting, such as the three great fasts during Lent, after Whitsun and in Advent. Theodore addressed his monks twice a week as well as on Sundays, and during times of fast every evening after Compline one of his sermons would be read to the community by a senior monk. The Studites had to make their confession at least once a fortnight and daily confession was considered advisable. Communion was usually received each Sunday, though Theodore himself advocated this daily, provided one came with a pure heart, and such was the custom of Symeon the New Theologian.

The day by day activities of the common life were centred in the Office. These liturgical hours, Orthros, Prime, Terce, Sext, None, Vespers, Compline (Apodeipnon) and midnight prayers, were held in the monastic church, and the climax of this corporate worship was the communion service, the Divine Liturgy, as it was called. The Office varied according to the day and season, and the canonarch arranged that the appropriate liturgical hymns and psalms and lessons were sung, instructed the novices in singing and apportioned duties among the brothers. He was assisted by the taxiarch who organised the choirs according to their voice and experience, and saw that the dead were entered on the diptychs for commemoration and the altar and holy vessels cared for. Thus the splendid ritual of the Eastern Church was faithfully performed and the special liturgical instructions of the founder observed. Sometimes monks were exempt from attending Terce, Sext and None on weekdays, perhaps because they were working in the distant fields. Solitaries might withdraw altogether; it was understood that they were in a different position, living as it were in a 'supra-liturgical' state, being more experienced than most in the *vita contemplativa*. Something of the implications and meaning of this coenobitic life for the ordinary monk can be realised when the instruction which was an essential part of their daily life is set side by side with the regulation of externals and the actual content of the daily liturgical hours. Such abbots as Theodore the Studite or Symeon the New Theologian were themselves far advanced in spirituality and yet admirably suited to guide communities of very varying quality, and practical administrators withal. Symeon evidently had to face considerable opposition from those who no doubt resented having their shortcomings and foibles held up to light, hence the angry crowd of his monks which rushed out of St Mamas to complain about him to the Patriarch. But the addresses to their brethren which both Theodore and Symeon have left were extensively used by later generations in Slav as well as Greek monasteries, and Symeon's were remodelled for this purpose and some personal references in his sermons were omitted in the edited version. Both Theodore and Symeon stressed the need for unconditional obedience. In his later days as head of a house Symeon may well have disapproved of his own conduct as a young man when he had to leave the Studite house because he did not see eye to eye with his abbot and refused to obey his command to change his spiritual father. In one of his sermons he maintained that the abbot must be obeyed even if he is openly leading an evil life. Like other monastic teachers, he had come to realise that it was only by complete submission that progress could be made towards 'perfection', the goal of monastic life.

Training in a coenobitic house was regarded by many as the best apprenticeship for monks, and for some it might be the only life which they would know. But from the earliest days of the Egyptian and Palestinian monks there continued to be other possibilities within the monastic framework. The *laura* and *kellion* allowed individuals to dispense with the set discipline of community life and to follow a more eremitic way under the general direction of a superior. In the later middle ages another type of community developed, the idiorhythmic, which is still followed by some of the monasteries on Mt Athos. It has been suggested that it grew up on the Holy Mountain because the common life was disrupted in the troubled days following the Fourth Crusade by such depredations as those of the Catalans or the Ottomans. These disturbances may have been a contributing factor, but at the same time the system has something in common with the life of a scete or lavra and some have attributed it to the development of hesychasm. In an idiorhythmic house the monks lived in small 'families' grouped under a superior. Some property was held in common and administered by two or three annually elected deputies (*epitropi*) but, in contrast to coenobitic practice, private ownership was allowed. Individuals lived in their 'family' except for very occasional common meals as at Christmas or Easter; they all took part in the services of the Office together in their chapel.

It was only occasionally that some kind of association developed between the different forms of monastic life found in the Eastern

Church. A coenobitic house might be given other monasteries as dependencies, or might set up its own *metochia* or scetes or individual hermitages. Groups of hermits might be federated under an elected superior sometimes called a *protos*. Often the relationship depended on the personality of a founder or leader and dissolved soon after his death. Sometimes an association arose during a crisis such as the iconoclast controversy. At this time districts in and around Bithynia were flooded out with refugee monks (and bishops) and there seems to have been some kind of central meetings or consultations, though not of a permanent character. The original Pachomian houses were grouped round the main house of Pabou to which they were affiliated. Amongst the various foundations of St Sabas in Palestine there appear to have been links which were sometimes filial, sometimes more in the nature of a confederation between autonomous houses. There were close ties between the house of Studius and the other four monasteries associated with St Theodore, but in this case it is clear that the monastery in Constantinople was regarded as the mother-house. Its head nominated and controlled the *hegumeni* of the other houses and its *oeconomus* (called ὁ μέγας οἰκονόμος) had charge of the administration of all five establishments. Like the Pachomian houses, this was an autonomous house with filial dependencies. The more lasting form of union was a confederation of equals under a freely-elected head. The houses of Mt Latros in Asia Minor, of Mt Athos, as well as later foundations of the Meteora in Thessaly or in Mistra in the Peloponnese, all had their *protos* or archimandrite. Evidence for Mt Athos shows first a group of anchorites and a lavra centred in Karyes, then from the tenth century onwards the establishment of coenobitic houses under imperial, and later, patriarchal, protection, as well as the continuance of other forms of monachism. The power of the *protos* on Mt Athos diminished as that of the coenobitic monasteries grew, as is evidenced by successive imperial rulings (1045, 1312, 1394, and 1406). In 1312 the *protos* was placed under patriarchal jurisdiction; in 1394 the *hegumenus* of the Great Lavra was to preside with the *protus* in the synod consisting of the other twenty-four *hegumeni*. With the development of idiorhythmic government the office of *hegumenus* lost all real authority and gave way before an oligarchical regime. But the medieval organisation on the Holy Mountain, with its administrative headquarters in Karyes, which had developed as a result of special circumstances, was that of a confederation which has survived to the present day.

Sources emphasise the variety of constitutional arrangements, even though the monastic *ordo* in the East retained a unity of purpose, and was not differentiated as in the West. This elasticity is reflected in the interdependence of the coenobitic and the eremitic way. For Byzantines the one did not preclude the other. It was usual for a monk to begin in the common life and with his abbot's permission to proceed to the more difficult eremitic path. Those who were experienced directors fully realised the dangers in the solitary life as well as the reward for those sufficiently advanced to sustain its discipline. Sometimes coenobites would withdraw from the community for a time, and then return; some abbots resigned their position in order to live in solitude, as Symeon the New Theologian did. Often men and women became recluses from the start and undertook particularly rigorous forms of asceticism which caught the imagination of their contemporaries. The dendrites lived in trees; such was David of Thessalonica who sat for three years in an almond tree, 'numbed by the cold, scorched by the sun, shattered by the winds, with his angelic countenance unchanged, looking like a rose to those who saw him'.[1] The stylites, such as St Daniel or St Symeon, stood on pillars, but not entirely out of reach, for ladders were erected and followers and admirers camped nearby; disciples would spend the night at the top of the ladder, and Daniel's body was brought down a spiral stairway. In his *Ladder to Paradise*, which was widely used in the middle ages, John Climacus remarked that those who had not yet known God were unsuited for solitude and likely to be choked by it; he also pointed out that the holy fathers of the coenobitic Tabennisi did not produce as many burning and shining lights as the desert of Scete did with its many solitaries. This reflects the medieval attitude. The lives of the saints show how deep and universal was the veneration of all classes in Byzantium for the solitary who could sustain the voluntary hardships of his chosen life, whose perpetual vigilance and sacrifice were rewarded by special charismata marking him out as the 'friend of God', as one who could mediate on behalf of his fellow Christians. It is the sanctity of such men which explains why Emperors could tremble before them and why the humblest shepherds had faith in the prayers of those whom they had watched celebrating the liturgy with angels.

Monasticism was perhaps the most vital single factor in Byzantine spirituality and an integral part of its life throughout its history, and indeed it steadily increased in importance. Innumerable houses, lavras and hermitages remain unchronicled, but it is known that the cities teemed with foundations; the number already traced in Constantinople alone is estimated as at least 300 monasteries, and the still only partially explored countryside in Asia Minor is strewn with

[1] *Leben des heiligen David von Thessalonike*, ed. V. Rose (Berlin, 1887), ch. 6, p. 5.

ruins awaiting the archaeologist.[1] Foundations made before 717 outside the bounds of the empire of the middle and late periods often
continued as living and frequented centres, as the lavra of St Sabas
in Palestine, or the monastery on Mt Sinai which is today still surrounded and protected by Justinian's massive fortifications, and
which was the goal of many pilgrimages. In the neighbourhood of
the capital across the Bosphorus near Chalcedon stood Mt Auxentius
with its hermit settlements and a *coenobium*, associated with St
Stephen the Young who was martyred by the iconoclast Constantine V, which can be traced into the late middle ages. In Bithynia
the region round Mt Olympus was from early times a favourite retreat
of anchorites, and lavras and houses were to be found on its slopes
famous for the beauty of their vegetation. It was to one of these
foundations that Michael Psellus hastily retreated when threatened
with political disgrace in the mid-eleventh century, only to find that
he heartily disliked the cloister, unlike his companion in disgrace, the
jurist John Xiphilinus, who discovered his vocation in the contemplative life. In and around centres such as Ephesus or Trebizond, on
Mt Latros near Miletus or hewn out of the vast limestone cones in
Cappadocia, lavras, hermitages and monasteries abounded. Every
province of the Empire shared this development. Rome, though outside the Byzantine Empire after the mid-seventh century, still had
its Greek houses and communities; further south, Greek monasticism
flourished in Sicily until the Arabs came, and in South Italy well into
the twelfth century. In the tenth century the mountains of Calabria
enjoyed a high reputation for their anchorites, particularly in the hills
above Rossano, whence St Nilus went in 1004 to found the Greek
house of Grottaferrata near Rome where the Greek rite and the
Byzantine tradition of music still survive.

   One of the best-known and most long-lived settlements was the Holy
Mountain of Athos, the precipitous narrow tongue of land running
into the Aegean east of Thessalonica, some thirty-five miles long,
culminating at its southern end in the splendid peak some 6000 feet
high which gives its name to the peninsula. Its early medieval history
is obscure. It was evidently first settled by hermits and in the ninth
century John Colobos attempted to set up a monastery nearby. But
it was not until about 961 that the first notable foundation was begun.
With the support of the Emperor Nicephorus II Phocas his friend and

[1] For Constantinople see R. Janin, *Les églises et les monastères* (Paris, 1953), and for
the country in Lycia north of Myra see R. M. Harrison, 'New Discoveries in Lycia',
Illustrated London News, 20 August 1960, and *Anatolian Studies*, x (1960), 26–8. For
further citation of individual foundations see the *Notitia Monasteriorum* in H.-G.
Beck, *Kirche und theologische Literatur im byzantinischen Reich* (Munich, 1959),
pp. 200 ff.

confessor, St Athanasius the Athonite, established a coenobitic house known as the Great Lavra, whose rules drawn up by Athanasius show the strong influence of the Studite house. The *typicon* was confirmed by the chrysobull of John I Tzimisces in 971–2, and the Lavra became the leading monastery on the Holy Mountain. From then onwards numerous settlements were made and every kind of monastic life flourished. This rapid growth had brought difficulties in the relationship between hermits and coenobites and certain laxities had also given rise to comment. Constantine IX confirmed the privileges and immunities granted by former Emperors to the coenobitic houses, and Alexius I instituted an inquiry into scandals which had arisen partly as a result of an influx of nomad shepherds. In spite of minor troubles, religious life on the Holy Mountain continued to develop and stood high in the eyes of contemporaries throughout the Christian world. The Amalfitans and the Georgians each had a house there; from the eleventh century onwards the Russians appear to have frequented Athos and their special houses were Xylourgou and Panteleimon; the Serbian Chilandari was founded by a prince of the Nemanjid family at the end of the twelfth century; and the Bulgarians in the later middle ages made Zographou their centre. Though a somewhat cosmopolitan federation of houses and anchorite settlements, Mt Athos remained predominantly Greek in character, venerated by the whole Christian world. In the difficult days of the Latin Empire of Constantinople, Innocent III in 1213 took the monasteries under his special protection, acknowledging that by reason of its spirituality Mt Athos was indeed 'outstanding amongst the mountains of the world'. It was a microcosm of Byzantine monasticism. As imperial authority diminished in the later middle ages, the strength of the Holy Mountain increased. It took a leading part in the spiritual movement in the Orthodox Church known as hesychasm. The hesychast contemplatives had a far-reaching influence on the life of the Church in their own and subsequent generations and their fourteenth-century leader St Gregory Palamas, who subsequently became archbishop of Thessalonica, is still particularly venerated in the Greek Church. Athos was accessible yet isolated, and to a great extent it preserved its autonomy and integrity at a time when the Byzantine provinces were rapidly falling under foreign domination—Latin, Slav and finally Ottoman.

Monks had a special place in the Byzantine world by reason of their sanctity. They also performed other services for the laity as part of their daily life. Responsibility for education did not fall to their lot to the same extent as in the early middle ages in the West, as other facilities were available for the better-off Byzantine boy. But they had need to ensure for themselves some degree of education, and the continued study of the Bible and the fathers could give ample opportunity for intellectual development. Most monasteries also had to perform some kind of social service. Their obligation to almsgiving and care of their neighbour was often specifically defined in their *typicon*. This might be some simple form of charity, such as was described in the *Life* of the eleventh-century Dorotheus in the countryside of Asia Minor, when on his deathbed the saint bequeathed some of his pots and pans to the villagers, or some more ambitious project provided for by the ample endowments of a wealthy imperial foundation, such as the Pantocrator monastery of John II Comnenus. The Pantocrator house was responsible for a hospital of fifty beds; minute regulations were laid down about the division into wards for different diseases and both men and women were provided for, and an adequate medical staff was attached to the hospital. John II's brother, the sebastocrator Isaac, also founded a house with a hospital of thirty-six beds and a special bath-house designed for the use not only of the sick but of the monks, travellers and neighbouring villagers, and reserved for the use of women on Wednesdays and Fridays. *Typica* and saints' lives illustrate the wide range of monastic service. Hospices for travellers, orphanages and homes for the aged, were administered. Mortuary chapels attached to the monastic church were built by wealthy patrons, and cemeteries provided by monasteries for the destitute pauper and others. Theodore the Studite founded a kind of fraternity to care for unwanted corpses which were to be buried in the Studite cemetery and commemorated twice a year.

Monastic houses were frequently used as prisons, penitentiaries, refuges from political storms, and even simply for retirement. A number of imperial and canonical rulings specify those who are to be punished by being sent to a monastic house: adulteresses or indiscreet deaconesses, fugitive monks, ecclesiastics who indulge in theatre-going or gambling, those illegally dissolving their marriage vows. In the *Euchologium* there were special prayers to be used for clothing novices of this kind. Statesmen in defeat or disgrace were commonly sent to monasteries; in 944 Romanus I Lecapenus was banished by his ungrateful sons to a house on Prote, one of the Princes Islands; after his voluntary abdication in 1081 Nicephorus III Botaneiates retired to the Peribleptos in Constantinople. When death was imminent it was usual to enter to take the monastic habit; when Manuel I Comnenus was clothed in this way it was found that the habit hastily provided for him was too short, for he was a very tall man, and onlookers wept at the pathetic sight. Sometimes men and women built and endowed monasteries as a retreat for their old age and villagers would join together for this purpose. Psellus speaks of a peasant who engaged on a co-operative enterprise of this kind and became a nun but fell into difficulties because she could not extract the sum due from one of her fellows. Alexius II's wife, Irene, added buildings equipped on a princely scale to her foundation in Constantinople, intending these for her own use and that of her daughters.

More important than the various social services, though often not so spectacular and perhaps more difficult to assess, was the place of monasticism in the spiritual life of East Rome. Monastic influence was no longer exercised through the actual presence of hordes of monks at conciliar meetings, as in the days of the early councils before ecclesiastical ruling had forbidden this. It remained nevertheless a potent factor whether exercised within or without monastic walls, by coenobites or by solitaries. Monks frequently acted as spiritual directors, both as confessor and as more informal consultant. Symeon the New Theologian in the early eleventh century was spiritual father to many noble families in Constantinople and even when living in exile across the Bosphorus under patriarchal ban, he had frequent visits from them. The range of Theodore the Studite's correspondence shows how widely he was consulted outside monastic circles, and the same is true of John Mauropous, monk and archbishop of Euchaita in Asia Minor in the eleventh century.

As well as in countless personal cases, monastic influence was exercised in wider issues. During the iconoclastic controversy the weight of monastic opinion generally, though not always, supported the veneration of icons. Monks such as John of Damascus or Theodore the Studite were powerful defenders of Orthodox tradition, as their writings demonstrate. With the restoration of the use of icons, Orthodox spirituality—contrary to the view sometimes held in the West—did not virtually come to a standstill. The role of the monks, who were the leaders in this spirituality, cannot yet be fully evaluated because work on this is in its early stages and some key writings still remain unpublished. But it is at least clear that from Symeon the New Theologian to Gregory Palamas and the other hesychasts of the fourteenth century monastic spirituality was a creative leaven with an influence far beyond the monk's cell. Though not theologians as such, through their contemplative life they developed what might be described as a 'monastic' theology. It was the monastic world which produced the countless hymns, troparia and canons which enriched the liturgy. It was the great monastic directors who left instruction and meditation on the spiritual life, such as the classics of John Climacus or Maximus the Confessor, or the equally widely used *Catecheses* of Theodore the Studite (a number of manuscripts of these were copied

in Sicily) or of Symeon the Young. Despite service to the secular
world, sometimes outside the monastery, the keynote of Byzantine
monastic life was retreat from the world in order to lead a contemplative life. The work of the East Roman monks was not primarily
missionary or pastoral, but by their constant striving for perfection
they deepened the Christian life of the polity and were regarded by
East Romans as being an essential, and indeed the highest, expression
of Christianity. To have to become Patriarch of Constantinople was
an anticlimax to the monk John Xiphilinus, for to him nothing could
be higher than the holy quiet of the monastery. Theodore the Studite
expressed the Byzantine view when he said: 'Monks are the sinews
and foundations of the Church.'[1]

[1] Theodore the Studite, *Catecheses parvae*, 114, ed. J. Cozza-Luzi, *Nov. Patr. Bibl.*
IX (1888), p. 266.

CHAPTER XXVI

BYZANTINE THEOLOGICAL SPECULATION AND SPIRITUALITY

The religious attitude of the Byzantines was dominated by the idea of orthodoxy. Orthodoxy was comprised in the patristic writings and the canons of the seven oecumenical councils. Founded on the historical basis of Christianity, these were less arbitrary than the heresies which they condemned, and which had sometimes made their appearance as broaching a more liberal faith; and they remained the roots of the religious life of Byzantium throughout its history. The intensity of their awareness of dogma is shown, not only by the general interest of the Byzantines in theology, and the spirituality of their ascetics, but also by art, which far more than in the West is a visual interpretation of dogma.

But, as with art, the stuff of Byzantine theology is complex, drawn from more than purely Christian sources—often from pagan philosophy, either directly or indirectly, from neoplatonist or Stoic-inclined Fathers. To a lesser extent, contemporary movements also influenced theology, as when in the fourteenth and early fifteenth centuries translations were made from the works of St Thomas Aquinas and in some circles there was a marked reaction against any such scholastic trends. Moreover, their devotion to orthodoxy did not make the Byzantines as a whole bigoted. Whether they found it in their religious principles or were taught by circumstances to be realists, they were usually tolerant of other creeds when it was feasible to be so. The Patriarch Nicholas Mysticus wrote in the tenth century to a Saracen amir: 'The Saracens and the Romans, like the two great luminaries of heaven, outshine all other powers. We ought therefore to live in friendship despite our different ways of life and worship.'[1]

Thus secular and religious elements were fused to produce the paradox of a Christian civilisation. Their reluctance to take life, their laws protecting the weak, their dazzling display of a civilised existence under the continual threat of overthrow by barbarian hordes—these show, equally with the lives of saints, the practical application by the Byzantines of the principles of moral theology, and their belief in order, an eternal order, of which this natural one is the shadow.

In the writings of the Greek Fathers the Byzantines had a great

[1] *MPG*, cxi, 28.

heritage, and it would not have been surprising if they had been content, on the whole, to live on such a patrimony, rather than strike out into new territories of thought. Indeed a certain conservatism found its champion at the outset in St John of Damascus (died 749): 'We do not change the boundaries set by our fathers.'[1] One of John Damascene's greatest works was *The Fount of Knowledge* (Πηγὴ γνώσεως). This is divided into three parts of which the first is entitled *Philosophical chapters* and lays the foundations of theology by exact definitions of metaphysical terms such as being, substance and accidents, genus and species. These terms often appear to be taken from Aristotle but usually through the medium of the Fathers. The Aristotelianism of John of Damascus should not be over-emphasised. Although he used his Aristotle, he was far from making it his only philosophical source, and ridiculed the Jacobite heretics for calling Aristotle the thirteenth apostle. Through the influence of the Pseudo-Dionysius and others he was imbued with Platonism as much as Aristotelianism, and what are found in his work are the basic notions of the *philosophia perennis*, such as are already evident in earlier Fathers. But the importance he attached to philosophy was nothing like that given to it by St Thomas Aquinas. John Damascene's real masters were the Church Fathers, and he himself was primarily a theologian though also, it should be remembered, one who above all stressed the value of the contemplative life.

In part two of *The Fount of Knowledge* he goes on to give an account of the various Christian heresies and refutations of them, drawn mostly from Epiphanius, with original sections on iconoclasm and Islam. The third part, *De fide orthodoxa*, is an exposition of the Christian faith, basically of the doctrines of the creed, and a synthesis of patristic comment on them. It opens with a discussion of the Trinity, and goes on to consider the creation in general. (This part is the least theological and contains a wealth of curious lore from ancient physics and astronomy, and natural science, including the information that alone among the animals, men and the monkeys are unable to wriggle their ears.) The next section is devoted to the Incarnation and Christology; and the last deals with a mixed variety of topics, from Antichrist and the Resurrection to customs of prayer.

The Fount of Knowledge became the great textbook of orthodoxy, regarded indeed as a well-spring of Christian doctrine and an armoury of apologetics, and to later generations the work of Damascene may have appeared to set the seal on the theology of preceding centuries, reflecting the general acceptance by the Byzantines of the idea that devotion to orthodoxy is the first duty of a Christian and the great

[1] *MPG*, xciv, 1297.

mark of the Church. He had however been concerned not only with handing on to future generations the inspired wisdom of the past, but also with defending it against a new threat—iconoclasm. In its theological aspect, the iconoclastic controversy was a debate about the nature and effects of the Incarnation in which both sides accused the other of falling into the errors of earlier Christological heresies. The iconoclasts held image-worship to be idolatry, and in particular they objected to pictures of the Saviour, as denying his divinity by showing the infinite as finite and 'circumscribed'. Jewish and Muslim influences are discernible in this attitude but it also represented a reforming zeal for a return to the simplicity of the Gospels, and as such testifies to the strikingly large part that the sacred icons already played in East Christian piety. That they were the Bible of the illiterate was an argument used by their defenders, but this idea, familiar in the West, scarcely explained the special sanctity and power attaching to them for the Orthodox, which had come to be so marked, and yet had not received the special attention of theologians, although it had already attracted some notice.[1] The iconoclasts set out to exterminate a practice for which they found no scriptural or patristic authority, but their policy raised up theologians as well as martyrs in defence of the images. John of Damascus, and after him Theodore the Studite (759–826), worked out a sacramental theology to justify what was already the immemorial practice of the Church, and in so doing gave form to a recurrent Christian impulse and established the sacred artist in a priest-like position as a dispenser of the means of grace.

The charge of idolatry was answered in full by John of Damascus. His chief argument was that images are not worshipped as things in themselves but as the image of God's saints. 'It is not matter I adore but the Creator of matter.'[2] The identity of prototype and image was a platonic doctrine adopted by the Fathers and developed in the Christological controversies. The same terminology was used to define the relationship of archetype and image as had been used to define that of Father and Son in the Trinity. Secondly, the worship paid to images differed from that paid to God. They received 'due salutation and honourable reverence but not the worship that belongs alone to the divine nature'.[3] At this point the argument was turned upon the iconoclasts, who objected to the material nature of images. The iconodules retorted that to do so was to reject the Incarnation: 'Was

---

[1] Cf. N. H. Baynes, 'The Icons before Iconoclasm', *HTR*, XLIV (1951), 93–106 (reprinted in *Byzantine Studies and other Essays*, pp. 226–39), and E. Kitzinger, 'The Cult of Images in the Age before Iconoclasm', *DOP*, VIII (1954), 83–150.

[2] *MPG*, XCIV, 1215.   [3] *MPG*, XCIV, 1356.

not the wood of the cross a tangible thing? Was not Calvary a real place?...Nothing of God's creation is to be despised. That is a Manichaean error.'[1] More than this, matter was not only good in itself, but certain material things were specially blessed: 'Why should the icons be isolated from every other material thing used in the church, the cross, the sanctuary, the gospel-book, the altar, the sacred vessels, the Eucharist itself?' Here the saint has brought in his sacramental theology: 'I adore the image, not as God, but as filled with his efficacious grace.'[2] Images were channels of grace, having sanctificatory power by virtue of the persons they represented.

To the charge of misrepresenting Christ by depicting his humanity, the iconodules replied that their enemies were falling into the error of all those heretics, such as docetists and monophysites, who had denied the reality of Christ's human nature, and therefore the efficacy of the Incarnation.

In the course of the controversy, both sides appealed to tradition, not only legitimately but also in the form of spurious authorities, folk-tales and quotations wrenched from their context to bear a distorted meaning, and to some extent this element continued to be found in Byzantine theological debate. Another feature, which remained a part of Byzantine life, was the alliance of monasticism with popular piety represented by the leadership of St Theodore the Studite, and the sufferings and constancy of the monks who supported him. In the Church as a whole, the effects of the iconoclast struggle were far-reaching and greatly influenced later speculation. The impiety and persecutions of the heretic emperors and their supporting Patriarchs had led Theodore the Studite, like John of Damascus before him, to denounce state interference in ecclesiastical affairs, to demand freedom for the Church, and even on occasion to try to bring pressure to bear by appealing to Rome. But this policy was not successful. When the images were restored first in 787 and then finally in 843, in each case the initiative was taken by an Empress acting as regent. The traditional relationship of Church and State remained unaltered and the appeal to Rome was frustrated. But the Byzantines had been able to give no effective political help to the West. The Popes had therefore turned to the Franks for support and in 800 Charlemagne was crowned Emperor at Rome. A rift had been made between the two Churches which slowly widened into schism.

The theological aspect of that schism may be mentioned here, for in the ninth century there began the polemic against certain practices of the Latins which was kept up throughout the duration of the Empire. This was partly concerned with Latin divergencies of cult

---

[1] *MPG*, xciv, 1215.   [2] *Ibid.*

and of church custom such as the use of azymes and the shaving of beards. Moreover the final separation was to some extent due to political antagonisms and ecclesiastical rivalries. These facts hardly support the contention that deep theological issues were always involved and that a contradiction between two quite opposite approaches to dogma was the hidden rock which finally sundered the unity of East and West. But though political factors played their part, it is also true that in the course of centuries both in theology and in spirituality East and West had developed different approaches to major doctrinal issues such as the trinitarian question. The addition of the *filioque* to the creed, which had officially committed the Latins to a belief in the double procession of the Holy Spirit, was a scandal to the Greeks, who held at the most that the Spirit proceeds from the Father *through* the Son. They laid stress on the operation of the Spirit in the Christian life, following St Irenaeus who wrote: 'Through the Spirit one ascends to the Son and through the Son to the Father.' They also held that by an unwarrantable innovation the Latins were jeopardising the belief, common throughout the Christian tradition, that God the Father was sole ultimate source of Godhead, both in the Son and Holy Spirit. Many treatises were written on the subject, from the ninth-century Patriarch Photius to the fourteenth-century Archbishop of Thessalonica, Nilus Cabasilas and beyond. The dispute as to the *filioque* figured largely in all attempts at reunion and was certainly one of the stumbling-blocks in the way of success.

In spite of much abusive controversy on both sides, attempts at reunion were sporadic throughout the medieval period, but they were only twice consummated at official councils of reunion. In both cases the success was apparent rather than real. The official union of the Second Council of Lyons in 1274 was a political bid, never accepted by the Byzantine people. The negotiations had been marked by the intransigence of the Latin theologians, and the politico-religious situation had been all too recently envenomed by the Latin atrocities at the sack of Constantinople in 1204, with the consequent intrusion of a Latin Patriarch into that see. After the failure of 1274, relations between the Roman Curia and Constantinople were broken off for some years. But from 1331 onwards a constant stream of ambassadors passed to and fro. The Byzantine Emperors needed military help, and the Pope remained the head of the crusading movement. There was a new spirit of sympathy too, apparent in the respectful letters to Avignon of the Emperor Cantacuzenus, and the names of many Byzantine families are to be found in papal correspondence of the time. Such were the Metochites and the Lascarids, known to be enlightened sympathisers. The Popes on their side recognised the importance of the Byzantine Empire as the bulwark of Christendom against the Turks, but they still regarded ecclesiastical reunion with the Greeks as an essential preliminary to the provision of western help. Thus in 1355 by a secret treaty made with Paul, Latin Archbishop of Smyrna and papal legate, John V Palaeologus had to promise the conversion of his people in return for military aid.

The decree of union of the Council of Florence in 1439 represents a more serious effort at mutual understanding. Though the political necessities of the Empire were once again a dominant factor, a number of Greek theologians, of whom the most famous was Bessarion, would seem to have had a strong desire for restoring union, and a number of Latin theologians were found who were ready to meet them in the search for formularies which would safeguard the traditions of both Churches. Even at times of greatest tension, there is evidence that down to 1453 some Byzantines at any rate could regard the Latins not as heretics but as brothers in faith with whom they disagreed.

Polemic against Jews, Muhammadans, and above all against dualist heretics was another recurrent exercise for theologians. The Byzantine Emperors themselves considered the conversion of the Jews a special duty, and often arranged conferences between bishops and rabbis. The first notable treatise against Islam, which was regarded as a Christian heresy, was written by John of Damascus, who knew Arabic and used the text of the Koran. Such refutations were still being composed in the last days of the Empire, but by then they had become purely formal exercises, such as the one written in the fourteenth century by the former Emperor Cantacuzenus. Dualist heresy, on the other hand, was seen as a constantly recurring and urgent danger.

The problem of dualist heresy was inherited by the Orthodox Church in the imperial provinces of Asia Minor. These had been the home of early Christian dualist sects such as the Gnostics, which had prepared a fertile ground for the spread of Manichaeism from Persia. The third-century Persian Mani had taught that there are two eternally opposite principles of good and evil: God, or spirit, and Matter, represented by Light and Darkness. This world is a mixture of both, brought about by the evil principle, in which particles of light, the souls of men, are imprisoned in the body in the darkness of matter. The divine will intends the separation of light from darkness, and man should co-operate by refusing to propagate his kind and by practising an extreme asceticism which, unlike Christian asceticism, is really aimed not at controlling the body, but at destroying it.

Early refutations of Manichaeism were written by John of Damascus in the eighth century and by Photius in the ninth. Photius particularly objects to the way in which these heretics 'behind the names of our dogmas perversely teach quite different things'.[1] This became a characteristic of the Manichaean sects and Anna Comnena complained that the Bogomils in the late eleventh century were particularly good 'at aping virtue'[2] and on the surface could scarcely be distinguished from the orthodox. For the basic doctrines of Mani penetrated deeply into orthodoxy itself, and in the seventh century there began a great revival of Manichaeism in a superficially Christian form, Paulicianism. The Byzantine government was at first concerned with the sect as forming the border populations of the Asian themes in Armenia and Asia Minor. After some persecution in the seventh century, in the following period they were on the whole left alone by the iconoclast Emperors, but in the ninth century greater violence was used, and massacres took place. They had become a religious and political menace and their armies made frequent raids into imperial territory, in 867 capturing Ephesus. In 869 an imperial ambassador, Peter of Sicily, was sent to treat with them. His peace proposals failed, and an expedition had to be sent against them in 871–2, when they were heavily defeated.

Peter of Sicily made use of his embassy to inquire into their doctrines and compiled a *History of the Manichees*[3] in which he gives an exposition of their teaching. Their belief in the intrinsic evil of matter led them to deny the reality of the Incarnation; thus they asserted that Christ's body was only a semblance of a real body. They rejected much of the written and oral traditions of the Church, including the whole of the Old Testament; but they particularly venerated the Pauline epistles (although this does not seem to be the explanation of the derivation of their name, which remains obscure). They rejected the priesthood, and the Eucharist, taking the words of the gospels which refer to the latter in a figurative sense.

The imperial policy had from time to time attempted to transplant colonies of the Paulicians to Thrace, in the hope both of breaking up their strength and exposing them to Orthodox proselytism, and of providing bulwarks against the Bulgarians. But in the eleventh century they again rose against the Empire and had to be put down by Alexius Comnenus. This Emperor was said to be a brilliant theologian, and he certainly took his role of maintaining and spreading orthodoxy very seriously. He held a long course of theological disputations with the three Paulician leaders in their stronghold of Philippopolis in 1114. Anna Comnena describes their vehemence: 'The three stood

---

[1] *MPG*, ciii, 524.   [2] *Alexiad*, xv, 8.   [3] *MPG*, civ, 1245–1304.

there sharpening each other's wits, as if they were boar's teeth, intent on rending the Emperor's arguments. And if any objection escaped Cusinus, Culeon would take it up; and if Culeon was at a loss, Pholuc in his turn would rise in opposition; or they would, one after the other, rouse themselves against the Emperor's premises and refutations, just like very large waves following up other large waves.'[1] Two of the leaders remained obstinate and died in prison, but the third was converted with large numbers of Paulicians, and a new city was built for them and great benefits conferred with it.

Paulicianism was greatly influenced by the sect of the Massalians which had arisen in the fourth century. The chief difference between them appears to have been in their ethical code. The Paulicians led an active and warlike life, and, probably because of this, did not practise extreme asceticism. The Massalians on the other hand were monastic and contemplative and advocated strict poverty; their ascetics often lived by begging, and abstinence from sexual intercourse was preached, although the 'perfect' were absolved from such restrictions, and noted for sexual excesses. They are described as an active danger, under the name of Euchitae, in a mid-eleventh-century work of Michael Psellus, *Dialogus de daemonum operatione*; but some of the doctrines there ascribed to them are characteristic of another sect, that of the Bogomils.

Bogomilism arose in the tenth century in Bulgaria, as a fusion of Paulician and Massalian teaching. With the destruction of the Tsar Samuel's empire, Bulgaria had become an imperial province by 1018, and Bogomilism, no longer restricted by any Byzantine frontier, began to spread throughout the Balkans and Asia Minor. It penetrated Constantinople itself and even had a great vogue among the aristocratic families. Alexius Comnenus held a trial of Bogomils in about 1110, and after failing to convert their leader, Basil, he had him executed by being burnt at the stake in the Hippodrome. But the Bogomilism of Constantinople was probably a rarefied form of the heresy, coalesced with mystical Massalian teachings also currently prevalent there, and no doubt owed its success to the attraction for the Byzantines of the occult, and of esoteric philosophy. In Bulgaria, the heresy in its original form presented no less a problem to the Empire, for though based on dualism it had the semblance of a simple ethical doctrine with a powerful appeal to the peasant masses. Therein lay its danger, for the oppressed Bulgarian people, ground down by Byzantine tax-collectors and denied their own ecclesiastical hierarchy, who had been replaced by Greeks, turned to Bogomilism almost as to a national religion, and it therefore took on the colours of

[1] *Alexiad*, XIV, 9 (trans. E. Dawes, pp. 387–8).

a popular nationalist movement. The Byzantine development of the heresy, though suppressed in the capital, was later carried back to Bulgaria where it further strengthened the sect.

The monk Euthymius Zigabenus was commissioned by Alexius Comnenus to compile a new guide to heresy, including Bogomilism, of which he gives a long account. It is clear from this that the Bogomils held a modified form of dualism. They attributed the creation of the world, not to an eternal evil principle, but to Satanael, the Devil, who was created, and will eventually be destroyed, by God. This dualistic cosmology was based on the Bible, but the biblical text was freely interpreted and adulterated with the Bogomils' own mythology. And, in common with nearly all dualist sects, they considered the Old Testament to be the revelation not of God but of Satanael. Equally typical was their docetist view of the Incarnation. They held a complicated demonology, believing that this world is entirely in the power of the demons, the agents of Satanael, whom they therefore honoured out of fear. Their ethical rule, based on the condemnation of matter, was generally marked by an extreme asceticism, at least for the elect.

From the tenth to the fourteenth century, Bogomilism remained an active danger to the Church. Later writers use the terms Bogomil and Massalian synonymously, and there does seem to have been a real coalescence of the two, which in the fourteenth century appears to have spread to Mt Athos in a mystical form, thus causing some confusion between the practices of the heretics and those of the hesychast monks. The latter were indeed dubbed 'Massalians' by their enemies; but, in fact, the monks convened a council to deal with any heretical growth in their midst, and the ringleaders were expelled from Athos.

While concerned in these ways to defend orthodoxy against its enemies, the Byzantines retained among themselves their passion for theological discussion. Between the ninth and the fourteenth centuries there may have been no such widespread interest among all classes as had accompanied the iconoclast and earlier monophysite controversies; but, freed from such pressing urgency, the court of Constantinople became the centre of sophisticated debate, sometimes with theologians from the Latin world. There was also an added zest from the element of rivalry between laymen and clerics. In contrast to the West, the ancient tradition of secular education had never died out in the East, and the civil dignitaries were classical humanists by upbringing, whereas high ecclesiastical posts usually went to monks, who often professed to hold all worldly knowledge in contempt, though they themselves had often had the usual education before entering the cloister. Before he was himself made Patriarch by the liberal-minded Caesar Bardas, Photius is said to have amused himself by starting the hare of a theory of two different souls in man, one earthly and prone to sin, the other immortal and impeccable—avowedly because he wanted to see how the Patriarch would deal with it without recourse to the dialectic he professed to despise. Similarly, Michael Psellus, the most famous figure of the eleventh-century revival of learning, also retorted with ridicule to the religious attitude of superiority towards human wisdom: 'I have heard tell by more accomplished philosophers that there is a knowledge superior to all demonstration and only accessible to a disciplined enthusiasm.... I read various mystical treatises...[but] as for wholly and satisfactorily grasping such matters I could not boast that I ever achieved it and I do not believe anyone else who says that he has.'[1]

Photius was the greatest figure in the ninth-century revival of learning. He was a pupil of Leo the Mathematician, and both taught at the university newly refounded by Bardas. He was especially interested in logic and dialectic, and his courses included such topics as the question of nominalism and realism. The iconoclast controversy had left a doubtful legacy in the intolerant party of monks and zealots who were fanatically devoted to orthodoxy, and suspicious of anything outside it. They made it a charge against Photius that he taught the profane sciences. As has been seen, he made light of such narrowness of mind. He was himself devoutly orthodox, and his famous library included even more of Christian theology than of classical authors. As Patriarch, he organised missions and refuted heresies. It is noteworthy that he preferred Aristotle to Plato, whom he regarded as primarily a maker of myths.

There would seem again to have been a classical renaissance under the Macedonians and Comneni which is reflected in their art and led to a closer familiarity with classical philosophy. But classical philosophy was conceived as a *philosophia perennis*: Plato and Aristotle were studied as parts of a single whole. Michael Psellus speaks in his *Chronographia* of 'the portals of Aristotelian philosophy and the symbols of Platonic teaching'.[2] Anna Comnena wrote in the preface to the *Alexiad*: 'I perused the works of Aristotle and the dialogues of Plato and enriched my mind with the quaternion of learning',[3] while a panegyric on Eustathius of Thessalonica, written shortly before 1200, notes that he had been a peripatetic both in the groves of Academe and in the Porch.[4]

---

[1] *Chronographia*, vi, 40 (i, p. 136, ed. E. Renauld).
[2] *Chronographia*, iii, 2 (i, p. 33, ed. E. Renauld).
[3] *Alexiad*, praef. i, 1.   [4] *MPG*, cxxxvi, 764.

But it was more especially Platonism which had coloured Christian theology in its early days, and even the exclusive claims of monasticism could find their source in Plato's teaching that philosophy was an active love of, and search for truth, involving a moral conversion, a turning from darkness to light. The idea is found in the second-century apologist Justin, who identifies philosophy with the pursuit of man's last end. It came to be equated with the Christian life, especially that of monks and hermits who are thus called 'philosophers'. But although not alien to Plato himself, Augustine's assertion 'Non dubitat [Plato] hoc esse philosophari amare Deum' is only justified by middle- and neoplatonism. Yet this syncretist philosophy of Plotinus, Proclus and Iamblichus was particularly fraught with dangers for the Christian theologian. In its later stages it had degenerated into theurgy, and the dabblings in magic which brought both Psellus and the Patriarch Cerularius under suspicion may be traced to it. Psellus himself describes a seance conducted by Cerularius in Constantinople on the lines, as he expressly states, of pagan theurgy, 'τοῖς Χαλδαίων λόγοις ἑπόμενος'.[1] Other dangers were to be revealed in the case of Psellus' pupil John Italus. His teaching was condemned at the instigation of the Emperor Alexius Comnenus, and ten articles against him were included in the liturgy of Orthodoxy Sunday. In the *Synodicon* read on this day he is accused of 'preferring the ancient philosophers and heresiarchs above the saints and doctors', and the list of heresies suggests that Plato and Origen seem chiefly to be envisaged, since he was accused, for instance, of believing in the pre-existence of souls, metempsychosis, the eternity of the ideas, the non-eternity of hell and a final purification which would result in the formation of a new world. Yet he is also accused of holding the eternity of matter and denying the creation, and this seems to indicate an Aristotelian bias, which is perhaps borne out by the fact that he wrote commentaries on Aristotle. The investigation and condemnation which overtook him show what happened when a Byzantine humanist went too far and, as the *Synodicon* puts it, 'sought truth, and not merely intellectual discipline, in classical literature'.

Psellus' pupil John Italus had apparently given the impression that he wished to revive neoplatonism in its integrity as the best rational explanation of dogma, thereby placing philosophy above theology. Psellus was more guarded, regarding the study of philosophy and rhetoric—considered by him as inseparable—less as an end in itself than as an instrument of education. He attempted a vast synthesis of human learning, that of the East as well as of the Greeks,

---

[1] *Scripta minora* (ed. E. Kurtz and F. Drexl, Milan, 1936), I, 237f.

including the occult sciences. Yet he gave special honour to Plato as a theologian, the precursor of Christianity; and his friend and teacher John Mauropous wrote an epigram pleading with Christ to spare Plato and Plutarch, whose doctrines were so near to the gospel teachings. This love of antiquity found its extreme expression in the fifteenth century in the works of Gemistus Plethon, who abjured Christianity and declared that the only hope for the survival of the Empire lay in a return to paganism, and drew up a system of religion based chiefly on the works of Proclus and Iamblichus.

The Empire of the later middle ages produced a revival of humanism (and this did not always clash with orthodoxy), as well as developments in the field of theology. The loss of the old imperial provinces appeared to have brought about a keener awareness of the classical past of Greece. It also seemed to encourage a new interest in Byzantine spiritual and monastic traditions, and once more the court became the centre of subtle theological debate. A controversy arose in the fourteenth century over hesychasm.[1] Although this was concerned with purely orthodox traditions of spirituality, it showed indirectly the influence of Latin scholasticism, and there was indeed a Byzantine scholastic movement which must be considered.

Many later Byzantine theologians were interested in western theology and wrote translations of Latin works or even adopted the methods of scholasticism. Such were Maximus Planudes (1260–1310) who translated the *De Trinitate* of Augustine and the *De consolatione philosophiae* of Boethius, and the theologians Nilus Cabasilas (died 1363), Joseph Bryennius (died 1430/31) and George Scholarius (died c. 1473). But the most important of these was Demetrius Cydones (c. 1324–1397/8), who translated into Greek the *Summa contra Gentiles* of Aquinas. His interest was first aroused as the result of personal experience. In his capacity as the private secretary of the Emperor John VI Cantacuzenus he was obliged to interview all kinds of people of varying nationalities. Many came from western Europe, among them ambassadors, papal legates, merchants, and Dominican and Franciscan friars who had houses of their order in Constantinople and the suburb of Pera. These people made their requests in Latin, through official interpreters. The latter proved unequal to their task, causing much confusion and delay, and finally irritation to the long-suffering secretary. He resolved to end the trouble by learning Latin himself, to the consternation of his acquaintances. A Dominican from Pera was found to teach him, and later gave him a work of Aquinas to translate. Demetrius wrote afterwards that he became far more interested in the matter than in the form of the language and was thus

[1] See below: pp. 197 ff.

led to the idea of undertaking a translation of the *Summa*. This work was welcomed on its arrival with great interest and Thomism almost became the fashion at court. Cantacuzenus was enthusiastic and urged Demetrius to continue his work. Cydones was later received into the Catholic Church, but his work shows him to have been in the main stream of Byzantine humanist tradition. He is perfectly familiar with classical authors and the ancient world, and classical allusions are found side by side with references to the Bible and the Fathers of the Church, both Greek and Latin. His brother Prochorus Cydones, who made a translation of Aquinas' *De ente et essentia*, was a monk of Mt Athos.

On the other hand, Barlaam, a Calabrian monk who had come to Constantinople after being educated in Rome, was condemned in 1341 for his sharp criticism, conducted on scholastic lines, of the mystical theology of Mt Athos, although he had previously been made welcome at the court and honoured as a man of letters. It was however more the object of his attack—the monks of Athos, powerful and revered—than its manner which had caused this revulsion, together with the fact that he himself was not of genuine Byzantine origin and might be regarded as a 'foreigner'. The leader of the hesychast monks, Gregory Palamas, was openly critical of secular learning and in particular of classical philosophy: he said that it was like poison from a snake, of value only when extracted from the dead and dissected reptile and then used as a healing drug.[1] Under pressure from his opponents he elaborated the doctrine of the divine energies or operations. However, the real significance of hesychasm is as a spiritual movement with a long and venerable history, and this fourteenth-century controversy can therefore only be understood in relation to the whole tradition of Byzantine spirituality.

The Byzantines often used the word 'theology', θεολογία, in a special sense, that of inwardness with God. Evagrius of Pontus wrote: 'If you are a theologian, you pray truly, and if you pray truly you are a theologian.' The life of prayer was led especially by the monks, and above all by the hesychasts. Hesychasm came eventually to mean a special discipline and technique of prayer, but the earliest use of the word was literally ἡσυχία, 'solitude', or 'holy quiet'. The earliest monks were solitaries, and later on, when some of them lived together in monasteries, they might still choose to go apart and live as hermits wholly given up to inner prayer, which they were allowed to do if they had been first tested in the coenobitic life and were sufficiently advanced in the spiritual life. Some elected to embark on this from the outset. As unknown country is mapped out, so guides to the life

---

[1] Gregory Palamas, *Défense des saints hésychastes*, i, 1, 20, ed. J. Meyendorff, i (Louvain, 1959), p. 57.

of prayer were written by its explorers, and these became more detailed and elaborate as time went on.

The theory of this kind of experience was named 'mystical theology' by the Pseudo-Dionysius the Areopagite. It is often stated that there are two schools of thought in the Byzantine tradition on the nature of contemplation, one deriving from Gregory of Nyssa and the Pseudo-Dionysius, which placed the highest degree of contemplation in a state of 'darkness' and unknowing; and the other deriving from Origen and Evagrius of Pontus, which considered this vision of God to be expressed rather as an illumination, although it is to be identified with higher prayer, which is above thought. Other early writers to be assigned to this second school are Diadochus and the Pseudo-Macarius, who both have this 'mysticism of light', and favour words like $αἴσθησις$, 'sensation', for religious experience, and describe 'spiritual sensations' (this sort of oxymoron is found in Origen). The Evagrian school exercised great influence, especially through Isaac of Nineveh, a late seventh-century Nestorian bishop, who, under the name of Isaac the Syrian, was translated into Greek and became one of the great masters of contemplative spirituality. Yet such an antithesis must not be overstressed. Inevitably, since both schools were committed to the formulae of St John, both held that the Son of God, the Logos, was essential Light, $φῶς$. The 'ray of divine darkness' of the Areopagite is essentially the result of an excess of light; the human intellect is blinded by it, like the night bird caught suddenly by the dawn. And it is noteworthy that although Maximus the Confessor (580–662) did much to establish 'Dionysius the Areopagite' as an orthodox source of spiritual teaching, his *Centuries on Charity* are to some extent Origenist and Evagrian in outlook.

The Evagrian tradition had also been prominent in the writings of John Climacus (525–605), which exerted a strong influence on later hesychasts. A long chapter of his *Ladder to Paradise* is devoted to $ἡσυχία$, considered as a state of soul necessary for $θεωρία$, the contemplation of God. He distinguishes between $ἡσυχία\ σώματος$, which controls sense perception, and $ἡσυχία\ ψυχῆς$, which imposes calm and holy tranquillity on the intellect. Climacus stresses, among the necessary dispositions, that the soul must be absorbed in God and must have the gift of tears. On these points he is closely followed by the eleventh-century Symeon the New Theologian.

For in the eleventh century a great development of this mystical tradition is to be found in the writings of Symeon (949–1022) and of his disciple Nicetas Stethatus. Symeon, canonised by the Orthodox Church and called the New Theologian, perhaps to associate him with the two other 'theologians', St John the Evangelist and St Gregory of Nazianzus, was an outstanding and influential figure, the greatest of the medieval Byzantine mystics. In his own day he was a well-known abbot and spiritual father in Constantinople, and through his works he exerted incalculable influence on later generations. One group of his outspoken monastic sermons, the *Catecheses*, circulated in a revised edition considered more suitable for a wide public. These and his other writings, particularly his *Loves of the Divine Hymns*, show him to be to some extent in the Evagrian tradition, much influenced by John Climacus, and certainly in the main stream of Orthodox development. But his works reflect a particularly individual quality born of personal experience.

With Symeon, as always in the Orthodox Church, the goal is deification. He constantly stresses the means whereby through grace this union with God may be obtained. Only through obedience and tears, penitence and constant prayer, could progress be made towards freedom from passions and a state of holy tranquillity (*apatheia*). Then, as he himself knew, deification might momentarily be experienced in this life, when the presence of God came to be felt, accompanied by a perception of the divine light. While stressing the apophatic nature of the Godhead, Symeon wrote again and again of the illumination by the Holy Trinity revealed in this way. 'Then the divine spark will light in the heart, illumine the soul and purify the mind and it will be borne upwards high in the heavens and will be united with the divine light. '[1] Often the emphasis is on the indwelling of the divine light described in terms of the Holy Trinity, though Symeon's own emphasis is at the same time markedly Christo-centric in that he sees the Trinity revealed through the Incarnate Christ. Unlike some of the earlier mystics, Symeon does not particularly stress the intermediate steps in the progress towards deification, tending to by-pass the stage known as the *theoria physica* ($\theta\epsilon\omega\rho\iota\alpha$ $\phi\upsilon\sigma\iota\kappa\eta$), found for instance in Maximus the Confessor. In this he is more akin to the later Palamites. His writings, which sometimes break into dialogue, are indeed marked by a compelling dramatic quality, by a sense of urgency, as he describes his possession of Christ through the sacraments or through a revelation of the divine light, and he unceasingly seeks to point out the way to these experiences to the brethren entrusted to him.

The fourteenth-century revival of hesychasm drew much of its inspiration from Symeon, although after him the practice of hesychasm seems to have somewhat declined. The revival, or rather spiritual renewal, really began in the late thirteenth century with Gregory of Sinai (died 1346), who was a famous teacher on Mt Athos.

---

[1] *MPG*, cxx, 558, *Div. Am.* 21 (Cod. Monac. gr. 177, f. 264r).

He is recorded as saying 'Read constantly the treatises on prayer and hesychasm such as those of Climacus, Isaac, St Maximus, the New Theologian and his disciple Nicetas Stethatus'. Through Gregory's work, Athos became again the home of numerous hesychast cells and in the following years physical techniques, though not all necessarily new, were stressed and developed in connection with the Jesus-prayer, particularly regulated breathing and fixing the eyes on the navel which was regarded as the seat of the heart. These physical devices were accompanied by the constant repetition of the Jesus-prayer, 'Lord Jesus Christ, Son of God, have mercy on me', which had long been used, certainly from the fifth century onwards. The aim of these exercises was to induce inner tranquillity and holy silence and a receptive state in which the mind might be emptied of all thoughts, however holy. It was however not only these particular practices but the whole tradition which was called in question in the fourteenth century.

In 1341 an attack was launched on the hesychast monks by Barlaam, a monk from Calabria. The first round in the conflict between Barlaam and Palamas had been over the use of syllogism in theology in connection with the procession of the Holy Spirit, and Barlaam's attempt to introduce scholasticism has already been mentioned. He had previously entered into correspondence with the theologian Gregory Palamas on the subject, maintaining that Aristotelian logic could usefully be applied to contemplative theology. Palamas, himself a hesychast, upheld the Athos tradition, which took account of only one mode of knowledge of God: the mystical way of asceticism and purification of the heart by which the divine light, the principle and source of all truth, presents itself to the soul.

Barlaam next wrote attacking the hesychasts as heretics, claiming that their physical methods of prayer and belief in 'spiritual sensations' showed them to be 'Massalians', that is, members of a Manichaean sect. In reply, Palamas repudiated rationalism, defended the hesychast prayer, and elaborated the doctrine of the divine light seen by the purified ascetics 'with the eyes of their senses'. Barlaam was condemned at a synod in Constantinople in June 1341, but there were others for whom these writings of Palamas seemed to exceed the limits of orthodoxy.

It was soon apparent that the immediate question of the validity of the hesychast prayer could not be settled without a discussion of its underlying principle, that of the deification of man. This doctrine was rooted in the tradition of centuries of monastic teaching and experience and of popular devotion to saints and holy men. Yet how did it accord with the absolute transcendence of God? Palamas' solution was to postulate a distinction in God between his essence, which remains unknowable and unparticipated (ἀμέθεκτος), and his energies or operations, which can be known by created beings and when perceived as 'the uncreated light' by the eyes of the purified ascetics represent a deifying grace raising them to union with the divine. This 'uncreated light', said to be identical with the light seen by the apostles at the Transfiguration on Mt Tabor, was perceived by the eyes of the body, which was as it were transhumanised by it. Such a doctrine sounded dangerously like the physical ecstasy indulged in by the Massalians, while an unknowable God with his divine energies even seemed to some to be reminiscent of the Platonic demiurge with his inferior gods, and of gnosticism, and thus led to a charge of polytheism.

A summary of the hesychast defence was given in the *Tomus Hagioriticus*,[1] put out by the monks of Athos in reply to the condemnation of Palamas by the Patriarch Calecas. This manifesto indicates the anti-rationalism of hesychasm. Reasoned arguments are not given, but statements are supported by patristic texts, some of which would seem to be of doubtful relevance. Nevertheless the authors of the *Tomus Hagioriticus* had behind them a long tradition when they stressed that the true monastic life belongs to the supernatural and not the moral order, and condemned those who said that grace was 'a habit of the rational nature, attained by imitation alone'. For, as the hesychasts maintained, 'virtue and the imitation of God may make the soul apt for the divine union, but its perfection is only realised by grace'.[2] This term, χάρις, grace, is constantly used for the deifying divinity, suggesting a comparison with the Thomist doctrine of beatification through supernatural grace. In contrast to St Thomas, however, they assert that this deification can and does take place in this life through a spiritualisation of the flesh which suggests the glorified body of the resurrection.

But the outstanding defender of hesychasm was Gregory Palamas, canonised by the Orthodox Church. In his *Defence of those living in holy tranquillity* (i.e. the hesychasts) he gives the lie to any who would regard Byzantine spirituality as merely repetitive and not an organic continuation of its great biblical and patristic heritage. Building on his predecessors, particularly the Cappadocians, the Pseudo-Macarius, the Pseudo-Dionysius and Maximus the Confessor, as well as on the living monastic tradition, he defends both Byzantine spirituality with its goal of deification and the doctrinal teaching with which this is linked.

It has been said that Palamas was attempting to formulate as

---

[1] *MPG*, CL, 1225–36. [2] *Ibid.* 1229.

much an anthropology as a theology of contemplation. 'No man shall see God.' Yet the hesychasts claimed to experience such vision, and Palamas, defending them, set out to explain in what way the human mind could be said to apprehend divinity. In his distinction between the knowable and the unknowable, he drew upon the mystical writers of the past: the 'mysticism of darkness' of the Pseudo-Dionysius, the 'mysticism of light' of Origen and Evagrius. Yet it seems that where, for them, the antitheses were left to be resolved, for Palamas the gulf was eternal between the unknowable Godhead and the created. But it could yet be bridged by the divine energies (ἐνέργειαι) of God, the 'uncreated' outgoings or operations which were active in creation. It was thus that deifying grace, the divine light, could descend upon the true hesychast. Yet this grace was not the unapproachable essence or substance (οὐσία) of the Godhead. Such explanations and terminology were criticised by the opponents of Palamism as cutting at the roots of the Christian doctrine of the Incarnation and the sacraments. And although the Byzantines closed their ranks against the attack made on the monks of their venerated Athos by Barlaam, an outsider, there were some amongst the Byzantines themselves who rejected the doctrines of Palamas and continued to combat them. The most important of these was Nicephorus Gregoras.

A pupil of the versatile polymath and statesman Theodore Metochites, Gregoras was himself a man of great learning and ability, and had published works on rhetoric and astronomy. Not primarily interested in theology but deeply devoted to orthodoxy he was drawn into the hesychast controversy by his own conviction that Palamas was teaching blasphemous heresy, of great danger to the Church. He was no friend of Barlaam, and in his secular days, before he plunged into these theological problems, he had met him as a rival. Barlaam appears to have challenged the scholars of Constantinople and a public disputation had been staged between the two, apparently on the subjects of the quadrivium. An independent account of this meeting contradicts that of Gregoras and attributes to Barlaam the victory on dialectic. Gregoras certainly opposed the other's Aristotelianism. This incident throws light on the position Gregoras later took up with regard to hesychasm: he wished to dissociate himself entirely from Barlaam and his scholastic methods of disputation. Palamas' writings were to be tested, not against the logic of Aristotle, but against the teaching of the Fathers of the Church. It was the contention of Gregoras and of the party which he led that, so tested, they would be revealed as innovatory, without a shred of patristic authority behind them, and therefore heretical.

All this speculation can only be understood in relation to its setting. The discussions did not take place in a vacuum, or simply in peaceful conferences on Mt Athos, but were usually the result of the public prosecution of one side or the other at different times. The councils which were called in Constantinople may seem minor domestic affairs, restricted in their numbers, remote or fantastic in their agenda, yet their tradition goes back to the first conference of Christian bishops called by the first Christian Emperor, and they are no less related to the needs of the Empire and Church as a whole. And in the fourteenth century the Emperor still retained his personal importance, and his own views naturally influenced imperial policy. When John Cantacuzenus was on the throne (1347–54), hesychasts held the Patriarchate and bishoprics, and their opponents were persecuted. Cantacuzenus appears to have been a sincere follower of Palamas' doctrine, and, as a usurper, he particularly needed the support of the monks, who were powerful allies as both numerous in themselves and possessing great influence over the people; they were moreover, like Cantacuzenus, great landowners.

The anti-Palamites had triumphed during the civil war of 1341–7 when the Queen Mother, Anna Palaeologina, still reigned. She was Anna of Savoy, Andronicus III's widow, and she was probably chiefly moved to suppress the Palamites because of their connection with the rebel Cantacuzenus. She herself was for a long time dominated by the bitter enemy and rival of Cantacuzenus, the Patriarch Calecas, who even appears to have thought of himself as uniting the offices of Patriarch and Emperor. Her Latin sympathies by birth were strong, but probably had less influence on the controversy during her own reign than during that of her son, John V Palaeologus (1354–91), who revived the discussions, apparently in the hope of reaching a compromise. It thus came about that one of the first points raised in the councils called on the subject soon came to be the validity of the acts of earlier councils and patriarchal decrees, a very confused question.

The Emperor, then, played a traditional part in these fourteenth-century debates, for theology still remained of vital interest to the state. What the Byzantines thought was also a matter of concern not only for the Patriarchate of Constantinople but for the Western Church. In 1355 the Latin archbishop, Paul of Smyrna, who came to Constantinople as papal legate to negotiate for the reunion of the churches, also had instructions to inquire into the question of hesychasm. 'For certain Byzantines had made known to the Lord Pope Urban V and his cardinals that the Greek Church had introduced into its teaching a theory of higher and lower divinities....'[1] John Palaeologus accordingly arranged for the archbishop to be present at

---

[1] *MPG*, CLIV, 835.

a disputation between Nicephorus Gregoras and Cantacuzenus (now the monk Joasaph); but this experience, and later personal discussions which he had with Cantacuzenus, only confirmed Paul in his opinion that Palamas held an 'impious doctrine'.

Nevertheless, Palamas' orthodoxy had been officially declared vindicated by the Byzantine Church at the council of 1351 and after his death he was honoured as a saint. But perhaps the real importance of hesychasm continued to be as a way of prayer and contemplation, and as such it has lived on in Orthodoxy, playing a great part in Russian spirituality. At first sight, this mystical hesychast prayer appears to offer a strange contradiction to the orthodox tradition of worship expressed through the sacraments of the Church, including the veneration of icons which were regarded as an important channel of grace. What could be more opposed to the icon, the visible paint or mosaic image of saint or divinity, with all the associations it presented to the mind of the gazing venerator, than this silence, this abandonment of the mind to nothingness and stifling of the senses? The Church has always recognised that for chosen souls there exists a direct means of communication with God, apart from the normal channels of grace. Yet in the Orthodox tradition the two ways are in reality not so totally distinct, for they are linked by the uncompromisingly physical basis of each. Matter is transcended in the achievement—the union of this world with the next; but the achievement is reached *through* matter. Just as the icon exists as a material object produced by the physical effort of the artist no less than his inner vision and is venerated by the physical action of its worshippers, so the prayer of the hesychast is considered as not being unrelated to a physical effort. Great stress is laid by the hesychasts on the physical means of their prayer—not only the control of breathing and bodily consciousness involved but the form of the prayer itself—its repetition of the uttered Word of the Holy Name. For this is to be made as a thing potent in itself, not because of the associations it would bring to the mind: these are expressly to be excluded.

In spite of the great traditions Byzantine mysticism, and the popular devotion to mystic saints, experience of this kind can only have directly affected a small minority in any period. But for all Byzantine Christians, whether monks or nuns or laymen, the central fact of their religious life was liturgical worship of God. This public worship centred in the offering of the Eucharist, the Divine Liturgy as it was called, a more rich and elaborate rite than the Latin mass. Symbolist or 'mystical' interpretations of its details were written by the Pseudo-Germanus, the twelfth-century Theodore, and, above all, by Nicholas Cabasilas in his *Explanation of the Divine Liturgy*. 'The

Church is represented in the holy mysteries', he wrote, 'not in figure only, but as the limbs are represented in the heart, and the branches in the root, and, as our Lord has said, the shoots in the vine. For here is no sharing of a name, or analogy by resemblance, but an identity of actuality.'[1] These mysteries are indeed the visible action of the Church, expressing its inner life, which is Christ. In his treatise *On Life in Christ* Nicholas Cabasilas gives a marvellously lyrical exposition of the doctrine of the Church as the mystical body of Christ. This 'life hidden in Christ' should be a constant secret source of joy to all Christians. It is by no means necessary to go into solitude or any other special place to seek it, for it is planted in the soul by baptism, and nourished by the other sacraments, especially by the Divine Liturgy. All Cabasilas' work is stamped with his intense conviction of the constant interplay of time and eternity, this world and the next. The liturgy was, for all Byzantines, the supreme realisation of this interplay. Certain icons, as well as a magnificent fresco at Mistra, show the mass being celebrated by angels. Thus the Byzantine church building was in a special way heaven upon earth. Christ was there, with the angelic host, and with his saints, present in their sacred images, and seeming, by the deliberate perspective of the artists, to project into the church itself their paradisaical world of gold and jewelled mosaic, and to commingle with the faithful.

The whole life of the people was brought into the ritual of the Church. The *Euchologium*, the equivalent of the Roman missal, contains not only the texts of the three liturgies, but many humbler rites, such as formularies for the blessings of houses, of cattle, and of wells. The shrines of saints (as formerly of pagan gods) marked the special sanctity of places, and cities had their guardian saints and patronal feasts. The belief in the intercession of saints shows that they were thought of as members of a single Church, existing both in heaven and on earth. Above all came the cult of *the Theotokos*, the Mother of God, who was constantly regarded as the mother and protectress of her people. It is this belief in the power of intercession, this awareness of the personal compassion binding the heavenly patron to his earthly client, that best explains the constant expectation of miracle which is apparent even in Byzantine political history, and has marked Byzantine iconography, where the saints are so often shown as wonder-workers. Things of nature were thought of not only as being permeated by the supernatural, but as being kept in existence by it, just as the sovereignty of the Emperor was maintained by the sovereignty of God; for whatever its defects, Byzantine civilisation was permeated by orthodox Christianity, and perhaps owed its existence to it.

[1] *MPG*, CL, 452 (trans. J. M. Hussey and P. A. McNulty, London, 1960, p. 91).

CHAPTER XXVII

BYZANTINE LITERATURE[1]

Byzantine literature reflects the intellectual life and climate of Byzantine society throughout the thousand years of its historical and cultural development, and reveals the curious dichotomy of the Byzantine mentality. Religious writings with a dogmatic and didactic tone stand well to the fore; their influence is also found in almost all secular literature, and they reflect the speculative, meditative and other-worldly outlook of Byzantine theology, the predominant intellectual force. On the other hand this does not preclude works (though very few are now extant) which crudely mock and satirise religion, and appear both frivolous and blasphemous. But anything in between these two extremes, such as the most simple joy in the divinely created world of nature, or even humour of a more subtle type, is almost entirely lacking. Byzantine literature has no really genuine secular lyric poetry; but the emotions could find some outlet in the erotic description of amorous adventures. They could also find expression in the mystical adoration of the Godhead and in the magnificent and varied beauty of the vast corpus of liturgical poetry, which bore witness to the genius of Greek spirituality and the adaptability of Greek literary forms. The Byzantines took a legitimate pride in being the sole possessors of an ancient culture; this, however, was not without its disadvantages. They were apt to concentrate too extensively upon merely preserving this heritage, for it was considered not only the summit of perfection but also the very medium of God's blessing. Providence had ordained that the Christian revelation, which had set a term to the eager inquiries of the human mind and rendered superfluous all further striving after knowledge, should be vouchsafed to mankind in the language of the Greeks. Caught up in this intellectual narcissism, the Byzantines ignored the new and vital spiritual forces at work on the peripheries of the central core of Greek territory. Such activities took the form of heretical movements and the revival of the old indigenous languages, and they were crushed with all the power at the command of the central authority. It was indeed by reason of this centralisation that Constantinople with the accumulated talent of its officials and higher clergy became the unique centre of literary activity in the service of court and Church, the privileged seat of a

---

[1] Full cross-references to authors mentioned in different sections of this chapter will be found in the Index.

noble culture slowly dying beneath the weight of tradition. But in the provinces—even in the cities—intellectual activity steadily declined.

Nevertheless, it was the lower classes in the provinces who in the later middle ages subsequently evolved new modes of expression for the imagination and the emotions, and for that perennial Greek urge to make poetry and to tell stories. The better-educated classes of Byzantine society did not in fact ever recognise as such this far superior part of Byzantine literature and thus denied its only means of acquiring permanence through being written down. The rare examples now extant of this popular Byzantine poetry date from a very late period, and certainly represent only a fraction of all that Byzantines must have made up and sung round the camp-fire or at the spinning-wheel. It was imperial and high ecclesiastical circles, vested with an authority emanating from the divinely appointed Emperor, which determined what could and what could not be permitted in literature. The result was an unwavering insistence on giving pride of place to form and a striving to emulate the style of classical models and to observe scrupulously a set of pedantic rules. In comparison with virtuosity in imitating classical models, no literary value was attached to originality of content, freedom of invention, or freedom in the choice of subject-matter, and in any case subject-matter was strictly limited by the narrow range of an uncompromising religious and political orthodoxy.

This is true not merely of literary forms but also of the development of the Greek language during the period. It is essential in the first place to consider the significance of this development and its effects upon Byzantine literature. Just as Latin developed into the various romance languages by way of vulgar Latin, through simplification of its structural basis and assimilation of irregularities into the regular morphological and syntactical systems, so the old Greek dialects from about the fourth century B.C. onwards combined to produce a single language (*koine*) with predominantly Attic characteristics which was spoken, written and understood throughout the Hellenistic world; and in time, by a similar process, this developed into the modern Greek of today. Henceforward the accent, instead of indicating the quantity of vowels and diphthongs now modified and treated as monophthongs, served to indicate where the stress should fall. Accidence and syntax tended towards simplification and assimilation. The vocabulary took over technical terms from Roman administrative and military life, and in more recent times has adopted from Arabic, Italian and Turkish innumerable expressions for the material objects of daily life, commerce and communications. Greek has undergone so many modifications in the process of becoming the spoken language of today that a modern Greek often has difficulty in understanding a text from the fourth century B.C. pronounced as in our present-day western schools. But official Byzantine literature did not use this new language. It was necessary to secure the approval of court and ecclesiastical circles and to do this it was necessary to keep to the rules of an Atticism that was academically fostered by gram- marians and rhetoricians, a form of expression artificially preserved and regarded as the language of Thucydides, Aristophanes and the great tragedians. The highest praise was given to the man who could extol the excellence of his imperial sovereign on ceremonial occasions in a speech composed of long rhythmic periods full of antiquarian terms and antitheses, supported by far-fetched comparisons and al- lusions to Greek mythology as well as to the Bible. It was of little consequence whether such a panegyric bore any relation to the actual state of affairs (usually far less glorious), provided that in style it adhered to the rules of encomium or *logos epideiktikos*. This was a pure delight in form, art for art's sake, a display of virtuosity in the use of artificial language that was comprehensible only to Byzantines of a similar level of education. It was obviously impossible for such an instrument to become the medium for the expression of genuine feeling, or to evoke that response from the majority of ordinary people without which the written word cannot become 'literature'. The Church, whose most influential representatives had usually passed through the schools of rhetoric, also supported this tendency towards classicism. Her aim was to preserve from 'corruption' the standard of the *koine*, in which God had conferred on mankind the final revelation of the New Testament and in which the Fathers of the fourth and fifth centuries, steeped in Attic culture, had set down its definitive interpretation. And so throughout the centuries the lan- guage of ecclesiastical literature in Byzantium remained more or less unchanged; it was Attic eloquence combined with biblical turns of expression, showing slight variations according to the particular genre (exegesis, sermon, religious poetry). Secular literature, bound by the laws of literary tradition, was written in the so-called 'pure' language; this was indeed a purist's style modelled on Attic literary traditions artificially perpetuated in the schools and centres of ad- vanced learning. When making a formal speech the orator would shrink from referring to any object in everyday use by its familiar name. Similarly, in a historical treatise the 'barbarous'-sounding names of contemporary races would be replaced by the names of tribes occupying the same territory in ancient times. In poetry the old metres persisted, although the quantitative principle on which they were based had long since disappeared.

It was only with the decay of political centralisation and the acquisition of power over a large area of the Empire by non-Byzantine rulers that a literature in the normally developed 'vulgar-Greek' vernacular came into being, from the thirteenth century onwards. The folk-epics and other works in the vernacular were set down in popular speech, though not in great numbers. After the collapse of Byzantine power in 1453 these writings became the most important spiritual factor in the preservation of Greek national feeling; circulated in the wretched typography known as 'Venetian print' they kept alive for the Greeks under Turkish rule an awareness of a common cultural tradition. But neither in the middle ages nor since have the Greeks produced any great figure like that of Dante who would have used this language, so free from the shackles of academic tradition, as the vehicle for a sublime theme, thus raising it to the status of the accepted literary medium.

And so it came about that, for the most part, Byzantine secular literature in proud self-satisfaction turned its back on all external influences, and showed a marked aversion to any form of change from within, thus remaining on the whole the esoteric concern of the upper classes, and contributing very little to the great literature of the world. Court, Church and university all alike fostered this sense of the exclusive possession of an ancient culture handed down by Greek forbears in a form valid for all time. This vivid awareness of tradition meant that Byzantine efforts to develop this ancient cultural heritage were confined to bringing it into harmony with Christian teaching and cultivating with the utmost care its more formal aspects.

It is, however, quite unjust to regard Byzantine literature, as it has for so long been regarded, as an arid collection of worthless and voluminous outpourings. Within these self-imposed limits the writers of Byzantium could produce works of considerable merit. In the field of ecclesiastical literature, there are for instance the Church Fathers of the fourth and fifth centuries, who had nearly all sat at the feet of the best teachers in company with the outstanding philosophers of the day; they were responsible for achieving that synthesis between neoplatonism and Christian teaching which first enabled Christianity to hold its own in intellectual circles. In christological disputes it was the patristic writers who defined their terms and articulated the literary forms in which such controversies were to be transmitted to the West through the Latin Fathers. Writing towards the end of the fifth century, the great unknown philosopher, the so-called Pseudo-Dionysius, with bold independence of argument and style transformed Plotinus' system of Emanations into the description of the ecclesiastical hierarchy and the return of the soul to God, and in so doing became the father both of Greek and of Latin spirituality. Then the art of story-telling found a frequent outlet in the Byzantine legends of the saints, with their innumerable heroes waging unceasing war on the evil spirits haunting the universe in diverse shapes, and these made a strong appeal to popular imagination and the widespread belief in miracles. Those capable of appreciating simple piety expressed in homely narrative may wander through the garden of Greek hagiography surrounded by brilliant, and sometimes exotic, blooms. Byzantine religious poetry contains, together with much that is artificial, passages of genuine literary merit and moving sincerity. And in secular literature many sparkling and witty lines are to be found in Byzantine epigrams, particularly of the early period.

One of the supreme achievements of Byzantium is its historiography. In an almost unbroken line down the centuries it carried on the finest traditions of the classical world and it is this particular literary form that is really indebted to the careful maintenance of the style and artistry of the historians of ancient Greece. Acknowledgement is also due to Byzantine grammarians and philologists, who rescued for later generations some of the most important poetical and prose works of antiquity, and whose erudition made a conspicuous contribution towards our understanding of them; but their work belongs to the history of civilisation rather than to literature. Those who require good literature to show original and individual quality may well give first place to the writings in the vernacular, not only to the countless romantic love-stories and the allegorical animal epics which have been preserved, but more especially to the epic of Digenis Akritas, which describes the heroic struggle of Christendom against the barbarians advancing from the East, and at the same time depicts the stirring adventures of the Byzantine marcher lord.

In the short survey which follows it is impossible even to name many Byzantine writings, and all that has been attempted is to select for brief mention the most important. The very fact already stressed, that the literary activity of the educated Byzantine was often somewhat artificial, an exercise in formal and technical skill rather than the result of direct inspiration or significant experience, meant that some Byzantine authors were active in many widely differing fields, religious and secular, poetry and prose, or they might at the same time be actively engaged as grammarians and philosophers, while in addition almost all cultivated the art of the epigram. It has however been impossible to consider each author as a whole in his own right, and literary figures have had to be split up for consideration according to their various works, for what is attempted here is only a general review of the main trends of Byzantine literature.

I. RELIGIOUS LITERATURE[1]

The foremost place in a history of Byzantine literature is rightly assigned to religious writings, for from the days of Constantine the Great, Christianity was the most important factor in the political and intellectual life of the Empire. As early as the third century it had already acquired a mastery of the literary forms of its pagan opponents—a mastery it owed to such mighty intellects as Clement of Alexandria and the towering genius of Origen. Furthermore, the secular works of Byzantine literature are themselves permeated with theological habits of thought to a far greater extent than is the case with the contemporary literature of the West.

(a) Doctrine and exegesis; polemical and homiletic writing

The overthrow of paganism, and still more the combating of heresies which were now particularly numerous and were for the most part defended by men of sound philosophical training, made the highest demands on the Christian theologians of the fourth and fifth centuries. It was fortunate for Church and State that the champions of orthodoxy were equal to these demands. The struggle called forth the best from both sides and the period up to the Council of Chalcedon (451), which witnessed also a late flowering of pagan literature, saw the greatest achievements of the Greek Fathers. It was at this time that theological terminology was fixed and the classic formulae of Christian ethics and dogma were worked out. In later periods, down to Theodore the Studite in the early ninth century, the monophysite and iconoclast controversies also produced important works in the fields of doctrine, exegesis and homiletics. As far as the eighth century is concerned, it is even possible to see homiletics blossoming in the form of ecclesiastical rhetoric. But by then, and indeed by the time of John of Damascus (first half of the eighth century), the creative period of Byzantine religious literature was really over and in subsequent centuries it fell a prey to that conservative traditionalism which so often characterised the Byzantine mentality. Then the writer's main aim was to preserve the authority of the early Fathers and he was not concerned with exploring new and original forms of thought and expression. Apart from a few outstanding minds such as Photius (ninth century) or Nicephorus Gregoras or Gregory Palamas (both fourteenth century), doctrinal works and exegesis were in the later period largely occupied with combating the Latin doctrine of the procession of the Holy Ghost. This is characteristically dealt

---

[1] See also above, Pt. I, ch. II and Pt. II, ch. XXVI.

with by the Greeks without dialectic, relying mainly on the cumulative effect of quotations from the Fathers (χρήσεις). In exegesis their method was to elucidate all the passages (περικοπαί) of Holy Scripture by means of appended catenae consisting of appropriate excerpts from early patristic writings.

Eminent amongst early ecclesiastical writers was Eusebius, Bishop of Caesarea (*c.* 263–*c.* 340), who came from Palestine and was the friend and champion of the Emperor Constantine the Great. He was educated by Pamphilus, who bequeathed to him his library and gave him the scholarly training which made possible his many-sided literary activities. Of these some of the most significant are his *Praeparatio evangelica* in fifteen books, in which he demonstrates the superiority of Judaism over pagan religions as a basis for Christianity; his *Demonstratio evangelica* in twenty books, in which he refutes the Jewish reproach that Christians do not observe the Law; his defence of Origen in which he collaborated with Pamphilus (the Greek original is lost); and his polemic against Marcellus of Ancyra (*Contra Marcellum*). Eusebius' style is highly rhetorical and tends to be turgid in expression. His historical works (see below, p. 225) were also of the utmost importance for western as well as eastern patristics.

Alexandria, the home of Christian scholarship, was the centre of the activities of its Patriarch Athanasius (*c.* 295–373). He was the staunch defender of the Nicene definition of the relation between God the Father and God the Son against the Arians; so unshakeable were his convictions that he went five times into exile rather than deny them. His most important polemical writings were those against the pagans and against the Arians, and his *Apologia* addressed to the Emperor Constantius II. Athanasius was no stylist, but he had at his command all the resources of rhetoric and knew exactly when to use them. His successor as Patriarch of Alexandria was Didymus the Blind (*c.* 313–98), chiefly known as an exegetist; he was succeeded (after Theophilus) by the masterful Cyril (Patriarch, 412–44). Cyril's main works are his *Contra Julianum Imperatorem*, which attacks paganism, and his various writings against Nestorianism, in which he attacks the Nestorian christological doctrine. His style is wordy and rhetorical and lacks a sense of form; even so, by reason of his ecclesiastical position he exerted an important influence on his age, especially at the General Council of Ephesus (431), and was also much used by later theologians. Nestorius, whose theological outlook had been influenced by his training in the catechetical school at Antioch, was appointed Bishop of Constantinople in 428. In the struggle between Nestorius and Cyril the rivalry between the Alexandrine and the Antiochene schools of thought comes to a head. The

Alexandrians preferred to interpret difficult passages of scripture in an allegorical sense, while Antioch favoured as far as possible the literal and historical explanation.

The three great Cappadocian Fathers, called by the Greeks 'the three hierarchs', belong to the Alexandrian school of thought. They are Basil the Great, Bishop of Caesarea in Cappadocia (*c.* 330–79); Gregory of Nazianzus, a writer of great sensibility with a turn for poetry, the great 'Theologian' (as he is called by later writers), for a short time Patriarch of Constantinople (*c.* 379–*c.* 390); and Gregory of Nyssa (died *c.* 394), brother of Basil the Great and Bishop of the small town of Nyssa, a profound thinker and versatile writer. Basil received his education at Constantinople and Athens, where he was a student with Gregory of Nazianzus. His writings and outlook show that complete fusion of Christianity with classical culture which may well be regarded as the mark of the Christian humanist in the highest sense of the term. All his works are distinguished by their fine style perfectly adapted to suit each shade of meaning. The most important are the three books against the Arian Eunomius (363–4) and the nine homilies on the creation (the *Hexaemeron*), which reveal so wide a range of knowledge that it even includes natural history. His famous homily to youth was of vital importance in determining the attitude of the Church towards the secular education inherited from a pagan past and may even be called the Magna Carta of Christian humanism. Gregory of Nazianzus was a close friend of Basil. A sensitive, perceptive, and widely read scholar, he was also a rhetorician with a bold pictorial style which must be described not as Attic but as Asian. Among his numerous addresses and sermons, which constantly served as an arsenal of ideas and expressions for the best Byzantine theologians, the five on the Divinity of the Logos are particularly famous. These were delivered in 380 in Constantinople when he was Patriarch. His poetry will be discussed later. Basil's brother, Gregory of Nyssa, had the greatest philosophical bent of the three Cappadocians, and the fewest literary gifts; his rhetoric reeks of the lecture-room. He too wrote against Eunomius, successfully defending his dead brother, and his work (379) on the creation of man is similarly regarded as a completion of the *Hexaemeron* of Basil. His main contribution to dogma is the *Oratio catechetica magna*. The great volume of his homilies links him with Gregory of Nazianzus, though he cannot compare with the latter for power of thought and vigour of expression. All three Cappadocians have left letters treating largely of doctrinal problems.

Another prominent scholar and churchman of the school of Asia Minor at this time was Eustathius, Bishop of Antioch (died *c.* 337), but only fragments of his very fruitful theological activity are now extant. The one complete surviving work is his treatise on the Witch of Endor, in which he fiercely attacks the allegorical exegesis of the Alexandrian school. Another contemporary of the Asia Minor group was Amphilochius of Iconium (340/5–after 394). He received the same kind of education as St Basil, and in 373 he became Bishop of Iconium. His writings are characterised by a skilful rhetorical method and are often presented in the form of a dialogue. He has left a number of sermons and a treatise on the suppression of sects. Another gifted and versatile writer was Apollinaris the Younger of Laodicea (*c.* 310–before 392), who produced commentaries on the Bible and apologetic. Despite his substantial services to the early Church— including his work as a poet—he was accused of heresy in 381 on account of his christological teaching.

Epiphanius, Bishop of Salamis-Constantia in Cyprus (*c.* 315–403), wrote, apart from many other works, the *Medicine Chest* (Πανάριον), a book of cures for those bitten by the serpents of heresy, and a work called *The Well-anchored* ('Ἀγκυρωτός) in which he gives an exposition of Christian teaching, especially that on the Trinity, and a refutation of heresy. His letter to Bishop John of Jerusalem condemning the representation of Christ on a curtain before the door of a church became famous during the iconoclastic controversy. Cyril, Bishop of Jerusalem (313–86), was one of the convinced champions of Nicene orthodoxy. Twenty-four catecheses have come down to us in his name, but the last five (the so-called μυσταγωγικαί) were probably written by his successor John of Jerusalem, mentioned above. Cyril's catecheses were very popular because of their liveliness and warmth of feeling. He did not write them down himself but they were taken down as they were delivered.

Another zealous champion of orthodoxy was Diodorus of Tarsus (died before 394), who founded the above-mentioned catechetical school of Antioch. Few of his fertile and varied literary productions have survived, for after his death he was accused of heresy by Cyril of Alexandria (see above, p. 212) and later condemned in 499. A similar fate overtook his pupil Theodore of Mopsuestia (died 428), a friend of John Chrysostom and the greatest exegete of the Eastern Church. He was suspected of Nestorianism and anathematised at the Council of Constantinople in 553. His many sober and unprejudiced works of theology and exegesis have practically all been lost; what remains is in the Syrian language, for he was the exegetist *par excellence* of the Syrian Church.

One of the most renowned preachers in the history of the Church was John, Bishop of Antioch, called Chrysostom (354–407), who studied with Theodore of Mopsuestia under the famous rhetorician Libanius (see below, p. 239). From 386 to 397 John preached in Antioch and was so idolised by the people that he had to be smuggled secretly out of the city when he left to become Patriarch of Constantinople in 398. His activities in Constantinople came to an end however owing to the hostility of the Empress Eudoxia, who considered that she had been personally attacked in his sermons, and Chrysostom was obliged to end his days in exile in Cucusus in the remotest corner of Asia Minor. The fine sermons on the Old and New Testaments which he delivered in Antioch stand out among the most distinguished examples of homiletic; like Cyril's catecheses they were taken down by people who heard them, and then published. Almost as remarkable are the twenty-one 'pillar' sermons—also delivered in Antioch after the statues of the Emperor Arcadius had been smashed by the populace. Five hundred sermons attributed to him are still extant, though many are spurious; his collected works fill eighteen volumes in the Migne edition. John Chrysostom combines the best rhetorical technique with the utmost sureness of touch in the use of bold metaphors and similes. He is an Atticist in the best sense of the word; in exegetical method he belongs to the school of Antioch.

Theodoret of Cyrus (*c.* 393–457/8), like his master Diodorus of Tarsus, was a friend (and pupil) of John Chrysostom. At first an adherent of Nestorius, he nevertheless subscribed to the Council of Chalcedon in 451, but was condemned in 553 as a heretic, as indeed was Diodorus. He wrote a number of commentaries on the Old and New Testaments, in a good lucid Attic style. Though he employed the sober literal method of Antiochene exegesis, he did not hesitate to embark on other and more symbolical types of exegesis. His most important work is called *Remedy for Pagan Diseases* (Ἑλληνικῶν θεραπευτικὴ παθημάτων), a manual in which pagan views on certain problems are set side by side with the true and more complete Christian solution. Proclus, Bishop of Constantinople from 434 to 446, belongs to this period. His sermons attacking Nestorius are chiefly interesting by virtue of their markedly Asian style; in them he employed phrases in rhyming couplets and, to stimulate his hearers, introduced the effective innovation of dialogues between his characters.

From the Council of Chalcedon onwards the contribution of Byzantine theologians to theology and exegesis is less extensive. Even so, there is an almost unbroken line of theologians and exegetes well into the eighth century, although they do not have the same originality as their predecessors. Very little is known of the life and character of Hesychius of Jerusalem (died after 451), in whose name survive many works of exegesis. The monophysite Basil of Seleucia (died *c.* 460) was an outstanding preacher, with a skilful and effective use of rhetoric; it is worth noting that despite Basil's heretical views one of his sermons was taken over word for word by Romanus the Melodus in one of his kontakia. The Patriarch Gennadius I of Constantinople (458–71) has left numerous commentaries on the Bible. Nemesius, Bishop of Emesa, is particularly significant because of the extent of his influence on medieval philosophy in the West. Though his exact dates are unknown, he certainly flourished about the middle of the fifth century. His treatise *On the Nature of Man*, sometimes found under Gregory of Nyssa's name, contains the first—and for centuries the only—Christian approach to anthropology, and it was translated into Latin, probably in the eleventh or twelfth century.

With the highly cultured theologian Leontius of Byzantium (first half of the sixth century) a new development appears. His all-embracing polemical treatise, *Against the Nestorians and Eutychians*, reveals an intimate knowledge of Aristotelian logic in its method of presentation, and resembles the work of the early schoolmen in the West. The treatise *De Sectis* attacking monophysitism and written between 547 and 553 is by Theodore from the monastery of Raithu (on the Red Sea) and not Leontius as was formerly supposed.

The problem of monophysitism, which was assuming increasing political as well as religious significance in the sixth century, called forth an imperial theologian, in the person of Justinian I. His unceasing activity for the welfare of the Empire included a series of theological pronouncements which dealt in some detail with the doctrinal problems of monophysitism and Origenism discussed at the Fifth General Council (553). His theological writings deserve more serious consideration than they have received. It is, however, just possible that the real author of these works may be Bishop Theodore Ascidas who was living at the imperial court in Constantinople.

In the sixth century biblical exegesis began to lose its originality and adopted the method of catenae, which relied on traditional interpretations. This method consisted in glossing a given passage from the Bible with a set of relevant comments taken from the early Fathers. Procopius of Gaza (c. 465–c. 538), the head of the famous rhetorical school of Gaza, began by using this method of disjointed catenae taken from older commentaries, though he did afterwards produce theological exegesis of a more independent and coherent nature, as well as secular works. And individuality is certainly found in the unique *Christian Topography* of the Alexandrian merchant Cosmas Indicopleustes. In describing his distant travels to the East, including Ethiopia and Ceylon, he tried to show that the earth was an oblong disk with the firmament arching over it like a bell-jar. The ultimate aim of his cosmography was to establish principles of physical geography which were in harmony with the Bible.

The commentary on the Revelation of St John by the philosopher and rhetorician Oecumenius (first half of the sixth century) is interesting because the Eastern Church did not include the Revelation among the canonical books until much later. This particular commentary used to be wrongly attributed to the tenth-century Bishop Oecumenius of Trikka in Thessaly. Andrew, Bishop of Caesarea in Cappadocia from 563 to 614, wrote another commentary on the Revelation which was much used and was expanded by Arethas (*c.* 895), a later occupant of that same see.

In the seventh century the monothelete heresy aroused violent disputes. The most prominent exponent of the doctrine of the two wills in Christ was Sophronius of Damascus (634 Patriarch of Jerusalem, died 638). Both rhetorician and theologian, he drew up the famous synodal pronouncement on this subject, and left a number of sermons; he also made his mark as a hagiographer and poet. A still more important theologian was Maximus the Confessor (Homologetes) of Constantinople (*c.* 580–662) and Sophronius' one-time travelling companion. He started as imperial secretary sometime before 613/14 and then took an active part in the monothelete controversy, which involved him in extensive journeys across Palestine, to Alexandria and to Rome. Eventually he was brought before an imperial court in Constantinople (662) and banished to Lazica in Colchis, where he ended his days. Maximus was an outstanding theologian and well trained in philosophical technique, and it was his reasoned arguments which presented the decisive theological refutation of the monothelete heresy, though he is however sometimes turgid in style and difficult to follow. His most important writings are the dogmatic and exegetical *Quaestiones ad Thalassium* and eleven dogmatic and polemical discourses and letters. His *Gnostic Centuries* belong to the literature of ascetical and mystical writings. Anastasius of Sinai is a kindred spirit (died shortly after 700); his *Guide* ('Οδηγός) is intended as an introduction to the refutation of heresies. He is also the author of an allegorical exposition of the *Hexaemeron* and may have compiled the so-called *Doctrina Patrum*, a comprehensive anthology to be used in the battle against monotheletism.

During the eighth century Byzantine theologians had to forge weapons against the obstinate and dangerous attack launched by the iconoclasts against icons, which were widely used in Byzantium as objects of popular piety. The Patriarch Germanus of Constantinople (died 733) was one who wrote in their defence and his opposition to imperial iconoclasm cost him his bishopric in 730. But the most important iconophile was John of Damascus (*c.* 675–?749), one of the great theologians of the Orthodox Church. He came of a distinguished Christian family who held high office under the Muslims in Damascus, and some time before 726 he entered the monastery of St Sabas near Jerusalem together with his adopted brother Cosmas. He is the last Orthodox theologian with a really comprehensive range of interest, for he was dogmatist, exegetist, ecclesiastical historian, hagiographer and hymnographer all at the same time and with equal success. His three *Discourses against those who reject the holy icons* are directed against the iconoclast Emperor Constantine V. But his most important work is his *Fount of Knowledge* (Πηγὴ γνώσεως, written after 742) which combines an introduction on the definition of terms in accordance with the principles of Aristotelian logic and an analysis of all known heresies with a hundred chapters called *De fide orthodoxa*, which consists of a comprehensive and lucid summary of Christian doctrine. There are also many polemical writings and other works which belong here. John's work was distinguished not only by its content but by its style of lucid simplicity and flawless Attic purity. A translation of the *Fount of Knowledge* appeared in the West as early as the twelfth century and was known to Peter Lombard and Thomas Aquinas.

During the second phase of the iconoclast controversy Nicephorus, Patriarch of Constantinople (806–15), and Theodore, abbot of the Studite monastery in Constantinople, were the most prominent of the polemical writers who supported the images. But the outstanding figure of the Eastern Church in the ninth century was Photius, a man of spiritual gifts and wide culture, who in 858 was raised to the Patriarchate of Constantinople by the liberal-minded Caesar Bardas. It is true that his importance for Church history and the development of humanism is greater than for dogmatics and exegesis. But his *Amphilochia*, which consists mainly of exegetical, theological and dogmatic questions and answers addressed to Bishop Amphilochius of Cyzicus, reveals him as a theologian of note, even though he takes considerable portions of his work word for word from his sources. It is now established that Photius also wrote various biblical commentaries. He is famous in the history of Christendom for his work *De Spiritus Sancti Mystagogia* which, though written after his reconciliation with the Pope, is directed against Latin doctrine on the procession of the Holy Ghost (the *filioque* controversy). He is also known for his work *On the Manichaeans* (against the sect of Paulicians in Asia Minor).

The statesman and philosopher Michael Psellus (1018–*c.* 1092) resembles Photius in his wide range of interest. He left theological commentaries and a theological didactic poem written for his pupil, the Emperor Michael VII, but his real literary significance lies in other fields. One of his contemporaries, Nicetas Stethatus, was responsible for a treatise on such teaching of the Latins as was condemned by the Eastern Church; this work was in readiness for the papal delegation which arrived in Constantinople in 1054, and was marked by the moderation of its tone. Archbishop Theophylact of Ochrida, who became Bishop of Bulgaria sometime before 1078, produced a number of biblical commentaries, based almost entirely on earlier patristic works. Euthymius Zigabenus was commissioned by the Emperor Alexius I (1081–1118), who was indefatigable in his war on heresies, to write a *Panoply* (Πανοπλία δογματική) against the various sects. Euthymius also produced works of exegesis.

In Manuel I Comnenus' reign a number of theological writers produced works connected with his plans (in part political) for promoting union with the churches in schism. Theorianus brought out two reports on the negotiations for union which he had had with the Armenians in 1170 and 1172, at the Emperor's request. Nicetas of Maronea, Archbishop of Thessalonica, wrote six dialogues on the Procession of the Holy Ghost, inclining towards the Latin doctrine on this point. Closely connected with the controversy aroused by Manuel's politico-ecclesiastical activities is the *Armoury* ('Οπλοθήκη) compiled on his suggestion by Andronicus Camaterus in about 1170/5; it is an arsenal of texts refuting the arguments of the Armenians and the Latins. The most comprehensive of these anthologies is the *Treasury of Orthodoxy* (Θησαυρὸς τῆς 'Ορθοδοξίας) compiled by the historian Nicetas Choniates (*c.* middle of twelfth century–1213), only part of which has been published.

The centuries following the Latin conquest of 1204 produced dogmatics and exegesis of an almost exclusively traditional nature, consisting of polemic attacking Latin doctrine and based not on dialectical disputation but on a constant repetition of the *chrēseis* of the early Fathers. There were also some theologians who were favourably inclined towards Latin doctrine and the union of the churches. One of these, also well known for his writings on philosophical subjects, was Nicephorus Blemmydes (*c.* 1197–*c.* 1272), the tutor of the Emperor Theodore II Lascaris. His imperial pupil (reigned 1254–8), who always had a strong interest in theological problems and even ascended the pulpit on occasion, wrote a polemic attacking the Latins. Later Michael VIII Palaeologus attempted to heal the schism between Rome and Constantinople, and his nominee to the Patriarchate, John Beccus (1275–82, died 1293), produced a number of works in defence of Latin doctrine. In so doing he aroused the opposition of Gregory of Cyprus, a theologian of inferior talent who succeeded him as Patriarch in 1283.

In the second half of the thirteenth century there is the first indication of Byzantine interest in western theological works with the translation of the Latin *De consolatione philosophiae* of Boethius by Maximus Planudes (before 1265–*c.* 1310), primarily a philologist but also a scholar of versatile talent.

The great theological controversy of the fourteenth century was provided by the dispute over hesychasm which concerned the 'uncreated' light of Mt Tabor and the extent to which the Godhead could be apprehended.[1] The main defender of orthodox teaching was Gregory Palamas (died in 1359), a monk from Mt Athos, who was consecrated Archbishop of Thessalonica in 1347 but was at first unable to take up residence owing to fierce local opposition. His works set out the theological implications of hesychast doctrine, which had already been attacked by Barlaam, a monk from Calabria well versed in western scholastic method. Meanwhile Barlaam and his Greek follower Acindynus were anathematised at the Synods of 1347 and 1351 convened by the Emperor John VI Cantacuzenus, whose interest in the case was political as well as theological. The Synods also condemned the gifted fourteenth-century scholar Nicephorus Gregoras, who wrote ten polemical discourses against the hesychasts and who constantly attacked their doctrinal views throughout his *History*. John VI Cantacuzenus, who abdicated in 1354, retired to Mt Athos as the monk Joasaph and himself composed several theological discourses, one of which attacked Islam. His son, the co-Emperor Matthew Cantacuzenus, also tried his hand at exegesis. Their outlook was characteristic of the extent to which Byzantine intellectual life during these final troubled years of the Empire was dominated by highly intricate theological problems.

The attacks on Barlaam, Acindynus and Nicephorus Gregoras were usually combined with a general attack on the Latins. In particular Patriarch Philotheus (1353–5 and 1364–76) was moved to write a lengthy polemical discourse against Nicephorus Gregoras. He also left a collection of sermons which was widely used. Increasing interest in the Latin world is another feature of this later period and is reflected in Demetrius Cydones' activities (*c.* 1324–1397/8). He was a sincere advocate of union, a man of wide culture with a knowledge of Latin and a familiarity with the scholastic theology of the West, who was frequently employed by the Emperor Manuel II in negotiating with the Curia. He composed several polemical works in favour of the Latin Church and is particularly remarkable for his translation

[1] See also above, ch. XXVI, pp. 197 ff.

into Greek of considerable portions of Thomas Aquinas' *Summa Theologica*.

The remaining dogmatists of the fourteenth and fifteenth centuries are of little special interest. The increasing prolixity of their works is matched by a corresponding poverty of thought. But the following deserve mention: Nilus Cabasilas (died 1363) with his polemical works directed against Barlaam and Acindynus and against the Latins; Manuel Calecas, grammarian, rhetorician and theologian (died 1410 as a Dominican on the island of Mytilene) whose systematic statement of Byzantine dogma shows scholastic influences; the Emperor Manuel II Palaeologus (1391–1425), author of a great defence of Christianity against Islam in dialogue form; Cardinal Bessarion of Trebizond (*c.* 1395–1472), famous for his activities in church politics and his work for the cause of humanism, who when Archbishop of Nicaea attended the Council of Florence and played a prominent role in achieving the union of the Church in 1439 by refuting his chief theological opponent, the metropolitan Mark Eugenicus of Ephesus, in his *Capita syllogistica*; and finally George Scholarius, Patriarch of Constantinople (1453–died after 1464), whose polemical writings show his transformation from a supporter into an opponent of union. However extensive the output of these later dogmatic, exegetical and homiletic writers, they did not provide a scholarly approach to theological problems and in both language and form they often lack literary interest and originality.

(b) Ethics, asceticism and mysticism

Christian asceticism with its complete renunciation of the world and Christian mysticism with its quest for direct and incommunicable union with God during this earthly life undoubtedly found their true home in Byzantium. And it was here in an atmosphere of contrasts, ranging from fervent exaltation to deep pessimism expressed in an uncompromising rejection of this world, that the earliest writings were produced in praise of these ideals and offering guidance as to how best they could be attained. There are fifty homilies which have been attributed to Macarius the Great of Egypt (*c.* 300–*c.* 390) and have given him the reputation of the first Greek mystic, though they are in fact from the pen of the Massalian Symeon of Mesopotamia who was condemned at the Council of Ephesus (431). As so often happens in the history of Greek patristics, writings which contemporaries judged significant—and justifiably so—took refuge behind an orthodox name and were thus preserved. The attribution of these works to Macarius, clearly not a literary man, may be due to the fact that his disciple in his desert retreat was Evagrius Ponticus (346–99), a monk surprisingly active in the literary field, the author of the *Sentences*, a set of directions for both educated and uneducated monks. Evagrius' own writings are preserved almost entirely in Syriac and Armenian, because he himself was condemned as a heretic in 553.

Of supreme importance for the development of monastic life in Eastern Christendom are the ascetical writings of the fourth-century Cappadocian father St Basil the Great. The *Longer* and *Shorter Rules* stressed the coenobitic, as distinct from the eremitic, way of life, and emphasised the place of the monastery in the ordinary everyday world in contrast to the solitary hermit living in the desert.

The three important fifth-century theorists of asceticism are: Nilus of Ancyra (died *c.* 430), a disciple of John Chrysostom and a man of great culture, who has left a series of ascetical and edifying writings together with one thousand and sixty-one epistles (not all of these works are genuine); his contemporary, Mark the Hermit (died after 430), who wrote treatises of similar content; and Diadochus of Photike in Epirus (known to be Bishop of Photike in 457), who wrote the so-called *Centum capita de perfectione spirituali* which influenced the development of mysticism and asceticism. More significant still was the unknown author of the four treatises *On the Divine Names, On the Celestial Hierarchy, On the Ecclesiastical Hierarchy* and *On Mystical Theology*, probably written in the late fifth or early sixth century. Wishing to claim apostolic authority for his views he took the name of Dionysius the Areopagite, one of St Paul's followers. He is usually referred to as the Pseudo-Dionysius. In an individual and somewhat artificial style he sets out a system based on Plotinus and on passages from Proclus (see below, p. 244) which he sometimes reproduces word for word. He held that God the One illuminated the whole universe which was arranged hierarchically, the ecclesiastical order on earth being a reflection of the celestial hierarchy in heaven, and that ultimately, after passing through various stages, the soul would find its unity with him. The author's assumption of Dionysius' name passed unquestioned and his works were translated into Latin during the ninth century by John Scotus Erigena and the abbot Hilduin, and by reason of their apparent apostolic authority they exerted an immense influence on philosophical, theological, mystical and liturgical developments in East and West alike. Another writer similar in outlook to the Pseudo-Dionysius is John Climacus (before 579–*c.* 649), a monk from Mt Sinai. He wrote the very widely used *Scala Paradisi* (Κλῖμαξ θείας ἀνόδου) which owes a good deal of its success to its more popular approach. It sets out the various stages whereby the ascetic may achieve union with God.

A number of works by Maximus the Confessor (Homologetes) should be included here; his *Mystagogy*, a symbolic interpretation of the liturgy, and his *Gnostic Centuries* made their own special contribution to ascetical and mystical literature. The *Sacra Parallela*, an important collection of scriptural and patristic passages predominantly ascetical and ethical in tone, is usually attributed (probably with justification) to John of Damascus. The *Magna* and *Parva Catechesis* by Theodore the Studite (759–826) is a collection of fine and moving addresses which the abbot delivered at regular intervals to his monks.

Quite a different spirit characterises the work of Symeon, abbot of the monastery of St Mamas in Constantinople, and it is significant that his own individual type of piety necessitated his early departure from the Studite house. He is known as Symeon the Young, the Theologian (c. 949–1022), and is usually regarded as the greatest Byzantine mystic. His works are only published in part. His Orations and particularly his *Loves of the Divine Hymns* (written in accentual verse) reflect his heartfelt adoration of the Creator of the universe. It is possible to see in his writings traces of pantheism, and it may have been partly this as well as the extreme individuality of his devotional life which caused offence in the official Church, so that he ended his days in voluntary exile. His biography was written by his faithful disciple Nicetas Stethatus, who himself left *Capita* on asceticism and ethics.

Of the later mystics three deserve especial mention. First comes the Metropolitan Theoleptus of Philadelphia (died c. 1324–5), spiritual father to Irene, widow of the Despot John Palaeologus, who took the veil after her husband's death. His letters to Irene and other edifying works bear witness to his deep piety and are not devoid of literary value. The last great Byzantine mystic is however Nicholas Cabasilas (1322/3–c. 1380), whose works *On Life in Christ* and *Explanation of the Divine Liturgy* are reminiscent of Thomas à Kempis. Nicholas, a nephew of Archbishop Nilus of Thessalonica (despite a widespread belief to the contrary Nicholas himself never held this office), was a follower of Gregory Palamas and an opponent of the Latin point of view in contemporary controversies. The long line of these great exponents of Byzantine mysticism ends with Symeon, Archbishop of Thessalonica (1410–29), and his exposition of the teaching of the Orthodox Church with special reference to the mystical significance of its liturgy.

(c) *Hagiography*

It was a genuine love of story-telling as well as a delight in miracles and the need to edify that produced the extensive and lively collection of Lives of the Saints which is one of the most characteristic achievements of Byzantine religious literature. Unfortunately, many of these no longer exist in their original homely and popular form. In the course of the literary movement under the Emperor Constantine VII Porphyrogenitus (913–59) many of these stories were rewritten by Symeon Metaphrastes, who is identical with Symeon Magister Logothetes the chronographer (see below, p. 235), in a form more in keeping with the dictates of classicism (hence his name of Metaphrastes); the original vernacular texts were thus consigned to oblivion. Even so a considerable number of these folk-tales with all their pious fantasy have been preserved.

The earliest examples of actual hagiography (the acts of the martyrs mostly belong to the period before the fourth century) were the biographies of monks. The model for these was the life of the hermit Antony by St Athanasius. A similar work is a collection of lives of monks by Palladius (died before 431) known as the *Historia Lausiaca* (Λαυσιακόν); it was immediately translated into Latin, as was the *Historia Monachorum in Aegypto* by Timothy, Archdeacon of Alexandria. These works also exerted great influence in the West. The lives and sayings of the monks who had retired into the desert to gain through their strivings special *charismata* or gifts of the Holy Spirit were of immense interest to contemporary readers. As gifted a theologian as Theodoret of Cyrus thought for instance that such men were well worth his attention, as he showed in his *History of the Love of God* which dealt with the lives of thirty famous ascetics. Similarly, Gregory of Nyssa in a delicate portrait of noble womanhood traced the likeness of his sister Macrina the Younger who had led a devout life as a nun. Cyril of Scythopolis, who finally became a monk in the monastery of St Sabas near Jerusalem (c. 514–c. 557), has left a complete and detailed series of biographies in his lives of Sabas the founder of the house and of other Palestinian monks. His presentation, though simple, possesses some linguistic merit and is also important as a historical source. The work of John Moschus (c. 550–619), a widely travelled monk, has a purely devotional aim, being a collection of edifying stories of monks, known as the *Pratum Spirituale*. In complete contrast to his simple, popular style is the writing of his friend and companion Sophronius (whose identity with the Patriarch Sophronius of Jerusalem (see above, p. 217) is dubious). His *Lives of John and Cyrus* and his *Mary the*

Egyptian are presented in a highly rhetorical style and somewhat pedantically rhythmical prose. Particular mention must also be made of Leontius, Bishop of Neapolis in Cyprus (*c.* 590–668), who wrote in the vernacular a most attractive and animated life of the Patriarch John the Almsgiver of Alexandria (611–19); he also wrote the life of Symeon Salus, the prototype of those who became 'fools for Christ's sake'.

The great days of hagiography were from the eighth to the tenth centuries, partly because the iconoclastic controversy provided special opportunities of paying tribute to the new martyrs and witnesses to the faith. Such were—to take only a few instances—the lives of Theodore the Studite, of the chronographer Theophanes the Confessor (Homologetes), of St Stephen the Younger and of St Gregory Decapolites, all of which are also important sources for the cultural life of the period. Special mention in this respect should also be made of the Life of St Philaretus (eighth century), those of the Holy Patriarch Tarasius (eighth century) and of the Holy Patriarch Nicephorus (ninth century) (both written by Ignatius the Deacon); the life of the Holy Patriarch Ignatius (ninth century; by Nicetas David of Paphlagonia), of the Holy Patriarch Euthymius (tenth century), of St Nicon Metanoite, the Apostle of the Peloponnese (tenth century), and of St Meletius the Younger (1035–1105). In the eleventh and twelfth centuries the fervour of religious life in Greek Calabria evoked a fresh flowering of hagiography with the lives of St Nilus of Rossano, founder of Grottaferrata, and other devout monks of these regions.

Apart from these, really creative hagiography comes to an end at this period. *Vitae Sanctorum* were produced by later writers such as George Acropolites and Patriarch Gregory of Cyprus in the thirteenth century, Nicephorus Chumnus and others, like Constantine Acropolites, known as the Second Metaphrastes (the son of the historian), and also Nicephorus Gregoras in the fourteenth century, but they are on the whole diffuse rhetorical exercises, often overloaded with theological erudition, and far removed from the spirit of earlier Byzantine hagiography.

(d) Ecclesiastical history

Once again the pioneer was Eusebius, the father of ecclesiastical historians (*c.* 263–*c.* 340). His *Ecclesiastical History* in ten books described the fortunes of the Church from her foundation up to Constantine the Great's victory over Licinius. This work was apologetical in tone in that its main concern was to prove the divine institution of the Christian Church. In the same way his championship of Christianity is clearly reflected in his orations on the consecration of the Church of the Holy Sepulchre at Jerusalem, and on the Tricennalia of the Emperor Constantine (both in 335). His *Chronicle*, a concise survey of the important events in the history of the empires of the ancient world from Abraham (2016/15 B.C.) to Roman times, consists mainly of parallel chronological tables and is without literary value.

Eusebius made a deep impression on his contemporaries and later generations, and his *Ecclesiastical History* was continued, as in the works of Gelasius of Caesarea (d. 395), Philip of Side and the Arian-minded Philostorgius (both fifth century), though these are all now extant only in fragments or extracts. Socrates Scholasticus (that is, a lawyer) from Constantinople (*c.* 380–after 439) recounted the events between 305 and 439, but did not confine himself to ecclesiastical history. Soon afterwards Sozomen, writing between 439 and 450, continued Eusebius' account of church history from 324 to 439. He owed much of his material to Socrates, but his far superior style reveals his training in the school of rhetoric at Gaza. Theodoret of Cyrus, the great exegetist (*c.* 393–457/8), wrote in exile (449–50) another continuation of Eusebius covering the years 325–428, which, though differing from Socrates and Sozomen, drew on the same sources. Theodoret ranges himself on the side of orthodoxy, though at the expense of objectivity. A compilation of these three continuators of Eusebius was made in about 530 by Theodore Anagnostes (reader in St Sophia), entitled *Historia Tripartita*; he then continued the history of the Church with an independent account of the years 439–527. His work is no longer extant but it was freely utilised by the historian Theophanes (see below). Another sixth-century church historian is Zacharias of Mytilene, a lawyer trained at Gaza (died before 553), who covered the period 450–90. The Greek text is lost (Zacharias was a monophysite) but fragments are extant in Syriac. A highly trustworthy history of the Church from 431 to 594, the period of the Nestorian and monophysite controversies, was written by Evagrius Scholasticus (*c.* 536–*c.* 600), who also gives some account of secular history.

From this point onwards there is a gap of some centuries in Byzantine ecclesiastical historiography, and information about the history of the Orthodox Church has to be obtained from the secular historians, who do indeed give considerable space to it, while much can of course be found in other sources, such as the Lives of the saints. It is not until the fourteenth century that a historian is found deliberately writing purely ecclesiastical history. This was Nicephorus Callistus Xanthopulus (*c.* 1256–1317), but even so he did not realise his aim of writing the history of the Church right up to his own day, for he only reached the year 610. It is now recognised that he did not utilise sources unknown to us for his compilation but relied on an older work, now lost, which went up to 911.

II. SECULAR LITERATURE

(A) LITERATURE IN THE 'KATHAREUOUSA'

(a) Prose

(1) *Histories*

The histories produced by the Byzantines were of two kinds. On the one hand there was the pragmatic presentation of events in polished Attic style, generally known as a History (ἱστορία); on the other hand there was the Chronicle, that is, the popular presentation of world history which was regarded as providing the setting for the Christian Roman Empire, and which recorded in homely language a medley of victories and campaigns, earthquakes and comets.

First in the long line of Histories which—in contrast to the Chronicles—were regarded as literature by the Byzantines themselves may be mentioned the historical writings of Eunapius of Sardis (c. 345–420), a supporter of the Emperor Julian, who carried on the work of the third-century Dexippus. He also wrote biographies of sophists as a continuator of Philostratus. His historical writings dealing with the period 270–404 have been preserved in fragmentary form. His work was continued by Olympiodorus (fl. 412–21), another pagan writer, who covered the period 407–25 and whose style has some rhetorical merit. Next came Priscus of Panion (Thrace), who in 448 went on an embassy to Attila. Fragments of his history are extant, dealing with the period 433–72; he succeeded in his literary ambition of becoming an Attic sophist. We only have fragments of Malchus, a Christian who wrote a history from Constantine the Great up to 480. The first complete historical work we possess is by Zosimus (second half of the fifth century), a neoplatonist and anti-Christian. He aimed at writing a history of the Emperors, and from Diocletian onwards gives a detailed account, but he failed to get any farther than 410. His history, published posthumously, was meant to show that the political and cultural decline of his day was a punishment sent by the neglected pagan gods.

Hesychius Illustrius from Miletus was also probably a pagan. In the first thirty years of the sixth century he composed a work extending from the beginning of the world to about 520 called a 'Chronicle' but which by reason of its nature and style cannot be included among the popular productions under this name. His *Onomatologos* is of

special value both for its wealth of reliable information and still more
for the literary history it contains, and the great lexicons of succeeding generations were greatly indebted to it. It was also very fashionable at the time to write the history of a particular city or region, but
most works of this kind have disappeared and are known only by their
titles. The Emperor Justinian's policy of restoration may well have
induced the imperial official John Laurentius Lydus (*c.* 490–*c.* 565),
who was also a professor at the university of Constantinople, to
pursue his antiquarian investigations into imperial institutions and
their Roman origin. His book *De magistratibus* may perhaps be described as 'antiquities of the Roman State', but as he had an imperfect
acquaintance with Latin, his work contained many serious errors.

In complete contrast to John Lydus was the imposing figure of his
contemporary, Procopius of Caesarea in Palestine (end of the fifth
century–after 562/3). He accompanied the general Belisarius on his
military expeditions and so was an eyewitness of most of the events
he related. His historical work in eight books gives detailed accounts
of Justinian's wars against the Persians, the Vandals and the Goths,
as well as a survey of events up to 554. In a special work, *De
Aedificiis* (? 553–555), he praised the Emperor as the creator of numerous buildings of all kinds, from churches to aqueducts and fortifications. For many years scholars have disputed whether he was the
author of the so-called *Anecdota* ('Ανέκδοτα), also known as *Historia
arcana*; it is however now established beyond doubt that this libel on
Justinian, Theodora, and Belisarius and his wife was written by him.
He composed it about 550, presumably out of thwarted ambition, and
it was published only after his death. Procopius' forceful, if somewhat
complex, style found many imitators. Far more rhetorical and stiff
in manner was his continuator Agathias (*c.* 536–82), the rhetorician
and poet, whose work embraced the period 552–8. Menander Protector imitated Agathias' method of presentation as well as his way
of life, and continued his work for the period 558–82, but only
fragments have survived. The last of this series of historians with any
claim to literary merit was Theophylact Simocattes (fl. *c.* 610–40).
Even so his style is artificial and florid in the extreme, with a pedantic
observance of the laws governing the rhythm of sentence endings.
A native of Egypt, where the Asian style had long been practised, he
turned his attention to history and the natural sciences. He wrote
eight books on the history of the Emperor Maurice (582–602) and he
gives the impression of having no special historical interest but of
simply using the events described as an occasion for rhetorical fire-
works, so much so that Photius thought him lacking in good taste,
and his chronology is certainly misleading.

After the development of an excessively erudite and rhetorical historical style there followed a gap of more than three hundred years, although some information on the period 602–813 was supplied by the *Chronicle* of Theophanes (see below, p. 235) and the *Breviarium* of the Patriarch Nicephorus (see below, p. 235), a work without any stylistic pretensions. The revival of historical writing with some claim to literary merit was due to the efforts of the Emperor Constantine VII Porphyrogenitus (913–59). After being relegated to the background in 920 by the energetic admiral who became the co-Emperor Romanus I Lecapenus he occupied his time with more academic pursuits, and wrote the life of his grandfather Basil I (867–86). This was in the form of a rhetorical encomium and made up the fifth volume of the work known as *Theophanes Continuatus*. It was meant to strengthen the claims of the Macedonian dynasty established by Basil after murdering his benefactors and so gives an idealised picture of its founder. Constantine VII also wrote a handbook on imperial government for his son Romanus. This was the *De administrando imperio*, which laid down principles of diplomacy for use in dealing with the various countries and peoples either under Byzantine rule or on her frontiers. In so doing it provided valuable information on their history and their individual differences. It is a unique source-book for the early history of the Slavs and Turkic peoples and its statements are increasingly corroborated by the findings of modern archaeology. Another work, *De cerimoniis aulae Byzantinae*, aimed at describing and maintaining time-honoured ceremonial at the imperial court, and this is equally important as a historical source. Constantine's *De thematibus* is also of value; it describes the division of the Empire into themes, or provinces, with historical observations on this development. These last three works contain whole sections which consist of material taken straight from the Byzantine archives and are characterised by a simple straightforward style; in fact the *De cerimoniis* is one of the earliest sources for Byzantine vernacular. Constantine VII did outstanding service to Byzantine historiography when he commissioned a history of the period ending with Basil I which was to begin where Theophanes had left off (813). It took the form of an account of the reigns of individual Emperors (that is, Leo V, Michael II, Theophilus and Michael III) and these four sections on the Emperors by an unknown author formed the first four books of the history which now goes under the title of *Theophanes Continuatus*. Constantine also initiated an extensive encyclopedist movement with the declared aim of extracting what was most significant from the multiplicity of published works and preserving this for posterity. Within the framework of this vast undertaking there were six special headings allotted to history, for example, *De legationibus* which was to comprise all the most important information on embassies. Unfortunately, these excerpts only exist in a fragmentary form. Though they preserved much that would otherwise have been lost (including work by Byzantine historians such as Nonnosus or Menander Protector), by their very nature they contributed to the disappearance of many texts.

The *Basileiai* by Joseph Genesius (written between 945 and 959) was composed at the instigation of this same Emperor. His account runs parallel to the first four books of Theophanes Continuatus and utilises many of the same sources. Genesius was credulous, biased and uncritical, while his style is uneven and slipshod. There was an appendix to this work and to the first five books of Theophanes Continuatus which consisted of an account of the reigns of Leo VI, Constantine VII, Romanus I and Romanus II (to 961), i.e. 886–961. Traditionally known as the sixth and last volume of Theophanes Continuatus, it was the work of Theodore Daphnopates, a patrician and high dignitary under Romanus II (959–63); its simplicity of style and arrangement make it a fitting sequel to the first four volumes of the so-called Theophanes Continuatus.

In 904 the city of Thessalonica was captured and sacked by the terrible Arab corsair Leo of Tripolis. This devastating event was portrayed by the cleric John Cameniates, an account which is also of value for other aspects of the city's history.

The series of imperial histories was continued by Leo the Deacon (*c.* 950–? 992), who accompanied Basil II on his Bulgarian campaign. Though at times in somewhat mannered Greek, Leo's narrative is none the less reliable; it covers events from 959 to 975, and was not written until 992. It was later continued by the statesman, philosopher and historian Michael Psellus (1018–*c.* 1092). In his *Chronographia* he dealt with the years 976–1077, that is, almost to the end of the reign of his imperial pupil Michael VII Ducas. Michael Psellus wielded considerable political influence under several successive Emperors and was thus able to penetrate behind the scenes and to give in his *Chronographia* an inside picture of contemporary history. He writes in the current classical manner, but without exaggerated rhetoric. A more mannered, equally thorough and fairly objective account is found in the parallel history of the period 1034–79 by Michael Attaleiates, lawyer, hippodrome judge and patrician (died after 1079). The concluding period of Psellus' *Chronographia* was also covered by that part of the *History* of Nicephorus Bryennius which achieved completion. Nicephorus (*c.* 1062–1138) was a gifted general who married Anna Comnena the daughter of Alexius I in 1097. He desired to immortalise the deeds of his father-in-law the Emperor, but he got no further than the period before Alexius came to the throne, which however he most conscientiously described with the help of reliable sources. His aim was fulfilled by his wife who survived him (1083– after 1148); her *Alexiad*, a monograph on her father Alexius I, was completed in 1148. This work of filial piety, covering the period 1069– 1118, set out to extol the virtues of her father whom she adored and admired above all others. Anna Comnena had received an excellent education; her narrative is composed in the elegant style of the humanist and is enlivened by reference to and quotation from classical authors. She drew on a variety of sources but she was writing of events which occurred some years before and her memory was often at fault in matters of detail.

Another contemporary work which contains a good deal of valuable historical material for the eleventh century was the *Strategicon*, although it makes no claim to be a history; it was written by Cecaumenus (probably the general Cecaumenus Catacalon from Armenia) between 1071 and 1078 and its purpose was to give advice to his son on military and administrative careers with special reference to contemporary events. It is written in the learned language though it is often somewhat clumsy in expression.

John Cinnamus (*c.* 1143–1203), secretary to the Emperor Manuel I, who went with him on his military expeditions, wrote a history of the period 1118–76 which was more or less an account of John Comnenus and Manuel Comnenus. Cinnamus' work is distinguished by the reliability of its sources; its value is enhanced by its author's use of documentary material and marked objectivity. In it the Byzantine claim to world domination is energetically defended against the western Emperors. The style is an impeccable, if painstaking, imitation of classical models. It is possible that Cinnamus' history was still in draft form on his death, and that we only possess extracts from this. His continuator, Nicetas Choniates (*c.* 1150–1213), formerly wrongly known as Acominatus, was certainly familiar with it, despite his assertion that a history of the period covered by Cinnamus had not yet been attempted. Nicetas was an imperial official who finally became Grand Logothete, and in 1189 (during the passage of the crusaders' army) he was commander at Philippopolis. His account deals with the twelfth century reign by reign and it covers the period 1118–1206. The part known as *De Statuis* is usually regarded as a separate work and is a description of the art treasures destroyed by the Latins when they took Constantinople in 1204. Nicetas is uncritical, and though he does attempt to be objective he shows a marked, if understandable, hostility to the Latins. Another act of

Latin aggression, the capture of Thessalonica by the Normans in 1185, was recounted, again in a classical style, by the humanist Archbishop Eustathius (Metropolitan of Thessalonica 1175–*c.* 1193/4), who is also well known for his wide range of literary activity (see below, p. 247).

The period 1203–61, for the greater part of which the Byzantine Emperor was in exile at Nicaea, was recorded by George Acropolites (1217–82) after the recapture of Constantinople from the Latins. He had received a first-rate education at the imperial court in Nicaea and became adviser to the Emperor John Vatatzes and his son Theodore II Lascaris; he was also given considerable responsibility by Michael VIII Palaeologus. His position thus gave him access to the fullest information on the events he described. He writes a simple but correct Attic Greek; like Nicetas Choniates, he was a rhetorician and poet as well as a historian. His own and Nicetas' historical work form the chief basis of a compilation by the Metropolitan Theodore Scutariotes of Cyzicus, who composed a history of the world in about 1182. George Acropolites' work was continued by the important ecclesiastical and secular official George Pachymeres (1242–*c.* 1310), who dealt with the period 1261–1308. He inaugurates that phase of Byzantine historiography when an overwhelming interest in ecclesiastical and dogmatic controversy tends to reduce the factual content of the narrative to a minimum. The difficulty of reading Pachymeres is further increased by his pedantic atticising—even the names of the months appear in their older Attic form.

The fourteenth century saw bitter dynastic feuds in the house of Palaeologus and civil war provoked by John VI Cantacuzenus. The two outstanding historians of the period each wrote from a different point of view. Nicephorus Gregoras (*c.* 1295–1359/60) was probably the outstanding scholar of the later middle ages. His history from 1204 to 1359 contains vital information for the period 1209–1328 which is not found in either Acropolites or Pachymeres. Nicephorus was the pupil of Theodore Metochites, chancellor to Andronicus II, and was therefore in a position to have first-hand knowledge of the period preceding 1328. He calls his work *Roman History* and gives a particularly detailed account of the years 1320–59. He wrote in the monastery of Chora in Constantinople, where he was imprisoned from 1351 because of his opposition to the hesychasts, whom John VI Cantacuzenus supported. His concluding volumes, written throughout in a style reminiscent of Plato, give the fullest detail on the theological disputes. The opposite point of view is found in the memoirs of John Cantacuzenus himself, who as John VI was Emperor from 1347 to 1354, before retiring as the monk Joasaph to Mt Athos;

he died in the Peloponnese in 1383. He makes an honest attempt at objectivity but the work, written in a simple classical style reminiscent of Plato, inevitably becomes an apologia for his own political activities (1320–56), and he concentrates on foreign policy and military campaigns rather than on the acute domestic controversies.

During the second half of the fourteenth century Byzantine historical writing almost ceases. We are forced to rely on meagre records of a purely chronological nature (the so-called *Short Chronicles* or cursory entries in manuscripts of the period), and on a wealth of correspondence. A few facts on this period can however be gleaned from the history by Ducas of Phocaea (*c*. 1400–*c*. 1470), secretary to the Gattilusi on Lesbos, but he is mainly concerned with the history of the Turks and only writes in any detail on the period after 1389. His work, which is also extant in a contemporary Italian translation, extends to 1462. Ducas possessed a sound classical education, and his knowledge of Italian and Turkish enabled him to give much valuable information. Another important source for the final half-century of the Byzantine Empire is George Sphrantzes (1401–*c*. 1478; hitherto erroneously called Phrantzes) of Corfu, who was the faithful supporter of Constantine XI, the last Byzantine Emperor, first in Mistra, then in Constantinople. The work in the learned language which has survived under his name is certainly not by him, but probably an expansion, and sometimes a distortion, of notes for the years 1401–77 which he set down in diary form and in the vernacular. The finished work is by Macarius Melissenus, Metropolitan of Monemvasia (died 1585), a pensioner of the King of Naples and of the Pope, who interpolated passages about his diocese and his family to impress his patrons.

The first Byzantine historian to recognise the Turkish authority as such was Laonicus Chalcocondyles (*c*. 1432–*c*. 1490). His history covers the years 1298–1463 and his style is a most painstaking imitation of his model, Thucydides. He certainly wrote with an eye to publication and his central theme is the origin and development of Turkish power. Critobulus of Imbros went much farther. He was the last Byzantine historian to use the learned language, and about 1470 he produced in the purest Attic Greek a history from the Turkish point of view which was virtually a panegyric of the great Turkish conqueror Muḥammad II.

During the later middle ages the separate Byzantine principalities also had their historians. A history of the Empire of Trebizond (1204–1426) was composed in a clumsy imitation of the classical style by Michael Panaretus of Trebizond (first half of the fifteenth century). Two monks, Comnenus and Proclus, wrote a history of the Despotate of Epirus (1328–1400) in an equally poor style which more nearly approached the vernacular. There is an account of the fate of Thessalonica, for long virtually independent as an 'imperial city', related by John Anagnostes, with the aid of numerous quotations from Homer and the Scriptures, telling of its capture by the Turks in 1430. Then John Cananus, writing in simple, almost popular Greek, describes the siege of Constantinople by the Ottoman Turks in 1422 and its subsequent relief, regarded as a miracle of the Mother of God.

(2) *Chronicles*

The chronicles, or more popular accounts, were usually written by priests or monks and were marked by their conscious attempt to justify Christianity. Their primary intent was to convince the reader that the Orthodox faith was divinely inspired and was specially manifested *sub specie temporis* in the Byzantine Empire (a fact clearly demonstrated by the course of world history). Thus they exercised very considerable political influence over the Byzantines, and in translation were also a powerful factor in moulding those countries which came under the influence of the Orthodox Church. They usually consisted of excerpts with no claim to any literary quality; a chronicler would take whatever he fancied from his predecessors, sometimes lifting whole passages at a time. The style of the chronicles was unpolished and never far from the vernacular; the compiler's aim was not a literary one but simply to tell a story which should ultimately serve to strengthen the reader's faith. These works of piety are nevertheless valuable historical sources, particularly for periods not covered by the ἱστορίαι.

Amongst the earliest Christian chronicles were those by Panodorus (fl. late fourth–early fifth century), and by Anianus (early fifth century), both now lost, which were modelled on Julius Africanus (third century). Then, in the sixth century, a highly successful Chronicle was written by John Malalas (*c.* 491–578), a Syrian rhetorician who may well be identical with the Patriarch John III Scholasticus (575–7). His work, published about 548 in eighteen books, stretches from the Creation to Justin II; seventeen books are monophysite, but the eighteenth, composed after 565, is orthodox dyophysite. It is a typical monastic chronicle, an undisciplined narrative without any pragmatic approach, interlarded with sensational accounts of extraordinary signs and wonders, teeming with gross inaccuracies, and in a slipshod style full of everyday expressions which made it readily intelligible to the people. This highly individual work has only survived in a mutilated form in a single manuscript (Oxon. Barocc. 128, XIIth century). Malalas' chronicle is one of a number which were translated into Old Slavonic and which, with other Byzantine works, exerted a powerful influence in the early development of the religious and political thought of the southern Slavs. John Malalas is not, as was long imagined, the same as John Antiocheus (early seventh century, after 610), whose chronicle is extant only in extracts of considerable length contained in later works, particularly in the collection of historical excerpts compiled by order of the Emperor Constantine VII Porphyrogenitus (see above, p. 229). These extracts under John Antiocheus' name fall into two groups and are clearly the work of two different authors (probably bearing the same name), one of whom produced a historical work in the literary language, the other a popular chronicle. The anonymous work known as *Chronicon Paschale* was written in Heraclius' reign; it originally went up to 629, though it is now extant only to 627. Its material is arranged chronologically, with dates calculated from the creation of the world (from now on typical of chronicle-writing). In the late seventh and early eighth centuries the Chronicle known as the *Epitome* was begun and was later continued up to 842. The work itself has not survived, but it was used extensively by the tenth-century group of chronicles produced by various authors such as Symeon Magister Logothetes (identical with Symeon Metaphrastes; see above, p. 224), Theodore Melitenus and Leo Grammaticus. It is sometimes found joined with the Continuation of George Monachus (see below, p. 236), and extending into the tenth and eleventh centuries.

We do however possess the *Chronicle* by George Syncellus (died after 810) who was the secretary of the Patriarch Tarasius. It is much concerned with problems of chronology, particularly with the underlying chronological relationship between the Creation, the Incarnation and the Resurrection (25 March). George Syncellus only brought his narrative up to 284. His work was taken up to 813 by his friend, the monk Theophanes the Confessor (d. 818), who wrote between 811 and 815 in his foundation, the monastery of Sigriane. This chronicle also arranges events schematically in chronological tables, and is written in a simple style for popular consumption. Both this work and the chronicle (the *Breviarium*) of Patriarch Nicephorus (Patriarch 806–15; died 829) are of first-rate importance because, using for long stretches at a time the same (unknown) sources, they provide the only continuous account of the seventh and eighth centuries (though Nicephorus only covers the period 602–769).

Apart from Theophanes, the historical work most widely read, and of the greatest importance in providing some conception of world history for the newly Christianised races, was the *Chronicle* of the monk George (Georgius Monachus or Hamartolus). This was a universal history from Adam to 842, in which the religious interest was particularly evident both in the construction of the work and in its interpretation of events. This chronicle was continued by various hands up to the eleventh century (and known as *Georgius Monachus Continuatus*); the continuation is sometimes found in manuscripts appended to the so-called *Epitome* (see above, p. 235) which also ended in 842.

The work known as *Theophanes Continuatus*, which stands midway between the history and the chronicle, was described above (see p. 229), and its only real connection with Theophanes is that it expressly continues where he left off (813). Another continuation of Theophanes is the *Historical Survey* from 811 to 1057 which bears the name of John Scylitzes, an officer of high rank (died towards the end of the eleventh century). His material is organised according to imperial reigns and, as the work relies on sources which have not survived elsewhere for the period after 961, it is of the greatest value for the history of the eleventh century. This chronicle was taken up to 1078 by an unknown writer (the so-called Scylitzes Continuatus); but this may well be an extract from Attaleiates (see above, p. 230). Scylitzes' work was used by George Cedrenus, probably an early twelfth-century monk. He compiled a world history based on Theophanes and other chronicles, and then for the period after 811 he used Scylitzes. His work has thus no independent authority.

Both in presentation of material and in style the historical manual (*Epitome historiarum*), written by the commander of the imperial bodyguard, John Zonaras (*c.* end of eleventh century–early twelfth century), stands on a considerably higher plane. Its scope is that of the chronicle for it goes from the Creation to 1118, but resembles the *historia* in its efforts at atticising. Its material is however used in a somewhat mechanical, often superficial, manner with occasional errors. Constantine Manasses, known for various poetical works (first half of the twelfth century), composed a *Chronicle* in 6,733 so-called 'political' verses (that is, lines of fifteen syllables). The poetical form of this work, and its continual emphasis on Manuel I Comnenus' revival of the Roman Empire, endeared it to a wide public. In 1340 the Bulgarian Tsar John Alexander even sponsored a Bulgarian version with illustrations.

Chronicles of the usual type continued to be written in the thirteenth century, and again some of them have preserved valuable information which has not survived elsewhere. For instance the work known as *Synopsis Sathas* ends with extracts from Nicetas Choniates and George Acropolites (under the name Scutariotes), but occasionally interpolated into this confused presentation of familiar texts is a certain amount of valuable original material from some otherwise unknown source. In about 1313 a writer named Ephraim composed another chronicle in verse which covers the period from Julius Caesar to 1261 and consists of 9,564 Byzantine twelve-syllabled lines. Here familiar texts have been skilfully put into verse by a mind steeped in the ancient classical authors, but there is little of independent value.

Far more lively, and outstandingly original, is the *Chronicle of the Morea* composed between 1325 and 1350 by an unknown Gasmul (that is, a Greek of Frankish origin). Written in decidedly demotic Greek, it gives an account of the Frankish rule in the Peloponnese from 1204 to 1292. The *Chronicle of Cyprus* was another piece of original work written in the Cyprian dialect by Leontius Machairas, secretary to King Janus of Cyprus. It describes the fortunes of the Lusignans in Cyprus from 1359 to 1432.

The fourteenth and fifteenth centuries did not show the same interest in producing world histories which had been so attractively provided in earlier ages for humbler folk and monastic circles. The difficult days in which men then lived were indeed more likely to move the devout to write *Threnoi*, lamentations, over humanity now suffering divine chastisement for its wickedness.

(3) *Geography. Warfare*

Byzantine literature is surprisingly lacking in geographical works. Questions of geography were usually discussed either in support of ecclesiastical teaching, or else for merely practical purposes, in which case the work hardly took a literary form. It was customary here, as in other Byzantine works, to lift material straight from a classical text and to incorporate it (not always very appropriately) into historical works. The Byzantine views on ethnography were particularly narrow. People from the Far East, the remote North or central Africa were all regarded as peculiar, as inferiors, as 'barbarians'. Their outlandish names were replaced by the corresponding names of antiquity in order to avoid offending the susceptibilities of ears used to the classical style. Races appeared under the names used by Herodotus, Xenophon or Dio Cassius to describe those tribes who had long ago occupied the territory in question; thus 'Scythian' varied in meaning in different authors and might signify Russian or Bulgarian or Rumanian or Caucasian. Descriptions of their appearance and customs also followed the accepted tradition of classical literature.

The most original Byzantine geographical work was the *Christian Topography* by Cosmas, the traveller to India (see above, p. 216), which contains interesting descriptions written in polished Greek. Apart from this work and from passages contained in historical writings already indicated (for example, Procopius, Constantine VII Porphyrogenitus, Nicephorus Gregoras), independent accounts of travels are rather rare. As examples of later Byzantine work one may mention Andrew Libadenus' description of his journey from Constantinople to Egypt and Palestine in the fourteenth century and Cananus Lascaris' record of his journey to Germany, Norway, Sweden and Iceland during the first half of the fifteenth century. In addition Byzantine literature contains geographical or topographical works of a practical nature. There were for instance lists of dioceses (known as *Ektheseis*) which were bare catalogues of names arranged in hierarchical importance. That by Hierocles (before 535) provided geographical information for Constantine VII Porphyrogenitus' *De thematibus*. There were also guide-books, pilgrims' itineraries and *portulani*, that is, guides to navigation. These last were usually written in a most colloquial style comprehensible only to a sailor. Sometimes topographical details are found incorporated into other works, mostly historical, by way of descriptive embellishment. The work known as *Patria Constantinopoleos* may however be regarded as a topographical account of Constantinople. It was once erroneously attributed to George Codinus (mid-fourteenth century), but was in fact composed in the tenth or at latest in the eleventh century. It is a compilation, drawing as a rule on reliable sources, and it describes the early foundation of the city, its monuments and buildings, freely interspersing facts with anecdotes of the guide-book variety.

Here mention must be made of the considerable achievement of the Byzantines in the field of military science.[1] They took over from the Romans (Arrian) their interest in a systematic scientific treatment of military tactics and were the only medieval Europeans to develop this. The treatise *Strategicon*, which went under the name of the Emperor Maurice (582–602) (Pseudo-Maurice or Urbicius), reveals in its references to military tactics the decided flair of the Byzantines for waging war, a flair evoked by the struggle against the various races of horsemen (Persian, Avar, Turkic) who erupted from Asia in the direction of Byzantium. This treatise was revised many times and it also appears under the names of the Emperors Leo VI (886–912) and Constantine VII Porphyrogenitus (913–59). An original contribution of the Byzantines to military literature is the manual providing an introduction to guerilla warfare (Περὶ παραδρομῆς πολέμου) ascribed to the Emperor Nicephorus Phocas (tenth century).

---

[1] See also above, ch. xx, pp. 42 ff. and below, ch. xxviii, pp. 303 ff.

(4) *Rhetoric and satire. Literature of an edifying nature*

Rhetoric has already been alluded to constantly in this chapter. Its treatment in a special section is justified in that the Byzantine regarded it not simply as an essential discipline but as a literary form of equal—or even superior—standing to poetry. One of the characteristics of Byzantine literature is that the functions of poetry and rhetoric are interchangeable. The modern sense of form finds this absurd, but it did enable a historical account or a sober description of events to be cast equally well in rhetorical verse or in poetic, stirring prose. A panegyric on the Emperor in a rhetorical style with long, complex rolling periods, and embroidered with mythological and biblical allusions, delighted the Byzantines quite as much as a well-turned epigram. The same predilection for rhetoric is seen in the correspondence of prominent Byzantines; almost every Church Father, historian, philosopher, rhetorician or poet of any importance has left us a comprehensive collection of letters almost always selected and arranged by the writer. Such letters have often been dismissed out of hand as mere verbiage. According to modern standards of literary criticism this view may perhaps be justified, but to the Byzantine every letter, however brief, sent by a friend, possibly along with some small gift, appeared as a present when rhetorical ornamentation was cherished as much as the exquisite chasing on a silver tankard. The Byzantine epistolary genre therefore deserves much closer attention than it has been given in the past.

One of the most important products of rhetoric, and indeed one with even wider scope, was oratory. During the fourth century the pagan rhetoricians of the older tradition were foremost in the field. Libanius of Antioch (314–c. 393), an orator of high reputation in cities throughout the Empire and a famous teacher of eloquence, has left a number of speeches of every class, 143 model specimens (προγυμνάσματα) as well as 1605 letters. He was a master of the Attic style for which he set the vogue. An occasional orator in equally great demand was his contemporary Himerius of Bithynia whose style was rather more Asian. Finally comes Themistius of Paphlagonia (c. 317–c. 388), a rhetorician of similar popularity who was also well versed in philosophy. These were admired and imitated by such disciples as the Emperor Julian (361–3) and also the Christian Fathers Gregory of Nazianzus, Gregory of Nyssa, Basil and John Chrysostom. Julian, himself a neoplatonist and rhetorician of considerable skill, holds a place in literature by his numerous speeches, satires, epistles and other rhetorical exercises. His attempt—the last in history—to annihilate Christianity and restore the pagan gods carried him to embrace the expedient of denying Christians any share in normal educational facilities, including of course philosophical and rhetorical training. But after his death they acquired complete mastery of these essential disciplines. From then onwards the Byzantine Church made constant use of this most persuasive art whose roots went back to the pagan sophistry of later classical times.

By the sixth century the famous school of rhetoric at Gaza was directed by Christians. Procopius of Gaza (died before 548) was head of this school and also an exegetist of considerable skill, and cultivated the purest Attic Greek in every type of speech; his pupil Choricius reached as high a degree of excellence as his master. They both observed the Byzantine ruling for periods, that is, the regulated sequence of stressed and unstressed syllables at the end of each clause.

In the centuries which followed there was scarcely any Byzantine author of repute who did not try his hand at one or two exercises of a rhetorical kind with an eye to literary renown. There are innumerable examples of this art, including many still unprinted: they include letters, *progymnasmata* (essays on fictitious, or sometimes grotesque, subjects), and speeches of every kind (imperial panegyrics, funeral orations, consolatory discourses). Some of the most prolific writers in this field were: Michael Psellus, Nicephorus Basilaces (mid-twelfth century), John Tzetzes (mid-twelfth century), Euthymius Malaces (late twelfth century), Eustathius of Thessalonica (late twelfth century), Emperor Theodore II Lascaris (mid-thirteenth century), Nicephorus Chumnus (thirteenth to fourteenth centuries; died 1327), Theodore Metochites (1260/1–1332), Theodore Hyrtacenus (thirteenth to fourteenth centuries), Demetrius Cydones (died 1397/8), and John Eugenicus of Trebizond (first half of fifteenth century). Particularly popular orations were those which a celebrated orator would occasionally deliver at Epiphany in the presence of the Emperor and his court, or funeral and consolatory discourses on the death of an eminent friend or relative.

Many important collections of letters have survived. The Emperor Julian and Libanius have already been mentioned; the three Cappadocians followed their example. St Basil left 365 letters to which one or two spurious ones were added, Gregory of Nyssa left twenty-five, and Gregory of Nazianzus 243, which rival his other compositions for polished elegance of thought and phrase. From Isidore of Pelusion we have no less than about 2000 letters, and from Synesius of Cyrene we have 156 including those written to friends and to Hypatia. Theodoret of Cyrus left 209 letters in Greek which are valuable not only as literature but for their historical information. Theophylact

Simocattes wrote numerous letters of varied content and they are as full of rhetorical subtleties as his historical work. Theodore the Studite's 550 epistles form a delightful addition to our knowledge of his attractive personality. After his day letters tend to be mere verbiage, indeed one may say they are almost entirely rhetoric. Often their Chinese puzzle of mythological, proverbial and biblical allusions is perplexing and even intolerable. So many comprehensive collections of correspondence have survived from the later Byzantine period that it is impossible to mention them all. Apart from those already noted, those writers whose letters are most valuable as historical sources are Procopius of Gaza (died before 548), Michael Psellus (1018–c. 1092), Theophylact, Archbishop of Ochrida (late eleventh century), Michael Choniates, Archbishop of Athens (died c. 1222), John Apocaucus, Metropolitan of Naupactus (died 1233), the Theodore II Lascaris (Emperor 1254–8), the learned Nicephorus Gregoras (c. 1295–1359/60), the diplomat Demetrius Cydones (c. 1324–1397/8), the theologian Manuel Calecas (died 1410) and the Manuel II Palaeologus (Emperor 1391–1425).

Anonymous satirical prose works also come under the heading of rhetoric. These are in the literary tradition of Lucian and they criticise contemporary conditions and personalities usually through the medium of dialogue. An unusual example of this kind of dialogue is the *Philopatris*, in which a Christian discusses with a pagan the gods of antiquity and holds them up to ridicule. But the second part of the dialogue reveals and criticises the ugly mood of the people against the Emperor Nicephorus II which ultimately led to his downfall in 969. The mid-twelfth-century dialogue the *Timarion* was also influenced by Lucian, and like the *Philopatris* is interlarded with classical quotations and allusions. In this work the main speaker Timarion describes the great festival and international fair of St Demetrius at Thessalonica; then follows the story of the journey to Hades which his soul was obliged to undertake on his way home to Constantinople. Here there is ample opportunity for satire, particularly against doctors. Later on there is a similar tale by Mazaris which can be assigned to the year 1414/15. This satirises the political, moral and social conditions of the day in open imitation of Lucian's *Necyomanteia*.

A more attractive type of Byzantine rhetorical writing is seen in the *Mirror for Princes*, which lays down a code of manners and morals intended for the sons of princes but to some extent applicable to any young man. There are various works of this kind, and they clearly reveal the Byzantine ideal of manhood. The classical model on which they are based is Isocrates' exhortation to Demonicus on the duties of a monarch. The earliest Byzantine *Mirror for Princes* was probably written during Justinian's reign by Agapetus. There are various other well-known examples: one was published under the name of the Emperor Basil I (867–86) although actually composed by a contemporary; then later Archbishop Theophylact of Bulgaria produced a treatise for Prince Constantine, son of Michael VII Ducas (1071–8), cast in a rather more ambitious form; and finally Nicephorus Blemmydes wrote the *Statue of an Emperor* ('Ανδριὰς βασιλικός) (*c.* 1250) for his pupil, later Theodore II Lascaris.

Besides these works intended for imperial princes there were other edifying writings of a popular kind, such as the story originating in India which Magister Symeon Seth translated into the Greek literary language in about 1080 at the request of Alexius Comnenus. This was one of a number of fables which reached Byzantium from India and later became popular romances known all the world over. It was the tale of the two jackals Calila and Dimna (in Greek they became Stephanites and Ichnelates), who instructed princes as to how men should behave. In Armenia about the same time another story of Indian origin about Siddhapati (Sindbad, in Greek Syntipas) was translated from Syrian into Greek. This particular tale was also exceedingly popular in the West as the tale of the seven wise men. On the advice of his tutor a king's son resolves to keep silence for seven days. His stepmother, whose advances he has repulsed (the Potiphar theme), makes use of this time to speak calumny of him to the king and have him condemned to death. But the seven wise men at court tell the king stories of woman's cunning until the prince's week of silence is over and he can reveal his stepmother's intrigues. Another popular oriental romance is the well-loved *Life of Aesop*, which usually prefaces his collection of fables; the Greek version is attributed to Maximus Planudes (see above, p. 220). The adventures it contains derive from the Hebrew Achikar story. This tale, like so many others, reached the Slavs by way of Byzantium.

The Romance of Barlaam and Joasaph was another well-known popular romance which came from India. It has no pretension to any rhetorical quality, but the skill and purity of its style give it considerable literary merit. It was originally a story about the Buddha but in its Christian form it tells of a king's son, in a completely pagan court, who was converted to Christianity by a hermit and who stood firm in the faith and finally became a monk in spite of determined opposition. This many-sided narrative contains not only parables, but provides a complete account of Christian faith and morals. The only Greek version now extant (there are Armenian and Georgian versions) was undoubtedly written by that great father of the Orthodox Church,

St John of Damascus.[1] The Greek story was translated into Latin as early as the eleventh century and had an immense circulation in the West.

(5) *Philosophy*

In Byzantium there was an intimate connection, both in the schools and university and in literary practice, between rhetoric and what was regarded as philosophy. After the establishment of Christianity conditions were not propitious for independent philosophical development divorced from doctrinal considerations. This was true in the West as well as in the East. The Christian revelation marked the term of all knowledge, and Christian faith and morals were so fully expounded by the early Fathers as to produce a body of doctrinal teaching which included both revealed truth and that which was ascertainable by human reason. And in formulating and expounding the central Christian dogmas, such as the nature of the Godhead or of Christ, they had incorporated into Christian thought the terminology of the earlier philosophers such as Plato and Aristotle and the Stoics. Anyone so misguided and presumptuous as to question this accepted teaching was anathematised and thus deprived of all influence in intellectual circles. Moreover, right up to the sixth century the Christian Fathers had had to wage a bitter war against pagan philosophy, which had absorbed much of Aristotelianism and Stoicism into a compact and unified neoplatonic system and was a formidable foe.

After Plotinus (third century), the last great pagan thinker and systematist, the neoplatonic system was further developed by his successors, the most important of whom were his pupil and editor Porphyry (died *c.* 303), author of the *Eisagoge* which was highly valued in the middle ages, Iamblichus (died *c.* 330), Proclus (410–85) and Damascius (died after 533). But their increasing emphasis on theurgy and their exaggeration of the dialectical method did much to lessen the attractiveness of their doctrine. The Emperor Julian's attempt to replace Christianity by neoplatonism as a universally accepted system was a failure. Meanwhile, in order to fight paganism and gnosticism, Christianity had been obliged to provide itself with a philosophical foundation. It had thus assimilated a good deal of neoplatonic thought, particularly in its formulation of the doctrine of the Logos (worked out by Origen, third century, and Gregory of Nyssa in the fourth century), and had paved the way for a conception of Christian revelation not as the contradiction but rather as the fulfilment of pagan philosophy. Meanwhile, the schools of philosophy

---

[1] [For other views see D. M. Lang, *Bull. School of Oriental and African Stud.*, xvii (1955), 306–25 and xx (1957), 389–407.]

in Athens and Alexandria continued to expound neoplatonic doctrine, though in Alexandria they had connections with the Christian catechetical school quite early on. Proclus of Athens composed various didactic works, including a commentary on Plato's *Timaeus*. He was not an original thinker, and is an important figure largely by reason of the potent influence which he exerted on the writings of the Pseudo-Dionysius Areopagites. The school at Alexandria numbered among its teachers Theon, Hypatia (Synesius' friend, murdered in 415) and John Philoponus (first three decades of the sixth century). The aim of philosophers in Alexandria was to demonstrate the compatibility of Aristotelianism and Platonism while laying the main emphasis on Aristotle. John Philoponus became a Christian in 520, but was later condemned as a monophysite by the Council of Constantinople in 680–1. His Aristotelian commentaries, of which seven are extant, inaugurated that long series of Christian commentaries on Aristotle which were to be the sum total of purely philosophical activity for years to come. The last representative of the Alexandrian school of philosophy, Stephanus, was appointed in 612 as professor at the University of Constantinople by the Emperor Heraclius, and he may be said to represent the final fusion of christianised Platonism and Orthodox theology. Leontius of Byzantium (*c.* 475–542/3), a profound thinker, decisively strengthened Orthodox theology by his skilful use of philosophical methods. With his usual sureness of touch and relentless vigour, he used the dialectical weapons forged in the school of philosophy in the battle against heresy, and may be regarded as the first Christian schoolman.

In the controversy with the Monotheletes, and particularly in the dispute over the doctrine of the soul, Maximus Confessor likewise stands out as a penetrating thinker of the Aristotelian school. He also did much to strengthen neoplatonic elements in Byzantine mysticism through his use of Pseudo-Dionysius the Areopagite. With John of Damascus (died 749?) came the end of one phase in the development of a Christian philosophy out of the various pagan schools of the Graeco-Roman world. In his *Fount of Knowledge* he created an entire ontology and system of logic deriving substantially from the Aristotelian tradition, and on this foundation he proceeded to build a system of Christian dogmatics. He thus produced the first real manual of Orthodoxy. The pressing need for the use of philosophical argument in refuting heresy, particularly the teaching of the iconoclasts, may well have impelled him to construct and publish this philosophical basis for the orthodox faith. He breaks no new ground, but summarises the work of his predecessors; his statement that he did not intend to add anything new was characteristic of the unswerving Byzantine faith in tradition which precluded any philosophical activity beyond the limits imposed by Christian dogma. Another factor which told against any such development was the spread of the monastic spirit which regarded pagan philosophy and its reliance on dialectic as inspired by the devil; in monastic eyes the true, and indeed the only, philosophy was the renunciation of the world. Moreover, after the settlement of the iconoclastic controversy there emerged little in the way of fresh heresies to be refuted by philosophical argument.

Even the re-establishment of the University of Constantinople by the liberal-minded Caesar Bardas and the activity of the Patriarch Photius did not stir up any philosophical revival but they did stimulate a humanist and literary movement with an erudite antiquarian bias. It was not until the middle of the eleventh century that the cause of philosophy found a vigorous and successful champion in Michael Psellus who taught philosophy in the reorganised University of Constantinople. He regarded Aristotle merely as a preliminary study to logic and physics, and he insisted on a study of Plotinus, Proclus and Plato as a preparation for metaphysics, the climax of the philosophical studies which would eventually lead to theology. He was accused of heresy because of his interest in Plato (in actual fact he was really more of a neoplatonist) but he was well able to refute the charge. He had a mind that ranged widely, touching on every conceivable branch of knowledge, yet his philosophical work showed little originality. Like all his predecessors he maintained that philosophical studies could only be justified as a preparation for theology with its immutable doctrine.

His successor in the chair of philosophy in Constantinople, John Italus, differed from him on this cardinal point. As his name showed, he had come over from Italy, where he had acquired a knowledge of scholasticism, which was then beginning to develop. His critical examination of many articles of faith led him to entertain doctrines such as metempsychosis and to expound heretical views on icons. He was thus brought into conflict with the ecclesiastical authorities and was excommunicated. This condemnation instigated by the orthodox fervour of Alexius I dealt the death-blow to any further philosophical progress in Byzantium. While the West saw a notable advance in scholastic philosophy, due in no small part to the basic principles passed on by Byzantium, in the East Roman Empire speculative philosophy—apart from a handful of isolated thinkers— was stilled for centuries. The humanist movement in the second half of the twelfth century was classical and literary in character rather than philosophical. In the middle of the thirteenth century the

theologian Nicephorus Blemmydes (*c.*1197–*c.*1272) produced a manual
on logic and physics which was popular both in the East and West,
but it was really only a skilful compilation containing nothing new.
This appears to be characteristic of the type of literature in the later
middle ages although more research still needs to be done in this
field. For instance, it is impossible to pass judgement on the comprehensive writings on philosophy by the historian Pachymeres
(1242–*c.*1310) until these are printed, though it is probable that they
followed the usual pattern. The philosophical encyclopaedia of Joseph
the Philosopher (*c.* 1330) is certainly a mere compilation. An exception to this seeming dearth of original philosophic thought is found in
the statesman Theodore Metochites (1260/1–1332). His *Miscellanea*,
a collection of widely varied essays, provide a critique of current
philosophical, political and social theories rather than a new philosophical approach; but they are original and shed a revealing light
on the intellectual life of Byzantium during Theodore's day. Metochites' pupil, the great encyclopaedist and historian Nicephorus
Gregoras, though called 'the philosopher' by his contemporaries only
deserved the name in its current meaning of 'scholar'. In the perpetual controversy in learned circles over the relative merits of Plato
and Aristotle Gregoras championed Plato, whom he sought to imitate
in his dialogue *Florentius*. It was Gregoras' doctrine of a universal
soul uniting heaven and earth which formed the core of George
Gemistus Plethon's teaching. This fifteenth-century scholar—perhaps
the last Byzantine philosopher—was a most ardent champion of
Plato. He even changed his name from Gemistus to the ancient
Plethon (which means exactly the same) so that it might resemble
Plato's. He taught philosophy at the court of the Despot of Mistra
in the Peloponnese and in 1438/9 accompanied the Emperor John VIII
and the Patriarch Joseph to the Councils of Ferrara and Florence.
An active but changeable mind, a fervent patriot as well as a political
and social reformer, this extraordinary writer at times foreshadowed
modern sociological conceptions. He was the first Greek philosopher
with the courage to criticise the whole body of Christian doctrine; like
Porphyry and Julian before him, he went so far as to demand the return
to the religion of the ancient Greeks, and while he was in Florence
persuaded Cosimo de Medici to found a Platonist Academy, thus
exerting an important influence on the history of ideas in the West.

(6) *Philology and grammar*

Byzantine preoccupation with philosophy and rhetoric carried with
it a great interest in classical Greek literature. The Byzantines thus
preserved much that the ancient world had discovered in the various

branches of knowledge and of technology, as well as handing down to posterity that classical culture which was based on these discoveries and was characterised by a brilliant literature. This was indeed one of Byzantium's greatest legacies to Europe. In contrast to the West where nearly all cultural activity went under for a time in the stress of the barbarian invasions, Byzantium, more securely defended, was well able to preserve its ancient Greek heritage, especially once the humanist element in Christianity had overcome those aspects of it which had been biased against intellectual activity.

Thus the educated Byzantine world gave a good deal of its time to the literature of ancient Greece, to textual emendation and commentaries and to the production of linguistic and other aids to its better understanding and appreciation. So strong was tradition that the best minds of Byzantium were constantly lavishing their time on absorbing this philological, exegetical and encyclopaedist work. One would hesitate to assert that such work necessarily precluded more original forms of activity; nor is there any proof that the Italian Renaissance came about as a result of activities of Greek humanists of the calibre of Maximus Planudes, Triclinius and Bessarion though they were certainly partly instrumental in preparing the way for it.

Philological textbooks and literary handbooks do not however constitute literature, and it must suffice to select one or two examples from the enormous number produced. Photius the great ninth-century Patriarch of Constantinople wrote a *Library* (also known as *Myriobiblon*) consisting of extracts from numerous secular and ecclesiastical authors he had read, most of them accompanied by penetrating judgements on their style. Such an approach broke new ground and remained unparalleled in Byzantine literature. John Tzetzes (born about 1110), a voracious reader gifted with an astonishing memory (occasionally at fault over details), has already been mentioned. He was enormously prolific, and indeed his mania for commentary extended not only to Homer, Hesiod and many other classics but even to his own erudite letters. The commentary on Homer by Archbishop Eustathius of Thessalonica (late twelfth century) is a discriminating work drawing on the best commentators of earlier centuries, with valuable additions of his own. It still forms the basis of modern commentaries. The fourteenth century produced scholars like Maximus Planudes, Manuel Moschopulus, Thomas Magister and Demetrius Triclinius in the field of textual criticism and commentaries on Homer, Pindar, Theocritus and the tragedians.

The urge which prompted the Byzantines to make collections, anthologies and commentaries, of which the most monumental was the massive *Excerpta* of Constantine VII Porphyrogenitus, also pro-

duced great dictionaries arranged alphabetically. These contained not
only linguistic (etymological) information but also factual and historical material, including excerpts from other collections. The most
important of these dictionaries is the tenth-century *Suda*. This is the
name of the actual work; previously scholars wrongly thought that
there was an author called Suidas. Another great lexicon dealing
principally with the etymological elucidation of lemmata is the
Etymologicum Magnum (a misnomer), which has much in common
with many other lexicons. The Byzantines took a special delight in
etymology, a fact probably connected with the belief that the name
of an object expressed its real nature, or that it was intimately connected with the essence of the object in both its genetic and logical
existence. Byzantine etymology lacked the most elementary knowledge of a scientific approach to the subject, though it would be
unfair to blame the Byzantines for this. Grammars were also indispensable for the teaching of the classics. The one by Dionysius
Thrax at the end of the second century remained in use in Byzantium
for many centuries. The canons by Theodosius of Alexandria (*c.* sixth
century) and the grammar by George Chocroboscus (between sixth
and tenth centuries) were also well used. The influence of Dionysius
Thrax was finally shaken off when the fourteenth-century humanists
introduced a new method of teaching languages which was particularly useful in Italy. This was the *Erotemata*, that is, teaching by
question and answer. This was the method taught by Manuel Chrysoloras, Theodore of Gaza and Demetrius Chalcocondyles, and it was
in this way that the western world learned its Greek in the fifteenth
and sixteenth centuries.

(b) Poetry in the 'Kathareuousa'

(1) *Poetry of an epic character: pseudo-drama, historical epics, the
ekphrasis, verse romances, didactic poetry.*

It has already been shown how the rhetorical and poetical forms
vied with each other when the Byzantine wished to give fitting expression to a lofty theme. Thus it came about in the field of church
poetry that some of the hymns known as *kontakia* were really sermons
slightly altered so that they fell into the metre of a hymn-tune. Still
more strange by modern standards is the Byzantines' lack of any
sense of what material is suited to poetic form. To us it argues a lack
of taste when Theodore Prodromus' undisguised begging is put before
the Emperor in verse, or when Michael Psellus produces for his
imperial pupil Michael VII a gloss on Latin legal terms in metre,
although none of this caused the Byzantines any embarrassment.

It has already been pointed out that one of the characteristics of Byzantine poetry is that it did not fall into the usual categories of drama, epic and lyric. Moreover, the close relationship between all forms of intellectual activity and the Christian religion did not encourage the portrayal of human beings as the victims of fate. The kind of situation found in Greek tragedy was frowned on by the Church. The development of the lyric was similarly hampered by the ascetic and other-worldly attitude implicit in the point of view of the Orthodox Church, which tended to regard nature as peopled by evil spirits, and earthly love as an instrument of the devil.

Thus the few works extant in what appears to be the dramatic form are really dialogues intended to be read, and were certainly never performed. They are: *Conversation between Adam and Eve and the Serpent* by Ignatius the Deacon (ninth century); a work called *Christus Patiens* (Χριστὸς Πάσχων; probably eleventh/twelfth century) which is a lament made up of lines clumsily put together from classical tragedy, chiefly Euripides, and erroneously attributed to Gregory of Nazianzus; and little sketches, *Dramatia*, by Theodore Prodromus (twelfth century) and Manuel Philes (fourteenth century). One possible explanation why Byzantium failed to develop a religious drama comparable to the western Miracle plays is that the people's craving for shows and pageantry was more than satisfied—in Constantinople at least by the splendid liturgical and court ceremonial which followed the Church's year and by the circus performances and races in the hippodrome which were closely connected with it. There is also ground for believing that the mime, half sketch, half operetta, which had supplanted tragedy and comedy during the later Roman Empire continued to persist underground in Byzantium throughout the middle ages. This kind of libretto was of course not written down— or at any rate none has survived.

Poetry in the *kathareuousa*, the only form of the language regarded as literary, is usually found in some kind of epic form, which was widely used for occasional verse. In the fourth and fifth centuries great popularity was enjoyed by 'historical' epics, thorough-going historical panegyrics extolling individual military expeditions by different Emperors. Stories of one's native city in epic form (*Patria*) were also popular. Only fragments of these are extant. Side by side with the new Christian poetry were over-subtle pagan poems which were not destined for a long life. In his *Dionysiaca* (c. 430–50) Nonnus of Panopolis revived the Dionysus myth in a massive epic in hexameters, full of the pathos of a world of dying gods. It is characteristic of this period that this same Nonnus also wrote a metrical paraphrase of St John's Gospel. As a final example by these later classicists there is the charming epic by Musaeus that tells of the unhappy love of Hero and Leander. From the technique of his verse the writer appears to be a disciple of Nonnus; the poem may well belong to the end of the fifth century.

Other writers were also influenced by Nonnus, particularly as regards his strict rules on the structure of the hexameter. Amongst these were two outstanding exponents of the independent descriptive epic or *ekphrasis*, Paul the Silentiary and John of Gaza. The former in 537 devoted exactly nine hundred hexameters to extolling the stupendous fabric of St Sophia built by Justinian; the latter devoted seven hundred hexameters to a picture of the world in the winter at Gaza, the seat of the famous school of rhetoric. Many years later, between 931 and 944, a descriptive poem on the Church of the Holy Apostles in Constantinople, also built by Justinian I, was written by an imperial official, Constantine of Rhodes. It consists of nine hundred and eighty-one Byzantine twelve-syllable iambic lines (this was a form of the classical trimeter based on the new metric rules and adapted to a stress accent). *Ekphraseis* (Ἐκφράσεις) in verse of a slighter kind, inspired by works of art, images of the saints and indeed almost every subject, can be found in the writings of practically any poet who coined an epigram. It was a literary genre with its roots far back in the classical period, and it survived throughout the middle ages.

Under the heading of 'historical' epic (more correctly historical encomium) there are weighty panegyrics by the deacon and chartophylax of St Sophia, George Pisides (first half of seventh century), on the victories won by Heraclius in his Persian campaigns (626). He wrote in the twelve-syllable metre which was from now on used for all Byzantine epic verse in the literary language. This was the metre employed by Theodosius the Deacon (first half of tenth century) for his panegyric on the expulsion of the Arabs from Crete by Nicephorus Phocas (962), and also by Constantine Manasses for his *World Chronicle* and for the description of his adventures when journeying as an ambassador to Syria (1160). There was also an astonishing crop of verse romances which suddenly sprang up towards the end of the twelfth century modelled on the romances of the third-century sophists. They were stories of adventure with unrestrained descriptions of love scenes, lovers' partings and lovers' meetings. The four romances of this kind came very close to one another in time and were the last example of such romances in the literary language; they were written by Constantine Manasses, Theodore Prodromus, Nicetas Eugenianus and Eustathius Macrembolites (who wrote in prose). The fact that they were written at this particular time is perhaps explained by the humanist movement that sprang up under Manuel I Comnenus (1143–80) when second- and third-century writers were used as rhetorical models for works often far removed from their prototypes in content and outlook.

This lack of taste was also responsible for a set of metrical compositions which strike us as being extremely odd verse, that is, didactic poetry, which was very common in Byzantine literature. Here the tradition that had grown up in the later Roman Empire was merely being continued. The poem written by Michael Psellus in order to teach legal terms has already been mentioned. The proverbial exponent of this genre is John Tzetzes (*c.* 1110–85) whose learned commentaries on a vast amount of ancient Greek poetry as well as other didactic works were written in verse. He even provided commentaries in verse to his own letters. Moral teaching in verse also enjoyed great popularity in Byzantium. The *Gnomic Stanzas* by Gregory of Nazianzus were widely known. The Patriarch Luke Chrysoberges of Constantinople (1157–1169/70) wrote a poem in support of asceticism, George Lapithes of Cyprus (fourteenth century) produced a lengthy piece of moralising verse. The vast allegorical didactic poem by Theodore Meliteniotes (second half of the fourteenth century) called *On Chastity* is of a more unusual nature. In this the lady Sophrosyne leads the poet through her kingdom, precisely as she does in contemporary allegorical poetry of the West; the many and varied descriptions introduced make the poem almost a kind of encyclopaedia in verse.

(2) *Poetry of lyrical character: epigrams, threnodies.*

The Byzantines may have failed to produce real lyrics in the *kathareuousa*, but they did achieve a good deal in a poetic form half-way between epic and lyric—namely, the epigram. Throughout the centuries the Greeks had retained their gift of seizing on a sharp antithesis and crystallising it in one, or more, couplets. It might serve as the elegant accompaniment of some gift, or as an inscription on a building or other work of art, or indeed as a delicate means of flattery, for wedding greetings, condolences or even for invective. The barbed wit grew increasingly blunt through the centuries, the underlying conception more and more objective and less 'lyrical' and the form began to lose its exquisite artistry. These miniature works of art gave enormous pleasure to the Byzantines as is demonstrated by their great anthologies of epigrams. One of the best known of these was the *Anthologia Palatina*, a re-edition—and the only surviving one—of an anthology composed by Constantine Cephalas in the ninth century from older collections and divided into books according to subject.

Together with many epigrams from the Hellenistic and Late Roman periods, it includes work by such Byzantine epigrammatists as Proclus of Athens (410–85), Palladas (end of the fourth century), Claudian (fifth century), Cyrus of Panopolis (mid-fifth century), Christopher of Coptus (end of fifth to beginning of sixth centuries), Agathias (sixth century), Paul the Silentiary (sixth century), George Pisides (seventh century) and Ignatius the Deacon (ninth century). Then in 1301 Maximus Planudes compiled a new collection, the *Anthologia Planudea*, on the basis of Cephalas' collection, cutting out a good deal but also adding several hundred poems.

There is scarcely a single Byzantine poet who did not try his hand at epigrams. Indeed one can say that their short 'lyrical' pieces almost all bear an epigrammatical character. This form was used even in monastic circles. The ninth-century Theodore, abbot of the Studite house in Constantinople, wrote a cycle of epigrams about monastic life and laid down in elegant verse the duties of each of his brethren, even including the doorkeeper. John Cyriotes (died after ?969), surnamed Geometres because he had been particularly interested in surveying, a science highly regarded in Byzantium, wrote some of the finest medieval epigrams. Other poets of this kind are Christopher of Mytilene (*c.* 1000–1050) who has left a number of pleasant satirical pieces, John Mauropous who taught philosophy about 1045 in the reorganised University of Constantinople and ended as metropolitan of Euchaita, Nicholas Callicles (end of eleventh to beginning of twelfth centuries) and the exceedingly versatile Theodore Prodomus (twelfth century). At this same period there was a contemporary revival of intellectual life in Magna Graecia under the Norman kings and later the Hohenstaufen which showed the same partiality for epigrams, as for instance in the verse of the Admiral Eugenius of Palermo or the Chartophylax George of Callipolis or John of Otranto, a notary at Frederick II's court. The popularity of the epigram was maintained to the end of the Byzantine Empire. By far the most prolific and the most skilful of its many exponents was Manuel Philes (first half of the fourteenth century).

Closely related to the epigram is the elegy or threnody. It was widely used in Byzantium, particularly to bewail the vanity of human life, to mourn the dead or to lament political calamity. These threnodies are an exact reflection of the asceticism, the renunciation of the world and the acute self-distrust which was so constantly emphasised by the Church and especially the monastic world. Many of these poems were modelled on Gregory of Nazianzus' elegies in elegiac couplets, called *On his own life* and *Lamentation on the weakness of his own soul*. An odd feature of these laments is that they were often written in anacreontic verse, the very form used for love lyrics and drinking songs by that bibulous classic who gave it his name. Nevertheless, effects of most moving pathos were produced in this metre, as when Constantine Siceliotes (first half of the tenth century) lamented the death by drowning of his whole family during a storm at sea. The elegy written in twelve-syllable lines by Archbishop Nicholas Muzalon of Cyprus (later Patriarch of Constantinople) on laying down his office (*c.* 1110) is in similar poetic style and contains valuable material. The cycle of elegies written in exile by Eugenius of Palermo is also interesting; it laments the decline of his fortunes as a courtier in the days of the Norman King William II (1168–89). One of the most famous elegies was written by Archbishop Michael Choniates of Athens on the deterioration of life in Athens at the beginning of the thirteenth century. There are also a good many of the so-called 'contrition' (katanyktic) alphabets which are verses on the theme 'to my own soul', usually by anonymous 'poets', who start each line with each letter of the alphabet in turn.

(3) *Religious verse: hymns in classical metres, kontakia, canons.*[1]

Secular verse was often written by ecclesiastics as well as laymen, and these poems themselves contain much that is of a religious character, yet Byzantium had as well a purely religious literature of first-rate quality. It was moreover in the field of hymnology, that is, verse intended for liturgical use, that new and individual forms were evolved.

Up to the beginning of the fifth century the writers of such religious hymns as have survived employed the older metres. But it is, however, difficult to believe that songs of this kind can have been used for congregational purposes during the service; they were doubtless intended merely as edifying reading. The *Banquet* by Bishop Methodius of Philippi (formerly known as Methodius of Olympus, died 311), which is modelled on Plato's *Symposium*, introduces virgins singing a hymn in praise of chastity. This poem was in stanzas with a refrain, thus already showing certain features which were to characterise the later kontakia. The last poet to employ classical metres in the writing of religious hymns appears to be Synesius, Bishop of Cyrene (*c.* 370/5–*c.* 413/14). His ten hymns in various classical metres (iambic trimeters, anapaestic dimeters and monometers) reveal unusual sincerity and deep religious feeling. He was a remarkable man, a valiant soldier in his country's cause, a bishop with certain reservations in the field of Christian dogma and law, a friend of the pagan philosopher

---

[1] See also above, ch. xxiv, pp. 140 ff.

Hypatia, and a courageous advocate for his flock at the imperial court in Constantinople. He was deeply influenced by both the Christian and pagan worlds and his neoplatonic Christian hymns with their profound sincerity stand as a symbol of the transitional period between the ancient pagan world and the Christian middle ages. At almost the same time pagan hymn-writing was brought to an end with the equally outstanding hymns of the neoplatonist Proclus of Athens (410–85).

Meanwhile, an entirely new form of hymn was being evolved for liturgical use, the kontakion. The metrical structure was not based on series of lines of equal length with long and short syllables alternating, but consisted of a number of stanzas made up of verses with lines of varying length which depended for their rhythm on the alternation of stressed and unstressed syllables. Each stanza was the same in metre and in the number of verses. The reason for the development of this rhythmic verse was that by the second century A.D. at latest vowels and diphthongs had ceased to be differentiated in length and were pronounced as though of equal quality (isochromy of vowels). The old quantitative metres were therefore losing their meaning and were succeeded by the principle of syllabic stress. The kontakia which were being written by the sixth century consisted of eighteen or twenty-two stanzas of similar structure with a refrain. The tunes of these hymns were closely related to the words, so that both words and music were composed by the same person, who was known as a Melode (μελῳδός). This new type of religious poetry probably originated in Syria and became known in Byzantium largely through the many Greek translations of the poet Ephraem of Syria (306–73). The arrangement of the Syriac service shows clearly that their hymns were used both as a dramatic sermon on the meaning of the festival and at the same time for congregational singing. This fact further supports the connection between Syriac hymns and the Byzantine kontakia, for some of the latter were certainly metrical versions of sermons preached on church festivals. The ease with which this form of hymn found a place in the Byzantine liturgy also reflects the Byzantine inability to distinguish between rhetoric and poetry.

This new type of rhythmical liturgical verse penetrated into Byzantium fairly late, not before the end of the fourth century, but after somewhat hesitant beginnings it rapidly reached its full flowering. The most outstanding exponent of the genre was the Syrian Romanus of Beirut (end of fifth to middle of sixth centuries). Legend has it that one Christmas Eve the Mother of God miraculously endowed him with the gift of poetry, and at once he mounted the ambo in St Sophia and intoned his famous Christmas kontakion. In the course of his life he is said to have composed about a thousand kontakia. Of the eighty-five that have come down to us in his name (hymn-writers often reveal their identity in an acrostic based on the opening words of each stanza), some sixty-five have been published. Romanus probably also wrote the famous Akathistos hymn (ἀκάθιστος ὕμνος), a song of praise to the Mother of God which is still used.

At the beginning of the eighth century a new form of liturgical verse developed from the kontakion. This was the canon, which was exceedingly popular throughout the Byzantine period and is still used in Greek services. The canon consisted of nine odes (following the practice of the early Christians who used in their services nine canticles taken from the Old and New Testaments); each ode consisted of the same number of metrically identical stanzas, constructed on the principle of the kontakion. Andrew of Crete (*c.* 666–740) is regarded as the creator of this new form. Theodore the Studite and Joseph the Hymnographer from Sicily (both ninth century) were chiefly famous for their canons, although they also wrote kontakia. John of Damascus wrote a number of canons of great linguistic beauty and metrical skill, many of which have found a permanent place in the Greek liturgy. His friend and adopted brother Cosmas, later Bishop of Maiuma (743), also used this form for his equally famous hymns, and the canon did indeed become the recognised form for liturgical verse. Metrophanes of Smyrna (ninth century), John Mauropous (eleventh century), John Zonaras (eleventh to twelfth century), Nicephorus Blemmydes (thirteenth century), not to mention Bartholomew, Arsenius and Joseph, the twelfth-century hymn-writers of the Greek monastery of Grottaferrata near Rome, all produced many such canons.

As well as the hymn proper, intended for liturgical use, there was a certain amount of other religious verse, such as the anacreontic hymns of Patriarch Sophronius of Jerusalem (*c.* 560–638), of Elias (eighth century?) and Michael (ninth century), both secretaries (*syncelli*) to the Patriarch of Jerusalem. These hymns were certainly not intended for liturgical use, but like the rhythmical poetry they have certain homiletic characteristics. The Emperor Leo VI (886–912) wrote a song of contrition with an acrostic; in fact many similar examples of the 'alphabet' literature already dealt with also fall within this category. George Pisides, who spread abroad the fame of the Emperor Heraclius (610–41), composed a *Hexaemeron* in 1894 trimeters, together with other minor religious poems. One of the last masters of the art of writing hymns intended as devotional reading-matter was Symeon the Young, the Theologian (*c.* 949–1022). His *Loves of the Divine Hymns*, most of which have only been published in

Latin translation, are marked by their simplicity and their profoundly meditative quality, and are a moving expression of spiritual experience of rare profundity. Symeon used not only the Byzantine twelve-syllable line but also the fifteen-syllable line which was the metre of popular verse; he was the first to make any general use of this metre for the composition of personal poetry in the pure language.

B. LITERATURE IN THE DEMOTIC

Didactic poems—Laments—Satire—Animal stories
Legends—Myths—Historical poems—Verse romances

Poetry written in the *kathareuousa* in artificial and archaic forms was doomed to wilt in the somewhat oppressive atmosphere of the capital. A less trammelled and more natural form of poetry grew up in the provinces, more precisely in Asia Minor and the islands of the southern Aegean. There, less troubled by the presence of erudite prelates or vainglorious court orators than in Constantinople, it was possible for man's age-old gift of story-telling to find its expression in the creation of genuine poetry, composed in the ordinary language familiar to every Byzantine. Such poetry also provided an outlet for certain characteristic features of the Greek popular imagination; the forces of nature, for instance, might play their part in the tale. Written down in the Byzantine provinces in the demotic language, it developed into a direct expression of popular thought and phantasy, but it did not spring entirely from the indigenous population. The Frankish ruling class (partly French but mostly Italian) which had settled in parts of Greece and the Aegean side by side with the native Greeks after the Fourth Crusade (1204) also exerted a considerable influence. This form of demotic literature which grew up in the provinces was constantly and arrogantly rejected by the writers of the metropolis: and it must be admitted that these productions in the demotic are often open to criticism. They show many of the worst features of poetry in the pure language: pedantically detailed descriptions in the rhetorical style, or the minute and pedestrian portrayal of the personal characteristics of main characters as though for police records, after the manner of late antiquity; or perhaps the wearying string of self-pitying complaints. This demotic poetry brought out far more clearly than did the literature in the pure language many Byzantine defects of character, particularly that fatal instability which accounts for the sudden change from sincere devotion to frivolous blasphemy, from self-sacrificing loyalty to base infidelity, from tender affection to devilish hatred. Most of the poems in the demotic are anonymous. One man would sing them, another would combine them with one or two more pieces, a third wrote them down, altering a line here and there, adding and omitting lines as he pleased. After all, these heroic songs and love stories were no one's property; they were not like the writings and orations of the Church Fathers and a word more or less made no difference. This means however that there are a good many problems, particularly of a textual nature, connected with the poems which have survived. For the most part they were written down in the fourteenth and fifteenth centuries and they are almost all in the popular fifteen-syllable line (called 'political' verse).

The poems in the demotic most nearly related to those in the *kathareuousa* both in aim and subject matter were those inculcating a moral. An instance of this is the so-called *Spaneas* by the co-Emperor Alexius Comnenus (1119–42), a poem instructing his nephew Alexius rather in the manner of a *Mirror for Princes*. The poem was so popular that its title became a generic term for all such advice in verse. Two late didactic poems by Stephen Sachlikis from Crete (second half of the fifteenth century) and by Mark Depharanas from Zante (beginning of the sixteenth century) fall into this category. The first begins by describing the poet's own roving existence, which landed him in a Venetian prison, and then proceeds to lay down rules of conduct for a friend's son; the second is an imitation of the first, and both are exceedingly coarse. These two poems are the crudest version of the *Spaneas* type, and incomparably more licentious than their prototype. An allegorical poem in certain respects like that of Meliteniotes (see above, p. 251) is the work in 776 lines called *Fortune and Misfortune*. Here a pilgrim sets out with the intention of learning the reasons for human misfortunes in the castle of Misfortune. On the advice of an old man, Chronos, who gives him a letter of introduction, he decides to banish from his mind all thought of Misfortune and to seek out Good Fortune who makes him her guest. Thus the lament so popular in poetry written in the pure language also provided writers in the demotic with full scope for their emotions. And when the imperial secretary Glycas was denounced by a friend and thrown into prison (1158–9) by Manuel I his moving complaint to his master was written in the demotic. Another lament called *Life Abroad* (Περὶ ξενιτείας) belongs probably to the fifteenth or sixteenth centuries. This outburst of bitter pain at all the sorrows of exile is a typically Greek theme, which for all its monotony and exaggerated pathos well illustrates the age-long nostalgia of the Greek for his own land.

Another Byzantine characteristic is found in a group of demotic poems which are full of criticism and spiteful mockery of inconvenient circumstances. The method used is a blend of complaint and satire. The poet who appears to have been particularly addicted to this kind of verse and who is regarded as its most typical exponent was Theodore Prodromus (born *c.* 1098) who was also a poet in the literary language. Doubts have been raised as to the authorship of his demotic verse and it is quite possible that poems by other hands, but in his manner, have been erroneously ascribed to him. These particular poems are addressed to the Emperor and other eminent figures and they begin with flattery but soon lapse into shameless begging. Ptochoprodromus or 'poor Prodromus' (as he sometimes calls himself) gives a highly coloured picture of his position as a 'man of learning', his economic wretchedness in contrast to the comfort enjoyed by the artisan, the grinding down of the simple monk by the despotic behaviour of the luxurious and princely abbot, and all this in the hope of eliciting some gift or assistance.

Some of the Byzantine animal stories are among the best productions of Byzantine folk poetry, at least from a purely literary standpoint. They are full of striking observations of animals, but under cover of this they severely criticise contemporary political and social conditions, attacking especially the cultural arrogance of the ruling classes and the hypocrisy of the clergy. A poem of this kind, which can be exactly dated to 1365, is the *Story of the Four-footed Animals*. In satirical vein it relates how King Lion, having promised to maintain the public peace, invites all the quadrupeds to assemble and air their mutual grievances as a prelude to inaugurating an era of perpetual peace. After a long argument in which individual animals all point out each other's merits and failings, the king gives the sign to end this truce. As usual, the large, powerful animals attack the weak. In the ensuing massacre the lion, the leopard and other fierce animals are killed by the weaker ones, to the immense satisfaction of the poet. A similar work is the *Pulologus*; instead of the lion it is the eagle, who as king of the birds invites his subjects to a similar discussion; and in the *Poricologus* the grape is condemned by king Quince. In the *Story of the Ass the Wolf and the Fox* the two beasts of prey join forces to entice the poor donkey, beaten black and blue by his master, out on to the open sea. There, by pretending to be shipwrecked, they hope to drive him to confess his sins and then to condemn him to death. But the ass cunningly reckons on the cupidity of the other two and succeeds in pushing them overboard. Thus the craft of the small provincial defeats the enlightened erudition and arrogant culture of the great, the 'philosophers'. The influence of Reynard the Fox may be traced in the fox and in the stories he tells.

An example of the crude blasphemy to be found in poetry, along-side the puritanical orthodoxy of the Byzantine Church, is the *Mass of the Beardless Man* (᾿Ακολουθία τοῦ ἀνοσίου σπανοῦ). This extraordinary work (thirteenth/fourteenth centuries), a thoroughly obscene piece of satire written in the metre of Byzantine liturgical verse, is known more fully as 'the mass of the profane and beardless son of a goat'. As is well known, a beardless man in the East means a eunuch, with all his unpleasant traits. In this parody of the celebration of mass the officiating priest gives this beardless man the hand of his daughter in marriage. The satire directed against the Byzantine clergy is obvious.

It is not surprising that the wealth of legend from ancient Greece has left its mark on the popular poetry of the Byzantines. Even during the decline of the Empire it roused the lively interest of various sections of the population. In Epirus in about 1330 the Despot John II Orsini commissioned Constantine Hermoniacus to make a compilation of stories from Homer. Admittedly the beauty of the original epic is lost in the process. The compiler has inexpertly pieced together pre-Homeric, Homeric and post-Homeric themes, and has moreover frequently misunderstood the original text, so that the 8800 trochaic eight-syllable lines read like a parody of the old epics. The *Trojan War*, an almost worthless translation of the Old French romance on Troy by Benoît de Saint-More, was even more feeble. A far more successful treatment is found in the *Achilleis*. In this version of the story of Achilles, the hero is shown as the perfect medieval knight who sallies forth with his twelve companions, who include Pandurclus (= Patroclus), to win Polyaina, the daughter of the hostile king. During a tournament held as part of the wedding festivities a Frankish knight unseats all Achilles' companions, even Pandurclus, until Achilles himself enters the lists and defeats the foreigner. After Polyaina's death Achilles marches against Troy, where he is slain by the cunning of Paris. This lively, charming poem (*c.* fourteenth century) shows how ancient native elements were fused with the themes of western chivalry. Similarly the legendary figure of Alexander the Great, who as the founder of a Hellenic world Empire still occupies an honourable place in the imagination of the Greek people, was worked into a vast epic of chivalry with all the romantic themes (Brahmins, Amazons, etc.) that had been spread throughout the world by the Pseudo-Callisthenes and Julius Valerius. The genuine exploits of the sixth century Belisarius, the great commander of Justinian I, have today faded from the Greek memory, as indeed they had already been forgotten in the course of the middle ages. The *Lay of Belisarius* attempts to portray the ravages of envy among mankind, and is little more than an elaboration of the theme of the fickleness of fortune and the intrigues of courtiers based on the legend of Belisarius, which did not appear in Byzantine poetry until the tenth century at the earliest. The poem may possibly contain some allusions to historical conditions at the beginning of the fourteenth century.

Then there is the mythical, and also symbolical, figure of the marcher-lord (Akrites) of the Euphrates frontier, the hero of the great epic *Digenis Akritas*, which is extant in several versions. It has often been regarded as the medieval national epic of the Byzantines, though without much justification. It is really the song *par excellence* in praise of the unknown frontier-warrior of the Empire, whatever his racial origin; for this same frontier protected Byzantine civilisation against the barbarian world, Christendom against the infidel. How little 'race' mattered is evident from the fact that the hero, Digenis Akritas, had an Arab amir as his father while his mother came from a famous Byzantine family. This amir had carried off the maiden but finally married her and became a Christian. The second part of the epic relates the heroic deeds of the child of this union, Digenis Akritas; how he captured and won a bride by many valiant feats, and how he ended his days in restful ease in a magnificent castle on the Euphrates, until Charon claimed him and led him down into the underworld. This great epic took shape about the middle of the tenth century. It drew on a series of minor epics some of which have been handed down orally and can still be recited from memory by the inhabitants of the Greek islands. Just as the main story of the epic was built round a nucleus of historical fact, so other independent sections of the Akritas cycle are based on actual events, for example, the song of Armuris and the song of Andronicus' son. All these show the genuine self-conscious folk epic, in which the valour and the strength of the hero gradually assume gigantic proportions in the imagination of the singer.

There are also some poems in demotic which set out to deal almost entirely with historical events, or to cover a considerable period of history. To a Byzantine, verse did not seem an inappropriate medium for material of this kind, and the verse chronicle written in the literary language by Manasses has already been mentioned. In the demotic in the fifteen-syllable line there is the *Chronicle of the Morea* which gives an account of Frankish rule in the Peloponnese during the period 1204–92, as well as the description of the battle of Varna (1444) by an anonymous writer, who praises the heroism of 'Iangus', that is, John Hunyadi. The *Capture of Constantinople* was based on the fall of the city to Muḥammad II in 1453 and the subsequent enslavement of the Greeks, coupled with the inevitable complaint about the behaviour of the western powers who are challenged to drive out the hated Turks.

Byzantine folk-literature is very rich in verse romances. These are love-stories displaying many of the characteristic motifs and devices of the romances of the late classical period, such as separation and reunion of the lovers, reunion through recognition (ἀναγνωρισμός), pirates or dreams. They constantly introduce descriptions (*ekphraseis*), or rhetorical love-letters, thus reflecting the Byzantine predilection for didactic treatment and the strength of the rhetorical tradition. A naïve pleasure in story-telling combined with phantasy reminiscent of the oriental world and a hero steeped in knightly chivalry gives the reader an attractive picture of the contemporary outlook which produced these verse romances. The oldest is *Callimachus and Chrysorrhoe*. A maiden imprisoned in a castle guarded by a dragon is set free by Prince Callimachus. But then another prince, after persuading a witch to give the first suitor a magic apple which sends him into a deathlike sleep (the Snow-White motif), abducts the girl. Callimachus is miraculously awakened by his brothers and, disguised as a gardener, he finds his beloved once more. The verse romance of *Lybistrus and Rhodamne* has a similar plot. Here Lybistrus after many trials delivers his beloved from the grasp of a Frankish rival. The plot gains in vigour by being interwoven with the subsidiary love-story of Clitobus, Lybistrus' friend, and the whole story is set in a narrative framework. The verse romance of *Imberios and Margarone* (the fair Maguelone) reveals even in its title its close connection with the vernacular romance so widespread in the West. This too is the story of two lovers, Prince Peter of Provence and Princess Margarone of Naples. It contains the usual motifs: abduction, the bride's capture by pirates, forcible removal of the hero to Egypt, and finally the reunion of the lovers by means of a ring found by Margarone inside a fish brought to her by fishermen. *Phlorius and Platziaphlore* was a very similar romance and was a version of the legend of Flore and Blanchefleur universally known in the middle ages. It was the Greek version of the fourteenth-century Italian *Cantare di Fiorio e Biancafiore*. The verse romance *Apollonius of Tyre* is another translation from the Italian. This is really a literary 'reversal' in that the Italian version is based on the Latin treatment (*c.* fifth to sixth century A.D.) of material derived from a Greek work now lost. The verse romance about *Ptocholeon*, or the wise old man, takes a short-story theme very common in literature, namely the test of sagacity. Ptocholeon, an aged father reduced to extreme poverty, is sold into slavery by his sons at the slave market and is bought by the Emperor, richly rewarded, and allowed to return home. The poem is exceptional in being written in trochaic eight-syllable lines.

Use of the familiar everyday language did afford opportunity for genuine, unrestricted expression of the most intimate emotions. Perhaps this freedom of expression was also fostered by the freer social code of the Frankish conquerors. However that may be, this demotic poetry brought out a capacity for the secular lyric. These love romances of the later middle ages themselves contain many passages of lyrical quality. And in the fourteenth to fifteenth centuries the so-called *Rhodian Love Songs* is a magnificent collection of most moving love-poetry. It tells the story of a knight of Rhodes who woos a Greek beauty. She finally promises to accept him if he can answer a hundred questions on love. His answers arranged as an alphabetical acrostic take the form of a number of love-lyrics of great ardour and beauty. This poem was later combined with others to form the whole collection which has come down to us.

In assessing the place of Byzantine literature in the general context of medieval literature, it is clear that it almost entirely lacked such important literary genres as drama or genuine lyric poetry. But it is equally clear that it was a formative influence in the spirituality of the middle ages. Quite apart from the enrichment of the liturgy by various forms of religious poetry, or writings on the spiritual life which appeared throughout the middle ages, the Greek Fathers of the fourth and fifth centuries were in this respect outstanding. They produced works which from the literary and philosophical point of view could hold their own with their pagan opponents; thus in their writings they transformed the tidings of redemption proclaimed to the poor and oppressed and ensured their survival and they supplied the philosophical concepts indispensable for the formulation of doctrine. Grammarians and rhetoricians fully recognised the aesthetic, literary and historical value of the works of antiquity despite their pagan character. They toiled indefatigably to preserve and elucidate these, with the result that they remain available for us today, together with the commentaries which are still often indispensable to their understanding. Byzantine scholars of the fourteenth and fifteenth centuries faithfully passed on these texts and their commentaries to the humanists of the West. Thus the knowledge acquired from ancient Greece was saved from being submerged beneath Turkish domination and was able to make its contribution to the development of the renaissance in the West. Byzantine historiography had a long and distinguished tradition. Its works provide comparatively full information, on the whole objectively presented, about the

Empire itself, and also about the history of neighbouring peoples and their relations with Byzantium. And, in conclusion, Byzantium added much to the rich store of medieval European folk tales, for it was the great clearing house of East and West. Moreover this folk literature contributed not a little to the proud sense of solidarity which enabled the Greeks to preserve their characteristics throughout the Turkish rule until the day of their liberation.

CHAPTER XXVIII

BYZANTINE SCIENCE

When the course of Byzantine history is surveyed as a whole, it will be seen that long periods of partial or complete neglect of the sciences alternated with periods of intensive activity. Thus, the sciences flourished under Justinian I, then again under Theophilus and Michael III, under Constantine VII Porphyrogenitus and Constantine IX Monomachus and finally under several of the Emperors of Nicaea and the house of Palaeologus, whose members, despite their political preoccupations, did not confine their patronage merely to those practical branches of science indispensable to the health of the national and private economy.

Byzantium is important in the history of science, and especially that of mathematics and astronomy (the two subjects about which there is more information, though the situation is similar for the other sciences), not because any appreciable additions were made to the knowledge already attained by the Greeks of the Hellenistic era, but because the Byzantines preserved the solid foundations laid in antiquity until such time as the Westerners had at their disposal other means of recovering this knowledge. It must be admitted, however, that the theoretical discoveries of the great figures of classical mathematics (Archimedes, Apollonius, Diophantus) were only understood by a few, whereas calculations and measurements with a practical bearing (as in logistics and geodesy), and the subjects of the Quadrivium (arithmetic, geometry, astronomy and music), found their way into educational curricula, both because of their practical importance in ordinary life and also as a preparation for courses in philosophy; both geometry and logic start with definitions, postulates and axioms.

Chronologically considered, Byzantine history shows three main periods of scientific activity, each of which opens with a spectacular, or at any rate a high, level of achievement, followed just as regularly by a perceptible decline. The beginning of the first period (from Justinian I to Michael II) saw the activity of Eutocius and Isidore of Miletus, who were responsible for preserving the work of Archimedes and Apollonius. But soon afterwards interest in higher education evaporated, and all the available energy was caught up in the state's struggle for existence in the face of external foes or consumed in ecclesiastical conflicts. However, intolerance towards the pagan schools and the Nestorians had the effect of sending eastwards to Syria and Persia a number of refugee scholars who were learned in antique science; under the Sassanids there was a cultural centre, with a medical school, at Jundishapur (in Chusistan), to which the Nestorians came after their expulsion from Edessa in 489, and the Neoplatonists from Athens in 529. The opening of the second period (from Theophilus to Alexius V) is marked by the appearance of Leo the Mathematician at the university of Bardas; without Leo, the revival of mathematical studies in the West based on Greek texts is well-nigh inconceivable. For it must be remembered that the Arabs, who by the end of the ninth century had already mastered the corpus of Greek science, could only influence the West through Latin and Hebrew translations. The cultural efflorescence of the reign of Constantine VII Porphyrogenitus was also beneficial to scientific studies, and mathematics and astronomy, chiefly as subjects of the Quadrivium, were once more sedulously cultivated at the university of Constantinople reorganised under Constantine IX Monomachus (1045). But the internal and external weakening of the state once more took its toll of the sciences, so that the period of interregnum between the Macedonians and the Comneni has nothing to show in the way of mathematical activity. Even the succeeding period, covering the revival of the Empire under Alexius I Comnenus up to the time of the Latin conquest, can boast of only a few names to prove that intellectual endeavour was not wholly absent. In the third period (1204–1453) there was a marked revival from the time of John Vatatzes onwards. In the thirteenth and fourteenth centuries mathematicians such as Pachymeres, Maximus Planudes and Theodore Metochites discovered once again the paths leading back to the ancients. From the beginning of the fourteenth century, Greek astronomical lore which had formerly been known only to the Arabs and the Persians began to return to Byzantium, where there is also evidence of Eastern medical and pharmacological knowledge at this period.

I. MATHEMATICS AND ASTRONOMY

(a) *Justinian to Michael II* (527–829)

There could have been no mathematics in Christian Byzantium but for the scientific work already accomplished in the pagan universities. The great classical thinkers had lived in Alexandria, and it was at Alexandria that their works were assembled and studied. Hypatia (died 415) was the last of the line of commentators who helped to preserve Hellenistic learning for the West, where the heritage was to be received centuries later by way of Byzantium and the Arabs. In the Academy of Athens, on the other hand, pride of place in mathematical studies was given not to the higher mathematics but to those branches which were regarded as necessary to the understanding of problems in philosophy and natural philosophy, such as the elements of geometry, 'Platonic figures' and neoplatonic arithmetic, which were studied by Proclus, Simplicius and others in conjunction with the writings of Plato, Aristotle, Euclid or Nicomachus. Byzantium was added to Alexandria and Athens as a centre of learning when Theodosius II in 425 revived an educational institution which had existed there in the time of Constantine. Admittedly, mathematics was not the central feature of the curriculum: there were thirty professors of languages and law and only one of philosophy. However, there is evidence that lectures were given on the subjects of the Quadrivium.[1] The school clearly had a good reputation, since Armenian students and scholars went there to study as well as to Athens and Alexandria. Subjects of practical application, such as logistics and surveying, were probably taught by private teachers; an edict of 425 makes a clear distinction between such private teachers and the professors of the state academy.

Close relations existed between these three schools, which were all within the Empire; there is even evidence of a conference being held. Proclus, born in 410 at Byzantium, studied at Alexandria and in Athens, where he succeeded his master Syrianus as head of the Academy. One of his pupils in Athens, Ammonius (died before 510), revived the school of Alexandria, which had sunk into insignificance after the death of Hypatia. Among Ammonius' followers in Alexandria were Simplicius and Damascius, who both worked later in Athens, migrating to Persia when the Academy of Athens was closed by Justinian in 529. Another of Ammonius' pupils in Alexandria, the monophysite John Philoponus, was one of the greatest scholars of this period of transition from Hellenistic to Byzantine science. Some of his mathematical and astronomical work has survived, a commentary on Nicomachus and a treatise on the astrolabe. In a commentary on Aristotle, John Philoponus dealt with quadrature of the circle and duplication of the cube.

Another pupil of Ammonius was Eutocius (born *c.* 480 in Ascalon), who, under the inspiration of his master, devoted himself to the study of classical mathematics; we are indebted to him for commentaries on some of the works of Archimedes. In his commentary on Book I, *On the Sphere and Cylinder* (dedicated to Ammonius), Eutocius gave a detailed account of all earlier solutions of the problem of duplication

[1] H. Usener, *De Stephano Alexandrino* (Bonn, 1880), pp. 5f.

of the cube,[1] and in doing so preserved certain precious fragments of ancient Greek mathematics, taken partly from the lost *History of Mathematics* of Eudemus (*c.* 340 B.C.). He was also successful in recovering a lost text of Archimedes (on the geometrical solution of the cubic equation) from an old Doric version. His commentary on Archimedes' *Measurement of a Circle* provides examples, otherwise rare, of Greek arithmetical methods. Eutocius also wrote a commentary on Archimedes' *Plane equilibriums* and on the first four books of Apollonius' *Conics*,[2] which he dedicated to his friend Anthemius of Tralles, the first architect of St Sophia. It is not known whether they became friends in Alexandria or whether Eutocius actually lived at Constantinople later in his life; in either case, Eutocius must have the credit of having introduced classical Greek mathematics into Byzantium.

Anthemius (ὁ μηχανικός, architect and engineer) can also be counted as a mathematician. In his work on the burning-mirror he outdistanced Apollonius on several points; he knew of the directrix-focus property of the parabola and the method of constructing ellipses known as 'the gardener's', and also described the construction of ellipses and parabolas from their tangents.

Serious work in mathematics and mechanics was also undertaken in the circle of Isidore of Miletus, who became responsible for the building of St Sophia after the death of Anthemius in 534. Under his direction, Archimedes' writings on measurement of a circle and on spheres and cylinders were published, together with Eutocius' commentaries; one of Isidore's pupils was responsible for the so-called 15th Book of Euclid's *Elements*, whilst Isidore himself was the inventor of a pair of compasses for drawing parabolas, and the author of a commentary on the lost 'Καμαρικά' (*On the Construction of Vaults*) of Hero, with its stereometrical and mechanical problems which were necessarily of interest to any architect. There is no clear evidence of a connection between Isidore and the state university.

The university was closed by Phocas (602–10) but revived as an oecumenical academy under his successor Heraclius (610–41) through the Patriarch Sergius. The direction of philosophical and mathematical studies was given to the scholar Stephen, summoned from Alexandria to Constantinople about 612, the author of an astronomical treatise *An explanation of Theon's method of handy tables by means of individual examples* (Διασάφησις ἐξ οἰκείων ὑποδειγμάτων τῆς τῶν προχείρων κανόνων ἐφόδου τοῦ Θέωνος).[3] Stephen also lectured on

---

[1] Archimedes III, ed. J. L. Heiberg (2nd ed. 1915), pp. 54ff.
[2] Apollonius II, ed. J. L. Heiberg (1893), pp. 168ff.
[3] Ed. H. Usener, *De Stephano Alexandrino*, pp. 38–54.

Plato and Aristotle and on the Quadrivium. This division of mathematics into the four branches, arithmetic, geometry, astronomy and music, which together with the Trivium comprised the seven liberal arts, was defended by Ammonius (against Proclus), although it originated at a much earlier date.[1] Later the Quadrivium was continued as the foundation of all mathematical instruction in the curriculum of the Byzantine and also of the western schools, where it was introduced through the writings of Martianus Capella and of Boethius, who was responsible for the name Quadrivium.

Little is known of the later activities of the oecumenical academy of Constantinople up to the time of its dissolution by Leo III the Isaurian in 726, and still less is known of scientific work in the following century up to the revival of learning under Theophilus. It is said that the Armenian Ananias of Shirak came to Constantinople towards the end of the seventh century to study philosophy, but found there no teacher of the subject; if this is true, it shows how deeply this branch of secular learning had declined. On the other hand, it is probable that the subjects of the Quadrivium continued to be taught and it is certain that there was never any interruption in the teaching of elementary arithmetic (logistics) and of geometry (geodesy), which at that time was regarded only as a branch of arithmetic; prescriptions were used without recourse to proof. These elementary subjects, indispensable to the life of the community, may perhaps have been taught privately or in church schools, which the Third Council of Constantinople (681) ordained that the clergy should establish 'per villas et vicos'. There are some collections of geometrical and stereometrical prescriptions for everyday use (they occur in a number of manuscripts from the ninth century onwards), many of which are ascribed to Hero; they are in reality only meagre extracts, in quality far below Hero's authentic writings. The knowledge of mathematics and mechanics necessary in building must have been handed down in the guilds of masons, just as merchants and craftsmen must themselves have undertaken the education of the rising generation. A few textbooks of logistics have survived from that period. The sixth- or seventh-century papyrus *Akhmîm*, found in Egypt,[2] contains an

---

[1] Proclus, following Geminus (c. 70 B.C.), distinguished eight branches of mathematics, two of which were on an elevated and advanced level (theoretical arithmetic and geometry) while six were lesser ones, concerned with the αἰσθητά (logistics, geodesy, optics, music, mechanics and astronomy). Varro in his scheme of education drawn up in 32 B.C. added medicine and architecture to the subjects later to be known as the seven liberal arts. After Apuleius (c. A.D. 150) and Martianus Capella (first half of the fifth century) Roman schools usually followed a plan of instruction based on the seven liberal arts, and this division must also have been the plan followed in the early Byzantine schools.

[2] Ed. J. Baillet, *Mém. miss. arch. française*, IX, 1 (Paris, 1892).

arithmetic book which includes amongst other things tables of fractions, exercises in division of fractions, and partnership rules. There is a wooden tablet from Cairo of the same period which gives tables of fractions and calculations of interest.[1] To logistics belong also the puzzles so popular as mathematical entertainment, which could be solved by algebra or arithmetic; a collection of these was made by Metrodorus (late fifth or early sixth century).[2] A similar collection 'for retailing at feasts' was made by the Armenian Ananias, who may have become acquainted with puzzles of this kind during his stay in Byzantium.

During the seventh century the Byzantine era, which fixed the creation of the world at September 5509 B.C., was introduced, an innovation which also soon came into use outside the Empire, to be superseded later by the Christian and Arabic eras.[3]

(b) *Theophilus to the Fourth Crusade* (829–1204)

A second epoch in the history of Byzantine science begins with Theophilus. His taste for splendour and luxury was itself a stimulus to building and the ornamental arts; but he was also anxious to make Byzantium the leading cultural force in the orient, impelled in this ambition, perhaps, by thoughts of rivalling Baghdad where the Caliph al-Ma'mūn (813–33), like his father before him, was seriously concerned to make translations of the Greek works preserved in Syrian monasteries or purchased from Constantinople available to Arab readers. al-Ma'mūn also tried to acquire for his court the man who was to preside over the revival of studies in Byzantium, Leo the 'philosopher' and 'mathematician'. From what we known of Leo's youth—he was born about 800, in Hypata (Thessaly)—it is clear that it was still possible to obtain some education even after the closing of the university in 726. Leo attended a school of grammar in Constantinople; he found a teacher of philosophy and mathematics on the island of Andros, where there was also a library. He later set up as a private teacher in the capital, dealing with all branches of learning. When Theophilus heard that Leo had been invited to Baghdad, he appointed him a state teacher, to lecture publicly at the Church of

---

[1] See D. S. Crawford, 'A Mathematical Tablet', *Aegyptus*, XXXIII (1953), 222–40; he thinks the *Akhmīm* is rather earlier. In addition to the tables of fractions mentioned by Crawford (p. 223) there are also similar tables from c. A.D. 600, published in W. E. Crum and H. I. Bell, 'Coptic and Greek Texts from the Excavations Undertaken by the Byzantine Research Account "Wadi Sarga"', *Coptica*, III (Copenhagen, 1922), 53–7.

[2] Published in P. Tannery's *Diophanti Opera*, II (1895), pp. 43 ff., and with an English translation by W. R. Paton in *The Greek Anthology*, v (1953), Book XIV (Loeb).   [3] On chronological problems see V. Grumel, *La chronologie* (Paris, 1958).

the Forty Martyrs. It was thus only when Leo was already advanced in years that he acquired enough influence to bring about a genuine advance in Byzantine scientific studies. In 863 Caesar Bardas made him rector of the newly established secular university in the Magnaura palace, where Leo, as 'chief of the philosophers', taught both philosophy and the subjects of the Quadrivium. He had as assistants his pupil Theodore, who taught geometry, and Theodegius, who taught astronomy. Amongst those who heard Leo lecture on Euclid were the deacon Arethas,[1] later Bishop of Caesarea, and Constantine (Cyril), the Apostle of the Slavs.

Apart from his work as a teacher of the Quadrivium, Leo merits an honourable place in the history of mathematics on account of his effort to preserve the work of the great classical mathematicians. It was during his time that most of the manuscripts forming the vital link in the line of descent from antiquity were written. The following are known to have been copied in the ninth century: a text of Euclid, written in 888 and at one time in the possession of Leo's pupil Arethas, who himself made a number of notes in it;[2] the now missing manuscript of Diophantus, on which the oldest existing codex (dating from the thirteenth century) is based;[3] two lost manuscripts of Apollonius, from which copies were made in two codices now in the Vatican (tenth and twelfth centuries);[4] and three manuscripts with the *Syntaxis* of Ptolemy, among them the magnificent Cod. Vat. Gr. 1594.[5] There was no full edition of Archimedes, since Isidore's was incomplete. Leo, however, had a collection made of everything still extant. Thus there came into being the archetype, lost during the sixteenth century, which in the twelfth century was in the library of the Norman kings of Sicily and after the battle of Benevento came into papal possession, to be used (together with an older manuscript containing writings on mechanics) by William of Moerbeke in his translation of Archimedes. From Leo's time also dates a manuscript of the short treatise on astronomy, interpretations of Archimedes based on Leo's teaching, as well as the oldest scholia on Euclid,[6] the

---

[1] See J. L. Heiberg, 'Der byzantinische Mathematiker Leon', *Biblioth. Mathem.* I (2. Folge, 1887), 33–6. A much more important contemporary was Photius, chiefly a theologian and philologist, who only quite incidentally concerned himself with medicine and natural science; there are extracts made by Photius from Nicomachus in Cod. Vat. Gr. 198, fol. 1.

[2] See Euclid, *Elements*, ed. J. L. Heiberg, V (Leipzig, 1888), p. xxviii: ἐκτησάμην ἀρέθας πατρεὺς τὴν παροῦσαν βίβλον νομισμάτων ιδ. (in Cod. Bodl. Dorvillian., x, 1, inf. 2, 30).

[3] *Diophanti opera*, ed. P. Tannery, II (1895), p. xviii.

[4] Apollonius, ed. J. L. Heiberg, II (1893), p. lxviii (Cod. Vat. Gr. 204 and 206).

[5] See also Cod. Vat. Gr. 1291 and Cod. Paris. Gr. 2389 (from Egypt).

[6] Euclid, ed. J. L. Heiberg, V (1888), pp. 714–5; ὑπόμνημα σχόλιον εἰς τὰς τῶν λόγων σύνθεσίν τε καὶ ἀφαίρεσιν Λέοντος. Going far beyond what was then the usual practice

pseudo-Heronian treatise *On measuring* ($\pi\epsilon\rho\grave{\iota}$ $\mu\acute{\epsilon}\tau\rho\omega\nu$), and many other texts.

Little is known of the fate of the secular university during the reign of Basil I though it is clear that learning as well as art flourished in the Amorian and early Macedonian periods. Basil I, and to an even greater degree his son, Leo VI the Wise, attached much importance to education.[1] Constantine VII Porphyrogenitus was well known for the stimulus which he gave to arts and sciences. He himself studied mathematics, astronomy, music and 'philosophy the queen of all', and appointed distinguished teachers, and there were clearly still notable scholars to be found. Constantine's intellectual endeavours (the compilation of comprehensive encyclopaedias and collections of excerpts) were also beneficial to mathematics. The *Suda* contains numerous biographical notices, the sources for which must have been available in the libraries of the time. The number of manuscripts originating in the tenth century shows that mathematical works were then being studied and sought after in the bookshops; these included the edition of the *Elements* of Euclid in Cod. Vat. Gr. 190[2] (based on a pre-Theon text) and other manuscripts of Euclid,[3] Eutocius,[4] Ptolemy,[5] and Nicomachus.[6] The famous Archimedes palimpsest which also contains the *Method* dates from this time.[7] Constantine Cephalas' edition of the *Anthologia Palatina*, with mathematical epigrams from two older collections and scholia which go back at least to Metrodorus, also dates from the tenth century, as does a *Geodesy* of a surveyor known as Hero of Byzantium.

After the death of Constantine VII Porphyrogenitus in 959 there followed almost a century in which scientific studies were neglected as far as imperial patronage went and the Emperors were occupied with the extension and consolidation of the Empire. Basil II, whose reign marked the highest point of Byzantine power, was notorious for his hostility to learning, but in spite of this scholars were still to be found, and the fruits of their work were seen in the marked intel-

---

by which letters were used for numbers (see J. Tropfke, *Geschichte der Elementarmathematik*, II (3) (1933), pp. 46 ff.), Leo employed letters in calculations such as $a \cdot \beta = \delta$ ('$\acute{o}$ $\mu\grave{\epsilon}\nu$ $\acute{\upsilon}\pi\grave{o}$ a, β $\acute{\epsilon}\sigma\tau\omega$ $\acute{o}$ δ'), or $a = \beta \cdot \gamma$ ('$\acute{\epsilon}\sigma\tau\omega$ $\acute{\alpha}\rho\iota\theta\mu\grave{o}\varsigma$ $\acute{o}$ a $\tauο\widetilde{\upsilon}$ β $\pi\omicron\lambda\lambda\alpha\pi\lambda\acute{\alpha}\sigma\iota\omicron\varsigma$ $\kappa\alpha\tau\grave{\alpha}$ $\tau\grave{o}\nu$ γ').

[1] For one of his mathematical puzzles see Nicomachus, *Introductio arithmetica*, ed. R. Hoche (1866), p. 151.

[2] The Euclid manuscript, which probably originated in Syria (see Euclid, VI, p. vi, ed. H. Menge, 1896) contains also the *Data* with Marinus' commentary on it, and Theon's memorandum on Ptolemy's tables.

[3] Cod. Flor. Laurentian. 28, 3 (*Elements* and *Phaenomena*); Cod. Vat. Gr. 204 (*Data, Optica, Catoptrica* and *Phaenomena*).

[4] Cod. Vat. Gr. 204 (commentary on the *Conics* of Apollonius).

[5] Cod. Marc. Gr. 313 (*Syntaxis*).   [6] Cod. Gottingensis Philol. 66.

[7] Cod. rescriptus Metochii Constantinopoli S. Sepulchri monasterii Hierosolymitani 355.

lectual activity of the mid-eleventh century. Moreover, private teachers and the church schools had seen to it that the subjects of the normal curriculum were still taught, as is shown by the Quadrivium of an anonymous writer (perhaps Gregory the Monk or Romanus of Seleucia) of the year 1008.[1]

Mathematics took on a new lease of life when Constantine IX Monomachus reorganised the university in 1045 with a faculty of law and a faculty of philosophy. The Emperor himself exhorted the young to the study of philosophy and mathematics. At the head of the faculty of philosophy was set the versatile genius Michael Psellus. He lectured not only on philosophy and the subjects of the Trivium but also on those of the Quadrivium. But he did not consider this the most essential part of his work. Like Plato and Proclus, he saw in mathematics the connecting link between material objects and ideas, a means of leading students into the realm of abstract thought. He also devoted some time to the mathematical portions of Aristotle. His treatise on numbers ($\pi\epsilon\rho\grave{\iota}$ $\mathring{\alpha}\rho\iota\theta\mu\hat{\omega}\nu$) betrays the influence of neoplatonic and oriental number mysticism. Among his surviving writings is an astronomical treatise on the movements of the sun and moon, their eclipses, and Easter calculations.[2] There is also a letter on the nature of geometry, scholia on Nicomachus (written by 'Soterichus') and a letter on the algebraic terms used by Diophantus, of whom he possessed a manuscript (perhaps the only one in existence at the time).

One of Psellus' pupils, and his successor as 'chief of the philosophers', was John Italus; he also lectured on the Platonic theory of ideas, on Aristotle, Proclus and Iamblichus. In 1082, under Alexius I Comnenus, Italus, who had taught 'the foolish wisdom of the heathen', was condemned as a heretic. The secular university continued, though it henceforth appears to be to some extent under the supervision of the Patriarchs; the first evidence of this is furnished by Nicholas Mesarites (c. 1200).[3] Now, as formerly, the Quadrivium (which had formed part of the education of Anna Comnena) was taught, and there is even evidence that it figured in the teaching of

---

[1] See A. Diller, 'Byzantine Quadrivium', *Isis*, xxxvi (1945–6), 132; this Quadrivium was published twice in the sixteenth century under the name of Michael Psellus (in 1533 and 1556). There is a modern edition by J. L. Heiberg in *Det Kgl. Dansk. Vidensk. Selsk. Hist.-fil. Medd.* xv, 1 (Copenhagen, 1929).

[2] In Cod. Vindob. Phil. Gr. 190; cf. *GBL*, p. 622.

[3] In the description of the courses given at the Church of the Holy Apostles there is no mention of astronomy, and medicine appears in its place (see A. Heisenberg, *Grabeskirche und Apostelkirche*, II (Leipzig, 1908), 17 ff. and 90 ff.). The Patriarch had the last word on debatable points: he was 'an arithmetician greater than Nicomachus, a geometer greater than Euclid and a musician greater than Ptolemy' (A. Heisenberg, *op. cit.* p. 95).

the patriarchal school, which had clearly somewhat extended its curriculum.[1]

That the study of the ancient authors had certainly not ceased is shown by the number of manuscripts originating in the eleventh and twelfth centuries and containing works of Euclid (the *Elements, Data* and *Phaenomena*), Proclus, Marinus, Ptolemy, Apollonius, Serenus and Hero. One eleventh-century manuscript[2] provides not only the genuine *Metrica* of Hero but also the compilations known as the *Geometrica* and *Stereometrica* as well as the pseudo-Heronian *Geodesy* and similar writings of Didymus and Diophanes.[3] Cod. Paris Suppl. Gr. 607 of the same period contains Hero's *Dioptra*, and the *Definitions* of Hero contained in Cod. Paris. Suppl. Gr. 387 (*c.* 1300) are also authentic and taken from an eleventh-century compilation.[4]

During the twelfth century, political and economic relations between Byzantium and the West had their effects on scholarship. In the reign of Manuel I (1143–80), who was well disposed towards astronomical and astrological studies, Aristippus conveyed a manuscript of Ptolemy (the *Almagest*) to Sicily, where it was probably translated by Adelard of Bath. At about the same time Leo's archetype of Archimedes and other Greek manuscripts reached the Norman court, to be translated by William of Moerbeke. Admittedly, there was little in mathematics that Byzantium could learn from the West at that date; however, it may well be that the Byzantines gained from the West their knowledge of Arabic numerals, which appeared in Byzantium for the first time in a twelfth-century scholium on Euclid.[5] It is noteworthy that Leonardo of Pisa (b. *c.* 1170), whose career marks the beginning of the renaissance of mathematics in the West, and who introduced Arabic numerals and methods of calculation with his *Liber abbaci*, is known to have visited Byzantium. As he himself tells us,[6] he became acquainted with a number of

[1] Michael Italicus (second quarter of the twelfth century) taught not only grammar and rhetoric but also 'the mathematics' (the Quadrivium including mechanics, optics, catoptrics, metrics, the theory of the centre of gravity) and theology; see H. Fuchs, *Die höheren Schulen von Konstantinopel im Mittelalter*, pp. 37 f. See also a letter written by the prolific writer Theodore Prodromus to Michael Italicus, περὶ τοῦ μεγάλου καὶ τοῦ μικροῦ, ed. P. Tannery, *Mém. sc.* IV (1920), 207–22.

[2] Cod. Constantinop. palatii veteris no. 1.

[3] Ed. J. L. Heiberg, 'Mathematici Graeci minores', *Det Kgl. Dansk. Vid. Selsk. Hist.-fil. Medd.* XIII, 3 (Copenhagen, 1927), 3 ff. and 25 ff. There is a French translation by P. Ver Eecke, *Les opuscules mathématiques de Didyme, Diophane et Anthémius* (Paris-Bruges, 1940).

[4] See Hero, ed. J. L. Heiberg, IV (1912), p. iv.

[5] Euclid, ed. J. L. Heiberg, V (1888), p. xix.

[6] The *Liber abbaci*, ed. B. Boncompagni (Rome, 1857), pp. 249 ff.: 'Questio nobis proposita a peritissimo magistro Musco Constantinopolitano in Constantinopoli.' Other examples (pp. 188, 190, 203, 274 and 276), as well as the measures used, point to Byzantium.

arithmetical and algebraic problems from his contact with several Byzantine teachers, which is evidence that such studies continued to be cherished among them.

(c) *The Latin Empire to the fall of Constantinople* (1204–1453)

During the rule of the Latin Emperors there is no evidence of intellectual activity, whether of a general or a mathematical nature, in Constantinople itself. Baldwin planned a university there, but it never materialised. The private teachers migrated, irreplaceable manuscripts were destroyed or scattered. Only the practical subjects seem still to have attracted attention; and at this time also the new Arabic numerals and methods seem to have slowly started to spread. An arithmetic book in which they are used, dating from 1252 (ἀρχὴ τῆς μεγάλης καὶ Ἰνδικῆς ψηφοφορίας) later came into the possession of Maximus Planudes.

The court of Nicaea, on the other hand, whither most of the Greek scholars had fled, became, especially during the reigns of John Vatatzes and Theodore II Lascaris, a centre of Greek intellectual life, in which the leading figures were Nicephorus Blemmydes (c. 1197–1272) and George Acropolites (1217–82). John Vatatzes founded a school of philosophy in Nicaea (under the direction first of Hexapterygus and later of Blemmydes) and also other schools, with libraries, in various towns. In the Nicaean Empire there was a serious attempt at making education comprehensive to a much greater degree than it was in the West at the time, though it must be admitted that in mathematics it was again the practical branches that primarily received attention; had it not been so, the mathematics professors of the time of John Vatatzes—like the teachers of philosophy, with their renowned disregard of money—would have received no payment from the state.[1]

Blemmydes, a doctor's son born in Constantinople, founded a school at Ephesus; he was the tutor of the future Emperor Theodore II Lascaris (the best educated Basileus since Leo VI), who established at Nicaea a school of grammar and rhetoric and himself discussed scientific—including mathematical—problems. The most important of Blemmydes' and Hexapterygus' pupils was George Acropolites, statesman and humanist (also a tutor of Theodore II). Michael VIII Palaeologus, who undertook the revival of the schools and hospitals

---

[1] Zachariae von Lingenthal, *Jus graeco-romanum*, Synopsis minor VI (1931), pp. 495 f. —always assuming that von Lingenthal is right in saying that the 'Synopsis minor', ascribed to Michael Attaleiates, belongs to the period of Vatatzes; see his *Geschichte des griechisch-römischen Rechts* (3rd ed. 1892), p. 40.

of Constantinople after the restoration of 1261, appointed Acropolites head of the reopened state university at St Sophia, which was much under the influence of the Patriarch, Germanus III. In addition to the university, and connected with it (probably as a school of preparation), was a grammar school, held in the orphanage of St Paul's Church, where the normal general curriculum (ἐγκύκλιος παίδευσις) was taught. Acropolites lectured on mathematics after Euclid and Nicomachus,[1] as part of a course on philosophy. Of his successors as *hypatus* in his chair of philosophy, John Pediasimus (fl. *c*. 1310) showed a special interest in mathematics. He wrote scholia on Cleomedes and Ptolemy, a geometry consisting of excerpts from 'Hero' and also *Some Observations*, consisting of explanations of musical points, such as the numerical names of the intervals. According to his own account, the gifted scholar and historian, George Pachymeres (born 1242 in Nicaea, died *c*. 1310), a pupil of Acropolites, also taught at the university, despite his preoccupation with his ecclesiastical and secular offices. Like all philosophers, he was interested in Euclid and Nicomachus, he knew the Arabic system of numerals, and was the author of a Quadrivium much superior to the others (*Handbook on the Four Sciences*); in the arithmetical section he clearly demonstrates his close knowledge of Diophantus, at that time something very unusual. Pachymeres also lectured on the mathematical portions of Aristotle; one of his pupils made a set of notes on these lectures.

Maximus Planudes (*c*. 1255–*c*. 1310), who was a monk from Nicomedia, taught neither at the state university nor in the patriarchal school but in a public institution connected with a monastery with a library. He edited and commented on Diophantus' *Arithmetic* and revised the *Anthologia Graeca*. His *Arithmetic after the Indian method* (*c*. 1300), which was based on the similar book of 1252 mentioned above, shows that the new numerals and methods were still spreading.[2] It seems that before the time of Planudes there was a monk called Neophytus who used the Arabic numerals but employed the zero merely as a 'kind of exponent' or index for representation of the value of the digits,[3] so that his work represents no real advance over the arithmetic in which the numerals were alphabetical.

George of Cyprus (identical with the Patriarch Gregory (1283–9))

---

[1] George (Gregory) of Cyprus gave an account of the teaching he received from Acropolites (printed in *MPG*, CXLII, 25).

[2] Although the western Arabic Gobar digits are used in an arithmetic book of 1252, Planudes used the east Arabic forms; this points to influences by way of Persia-Trebizond-Constantinople. See P. Tannery, 'Les chiffres arabes dans les manuscrits grecs', *Mém. sc.* IV (1920), 199–205. Planudes received the book from George Beccus.

[3] The zero was denoted by a dot, or small circle, placed over a numeral, one dot indicating that the numeral was multiplied by ten, two dots by one hundred, three by one thousand, and so on [I am indebted to G. J. Whitrow for this note].

taught at the same monastery as Planudes, and was stimulated by his teacher Acropolites to the study of Euclid and Aristotle. Manuel Moschopulus, who wrote a treatise on magic squares, from a purely mathematical rather than mystical standpoint, was a pupil and friend of Planudes.

In the first half of the fourteenth century, a period very favourable to the pursuit of serious studies, the tutelage of the sciences at Byzantium passed into other hands. Among those who now came to the fore were some high officials of the civil service, who gathered round them a number of pupils to whom they handed on the intellectual achievement of the ancient world. Among such officials was Theodore Metochites (*c.* 1260–1332), who was deposed from the position of Grand Logothete in 1328, a man of wide education with a deeply ingrained love of learning. In his description of his course of study, he mentions that mathematics had for many years been in a perilous situation, lacking both teachers and students.[1] The only parts of Euclid and Nicomachus still studied were those relevant to philosophy, but did not include the tenth book of the *Elements* or the *Stereometry* or even the *Conics* of Apollonius or those of Serenus. Metochites eventually found a teacher to initiate him into the *Syntaxis* of Ptolemy; this was Manuel Bryennius, professor of astronomy and author of a book on harmony. He later studied Euclid (including the *Stereometry*, *Optics*, *Catoptrics*, *Data* and *Phaenomena*), Theodosius, and also, 'with much toil', Apollonius.

Metochites was the author of an introduction to Ptolemaic astronomy (*The Elements of Astronomy*), a treatise on the mathematical (harmonic) form of philosophy, and of many commentaries on Aristotle. The revival of higher mathematics at this period is attested by the numerous manuscripts of the thirteenth and fourteenth centuries, many of which certainly emanated from the circle of Manuel Bryennius and Theodore Metochites. Among them are included all the authors instanced by Metochites in his account of his studies (Euclid, Theodosius, Apollonius, Ptolemy), and many others (Eutocius, Theo, Pappus, Proclus, Geminus, Marinus, Autolycus and Aristarchus). Thus, while there is only one twelfth-century manuscript of Ptolemy's *Syntaxis* there are many surviving from the thirteenth and fourteenth centuries, including two with scholia 'by Bryennius', as Demetrius Cydones records.[2]

Metochites was responsible for introducing the encyclopaedic scholar and historian Nicephorus Gregoras (b. *c.* 1295 at Heraclea in Pontus, died *c.* 1360) to the study of astronomy and of the Greek

---

[1] C. N. Sathas, Μεσ. Βιβ. ι, πϛ´ f. (Venice, 1872), pp. 139–95.
[2] Cod. Paris Gr. 2390 and Cod. Flor. Laurentian. 28, 1.

mathematicians such as Nicomachus. Nicephorus Gregoras gave some private lessons at the Chora monastery, but he chiefly lectured before the learned audience of the court of Andronicus II. He was the author of a moderate work on the formation of square numbers, of two essays on the astrolabe and of various other astronomical writings, in which he sets out his own ideas (as also did Plethon, *c.* 1355–1452). His proposals for a reform of the calendar in 1324 went unregarded. By 1328 he seems to have stopped teaching, to resume his courses later, after his victory in a disputation with the Calabrian monk Barlaam (died *c.* 1350), a man well versed in scholastic dialectics, who had been appointed by John Cantacuzenus as teacher of theology and exponent of Aristotle; this success seems to have been due to Gregoras' superior ability as a mathematician. About 1358 Gregoras seems to have been living on Mt Athos, where there is evidence of an interest in mathematics and Aristotelian physics at this period. Many of the manuscripts found at Mt Athos have notes written in by Gregoras himself, which show that he was expert in the subjects treated. Barlaam, mentioned above, was the author of a commentary on the second book of Euclid's *Elements* and also of a work on logistics, in which calculations with vulgar and sexagesimal fractions and with ratios are taught. The fourteenth-century Cod. Marc. 310 contains an astronomical treatise by Barlaam on solar eclipse.

Another contemporary was Nicholas Rhabdas (fl. 1351); he knew Diophantus and was familiar with the 'Indian' methods of calculation. In two letters in which he employs the old numerical symbols Rhabdas expounds finger-symbolism and methods of arithmetic (including roots) and so brings together examples of problems in political arithmetic (rule-of-three, mathematical puzzles), which give us some insight into the old problems of logistics. Similar examples of arithmetical problems—some of them identical—appear in Cod. Paris. Suppl. Gr. 387 of the year 1303 as Ψηφοφορικὰ ζητήματα καὶ προβλήματα (Arithmetical questions and examples).

There was also a revival of astronomy in the first half of the fourteenth century. In this case the stimulus came from Trebizond, with which Byzantium had always maintained political, economic and cultural relations. Trebizond was the terminus of the important trade-route leading out of Persia. Gregory Chioniades (who died in Constantinople at the end of the thirteenth century) had made contact with Persian and Arabic science whilst living at the court of Trebizond; he travelled to Persia, learned the language, collected books, particularly on astronomy, and brought them back to Trebizond, where he founded a kind of academy. Cod. Vindob. Theol. Gr.

203 contains letters from Chioniades, including many addressed to
the mathematician and *protonotarius* and *protovestiarius* Constantine
Lukytes (not Lykytes), to whom he probably left his library. There
is also a free translation (dated 1323) of a work of a Persian astronomer writing in Arabic (Shams al-Bukhārī, died *c.* 1339), known as
Σὰμψ μπουχαρής. A cleric of Trebizond, Manuel (otherwise unknown),
was the teacher of the physician, astronomer and geographer George
Chrysococces. Manuel based his instruction on the books collected
by Chioniades, which he translated. Chrysococces was himself the
author of a *Commentary on the Persian Astronomical System* (1346),
and of other astronomical works. Thus by a circuitous route the
learning of Greek antiquity returned to Byzantium.

Still under the Persian influence were Isaac Argyrus (*c.* 1310–after
1371) and Theodore Meliteniotes (fl. 1360–88). Argyrus, a pupil of
Nicephorus Gregoras, probably also lived in Constantinople; in 1367
he wrote a treatise on the astrolabe, possibly based on a similar work
by his teacher. He is also regarded as the author of two astronomical
treatises (1371) and of two computi. The following mathematical
works of his have survived: an essay on square roots, scholia on
Euclid (six books of the *Elements*) and on the arithmetic of Planudes
in Rhabdas' edition, a new edition of Nicomachus' commentary by
Proclus and Philoponus and finally an unpublished geodesy in the
style of the pseudo-Heronian compilation.

Theodore Meliteniotes, the *megas sacellarius* and chief instructor,
one of the teachers at the patriarchal school in Constantinople, studied
Euclid and, besides the astronomical writings coming from Trebizond,
also once again read Ptolemy and Theo in the original. His *Astronomy*
in three volumes ('Αστρονομικὴ τρίβιβλος) of 1361 is the most comprehensive and learned work of this kind in existence. It cannot be
clearly established whether this depended on a similar work of
Argyrus or vice versa, since both have much in common and use
the same sources. The hesychast Nicholas Cabasilas (born 1322/3
in Thessalonica, died *c.* 1380) also studied Ptolemy and Theo of
Alexandria, whose commentary on the third book of the *Syntaxis* (on
the length of the year and the mean velocity of the sun) he tried to reconstruct. A friend of Cabasilas (and also of Nicephorus Gregoras) was
Demetrius Cydones (died 1397/8), who is known as one of the first
translators from Latin into Greek. His scholia on Euclid have survived,
as have also those of John Cabasilas (a relative of Nicholas).

There is little to be said on mathematical studies in the last decades
before the fall of the Empire. Nothing more is heard of Archimedes,
Apollonius and Diophantus. However, as is shown by the numerous
array of new manuscripts still being written, an interest was taken in

the elementary Quadrivium, which was still taught within the framework of 'the seven branches of learning' as they are called by Joseph Bryennius, who was teaching at the patriarchal school in 1396;[1] attention remained focused on geodesy and logistics. An arithmetic book with numerous exercises similar to those in Cod. Paris Suppl. Gr. 387 of 1303 is preserved in Cod. Vind. Phil. Gr. 65;[2] throughout this work calculations are made using the new Arabic decimal methods, although it is occasionally obvious that the scribe had not reconciled himself to these numerical forms, since he uses in their place the Greek alphabetical numerals from 1 to 9 and a symbol for zero; calculations can be conducted quite satisfactorily in this manner since the form of the ten symbols is unimportant.[3]

Private, public and ecclesiastical libraries still had a rich store of books, which were much coveted and bought by the increasingly large number of Latins who had come to Constantinople to learn Greek and to gain acquaintance with Greek culture. It was men such as Filelfo and Bessarion of Trebizond (fellow-students at the feet of Chrysococces), and George of Trebizond, himself the director of a school, who took Greek manuscripts back with them to Italy. The study of such manuscripts and of earlier arrivals in Italy, taken together with the Latin and Hebrew translations made from Arabic editions, brought to its full flowering the mathematical renaissance in the West which had begun with Adelard of Bath, Leonardo of Pisa, Jordanus Nemorarius and William of Moerbeke.

II. PHYSICS (MECHANICS)

The Greek concept of physics did not coincide with our modern ideas of physical science as the theory of the forces in nature. The Greek idea was much more comprehensive, especially in respect of particular

[1] His library included, amongst other things, a geometry in fifteen books (obviously Euclid's *Elements*), Nicomachus' arithmetic, the *Great Syntaxis*, and also a book on music (Manuel Bryennius and Ptolemy). See A. Papadopulos-Kerameus, *Varia Graeca Sacra* (St Petersburg, 1909), pp. 295 f.

[2] J. L. Heiberg, 'Byzantinische Analekten', *Abhandl. z. Gesch. d. Mathem.* IX (1899), i, 163–9. In iii, 172–4, Heiberg publishes a series of various digit forms (Indian and Herodian) from Cod. Marc. Gr. 323. For Byzantine arithmetical problems in western textbooks see K. Vogel, *Die Practica des Algorismus Ratisbonensis* (Munich, 1954), pp. 206 ff.

[3] In Cod. Vind. Phil. Gr. 65 the decimal fraction is already in use, for the writer says that this is the method which has been current 'since the Turks have been ruling our country'. Clearly we can see here the influence of al-Kāshī, the inventor of the decimal fraction system described in his *Key to Arithmetic* (Samarkand, 1427). See H. Hunger and K. Vogel, *Ein byzantinisches Rechenbuch des 15. Jahrhunderts* (Osterreiche Akad. der Wissenschaft, phil.-hist. Kl. Denkschriften, Bd. 78, Abh. 2, Vienna, 1963).

concepts, such as that of motion (= change). Likewise meteorology
was not confined, as it is today, to the study of atmospheric phenomena, but included subjects which are now considered more proper
to astronomy, physical geography, geology, or even chemical technology. But above all the fundamental attitude was different; the
Greeks achieved their results by means of speculative deductions
made on the basis of chance observations and perceptions. The idea
that nature by means of experiment might be made to speak for herself was for the most part alien to the Greeks.[1] Scientific results were
occasionally achieved, in subjects already amenable to mathematical
treatment (for example, mechanics, geometrical optics, acoustics);
otherwise, however (for example, in heat, magnetism, physiological
optics, meteorology), activity was confined to observation and descriptive writing.

All this applies equally to Byzantium, which has scarcely anything
to its credit in the advancement of physical theories, although there
was a widespread interest in the application of physics to technical
problems. The contribution of Byzantine scholarship in physics, as in
mathematics, consisted in preserving the old texts and in making
new editions and commentaries; and also in ensuring the dissemination of some knowledge of physics through the teaching of the universities, where Aristotelian physics and meteorology were taught as
part of philosophy, while acoustics and optics (which formed a part
of geometry) came within the framework of the Quadrivium. Thus
was made possible the later transmission of this inheritance, first to
the Syrians and the Arabs, and afterwards, particularly in the twelfth
and thirteenth centuries, to the West.

There is evidence of serious work in mechanics, mathematically
based, in the sixth century, a period of great importance in the
transmission of Greek learning. Eutocius, who commented on Archimedes' *Plane Equilibriums*, was familiar with the first book of Hero's
Introduction to Mechanics,[2] which was to be preserved only in Arabic
versions; and it is not surprising to find that Isidore of Miletus, the
second architect of St Sophia, was also interested in the works of
Archimedes and Hero. And although there are only occasional references in later periods to the teaching of mechanics or centre-of-
gravity problems, there can be no doubt that the master-builders
themselves took care that the important writings of Antiquity on
these subjects should be preserved. This is proved by the fact that the

---

[1] Ptolemy, with his optical experiments, is a famous exception. For an experiment
by which Gregory of Nyssa sought to demonstrate the emergence of the cosmos from
the chaos see S. Günther, *Geschichte der Erdkunde* (Leipzig–Vienna, 1904), p. 38.

[2] *Heronis opera*, I, ed. W. Schmidt (Leipzig, 1899), *Supplementum*, p. 68.

Greek manuscripts which reached the West in the time of the Normans and Hohenstaufen included the classic works on mechanics.

There is much richer evidence of a continued interest in Aristotelian physics. In the sixth century there lived two of the greatest commentators on Aristotle after Alexander of Aphrodisias, Simplicius and Philoponus; in a few of his ideas Philoponus even advanced beyond Aristotle. He suggested (on the basis of experiment?) that heavy bodies do not fall more quickly than lighter ones, and the possibility of a vacuum. He also seems to have come closer to the concept of inertia.[1]

Of the Byzantine scholars of the ninth century, Photius, in his *Bibliotheca*, busied himself with a number of physical questions, and Leo the Mathematician concerned himself with technical applications. The school of Aristotelian physics reached its full flowering in the university of the eleventh century, whose moving spirit, Michael Psellus, wrote copiously on physical subjects (such as matter, colour, motion, echo, rain, thunder and lightning) in his *Omnifaria doctrina* and in his other works. He was also the author of a treatise on meteorology, and a commentary on Aristotle's *Physics*. The *Short Solutions of Physical Questions* which go under his name are not really by Psellus; they are in fact the first three books of the *Conspectus rerum naturalium* of his contemporary, Symeon Seth, who, like Psellus in his *Omnifaria doctrina*, makes this work on natural science the occasion for a number of reflections on heaven and earth, matter and form, place and time, soul and spirit, and the five senses. Physics and meteorology were also taught under Manuel I at the academy of Michael, later Patriarch, and probably also at the school of the Church of the Holy Apostles. The dialectical treatment of physics at this school is of interest: anyone who pronounced on the laws of nature themselves (instead of relying on ambiguous premises) was no philospher.[2]

The Greek manuscripts from Byzantium which reached the Norman court in Sicily during the reign of Manuel I included a number on physical subjects. Aristippus (died *c*. 1162) translated the so-called 'fourth book' of Aristotle's *Meteorology*; and he is known to have had Hero's *Pneumatica*, also translated at that time, in his possession. The *Institutio physica* of Proclus (Στοιχείωσις φυσικὴ ἢ περὶ κινήσεως) was at that period in the hands of Adelard of Bath, and seems to have been translated by him. A century later William of Moerbeke was at

---

[1] See E. Wohlwill, 'Ein Vorgänger Galileis im 6. Jahrhundert', *Physik Zeitschr.* VII (1906), 23–32. The originality of Philoponus was questioned by A. E. Haas in *Biblioth. Mathem.* VI (3. Folge, 1905–6), 337 ff.

[2] *Apostelkirche*, ed. A. Heisenberg, p. 90.

work on his numerous translations, which included versions of Hero's *Pneumatica*, Archimedes' writings on mechanics (*De insidentibus aquae* and *De planis aeque repentibus*, the latter with the commentary of Eutocius), and the four books of Aristotle on meteorology (partially a revision of earlier translations) as well as other works of Aristotle. William of Moerbeke also revised an older Latin translation from the Greek of Aristotle's *Physics*, which itself preceded the oldest Latin translation from the Arabic (made by Gerard of Cremona).

Nicephorus Blemmydes, Nicephorus Chumnus, and above all Theodore Metochites, bear witness to the continuance of physical studies in Byzantium in the thirteenth and fourteenth centuries; Metochites included the *Physics* and *Meteorology* in his commentaries on Aristotle (see above, p. 276). His pupil, Nicephorus Gregoras, was also interested in Aristotelian physics. There is a final reference to scientific education at Byzantium during the reign of the Emperor Manuel II (1391–1425), who brought about a brief scholarly revival. Thereafter came the end.

III. OPTICS

The ideas of the Greeks on the nature of vision and their mathematically formulated view of the paths of light rays are set down in the works of Aristotle, Euclid, Hero, Theo of Alexandria and others, and most fully in the *Optics* of Ptolemy.[1] Ptolemy, working from observation and experiment, achieved sound results in measuring the angle of refraction at the entry of a ray of light into another medium. Only one advance on existing knowledge can be credited to Byzantium, and this falls into the earliest period (sixth century), being the work of the architect Anthemius of Tralles (see above, p. 276). His treatise *On Curious Mechanisms* contains a passage on burning-mirrors. This treats of plane mirrors forming tangents to an ellipse.[2] It was once again the Arabs who, from the ninth century onwards, preserved the Greek legacy. Thus it came about that the original text of the lost *Optics* of Ptolemy reached the West in a Latin translation from the Arabic made by the Norman admiral Eugenius in 1154; he also had in his possession the *Optica* (known also to Aristippus) and *Catoptrica* of Euclid. Both these works were studied by the

---

[1] The most important works are: Aristotle, *Meteorologica*, Euclid's *Optica* and its revision by Theo of Alexandria; the Pseudo-Euclidian *Catoptrica* of Theo of Alexandria, Ptolemy's *Optica*, the Pseudo-Ptolemaic *Catoptrica* of Hero and the *Optica* of Damianus of Larissa (fourth century A.D.). The earlier authorities make a distinction between optics (passage of light rays in direct vision) and catoptrics (refraction in mirrors); Ptolemy and Damianus, however, include both under the heading of optics.

[2] See T. L. Heath, 'The Fragment of Anthemius on Burning Mirrors and the "Fragmentum mathematicum Bobiense"', *Biblioth. Math.* VII (3. Folge, 1906–7), 225–33.

author of the translation of the *Almagest* made in Sicily *c.* 1160
(probably Adelard of Bath) and were perhaps translated by him. The
now lost manuscript of Hero's *Catoptrica* which William of Moerbeke
used as a model in Viterbo in 1269 was certainly also among the Greek
manuscripts in circulation in Sicily and southern Italy at that date.

At Byzantium, from the time of Philoponus onwards, there was
some interest in the physiological aspects of optics (vision, colour,
rainbows, solar coronas and so on) as treated in Aristotelian physics;
the subject was discussed both in works on meteorology and in special
studies. Psellus made some observations on the subject in his *Omnifaria doctrina*, but there is a more detailed survey in Symeon Seth's
note *On Optics* which also contains some remarks on refraction. The
classical writings on mathematical optics were still being copied. In
addition to the many manuscripts of similar nature from the twelfth
and thirteenth centuries and later there have survived a manuscript
of Theo's revision of Euclid's *Optics*, written in the tenth century, and
a manuscript of his pseudo-Euclidian *Catoptrica*; both have scholia.
It is known that Nicephorus Blemmydes, who as a young man
experienced the extreme poverty into which scientific education had
fallen in Latin Byzantium, learnt optics and catoptrics (together with
mathematics and astronomy) at Skamandros (Troas) from a teacher
called Prodromus. Pachymeres included an extract from Euclid's
Optics in the section on geometry in his Quadrivium. In the later
period there are only sparse references to mathematical optics; Theodore Metochites (later thirteenth century) refers to it in his curriculum, and Joseph Bryennius (*c.* 1400) had a book on optics (Ἐποπτικά)
in his library.

IV. ACOUSTICS

The practice of music at Byzantium took on a new lease of life from
the time of John of Damascus (eighth century) and was further
developed to meet the requirements of the Christian liturgy. One
crying need was the development of a form of notation, and from the
tenth century onwards the simple system of dots and lines was further
improved until a form was evolved which marked not only the notes
themselves but also the tone intervals (thus: two higher, five lower)
as well as the length of the note, stress, key, rhythm, tremolo and so
on.[1] Musical theory, on the other hand, remained where the ancients
had left it, both as regards the nature of sound and hearing and the
mathematical treatment of intervals. In contrast to the practical
thinkers, such as Aristoxenus (fourth century B.C.) who relied on the
ear, the Pythagoreans based their mathematical theories on the

---

[1] See also chapter XXIV by E. Wellesz.

numerical laws of the tetrachord. These Pythagorean doctrines continued to flourish at Byzantium and were taught in the portion of the Quadrivium designated as 'music' or 'harmony'. Michael Psellus concerned himself with questions of acoustics more than once. In his treatise *On the Resounding Hall in Nicomedia* he describes a covered building constructed of four walls set in a semicircle, which had a remarkable echo effect which he sought to explain without reference to sorcery or mechanical devices.[1] In this connection he was led on to discuss thunder and lightning and advances the curious idea that the eye detects it before the ear because it 'protrudes' and is 'not hollow'.[2] His contemporary, Symeon Seth, has a better explanation: sound needs time, whereas sight is independent of time.[3]

At the beginning of the thirteenth century music was being taught at the Church of the Holy Apostles in both its practical and theoretical aspects. In the preparatory school the psalmodists practised with the pupils, with pleasantly harmonious results, and sound and key formed part of the mathematical instruction of the university, together with some discussion of intervals. Pachymeres (d. c. 1310) in his teaching of the Quadrivium treated music in great detail, illustrating the intervals (the lengths of the strings in the tetrachord, in the Pythagorean octachord, etc.) with numerous diagrams. His teaching of music was thus much more advanced than that of Gregory the Monk (1008) who discussed it only very briefly in his Quadrivium. Manuel Bryennius made a comprehensive compilation called *Harmonics* which drew on the old theorists and practitioners and also on Pachymeres, only slightly his senior; Bryennius' contemporary Pediasimus wrote *Some Observations* (see above, p. 275). More important was Nicephorus Gregoras (died c. 1360) who in music, as in his astronomical studies, went back to Ptolemy, commenting on his unfinished work on harmony and even attempting to complete it. In conclusion, mention must also be made of Joseph Bryennius, whose library, which he bequeathed to St Sophia, contained the works of Ptolemy and Manuel Bryennius on musical subjects.

v. zoology

Byzantine scholars for the most part ignored the deeper questions of zoology such as were treated by Aristotle (the development of organisms, the physiology of organs and their purpose); the most that was done, and that only rarely, was to make a study of Aristotle himself.

---

[1] ἠχεῖα was used also to denote acoustic vases which might be built into the floor of a theatre to act as resonators.

[2] J. F. Boissonade, *Psellus*, p. 60.   [3] A. Delatte, *Anec. Athen.* ii, p. 31.

There is an *Epitome of Aristotle's Zoology* dating from the time of Constantine VII Porphyrogenitus, and a commentary on the *De partibus animalium* is ascribed to John Tzetzes (1100–80). Further evidence of an interest in Aristotle is furnished by the Greek manuscripts used by William of Moerbeke for his Latin translation in 1260 of the *History of Animals* and of the *Generation of Animals*.

On the other hand, there was great interest in practical zoology, the description of animals, their characteristics and diseases, which was often mingled with ancient fantastical and occult ideas. Material relevant to the household and to agriculture and hunting was observed and written up; thus the *Hippiatrica* treats of horses, and the *Geoponica* of domestic animals (including bees), fish, and vermin. Medical writings (see below, p. 288) contain accounts of useful and noxious animals (leeches, poisonous creatures, parasites, worms) and also indicate the value of animal products as food and in making medicaments.

There is a bestiary compiled by Timothy of Gaza dating from the reign of Anastasius I (491–518). During the sixth century Cosmas Indicopleustes travelled widely in Africa and Asia (Arabia and Ceylon); his *Christian Topography* contains descriptions, accurate for the most part, of African and Indian beasts. The introduction of the silk-worm probably from central Asia (Sogdiana) in 553–4 was of great importance for Byzantine, and later also for Italian, industry.

A remarkably detailed work on falconry (*On the Breeding and Care of Falcons*), which used sources different from those drawn on for Frederick II's famous book on the subject, was written by a doctor named Demetrius Pepagomenus during the reign of Michael VIII Palaeologus (1259–82). It has some exact observations concerning the presence of worms in the eyes of falcons. It is uncertain whether Demetrius was also really the author of a mediocre book on dogs (*Kynosophion* or *The Care of Dogs*). Three other anonymous books on falconry also belong to this period: a book on birds (*Wild Birds*) which describes their diseases and their treatment; *The Management of Birds*, written for Michael VIII, and, based upon it, a *Treatise on the Management of Hawks*.

Manuel Philes (1275–1345), a friend of Pachymeres and Maximus Planudes, wrote the *Brief Description of the Elephant*, and a rather mediocre didactic poem *On the Characteristics of Animals* which describes not only authentic birds, fishes and four-legged beasts, but also fabulous creatures (unicorns, jumars). Among his sources was the *Physiologus*, the most important medieval work on natural history. The *Physiologus* is of anonymous origin, and dates from some time during the earliest centuries of Christianity; it found its way into the literature of many nations, though the stream of its Byzantine tradition can only be followed closely from the eleventh century. The zoological portion contains descriptions of actual and fabulous beasts (as basilisks, centaurs, the phoenix, dragons), with religious and allegorical interpretations of their actual or imaginary properties.

VI. BOTANY

There is little evidence of any scientific study of botany (for example, systematic botany, the physiology and biology of plants) at Byzantium. The high standard of a Theophrastus, who conducted his investigations in the spirit of Aristotle, was no longer maintained. It is true that Basil of Caesarea (*c.* 330–79) shows in his *Homilies on the Hexaemeron* (the Creation) that he had some accurate ideas concerning the way things happen in the world of plants, but from him the tradition seems to have passed to the West (via Ambrose) rather than to Byzantium.

As in zoology, Byzantine interest in botany was confined to descriptions and to its practical applications in agriculture, horticulture, household matters (for example, cooking), medicine and pharmacology. Some information on the subject is to be found in geographical and historical works, in Photius, the *Suda* and Psellus. The *Geoponica* has an account of the useful plants and their cultivation (cereals, vegetables, fruit and olive trees, the vine); the section on viticulture was translated into Latin by Burgundio of Pisa (died 1193), who from 1136 onwards made frequent visits to Byzantium. The number of surviving manuscripts of Dioscorides, some with illustrations (the first dates from *c.* 512), shows the respect in which the memory of this encyclopaedist of the first century A.D., who described about 600 plants, was long held.

Michael Glycas (fl. mid-twelfth century) took some descriptions of plants from the *Physiologus*, which was also known to Manuel Philes (1275–1345), who composed a number of poems on plants, fruits and flowers. Botanical *lexica*, mostly of unknown origin, were also generally current and survive in manuscripts of the thirteenth and fourteenth and later centuries.

VII. MINERALOGY

In the pre-Byzantine period some attempts were made at treating mineralogy scientifically by defining, systematising and interpreting the data. Theophrastus (late fourth century B.C.) in his work *On Stones* describes many stones (including precious stones) and types of soil, giving an account of the places where they are found and their uses. Some fragments of a work *On Minerals* are also ascribed to him. Straton, rather later than Theophrastus, was probably the author of the so-called fourth book of Aristotle's *Meteorology*, which could be described as the first textbook of theoretical chemistry (see also below); minerals were dealt with in the authentic fourth book (τὰ μὲν ὀρυκτὰ τὰ δὲ μεταλλευτά) and, like the meteorological phenomena treated in the first three books, were held to derive from the moist and dry rising vapours. This now lost book (μονόβιβλος περὶ μετάλλων) was still known to Olympiodorus and Simplicius and continued to be written about, above all by Philoponus.

Byzantium made no advances in this subject: quite the reverse, since scientific mineralogy was all but destroyed by the superimposition of occult imaginings. Even the knowledge which continued to be gained as a result of mining operations and the observation of nature was no longer regarded as of any theoretical value. There was still an occasional interest in the practical applications of the subject in technology (see below, p. 299), medicine and pharmacology: minerals might be taken in powder form or applied externally. The books produced in later periods, also under the title *On Stones*, deal first and foremost with the magical powers innate in minerals (and especially precious stones, see below, p. 298). The only useful accounts are those to be found in the descriptions which occur incidentally in a few of these writings, some of them lexigraphical in character: for example, the enumeration of stones in Theodore Meliteniotes' poem 'To moderation'.

VIII. CHEMISTRY

Chemical processes in nature, such as fermentation, coagulation, putrefaction, oxydisation, have been observed at all periods—the Greeks were not alone in this—and some processes are utilised in day-to-day living, in making bread, beer, oil, and vinegar, and in tempering and purifying metals. But chemistry only made its appearance as a theoretical subject with the author of the so-called fourth book of Aristotle's *Meteorology* (Straton, see also above), which sought to explain chemical processes by the combination and dissociation of substances. There can be no doubt that this, the oldest textbook of chemistry, was still known in the time of Philoponus; it also survived in some Aristotelian manuscripts and was among the first works of Greek origin to reach the West. It was translated in the twelfth century by Aristippus and a hundred years later by William of Moerbeke. But Theodore Metochites recognised that this

'Fourth Book' could not have been by Aristotle, as he stated in his commentary on Aristotelian physics.

At Byzantium, however, the chief interest in chemistry was in its practical use in technology (as metallurgy, production of dyes, drugs, glass, chalk) and its household applications; this is evident in numerous, mainly alchemical writings, in which, indeed, unscientific, not to say occult, ideas are frequently uppermost.

IX. MEDICINE, DENTISTRY AND VETERINARY MEDICINE

As in the other sciences, the main Byzantine contribution to medicine was the preservation of the classical and Hellenistic heritage and its transmission to both East and West. But there was an advance in the field of organisation, which was connected with the Byzantine social sciences: both State and Church concerned themselves to a high degree in everything connected with health: hospitals were organised, the education of doctors regulated and their livelihood guaranteed, and there were even rules for the preparation and safe custody of medicines.

As in the case of astronomy, it can be shown that during the later period some of the classical learning concerning medicine was reintroduced into Byzantium from the East, where Jundishapur was a famous centre of medical studies. In the East itself the only new discoveries concerned *materia medica* and methods of treatment.

The point which marks the transition from Hellenistic to Byzantine medicine coincides with the career of Oreibasius of Pergamum (325–c. 400), the personal physician and friend of Julian the Apostate. In his magnificent encyclopaedia (*Corpus of Medicine*) he not only handed down the learning of Hippocrates and, above all, of Galen, but also, by his careful citation of sources, rescued from oblivion much that would otherwise have been lost. All later Byzantine authors base themselves on his work. Only twenty-seven of the seventy books of his *Corpus* (*Synagogai*), together with a fragment of another, have survived; the contents of the lost books can be deduced from a *Synopsis* which he made for his son. It is remarkable that surgery is omitted as being a subject for specialists. Contemporaneous with Oribasius were Philagrius and Posidonius, two doctors who were particularly interested in diseases of the brain, and Nemesius, Bishop of Emesa, whose treatise *On the Nature of Man* was later translated into Latin, first c. 1050 by Alphanus of Salerno, and later by Burgundio of Pisa (c. 1110–93).

Medical lectures were given at the Theodosian university within the framework of the philosophy course. The philosopher Agapius was summoned thither from Alexandria, the centre of medical teaching and research, to be lecturer in medicine. Aetius of Amida, physician at the court of Justinian I, was also educated at Alexandria. The section on ophthalmics in his encyclopaedic sixteen volumes on *Medicine* (based on Archigenus and Galen) is one of the best of antiquity. A slightly younger contemporary, Alexander of Tralles (*c.* 525–605), a brother of the mathematician Anthemius, stands out for the independence of his opinions, based on his own experience. His work on pathology and therapeutics, in twelve books, was widely known; he was also the author of some monographs, on diseases of the eyes, fevers, and intestinal worms.

The last of the four great early Byzantine scholar-physicians was Paul of Aegina (fl. 640), who stayed on in Alexandria after its capture by the Arabs. Through his textbook on diseases and their treatment (entitled *Memorandum*), based on Galen and Oribasius, he became the teacher of the West on medical matters, and, through his studies on surgery and obstetrics, exerted a great influence on Arab medicine. Another of Paul's contemporaries, also from Alexandria, was Aaron, who deserves mention for his description of smallpox in his *Compendium of Medicine*.

During the reign of Heraclius (610–41) medical lectures were being given at Byzantium by the *protospatharius* Theophilus, and some of his works have survived. Stephen of Athens, a pupil of Theophilus, wrote on the effects of drugs on fevers and on urine, as well as on other subjects. He also wrote commentaries on Hippocrates and Galen as did his contemporary John of Alexandria (fl. *c.* 627–40), who remained in Alexandria after the capture of the city by the Arabs and who, like Paul of Aegina, had a considerable influence on Arab medicine. In fact, John's epitome of Galen (*The 16 Books of Galen*) has survived only in an Arabic translation.[1] Sophronius (Patriarch of Jerusalem in 634) in his 'Letter to Joseph' gives us some incidental information concerning diseases and their treatment at this period, including the fact that doctors who wanted payment were distrusted.

During the next few centuries there was little original work done in medicine at Byzantium. Nicholas, an expert in the medical field of learning, was giving lectures during the time of the Emperor Philippicus (711–13); the Phrygian monk Meletius (somewhere between 600 and 800), the author of an unremarkable work on anatomy, also probably belongs to this period. Much more considerable, especially on the surgical side, is the *Epitome of Medicine* of the early ninth century of Leo, mathematician and 'learned physician' (ἰατροσοφιστής). His treatise *On the Characteristics of Human Beings*

---

[1] British Museum, MS. Arundel Or. 17.

has also survived, and a still unpublished *Epitome on the Nature of Human Beings* similar to that of Meletius. About the same time, and not, as is often thought, in the eleventh century, lived Nicetas, who collected together a number of older surgical treatises (for example, of Palladius, Soranus, Paul of Aegina). There are also many medical chapters in Photius' *Bibliotheca*.

Among the encyclopaedias produced at the behest of Constantine VII Porphyrogenitus was a *Medicine* by Theophanes Nonnus, compiled from the works of the four Byzantine classical writers on medicine. A work on the pulse, by an otherwise unknown Mercurius, also belongs to the tenth century. To the same century, or perhaps the eleventh, belongs a Greek translation of an Arabic text by Abū Jaʿfar Aḥmad ibn Ibrāhīm ibn al-Jazzār (died 1009) entitled *Viaticum for travellers*, which contains amongst other things descriptions of the plague, smallpox and measles. A short work of a certain Damnastes *On the Care of Pregnant Women and Infants* also belongs to this period.

The eleventh century is represented by two highly important figures, Michael Psellus and Symeon Seth. That talented and versatile scholar Psellus expressed opinions on a variety of medical topics in both prose and verse. He was the author of a dictionary of diseases, a 'Work on Medicine' (in 1373 trimeters) and another 'On Baths' and also of some humorous verses on scabies, of which he had personal experience. There is also much medical and physiological material in his *Omnifaria Doctrina*. Symeon Seth's most important work is a lexicon of the healing powers of various foods (*Lexicon on the Properties of Foods*), in which the names of a number of oriental drugs are met with translated into Greek for the first time.

The twelfth century is characterised by an intensification of state activity in the care of the sick. John II Comnenus and his wife Irene founded hospitals, laying down precise regulations for their management. The centre of medical teaching was the hospital founded by the Empress in 1136 at the Pantocrator monastery, where Michael Italicus was appointed medical instructor (διδάσκαλος ἰατρῶν). In his lectures he expounded Hippocrates and Galen and also used cases in illustration of various diseases. The children of the hospital physicians were also trained to follow the profession. A pupil of Italicus, Theodore Prodromus, gives a good description of smallpox. A certain Callicles is also described as 'teacher of the doctors' at this period. There is a lively sketch from the pen of Mesarites of the conduct and teaching of the school at the Church of the Holy Apostles about the year 1200.[1]

[1] See A. Heisenberg, *Apostelkirche*, pp. 91f.; a translation is published by K. Sudhoff in *Mitteilungen z. Geschichte der Medizin, der Naturwissenschaften und der Technik*, XXIII (1924), 189f.

Medicine also had its share in the revival of studies at the imperial court of Nicaea and at Byzantium under the Palaeologi after the restoration. Nicephorus Blemmydes wrote a little on medical subjects. Nicholas Myrepsus (= *unguentarius*) was court physician (ἀκτουάριος) at Nicaea under John Vatatzes and wrote a work on *materia medica* (Δυναμερόν) which was still influential as late as the seventeenth century. Demetrius Pepagomenus (physician to Michael VIII) wrote a useful book on gout, which was used by a somewhat later writer on the same subject, John Chumnus. Much more important was John Actuarius, court physician to Andronicus III. He is the last great Byzantine doctor of the school of Galen with personal clinical experiences. He wrote a book *Methods of Treatment* (diagnosis, pathology, therapeutics, pharmacology), and a detailed treatise on urine which was of considerable importance in medieval uroscopy. A third work is of significance in the history of pneumatism and psychopathology. It consists of two books on the three kinds of pneuma. The first book deals with the powers of the mind and their disorders, and the second lays down rules of hygiene. He is the first writer to describe the whipworm (*trichocephalus dispar*, a parasite of the human intestine), which he may have himself discovered.

During this period medicine, like astronomy, was clearly subject to eastern influences. Constantine Meliteniotes translated a Persian work;[1] there are two anonymous and undated treatises of Syrian and Persian origin on urine, and Persian influence can also be seen in another anonymous work, on diagnoses made from the blood. There is also a Greek translation of a treatise on urine by Ibn Sīna (980–1037).

Medical teaching at Byzantium ended with John Actuarius and the practice of medicine passed to Jewish doctors. This is explicitly stated by Joseph Bryennius (fl. 1387–1405) who tried to discover the reasons for the decline. But in any case, all the material which was important for posterity was now in other hands. Alexander of Tralles and Aetius of Amida, like Galen, had already been translated into Syrian and Arabic, while the tradition of John of Alexandria and Paul of Aegina was kept alive at Alexandria by the Arabs; but long before the West became acquainted with Arab medicine, Greek medical texts were available to the Latins. Oribasius was translated as early as the sixth century, and the partial translations of the works of Paul of Aegina which originated in southern Italy in the eighth or ninth century seem to have been influential in the early development of

---

[1] A. P. Kuses, 'Quelques considérations sur les traductions en grec des œuvres médicales orientales et principalement sur les deux manuscrits de la traduction d'un traité persan par Constantine Melitiniotis', *Praktika Akad. Athen.* xiv (1939), 205–20.

Salerno. By the time medical learning at Byzantium had totally declined, the study of the classical works of the Greek medical authorities in the West had already reached its fullest flowering in Italy, France and Spain.

As was usually the case in antiquity and the middle ages, dentistry was not regarded at Byzantium as a special profession. The collected writings of the four great Byzantine medical authorities, Oribasius, Aetius of Amida, Alexander of Tralles and Paul of Aegina, all contain passages devoted to diseases of the teeth and gums and to methods of treatment (extraction, filing, ointments and other remedies). The subject is also treated by many of the doctors of later centuries and by writers on medical subjects.

The Greeks had already much concerned themselves with the care in sickness and health of those animals indispensable to man as food, means of transport and in riding and hunting. Farmers and soldiers were naturally those most interested in the subject. The compendium collection made under Constantine VII Porphyrogenitus entitled *Hippiatrica* (see above, p. 285), composed of more than 400 existing fragmentary writings, included the corpus of knowledge concerning the care of horses and their diseases which had been assembled during the Hellenistic and early Byzantine periods.[1] A principal source was the writings of Apsyrtus, chief army veterinary surgeon to Constantine the Great, who was the author of two books on the treatment of sick animals. One of the best of the veterinary doctors of late Antiquity was Hierocles (*c.* 400); he wrote a book *On the Care of Horses* and is represented by 107 fragments in the *Hippiatrica*, which also contains writings by Theomnestes (fourth century) and others. The *Hippiatrica* also indirectly enshrines the experience in the art of healing animals gained by other peoples: for example, Apsyrtus was acquainted with Sarmathian, Syrian and Cappadocian practices, Theomnestes knew Armenian ways, and it seems that the thirty-six passages attributed to 'Hippocrates' are really the work of an Indian author of the sixth century. The *Geoponica*, also compiled under Constantine VII Porphyrogenitus (see above, p. 286), contained a certain amount on the ailments of horses, dogs, cattle and sheep, goats and pigs.

---

[1] Cf. Plate 25.

X. PHARMACOLOGY

Pharmacology as an independent branch of study was unknown at Byzantium; the doctor acted as his own apothecary[1] and did not shrink from travelling far and wide seeking out the substances used as healing agents (plants, ores and so on) in foreign lands, collecting and testing them for himself. The writings of doctors on therapeutics therefore usually include prescriptions for the remedies to be employed. It was only later, with the increased intervention of the state in affairs of health, that some order was introduced into pharmacy and rules laid down for the production and storage of medicines.

The Byzantines were able to make some advances on the knowledge amassed by Nicandrus, Dioscorides and Galen, since they gradually added remedies from the east, from Arabia and Persia, to those obtained from their native flora and fauna.

A large part of the literature of the subject was taken up with works on dietetics, either as separate monographs or incorporated into general medical textbooks, a fact which emphasises the importance attached to correct nourishment in both sickness and health. These treatises describe the characteristics and properties of the various items of diet, and often give advice on their preparation; this subject is in fact dealt with in the first five books of the *Synagogai* of Oribasius. There is a very illuminating letter entitled 'De observatione ciborum', addressed to the Frankish king Theodoric by Anthimus, a Greek physician exiled from Byzantium and living at the court of Theodoric the Ostrogoth. Others to write on the subject of diet were Theophanes Nonnus, Michael Psellus, Symeon Seth and John Actuarius, and there are also a number of anonymous writings. Of all these the most important is Symeon Seth's *Lexicon on the Properties of Foods*. He is the first to mention substances of oriental origin, such as cloves, nutmegs, and hemp-seed (hashish).

Dietary rules were often laid down for the four seasons or even for the different months of the year. One such treatise, by the sophist Hierophilus (twelfth century), has the title *On various foods for each month and their use*; there are a number of different versions. A poem of similar content, 'Verses on the twelve months', was written about this time by Theodore Prodromus.

Medical writers such as Oribasius, Aetius of Amida, Paul of Aegina and Theophanes Nonnus compiled lists of remedies, both household

---

[1] The first record of a distinction being made between doctors and apothecaries comes from the reign of the Emperor Frederick II (see E. Kremers and G. Urdang, *History of Pharmacy* (Philadelphia, 1951), pp. 555–6).

medicines and those manufactured professionally. Stephen Magnetes
(eleventh century) made an alphabetical list. Symeon Seth's book on
the properties of various foods, already mentioned, also refers to
other remedies. The most detailed *antidotarium* of all, and one whose
influence with western apothecaries remained strong until the seventeenth century, was the *Materia Medica* (*c.* 1280) of Nicholas Myrepsus (see above, p. 291); of the 2656 recipes contained therein, about 150
are taken from Salerno (*antidotarium parvum*), whilst others are of
oriental origin. John Actuarius' *Methods of Treatment* has two books
devoted to the preparation of remedies. With Actuarius, the last
important Byzantine physician writing from personal experience,
independent works on pharmacology also come to an end. As in the
case of medicine and astronomy, Persian influences for a time became
dominant. George Choniates composed a book, *Antidotes culled from
Persia and translated into Greek*, perhaps based on one of the works
brought out of Persia by Chioniades (see above, p. 277). Constantine
Meliteniotes (see above, p. 291) translated a similar *antidotarium*
from the Persian. But even this Perso-Byzantine renaissance was
short-lived; during the succeeding ninety years' long gradual decline,
there is no further scientific activity to record, apart from the doings
of the scribes, who still continued to copy and compile pharmacological texts and encyclopaedias.

XI. GEOGRAPHY

The work of Eratosthenes, Strabo and Ptolemy stands as testimony
to the noteworthy discoveries already made by the Greeks in geography, both in its physical and mathematical aspects (the figure and
measurement of the earth, position co-ordinates, map projection).
The Byzantines made little use of such concepts, with the result that
they made no further advances in this direction. It is true that a
number of thinkers discussed the composition of the earth in their
general treatment of natural philosophy: for example, Symeon Seth
in the first book of his *Epitome of Physical Treatises*. But it also
happened that some discoveries, long well-established, were brushed
aside. Thus Cosmas Indicopleustes (see above, p. 216) in his *Christian
Topography* rejects the 'extravagant Greek notion' that the earth is
spherical; he considers that the universe rather resembles in form
Moses' tabernacle. It was important for astronomers to have a
knowledge of the position of their observation points and the seven
climata (or belts of latitude). For this Ptolemy, who was never forgotten, sufficed; his *Guide to Geography*, for example, was in the
library of Joseph Bryennius. Apart from Agathemerus (fifth to sixth

century), who wrote a very modest *Outlines of Geography*, the only writers on geographical subjects worth mentioning are Nicephorus Blemmydes and Nicephorus Gregoras. Blemmydes, drawing on Dionysius Periegetes (? 2nd c. ? late 3rd c. A.D.) wrote a *Comprehensive Geography* and a small work entitled *Various Accounts of the Earth*, which treats of the size of the earth and its spherical shape, as well as the seven *climata*. Nicephorus Gregoras was the author of some maps and of a commentary on the geography of Ptolemy.

On the other hand, there was great interest at Byzantium in geographical knowledge with a practical bearing or which might be needed for ecclesiastical or political purposes: for example, maps, travel narratives, or lists of place names. The Ptolemaic maps, whose line of descent can be traced back to the third century, had a long life (they are to be found, for example, in a manuscript from Mt Athos of the mid-thirteenth century). Among the early authors who wrote descriptions of their travels was Cosmas Indicopleustes, already mentioned, who is the first to give definite information concerning China. The dates of a certain Marcian of Heraclea, the author of several *Peripli* (voyages), are unknown. A *Periplus Ponti Euxini*, formerly ascribed to Arrian, cannot be earlier than the second half of the sixth century. A series of Greek *portulani* of later date probably originated in Italy; the *Stadiasmus or Voyage in the Great Sea*, however, in a tenth-century Madrid manuscript, is certainly Byzantine.

Of particular importance to both Church and State were the statistical registers of districts and places. Stephen of Byzantium probably compiled his geographical dictionary as early as the reign of Justinian I; fragments of it are preserved in the works of the otherwise unknown sixth-century Hermolaus and in those of Eustathius of Thessalonica (died *c.* 1193). Hierocles' *Handbook*, in which are listed sixty-four provinces of the Empire and 912 towns, also comes from the reign of Justinian, and George of Cyprus compiled a similar work at the beginning of the seventh century. Constantine VII Porphyrogenitus drew primarily on both Hierocles and Stephen of Byzantium for his statesman's handbook *On the Themes*. A concordance of town names (*On Names of Cities and Places*) made by George Chrysococces has also been preserved. Just as in the land and sea itineraries, travellers' narratives and books of pilgrimage, geographical information is also recorded in the descriptive poems (*ekphraseis*) in which the praises of individual cities and landscapes are sung. Apart from these, there are some passages in the works of the historians dealing with ethnographical topics, and some information on plant and animal ecology may be gathered from the authors on biological subjects.

XII. SUPERSTITION AND PSEUDO-SCIENCES

Superstitious and mystical ideas were deeply rooted in Byzantine popular thinking, as they always have been among the ordinary people at all periods. They were nourished by the fear of illness and death. Incantations against disease, magic formulae, amulets, all might be of some avail. Attempts were made to counteract the uncertainty of mortal destiny by consulting oracles of all kinds or by trying to determine which days were favourable or unfavourable; it was not only a question of predicting illness and death but also of making forecasts concerning a great variety of events likely to arise in everyday life, such as the success of business transactions, the victory of a horse, the flight of a slave, or the arrival of a friend. Predictions were made from the stars, numbers (the numerical value of certain words), geometrical figures, dreams, thunder and much else. When such serious thinkers as Aetius of Amida, who was already Christian enough to use Christian forms of incantation, Alexander of Tralles and even Michael Psellus could indulge in such notions, the extraordinary conjunction of piety and superstition is not to be wondered at. There were others, however, such as Oribasius, Theophanes Nonnus and Nicholas Myrepsus, all of them doctors, who attacked such irrational ideas, and on occasions even the state took action against them; the destruction of alchemical texts ordered by Diocletian (c. A.D. 290) entailed the loss of much valuable technological material. In a passage of Graeco-Roman law already cited (above, p. 274, note 1) a strict distinction was made between doctors and those who mingled medicine and astrology (*iatro-mathematikoi*), exorcisers of diseases, who made use of evil practices and therefore should not receive payment.

With the exception of astrology and alchemy, none of these pseudo-sciences made any contribution to the advancement of knowledge; they must be mentioned, however, since they were then counted as authentic sciences (alchemy was even described as 'the great and holy art'). There was indeed much more to astrology than the making of horoscopes; it was almost a whole philosophy and religion in itself.

According to the astrologers, mankind was subject to numerous influences emanating from the cosmos. Pre-eminent were the seven heavenly bodies (the moon, Mercury, Venus, the sun, Mars, Jupiter, Saturn), to which corresponded the seven days of the week, the seven metals (silver, quicksilver, copper, gold, iron, tin and lead), the seven vowels, colours, tones (intervals), minerals, plants, parts of the body and orders of animals; these heavenly bodies, or the gods identified with them, sent out rays or forces which worked for good or ill on the various parts of the human body, or even on whole groups of men or states, and 'became interwoven with them'. Since the size and distance of the heavenly bodies, and above all their respective positions in the zodiac played an important role, astrological speculations presuppose an exact knowledge of astronomy; they thus served to preserve and also to propagate existing knowledge and even helped towards further scientific inquiry.

Alchemy, which had its origins in the practices of Egyptian goldsmiths and craftsmen of the pre-Christian era, becoming only later (second and third centuries) intermingled with magical ideas and mystical symbolism, also had a double aspect. On the one hand, the texts give technical instructions, mostly quite clear, for metallurgical processes such as the manufacture of alloys and pigments, tempering metals, or glass-making (see below, p. 301); on the other, they are also full of fantastic and valueless notions concerning the sympathetic influences of minerals, the correspondence of metals, plants, animals and parts of the body to the planets or the signs of the zodiac, the Philosopher's Stone and the art of making gold.

Astrology and alchemy flourished greatly in Roman Egypt. It was texts from this period which had a preponderant influence on the Byzantine astrologers and alchemists: Ptolemy's comprehensive *Astrology* (*Tetrabiblos*), the third-century work of Hermes Trismegistus on illnesses influenced by the stars, the treatise of Pseudo-Democritus *Physica et mystica*, in which the magical element predominates, and the *Alchemy* of Zosimus, in which the technical element predominates. The influence of these writings was particularly strong in the early period, but then receded, to be revived to a considerable extent in the eleventh century when the work of Hermes Trismegistus probably became known in Byzantium, arriving by a devious route via Syria and the Arabs.

Among the early commentaries (fifth or sixth century) are those of an anonymous writer and of a 'Christian' philosopher, who even tried to reconcile Christian teaching with astrology. The prophecy concerning Muhammad and the future of Islam ascribed to Stephen of Alexandria is apocryphal; there is also a much commented on alchemical writing *On Making Gold* which goes under his name. Hopes of finding in it a sovereign recipe for making gold are doomed to disappointment, for it is nothing but a confused hotch-potch of occult ideas. Astrological, alchemical and magical writings were first assembled into a single corpus containing the works of the older authorities and their commentators in the seventh or eighth century, and this collection appears in an extended form in the *Encyclopedia* of Constantine VII Porphyrogenitus.

Michael Psellus and Symeon Seth must be included among the authors of pseudo-scientific works of the eleventh century. Seth wrote on the influence of the heavenly bodies and Psellus on making gold and on other occult matters. Astrology continued to flourish under the Comneni. Theodore Prodromus wrote a poem on the subject. The Emperor Manuel I, in his *Pittakion,* himself defended astrology against a dissentient monk and was supported in his opinions by John Camaterus, the author of two astrological poems, though Michael Glycas, the historian, declared himself in a letter opposed to the Emperor's views.

Further alchemical writings have survived from the time of the Palaeologi, for example, Nicephorus Blemmydes' treatise *On Making Gold* and an *Interpretation of the Science of Making Gold* of a monk called Cosmas. A worthless concoction of John Canabutzes (early fifteenth century) has much alchemical matter (transformation of metals, the Philosopher's Stone). An ancient link between astronomy and music is once again brought to light by Manuel Bryennius.

The magic of stones and plants, which was connected with the planets, played an important role in Byzantine superstition. In Michael Psellus' *On the Properties of Stones,* there are not only descriptions of the external appearance of precious stones but also an account of their sympathetic powers of healing; they were particularly effective as amulets. Special rules and magical rites had to be observed when gathering plants as food or for use as drugs; for example, they should be dug up at night during a full moon.

Numbers and numerical relations were particularly important in the doctrines of the Pythagoreans and Neoplatonists. Some numbers were preferred as being particularly lucky, many had magical properties and influences. Such ideas were kept alive by the Byzantines and even formed part of the school curriculum. Mesarites, for example, describes the teaching on this subject given at the Church of the Holy Apostles; the even numbers were masculine, odd numbers feminine; in months which become uneven when divided by some power of two (περισσάρτιος), for example, in the sixth month, there could be no fear of premature births occasioned by a sudden fright. In the vast corpus of prophetic literature numbers play a large part as the instruments of soothsaying. Oracles were pronounced based on the numerical value of letters (onomatomantics), as, for example, the determination of the sex of an embryo. A text from the early fourteenth century states that those who wished to prognosticate by this arithmetical method what sex a woman's embryo will be should add the value of the letters forming the names of the parents to that of the month of conception and divide the result by three; if the remainder were one, the child would be a boy, if two a girl: there is no mention of what might be expected where there was no remainder. There was even a table for the geometrical figures formed by the combination of stones as they lay in their different 'houses'.

The lowest level of soothsaying was reached with the *Oracle Book* in which a passage from a book selected at random was supposed to give significant information on the subject on which advice was sought. Another method made use of thirty-eight different passages from the Bible: a number from 1 to 38 was chosen, and the corresponding text gave the answer. Oracle books with prepared answers also belong to this category.

Further degenerate forms of soothsaying included catoptromancy (which involved mirrors), lecanomancy,[1] hydromancy, prophecies from wine and oil, prophecies from dream-books, thunder-books and much else. There is no need to go into these further, since such methods had not the slightest affinity with the sciences.

XIII. TECHNOLOGY

Although there was little discussion of the subject in the ancient world, in many branches of technology advances had been made to the full limit of what was possible in the given circumstances. Life was not from hand to mouth, but was lived with conscious control over the means of subsistence and its preparation as food, habitation and clothing. There was also the possibility of leading a fuller existence than that of mere survival. Here the contributory skills were those of the fine arts (music, painting, the decorative arts, as applied to *objets d'art*), and of architecture and engineering (aqueducts, baths, theatres, centres of worship), together with the talent which went into the devising of tools for scientific purposes (for example, surgical instruments) or for constructing them on a scientific basis (instruments and machines based on mathematical, astronomical, physical or chemical knowledge). Technology also played a part in providing man with defences against his enemies, including disease, and with the means of waging war against them (weapons, fortifications, warships, medicaments). All these activities required the proper preparation of the materials, smooth working of the tools and machines and the creation of the necessary means of transport and lines of communication (trucks, roads, bridges, ships and harbour-works).

The outcome of all these endeavours usually owed little to scientific principles, but rather represented the empirical discoveries of anony-

---

[1] A mode of divination by throwing three pieces of stone into a bowl or basin and invoking the aid of a demon.

mous workmen. A variety of skills, acquired as they were needed in the course of daily life, were handed down within the circle of the family and of manual workers, amongst whom there was very little specialisation at that time. Such work, usually done by slaves, was held in low esteem, and it is understandable that in a society which held that mechanical work led to a lower form of intelligence there were very few writers (among them were Archimedes, Hero and some of those who wrote on siege-warfare) who concerned themselves with technical questions. Even those who did mostly confined themselves to the description of single machines and pieces of apparatus. Pappus of Alexandria, it is true, envisaged the problem as a whole, as the Roman Vitruvius had before him. In the introduction to the eighth book of his *Synagoge* he outlines the intellectual and practical equipment necessary for an architect or engineer (*architekton*). Such a man must be a mathematician and have mastered the subjects of the Quadrivium; in addition he must understand the working of metals, building, carpentry and painting. If he was proficient in all these, then he could be called a creative engineer and architect. Pappus also enumerated the important contributions of engineers who specialised in certain branches; their constructions included levers, catapults, water-raising machines, automata, sundials, water-clocks, and celestial globes activated by water. It will be seen that even Pappus, despite his informative discourses, does not cover all possible branches of technology.

At Byzantium the modest sum of the written knowledge of Antiquity concerning technology was preserved and in some particulars extended: for example, in the fields of apparatus and instrument construction, and of military, pharmacological and chemical technology.

The Byzantines had little written authority to guide them in solving the primary problems of providing food, clothing and shelter; for those who had to deal with these matters, the necessary knowledge was obvious and familiar, and was handed down by oral tradition. Much information concerning both private life and technological activity can be found in a variety of sources, both literary and otherwise. Contemporary illustrations include houses and house-building, baths, furniture, eating utensils, ploughs, weapons, clothing, implements for hunting and fishing, and musical instruments, and there are scenes depicting smiths at work, the harnessing of horses and the taking of land measurements. We can reconstruct something of the different methods of obtaining food (agriculture, hunting, fishing, bee-keeping, horticulture, fruit-growing, viticulture), and the arrangement of the house, with special attention to its heating and plumbing, its kitchen, crockery and utensils, as well as clothing, shoes, and

much else pertaining to family life. There are also specialised monographs dealing with the cloth and silk industries. Much information
can be gathered from the *Geoponica* concerning the techniques of
agriculture, the cultivation of fruit, vines and olives, and their pro-
cessing (for example, oil-presses), on granaries and methods of preserving (in cellars, casks, brine) and on the ways of procuring materials
such as pitch and lime. Of importance also are the chemical techniques used in the household and described by the alchemists, for
example, the manufacture of soap and lye, of size for glasses and pots,
and methods of making beer.

The *Corpus* of alchemical writings is especially informative on the
technical aspects of the fine arts. Here may be found the valuable
results of chemical experiment as applied to the creation of useful and
ornamental objects, particularly in the fields of metallurgy, dyeing,
manufacture of glass and ornaments. The rules for handling metals,
which provided instruction for metalworkers and gold- and bronze-
smiths, covered soldering, tempering ($\beta\alpha\phi\acute{\eta}$), purifying and separating,
the production of alloys (for example, white gold) and methods of
testing the fineness of an alloy, which was of great importance in the
coinage. Admittedly, it was not possible to produce gold from inferior
metals by the methods of alchemy, but by tinting and refining some
metamorphoses could be achieved so that copper or iron, for example,
could be given the appearance of gold. There are further prescriptions
from a later period for the production of sheet metal (lead and gold
leaf) or metal thread and for making hollow and embossed moulds.
The early Byzantine alchemists give recipes for making colours used
in painting and textiles (for example, from purple and cinnabar), for
inks, and for dyeing wool. This earlier knowledge of colouring techniques is reproduced in the *Painter's Handbook* of Mt Athos. In the
Suda (c. 976; the manuscript dates from the eleventh century) there
is also information about the mixing of colours, a practice already in
use among craftsmen.

Writings on alchemy are also a rich mine of information concerning
the manufacture and treatment of glass. There are directions for
making vases and beakers, for glass-painting and for tinting glass,
pearls and precious stones, and for the manufacture of cultivated
pearls. For their ornamental work Byzantine goldsmiths used not
only metals and jewels, but also amber, alabaster and pearls, and
were particularly skilled in working gold and ivory and in enamelling.
The alchemical works also describe, with diagrams, a number of
pieces of apparatus, for example, phials, retorts, distilling apparatus
and ovens.

Technology further added to the richness of life by its contribution to architecture, that is, to building on a larger scale than that required for the simplest forms of dwelling. In addition to the churches and the often many-storied private edifices, special mention must be made of the constructions which were of common utility and enjoyment: the roads (with footpaths often built in tiers), bridges and harbour works supplying the needs of transport, aqueducts and canals, baths and theatres. A building edict of the Emperor Leo I of the year 469 restricted the height of houses to 100 feet (29 metres). The 23 metres high and 1170 metres long aqueduct built under Valens in 368 was restored by Justinian II in 567 and is still in being. There was immense architectural activity under Justinian I; its crowning glory was the famous domed cathedral of St Sophia, which was the work of two architects, Anthemius of Tralles and Isidore of Miletus.

Among the greatest achievements of ancient technology, apart from the construction of ordnances, was the invention of tools and instruments based on scientific principles or made for scientific purposes, some of which, indeed, were of service in the arts and entertainment. Some of them are already mentioned by Pappus in his curriculum for engineers and architects (automata, clocks, celestial globes). The classical description in Antiquity of automata, in which simple machines (levers, rollers and so on) work under hydraulic or pneumatic pressure, is that of Hero. The Byzantines further developed these mechanisms, as the men of the Renaissance were later also to find pleasure in doing. Leo the Mathematician made a whole series of them for the Magnaura Palace (as singing birds, or a roaring lion). There is an *Ecphrasis Horologii* on a clock of Gaza from the time of Justinian I. Leontius, an engineer, wrote a treatise *On Preparing a Sphere of Arateia* describing the method of making a celestial globe with the latitude of Byzantium (seventh or eighth century). From what is known of the level of astronomical knowledge at that time one might have thought that Leontius was a contemporary of Leo (ninth century).

Other scientific instruments requiring a finely developed mechanical skill were the dioptra and the astrolabe. Hero had already described the building and uses of dioptra, which were employed in surveying and observing the heavens, and which had a level and a micrometer screw for fine adjustment. Hero the Younger's work on land-measurement (see above, p. 273) is also based on these methods. Philoponus, Nicephorus Gregoras, Isaac Argyrus and others all concerned themselves with the astrolabe, the instrument indispensable to astronomical measurement. Anthemius of Tralles who wrote on burning-mirrors also described a heliostat, which, while remaining at rest, directed the rays of the sun, despite their continual change of direction, always to the same point. In acoustics mention must be made of the numerous musical instruments and of the ἠχεῖα, acoustic resonant vessels which were in use in Asia Minor. It will also be remembered that a number of instruments were evolved by doctors; many were already described by Oribasius. Finally, mention must be made of the most important of all instruments of measure, weights and balances, of writing materials (ink, parchment, paper) and of the apparatus used by the alchemists, already referred to (see above, p. 297).

Defence against the enemy is the special responsibility of the military and in particular of those branches which deal with equipment and armaments, fortifications, intelligence and communications. It is often held that military science can teach men how to organise an army and the tactics and strategy of its deployment. As sciences, however, these branches of learning lack the attributes of an absolute authority which can pronounce infallibly; the subject-matter is too much at the mercy of the prevailing techniques, so that one should speak rather of the 'art' of war, an art which, historical questions apart, scarcely admits of scientific method. But since the Byzantine writers on warfare also deal with technical matters they merit a place here. After the older writers on siege warfare and tactics of the Alexandrian period the first authors to be mentioned are two who are anonymous, one from the time of Justinian I, who wrote *On Strategy*, and another who wrote the *De rebus bellicis*. A number of later works go under the name of the Emperor of the day, who, understandably enough, was usually particularly well disposed to this branch of literature. There is thus a *Strategicon* of 'Maurice' and the *Tacticon* of Leo VI, perhaps the most important of all Byzantine writings on warfare, which includes a section on naval warfare. There is a juvenile work of Leo VI in the *Problemata*, but the *Sylloge* which goes under his name is not by him but is a tenth-century work. Further works include an unimportant essay by Psellus and a number of anonymous treatises such as the *Strategemata* contained in a Milan manuscript, the *Extracts from the Strategica*, a treatise on siege-warfare once ascribed to Hero of Byzantium, and a brief military dictionary. The last of the line of military writers was Nicephorus Uranus, general of Basil II (976–1025), who painstakingly compiled a *Tacticon* from the works of a number of authors.

These works also contain some discussion of military technicalities. These include equipment and armament, hand-weapons, war-engines and ordnance. Pappus had already classed the construction of catapults among the more important duties of an architect. The Byzantines probably made no advances over knowledge already acquired by the Alexandrians and recorded by Hero, Bito and Philo concerning the building of cannon. Siege-engines ('tortoises' and battering-rams), for example, were described by the Anonymous who wrote in the sixth century. Orbicius (sixth century) made a suggestion for mobile battering-rams. There were special firing rules for bow-men.[1] The most important Byzantine weapon, which to begin with was their monopoly and therefore had a decisive influence in their favour, was Greek Fire which is discussed in Leo's *Tacticon*. It appears to have been discovered by Callinicus (c. 673), an architect from Heliopolis in Syria. This substance, compounded of naphtha, sulphur and quicklime, was combustible in water and exploded by contact with it, and was launched against the enemy either with lances or by means of pressure (from a siphon). Greek fire was an especially powerful weapon in naval warfare; as is shown in illustrations, the 'siphonarius' stood in the bows and turned the mouth of the siphon in the direction of the enemy. Earthen vessels filled with the fiery material were used as hand-grenades, designed to go off on reaching their target. The tacticians also had to consider the techniques of fortification and siege-warfare. An important role was played by ramparts and walls, for example, the great land-walls of Constantinople. The sixth-century Anonymous discoursed at length on the construction of a town and its defences from the military point of view.

Among intelligence techniques mention must be made of the signalling system and of the optical telegraph of Leo the Mathematician; in naval warfare signalling was by flags, smoke and flashes. Communications were facilitated by military bridges and other forms of transport across rivers, although on land ordinary civil means were used.

Technology also had a part to play in the defence of men against illness, and an important weapon was the manufacture of pharmaceutical drugs, recipes for which are given in books compiled especially for the purpose (see above, p. 293). The information is detailed: thus in a description of a universal nostrum used as a prophylactic ($\tau\grave{o}$ $\delta\omega\delta\epsilon\kappa\acute{a}\tau\epsilon o\nu$), the healing effects are first retailed, then the names and quantities of the twelve ingredients and finally the method of taking the preparation: in this case all food was to be dipped in the medicine.

As a conclusion to this survey of Byzantine technology some reference should be made to the methods of procuring the materials required in the work of the household and by all manual workers, whether farmers, builders or artists, and to the tools and apparatus

---

[1] Given in Leo's *Tacticon* and in the *Sylloge*. See the edition by C. Schissel, 'Spätantike Anleitung zum Bogenschiessen', *Wiener Studien*, LIX (1941), 110–24, and LX (1942), 43–70.

necessary for their preparation. But practically none of the texts deals with these subjects as such. On the other hand, much information is to be gained from a wide variety of sources (the *Geoponica*, the doctors, alchemists, works on siege-warfare), and from such contemporary illustrations and tools as have survived. In addition to the age-old tools of handworkers and peasants (the hammer, chisel, drill, saw, knife, chopper and plough) the Byzantines also knew several simple machines (levers, rollers, cog-wheels, wedges, inclined planes, screws and pulleys) which were used mostly as parts of big machines (capstans, tread-wheels, scooping-machines, weight-lifters and catapults), as is clear from the works of Hero and the writers on military technology. Among individual technical devices mention may be made of Cardan's suspension and the micrometer screw. There is almost complete silence concerning means of transport; though as exceptions may be cited innovations in harnessing horses and cattle, and shipbuilding, which, on account of their military importance, are referred to by many of the authorities. There has been some recent work on these particular topics; but much research on the subject of Byzantine technology still remains to be done.

CHAPTER XXIX

BYZANTINE ARCHITECTURE
AND ART

THE FOURTH TO THE SEVENTH CENTURIES[1]

The period between late antiquity (*c.* 300) and the middle ages is characterised so far as the arts are concerned by a process of continuous limitation. Art was gradually restricted in the variety of its forms and reserved for objects and occasions of an increasingly specialised nature. Moreover, certain forms (such as monumental sculpture, painting on glass, and intarsia) were wholly abandoned, while more and more sections of the community found that they could no longer afford the luxury of artistic possessions. Works of art tended to become the privilege of a minority still able to pay for and appreciate them. The size of this active minority varied with place and period, as did its influence and effect on artistic output and standards; a really powerful monarch with constructive ideas, such as Justinian I, could give a quite exceptional impetus to artistic creativeness.

When economic power becomes more and more concentrated in the hands of those who wield political authority there is a great temptation to use it for some propagandist purpose. This tendency in itself is nothing novel, but it can lead to a situation in which the only art tolerated will be that 'directed' from above, to the exclusion of all else, especially where artistic production is already on a limited scale. This exclusiveness becomes absolute when the 'direction' is concerned with religious art and particularly harsh when it is imposed, as the iconoclasts imposed it, on a population resolutely hostile to its aims. Patronised though it was by the aristocracy and the government, the art of the early Byzantine period would have had little outlet for expression had it not found another patron in the Christian Church, which from the fourth century at the latest never wavered in the conviction that art could enhance the dignity of God's house. Admittedly, as impoverishment became general, a growing number of the faithful, within the bosom of the Church itself, could no longer contribute to this work of pious glorification: on the contrary, artistic effort was to become increasingly concentrated in the hands of a powerful *élite*, the Emperors and the dignitaries of Church and State.

[1] Although in the general plan of this series the volume on the Byzantine Empire begins in the year 717 any account of Byzantine architecture and art must necessarily include some consideration of developments from the fourth to the seventh centuries.

But the fact remains that works of art commissioned for the Church —counted among the most meritorious acts of piety in the highest circles of the time—helped to preserve through the less richly endowed centuries many of the modes and techniques of the great art of the past.

The initiative lay with religious rather than secular art because ecclesiastical communities could often undertake artistic enterprises on a vaster scale than was possible for individuals afflicted by economic hardship and social or racial insecurity. But the price for entrusting the survival of art and its traditions mainly to the Church was high: besides the arts fostered by the patronage of princes, only those forms of art which would serve the cause of the Christian religion were maintained and promoted (though their scope was variously and sometimes generously interpreted). All else was abandoned and soon forgotten, though the process was never systematic, and as a result certain heterogeneous fragments of the heritage of classical art occasionally survived unscathed among the ruins. This process of limitation, which started before Constantine, or at the latest in the fourth century, reached its peak in the period between the end of the sixth and the end of the ninth centuries.

Restriction and limitation are usually negative in their effect and one would hardly expect them to produce the conditions necessary for a flourishing art. But in art, as in all else, limitation has its own advantages, and this was particularly true of the artistic activity at present under discussion. Thus by concentrating on propaganda, whether governmental (imperial art) or religious (ecclesiastical art), the art of the Byzantine period gained in intensity: in its power of expression it compares strikingly with the somewhat neutral and unemphatic productions of the immediately preceding period.

It was the task of the new art to convince the mass of anonymous beholders; and its greatness, as is strikingly obvious, arose from the need to thrust itself on the collective aesthetic consciousness by means of a few forceful impressions—impressions which retain their vitality to this day, and which, because of their somewhat brutal clarity, lent themselves readily to reproduction by technical processes of an almost mechanical nature. Floor mosaics, decorative mural paintings, pictures on jewellery and other media in current use could be copied from the original work for the benefit of a large number of customers. Such works are the best representatives of the true quality of early medieval art: but when the same methods were employed to produce imitations of pictures of more individual workmanship and appeal the results are highly unsatisfying (witness the mediocre imitations of classical paintings in the floor mosaics at Antioch and in many of the mural frescoes of Pompeii). The techniques involved were little suited to the imitation of work of an individual style but were well adapted to impressing the aesthetic susceptibility of the masses; and the very fact that the choice of appropriate themes and techniques was limited made for the creation of fresh aesthetic values, directly inspired by the function of art as propaganda directed at the masses.

The impoverishment of society also favoured certain modes of aesthetic expression which conformed to the limitations imposed by restriction and economy of choice. Forced to make the best of the materials to hand, often mediocre, the craftsmen adopted new methods which could not fail to affect the aesthetic content of their work. The declining standard of technical training, due to the same cause, produced similar effects; methods of improvisation replacing professional techniques were sometimes responsible for the birth of aesthetic values.

Everything said so far applies to all the art of the fourth to sixth centuries produced in the Mediterranean lands within the Roman Empire, and there can have been little to distinguish Byzantine work from the rest. In fact the Byzantine art of this period (of which very little has survived) had less individuality than that of certain other parts of the Roman world, for example Syria or Egypt; this was only natural since Constantinople had no artistic tradition of its own until Constantine made it the capital of the Empire. Byzantium thus asserted itself artistically only by becoming, in affirmation of its new political role, a magnet for artists and a centre for artists' workshops. From the fourth century onwards there was re-enacted at Constantinople, the New Rome, the process which had taken place six centuries earlier in the old Rome; Byzantium, as the capital of a vast Mediterranean state, became a leading artistic centre, an ascendancy favoured by the prevailing autocratic regime. But in spite of the advantages of its political eminence it was not easy for Constantinople to achieve distinction as a centre of independent and original art, since there were many places within the Byzantine Empire which enjoyed a longer artistic tradition. First under the Hellenistic kings and later under the Romans, the Greek cities on the eastern shores of the Mediterranean had been the scene of intensive artistic activity.

At the beginning of the fourth century Thessalonica, Alexandria, Beirut, Antioch, Ephesus and other towns in Syria and Asia Minor still possessed ateliers capable of meeting the demands of a large circle of customers. It was the artists of these workshops and those of Rome itself who were called upon when Constantinople was raised by Constantine to the dignity of a capital city, and it took time to redress the balance and make Syria and Egypt receptive to the inva-

sion of an art inspired by Constantinople. Because the monuments
have been so largely destroyed it is impossible to elucidate either the
various stages in the evolution of a distinctively Byzantine art from
imported models or the gradual progress of its extension to the provinces of the Eastern Empire. But some observations can be made
concerning those monuments which have survived, supplemented by
information drawn from literary and epigraphical sources. More
attention will be given to the monuments of the eastern provinces
than to those of Constantinople, partly because, with the exception
of the surrounding walls, almost nothing has survived at Constantinople which is earlier than the sixth century.

(a) Architecture

At the time when Constantine, almost at a single stroke, relaxed
the restrictions on the open practice of Christianity, to the point even
of encouraging the construction of churches, and laid the foundations
of the future Byzantine Empire by transferring his capital to the
Bosphorus, the most important works of architecture were beyond
doubt the imperial palaces. The Tetrarchy was particularly favourable to this type of courtly art, each Emperor and Caesar having his
own residence to cherish as a worthy monument to his power and
ambitions; and each prince might have several such palaces, either
at one time or in succession. Unfortunately, the fourth-century
palaces of Constantinople, Nicomedia, Antioch and Milan have entirely disappeared, and these were the most important. But some
suggestive fragments of the imperial palace of Galerius have survived
at Thessalonica and the fortified palace of Diocletian at Spalato still
retains a large part of the original building.

Certain features of this palace architecture in the grand style are
apparent from the reflections of them which can be discerned in the
buildings grouped together to form the great fortified camps of Diocletian, as revealed by excavations (for example, Palmyra). The
excavations of a fifth-century courtyard enclosed by porticoes within
the precincts of the Great Palace of Constantinople, and of a slightly
later palace at Ravenna (known as the Palace of the Exarch) provide
similar evidence. But to get a proper idea of what the imperial
palaces of the fourth century, and in particular those of Constantine
and his heirs at Constantinople must have been like, it is necessary
also to study the surviving remains of other buildings of the wealthy
cities of this period: to the examples preserved at Rome it is now
possible to add those of Antioch, of Piazza Armerina in Sicily, and
the cathedral ruins at Bosra and Side.

The great public buildings erected at Constantinople contemporaneously with the Great Palace, that is immediately after the capital of the Empire had been moved to Byzantium, have all disappeared. But a certain chance discovery has revealed the ruins of an important group of civic buildings of the fifth century near the Hippodrome of Constantinople; behind a semicircular portico, with columns at the entrance, was a group of rooms varying in size and shape, some circular, some polygonal. Another group of civic buildings of similar type and showing the same technical qualities has been discovered not far from Constantinople at Rhegium on the Sea of Marmora. An even higher degree of skill was displayed by the men who, in the decades following the sack of Rome by Alaric, built the walls surrounding Constantinople, to be its bulwark against all comers until the invasion of the crusaders in 1204 (Plate 1). These walls, like the rest of the public civic architecture which was undoubtedly being erected at Byzantium from the time of Constantine onwards, were conceived in accordance with the traditions of Roman military architecture. But the engineers working at Constantinople at the beginning of the fifth century added so many fundamental improvements to their received Roman models that their achievement, as skilful in technique as it is imposing in appearance, can justly claim to be regarded as being distinctively Byzantine. Thus, since these walls are earlier than any of the surviving ecclesiastical buildings, Byzantine architecture as we know it begins with a magnificent example of the art of military construction. The walls of Constantinople had their proper successors in the military works of generations of experienced architects who in each reign, but notably under Justinian, erected countless Byzantine forts: in Africa, Spain, Lombardy, the Balkans, the Crimea, Asia Minor, Syria and Mesopotamia, the imposing ruins of these fortifications, which the Muslims and crusaders were to study and imitate in their turn, remain standing to this day.

There must undoubtedly have been some examples of new buildings for pagan religious cults in the fourth century, but none has survived, except perhaps at Rome in the walls of the Sanctuary of the Syrian gods on the Janiculum, attributed to the reign of Julian the Apostate. Since the proclamation of the Peace of the Church coincided with the foundation of Constantinople as the capital city of the Empire, the first examples of church architecture on the grand scale must go back to the time of Constantine. But throughout the whole extent of the 'Byzantine' part of the Empire, the *pars orientalis*, only one such building has survived (apart from the ground plans of a few basilicas of the late fourth century which have been established by excavation, for example, at Corinth and St Menas near Alexandria): this is the

Church of the Nativity at Bethlehem, founded by St Helena, though only the five naves are original, the trefoil choir being the result of sixth-century alterations. In the earliest building (as can be seen from the plan uncovered by excavation) the place of this choir was occupied by an octagon standing over the grotto of the Nativity. The church at Bethlehem thus combined two types of Christian building, which were elsewhere juxtaposed or widely separated from each other, and which were both very common in early Christianity (though not in the middle ages): a church proper, a place for the celebration of the Eucharist, and a *martyrion, martyrium* or *memoria*, which was reserved for commemorative acts of worship (for the cult of a martyr, whose body, or a portion of it, might be preserved there, or of a special object or of a place deserving particular veneration).

The churches were elongated and rectangular halls. From the middle of the fourth century they were built for preference in the basilican style, that is, in the form of a hall divided lengthwise into three (or more rarely five) parallel aisles, that in the middle being broader and higher than the rest and lighted directly by windows opening above the lateral aisles; an apse enclosing a raised dais or tribune was added to this middle aisle at the end opposite the entrance. The priest presiding at the service and his assistants, if any, sat at the back of the tribune and in its centre was placed the altar table. Recent excavations and detailed study of the churches which have survived have revealed the great variety that existed among these early basilicas, but it is at least as important to recognise that throughout the vast extent of the fourth-century Empire the same basic architectural formula for a basilica was adopted by all Christians. The most plausible hypothesis for the derivation of the Christian basilica is that which links it with the halls of public buildings, for example the judicial basilicas and the imperial audience chambers. Other religious communities in the Empire, Jews, Mithraists, Semitic worshippers of the astral deities, followed the same exemplars, and the architecture of their centres of worship was also to a greater or lesser extent indebted to the halls of Roman public buildings. The internal arrangements of the bigger churches also adhered to the same pattern: the eastern end was raised and a barrier or chancel-rail stood in front of the tribune (during the middle ages in Byzantium this was transformed into the iconostasis), while a ciborium or baldacchino covered the altar or the ambo.

In contrast to the churches proper, the *martyria* or *memoriae*, commemorative and more specifically funereal in function and inspired by Roman architecture, were usually constructed on a central plan: circular, polygonal, trefoil or square in the form of a cross (cf. Bethlehem), although the simple rectangular form of the basilican hall was not excluded and in certain regions, particularly in the Latin countries, was frequently adopted. The central plan of the *martyrium* allowed of its being roofed by a dome, in wood or stone, and this was also in the tradition of Roman funerary art. The rotunda of the Holy Sepulchre at Jerusalem (built under Constantine or in the second half of the fourth century) was the most famous of the early Christian sanctuaries to adopt this type of architecture. From that time onwards and particularly in the fifth and sixth centuries examples of the domed *martyrium* built on a central plan could be found on the outskirts of every city of the Byzantine Empire. In the sixth century they had begun to penetrate *intra muros* and were tending to become fused with churches proper (see below, p. 317).

Early Christian architecture is also characterised by a third type of building, the baptistery. During the fourth and fifth centuries baptisteries were as common in the countries of the Eastern Empire as they were in Italy, Provence, Spain and Africa. But, in contrast to the practice in the West, those in the Greek and Semitic regions of the Empire were rarely free-standing structures but rather rooms adjoining a church where the liturgical furnishings and not the architecture served to define their purpose. In the East, as in Syria (where the baptistery was in fact a separate building), the baptisteries were small and showed few distinguishing architectural features. Again in contrast with the West, in Byzantine countries after the sixth century the baptistery disappeared altogether, that is to say more or less about the same time as the free-standing *martyrium*: the church proper henceforth was to shelter under its own roof both the reliquaries, usually containing portions of the bodies of saints, and the font (only infants were now being baptised).

There are too few buildings of the period of early Christianity surviving in Egypt to form a definite idea of the characteristics of church architecture in that province. But enough is known to be able to say that side by side with monuments Graeco-Byzantine and Syrian in inspiration there existed an architecture peculiar to Christian Egypt. The most imposing groups of buildings are the two churches of the Red and White monasteries at Sohag, belonging to the early fifth century, which the great Coptic saint Shenudi visited soon after their foundation. The basilican naves, the trefoil eastern end, the mural decorations consisting of a veneer of polychrome marble, the arches and columns are recognisably borrowings from the current repertoire of early Christian architecture in the Mediterranean lands. But the treatment of the masses as a whole, the porch with its heavy inclined walls reminiscent of the pylons of the temples of the Pharaohs, the method of supporting the columns of the naves by means of the wall enclosing the basilica (possibly the only original part of this wall is in the sanctuary) and the interior façade of the sanctuary or *haikal* itself, all have their origins in the art of ancient Egypt. From about 400 onwards this style of Christian architecture has a distinctively regional—one might say Coptic—aspect.

Syria, that is to say the provinces of the Empire lying between Egypt and Asia Minor, is the only region in which a large number of churches has survived which are in some cases dated; and there are others which have been revealed by excavations. These churches (apart from the *martyria* which are on the centralised plan with wooden domes) are basilican in plan, roofed sometimes with timber and sometimes with slabs of stone placed flat on the walls and on transverse rib-arches. Separated by piers, the naves lead into an apse rarely visible from the exterior and flanked by two small symmetrical rooms, one being the sacristy and the other often serving as a *martyrium*, a chapel where relics were preserved (as at Brad). In the sixth century this became the site of the prothesis, the place reserved for the offerings and also the point of departure for the procession of the Great Entrance, introduced at this time, which in the Greek liturgy conveys the Sacred Elements to the altar for their consecration. The entrances to the church are in one of the longitudinal walls of the basilica; they are sometimes sheltered by a long passage running the length of the walls. In some rare cases, and then only in the sixth-century churches, the entrance to the nave is through a porch opposite the apse and flanked by two towers (as at Qualb Louzeh). The façades of these churches must be admired for the careful workmanship of the walls and mouldings and of the decorative columns engaged to the apse, though these are more rare. The decoration, which is very restrained, is partly classical and partly Semitic in inspiration: geometrical motifs, continuous convex mouldings which curve round to frame the doors and windows.

The Christian architecture of Syria extended its influence northwards into Mesopotamia (Byzantine and even Persian) and westwards into Asia Minor. In Mesopotamia this influence can be seen at the great sanctuary of St Sergius at Resafa and at St James of Nisibis. It is also evident in the decoration of a number of other monuments which are however of a very local character. These buildings are rectangular, wider than they are long, with an apse on one of the long walls and an entrance built into the opposite wall. They are generally roofed with a heavy transverse barrel vault and are very feebly lighted. Internally their walls present a continuous unbroken surface without decoration.

The churches of the Holy Land and southern Palestine have their own distinctive features and are more closely related to the buildings of the south coast of Asia Minor or even those of Greece and the Greek islands. In all these maritime provinces the most common type found is a colonnaded basilica with a single apse roofed with timber. A porch and even an *atrium* may be placed before the naves; while the naves themselves usually extend right up to the apse. All along the Mediterranean coast-line, however, from Palestine (the so-called church of the Feeding of the Five Thousand) through southern Asia Minor (Perge and Side, in Pamphylia) up to Macedonia (Philippi) there are examples of basilicas in which a transverse space has been interposed between the naves and the apse. This is in fact a kind of transept, but one which in many cases is not extended beyond the lateral walls of the basilica and which may even, as at St Demetrius in Thessalonica, be traversed by the two rows of columns dividing the naves from each other. This last peculiarity distinguishes this type of transept from those of St Peter's and St Paul's at Rome, where the colonnades of the naves stop short at the junction with the transverse space, but it has affinities with that in the church of St Thecla at Milan (the second cathedral). Cruciform churches of this type soon disappeared in the east but were often favoured during the succeeding centuries in Latin Europe.

Asia Minor undoubtedly played an essential part in the history of the earliest Christian architecture. But in view of the wholesale destruction which the monuments have suffered and the small number of excavations of ecclesiastical sites this statement must be supported by conjecture rather than by ascertained fact. However, enough is known for it to be certain that Asia Minor presents no uniformity in this kind of architecture. In its eastern provinces, on the central plateau and its flanks, basilicas were built reminiscent of those of northern Syria and neighbouring Mesopotamia. But in the cities on the coast buildings were in a style more purely Greek and may be admired both for their technical and their aesthetic qualities. One day it may be possible to trace not a few of the distinguishing features of Syrian churches back to their models at Antioch or the wealthy cities of the Mediterranean coast of Asia Minor. The churches of those regions impress by their number, their size and the technical perfection of their construction, while the variety and originality of their architectural forms (for example the domes of Meriamlik and Koja-Kalessi (Alahan Kilisse) in Isauria, the baptistery of Side with its monumental ciborium and the transepts of Perge) are equally striking. The excavations at Ephesus have been particularly revealing in this respect: the basilican cathedral dedicated to the Virgin provides a suggestive example of the adaptation of a pagan civic building to Christian architecture, and St John's is a cruciform *martyrium* which anticipates the Church of the Holy Apostles at Constantinople; finally, at the Seven Sleepers there is a hall roofed by an enormous brick vault which on the one hand recalls the mausoleums (the vaulted hall sheltered thousands of tombs, crowded together above the Grotto of the Seven Sleepers) and on the other is reminiscent of the brick vaults of the capital, where they are to be found from the fifth century onwards, in the towers of the encircling walls and in the rotunda of the *martyrium* of Sts Carpos and Babylas.

In the interior of the peninsula, in the regions where wood for building was lacking, a fully vaulted type of church was evolved, the first examples of which certainly belong to the fourth or fifth century. Constructed in dressed stone, these buildings are solid if rudimentary. They follow the form of the basilican and cruciform structures, using both the Latin and the Greek cross for their plan, and seem to prefigure the Romanesque churches of the West. The relationship is authentic, but it can hardly be explained by supposing that the western architects were in any way directly influenced by the churches of the remote provinces of Cappadocia or Phrygia, such as those at Bin Bir Kilisse or Tomarza: rather, these churches must themselves have been based on the models provided by the great cities of the coast, as far as was possible for local craftsmen working with the materials and the knowledge at their disposal.

The great cities of Asia Minor, which continued to flourish up to the time of the Persian and Arab invasions, undoubtedly attracted the best architects of the period and it was not by chance that the architects employed by Justinian for building St Sophia came originally from towns of Asia Minor (Anthemius of Tralles, Isidore of Miletus and his nephew of the same name): and many craftsmen trained in the workshops of these cities could have gone from them to the capital. But does this imply that the architecture of Constantinople in its essentials derived from that of Asia Minor? This is likely enough, but it would be wrong to leave out of account altogether the influence on Constantinople of its European hinterland, including Greece and the Greek islands.

Few of the early Christian churches of these provinces are still standing. But there are several at Thessalonica—the round church of St George, the fifth-century basilica of the Acheiropoietos, the little oratory of Christ of the Latomos (Hosios David), also fifth-century, and the basilica of St Demetrius, of the fifth to seventh centuries; and a church at Paros which was adjoined by a sixth-century baptistery was only recently destroyed by fire. In the northern Balkans the impressive ruins of a number of magnificent sixth-century churches can still be seen, for example at Sofia (St Sophia), and at Peruštica. Finally, extensive excavations in all the Balkan countries have uncovered the foundations of about a hundred churches of early Christianity. In the Eastern Empire the European provinces were as rich in Christian monuments as those of Asia, and the architectural forms employed were identical with those of the Greek cities of the Mediterranean coast: colonnaded basilicas with timber roofs, vaulted basilicas with one or three naves, domed basilicas, cruciform buildings and structures on the square or round plan vaulted throughout. It is no longer possible to give all the credit to the architects of Asia Minor or Mesopotamia for the initiative in inventing the various types of vaulted churches, which were being constructed at an equally early date at Thessalonica and in the northern Balkans.

It seems likely, however, that before long the focal point from which the influence of this monumental art emanated came to be Constantinople. The Christian architecture of Constantinople, like its secular counterpart, seems to have had complex origins, which the state of the monuments has so far failed to elucidate. The rotunda of Sts Carpos and Babylas and the colonnaded basilica of St John of Studius (Plate 2), dated to 463, are the oldest known ecclesiastical structures in Constantinople. But at the time they were being built many of the salient features of Byzantine architecture, including the dome, were already established by more than a century of development; so that these buildings provide little evidence about the origins of Christian architecture in Constantinople.

Hundreds of churches are known to have been built there between the fourth and the seventh centuries but only three or four of them have survived in their entirety, apart from a small number of ruins. Chance has ordained, however, that among the survivors is included the great masterpiece of Byzantine architecture, St Sophia (Plates 5, 6). It was built, at the orders of Justinian, between 532 and 537. The main structure, approached through an *atrium* and a one-storeyed porch or narthex, consists of one enormous and virtually square hall (77 × 71·7 metres) surmounted by a hemispherical dome supported, on the east–west axis, by two half-domes. A sanctuary apse and four exedrae soften the straight lines and hard angles of the rectangular hall, which is flanked laterally by galleried aisles. The predominating effect is that of the dome, which seen from the outside sharply defines the summit of the pyramidal silhouette and within forms a harmonious crown to the mass and lines of the walls and arches. This is not the place to discuss the technical skills which went to the construction of St Sophia: as a feat of engineering it is above all remarkable for the astonishing mastery displayed in brick vaulting, which involves achieving an equilibrium of thrusts in opposition. Abandoning the Roman method of 'concrete' vaults, the architects of St Sophia everywhere constructed their vaults from bricks and without centering (this was to remain the favourite Byzantine method). The architects of St Sophia—experimenting as they built—succeeded in resting the dome, 51 metres in diameter, on four piers, supporting the outward thrust by means of half-domes on the east and west and massive abutments on the north and south. In so doing they managed to detract attention from the crushing weight of the huge vault and its bulky supports (in its first version the dome proved too insubstantial, and between 558 and 562 it was replaced by the present one).

Neither before nor afterwards was there any attempt at emulating the experiment, nor did the Byzantines make a general practice of erecting domed buildings on a comparable scale. On the other hand, however, in one somewhat surprising feature the architecture of St Sophia does exhibit a tendency which was to be typical of Byzantine architecture proper. St Sophia is essentially a building on the centralised plan and the centralised elevation. But the central domed hall is flanked by aisles as though it were a basilica, and despite the danger to its stability the dome is not buttressed by half-domes on the flanks pendant to the two half-domes on the east and west. It was typical of Byzantium in the time of Justinian that there should have been this desire to combine two types of church hitherto distinct: the basilica and the centralised building. Admittedly, churches of a distinctively centralised plan continued to be built, as, for example, Sts Sergius and Bacchus at Constantinople, which is actually a votive *martyrium*, built by Justinian. Here an octagonal structure is enclosed in such a way as to relate its plan to that of a square building, while in elevation it resembles the memorial buildings of cube shape crowned by a dome. In other cases, as with St Sophia itself, a similar effect is achieved but starting from the superimposition of a dome on a basilican nave more or less shortened in length. From the sixth century, one of the essential peculiarites of Byzantine ecclesiastical architecture (as opposed to that of other Christian communities) was this very habit of adapting for ordinary churches the forms of the *martyria* or rather of a certain type of *martyrium*, which produced the combination of an almost square ground plan with a central dome.

(b) Mosaics and frescoes

Among the figurative arts painting was more important than sculpture. Already gaining ground in the first centuries of our era, painting really came into its own with the advance of Christianity, for sculpture had too many associations with paganism: the Church tolerated and later encouraged mosaic and painting more readily than the plastic arts. But since painting is unhappily the most fragile of all forms of art very few examples from the early centuries of Christianity have survived.

The buildings of this period commonly had a mural decoration of mosaic. But from the vast number of palaces and religious buildings so ornamented very little of such work is preserved. At St Sophia in Constantinople the sixth-century mosaics of the arches and vaults make an arresting impression despite their sobriety. There are no figures, only crosses and decorative motifs. Thessalonica has the distinction of possessing three groups of mosaics from before the time of Justinian: in the Church of St George (*c.* 400) the upper part of the dome has a large composition showing Christ surrounded by angels, prophets(?) and martyrs; in the Church of the Virgin Acheiropoietos (fifth century) the arches are richly decorated; and at the Christ of the Latomos (fifth century) there is Ezekiel's vision of Christ in glory (Plate 9). The destructive hand of fate has spared none of the mural mosaics of Asia Minor, Antioch and Alexandria, but two sets of mosaics are preserved in Cyprus, each in the apse of a church and each depicting the Virgin and Child with angels. At Sinai another apsidal mosaic, of slightly later date, shows the theophany of the Transfiguration. The influence of Byzantine art must have been very strong at Ravenna in the fifth century and even more so in the sixth. This fact makes it reasonable to include in this survey the famous mosaics of that city, while freely admitting that not everything there is Byzantine in inspiration. In the absence of comparable Byzantine work there is nothing to be gained by discussing the mosaics of the oratory known as the mausoleum of Galla Placidia or those of the baptistery of the cathedral (also known as the baptistery of the Orthodox or of Neon): they could well have derived from the art of the Western Empire. On the other hand, the miniature scenes from the Gospels of the mosaics of St Apollinare Nuovo, some showing Christ bearded according to the eastern type, and probably also the Christ and Virgin enthroned at the foot of the same walls, reflect Greek models from Constantinople or Palestine. Finally, the portraits of Justinian and Theodora in San Vitale (Plate 8) and also of Constantine IV and his sons in St Apollinare in Classe certainly belong to the Byzantine tradition, as may also the other mosaics of these two churches. The two panels of San Vitale are indeed among the greatest achievements of Byzantine mosaic art of the sixth century. They are marvellous in the richness of their composition and skilful harmony of colouring, while the realism of the heads and details is emphasised by the artist's indifference to space and volume.

From the fourth to the sixth centuries floor mosaics were quite common in the Byzantine world, but this fashion did not last. Aesthetically such mosaics are rarely above the level of artisan work. The most remarkable exception is the pavement of an interior court revealed recently by excavations inside the Great Palace of Constantinople (Plates 10, 11). This work, perhaps of the fifth century, depicting pastoral idylls and hunting scenes is still in the classical tradition, but the style, as for instance the idealisation of the faces, is Byzantine.

The taste for mural decoration in colour was so prevalent that those who could not afford the expense of mosaic regularly had recourse to fresco-painting. But frescoes do not stand up to the passage of time, which explains why so few of the surviving wall-paintings have retained the freshness of their original colouring: those which have are usually to be found in places for centuries hidden from the light of day and protected from changes of temperature, such as hypogea and ruined buildings buried under the earth. A protective layer of soil has preserved the remarkable second- and third-century frescoes discovered at Dura-Europos on the Euphrates. These are obviously pre-Byzantine, but they foreshadow the development of specifically Byzantine art in their technique and style. They therefore deserve a place in any survey of Byzantine art. The paintings of Dura decorate the walls of a number of pagan sanctuaries, as well as a synagogue and a Christian baptistery. Despite the variety of themes and styles, they all present that blending of the classical tradition with a Semitic interpretation which was later to characterise the Christian paintings of the Levant: in this respect Coptic and Syrian art are closely linked. In the region within the orbit of Constantinople proper there survive only a few sepulchral frescoes (at Thessalonica, Sofia, Niš) and some important fragments of wall-paintings of the sixth century in a ruined church at Peruštica near Philippopolis. Although faded and partially obliterated, these paintings are valuable evidence for this type of art at Constantinople in the time of Justinian; they depict the Childhood of Christ, the Lamb and Angels, and scenes from the Old Testament and lives of the martyrs. In Egypt there are some other valuable examples, for instance at Bagawat, where painted domes of mausoleums of the fourth and fifth centuries are still standing, showing scenes from both Testaments. Excavation of a hypogeum at Antinoe has uncovered some excellent sixth-century paintings: a Christ enthroned, and a dead woman being conducted into the presence of God by Mary and a local saint. Much more numerous are the frescoes revealed by excavation on the site of the Coptic monasteries of Bawit and Saqqara. Here there are paintings in many chapels; the apse usually has a theophany, showing Christ in glory with the Virgin and apostles, while the walls of the nave depict rows of local saints and deceased monks. Scenes from the Gospels are rare. The numerous inscribed prayers suggest that these paintings were regarded as the iconographical accompaniments of invocations to God and the saints. But the iconography of the apse had also associations with the Eucharist which must have been celebrated in these monastic chapels.

Some of the Bawit frescoes reproduce portable pictures of saints in their frames. Several early examples of such easel paintings of religious subjects have been recovered in Egypt and Sinai, depicting the Virgin and saints. At Rome, after removing layers of later painting, two icons of the Virgin have been revealed (at St Maria Nuova and St Maria in Trastevere). These are painted on wood in the encaustic technique, the colours being melted in a wax paste. In others, however, the tempera technique has been used, a method perpetuated in the icons of medieval Byzantium.

(c) *Miniature painting*

Illustrated books must have been numerous during the period under discussion, judging by the copies of them made later and the reflections of their style to be found in the miniatures of the middle ages. In the early days of Byzantium painted illustrations in books were still a relative novelty, though they had already been used in scientific treatises and histories and to illustrate Homer and Euripides. The practice was continued at Byzantium, and it seems that from the fifth century onwards contemporary historical works were also being illustrated, such as those of Socrates, Sozomen, or the Alexandrine Chronicle.

Two examples of books in the luxury class, illustrated at Constantinople in the early sixth century, have been preserved: an Iliad in a fragmentary condition in the Ambrosian Library, Milan, and a treatise on medicinal plants of Dioscorides the physician. It is not known when religious books first began to be ornamented. It is almost certain that the Jews did this before the Christians, by illustrating the historical books of the Bible, and these compositions must have been imitated and later filled out by the Christians. But the oldest surviving examples of a Christian illustrated Bible go back no farther than the sixth century. The small pictures which decorate the Genesis manuscript in the National Library in Vienna are in a gracious style with an eye for detail, purely in the classical tradition. Similar illustrations and also some on a purple background are to be found in two sixth-century manuscripts of the Gospels, the Codex of Rossano in Calabria, and the fragment of the so-called Gospel of Sinope in the Bibliothèque Nationale in Paris. It is certain that the Gospels were being illustrated earlier than the sixth century (a manuscript of the Alexandrine Chronicle on papyrus in Moscow has a number of paintings on Christian subjects which are fifth century), but no older example is known. The miniatures of the Gospels of Rossano and Paris, which are similar in inspiration, are not restricted to illustration of the scriptural text but go farther by adding a theological or didactic interpretation of the subject-matter; thus the prophets of the Old Testament appear in the pictures of the gospel events which they foretold. A similar purpose informs the paintings of a Gospel in Syriac, the so-called Gospel of Rabula, dated to 586, in the Laurentian Library at Florence. Here the illustrations are grouped together to form as it were a 'symphony' of the four Gospels in the margins of the Tables of the Canons of Eusebius. The prophets are also depicted, although the manuscript only contains the text of the Gospels. Although the text is in Syriac, the art of the miniatures is Greek in tradition, as also in another sixth-century Syriac Gospel (Paris, Bibl. Nat. syr. 33). The Syrians of this period used a Greek style in their religious paintings and did no more than add some nuances in their own idiom to an art essentially classical in inspiration. From the third century the artists of Dura-Europos were doing the same for mural paintings. Valuable evidence concerning the presence in Syria of models of Greek painting (probably very numerous) is afforded by the early eighth-century mosaics of the Great Mosque of Damascus (see below, p. 324): it is all the more remarkable that they should show the classical tradition still so much alive since they are the work of Muslims and chronologically yet more remote from antiquity.

(d) *Sculpture and other works of art*

It has been said that the Peace of the Church hastened the decline of sculpture evident in Rome from the third century, and earlier in the eastern provinces. But the advent of the Christian Empire did not mean the total prohibition of sculpture: indeed it was the Christian monarchy itself, both in Rome and in Byzantium, which was careful to preserve over the centuries, along with other imperial traditions, that of the portrait statue. As under the pagan dispensation, official statues of the Emperors and imperial dignitaries of sufficiently high rank continued to be made. The statues in marble of Valentinian in the Museum of Istanbul and in bronze of an anonymous Emperor at Barletta in Apulia, as well as those of various dignitaries at Istanbul, Smyrna and Athens, show that these works had a style of their own and a dignified grandeur. It is known from the texts that the public places of Constantinople were filled with imperial statues from the fourth to the seventh centuries; the most popular charioteers of the Hippodrome were equally honoured in triumphal effigies. Moreover, Theodosius II, for all his well-attested piety, did not refrain from covering the façade of the Golden Gate of Constantinople (which was built in his reign) with a series of reliefs of mythological subjects. An Emperor could thus revive an apparently condemned art. Court patronage was also responsible for the historical bas-reliefs which adorned large triumphal monuments, such as the figured columns of Theodosius and Arcadius (known only from a few fragments and some drawings) and the base of an obelisk of Theodosius in the Hippodrome.

Side by side with this sculpture, imperial in inspiration, was that of religious intention. Statuary was a part of early Christian sculpture. Eusebius, Constantine's contemporary, describes a celebrated example, the group in high relief which stood in a square in the small town of Paneas in Palestine representing Christ and the woman with an issue of blood. At the same period a number of statues, one of them showing Daniel surrounded by the lions, were being erected to decorate a fountain in the imperial palace at Constantinople. But Byzantine statuary, both imperial and to an even greater extent Christian, was only a continuation of the practices of antiquity which carried on because none dared to suppress them completely. Statuary finally disappears only about the seventh century: it thus had a longer life in Byzantium than in the West. But never during the middle ages did it experience a revival in the East comparable to its brilliant renaissance in western Europe.

Christian relief-sculpture had no greater success in Byzantium, even during the fourth, fifth and sixth centuries. The writer knows only one example applied to the façade of a church, though that is a remarkable one: the ranks of sheep in relief on marble which once decorated the entrance wall of the pre-Justinian church of St Sophia (now in front of the existing church). Otherwise, reliefs with Christian subjects were used only for church fittings, such as chancel-screens, ambos, or receptacles for holy water. Among the best pieces in this category are the group of Christ and two apostles from Constantinople (fifth century) preserved in the Museum of Istanbul: the figures make a strikingly monumental effect, placed as they are in front of a niched façade reminiscent of the sarcophagi of Sidamara. Another fine piece is the ambo of St George of Thessalonica, now in the Museum of Istanbul, with an Adoration of the Magi in which the figures are placed each in its own niche.

At this same period some sarcophagi at Constantinople were decorated with rather primitive reliefs of subjects taken from the Gospels. But this fashion did not last, although at Ravenna such sarcophagi were still frequent in the fifth century; and it is significant in this respect that the green or red porphyry tombs of the Emperors and members of the imperial family were ornamented only with crosses. The most graceful figured reliefs of this period are those of a child's sarcophagus in Constantinople, and the gospel scenes on the borders of marble basins found in all Byzantine countries. But these are works on a small scale, inspired by classical and perhaps bacchic models of the same type. From the end of the early Christian period Byzantine reliefs are usually of small dimensions and the most numerous and remarkable of these are in ivory. The subjects of some of these are governmental in theme and are carved on 'official' objects such as imperial or consular diptychs, though they do not appear before the fifth century. Other reliefs are found on furniture, such as episcopal thrones (the *chef d'œuvre* of this style of Byzantine work, perhaps Alexandrine in origin, is the throne of Maximian, Archbishop of Ravenna and contemporary of Justinian), and on liturgical vessels, pyxes or caskets. Ivory was much in vogue during this period and was probably being worked in several towns, in Constantinople itself, in Alexandria and cities of the Levant as well as in Italy and Gaul.

This same taste for sculpture on a small scale applied to portable precious objects is shown in gold and silver work. As always, objects in precious metals are rare. Even so there exists a considerable series of plates, vases and caskets in silver which can often be dated to a particular reign by their punch marks. This series runs from the fourth to the mid-seventh centuries and includes the productions of different workshops (Constantinople, Syria, Rome). The reliefs in repoussé decorating these objects make it possible to distinguish between those intended for ecclesiastical and those intended for secular use. Among the former are some Syrian works: a vase from Emesa in the Louvre, the paten of Riha at Dumbarton Oaks, Washington. Among the latter are the Treasure of Kyrenia, Cyprus, in the Museum of Nicosia (Plate 39) and in the Metropolitan Museum and silver vessels from the palaces, plates, cups, ewers with mythological subjects, in the Hermitage collection in Leningrad (Plate 38). This figured silverwork strikingly demonstrates the continuation well into the seventh century of an ancient tradition of the silversmith's art. The imitation of classical and pagan models is also remarkable a century later in the mosaics of the Great Mosque of Damascus: and it is no less interesting to find that the more recent pieces, dating from the time of Heraclius and the great Arab invasions, are among those most faithful to the ancient style.

Slightly earlier, in the sixth century, it was already becoming a widespread practice to decorate with Christian themes a great variety of objects, above all those connected with pious observances, however humble. In the Holy Land, for example, ampullae of silver and lead were being manufactured for the use of pilgrims, to contain holy oil from Jerusalem. These ampullae were decorated with minute scenes in repoussé work representing the gospel happenings as commemorated in Palestine by the pilgrimages. These representations formed a unique collection of very ancient iconographical formulae which spread from Palestine throughout all Christian territories to become the basis of a universal Christian iconography.

Figured textiles were very fashionable in the later Roman Empire, and despite the opposition of the clergy which became manifest from the fourth century, Christians made frequent use of them for clothing, curtains, and other purposes. This fashion continued at least until the sixth century: the cloak of Theodora in the mosaic in San Vitale at Ravenna, for instance, is decorated with a picture of the Adoration of the Magi. Pagan and Christian subjects, embroidered or woven, were equally favoured, and in Egypt remained in vogue even after the Arab conquest. In Egypt, too, many such fabrics must have been made from cotton or wool: examples in silk must either have been imported from Sassanid Persia or imitated from Persian models. But, as with all the arts associated with luxury articles, these fabrics must have been in production in the capital of the Empire from a very early date. There is known to have been a workshop at Heraclea in the Propontis, close to Constantinople, where clothes were being woven for the imperial court from the fourth century. But the sample in the Textile Museum at Washington, which on account of an inscription is attributed to this workshop, was found in Egypt. This Propontid workshop thus exported its products, and its successful expansion was probably due to its proximity to the capital. The cloth has pictures of *putti* holding crowns. It is entirely classical in inspiration and in this respect is connected with the whole corpus of Egyptian figured textiles. This artistic industry, like all the arts in Byzantium during its earlier period, continued the practices of the age immediately preceding it.

The Arab invasions affected the artistic life of Byzantium in many and various ways. The separation of the eastern provinces from those which continued to be governed from Constantinople set a barrier between the art of Syria and Egypt and that of Byzantium. Admittedly, Byzantium like Italy received many Christian refugees fleeing from Islam, and these *émigrés* influenced the religious art of all the countries still outside Muslim rule, notably Byzantium. But this had only a temporary effect, while the separation of Syria and Egypt from Byzantium was permanent; the religious art of Byzantium had now to develop independently, without the hitherto regular contribution of these provinces. For not only had these countries been exceptionally active artistically, but their craftsmen had been working for export and their products, which had travelled far and wide, had popularised Egyptian and Syrian forms and practices, the work of the Levant being particularly acceptable on account of the prestige attaching to the Holy Land.

After 650 both Byzantium and the West were largely deprived of the influence of these regions; but this very fact hastened their own artistic emancipation. If the implications of Pirenne's hypothesis of the economic effects of the Arab conquests on European countries have had to be modified, and with good reason, the revolutionary consequences in the field of art can be stressed by way of compensation. Moreover, the importance of Syrian and Egyptian work in Mediterranean art at the end of the early Christian period is confirmed by the fact that, despite Muslim rule, the contribution of these provinces to the art of Christian countries, both Greek and Latin, was renewed even before the Crusades; and, although their contribution to European art might henceforth consist only in supplying the deficiencies of the Christian workshops in the art of *décor* and ornamentation, the fact remains that they resumed the place which they had formerly occupied in the network of interchange between the various Mediterranean schools.

In an Empire with its eastern provinces amputated and deprived of the influence of Syrian and Egyptian artists, the arts must soon have lost those distinguishing features so characteristic of the early middle ages. Unfortunately, the history of the development of Byzantine art in the period immediately after the Islamic conquests is but little known because of the large-scale destruction of seventh- and eighth-century works, even though certain traces of its style may be observed in those monuments of the ninth century which were consciously inspired by pre-iconoclast models. Nor was artistic activity during the period between Justinian I and Justinian II (565–705) very vigorous. The general conditions were highly unpropitious for a flowering of the arts; and if, in spite of all, some palaces and churches were built and some painters and mosaic workers and silversmiths employed (witness the celebrated silver pieces from the time of Heraclius, Plates 38, 39), this was mainly because the exercise of imperial power and the practice of religion continued inevitably and by their very nature to require the services of artists and their works.

THE ICONOCLASTS

The iconoclast Emperors in particular continued to employ the services of artists. Their attitude to art, though hostile to religious imagery, was not, as is generally supposed, purely destructive. They founded churches, built palaces, and decorated their new buildings no less than the old ones whose walls they had previously stripped of representational images. The iconoclasts had, in short, a positive programme of art which deserves to be better known. Unfortunately, after their fall their enemies followed the example which they had themselves set by striving to eradicate all traces of the art of these Emperors and their associates. But contemporary texts and Islamic work give an idea of some aspects of this art which, it must be remembered, could find original expression only in the official imagery of the palaces, as in coin portraits, and in the scenes approved for inclusion in the decoration of churches, liturgical furniture and manuscripts. The texts only mention some of the decorations in iconoclast churches. They reveal, in particular, that the iconoclast Emperors excluded all representation of Christ and of the saints, but allowed scenes from the Hippodrome or from the chase, or scenes of animals and birds in the midst of gardens and orchards to be represented.

At first sight this policy would seem to be aimed at confining decoration to purely ornamental motifs. On closer analysis, however, its products are seen to be connected with that cycle of secular art which, at the close of antiquity and in the early middle ages, had been favoured by many generations of princes and nobles in all Mediterranean countries. It appears in fact that the iconoclast Emperors extended to their churches the style of decoration adopted in their palaces. In this respect, the inclusion of scenes from the Hippodrome races is significant, since these could clearly not be taken as symbolic of Paradise as could, perhaps, the pictures of gardens and animals. The Hippodrome scenes evidently belonged to the cycle of secular art adopted for decoration of the palace. It is indeed probable that these secular paintings adorned not the churches themselves, but the buildings adjoining the church, as in St Sophia at Kiev in the eleventh century: in Constantinople they were sometimes put in the rooms used by the Emperors. This is in fact the case in the Palace of the Blachernae, in which the Emperor Constantine V had one of these cycles painted. On the walls of the Milion, a public building in Constantinople from which all the great roads of the Empire radiated, the same horse races at the Hippodrome were substituted for the pictures of Church Councils (the complete series of which represented the triumph of the *credo* of Orthodoxy). The victories at the Hippodrome, it is known, recalled the triumphant valour of the Emperors, and because of this images of this nature were multiplied at the time of the iconoclast Emperors. As a result the iconoclasts were accused by their enemies of over-emphasising their own auto-cratic power to the detriment of Christ the Pantocrator, and of appro-priating to themselves an iconography normally reserved for Christ.

Granted that the art of the palace was extended to the churches in this manner, some idea of the *décor* of the iconoclast churches may be gained by appealing to the evidence of the decoration, both in paint and in sculpture, of the contemporary Umayyad castles. Since the imperial palaces themselves were destroyed, the *décor* of these Umay-yad buildings, deriving as it does from similar traditions (Greco-Latin on the one hand and Sassanid on the other), may serve to give some impression of the royal residences of that period. As a result of recent excavations at Kasr el-Heir and at Khirbet el-Mefjar and thanks to the murals at Kusejr Amra it is now known that the Umayyad residences had cycles of images intended to glorify and divert their princely owners; their own effigies, the relation of their great deeds and their horoscopes held a central position. There can be no question of Muslim influence on the art of the iconoclasts, in so far as profane ornament in churches is concerned, since Islam did not extend to its mosques the type of decoration used in its palaces. The *décor* of the Muslim palace with its representational images was thus in contrast to that of the mosque; the iconoclasts on the other hand brought the forms of palace and church decoration closer together.

None the less, Islamic art left its mark on Byzantium under the iconoclasts. Thus almost contemporary chroniclers mention the founda-tion by the last iconoclast Emperor, Theophilus, of a suburban palace at Bryas which, they relate, was built and decorated after the model of the residences at Baghdad, and was brought to completion with the help of the descriptions, and under the direction, of an imperial ambassador who had returned with enthusiasm from the capital of the Caliphs. It is probably to this reign that there should be attributed the peculiar fittings of the audience-chamber at Constantinople, which had a throne that moved up and down, a silver tree thronged with birds which fluttered and sang, and lions which roared at the foot of the throne. The automata of the palaces of Baghdad and Samarra were the models for these extravaganzas. Finally, it is very probable that the strong oriental influences which mark Byzantine decorative art immediately after the iconoclasts had already appeared under the iconoclast Emperors: the model of the Caliphate court and of its dazzling decorative art may well have made a strong impression on these rulers, insistent as they were on the majesty of the imperial position. From the information at present available, however, it is impossible to judge the extent to which the iconoclasts were responsible for the introduction of those oriental features which abound in the secular and even in the religious art of Byzantium under the Macedonian Emperors. The taste for ornamental decoration which becomes common in Byzantium after the iconoclast crisis would seem most naturally attributable, and has indeed been attributed, to the iconoclasts. But the development of decorative art was at least as marked, during the middle ages, in the West, where the iconoclasts exerted no influence. The sudden flourishing of Muslim art between the eighth and the thirteenth centuries certainly contributed more than iconoclasm in itself to the spread of ornamental art in all the countries of the Mediterranean, in Byzantium as elsewhere.

FROM THE RESTORATION OF ORTHODOXY TO THE CONQUEST OF CONSTANTINOPLE BY THE CRUSADERS (843–1204)

(a) Architecture

The Byzantine style of architecture during the middle ages shows a remarkable uniformity: throughout this long period the same types of buildings were constructed, using the same methods and forms. It is true that between the ninth and the twelfth centuries the proportions of the buildings progressively changed and that certain details of construction and decoration were modified. But it is hardly possible to speak of a general evolution in Byzantine monumental art during this period, for architects did not as a rule go beyond some more or less special application or some original combination of accepted motifs. In this respect the architecture of western Europe was quite different with its innumerable experiments and inventions and its very varied creations produced at different times and in different regions. In accounting for this difference it must be remembered that western architecture was then only at the beginning of its almost miraculous development, and was bringing into being a new art for a society itself in the process of formation; whereas Byzantine medieval architecture was required to fulfil a traditional function in an already very stabilised society. This at least is the case with ecclesiastical architecture, which is the only type of building fairly well represented. The rise of the provincial nobility during this period certainly had its effect on the architecture of aristocratic dwellings, such as castles and palaces. But this secular art has almost entirely disappeared, while in ecclesiastical architecture, much of which has survived, it is evident that no considerable changes were necessary, since the forms of worship remained essentially the same during this period. Even from as early as the sixth or seventh century the settled order of Byzantine worship and the Byzantine liturgy had determined its own most suitable architectural forms and defined the appropriate type and arrangement of building. A degree of technical perfection in construction was also attained very early, and the Byzantines of the middle ages, unlike their Latin contemporaries, had not to embark upon technical inventions, beginning with the problems of the partial or complete vaulting of their churches. In the ninth century therefore the Byzantines began at a stage which was not generally reached in western Europe until the twelfth century, after a lengthy process of trial and error. If the religious architecture of the West showed a variety of invention, it was because it was developed independently in the different countries under the patronage of both monastic and urban communities, and by individuals whose training differed widely.

In Byzantium the undivided Empire was a leveller of taste: the absolute monarchy habitually gave to the court a leading role which stifled any individual enterprise, while the Church, also centralised, acted in the same way: and even the monks, in spite of their number and moral power in Byzantium, exercised less direct influence on art than is generally supposed. Or rather their influence was exerted after the Byzantine fashion, not by creating a special art with its own system and aesthetic code, but by imposing their taste on work executed under the patronage of Church and State. Moreover, the absence of distinct monastic orders each with its independent organisation, its network of religious houses and workshops with trained workers, prevented Byzantine monasticism from developing and spreading particular types of artistic work. There are no Byzantine counterparts of the monastic schools of architecture of the Cluniacs or Cistercians. Nor does one find in Byzantium lay communities such as guilds or fraternities, which would undertake the construction or adornment of important buildings.

The initial conception and creation of buildings which were works of art, whether ecclesiastical or secular, depended entirely on individuals, which in practice usually meant the rich who were for the most part those in power, beginning with the Emperor and his dignitaries. Under this monarchy the rest of the Emperor's subjects had little influence, being unable to act individually for lack of financial means, or collectively for lack of organisation. This was one of the factors contributing to the elimination of monumental buildings on a large scale, such as those of the Roman period and even of the reign of Justinian, or those built in western Europe from the Carolingian epoch onwards. The desire to multiply religious foundations—typical of Byzantium—was strengthened by the same considerations: the Emperors confined themselves to building churches (and probably palaces) which were quite small, while decorating them lavishly. This fashion for buildings on a modest scale was also probably a question of taste, judging by the illuminated Byzantine books of the same period (eleventh to twelfth century) which favour minute illustrations. Behind these somewhat precious refinements one glimpses the influence of individual patrons, who do not however seem to have extended their demands for technical perfection to the masonry of the buildings they founded. Construction was generally in brick, or in alternate rows of brick and stone: but from the technical point of view the contemporary building of the western Europeans or of the Armenians, Georgians or Seljuqs is more careful and sometimes more scientific. The small Byzantine buildings, however elegant in their proportions, posed no new technical problem and could easily be constructed, even to the vaulting and domes which were considered essential as the crowning touch. Bearing in mind the scale and the fact that their predecessors had, under Justinian, constructed far more daring vaults, it can scarcely be claimed that the medieval Byzantine architects showed any marked inventiveness or any novel technical ability. This does not mean that the average builder did not attain to a good level of skill and taste. Nothing is known of the training of these master builders nor of the organisation of the work by which their plans were carried out. The relative simplicity of the buildings, following a small number of recognised patterns, made it possible for apprentices to be trained on the actual site; and it seems probable that teams of builders generally confined their activities to a particular district, only rarely moving outside its boundaries. This can be argued from the existence of regional schools of architecture, such as those of Thessalonica, the Greek mainland, or Macedonia.

The downfall of the Empire dealt a fatal blow to large-scale secular buildings in Constantinople, in the other towns and in the Byzantine country districts. The Turkish conquerors, who preserved certain churches by transforming them into mosques, showed no respect for the imperial palaces nor for the public buildings of the Christian Empire, and left the castles of the great Byzantine families to fall into ruin. Of the humbler private houses very little is known, and that little mainly from certain echoes of their style traceable in the houses of the Turkish period. Old secular buildings are in any case rare since they were built of wood and have mostly disappeared without leaving any trace. One might have expected to find representations of medieval secular buildings in contemporary painting. But Byzantine painting is rarely realistic in material detail, so that this source of information is neither as productive nor as reliable as might have been hoped. The main fact to be gleaned is that the house of the wealthy Byzantine had two storeys; on the upper floor, above the arcaded ground-floor chambers, was a series of rooms communicating with the outside by a number of windows and by open galleries. The upper storey, which must often have been built of wood, was decorated with carving, and when it was of masonry the decoration was carried out in a combination of stone, brick and glazed pottery. The ruin of a substantial building which still exists at Constantinople near the site of the Blachernae church and which is known as Tekfour Serai (or Palace of Constantine Porphyrogenitus) gives some idea of this type of ornamentation and of the general form of a small medieval palace: arcaded ground floor, first floor lit by large windows, decorated exterior (Plate 4). The inside arrangements of this impressive building cannot be reconstructed and its date remains uncertain. In the opinion of the writer it should be attributed to the time of the Palaeologi (see below, p. 349), but the evidence which it provides about secular architecture is valid for the whole medieval period, apart perhaps from the detail of motifs used in the decoration of the façade of the upper storey, which almost certainly belong to a date later than 1204.

More information about Byzantine secular architecture will only be forthcoming with more extensive excavation of residential districts and palaces. The imperial residences, the Great Palace and the Palace of the Blachernae, may then yield their vital evidence. The little that is known from the texts (from the Continuator of Theophanes or the *Life of Basil I* by Constantine Porphyrogenitus) suggests that architecture in some respects continued the traditions of the last centuries of antiquity, as represented by the royal palaces of that period, built on a centralised plan and covered by a dome; in other ways it was influenced by the style of the Muslim residences, with their garden pavilions and polychrome interior decoration. In the time of Basil I, who at the end of the ninth century carried out an ambitious programme of building in the Old Palace of the capital, and in the following centuries, Byzantine palace architecture at Constantinople still showed much affinity with ecclesiastical architecture, and both had their roots in the art of late Antiquity. This is a remarkable fact, when one recalls the correspondingly rapid development of separate styles of ecclesiastical and secular architecture in western Europe in the middle ages. The unity of inspiration and forms in Byzantine medieval architecture finds its counterpart rather in contemporary Muslim architecture (palaces, madrasas and mosques), which also derived from the traditions common to the Mediterranean region in the last centuries of Antiquity.

Basil I restored and constructed not only palaces but also churches. None of these has survived, but one would assume that the churches built by this Emperor at Constantinople must have been of considerable significance in the history of Byzantine art: they were the first important constructions after the end of iconoclasm and the first to which the founder of the Macedonian dynasty gave his name. Whether he perpetuated in these buildings traditions of church architecture which were growing up before his time or whether he himself originated new forms, the fact remains that the churches of Basil I are the first and most important in the succession of post-iconoclast Byzantine churches. One of them in particular, the 'New Church' of the Palace, with its five domes, appears to have inspired numerous churches during the next few centuries, although this cannot be proved conclusively, since it has disappeared and there are no texts which refer to its influence. It is indeed extremely difficult to assess this presumed and probable influence in view of the fact that the iconoclasts did not forbid the construction of churches in the way that they forbad the making of sacred images. There was thus no complete break in the development of religious architecture as there was in that of religious art of a representational character. Basil I did not have to make a fresh start in the building of his churches, and the measure of originality in their architecture was thereby reduced. This fact is confirmed, for instance, despite the destruction of the churches of Basil's own reign, by the obvious thread of connection that unites churches of certainly earlier date (such as the Christ of the Latomos in Thessalonica of the fifth century, or St Andrew in Krisei at Constantinople of the eighth century) with those of the ninth or early tenth centuries (such as the Christos Akataleptos, or the Church of the Mother of God at Constantinople founded by Constantine Lips).

Under the Macedonians and Comneni Byzantine churches sometimes harked back to the basilican plan and wooden roofing of the early Christian churches; such conscious archaising was adopted for some provincial cathedrals, such as those of Mesembria or Serres, probably out of a desire to revert to the more ancient style of the episcopal church. In other churches, no doubt for similar reasons, the centralised plan was revived which had enjoyed a certain popularity in the first centuries of Christianity, in *martyria* and baptisteries; it makes its appearance in cruciform plans of various types with three or four bays, trefoil or quatrefoil, as in the Panagiotissa at Constantinople, at Peristera near Thessalonica, and at Vodoca in Macedonia. But the great majority of churches were built on a rectangular plan approximating in greater or lesser degree to a square. The entrance is through a transverse portico or narthex, and the nave usually terminates in three apses; the church is vaulted throughout, and has a central dome supported on a drum (sometimes flanked by two or four smaller domes) which rises above the whole building. From the outside the level of the building slopes gradually upwards to the top of the dome, and from the base of this at roof level radiate the four arms of a cross, distinguished by the higher elevations of their vaulted roofs. All these buildings, or almost all, may therefore be defined as 'a cross described within a square'. But the actual construction of these churches is far from being the same everywhere. It is true that the central dome is a regular feature, but it may be built up either on four pendentives (triangular sections of the spherical surface of a dome supported on four piers) or else on four squinches resting on eight points of support. The first is the more widespread type; the other, which allows a greater central space to be kept clear, is characteristic of a group of well-known churches in Greece such as that of Sts Theodore at Athens or that at Daphni (Plate 3). Other vaulted roofs were grouped all round the dome, and the studies of Gabriel Millet have demonstrated that the choice of barrel vaulting, groin vaulting or flattened domes ('calottes') for a particular part of the structure, as well as the direction of the barrel vaults and the methods of vault construction, may vary considerably while still adhering to an accepted general plan. The persistence with which the Byzantines, from the iconoclast period on, sought to accommodate the external appearance of their churches to the 'cross-in-square' formula suggests deliberate symbolism; for the effect is contrived and is not necessarily imposed by the form of construction. The type of the cube-shaped church with a dome seems indeed to have been favoured for the very reason that it imitated the form of the universe.[1] One is conscious

---

[1] This idea was put directly into words in a text of the sixth or seventh century, of pseudo-Dionysian inspiration, the 'Suhita' or Syriac hymn in honour of the church of St Sophia at Edessa.

of the preference shown for this type of church-building from the period of Justinian, beginning with St Sophia at Constantinople. In the period after the iconoclasts it was almost exclusively adopted, and the iconographical schemes of interior decoration employed at that time (see below, p. 337) tend to support the hypothesis that the structure was designed to symbolise the universe.

It is in the arrangement and technique of the vaults that the old traditions were longest preserved: the barrel vaults which in the aisles run parallel to the main axis of the church are relics of basilican buildings; the grouping of the vaults, with frequent recourse to cross-vaulting, symmetrically around the central dome shows a faithful adherence to the tradition of the centralised plan. The same tradition also dictated that the nave of the church should form a square whose centre was marked by the dome; to the eastern side of this square a transverse bay was added to accommodate the choir or sanctuary. But in the Byzantine provinces this addition was not always made, and the eastern side of the square itself became the sanctuary. The former solution allowed the two essential elements of a church, the sanctuary and the space for the worshippers, to be very distinctly articulated. In the best Byzantine buildings of the period under consideration this principle of clear articulation was extended to the outward aspect of the church: the whole structure of the building and its components can be clearly seen from the outside. Apart from occasional uncarved stone or brick designs set flush to the wall the façades of these churches were undecorated. Their aesthetic effect depended entirely on the proportions and harmony of the lines and masses which rose gradually towards the summit of the central dome.

It is in the proportions of buildings that any architectural development is most apparent in the period between 843 and 1204. Buildings tended to grow in height while the outer walls and free supports within the nave became less massive. This development can best be observed by comparing a pre-iconoclast church such as St Sophia at Thessalonica with one of the tenth or eleventh century. The Church of the Virgin founded by Lips and that of the Myrelaion built by the Emperor Romanus Lecapenus, for instance, show even in the tenth century a slender elegance in their proportions which became still more pronounced later on. The somewhat reduced scale of all these churches certainly simplified the task of the Byzantine architects of the period. But they were not thereby deprived of opportunities for demonstrating their consummate skill, as the two last-named churches testify. To appreciate this fact one need only observe how apparently fragile are the supporting members and how great is the proportion of open space to solid masonry in the walls of a church such as that of Lips, in spite of its being vaulted throughout. By their own special methods, and by drawing on traditional knowledge based on experiments begun in the sixth century or even earlier, the Byzantines under the Macedonians and the Comneni created buildings which were allied in general appearance to Gothic and particularly to the Romanesque constructions in Burgundy: there is the same tendency to vertical lines and slenderness, and the same audacity of construction in the vaults and their delicate supports.

The little cube-shaped churches of the Byzantines with their hemispherical domes were widely distributed. The Empire was still fairly extensive and this type of architecture was in use even in the most distant provinces such as southern Italy. Later it passed beyond the frontiers and was found wherever the political and economic influence of Byzantium had penetrated: in Syria in the tenth century, in the Holy Land in the twelfth, in Venice and in Sicily—this last in spite of, indeed owing to, the hostility of the Norman princes towards the Emperors, whom they imitated the better to overthrow. Above all the religious influence of Byzantium, which was by no means divorced from political and economic pressure, was the most important instrument in spreading the precepts and practices of Byzantine architecture, which were introduced and adopted wherever this influence was exercised: in Bulgaria, Serbia, Russia, on the west coast of the Black Sea, in Georgia and Abhasia. Byzantine architectural influence in these countries was at its strongest during this period; it progressively diminished with the later rise of Gothic architecture in all the Latin countries. After this period it only survived in regions connected with the Empire by the ties of common religion: the Slav countries, Georgia, and also the Rumanian principalities on the Danube.

(b) *Mosaics and frescoes*

The return to representational religious art after the iconoclast crisis (843) must have been a slow process, and the great period of medieval art only really begins towards the end of the ninth century. The few works which remain to illustrate this period of readaptation to representational art after the long break show that it was obliged to turn for inspiration to very ancient models, pre-iconoclast in date, and that craftsmen had to re-learn their trade. The miniatures of the ninth century are almost all reproductions of illustrations in pre-iconoclast books, for example, the manuscript of Cosmas Indicopleustes in the Vatican, the so-called Chludov Psalter in the Historical Museum at Moscow, or the Homilies of Gregory of Nazianzus in the

Bibliothèque Nationale in Paris (gr. 510); the variety of their styles reflects the diversity of the originals on which they were modelled. The few mosaics of the ninth century which survive reinforce this impression of an art still lacking in self-assurance: examples are the fragments in the south-west room and the scene in the tympanum of the main door of St Sophia at Constantinople, and others in the conch of the apse and in the dome of St Sophia at Thessalonica (Plate 7), and the mosaic, destroyed in 1922, in the apse of the Church of the Dormition at Nicaea. But the style of this period varies considerably from one work to another, and through lack of experience the creators of these large-scale mosaics did not know how to avoid the distortion which affects images applied to concave surfaces (all the examples just quoted show this). Their draughtsmanship is often imperfect (there is frequent acromegaly), even in the mosaics of the greatest churches of the Empire, such as those above the door of St Sophia at Thessalonica. It was only towards the beginning of the tenth century that Byzantine artists recovered complete freedom of expression. Once in full command of their medium they were able to abandon their ancient models and attempt new experiments. Maturity in medieval Byzantine painting began in the tenth century.

Among the creations of Byzantine artists in this period wall-mosaics hold pride of place. Some are known to have been executed in the imperial palace in the reign of Basil I (867–86). But with the exception of a few portraits no secular work has been preserved and only a very few church mosaics have survived. The ninth and tenth centuries are represented only by a number of panels in the Church of St Sophia in Constantinople, and in actual practice this essentially Byzantine art can only be judged from the work of the eleventh and twelfth centuries. Whole interiors decorated with mosaics of the eleventh century survive in Hosios Loukas in Phocis (Plate 18), in Nea Moni on the island of Chios and at Daphni near Athens. To these complete series must be added what remains of the mosaics in the sanctuary and central vaulting of St Sophia at Kiev and also the narthex of the Church of the Dormition at Nicaea. In the twelfth century the sanctuaries of the churches at Serres and of St Michael at Kiev (both, as also the church at Nicaea, destroyed within living memory) provided the best examples of mosaics; and there are certain surviving fragments at Gelat in Georgia, at Bethlehem, and on Mt Athos. But the most impressive examples both from the aesthetic and from the iconographical point of view are in Sicily, in the churches founded by the Norman kings in the second half of the twelfth century—at Cefalù, in the Palatine Chapel and the Martorana in Palermo itself, and at Monreale just outside the city. The mosaics of the

1. Constantinople. The land walls. 5th century.

2. Constantinople. Church of St John of Studius. 5th century.

3. Daphni. The monastery church. Late 11th century.

4. Constantinople. The palace of Tekfour Serai. Probably 13th century.

5, 6. Constantinople. Church of
St Sophia. 6th century.

7. Thessalonica. Apostle. Mosaic from the dome of the church of St Sophia. 9th century.

8. Ravenna. Justinian and his retinue. Wall mosaic in the church of San Vitale. 6th century.

9. Thessalonica. Ezekiel's Vision. Apse mosaic in the church of Hosios David. 5th century.

10, 11. Constantinople. Details of floor mosaic in the Great Palace. 5th or 6th century.

12. Vladimir. Detail from Last Judgment. Fresco from the church of St Demetrius.

13. Constantinople. The Emperor Constantine IX. Wall mosaic in
the church of St Sophia. 11th century.

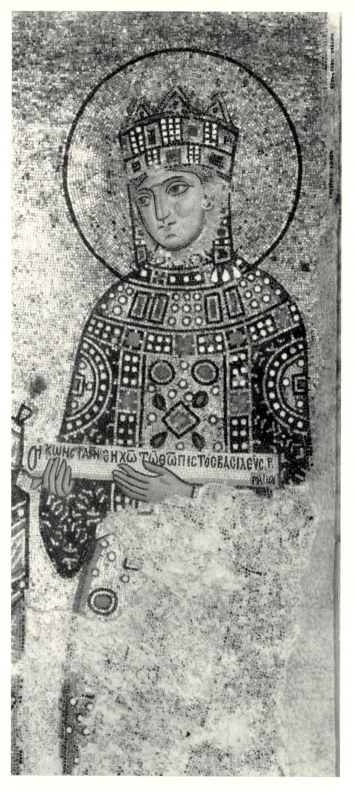

14. Constantinople. The Empress Zoe. Wall mosaic
in the church of St Sophia. 11th century.

15. Constantinople. Joseph's departure. Wall mosaic in
Kariye Camii. 14th century.

16. Constantinople. Theodore Metochites. Wall mosaic in
Kariye Camii. 14th century.

17. Constantinople. Virgin and Child. Mosaic in Kariye Camii. 14th century.

18.   Greece. The Washing of the Feet. Wall mosaic in the church of
Hosios Loukas in Phocis. 11th century.

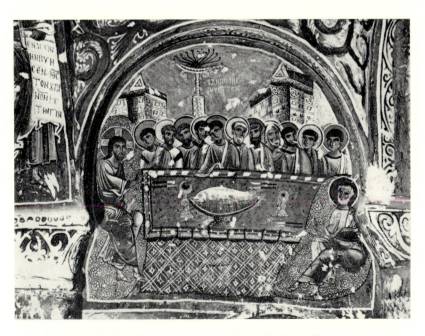

19.   Cappadocia. The Last Supper. Fresco in Karanlik (Qaranlek).

20. Macedonia. Pietà. Fresco in the church at Nerezi. 12th century.

21. Cappadocia. Scenes from the Life of the Virgin. Fresco in Kiliclar (Qeledjlar).

22. Constantinople. The Descent into Hell. Fresco in Kariye Camii. 14th century.

23. Peloponnese. The Raising of Lazarus. Fresco in the church of
the Pantanassa in Mistra. 15th century.

24. Macedonia. Girl with pitcher. Fresco in the church of
St Demetrius at Peć. 14th century.

25. Miniature from a treatise on Veterinary Medicine. 14th century.

26. Miniature. The Conversion
    of St Paul. 9th century.

27. Miniature from a monastic
    typicon. Community of nuns.
    Late 14th century.

28. Miniature. The Emperor John VI Cantacuzenus. 14th century.

29. Silk shroud of St Germain at Auxerre. Late 10th century.

30. Ivory casket. Troyes. 11th century.

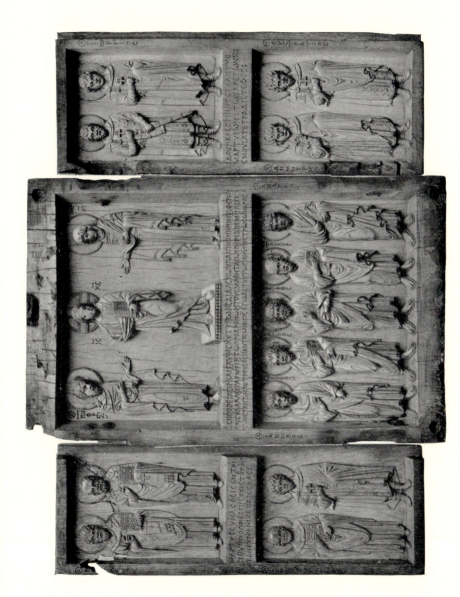

31. Ivory triptych. Palazzo Venezia, Rome. 10th century.

32. Marble relief. The Virgin. Archaeological Museum, Istanbul. 11th century.

33. Copper relief. Virgin and Child. Victoria and Albert
Museum, London. 12th century. (*Crown copyright*)

34. Silver reliquary lid. The Women at the Tomb.
Louvre, Paris. 12th century.

35. Enamel book-cover. The Archangel Michael.
St Mark's, Venice. 12th century.

36. Enamelled icon. The Entry into Jerusalem. St Mark's, Venice. 11th century.

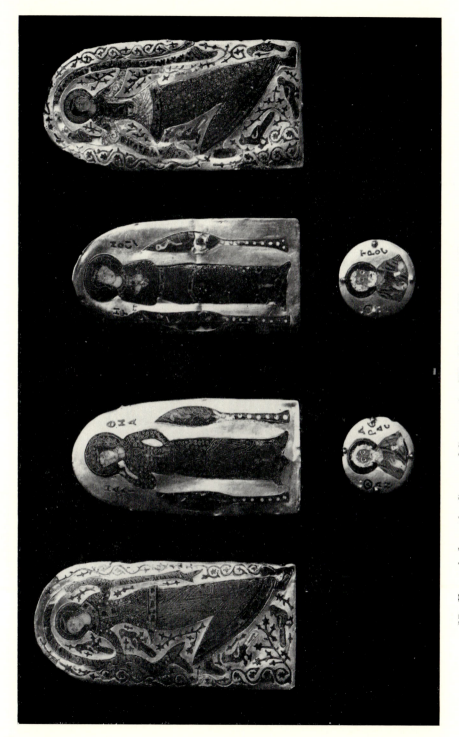

37. Enamels from the Crown of Constantine IX. National Museum, Budapest. 11th century.

38. Silver dish. Silenus and maenad. Hermitage Museum, Leningrad. 7th century.

39. Silver plate. Marriage of David. Archaeological Museum, Nicosia. 7th century.

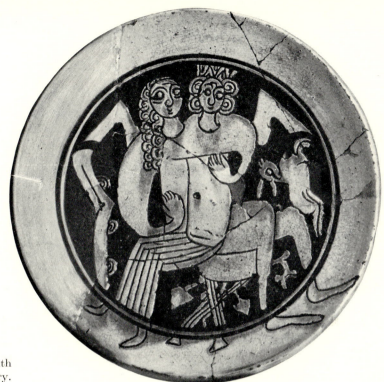

40. Incised plate. Corinth
Museum. 12th century.

41. Sgraffito plate. Agora
Museum, Athens. 12th
century.

1 2 3 4 5

6 7 8 9 10

11 12 —— 13 —— 14

15 16 (Æ) 17 18 (Æ)

42. Coins (selected by P. D. Whitting).

nave of St Mark's in Venice were also inspired by the same art of Byzantine mosaic work of the twelfth century, although they are probably of a slightly later date (the mosaics in the north narthex show a fusion of Byzantine art of the Palaeologian period with the local Gothic). A few imperial ex-votos with fine portraits of Emperors and Empresses have also been discovered in the south gallery of St Sophia at Constantinople (Plates 13, 14).

All the schemes of mosaic decoration follow a similar iconographic plan. This, although it originated earlier, seems to have been given definite shape and to have come into general use only from the end of the ninth century or the beginning of the tenth century, and in Constantinople itself. This plan aimed at gathering together on the vaults and walls of a church a series of carefully grouped pictures showing the Kingdom of God and its inhabitants—a theme to be distinguished from that of Paradise, which predominated in Early Christian times. Within the limits of this plan the artists also endeavoured to adapt their cycle of pictures to the architecture of the churches which, as has been remarked (p. 334 above), were themselves designed to symbolise the structure of the universe, as popularly imagined at the time. The mosaics of such churches were meant to illustrate the Christian universe, the new and ideal Cosmos which came into being when the Church was created and which, geographically speaking, was 'constructed' on the model of the visible Cosmos, that is to say in the form of a cube surmounted by a dome. While the actual building of the church imitated this cosmic form the symbols were arranged in it according to the place which belonged to each member of the Christian community in this visible universe. Thus Christ and his angels were represented right at the summit, in the highest spheres, then the different classes of saints who have their dwelling near to God. To these citizens of the Christian universe governed by Christ himself scenes from the Gospels were added, corresponding to the great festivals of the liturgical year. They had their place in this evocation of Christ's universal kingdom, since it owed its very existence to the work of incarnation which these scenes commemorated. Their presence was the more meaningful because each time the eucharistic liturgy was celebrated in the church there was a sacramental re-enactment of the story of the Redemption.

Iconographically these mosaic decorations developed little from the ninth to the thirteenth century. It is possible, however, that originally only Christ and his saints were shown and not the gospel scenes. Yet a description of a church at Constantinople from the reign of Leo VI the Wise (886–912) proves that by his time the historico-sacramental cycle had already found its way into decorative schemes of the 'Cosmic' type. Aesthetically, however, there was certainly some artistic development between the tenth and thirteenth centuries, although there appear to have been no very fundamental changes. The precise adaptation of the pictures to the supporting architectural features, and the predominance of the human figure above all other subjects, including landscape and purely ornamental compositions, remained constant features of this period. In contrast to the contemporary mural painters of the West the Byzantine artist in mosaic rarely presented grouped compositions within a frame, but preferred isolated figures against a background of plain gold. In the tenth century, in St Sophia, the figures in mosaic are large and heavy, always presented full-face and somewhat lacking in depth. In the following century several different styles sprang up simultaneously: Hosios Loukas (c. 1000) carried on the traditions of the tenth-century figures at St Sophia, but one can glimpse the first faint signs of a more supple manner inspired by classical models (Plate 18). This manner found its most noble expression at Daphni towards 1100, and throughout the twelfth century there was a partiality for this 'classical' style which tended to give mosaics the appearance of coloured reliefs. Yet certain mosaics of the eleventh century, particularly those at Chios, about 1050, stand completely aloof from this 'humanist' trend and take pleasure in stressing, with a surprising verve, dramatic expressions and gestures and the incisiveness of bright colours. The mosaics of Chios, with their sweeping outlines and heavy shadows, stand opposed to the mosaics of the twelfth century. They have an 'oriental' look about them, although this may be due only to the absence of the revived classical influence. In the twelfth century under the Comneni, and in the territories of the Norman kings, no mosaicist attempted to resist this influence, and the pseudo-classical manner reigned supreme, although the imitation of classical models was not actually carried any farther.

Progress at this time did however show itself in another branch of architectural decoration—fresco or mural painting. After the end of iconoclasm, the walls of churches were freely covered with mural paintings on religious themes. The iconography and arrangement of these were exactly the same as those of mosaics, with one exception: whereas wall mosaics were confined to the surfaces above the cornice of the arches, wall paintings covered the surfaces of arches and walls alike right down to ground level.

One of the oldest examples of these complete iconographic decorations is preserved in the crypt (or rather the lower chapel) of Hosios Loukas in Phocis. But it is in Cappadocia, in the churches and rock-cut chapels of the little deserted monasteries, that the most numerous examples of these mural paintings have been brought to light. Obviously these are provincial, even primitive productions; but they reflect the art which was flourishing in the Empire, particularly in Constantinople, at the same time or a little earlier, and which was brought to Cappadocia after the reconquest of this part of Asia Minor in the tenth century. It is in Cappadocia that the differences between two types of decorative schemes can best be seen: the one (illustrated in Toquale I and Guereme) using narrative cycles set out in superimposed bands, following a fashion which dates back to the time of the basilicas, the other (represented in Toquale II and Elmale Kilisse) using decorations set out according to their function, with their cycles representing the festivals of the liturgical year, as in the cruciform or cross-in-square churches. These Cappadocian frescoes also display a very considerable iconographical range and provide a foundation of evidence on which to base the first stage in the history of medieval Byzantine iconography (Plates 19, 21). There is obviously no question of the monastic painting of remote Cappadocia having any influence on the methods of western iconographers, yet the iconographical types found in Cappadocian frescoes of the tenth, eleventh and twelfth centuries may help to assess the Byzantine share in the evolution of western Christian iconography, which, as is well known, rapidly becomes much richer in the twelfth century, drawing on various earlier experiments and particularly those of the Byzantines.

The best Byzantine frescoes were certainly produced at Constantinople. But the only surviving examples of this period are to be found in places outside the capital, although directly indebted to its influence; and a few such works, like the frescoes at Nerezi in Macedonia, dated to 1164, or in the Church of St Demetrius at Vladimir in north-east Russia, of 1198, can be classed among the masterpieces of Byzantine art (Plates 20, 12). These wall-paintings are particularly notable for their successful attempts to portray the human form, to express noble and gracious character by individual treatment of the heads, and to show convincingly the most moving scenes of suffering and death from Christ's Passion. Other painters of the twelfth century were less original. But all the wall-paintings of this period, from the eleventh century at the latest, are distinguished by their balance and restraint, and by the skill with which they are adapted to each wall they are to cover, to each church interior they are to adorn. Even the most modest of these works leave an impression of calm grandeur.

(c) *Miniature painting*

Miniatures originated in the *scriptoria* where manuscripts were produced, and scribes engaged in copying texts had a natural tendency to reproduce in their copy illustrations from the manuscript which served as their model. In the illumination of manuscripts there was thus established a link from one copy to another between illustrations of the same text, which proved stronger than any other ties of continuity such as the period or the school of painting. The critic has therefore to consider miniatures in a separate category from monumental paintings and icons.

As has been said above (p. 335), painting in the books of the ninth century lacked any artistic uniformity of its own because the artists of that time had not been able to assimilate the lessons of their models sufficiently to become emancipated from them in their various styles. Thus the marginal illustrations of the Psalters preserve, well into the ninth century, the vigour of the incisive work of some anonymous and probably oriental painter of the sixth or seventh century. To this same period belongs, to all intents and purposes, the style of the celebrated miniatures of the *Christian Topography* of Cosmas Indicopleustes, the author himself having illustrated his original manuscript in sixth-century Alexandria. But in this case the illustrations are monumental in their conception, placed within a framework, grave ponderous figures and narrative pictures created by an artist who was also a scholar (Plate 26). The manuscript of the *Homilies* of Gregory of Nazianzus in the Bibliothèque Nationale (gr. 510) which was executed for the Emperor Basil I (867–86) is in itself a complete gallery of copies taken from various originals. But whereas the copyists of the Cosmas miniatures were reasonably skilled, those of the *Homilies* seem consistently to have produced work much clumsier than their models, which were mainly paintings in books of various kinds, but almost certainly included also some monumental paintings (for example, the scenes of the visions of God). Taken all in all these works give an impression of diversity, but this should really be put to the credit of the models rather than of the Byzantine miniaturists of the day. This view may be confirmed by comparing the productions of the period immediately following, which, if less diverse, are at the same time more original. In fact by the end of the tenth century it would appear that the whole output of the Byzantine *scriptoria* was characterised by a single style. There are several well-known works, however, which antedate the completion of this process of standardisation: among them are the Psalters with large-scale illustrations in the classical style (Paris, Bibl. Nat. gr. 139; Vatican,

Reg. gr. 1) and the Joshua Roll in the Vatican, no less classical in taste yet quite distinct in style. These works bear the stamp of their originals; their individuality derives from individual prototypes. But the prototypes have been subjected to a process of interpretation which lends to the new works a character of their own peculiar to the Byzantine art of this period and destined to persist. The miniatures in a collection of Lives of the Saints, the *Menologion* of Basil II in the Vatican, give some idea of the kind of Byzantine miniature-painting which was produced for court patrons about the beginning of the eleventh century. The artists in the studios of the capital were by then in complete mastery of a balanced style which had but recently become standardised, and which was, with certain inevitable variations, to predominate in Byzantium until the sack of Constantinople by the crusaders in 1204. This style finds its closest large-scale counterparts in the mosaics of St Sophia at Kiev, in the narthex of the Church of the Dormition at Nicaea (now destroyed) and above all at Daphni. Possibly it is only because monuments are more vulnerable to the hazards of destruction that no mosaics or frescoes survive of the same style as the *Menologion* in the Vatican and closer to it in date. Or on the other hand it may be that this new style was first developed in manuscript illustrations; for it is a style which strikes a certain balance between motifs borrowed from the classical tradition and elements which were essentially Byzantine, such as the composition, the treatment of space, and the inner spirituality of the human figures. Whatever the case, it is certainly true that the eleventh and twelfth centuries were very productive of this delicate art, turning out illuminated manuscripts in great profusion and increasing the number of illustrations in each manuscript. It is in the eleventh century that manuscripts of the Gospels appear in which each sentence of the text is accompanied by a picture (Paris, Bibl. Nat. gr. 74; Florence, Bibl. Laurent. VI. 23), and some of these illustrations were not based on earlier models. The Bibles, Psalters and collections of homilies of the eleventh and twelfth centuries are most lavishly illustrated and besides adaptations of older paintings they contain entirely fresh creations, compositions either completely new or made up of elements taken from an earlier repertory. Such, for example, are the numerous vivid and sometimes genuinely moving paintings of James of Kokkinobaphos illustrating the twelfth-century collection of homilies on the Virgin in the Vatican Library and in the Bibliothèque Nationale in Paris.

Two tendencies deserve special notice in the miniatures of the eleventh and twelfth centuries: in the illustrations just mentioned and in the Bible miniatures there is a taste for the picturesque, even the exotic, which shows itself in oriental figures, rich costumes and landscapes of fantastic trees; mingled with it are flashes of realism, and a strong partiality for emotional themes, such as the tenderness of children or the grace of angels. This tendency has affinities with the experiments of certain mural painters already noted at Nerezi (Plate 20) and Vladimir (Plate 12). The other special characteristic is of a very different kind: in the eleventh and twelfth centuries a type of book illustration for the connoisseur was produced which had no precedent. The paintings are on a minute scale, some enclosed in borders ornamented with patterns like those of carpets, others delicately inserted in the margins or even woven round the initials. These works are distinguished by a wealth of gold and bright but harmoniously blended colours imitated from contemporary enamel works. Painting and calligraphy combine to heighten the decorative effect of each page of the manuscript, and the result is notable not so much for the feeling the work inspires or the intellectual concept behind it as for its exquisite taste and unerring execution. Several manuscripts of this description were produced in the *scriptoria* of the great monasteries of the capital, like those of Studius or of the Pantocrator. While mural painting and other forms of book illustration were breaking new ground through the observation of nature, this delicate art of painting on a minute scale achieved its effect by technical perfection and preciosity.

(d) Enamels, ivories and other works of art

Never since the early days of Christianity had representational art, and especially the portrayal of the human form in religious contexts, been so common as in the Byzantine Empire after the iconoclast crisis had ended. Neither previously in Byzantium itself, nor in any country of western Europe, had representations of Christ, the Virgin, the saints and scenes drawn from Scripture and other Christian sources been produced in such prolific quantities; and indeed, from the tenth or eleventh century, copies of these holy pictures (along with figured silks) were among the most important of Byzantine art exports (Plate 29).

This artistic prodigality is also seen in the application to religious imagery of a craft which was raised to the level of a great art in the period between the beginning of the tenth and the end of the eleventh centuries. The art of cloisonné enamel attained to a particular brilliance and to an unprecedented technical perfection at this time, and consequently must be classed as a separate branch of Byzantine painting. It owed its special qualities to the clear effect of the coloured enamel. As in the mosaics and in the stained-glass windows contemporary with these enamels, there is an infinite play of light within the image which gives it an extraordinary effect of luminosity. Among the masterpieces of Byzantine enamel are the tenth-century reliquary for a fragment of the Cross in the Cathedral of Limburg-on-the-Lahn, the Pala d'Oro in St Mark's at Venice (Plate 36), with its enamels of the eleventh and twelfth centuries, and the eleventh-century icon of the Virgin in the form of a triptych at Khakhuli in Georgia. Many objects including liturgical vessels, icon-frames, large and small reliquaries, crosses, rings and ear-rings were also decorated with figure-motifs carried out in these enamels (Plate 37). At the time of the crusades many found their way to western Europe, and after 1204 much fell into Venetian hands: the Treasury of St Mark's possesses the finest known collection of Byzantine enamels (Plate 35).

While enamel work has some connection with painting it is more closely related to goldsmith's work. This craft was as flourishing at Byzantium in the tenth, eleventh and twelfth centuries as was that of mosaic. But naturally gold and silver objects, easily plundered or melted down, did not escape the misfortunes which later befell Byzantium. For this reason there is only a relatively small number of specimens from which to judge their quality. Technically they are usually excellent and their design and detail distinguish them from the work of other schools, making it obvious that behind these rare specimens stands a long and solid tradition of well-equipped work-shops. Here too iconographical images were employed for decorative purposes. There are repoussé reliefs, generally small, though some include figures several inches high, such as the icons in relief of the Archangel Michael, now at St Mark's (Plate 35). Such works can be classed as real pieces of sculpture. The most noteworthy examples are icons; others decorate icon frames or liturgical objects such as chalices or reliquaries (Plate 34). The influence of classical sculpture, notice-able in the treatment of the human figures, appears side by side with that of Muslim techniques of metalwork. From the tenth or eleventh century onwards eastern ornamental motifs, such as the arabesque or the Sassanid palmette, and decorations such as backgrounds covered with fine tracery, disks and bosses with perforated designs, became quite common in Byzantium. Besides caskets and censers of the usual shapes Byzantine workers in precious metals created some in the form of pavilions and chapels and reproduced in miniature real buildings both secular and ecclesiastical: examples are to be seen in the Treasury of the Cathedral at Aix-la-Chapelle and in St Mark's, Venice.

This repoussé work on objects in precious metal was only one branch of Byzantine sculpture. There were several others, although sculptured figures never had a very important place in Byzantine art in the middle ages. Bronze was commonly used to make small icons like the Torcello Virgin in London (Plate 33), but they were seldom of a high artistic standard. It is still rare to find great artistic merit in the carved steatite icons which were produced in large numbers. On the other hand the marble bas-reliefs of the eleventh and twelfth centuries, intended to be attached to iconostases or placed against the inner or outer walls of churches, are often of great beauty and very skilful workmanship, while their scale brings them closer to the category of monumental sculpture: examples of such work are to be seen in the Christ and Apostles from Fenari Isa Camii and the Virgin from the Mangana district now in the Archaeological Museum at Istanbul (Plate 32); and at Venice there are several reliefs of the Virgin and saints built into the façades of St Mark's. Some reliefs in Venice and at Dumbarton Oaks showing an Emperor, and others at Kiev and at Torcello prove that works of this nature were not produced for religious purposes only. Nevertheless, the aims and technical methods of Byzantine sculpture were strictly limited after the iconoclast period. The victorious iconophiles were particularly anxious to make a clear distinction between a Christian icon and an idol; and so the connection between sculpture and idolatry led them to discard the one in order to avoid the other.

It is clearly significant in this respect that among the types of sculpture on a small scale which were considered innocuous was that of ivory carving, which had been employed in secular no less than in ecclesiastical contexts, for pagan as well as for Christian themes. The art of ivory carving undoubtedly flourished in Byzantium between the tenth and the thirteenth centuries. There can be no disputing the fact that secular and ecclesiastical ivories constitute two very distinct groups, even from the purely aesthetic point of view. Ivories carved with religious subjects have their counterparts in other categories of Byzantine art, such as reliefs in gold, silver or marble, or even paintings; they can thus be connected with known works in other media and dated with fair certainty. Among the masterpieces are the Descent from the Cross in the Victoria and Albert Museum, the Utrecht Madonna, the so-called Harbaville triptych in the Louvre, and another similar to it in the Palazzo Venezia in Rome (Plate 31). On the other hand, caskets and oliphants decorated with secular subjects have too few characteristics in common with other categories of known Byzantine works to be fitted so easily into any general classification. Like the specialised book illustrations the decorations of these objects for secular use follow distinct traditions of their own and remain to some extent a law unto themselves. The oldest examples of the secular ivories would seem to belong to the iconoclast period, and their art has affinities with the sculptured ivories of very late Antiquity, whether in the Hellenistic style of Syria or Egypt or the Sassanid type (see the caskets in the Victoria and Albert Museum and the Musée de Cluny, and the Byzantine oliphants in the Copenhagen and British Museums). The fact that the reliefs which decorate these objects belong to a tradition of their own is true of the themes they illustrate no less than of their style. The style varies between two extremes, the Iranian and the Hellenistic; but the ivory carvers following classical models subjected them to a different interpretation when depicting religious subjects. This different treatment is particularly obvious when objects of a similar shape are compared, as for instance the caskets with borders of rosettes bearing reliefs of biblical subjects on the one hand and of Bacchic themes on the other. The repertory of themes in secular work is rich but apparently unsystematic, although this may well be due simply to the absence of any major works showing a complete cycle of any theme. The commonest subjects are representations of amusements—hunting, games in the circus and hippodrome, acrobats and animals, mingled with fragments from the stories of Bacchus and Hercules, which ever since the late classical period had commonly been used for the decoration of small luxury articles (Plate 30). These cycles of pictures showing entertainments never ceased to be used for the decoration of palaces and noble houses, and in Byzantium itself were doubtless fostered by court patronage. The floor mosaics in the Great Palace of Constantinople long before the iconoclast period showed scenes which belonged by tradition to these cycles (Plates 10, 11); while in the eleventh or twelfth century the creators of the frescoes on the staircase walls of St Sophia in Kiev, and of the miniatures in the codices Sinait. 339 and Paris. gr. 64 and 550 each make independent use of characteristic elements taken from this repertory.

It is from these works and others like them, still insufficiently studied, that it will eventually be possible to judge the importance of secular artistic work at Byzantium and particularly that of the imperial palaces. Although such work was largely destroyed, one can hazard a guess at the part it played in the general development of Byzantine art, and especially its prime importance in relation to the ecclesiastical art which alone is fairly well represented today. It is not surprising that the court, under an absolute monarchy such as that of Byzantium, should have exercised so great an influence on art; and it was natural that this influence should extend to the ecclesiastical sphere, since the ruler claimed direct authority from

Christ, and in this capacity constantly intervened in the affairs of the Church. On the artistic plane the Byzantine Emperors, like so many other princes, generally showed eclectic tastes and were interested not in a particular standard of aesthetic values but in a general artistic scheme and in the technical perfection and the material value of the works produced, that is to say their rarity, which was flattering to the imperial vanity. Moreover, secular works in Byzantium often adhere to well-established cycles of topics, but without using any discrimination between the style of the Greeks and Romans of the first centuries of our era, and that of the Sassanid Iranians, or even that of the Persians and Arabs of the early Muslim period. Elements from different sources mingle in the secular works of art favoured in court circles; and the Muslim tradition particularly, with all the older oriental elements it included, is seen in many ornamental works and especially in the patterns on figured textiles and in the garments made from these for ceremonial use by the dignitaries of the court. The court favoured the Hellenistic and Roman style as well as the oriental; but it was nevertheless the principal centre of the influence of oriental art in Byzantium between the ninth and the twelfth centuries. This influence spread from one royal household to another, each anxious to maintain its own prestige, and the prodigality and munificence of the Muslim princes (Umayyad and still more Fatimid, Abbasid, Samanid and others) made their palaces something to be envied and copied by all Muslim and Christian potentates. Without abandoning their own traditions of secular art, inherited from Rome and the Hellenistic capitals, the Byzantine Emperors were the first to take advantage of early Muslim art in its production of luxury goods. Thus from the iconoclast period onwards, Byzantine art gradually acquired an increasing number of elements foreign to classical culture. This oriental contribution was of course no more obvious in Christian representational art than in the literary language of writers, for both artists and authors made deliberate efforts to imitate classical work and clung to the tradition of the early centuries of the Christian era. But in pure decoration, as in industrial and secular arts, the non-classical element gained ground steadily. In religious art Byzantium led the field, but in secular art the Empire followed the lead set by artists working in other countries, particularly in the neighbouring capitals of Islam. Consequently, Byzantine art became in many respects dependent on centres beyond its frontiers, a dependence which increasingly affected more and more branches of artistic and semi-artistic activity.

THE AGE OF THE PALAEOLOGI

Up to 1204 the fate of Byzantine art was closely bound up with that of the Empire. Art reflected its ideas and its greatness, lived under its protection and on its riches. Exported beyond the frontiers of the Empire it proclaimed everywhere its Byzantine origin and, whether in Sicily or in Russia, spoke the language of Constantinople.

After 1204, in spite of the return of the Emperors to Constantinople in 1261, the situation was never again the same. Certainly a remarkable art flourished in the capital, bearing witness to the power of the Byzantine tradition and the intensity of life on the Bosphorus and in the Balkans at the end of the middle ages. It bears witness also to the importance that Constantinople managed to preserve even when robbed of her hinterland in Europe by the Slavs, in Asia by the Turks, and bled white by the Italian merchants. In art as in literature it was there, in the capital, in the heart of the Greek society of Constantinople and imbued with the Greek tradition, that there was again an upsurge of creative activity. But this vigorous outburst no longer evoked the greatness of an Empire, for the Empire was a thing of the past. With its much narrowed boundaries it could no longer contain nor command the talents of all those who might have served its greatness, nor could it offer them more than a fraction of the material resources necessary if they were to be fruitfully employed. This artistic renaissance, which received its impulse in the Constantinople of the Palaeologi, spread to the Greek provinces and flourished there—in Trebizond, in the Crimea, in Mistra and in the islands; that is to say in cities and districts inhabited by Hellenes but belonging either to Greek princelings, or to the Italian city states, the Franks or the Turks. On the other hand in Bulgaria, Serbia, Wallachia, Moldavia, Georgia and Russia non-Hellenic peoples adopted this same art, which thus became the accepted art of the Orthodox Church in all its national branches. Thanks to this position of vantage it spread its influence over a territory far more extensive than that of the Empire at the height of its power. Its extent is all the more impressive in view of the territorial insignificance and precarious political situation of the contemporary Byzantine state. It must be remembered, however, that this artistic (and religious) revival of Byzantium under the Palaeologi has its roots in foundations laid before 1204.

It is somewhat surprising to see that Byzantium was still capable of inspiring an artistic movement destined to exert a lasting influence among peoples so different, and in the face of the rapid progress of western experiments in art. This success is no doubt partly accounted

for by the large numbers of craftsmen in the great city on the Bosphorus, unrivalled by those of any other town or region of eastern
Europe at that time. But the main reason is to be found in its
position as the centre of Orthodoxy which it always retained; this
gave it a prestige which was reflected in all it produced, especially in
its religious art. The great work of the Palaeologian period is almost
exclusively ecclesiastical, and for this reason, quite apart from any
aesthetic considerations, it was welcomed with open arms in all
countries looking to Constantinople as the capital of their faith. Yet
it was not a uniform art which thus radiated outwards from Byzantium: it was continually subjected to local influences and acquired in
varying degrees a specialised and localised character. Thus, in the
thirteenth century the development of autonomous schools began,
not only in Serbia and Bulgaria but also at Mistra and perhaps in
Macedonia, that is to say in both Slav and Greek countries. The
capitals of little principalities and the palaces of their rulers, of differing races but united by their Orthodox faith, became for a time centres
of a flourishing religious art which, within the general Palaeologian
framework, showed distinct variations—local dialects rather than
separate languages. This regrouping of creative artistic forces widened
the Byzantine outlook in a way unknown in the previous period.
But one must beware of exaggerating the local or national peculiarities of this medieval art of the Balkans. Generally they are less
marked than, for instance, the respective characteristics of the different schools of Ottonian miniature, or those of Italian painting of the
Dugento or Trecento. This indicates that there was but relatively
little progress in the differentiation of artistic styles and methods in
the Orthodox world of the Balkans, and in any case that progress was
once again to be retarded under Turkish rule. The Ottoman Empire
was to tolerate Christian art, but to reduce it to a certain uniformity,
while fixing for it a much more modest level of production than in the
days of the great Byzantine Empire. In such circumstances Byzantine influence was not able to affect surrounding countries so easily
and the importance of its guiding role in secular and decorative art
was still further diminished. In the late middle ages the Byzantines
came increasingly under the influence of fashions from abroad;
this is shown by glazed pottery, textiles, or work in precious
metals. Byzantium was now only a single province in a very vast
artistic world which had as its leading centres distant, even remote
towns in Persia, in Egypt, in Italy, in France. During the Palaeologian period material resources were never sufficient to allow the
construction of important artistic buildings, or even of indispensable
large-scale works of military architecture. But the forms of worship

remained unchanged at Constantinople, and numbers of churches and religious houses continued to be built, and these new sanctuaries were planned on the same lines and given the same modest dimensions as formerly. Aesthetically, too, the churches of this period are not easily distinguishable from earlier buildings, although a tendency to more picturesque effects can be noted. They vary in their proportions with a preference for increased height; extra elements were added to buildings giving them a greater personality and lending more fantasy to their appearance both outside and inside; there is richer decoration of the outer walls through the use of bricks and small pieces of glazed pottery; and above all there is a more individual interpretation of the forms in everyday use. The most famous examples of churches of this period are at Thessalonica (the Holy Apostles), in Macedonia (at Kastoria, and St Clement at Ochrida), at Mistra (where there is a variety of churches of every type of plan, some with oratories built on, some with a narthex attached, or whole groups of monastic buildings), at Arta (the Church of the Panagia Parigoritissa) and at Mesembria (St John Alitourgitos and others). At Constantinople this same art, in its Constantinopolitan version, can be seen in the church known as Fetiye Camii with its chapel, in the narthex of Kilisse Camii, and in the funerary chapel of the Palaeologi at Fenari Isa Camii. The palace of Tekfour Serai (called 'of Porphyrogenitus') still recalls the splendours of earlier palace architecture: although the interior of the building has been entirely destroyed, its façade, ornamented with bricks and glazed pottery, is a remarkably successful piece of architectural decoration (Plate 4). This is the same type of decoration as that which began to be applied to the façades of churches about the eleventh or twelfth century and which can be seen in Constantinople itself, in Greek and Slav Macedonia and throughout the Balkans, as well as in southern Italy. The present writer believes it to have been inspired by Muslim models; it may be compared to the similar but richer and more skilful examples of decoration in the Seljuq architecture of northern Persia, between the tenth and thirteenth centuries.

Besides the groups of churches mentioned above, and several others in Greek cities and provinces, reference must be made to those of Serbia, Bulgaria and the Rumanian principalities. Here the religious fervour of the princes, their wealth and their desire to display their new power were the source of intense artistic activity. Local peculiarities rapidly appeared and they are to be explained in part by the varied aptitudes and different national tastes of the artists. It would however be an anachronism to consider such peculiarities as heralding the emergence of national schools of art; they did not survive long and sometimes, as in Serbia, the special characteristics of artistic work showed considerable variations between one generation and the next or even simultaneously between one province and another. In fact such characteristics and variations were determined more by local conditions and provincial customs, both social and economic, than by the influence of nationality in the wider sense. Extreme examples of local peculiarities of this kind are seen in the type of art found in thirteenth-century churches in the province of Rascia in medieval Serbia, and in churches of the twelfth and thirteenth centuries in north-east Russia, in the province of Vladimir-Suzdal.

It was in religious painting that the most beautiful and noteworthy work was produced under the Palaeologi. This art is seen at its most brilliant and original in the few complete series of wall-mosaics and in the frescoes of churches (Plates 15, 16, 17, 22). Portable icons (in mosaic or paint) for placing on iconostases or for the use of private worshippers were also produced on an extensive scale. Manuscript illustrations on the other hand, although not invariably of poor quality, fell short of the high standard attained in the eleventh and twelfth centuries. It was the discovery of the mural paintings of the fourteenth century some fifty years ago which revealed the Byzantine 'renaissance' under the Palaeologi—a rebirth of the arts after the interruption of the years of the Latin Empire. Today there can be no doubt of the specific character of this artistic revival, confined though it was to painting and mosaics.

When compared with earlier Byzantine work these paintings show many of the characteristics which have been noted in certain frescoes and illuminations of the twelfth century; they recall in particular the naturalistic treatment and realism observed in the frescoes at Nerezi (Plate 20) and Vladimir (Plate 12). From about 1150 onwards some painters tried to imitate more exactly the material reality of objects and of living creatures and to affect the spectator by accentuating the emotional quality of their themes, such as the tenderness of childhood, or the pathos of suffering and death. This trend was continued by the Orthodox Greek, Serbian and Bulgarian painters who decorated with frescoes several churches of the thirteenth century founded by the kings of Serbia and the princes of Bulgaria. The most remarkable of these paintings are at Mileševo (about 1235) and at Sopoćani (about 1265) in the north-west of the Serbian kingdoms of the period, not far from the Dalmatian coast, and at Boiana (1259) near Sofia in Bulgaria. Between the work at Nerezi and that at Sopoćani, an interval of about a hundred years, noticeable progress was made in the way of naturalistic representation; artists acquired a greater feeling for substance, weight and volume, and for the individual appearance of objects and living creatures. The Byzantine tradition and the lessons of antiquity assimilated in the eleventh and twelfth centuries were by no means abandoned by these artists; but they imparted to them a new value, enlivening the classical forms by their personal observation of nature—as in the portrait of King Vladislav and the angel of the Resurrection at Mileševo, or the scene of the Dormition at Sopoćani. At the same time the new trend was marked by a reversion to old models such as the early mosaics; in the same churches there are large figures drawn in sweeping outlines against a yellow background imitating mosaic. It was shown again by the desire to widen the range of the iconography and to hold the attention of the spectator and rouse his imagination by displaying before him large numbers of descriptive and dramatic pictures.

This also led the artists, and those under whose orders they were working, to turn to very early models, notably to the paintings of pre-iconoclastic times. Thus painting under the Palaeologi brought about a revival of an early Christian type of art, impregnated with classical forms and motifs—religious narrative cycles, full of drama and detail, landscapes composed of hills and buildings, rich ornament Hellenistic and Roman in origin, decorative schemes made up of series of pictures one above the other, or of rows of portraits of saints framed in medallions.

Yet the most striking thing about the works of the thirteenth and early fourteenth centuries, particularly in the very numerous mural paintings which are known to be of this period, is the extent to which each artist impressed his own personality on his work. Every large-scale scheme of decoration in a church has its own individuality pointing to a single, though usually anonymous artist. (A few names of artists are in fact known, but anonymity was the general rule.) In the thirteenth century, especially at Mileševo and Sopoćani, the personality of the painter asserted itself most markedly in the treatment of human figures, the delineation of features and hairstyles, in draperies and certain everyday objects such as utensils. But from the beginning of the fourteenth century, in the mosaics of Kariye Camii at Constantinople, although retaining his individuality and preserving that of his models, the artist cultivated above all elegance of design, charm of expression, and picturesque detail (Plates 15, 16, 17). A similar tendency can be seen in other mosaics of the same period, in the narthex of Kilisse Camii at Constantinople, and in the Church of the Holy Apostles at Thessalonica. It is the beginning of a new 'academic' approach, which rediscovered the methods of the past and simply applied them to painting or mosaic enriched by the bolder experiments of the artists of the twelfth and thirteenth centuries.

This academic attitude, with its innumerable variations of style deriving from different schools and workshops and from individual painters of the fourteenth and fifteenth centuries and even of the sixteenth century, had come to stay in Byzantine religious painting. The frescoes of the churches of Mistra, of Kastoria, of Verria and particularly of those of Serbia (at Nagoričino, Gračanica, Lesnovo Dečani and Peć) provide examples, the majority of them aesthetically satisfying and most instructive from the iconographical point of view (Plates 23, 24). To this same type of art belong other collections of frescoes, in all the Orthodox countries: for example, at Zemen and in the rock chapels of Ivanovo in Bulgaria, at Curtea de Argeş and in many other post-Byzantine churches in Rumania, at Zarzma in Georgia, and at Volotovo (destroyed in the last war) and in the Church of the Transfiguration at Novgorod in Russia.

The paintings of the thirteenth century held promise of further progress: the first steps had been taken towards the creation of an art more naturalistic in style and more emotional in content. But this movement, which corresponds to the art of the Dugento in Italy, contact with which can scarcely be denied, lost its first impulse and soon came to a complete stop, in conditions which have still to be satisfactorily explained. It is probable that the return to conservatism in the early years of the fourteenth century, which was still more marked in the following decades, must be connected with the growing influence of the monks, who strongly mistrusted secular knowledge, that is to say classical learning, and no doubt everything which came under the heading of rational knowledge as opposed to revelation. This mistrust was further increased by the rise of science and experimental methods in the contemporary Latin world. The hesychast movement which triumphed at Constantinople at the Council of 1351 can provide some indication of the attitude of mind which curbed the creative impulse of the Byzantine painters of the twelfth and thirteenth centuries and led to a return, at the beginning of the fourteenth century, to a conception of art more closely based on tradition. This was full of charm and extremely sensitive, like that which preceded it. It was, however, clearly unfitted to retain the leadership of the European schools of painting which it had held for a short while in the thirteenth century. Its growth was arrested and it was surpassed by the arts of the Latin countries, and thereafter it never recovered from its fatal loss of vitality. It finally became what it was during virtually the whole of the Palaeologian period, an art almost exclusively intended for the service of religion and having as little reason to change as the forms of worship it served. Like mural paintings, but to an even greater extent, icons on wood were to preserve intact for centuries the forms and fashions of art of the Palaeologian period. Miniature painting, in decline since the thirteenth century, is still found in the fourteenth century in a few works executed in Constantinople, chiefly for the court—witness the illustrations in the *typicon* of the Theotokos of Good Hope, or in the theological treatise of John VI Cantacuzenus (Plates 27, 28).

Except for architecture and religious painting Byzantium was no longer one of the artistic capitals of Europe at the end of the middle ages. Muslim power was advancing triumphantly towards the West, and its civilisation flooded what still remained of the Byzantine Empire and overflowed into other Christian countries of eastern Europe, imposing its taste and artistic productions upon them. Goldsmiths' work, art pottery, rich textiles, costumes and head-dresses were either imported from Muslim countries or else made in Italy according to oriental patterns and brought to Byzantine markets, or yet again made at Byzantium but according to Muslim fashion, either Turkish or Persian. Thus at the end of the middle ages the Byzantines wore several types of garment and hair-styles of Persian or Turkish origin; their ceremonial dress was made from silks which might just as well have been manufactured in one of the Italian towns or in the 'tiraz' of a Muslim prince as in Byzantium itself. The decorated pottery of Constantinople merely reproduced, detail for detail, contemporary Persian models: indeed, where pottery is concerned it is very difficult to identify the specifically Byzantine products of this period as such, because everywhere the design was Muslim. Finally, in goldsmiths' work, for example in picture-frames, the Byzantines borrowed themes and techniques from the style already common for centuries in central Asian countries, characterized by its use of perforated bosses and patterns reminiscent of carpet-designs.

CHAPTER XXX

THE PLACE OF BYZANTIUM IN THE MEDIEVAL WORLD

It is sometimes difficult for students of western European history to realise the impression that Byzantium made upon the world of the middle ages. Not only was the Empire regarded by everyone in the early middle ages as the continuation of the Roman Empire and Constantinople as New Rome, the imperial capital to which Constantine the Great had transferred the government of the *oikoumene*, but also Constantinople itself was, at least till the thirteenth century, by far the richest, most splendid and most populous city in Christendom.

Till the time of the coronation of Charles the Great the right of the Byzantine ruler to be considered as Emperor and heir to the Roman Emperors was never questioned in the West. Justinian's reconquest of the western provinces was regarded, not only legally, as a resumption of rights; and even in lands such as France where imperial control was never likely to return, or in lands such as Germany beyond the *limes*, where it had never been, the Emperor was still acknowledged to be the supreme sovereign on earth, and local monarchs like Clovis were glad to receive titles of honour from him. The Popes continued to date their bulls and letters by the Emperor's regnal year and to have their elections confirmed by the Emperor or by his viceroy at Ravenna.

That this was modified was largely the fault of the Byzantines themselves. In the middle of the eighth century, when Rome was threatened by the Lombards, the Popes, ignoring their religious differences with the iconoclastic Emperors of the Isaurian house, asked for protection from Constantinople; but none was forthcoming either from the Emperor or his viceroy. Rome therefore called in the Franks. The Frankish king received from the Pope the rather vague title of 'Patrician of the Romans' and after 772 the regnal year of the Emperor is no longer used for dating papal documents.[1] The imperial coronation of Charles the Great followed three decades later. Whatever was meant by the coronation—and the Pope, the new Emperor and his adviser Alcuin all seem to have interpreted it in a slightly different way—the ceremony seems to have been a rough copy of a coronation ceremony at Constantinople, while at Rome at least emphasis was laid on the fact that there was no Emperor at the time

---

[1] See P. Jaffé, *Regesta Pontificum Romanorum* (Leipzig, 1885), II, 289.

reigning at Constantinople, only an Empress. Charles was therefore the successor of Constantine VI. But Charles himself was unhappy about it. He was prepared to pay heavily for the recognition of his title at Constantinople, by abandoning conquests in Venetia; and not until ambassadors from Constantinople had saluted him by it did he make any arrangements for its transmission to his son.[1]

The existence of an Emperor whose position depended on a papal coronation inevitably lowered the rank of the Emperor at Constantinople in the eyes of western Europe. At best he was a co-Emperor, at the worst a usurper. The Papacy inclined to the former view. Till the mid-eleventh century letters to the eastern ruler from Rome gave him the imperial title without qualification. Pope Leo IX addresses Constantine Monomachus as 'Imperator' without adding a territorial designation, and Victor II addresses Theodora in 1055/6 as 'Imperatrix Augusta'.[2] But by the end of the eleventh century the papal protocol has changed, and the eastern Emperor is henceforward qualified by the epithet 'Constantinopolitanus'.[3] The imperial court of the West naturally always qualified the eastern Emperor's title. Liutprand of Cremona, who had twice visited Constantinople during the interval between the Carolingian and Ottonian Empires and had been well received there, and who speaks of the Byzantine rulers as Emperors without qualification in his *Antapodosis,* found himself in difficulties when he went to Constantinople as Otto I's ambassador with letters addressed to the 'Imperator Graecorum'. Later the practice of western lay authorities seems to have been to address the eastern Emperor as 'Constantinopolitanus' if they wished to be polite and as 'Graecus', 'Graecorum' or even 'rex Graecorum' if they wished to be offensive. After Carolingian times the East never addressed the western Emperor by any title higher than 'rex'.[4]

The West might grudge the eastern Emperor his claim to be the sole legitimate Emperor, but until the time of the Fourth Crusade it remained deeply impressed by the dignity and prestige of the court of Byzantium. No other court could compete with its ceremonies, in which the imperial and the ecclesiastical were so perfectly blended; and though visitors might resent the clockwork devices and theatrical

---

[1] *Annales Regni Francorum,* ed. F. Kurze (Hanover, 1895), p. 138. See also G. Ostrogorsky, *History of the Byzantine State* (Oxford, 1956), pp. 164, n. 2; 165, n. 1.

[2] Jaffé, *op. cit.* pp. 548, 550.

[3] *Ibid.* p. 627 (Gregory VII's excommunication of Nicephorus Botaneiates, using the epithet 'Constantinopolitanus').

[4] Liutprand of Cremona, *Legatio,* ed. J. Bekker (Hanover, 1915), II, 176–7; XLVII, 200–1; L, 202; Otto of Freising, *Gesta Friderici,* ed. G. Waitz (Hanover, 1912), I, 25 (John II addressed as 'Imperator Constantinopolitanus'), p. 27 (Manuel I addressed as 'rex Graecorum', both in letters from Conrad of Germany).

tricks with which the Emperor enhanced his grandeur, they could not avoid a feeling of awe. Behind Liutprand's determination to decry everything he saw at the court of Nicephorus Phocas, an Emperor who had a certain reputation for meanness, there lurks an angry admiration. A more honest impression is given in the letter written to his wife by Stephen, Count of Blois, on his way to the First Crusade, to boast of the splendour of his host, the Emperor Alexius, and the graciousness of his reception.[1] Western monarchs were always eager to achieve a marriage-alliance with the imperial family. One of the chief objects of Liutprand's unfortunate embassy had been to secure a Byzantine bride for his master's son; and Otto III sought anxiously to win one for himself.[2] And the Emperor's prestige was known even further afield, in the far north-west. It was the ambition of every enterprising young Scandinavian to serve in the Imperial Guard at Constantinople; and he would return to tell his kinsfolk in Iceland or the Orkneys of the splendour of the imperial court.[3]

In the East the Emperor had no rival as head of Christendom. There, right on till the fall of the Ottoman Empire, nationality was a matter of religious rather than of territorial status. The Orthodox, even in lands controlled by the Muslims, considered the Emperor as their ultimate sovereign. St John of Damascus, though he had been a civil servant in the Caliph's administration, always addressed the Emperor as his master, referring to the Caliph only as 'the amir'.[4] The Muslims themselves recognised this attitude. It was an accepted method of the Caliph to put diplomatic pressure upon the Emperor by threatening to persecute the Orthodox in the lands of the Caliphate. When the Fatimid Caliph, al-Ḥākim, destroyed the Church of the Holy Sepulchre, the Emperor saw to its rebuilding; and it seems that he was allowed to keep his own officials in the church to extract tolls from pilgrims to pay for the work. The Emperor was not in fact able to exercise any direct control over the Orthodox *in partibus infidelium*, though the recovery of Antioch in 969 gave him an indirect influence over the lands of the Antiochene Patriarchate that lay outside his frontiers, and we find Patriarchs of Jerusalem in the eleventh century paying long visits to his court. The Orthodox—the Melkites or the Emperor's men—undoubtedly had an advantage over their heretic brothers because they could call upon his protection. The crusades somewhat impaired the Emperor's monopoly to protect the Christians in the East, which had only hitherto been interrupted

[1] H. Hagenmeyer, *Die Kreuzzugsbriefe* (Innsbruck, 1902), pp. 138–40.
[2] J. Gay, *L'Italie méridionale et l'empire byzantin* (Paris, 1904), pp. 389–95.
[3] P. Riant, *Expéditions et pèlerinages des Scandinaves en Terre Sainte* (Paris, 1865), pp. 41, 49: V. G. Vasilievsky, *Trudy* (*Works*), I (St Petersburg, 1908), 184 ff.
[4] St John Damascene, letter in *MPG*, xcv, 380–1.

rather ineffectually by Charles the Great.[1] But after Saladin's recapture of Jerusalem the Emperor Isaac Angelus took charge of the
negotiations with the Muslims to restore the rights of the native
Orthodox at the Holy Places.[2]

The Christian countries to the north and east of the Empire seem
always to have recognised the Emperor as their superior, even if they
did not allow him any political control. Recognition by Byzantium
was always of supreme importance, even in the Balkans in the later
middle ages when the political power of the Empire had sunk low.
To the Russians Constantinople was the capital of Christendom till
its fall to the Turks; and the conception of Moscow as the Third
Rome arises out of this. The Tsars of Muscovy wished to inherit the
oecumenical position that they had previously attributed to the
Emperor; hence the attempts of later Russian rulers such as Catherine
the Great to be recognised as having the right to interfere in matters
concerning the Orthodox in Turkey.

To the East, Christian and Muslim alike, there was no question
that Byzantium was not Rome. The Patriarch's title 'of Constantinople which is New Rome' exemplified the attitude of the Orthodox
world, while the Arab courts always referred to the Byzantine Emperor as the monarch of Rūm. The word even acquired a false geographical meaning; the Seljuq sultanate set up in the heart of the old
imperial provinces of Anatolia was popularly known as the Sultanate
of Rūm, though the Ottoman Turks only used the adjective *Rumeli*
to describe their European as opposed to their Asian territory.[3]

The Emperor's prestige was largely due to the splendour of his
capital. There was nothing like it in Christendom. In everything,
wrote Eudes of Deuil at the time of the Second Crusade, after describing its size, its beauty, its wealth and its squalor, 'it exceeded
the measure'. To Villehardouin half a century later it was the
'sovereign of cities', whose glories had to be seen to be believed.[4]
Moreover, however much the West might dislike its Greek owners, it
was New Rome, the imperial city founded by the great Constantine.
Jordanes, himself probably an Alan, writing in the sixth century,
tells of the impact that the glories of the city made upon western
visitors. It was no wonder that they thought its ruler to be a god

---

[1] See S. Runciman, 'Charlemagne and Palestine', *EHR*, L (1935), 606 ff., and 'The
Byzantine "Protectorate" in the Holy Land', *B*, XVIII (1946–8), 207 ff.

[2] *DR*, 1608.

[3] See article 'Rum' by F. Babinger, in *Encyclopaedia of Islam*, IV (Leyden/London,
1936), 1174–5.

[4] Etudes de Deuil, *La Croisade de Louis VII*, ed. H. Waquet (Paris, 1949), IV, 44–5;
G. de Villehardouin, *La conquête de Constantinople*, ed. E. Faral (Paris, 1938), I,
cxxviii, p. 130.

on earth.[1] Amongst Charles the Great's most prized possessions were
two silver tables on one of which was engraved a plan of Rome and
on the other Constantinople. He bequeathed this latter to the Church
of St Peter at Rome.[2] Large numbers of pilgrims on their way to the
Holy Land made a point of visiting Constantinople, attracted above
all by the stupendous collection of Christian relics there. All those
who wrote accounts of their journeys spoke with awe of the great
city. The first crusaders regarded the city as being particularly holy.
Robert the Monk calls it the equal of Rome in holiness and majesty,
Guibert of Mogent describes it as being worthy of the whole world's
respect, and Ekkehard of Aura as deserving its divine protection.[3]
But by the end of the twelfth century, when relations between Greeks
and Latins were worsening, there appears in Latin travellers a note
of resentment that so many precious objects should be in Greek
hands.[4]

To the Slavs Constantinople was Tsarigrad, the city of the Emperors and the capital of the earth. The Scandinavians called it
Mikligardr or Micklegarth, the great city, whose wealth and whose
holiness alike impressed them. Its splendour shines in the Icelandic
sagas. It was a venerable city, the equal of Rome, and even greater,
for from it came the red gold of the Emperor. They called the Bosphorus Sjávidarsund, the Narrows of the Pious. The *Book of Skál-
holt*, based on the tales of returned travellers, praises St Sophia
(*Aegisif*) as the most glorious temple in the world, and enumerates all
the relics within the city walls.[5]

The Muslims were better accustomed to great cities. There were
times when Baghdad, Cairo and Cordova were each larger and more
populous than Constantinople. But the imperial city had a special
fascination for them. An early tradition reported that the Prophet
himself had ordained that it must be conquered for the Faith and had
promised a special place in Paradise for its first Islamic conquerors.[6]
Arab travellers such as Hārūn ibn Yaḥya, Masʿūdi and Idrisi give
detailed and laudatory descriptions of the city; and the geographer

[1] Jordanes, *Getica*, ed. H. Mommsen (Hanover, 1882), xxviii, p. 98.

[2] Einhard, *Vita Caroli Magni Imperatoris*, ed. L. Halphen (Paris, 1947), xxxiii, p. 98.

[3] Robert the Monk, *Historia Hierosolymitana, Rec. Hist. Cr., Historiens Occiden-
taux*, III, 750; Guibert of Nogent, *Historia Hierosolymitana, ibid.* IV, 132; Ekkehard of
Aura, *Hierosolymita*, ed. H. Hagenmeyer (Tübingen, 1877), pp. 69–70.

[4] For the western attitude, which was adduced as a reason for the diversion of the
Fourth Crusade, see P. Riant, 'Les dépouilles religieuses enlevées à Constantinople par
les Latins', *Mémoires de la Société Nationale des Antiquaires de France*, XXXVI (1875),
1–14.

[5] P. Riant, *Les Scandinaves en Terre Sainte*, pp. 67–9. The Norse already identified
Constantinople with the legendary Asgard (*ibid.* p. 17).

[6] For this tradition see article 'Constantinople' by J. H. Mordtmann, in *Encyclopaedia of Islam*, I (Leyden/London, 1913), p. 867.

Ibn Hauqal found his fellow-Muslims so full of admiration for the city and the Empire that he thought it his duty to say that Byzantium was not nearly so rich and powerful as they supposed.[1] But Ibn Battuta, who visited Constantinople during its decline in the fourteenth century, wrote of it with an enthusiasm that was only matched by his disappointment with Baghdad.[2] Amongst its other admirers was the Spanish Jew Benjamin of Tudela, who visited it in the gorgeous days of the Emperor Manuel Comnenus. He was not unaware of its sordid quarters, but he was deeply struck by the loveliness of its public buildings. To him St Sophia was the most beautiful ecclesiastical building in the world, and the Emperor's newly decorated Palace of Blachernae the most magnificent of royal residences.[3]

Only few of the visitors to Constantinople wrote down their impressions. What struck them all was the diversity of peoples from all over the world to be seen in its streets. There were constant embassies visiting the city from foreign capitals; and Byzantine protocol laid down how each should be received and addressed. Only a few of the ambassadors, such as Liutprand or William of Tyre or the Arab Naṣr ibn al-Azhar, wrote down accounts of their missions, but hardly a year passed without some ambassadorial party arriving at the capital. There was a constant stream of foreign merchants coming and going. Every year Russian merchants descended on the city, with the furs, the honey and the slaves that the north produced. There were merchants from the Khazars and countries farther away, bringing goods from the extreme orient. By the tenth century Arab merchants came in sufficient numbers for them to be given a mosque for their worship, and by the twelfth century there was an Arab quarter established by the Golden Horn. Italian merchants began to come in great numbers from the tenth century onwards, till by the twelfth they had their own prosperous quarters in the city and had captured most of its foreign trade. The Emperor's foreign mercenaries, especially the Norsemen and Englishmen of the Varangian Guard, added to the colour on the streets; and pilgrims from every country of the West were to be seen, pausing to examine the city's relics on their way to Jerusalem and back, and a few pilgrims coming in the other direction, natives of the Holy Land or of Georgia. There were Jewish travellers, though the resident Jewish colony was never very

---

[1] For Hārūn ibn Yaḥya and Mas'ūdi see extracts given in A. A. Vasiliev, *Byzance et les Arabes*, ed. H. Grégoire and M. Canard, II, 2, pp. 382–408, and for Ibn Hauqal, *ibid.* pp. 411–19; for Idrisi, *La géographie d'Edrisi*, trans. P. A. Joubert (Paris, 1840), II, 293–9, 383–5.

[2] Ibn Battuta, *Travels*, transl. H. A. R. Gibb, I (London, 1962), pp. 326–35, 504–12.

[3] Benjamin of Tudela, *Itinerary*, ed. M. N. Adler (London, 1907), pp. 11–14.

large. There were vast numbers of men and women from the Empire's vassal-states, Armenians, Caucasians and Slavs.

We are apt to forget how frequently men and women travelled in the middle ages. The historians and chroniclers of the time were not interested in such matters. They only tell us of the movements of the great. It is when we read the stories of pilgrimages or the lives of the saints that we realise how much intercourse went on between people on a humbler level. The journeys were almost all made for purposes of trade or religion. But there were many merchants, and good fortunes to be made by commerce; and almost everyone was religiously minded. Wherever merchants went, they had to make friends, in order to conduct their business, unless, like the Russians in the tenth century, they came in parties under strict police supervision. Similarly the pilgrims that travelled in large parties cannot have had much contact with the natives of the lands through which they passed. But many came singly or in small groups. Sometimes they had friends already established in foreign parts. Norse pilgrims often found a kinsman at Constantinople serving in the Varangian Guard. Italians often had relatives in the merchant-colonies. And many others made friends without such help. We hear of a western bishop who came to Constantinople in about the year 1000 on a journey of expiation, after having accidentally killed his nephew. He already had a friend there in the person of a Byzantine patrician who introduced him to St Symeon the New Theologian; and he entered the saint's monastery.[1] Another western cleric, the Norman William Firmat, made himself so well liked in Constantinople that he was said to have been offered a bishopric there.[2] The Byzantine pilgrim John Phocas tells us of an Iberian monk whom he first met as a hermit living on a rock near Jerusalem.[3] Many Byzantine pilgrims visited Rome. In 1080 they were so numerous that Robert Guiscard had no difficulty in finding amongst them a scoundrel to impersonate the fallen Emperor Michael VII.[4] Other individual Greeks attained more reputable honours. There was a boy called Nicholas who was born in Achaea and crossed the Adriatic at the age of seventeen and died at Trani in 1094 as the most venerated man in southern Italy. Pope Urban II canonised him four years later. There was a Symeon of Syracuse about the same time who was educated at Constantinople, became a guide at Jerusalem, then retired to Mt Sinai, emerging after a few years to travel in the West. He settled first in Normandy, then went

[1] *Vie de Syméon le Nouveau Théologien*, ed. I. Hausherr (Rome, 1928), pp. 68–76.
[2] See B. Leib, *Rome, Kiev et Byzance* (Paris, 1924), pp. 85–6.
[3] Joannes Phocas, *A Brief Description*, trans. A. Stewart, *Palestine Pilgrims' Text Society* (London, 1896), p. 29.
[4] Anna Comnena, *Alexiad*, I, xii (ed. B. Leib, I, p. 45).

to Verdun and died eventually at Trier. Another Symeon, an Armenian, went from Jerusalem to tour western Europe as far as England and Santiago de Compostella in Spain. He ended his days in a monastery near Mantua.[1] There were already Greek religious communities in Lorraine and Provence; and in Germany there had been itinerant monks from Byzantium since the days of Otto II and his Greek Empress Theophano. Many of these monks seem to have been craftsmen as well.[2]

The merchants left fewer written traces; their lives would have been of little interest to the pious readers of the time. Not many Greek merchants travelled abroad. The imperial government discouraged them, preferring to control the sale of the Empire's finest manufactures and to oblige foreigners to visit the markets within the Empire for even the less precious wares. But there were several Byzantine merchant-vessels which sailed beyond imperial waters, such as the ship which rescued Otto II after his defeat by the Saracens near Stilo in Calabria; while till the time of the Latin empire the far eastern trade that arrived at Cherson or Trebizond was carried across the Black Sea in Byzantine ships. There were still a few Byzantine merchantmen in the days of the Palaeologi. One of them even broke the Turkish blockade during the final siege of the city.[3]

A certain number of Byzantine craftsmen travelled abroad. We hear of mosaicists from Constantinople working for the Umayyad Caliph and engineers at Baghdad, such as the ambassador Tarasius, who was said to have designed a water-mill for the Caliph Mahdi.[4] Manuel Comnenus sent artists to decorate churches in the crusader kingdom of Jerusalem.[5] There were also the Greek monks who worked in Germany in the late tenth and early eleventh century. The chapel of St Bartholomew in the cathedral at Paderborn was built by them, and a little later there were so many of them in the diocese of Hildesheim that the bishop forbad them to stay for more than two days in any of his hospices. But some of the craftsmen made their journeys involuntarily, like the silk-weavers whom Roger II of Sicily kidnapped from Thebes and Corinth in 1147.[6]

The Italian merchants who operated within the Empire were soon too numerous and too prosperous to create good relations with the

---

[1] Leib, *op. cit.* pp. 96–9; J. Ebersolt, *Orient et Occident* (2nd ed., Paris, 1924), p. 55.

[2] See E. Muntz, 'Les artistes byzantins dans l'Europe latine', *Revue de l'art chrétien*, XXXVI (Paris, 1893), pp. 183 ff.

[3] See S. Runciman, 'Byzantine Trade and Industry', *Cambridge Economic History of Europe*, II, 96–7, 102–3.

[4] J. H. Bury, *History of the Eastern Roman Empire* (1912), pp. 241–2.

[5] Joannes Phocas, *op. cit.* pp. 19, 27, 31. See also S. Runciman, *History of the Crusades* (Cambridge, 1954), III, 380–1.

[6] See Pt. I, chapter V, p. 428.

peoples that they exploited so successfully. Indeed, their arrogance was one of the main factors in embittering the Byzantines against the West. Intellectual exchanges were more fruitful. There was a long tradition of not unfriendly cultural rivalry between Constantinople and Baghdad and Cairo. The Abbasid Caliph al-Ma'mūn was famed for his passion for everything Greek, which he satisfied by sending savants to collect books in Byzantium. The intellectual prowess of Leo the Mathematician was known in Baghdad from the impression made by one of his pupils who was taken there as a prisoner; but he refused tempting offers to lecture in the Muslim capital. The Emperor Theophilus was in his turn fascinated by Muslim culture, and rebuilt much of the imperial palace from plans brought back from Baghdad by his ambassador John the Grammarian, the future Patriarch.[1] Byzantine doctors studied Arab medicine, while Psellus numbered amongst his pupils at Constantinople some Arabs, Persians and Ethiopians and one man from Babylon.[2]

With western Europe in the middle ages Byzantine cultural exchanges were inevitably few. The West had little to offer to Byzantine learning, and few Byzantine scholars travelled there. Charles the Great engaged a Byzantine tutor called Elissaeus to teach his daughter Rothrud Greek when she was betrothed to Constantine VI; but Elissaeus' classes at Aachen were not very successful.[3] Otto III acquired a knowledge of Greek from his Greek mother and his Italo-Greek tutor;[4] and according to Roger Bacon there had always been a certain number of students of Greek in the West.[5] But the West, when it became interested in ancient Greek learning, sometimes preferred to use Muslim Spain as the channel, sending scholars to the schools of Toledo to make Latin translations from Arabic translations of the original. A Greek manuscript of Aristotle's philosophical works reached Paris in 1200, but it was not till Michael Scot published a few years later his Latin translation of the Metaphysics, with Averroes' commentaries, that Aristotelian philosophy began to have any influence.[6] There was, however, a feeling that wisdom could be acquired in the Greek East. John of Basingstoke, who flourished in the late twelfth century, claimed to have been instructed at Athens, with

---

[1] G. E. von Grunebaum, *Medieval Islam* (Chicago, 1946), pp. 54–5; Bury, *op. cit.* pp. 436–9.

[2] Psellus, Letter to Michael Cerularius, K. N. Sathas, *Bibliotheca Graeca Medii Aevi*, v, 508.   [3] Theophanes, *Chronographia*, i, 455 (ed. C. de Boor).

[4] P. E. Schramm, *Kaiser, Rom und Renovatio* (Leipzig, 1929), i, 101.

[5] Roger Bacon, *Opus Tertium*, ed. J. S. Brewer, Rolls Series (London, 1859), pp. 32–4. His own Greek grammar is preserved in the library of Corpus Christi College, Oxford.

[6] A. Guillaume, 'Philosophy and Theology', *The Legacy of Islam* (Oxford, 1931), pp. 246 ff.

the lovely daughter of the Archbishop as his tutor;[1] and according to the medieval legend, the Englishwoman who became Pope Joan also received her education at Athens.[2]

There was however in South Italy and Sicily an area which could serve as an intermediary. Till long after the Norman conquest there, many of its inhabitants were Greek-speaking and in constant touch with Constantinople as well as with the West. Venice, which had a Greek colony and Byzantine traditions, provided another link. Italy therefore never entirely forgot its Greek. When John of Salisbury wanted to learn Greek he engaged a Greek from Benevento. Roger Bacon, who disliked dependence on translations from the Arabic, maintained that Greek teachers could be obtained in Italy, if not from further east. The crusades in the East, for all the political harm that they did, brought the westerners in closer contact with a living Greek tradition. There had always been a few western immigrants settled in Constantinople, but they had for the most part been soldiers employed in the imperial army; though Psellus claimed to have 'Celts' amongst his pupils.[3] But one of the few fortunate results of the Fourth Crusade was that it brought large numbers of westerners to live in Byzantine lands and to learn about Byzantine civilisation. By the time that the Italian renaissance got under way, Italian scholars had begun to realise that Byzantium had something to teach them. Petrarch, like John of Salisbury, did not make much of a success of learning Greek, but at least he tried.[4] Above all it was the concourse of Byzantine scholars who attended the Council of Florence in the early fifteenth century which introduced Italy to the richness of Byzantine contemporary intellectual life. Thenceforward Byzantine savants discovered that they could make a career full of honours by lecturing in Italy; and the story of men such as Manuel Chrysoloras and Cardinal Bessarion showed how productive such intercourse could be.[5]

When we try to assess the place of Byzantium in the medieval world we must do so on two levels. There is first the sphere of world politics, in which it was the role of Byzantium to act as a bulwark of Christendom and as a civilising force for the nations of the Slavs. There is secondly the sphere of culture; and here, though Byzantine culture would never have flourished and endured for so long had it not been for the strength and vitality of the political structure of the

[1] Matthew Paris, *Chronica Majora*, ed. H. R. Luard, Rolls Series (London, 1880), v, 284–7.

[2] Martin Oppariensis, *Chronica Pontificum, MGH, Script.* XXII, p. 428.

[3] Psellus, *op. cit., loc. cit.*

[4] See E. Gibbon, *Decline and Fall of the Roman Empire*, ed. J. B. Bury, VII, 118–20.

[5] *Ibid.* p. 123. See K. M. Setton, 'The Byzantine Background to the Italian Renaissance', *Proc. Amer. Philosophical Soc.* C (1956), 1–76.

Empire, the disseminating force was to be found rather in the fact that Constantinople was an international centre and that merchants, craftsmen, scholars and pilgrims travelled to and from all the neighbouring lands.

The main political role of Byzantium was to provide a continuous link between the ancient world and medieval Christendom and at the same time to protect medieval Christendom from onslaughts from the East. It is unprofitable to make conjectures about what might have happened in history had things taken a different course; but it is safe to say that if the eastern half of the Empire had not survived the barbarian invasions in which the western half collapsed, it would have been far harder for the whole of Christendom to remake order out of the chaos. The Church of Rome succeeded in establishing some sort of cultural unity in the West, but it could never have achieved its object but for the existence of the example, the prestige and the actual physical power of the continuing Empire at Constantinople. Justinian's reconquest of the West, though it brought little immediate advantage either to Constantinople or to the reconquered provinces, did reassert the authority of the Empire and had the practical result of confirming the ineradicable continuance of Roman law in Italy, with an effect that was only fully felt at the close of the middle ages. The creation of a Western Empire and the growth of the power of the Papacy, together with the Byzantines' own preoccupation with eastern problems, gradually alienated western from eastern Christendom, so that in the later middle ages it was easy to forget what the Empire had meant in darker times.

Nor was the influence of the Empire restricted to vague matters of prestige. There were many states and institutions in the West which profited by the example of Byzantine administration and organisation. The history of the development of papal institutions lies outside the scope of this volume; but not only did western canon law owe a great deal to Roman-Byzantine models, but the papal chancery shows many instances of the influence of the governmental system of Constantinople. Titles such as *vestiarius* and *sacellarius* are Latin words but the functions of their holders were those that men of similar titles held at the imperial court. The charitable institutions run by the medieval Popes almost all had Greek names, *xenodochia*, *ptochia*, *gerocomia* and *brephotrophia*, and were copied from those run by the Byzantine state. It should be remembered that Gregory the Great, who was responsible for most of the organisation of papal charities, spent some years as papal representative at Constantinople.[1]

---

[1] See A. Dumas, 'Les institutions pontificales', in A. Fliche and V. Martin, *Histoire de l'église*, VII (Paris, 1940), 153 ff.; also L. Homo, *Rome médiévale* (Paris, 1934), p. 285.

Charles the Great and Otto the Great, in spite of their imperial titles, each tried to administer their Empire on their old tribal systems; but Otto III's brave attempt to reorganise and integrate his Empire on a more theocratic and Roman basis was undoubtedly inspired by the Empire from which his mother Theophano had come.[1] His efforts had no lasting result; and later western Emperors, knowing that their power was based on Germany, preferred not to break too far with Germanic traditions. But Byzantine methods were remembered in Italy, not only in Rome but also in Venice and, to a lesser extent, the other Italian maritime cities. The constitutional development of the Venetian Republic did not offer scope for a copy of the imperial court; but the use of administrative and ceremonial titles shows the interest that the Venetians took in Constantinople.

Further south the restoration of Byzantine power in southern Italy in the late ninth century had a considerable effect on the later history of the country. When the Normans established their somewhat eclectic system of government there two centuries later, they made much use of the Byzantine system. In religious matters the king of Sicily tried, as far as his special relationship with the Papacy permitted, to copy the divine authority of the *Basileus*. In the mosaics of the Church of the Martorana Roger II is seen receiving his crown from Christ in an attitude directly taken from Byzantine models. The Norman High Court was Franco-Norman in origin; but the palace officials usually had Byzantine titles and performed the same functions as similar officials at Constantinople. The Ministry of Finance was of half-caste origin; it was called the *dohana de secretis*, from the Arabic word *diwan* and the Byzantine-Greek *sekreton*; and the minister was served by *sekretikoi*. Almost every official had an alternative Greek title as well as a Latin one. In provincial government catepans and turmarchs survived from Byzantine times, though their functions seem gradually to have altered.[2] This Byzantine tradition was reinforced by Frederick II as king of Sicily. Indeed, his whole attitude towards his position as Emperor as well as king was far closer akin to that of a Byzantine Emperor than to that of his German ancestors, though he never ventured to introduce Byzantine systems into his German or north Italian possessions.[3]

The extent to which the Ottoman sultans drew from Byzantine

[1] A. Fliche, *L'Europe occidentale de 888 à 1125* (Paris, 1930), pp. 219–32.
[2] See F. Chalandon, *Histoire de la domination normande en Italie* (Paris, 1907), II, 611 ff.
[3] There is no good account of Frederick II's government giving any attention to Byzantine institutions inherited or copied by him (see *Cambridge Medieval History*, VI, ch. 5 (by M. Schipa)). The best brief modern summary is in E. G. Léonard, *Les Angevins de Naples* (Paris, 1954), pp. 27–36.

experience is a matter of controversy. It was probably slight; for the Ottoman government never managed to build up a centralised civil service, such as formed the basis of Byzantine administration. The Patriarch of Constantinople as head of the Orthodox Christian *milet* surrounded himself with a court of officials as like as possible to that of the Emperors; and when two centuries after the fall of Constantinople the sultan found that some sort of organised civil service was necessary for the conduct of foreign affairs and of finance, he employed Phanariot Greeks trained in the patriarchal court. When these Phanariots took over the government of the principalities of Wallachia and Moldavia, the same model was employed.[1]

The greatness of the part played by Byzantium in preserving Christendom from the onslaught of the East is less disputable. It was not a consciously altruistic part. The Byzantines were only concerned in preserving their Empire; but they believed that their Empire was the *oikoumene*, the Christian world. They were not entirely wrong; for not only was Constantinople the cultural centre of Christendom during the early middle ages, but geographical considerations made it clear that so long as the city and the Straits were held inviolate, no Asian power could penetrate into Europe, and a certain check could be kept on invaders from the steppes of South Russia and on any fleet which attempted to dominate the eastern Mediterranean Sea. If Constantinople had fallen to the Persians and Avars in the time of Heraclius, the Persians themselves might not have drawn much lasting profit from it, but in the chaos that would have followed the road would have been open for later invaders, Arab, Slav or Turk. The preservation of the city against the Arabs was equally vital for Europe. The victory of Charles Martel saved France from the Arabs of Spain, but it is doubtful if in fact it was ever in their power or even their intention to establish a permanent dominion in France. They were operating far from their base, with the hostile population of northern Spain intervening. Constantinople, however, was their most coveted goal. It was a world-capital which they wished to use as the capital of their world-empire. When we reflect how easily the population of Syria and Egypt adapted itself to Arab rule, once the Byzantine armies had been defeated and dislodged, it is difficult to be sure that the population of Asia Minor, though less discontented and less heretical, would have resisted absorption much more vigorously. Islam might well have spread into central Europe from the Balkans, on a firmer foundation than the Ottoman Turks were later to possess, because Byzantium had not yet won those lands for Christendom. Moreover with Byzantium gone, there would have been no check on

[1] See N. Jorga, *Byzance après Byzance* (Paris, 1934), *passim*.

the attacks by the African Muslims on the coasts of Italy. Rome herself might not have survived the ninth century. By the time of the Seljuq threat to Constantinople the West was better organised to resist an onslaught from Islam, but a statesman of the calibre of Pope Urban II could well realise the disaster that it would be to Christendom if the city fell into Muslim hands. Unfortunately the Normans were less far-sighted and did their best to embarrass the Empire; and the crusade that Pope Urban launched to save eastern Christendom became largely a Norman adventure. The whole movement of the crusades, apart from giving Byzantium some immediate relief at the outset, did increasing harm to the Empire and led in the end to the disaster of 1204. In capturing Constantinople and breaking up its imperial organisation the West destroyed its protector. Byzantium never recovered from the blow. The revived Empire was powerless in the next century to prevent the Ottoman Turks from crossing the Straits into Europe. The capital itself held out for nearly a century longer; and so long as it was uncaptured the sultan could not venture to advance too far into Europe. But no practical help came to it from the West. Western Europe was by that date organised into powerful states which had reached the forefront of civilisation. Yet the Turks penetrated to the gates of Vienna, and long wars were needed to drive them back again into the Balkans; and the outcome of these long wars was decided more by the failure of the sultans to establish a firm and efficient governmental system than by the prowess of western arms. It is therefore alarming to calculate what the fate of the West would have been had such an invasion occurred at an earlier time, while its people still lagged behind the East in the resources of civilisation.

Western Europe owes a heavy debt to the walls of Constantinople; and the debt is not confined to the great issues of world politics. They preserved Christendom from being swamped by Islam, and they also preserved Greek civilisation. Our knowledge of the culture of ancient Greece would be infinitely smaller had it not been for the scholars, the librarians and the scribes of Byzantium. Many classical texts would have been lost to us but for Byzantine copyists. Of others we should know little but for works such as the *Bibliotheca* of Photius. We may speak scathingly of the pedantic devotion of the Byzantine writers to the classical past, which sterilised so much of their own work; but scholars of the classics who are contemptuous of the Byzantines should remember that if the Byzantines themselves had not shared a taste for the classics, classical scholarship would be a slighter affair today.

The transmisson of this learning to the West was done not on a governmental but on a personal level, as western scholars came gradually to realise the treasures to be found in Byzantium. So, too, the spread of the Byzantines' own civilisation was mainly due to the intercourse of travellers and traders. Political actions occasionally had a hand in it. Gifts made by the imperial court to foreign potentates and shrines, such as silks and enamel-work from the palace factories, undoubtedly had an effect on the art of the countries to which they were sent. But the imperial authorities were unwilling, for questions of prestige, that foreigners should learn too much about arts and crafts in which Byzantium specialised. The ambassador Liutprand tried to export some purple silk, and, to his fury, had it confiscated from him.[1] Occasionally too the travels of great personages might introduce Byzantine fashions to other lands. The Byzantines themselves derived their ceremonial robe, the *tzitzakion*, from the Khazar princess Chichek, or 'Flower', who became the Empress of Constantine V.[2] The Byzantine-born Theophano, wife of Otto II, does not seem to have succeeded in introducing to Germany the habits of personal cleanliness that she affected, and for which a pious nun subsequently saw her suffering in Hell; but the use of forks at meals was brought to Venice by her cousin Maria Argyrou, wife of the Doge Giovanni Orseolo. St Peter Damian disapproved; but the practice soon spread from Venice throughout Italy.[3]

It was however in the field of art that Byzantium gave its most valuable and lasting gifts to its contemporaries. During the long period from the sixteenth to the twentieth centuries western Europe lost its taste for Byzantine art, so that it is easy now to forget the domination that it exercised over the early medieval world. Byzantine art is a wide and loosely employed expression. The early Christian art of Italy which we usually include in it had little to do with Constantinople itself, but was the product of the same forces and influences that created the early art of Constantinople. Its oriental sources came directly from Syria and Antioch or from further to the East. But after the age of Justinian the creative centre was Constantinople. The area that depended artistically upon Byzantium was considerably larger than the Empire. Venetian art was essentially Byzantine till the close of the twelfth century. The cathedral of St Mark was architecturally a rough copy of Justinian's church of the Holy Apostles at Constantinople; and its earlier mosaics, and still more those of the neighbouring island of Torcello, are in so pure a Byzantine style that it is tempting to attribute them to Byzantine-

[1] Liutprand, *Legatio*, liii–liv, pp. 203–4.
[2] Gy. Moravcsik, 'Proischoždenie slova Τζιτζάκιον', *Sem. Kond.* IV (1931), 69–76.
[3] Petrus Damianus, *Epistulae*, *MPL*, CLXXV, 744.

born artists. It is only at the end of the twelfth century that the later mosaics in St Mark's begin to show a sort of western naturalism which is out of keeping both with the Byzantine tradition and with mosaic technique. Thenceforward Venice developed a mixed Gothic and Byzantine art peculiarly its own.[1]

In Rome the influx of refugee iconophile artists in the eighth century established Byzantine influences so strongly that more than a century later mosaics were being made there in a style that was already out of date in Constantinople.[2] This influence was renewed in the early tenth century when everything Byzantine was so fashionable at Rome that Roman aristocrats gave Greek names to their children. It declined when the city fell under the power of emperors from Germany and pontiffs from France or Lorraine. In the artistic sphere we find a native school arising, even of mosaicists, though in the early thirteenth century Pope Honorius III reverted to older fashions and imported from Venice mosaic artists trained in the Byzantine style.[3]

The Norman kingdom of Sicily was as eclectic in its art and civilisation as in its administration. In art Byzantine influences dominated at first. The first great Palermitan church of the period, the Martorana, built by the Greek-born admiral George of Antioch, was, before fifteenth-century alterations, built in a Byzantine style, probably modelled on some Greek church in southern Italy; but its mosaic decorations seem to have been made by Greek artists working in the imperial style of Constantinople. These same artists went on to work in the cathedrals of Cefalù and Monreale and in King Roger's Capella Palatina and at the same time trained native Sicilian mosaicists. The later mosaics at Monreale are of Sicilian workmanship, and show a falling-off from pure Byzantinism; they are at the same time cruder and fussier, overladen with inappropriate arabesque ornamentation. The architecture of these churches, unlike that of the Martorana, is basically western.[4]

Very little remains that can be definitely ascribed to Greek craftsmen working in Germany. The Saxon and Romanesque architecture there bears a striking likeness to that of medieval Armenia; and it is tempting to assume that the Greek monks working in Germany were in fact Armenians. Armenian architects, unlike those of Constan-

[1] See S. Bettini, *Mosaici Antichi di San Marco a Venezia* (Bergamo, 1944), *passim*; also O. Demus, *Byzantine Mosaic Decoration* (London, 1948), pp. 67–73.

[2] A. Grabar, *Byzantine Painting* (Geneva, 1953), pp. 77–81. The frescoes at Castelseprio in northern Italy (*ibid.* pp. 83–6), which show an extraordinary Byzantine influence, should be mentioned, though their dating is still a matter of controversy (see D. Talbot Rice, *The Beginnings of Christian art* (London, 1957), pp. 103 ff.).

[3] L. Homo, *Rome médiévale*, p. 283. The mosaics of Santa Maria Nuova (late twelfth century) are completely Byzantine in style.

[4] O. Demus, *The Mosaics of Norman Sicily* (London, 1950), pp. 3–148.

tinople where bricks provided the main building material, were accustomed to work in stone; and it may be that German builders, trying to reproduce in stone lessons learned from Byzantine architecture, achieved much the same results as those achieved in Armenia. On the other hand the Armenians have always been a restless and enterprising race, and it is known that many of them penetrated to the West throughout the early middle ages.[1]

The indirect artistic influence of Byzantium was widespread. Anglo-Saxon art shows Mediterranean affinities that were probably derived from Italy, with which the Anglo-Saxon rulers were in close touch, and thus may have links with the East.[2] Carolingian art was certainly revolutionised by Charles the Great's conquest of Italy and particularly by what he found at Ravenna. His cathedral at Aachen was modelled upon the church at San Vitale there.[3] The domed churches of south-western France present a problem that has not been satisfactorily solved; but the Byzantine elements in them seem to have come from northern Italy and Venice and only at secondhand from Constantinople.[4] In French and English fresco and miniature painting there was a remarkable revival of Byzantine styles in the middle of the twelfth century. It is clearly noticeable in works such as the Winchester Bible, whose later illuminations show a clear Byzantine influence. This was undoubtedly due to the close connection which Normandy and Norman England maintained with the Normans in Sicily.[5]

After the triumph of the Gothic style in the West, Byzantine influences declined, except perhaps in painting. It would be rash to say how far Italian painters of the early renaissance were affected by the great renaissance in Byzantine painting, which came to full fruition at the end of the thirteenth century; but some connection seems certain. The final and perhaps the most splendid Byzantine contribution to the development of European painting was made after the fall of Constantinople. Domenico Theotocopoulos was born a Venetian subject in Crete, and most of the characteristic traits which he bequeathed to the art of his adopted country Spain came from his Venetian training. But he remained to the last a Byzantine icon painter not only in his use of colour but still more in his treatment of

[1] See O. M. Dalton, *East Christian Art* (Oxford, 1925), pp. 63–4, and S. Der Nersessian, *Armenia and the Byzantine Empire* (Cambr., Mass., 1945). The question of Armenian influences in the West needs further study.

[2] D. Talbot Rice, *English Art, 871–1100* (Oxford, 1952), pp. 28ff., possibly somewhat exaggerating Byzantine influence.

[3] R. P. Hinks, *Carolingian Art* (London, 1935), *passim*.

[4] See A. W. Clapham, *Romanesque Architecture in Western Europe* (Oxford, 1936), pp. 87–9.

[5] W. Oakeshott, *The Artists of the Winchester Bible* (London, 1945), pp. 10–16.

light and shade, eschewing the ephemeral brightness and shadow caused by the sunshine and preferring an everlasting interior light.[1]

Eastern Europe obtained its whole Christian civilisation from Byzantium; and art formed part of the gift. The art of the Balkans must be considered as a branch of Byzantine art. Patriotic Bulgarian historians talk of a proto-Bulgar art, brought from the steppes; and it is certain that Armenian craftsmen were working at the Bulgar court before King Boris's conversion. But, whether or not the legend is true that Boris was converted by the sight of an alarming picture of Hell painted by a Byzantine artist, the acceptance of Christianity from Byzantium brought Byzantine art in its train. The new religion required churches to be built and decorated, and the newly Christian monarch required palaces suitable for a civilised potentate. The art of the first Bulgarian Empire, to judge from the little that has survived, was purely Byzantine.[2] By the time of the second Empire the artists were native and certain local characteristics appear, particularly in painting; Bulgarian painters had their own taste in colour combinations and came to like a black background to their work.[3]

Serbia from the thirteenth century onwards produced a considerable art. The Serbian churches are architecturally in the Byzantine tradition but soon showed a national tendency to increase the height of their buildings beyond the canon of Byzantine proportions, exaggerating in this a taste that appears in twelfth-century Byzantine architecture. Apart from the early frescoes at Ochrida, which were painted by Greek artists at the time of the Bulgarian occupation in the early eleventh century, Serbian painting stems from the frescoes painted at Nereži near Skoplje by a Greek artist in 1164 on the order of a prince of the Comnenian dynasty. These poignant humanistic paintings seem to have had an enormous effect on the Serbian artists of the following century, who probably kept in touch with the schools of Thessalonica.[4]

Byzantium also provided the basis for the art of Christian Russia. The cathedral of St Sophia at Kiev, built and decorated by Greeks from Byzantium, was the model for later Russian architecture and decoration, while Russian icon-painting began with the arrival in Russia in the early twelfth century of the Byzantine icon later known as Our Lady of Vladimir. But the Russians quickly developed their own style. The classicism of Byzantium gave way to a certain fantasy.

---

[1] R. P. Hinks, *El Greco* (London, 1954), introduction.

[2] A. Grabar, *Les influences orientales dans l'art balkanique* (Paris, 1920), *passim*, esp. pp. 16, 53; Dalton, *op. cit.* pp. 50-2, 146-8.

[3] B. Filow, *Geschichte der Alt-Bulgarischen Kunst* (Berlin, 1932), pp. 46-91.

[4] A. Grabar, *Byzantine Painting*, pp. 139-52; A. Xyngopoulos, *Thessalonique et la peinture macédonienne* (Athens, 1955), pp. 45-57. See D. Talbot Rice, *Beginnings of Christian Art*, p. 181.

More even than the Serbians, the Russians liked to exaggerate the height of their buildings. Either owing to influences from Persia or because it was more suited to a land where the winter snowfall was heavy, the onion-shaped dome usually replaced the rounded dome of Byzantium. While later Byzantine painting began to return to a more naturalistic style, Russian painters tended more to a stark emotionalism which is more akin to Byzantine provincial monastic schools, such as the Cappadocian, than to the imperial style of Constantinople.[1]

The Christian countries to the east of the Empire, Armenia and Georgia, were in constant touch with Constantinople, but also with Persia and the farther east. They therefore developed local styles of their own. But the Armenians were excellent craftsmen. Many of them worked in Constantinople and, still more, in the Byzantine provinces, especially in Greece; and some went even further to the west. Where they went they brought some of their own characteristic traits.[2] On the Muslim world Byzantium did not have much artistic influence after the first centuries of Islam. Umayyad art is a continuation of Christian Hellenistic art, reinforced from contemporary Constantinople; but with the triumph of the Abbasids and the removal of the Caliphate to Baghdad, Islamic art looked more towards Persia and India. It was only in such practical matters as fortification and works requiring engineering skill that the Arabs consulted the Byzantines. It is probable, for instance, that the Fatimid fortifications of Cairo, which were largely constructed by Armenian architects from Edessa (Urfa), were inspired by the fortifications that the Byzantine general George Maniaces had recently erected there.[3] After the fall of Constantinople Ottoman architects and decorators were inevitably influenced by the great buildings that they saw there. The most important of Ottoman architects, Sinan, made a careful study of St Sophia before he developed his own style.[4]

The spread of Byzantine art-influences beyond the frontiers of the Empire shows how wide and profound was the impression made by Byzantium on the contemporary world. The spiritual outlook which lay behind this art might not be understood by foreign peoples; but they saw and admired the concrete results. They appreciated still more highly the commercial products of the workshops of the Empire,

[1] The fullest account of the origins of Russian Christian art is given in *Istorija russkogo iskusstva* (*History of Russian Art*), ed. V. N. Lazarev and others (Academy of Sciences of the U.S.S.R., Moscow, 1953), I, 111–232.

[2] See S. Der Nersessian, *Armenia and the Byzantine Empire* (Cambr., Mass., 1945), pp. 55–136.

[3] See K. A. C. Creswell, *The Muslim Architecture of Egypt* (Oxford, 1952), for the Armenian architects working in Cairo.

[4] There is no good study of Sinan. See A. Gabrieli, *Les mosquées de Constantinople* (Paris, 1926).

the rare silks that were put on the market, the carpets from Anatolia
and the Peloponnese, the enamels, the metalwork and the jewelry
made in the greater cities. Byzantine exports were almost entirely
objects of luxury; and their quality added to the glamour of their
land of origin.

In less concrete matters Byzantium exported little. Byzantine
thought was not understood by the world beyond the frontiers. On
lower levels there might be sympathy. The outlook on life of the
Anatolian peasant was not so different from that of the peasant of
medieval France, though the difference in language prevented understanding when they met, as during the crusades. In southern Italy,
where Greek was known, the wandering Byzantine pilgrim could feel
himself at home. It is significant that popular heresy such as that of
the dualists could pass easily from Constantinople and the Balkans
into Italy and France. But Byzantine thinkers, philosophers and
theologians were not understood abroad. The Muslims paid respect
to Byzantine mathematicians and medical doctors; but the West
took its mathematics and medicine directly from the Arabs. In
theology the last Greek Father to be known at all in the West was
St John of Damascus. Eastern theology tended increasingly towards
a mysticism of a type that the western found alien. The last Greek
mystic to influence the West was the Pseudo-Areopagite, who probably wrote towards the end of the fifth century. Byzantine Platon-
ists such as Psellus were never known outside Byzantine intellectual
circles. It was only the Platonic scholars of the fifteenth century,
with George Gemistus Plethon at their head, who had any effect in
the West. Plethon's presence at the Council of Florence resulted in
the foundation of the Florentine Platonic Academy. But even there,
western students preferred to examine the ancient philosophies without the commentaries of Byzantine scholars.

There has always been a tendency amongst western historians to
neglect Byzantium because it seems to them to stand a little apart
from the main course of the history of our Christian civilisation.
Events of recent years seem to confirm their view; for it is those
countries which owed their civilisation to Byzantium that now stand
divided from the West by an ideological curtain. This is a facile view
which ignores much subsequent history. Greece and Turkey, the two
geographical heirs of Byzantium, have not passed behind the curtain;
and if Balkan countries have accepted another ideology, it has not
been an entirely voluntary acceptance. Russia presents another
problem. The Tsar of Muscovy certainly saw himself as the Emperor
of the Third Rome. But there was a great difference between the

Third Rome and the Second. The Tsar's subjects were of racial origins
and traditions quite unlike those of the Basileus' subjects. They were
of a simpler and less independent stock than the Greeks and the
hellenised Anatolians. They underwent two centuries of Mongol rule,
and the Asian element steadily increased. Nor did the Russian
Church ever possess the influence or the culture of the old Byzantine
Church. The term Caesaropapism is not quite accurate if it is applied
to the imperial government of Byzantium, where the Patriarch was
officially recognised as the second head of the Commonwealth. But the
Russian Tsar was fully caesaropapist. Even during the short periods
when he permitted the existence of the Moscow Patriarchate, he kept
it well under his control. It may be that the Byzantine system which
Russia inherited lent itself to such a development; but Byzantium
cannot be wholly blamed for the subsequent course of Russian history.

It is true that, with the great exception of Justinian's codification
of the law, which is still a dominant influence on European legal
systems, Byzantium contributed little to the political theory or the
constitutional practice of the West. It is true that its contribution
to western thought and spiritual life has been small and that its
contribution to western art has been in the main indirect, at least
till modern times, when at last there is a better understanding of the
aesthetic aims of the Byzantines. Nevertheless, Byzantium played a
vast and at times a decisive part in European history. Gibbon, whose
flashes of historical insight often pierced through his eighteenth-
century prejudices, declared roundly that the historian's eye must
always be fixed on the city of Constantinople.[1] He made it clear that
he himself did not much enjoy fixing his eyes there; but his judgement was sound. The great fortress-city stood for centuries as the
bulwark of Christian civilisation against the forces of the East. Its
citizens by their respectful devotion to past standards of civilisation
preserved traditions that would otherwise have been lost to us. These
two achievements played an essential part in the story of our civilisation. And in its own right Byzantine civilisation has enriched our
understanding of mankind and of the universe.

There is much that we can deplore about the Byzantines. Their
story is full of selfish intrigue, of callous murder and bloodthirsty
riots. The Byzantine had a strange and contradictory character. He
had a quick mind and a practical common sense. He was a passionate
individualist, sure of himself and his standards and eager to assert himself. He was cynical, unscrupulous and intolerant towards foreigners.
He was impatient and short-sighted in his search for worldly honours.

[1] E. Gibbon, *The History of the Decline and Fall of the Roman Empire*, ed. J. B.
Bury, v, 171.

But he had an overriding sense of religion. This might take a selfish form; he was very ready to renounce the world and retire into solitude to save his own soul, with no regard to the rest of mankind. Yet when we read the lives of the hermit-saints we find them always ready to give advice and practical help to their neighbours. For all his individualism the Byzantine had a deep respect for the institution of the Christian Empire. He accepted its controls and its desire for uniformity; and when he rose in rebellion against the government it was because the government had offended against his sense of propriety or because by its failures it showed itself no longer to have the approval of Heaven. He had a deep devotion towards his Church and its ceremonies. The Divine Liturgy was to him the great experience of his regular life, and his loyalty to it was unbounded. Byzantine life was full of squalor. Mutilated ex-criminals made an ugly impression in the city streets; but mutilation was the first step towards the humanisation of the criminal code. There were beggars in plenty. But no medieval city had such efficient and disinterested charitable organisations. There was throughout Byzantium a sincere conviction that this life was only a pale prelude to the life to come, and that the Christian Empire should copy, as far as fallible humans could do so, the Empire of God. The ceremonies of the court and Church were blended to be a great sustained act of worship. But the ritual, for all its formality, was integrated into daily life; there was nothing self-consciously remote about it.

It is, perhaps, this overwhelming sense of religion that makes, and always made, the Byzantines difficult for the West to comprehend. They loved beauty. They admired handsome men and women and liked to see them moving in shimmering silks through the glittering halls of their palaces. They delighted in gardens and fountains and the lordly colonnades of their city. But they loved more than all that the humble saint who renounced such splendour and lived in utter squalor close to God. Yet it is noticeable that hardly a monastery or a hermitage was not placed in a site from which the natural loveliness of God's world could not be admired. But the world was a transient thing; life was hard and difficult, and numberless dangers lurked around. Byzantine civilisation was tinged with melancholy. The Empire assuredly could not last for ever. The columns and the wise books kept in the city all foretold of the days when there would be no more Emperors and when anti-Christ would triumph. But till that day the Empire would proudly do its duty of defending Christian civilisation on earth, and its citizens would keep in touch with Heaven through the mysteries of the Divine Liturgy.

BIBLIOGRAPHIES

LIST OF ABBREVIATIONS

AASS	*Acta Sanctorum Bollandiana* (see Gen. Bibl. IV).
AB	*Analecta Bollandiana* (Paris and Brussels, 1882–).
AcadIBL	*Académie des Inscriptions et Belles-lettres.*
AcadIP	*Académie Impériale de St Pétersbourg.*
AHR	*American Historical Review* (New York and London, 1895–).
AIPHO	*Annales de l'Institut de Philologie et d'Histoire Orientales et Slaves de l'Université de Bruxelles* (Brussels, 1932–).
AJT	*American Journal of Theology* (Chicago, 1897–).
AKKR	*Archiv für katholisches Kirchenrecht* (Innsbruck, Mainz, 1857–).
AMAP	*Atti e memorie dell'Accademia patavina di scienze, lettere ed arti* (Padua).
AMur.	*Archivio Muratoriano* (Rome, 1904–22).
AOC	*Archives de l'Orient Chrétien* (Bucharest, 1948–).
Arch. Praed.	*Archivum Fratrum Praedicatorum* (Rome, 1930–).
Arch. Ven.	(and *N. Arch. Ven.*; *N. Arch. Ven.* n.s.; *Arch. Ven.-Tri.*; *Arch. Ven.* ser. 5). *Archivio Veneto*, 40 vols. (Venice, 1871–90); continued as *Nuovo Archivio Veneto*, 20 vols. (1891–1900); *Nuovo Archivio Veneto*, nuova serie, 42 vols. (1901–21); *Archivio Veneto-Tridentino* (1922–6); *Archivio Veneto*, quinta serie (1927–).
ASAK	*Anzeiger für schweizerische Alterthumskunde* (Zurich, 1869–1938).
ASBM	*Annales ordinis Sancti Basilii Magni* (Rome, 1949–).
ASI	*Archivio storico italiano* (Florence). Ser. I, 20 vols. and App. 9 vols. 1842–53. Index 1857. Ser. nuova, 18 vols. 1855–63. Ser. III, 26 vols. 1865–77. Indexes to II and III 1874. Supplt. 1877. Ser. IV, 20 vols. 1878–87. Index 1891. Ser. V, 49 vols. 1888–1912. Index 1900. Anni 71, etc. 1913– , in progress (Index to 1927 in *Catalogue of the London Library*, I, 1913 and Supplts., 1920, 1929).
ASL	*Archivio storico lombardo* (Milan, 1874–).
ASP	*Archiv für slavische Philologie* (Berlin, 1895–1929).
ASPN	*Archivio storico per le province napoletane* (Naples, 1876–).
ASRSP	*Archivio della società romana di storia patria* (Rome, 1878–).
Atti Ist. Ven. S.L.A.	*Atti Istituto Veneto di Scienze, Lettere ed Arte* (Venice, 1841–).
AU	*Archiv für Urkundenforschung* (Berlin, 1907–).
B	*Byzantion. Revue Internationale des Etudes Byzantines* (Paris and Liège, 1924–9; Paris and Brussels, 1930; Brussels, etc., 1931–).
BA	*Byzantinisches Archiv* (at intervals; Leipzig and Munich, 1898–).
BBI	*Bulletin of the Byzantine Institute* (Paris, 1946–).
BEC	*Bibliothèque de l'Ecole des Chartes* (Paris, 1939–).
Beck	Beck, H.-G., *Kirche und theologische Literatur* (see Gen. Bibl. I).
Bess.	*Bessarione* (Rome, 1896–1923).

BHE	*Bibliothèque de l'Ecole des Hautes Etudes* (Paris, 1839–).
BHG	*Bibliotheca hagiographica graeca* (see Gen. Bibl. IV).
BIDR	*Bullettino dell'Istituto di diritto romano* (Rome, 1888–).
BISI	*Bullettino dell'Istituto storico italiano* (Rome, 1886–).
BM	*Byzantina Metabyzantina*, I (New York, 1946); II (1949).
BNJ	*Byzantinisch-neugriechische Jahrbücher* (Berlin, 1920–5; at intervals, Athens, 1926–).
BS	*Byzantinoslavica* (Prague, 1929–).
BSA	*British School (of Archaeology) at Athens. Annual* (London, 1895–).
BSOAS	*Bulletin of the School of Oriental and African Studies* (London, 1917–).
Budé	*Collection byzantine publiée sous le Patronage de l'Association Guillaume Budé* (Paris).
BUniv.	*Biographie universelle* (see Gen. Bibl. I).
BZ	*Byzantinische Zeitschrift* (Leipzig, 1892–).
CAH	*Cambridge Ancient History* (Cambridge, 1923–39).
CH	Langlois, V., *Collection des historiens anciens et modernes de l'Arménie*, 2 vols. (Paris, 1868–9).
CHJ	*Cambridge Historical Journal* (Cambridge, 1924–57).
CHM	*Cahiers d'Histoire Mondiale* (Paris, 1953–).
CM	*Classica et Medievalia* (Copenhagen, 1938–).
CMH	*Cambridge Medieval History* (Cambridge, 1913–).
CR	*Classical Review* (London, 1887–).
CSCO	*Corpus scriptorum christianorum orientalium* (see Gen. Bibl. IV).
CSEL	*Corpus scriptorum ecclesiasticorum latinorum* (see Gen. Bibl. IV).
CSHB	*Corpus scriptorum historiae Byzantinae* (see Gen. Bibl. IV).
D	Δελτίον τῆς ἱστορικῆς καὶ ἐθνολογικῆς ἑταιρείας τῆς Ἑλλάδος (Athens, 1883–).
DA	Δελτίον τῆς Πατριαρχικῆς Βιβλιοθήκης τῆς Ἀλεξανδρείας (Alexandria, 1948–).
DACL	*Dictionnaire d'archéologie chrétienne et de liturgie* (see Gen. Bibl. I).
DAI	Constantine Porphyrogenitus, *De administrando imperio*, ed. Gy. Moravcsik and R. J. H. Jenkins (see Gen. Bibl. IV).
DDC	*Dictionnaire de droit canonique* (see Gen. Bibl. I).
DHGE	*Dictionnaire d'histoire et de géographie ecclésiastique* (see Gen. Bibl. I).
DOP	*Dumbarton Oaks Papers* (Cambridge, Mass., 1941–).
DR	Dölger, F., *Regesten der Kaiserurkunden des oströmischen Reiches* (see Gen. Bibl. IV).
DS	*Dictionnaire de spiritualité* (see Gen. Bibl. I).
DTC	*Dictionnaire de théologie catholique* (see Gen. Bibl. I).
DZG	*Deutsche Zeitschrift für Geschichtswissenschaft* (Freiburg-im-Breisgau, 1889–98) (continued as *Historische Vierteljahrsschrift* [*HVJS*], q.v.).
DZKR	*Deutsche Zeitschrift für Kirchenrecht* (Tübingen, 1861–1917).
EB	*Etudes Byzantines*, I–III (Bucharest, 1943–5) (continued as *Revue des Etudes Byzantines* [*REB*], q.v.).
EcfrAR	*Ecoles françaises d'Athènes et de Rome* (Paris).
ECQ	*Eastern Churches Quarterly* (Ramsgate, 1936–).
EEBS	Ἐπετηρὶς Ἑταιρείας Βυζαντινῶν Σπουδῶν (Athens, 1924–).

EHR	*English Historical Review* (London, 1886–).
EO	*Echos d'Orient* (Constantinople and Paris, 1897–1942) (continued as *Etudes Byzantines* [*EB*], q.v.).
Ersch–Gruber	Ersch, J. S. and Gruber, J. G., *Allgemeine Encyklopädie* (see Gen. Bibl. I).
FHG	Müller, C., *Fragmenta historicorum graecorum* (see Gen. Bibl. IV).
Fonti	*Fonti per la storia d'Italia* (see Gen. Bibl. IV).
GBL	K. Krumbacher, *Geschichte der byzantinischen Litteratur* (see Gen. Bibl. V).
Glas	*Glas Srpska Akademii Nauka* (Belgrade, 1949–) (continuation of *Glas Srpska Kraljevska Akad.*, Belgrade, 1888–1940).
Gn	*Gnomon*, I–XX (Berlin, 1925–44); (Munich, 1949–).
GOTR	*Greek Orthodox Theological Review* (Brookline, Mass., 1954–).
GR	Grumel, V., *Les Regestes des Actes du Patriarcat de Constantinople* (see Gen. Bibl. IV).
HJ	*Historisches Jahrbuch* (Görres-Gesellschaft) (Munich, 1880–).
HTR	*Harvard Theological Review* (Cambridge, Mass., 1908–).
HVJS	*Historische Vierteljahrsschrift* (continuation of *Deutsche Zeitschrift f. Geschichtswissenschaft* [*DZG*]) (Leipzig, 1898–).
HZ	*Historische Zeitschrift* (von Sybel) (Munich and Berlin, 1859–).
IRAIK	*Izvestija Russkago Archeologičeskago Instituta v Konstantinopole* [*Transactions of the Russian Archaeological Institute at Constantinople*] (*Odessa*, 1896–).
JA	*Journal Asiatique* (Paris, 1822–).
Jaffé	Jaffé, P., *Regesta Pontificum Romanorum* (see Gen. Bibl. IV).
JEH	*Journal of Ecclesiastical History* (London, 1950–).
JHS	*Journal of Hellenic Studies* (London, 1880–).
JOBG	*Jahrbuch der österreichischen byzantinischen Gesellschaft* (Vienna, 1951–).
JRAS	*Journal of the Royal Asiatic Society of Great Britain* (London, 1833–).
JRS	*Journal of Roman Studies* (London, 1911–).
JTS	*Journal of Theological Studies* (London, 1900–).
KAW	(*Kaiserliche*) *Akademie der Wissenschaften* (Vienna).
LTK	*Lexikon für Theologie und Kirche* (see Gen. Bibl. I).
MA	*Le moyen âge* (Paris, 1888–).
Mansi	Mansi, J. D., *Sacrorum conciliorum collectio* (see Gen. Bibl. IV).
MEC	*Mémoires et documents publ. par l'Ecole des Chartes* (see Gen. Bibl. IV).
Med. Hum.	*Medievalia et Humanistica* (Boulder, Colorado, 1943–).
Med. Stud.	*Medieval Studies* (Pontifical Academy of Toronto) (Toronto, 1939).
Mém. Acad. IP	*Mémoires de l'Académie impériale des sciences de St Pétersbourg.*
MGH	*Monumenta Germaniae Historica* (see Gen. Bibl. IV).
MGT	*Magyar-Görög Tamulmányok*, Οὐγγροελληνικαὶ Μελέται (Budapest, 1945–).
MHP	*Monumenta historiae patriae* (Turin) (see Gen. Bibl. IV).
MHSM	*Monumenta spectantia historiam Slavorum meridionalium* (see Gen. Bibl. IV).
MIOG	*Mittheilungen des Instituts für österreichische Geschichtsforschung* (Innsbruck, 1880–).

MM	F. Miklosich and J. Müller, *Acta et diplomata graeca medii aevi sacra et profana* (see Gen. Bibl. IV).
MPG	Migne, *Patrologiae cursus completus. Ser. graeco-latina* (see Gen. Bibl. IV).
MPL	Migne, *Patrologiae cursus completus. Ser. latina* (see Gen. Bibl. IV).
NE	Νέος Ἑλληνομνήμων (Athens, 1904–27).
Neu. Arch.	*Neues Archiv der Gesellschaft für ältere deutsche Geschichtskunde* (Hanover and Leipzig, 1876–).
NRDF	*Nouvelle revue historique du droit français* (Paris, 1877–1921).
OC	*Oriens Christianus* (Leipzig, 1901–).
OCA	*Orientalia Christiana Analecta* (Rome, 1935–).
OCP	*Orientalia Christiana Periodica* (Rome, 1935–).
ÖstCh	*Östliches Christentum* (Munich, 1923–).
Pauly–Wissowa	Pauly, A., Wissowa, G. and Kroll, W., *Real-Encyclopädie der classischen Altertumswissenschaft* (see Gen. Bibl. I).
PAW	*Königliche preussische Akademie d. Wissenschaften* (Berlin).
PO	*Patrologia Orientalis* (Paris, 1907–).
PR	Potthast, A., *Regesta Pontificum Romanorum* (see Gen. Bibl. IV).
QFIA	*Quellen und Forschungen aus italienischen Archiven und Bibliotheken* (Rome, 1897–).
RA	*Revue archéologique* (Paris, 1844–).
RAAD	*Revue de l'Académie arabe (de Damas)* (Damascus, 1921–).
RAC	*Reallexikon für Antike und Christentum* (see Gen. Bibl. I).
RBén	*Revue bénédictine* (Maredsous, 1890–).
REB	*Revue des études byzantines* (Bucharest and Paris, 1946–).
Rec. hist. cr.	*Recueil des historiens des croisades* (see Gen. Bibl. IV).
REG	*Revue des études grecques* (Paris, 1888–).
RH	*Revue historique* (Paris, 1876–).
RHC	*Revue d'histoire comparée* (Budapest, Paris, 1943–8).
RHE	*Revue d'histoire ecclésiastique* (Louvain, 1900–).
RHSE	*Revue historique du sud-est européen* (Bucharest, 1924–).
RISS	See Muratori in Gen. Bibl. IV.
RN	*Revue numismatique* (Paris, 1836–).
ROC	*Revue de l'orient chrétien* (Paris, 1896–).
ROL	*Revue de l'orient latin* (Paris, 1893–).
RP	Rhalles, G. A. and Potles, M., Σύνταγμα τῶν θείων καὶ ἱερῶν κανόνων (see Gen. Bibl. IV).
RQCA	*Römische Quartalschrift für christliche Altertumskunde und Kirchengeschichte* (Rome, 1887–).
RQH	*Revue des questions historiques* (Paris, 1866–).
RSI	*Rivista storica italiana* (Turin, 1884–).
SBAW	*Sitzungsberichte der bayerischen Akademie der Wissenschaften* (formerly *Königlichen Akad. der Wiss.*) (Munich, 1860–70) Separate *Phil.-Hist. Klasse* (Munich, 1871–).
SBN	*Studi Bizantini e Neoellenici* (Rome, 1924–).
SEER	*Slavonic and East European Review* (London, 1922–).
Sem. Kond.	*Seminarium Kondakovianum* (Prague, I–VIII, 1929–36). Continued as *Annales de l'Institut Kondakov* (Belgrade, 1937–40).
SGUS	*Scriptores rerum Germanicarum in usum scholarum* (see *Monumenta Germaniae Historica* in Gen. Bibl. IV).
SHF	*Société d'Histoire Française* (Publications). Paris, 1888–).

SKAW	*Sitzungsberichte der (kaiserlichen) Akademie der Wissenschaften. Philosoph.-hist. Classe* (Vienna, 1848–).
SP	*Speculum* (Cambridge, Mass., 1925–).
SPAW	*Sitzungsberichte der königlichen preussischen* [after 1944 called *deutschen*] *Akademie der Wissenschaften* (Berlin, 1896–).
SRH	*Scriptores rerum Hungaricarum* (see Gen. Bibl. IV).
Trad.	*Traditio* (New York, 1943–).
TRHS	*Transactions of the Royal Historical Society* (London, 1869–).
VV	*Vizantijskij Vremennik*, old series I–XXV (St Petersburg, 1894–1927); new series (Leningrad, 1947–).
WMBH	*Wissenschaftliche Mittheilungen aus Bosnien und der Hercegovina* (Vienna, 1893–1912).
ZCK	*Zeitschrift für christliche Kunst* (Dusseldorf, 1888–1921).
ZDMG	*Zeitschrift der deutschen morgenländischen Gesellschaft* (Leipzig, 1846–).
ZKG	*Zeitschrift für Kirchengeschichte* (Stuttgart, 1876–).
ZKT	*Zeitschrift für katholische Theologie* (Innsbruck, 1877–).
ZMNP	*Žurnal ministerstva narodnogo prosveščenija* [*Journal of the Ministry of Public Instruction*] (St Petersburg, 1834–).
ZR	*Zeitschrift für Rechtsgeschichte* (Weimar, 1861–78) (continued as *ZSR*, below).
ZSR	*Zeitschrift der Savigny-Stiftung für Rechtswissenschaft* (Weimar, 1880–).
ZWT	*Zeitschrift für wissenschaftliche Theologie* (Jena, etc., Frankfurt-am-Main, 1858–1914).

Abh.	Abhandlungen.	n.d.	no date.
antiq.	antiquarian, antiquaire.	n.s.	new series.
app.	appendix.	publ.	published, publié.
coll.	collection.	R.⎱ r. ⎰	reale.
diss.	dissertation.		
Ge., Gé.	Georgia, Géorgie.	roy.	royal, royale.
hist.	history, historical, historique, historisch.	ser.	series.
		soc.	society, société, società.
Jahrb.	Jahrbuch.	subs.	subsidia.
k.	kaiserlich, königlich.	supplt.	supplement.
mem.	memoir.	*TU*	*Texte und Untersuchungen.*
mém.	mémoire.	Viert.	Vierteljahrsschrift.

GENERAL BIBLIOGRAPHY

A classified bibliography of works on Byzantine history and civilisation published from 1892 onwards may be found in the periodical *Byzantinische Zeitschrift*.

A number of works cited have been reprinted unaltered; such reprints are not generally noted here.

I. DICTIONARIES, BIBLIOGRAPHIES AND GENERAL WORKS OF REFERENCE

Altaner, B., *Patrologie*, 5th ed. (Freiburg, 1958); English transl. H. C. Graef (New York, 1960).

American Historical Association's Guide to Historical Literature, ed. by G. F. Howe and others (New York, 1961).

Beck, H.-G., *Kirche und theologische Literatur im byzantinischen Reich* (Munich, 1959). [Beck.]

Bernheim, E., *Lehrbuch der historischen Methode und der Geschichtsphilosophie* (5th and 6th enlarged eds., Leipzig, 1908).

Bibliografia storica nazionale [on works since 1939] (Giunta Centrale per gli Studi Storici: Rome, 1942–9; Bari, 1950–).

Biographie universelle, ancienne et moderne, 45 vols. (Paris, ed. L. G. Michaud and others, 1843–65). [Greatly improved ed. of earlier work, 1811–28, and its supplements, 1832–62.] [*BUniv.*]

Bresslau, H., *Handbuch der Urkundenlehre für Deutschland und Italien*, I and II, pt. 1, 3rd ed. (Leipzig, 1914); II, pt. 2, by H.-W. Klewitz, 2nd ed. (Leipzig, 1931); 2 vols. and Index vol. (Berlin, 1958–60).

Capasso, B., *Le fonti della storia delle provincie napoletane dal 568 al 1500*, ed. E. O. Mastrojanni (Naples, 1902).

Ceillier, R., *Histoire générale des auteurs sacrés et ecclésiastiques*, 23 vols. (Paris, 1729–63); new ed. 19 vols. (Paris, 1858–70).

Chevalier, C. U. J., *Répertoire des sources historiques du moyen âge. Biobibliographie* (Paris, 1883–8; rev. ed. 2 vols. 1905–7). *Topo-bibliographie* (Montbéliard, 1894–1903).

Colonna, M. E., *Gli storici bizantini dal IV al XV secolo. I. Storici profani* (Naples, 1956).

Cross, F. L. (ed.), *The Oxford Dictionary of the Christian Church* (Oxford, 1957).

Demetrakos, D. B., Μέγα λεξικὸν τῆς ἑλληνικῆς γλώσσης, 9 vols. (Athens, 1933–51).

Dictionnaire d'archéologie chrétienne et de liturgie, ed. F. Cabriol and H. Leclercq (Paris, 1907–1953). [*DACL.*]

Dictionnaire de droit canonique, ed. R. Naz (Paris, 1935 ff.). [*DDC.*]

Dictionnaire de spiritualité, ed. M. Villier, F. Cavallera and J. de Guibert (Paris, 1937 ff., in progress). [*DS.*]

Dictionnaire de théologie catholique, ed. A. Vacant, E. Mangeot and others, 15 vols. in 18 (Paris, 1905–50). [*DTC.*]

Dictionnaire d'histoire et de géographie ecclésiastiques, ed. A. Baudrillart, A. Vogt, U. Rouzies and others (Paris, 1912 ff., in progress). [*DHGE.*]

Dix années d'études byzantines. Bibliographie Internationale 1939–1948. Publ. by the Association Internationale des Etudes Byzantines (Paris, 1949).

Dölger, F. and Schneider, A. M., *Byzanz* (Berne, 1952).

Du Cange, C. du Fresne, *Glossarium ad scriptores mediae et infimae Latinitatis,* eds. of G. A. L. Henschel, 7 vols. (Paris, 1840–50); and L. Favre, 10 vols. (Niort, 1883–8).

Du Cange, C. du Fresne, *Glossarium ad scriptores mediae et infimae Graecitatis,* 2 vols. (Lyons, 1688).

Enciclopedia Italiana di scienze, lettere ed arti (Rome, 1929–36; and later supplementary volumes).

Encyclopaedia Britannica, 11th and later eds. (Cambridge, London and New York, 1910 ff.; new ed. in progress).

Encyclopedia of Islam. A Dictionary of the Geography, Ethnography, and Biography of the Muhammadan Peoples, 4 vols. and supplement (Leiden, 1913–48); 2nd ed. B. Lewis, C. Pellat and J. Schacht (Leiden and London, 1954 ff.). [In progress.]

Ersch, J. S. and Gruber, J. G., *Allgemeine Encyklopädie der Wissenschaften und Künste* (Berlin, 1818–90; incomplete). [Ersch–Gruber.]

Ghellinck, J. de, *Patristique et moyen-âge,* 3 vols. (Paris and Brussels, 1947–9).

Giry, A., *Manuel de diplomatique,* reprinted in 2 vols. (Paris, 1925).

Jugie, M., *Theologia dogmatica Christianorum orientalium ab ecclesia catholica dissidentium,* 5 vols. (Paris, 1926–35).

Krumbacher, K., *Geschichte der byzantinischen Litteratur.* [See below, v.]

Langford-James, R. L., *A Dictionary of the Eastern Orthodox Church* (London, n.d.).

Lexikon für Theologie und Kirche, ed. M. Buchberger; 2nd ed. J. Hofer and K. Rahner (Freiburg, 1957 ff.). [*LTK.*]

Λεξικὸν τῆς ἑλληνικῆς γλώσσης. Α΄. Ἱστορικὸν λεξικὸν τῆς νέας ἑλληνικῆς τῆς τε κοινῆς ὁμιλουμένης καὶ τῶν ἰδιωμάτων (Athens, 1933–).

Maigne d'Arnis, W. H., *Lexicon manuale ad scriptores mediae et infimae Latinitatis* (publ. Migne) (Paris, 1866).

Meester, P. de, *De monachico statu iuxta disciplinam byzantinam. Statuta selectis fontibus et commentariis instructa* (Vatican City, 1942).

Milaš, N., *Das Kirchenrecht der morgenländischen Kirche,* 2nd ed. (Mostar, 1905).

Moravcsik, Gy., *Byzantinoturcica,* 2 vols., I: *Die byzantinischen Quellen der Geschichte der Türkvölker;* II: *Sprachreste der Türkvölker in den byzantinischen Quellen,* 2nd ed. (Berlin, 1958).

Oudin, Casimir, *Commentarius de scriptoribus ecclesiae antiquae illorumque scriptis tam impressis quam manuscriptis adhuc extantibus in celebrioribus Europae bibliothecis a Bellarmino, etc., omissis ad annum MCCCCLX* (Frankfurt and Leipzig, 1722).

Paetow, L. J., *Guide to the Study of Medieval History,* rev. ed. (London, 1931) [a supplement for the years 1930–60 is in preparation].

Patristic Greek Lexicon, ed. G. W. H. Lampe (Oxford, 1961 ff.). [In progress.]

Pauly, A. F. von, *Real-Encyclopädie der classischen Alterthumswissenschaft* (Vienna, 1837–52); new ed. G. Wissowa, W. Kroll and others (Stuttgart, 1893 ff.). [Pauly–Wissowa.]

Philips, C. H., ed., *Handbook of Oriental History* (London, 1951).

Potthast, A., *Bibliotheca historica medii aevi. Wegweiser durch die Geschichtswerke des europäischen Mittelalters bis 1500,* 2nd ed. 2 vols. (Berlin, 1896) (see below, *Repertorium*).

Quasten, J., *Patrology*, III (Westminster: Maryland, 1960).

Reallexikon für Antike und Christentum, ed. T. Klausner, F. Dölger, H. Lietzmann and others (Stuttgart, 1950 ff.). [In progress.] [*RAC*.]

Repertorium Fontium Historiae Medii Aevi, primum ab Augusto Potthast digestum, nunc de cura collegii historicorum e pluribus nationibus emendatum et auctum. I. *Series Collectionum* (Istituto Storico Italiano per il Medio Evo, Rome, 1962).

Sophocles, E. A., *Greek Lexicon of the Roman and Byzantine Periods* (B.C. 146 *to A.D. 1100*) (Boston, 1870); ed. J. H. Thayer (New York, 1887 and 1893).

Stephanus, H., *Thesaurus linguae graecae*, ed. C. B. Hase, G. Dindorf and L. Dindorf, I–VIII (Paris, 1831–65).

Überweg, F., *Grundriss der Geschichte der Philosophie*, I, 12th ed. by K. Praechter; II, 11th ed. by B. Geyer (Berlin, 1926, 1928).

II. ATLASES AND GEOGRAPHY

Anderson, J. G. C., *Map of Asia Minor* (Murray's Handy Classical Maps, ed. G. B. Grundy) (London, 1903); partially revised by W. M. Calder and G. E. Bean, *A Classical Map of Asia Minor* (London, 1958).

Banduri, A., *Imperium orientale sive antiquitates Constantinopolitanae*, 2 vols. (Paris, 1711).

Bischoff, H. T. and Möller, J. H., *Vergleichendes Wörterbuch der alten, mittleren, und neuen Geographie* (Gotha, 1829).

Deschamps, P., *Dictionnaire de géographie* [supplt. to Brunet, J. C., *Manuel du Libraire*] (Paris, 1870); 2nd ed. 2 vols. (1878–80).

Dictionnaire d'histoire et de géographie ecclésiastiques [see above, I].

Du Cange, C. du Fresne, *Constantinopolis Christiana* (*Historia Byzantina*, pts. II and III). [See below, v.]

Freeman, E. A., *Historical Geography of Europe* [with Atlas] (London, 1881); 3rd ed. rev. and ed. J. B. Bury, 2 vols. (London, 1903).

Grässe, J. G. T., *Orbis Latinus* (Dresden, 1861, with index of modern names); 2nd ed. F. Benedict (Berlin, 1909; reprinted Berlin, 1922).

Hazard, H. W. and Cooke, H. L., *Atlas of Islamic History*, 3rd ed. (Princeton, 1954).

Heussi, K. and Hermann, M., *Atlas zur Kirchengeschichte*, 2nd ed. (Tübingen, 1919).

Honigmann, E., *Die Ostgrenze des byzantinischen Reiches von 363 bis 1071* (see Gen. Bibl. v).

Janin, R., *Constantinople byzantine: développement urbain et répertorie topographique*, 2nd ed. (Paris, 1964).

Janin, R., *La géographie ecclésiastique de l'empire byzantin*, part I: *Le siège de Constantinople et le patriarcat oecuménique*, vol. 3: *Les églises et les monastères* (Paris, 1953).

Kiepert, H., Πίναξ τοῦ μεσαιωνικοῦ Ἑλληνισμοῦ κατὰ τὴν δεκάτην ἑκατονταετηρίδα. Published by the Athenian Σύλλογος πρὸς διάδοσιν τῶν Ἑλληνικῶν γραμμάτων (Berlin, 1883).

Le Strange, G., *Palestine under the Moslems* (Cambridge, 1890).

Le Strange, G., *The Lands of the Eastern Caliphate: Mesopotamia, Persia and Central Asia, from the Moslem Conquest to the Time of Timur* (Cambridge, 1905).

Le Strange, G., *Baghdad during the Abbasid Caliphate, from Contemporary Arab and Persian Sources* (London, 1900).

Meer, F. van der and Mohrmann, C., *Atlas of the Early Christian World*, transl. and ed. by M. H. Hedlund and H. H. Rowley (London, 1958).

Mordtmann, A., *Esquisse topographique de Constantinople* (Lille, 1892).

Philippson, A., *Das byzantinische Reich als geographische Erscheinung* (Leyden, 1939).

Philippson, A. and Kirsten, E., *Die griechischen Landschaften*, i–ii in 4 pts. (Frankfurt, 1950–2, 1956–8).

Poole, R. L. (ed.), *Historical Atlas of Modern Europe* (Oxford, 1902).

Putzger, F. W., *Historischer Schul-Atlas*, ed. A. Baldamus and others (Bielefeld and Leipzig, various editions).

Ramsay, W. M., *Cities and Bishoprics of Phrygia*. 1 vol. in 2 (Oxford, 1895–7). [All publ.]

Ramsay, W. M., *Historical Geography of Asia Minor* (Roy. Geog. Soc., Suppl. papers, 4) (London, 1890).

Roolvink, R. and others, *Historical Atlas of the Muslim Peoples* (Amsterdam, 1957).

Setton, K. M., 'The Archaeology of medieval Athens', *Essays in Medieval Life and Thought presented in Honor of Austin Patterson Evans* (New York, 1955), 227–58.

Shepherd, W. R., *Historical Atlas*, 8th ed. (Pikesville: Maryland, 1956).

Spruner–Menke, *Hand-Atlas für die Geschichte des Mittelalters und der neueren Zeit* (Gotha, 1880) (3rd ed. of K. von Spruner's *Hand-Atlas*, etc., ed. T. Menke).

Tafrali, O., *Topographie de Thessalonique* (Paris, 1913).

Van Millingen, A., *Byzantine Constantinople: the Walls of the City and adjoining Historical Sites* (London, 1899).

Van Millingen, A., *Byzantine Churches in Constantinople* (London, 1912).

Vasmer, M., *Die Slaven in Griechenland*. (*Abh. d. Preuss. Akad. d. Wissensch., philos.-hist. Kl.*, 12) (Berlin, 1941).

Vivien de Saint-Martin, L., and others, *Nouveau dictionnaire de géographie universelle*, 7 vols. (Paris, 1879–95); supplt. by L. Rousselet, 2 vols. (1895–7). [Contains short bibliographies.]

III. CHRONOLOGY, EPIGRAPHY, NUMISMATICS, GENEALOGY AND DEMOGRAPHY

(A) CHRONOLOGY

L'art de vérifier les dates et les faits historiques, par un religieux de la congrégation de St Maur, 4th ed. by N. V. de St Allais and others, 44 vols. (Paris, 1818–44).

Cappelli, A., *Cronologia, cronografia, e calendario perpetuo dal principio dell'era cristiana ai giorni nostri*, 2nd ed. (Milan, 1930).

Chaine, M., *La chronologie des temps chrétiens en Egypte et en Ethiopie* (Paris, 1925).

Dulaurier, E., *Recherches sur la chronologie arménienne*. i: *Chronologie technique* (Paris, 1925).

Gams, P. B., *Series episcoporum ecclesiae Catholicae* [with supplt.] (Ratisbon, 1873, 1886); reprinted (Leipzig, 1931).

Ginzel, F. K., *Handbuch der mathematischen und technischen Chronologie*, 3 vols. (Leipzig, 1906–14).

Grotefend, H., *Taschenbuch der Zeitrechnung des deutschen Mittelalters und der Neuzeit*, 10th ed. by T. Ulrich (Hanover, 1960).

Grotefend, H., *Zeitrechnung des deutschen Mittelalters und der Neuzeit*, 2 vols. (Hanover, 1891–8).

Grumel, V., *La Chronologie* (*Traité d'études byzantines*, ed. P. Lemerle, I) (Paris, 1958).

Haig, T. W., *Comparative Tables of Muhammadan and Christian Dates* (London, 1932).

Ideler, C. L., *Handbuch der mathematischen und technischen Chronologie*, 2 vols. (Berlin, 1825–6); new ed. (Breslau, 1883).

Kubitschek, W., *Grundriss der antiken Zeitrechnung* (*Handbuch der Altertumswissenschaft*, I, 7) (Munich, 1928).

Lane-Poole, S., *The Mohammedan Dynasties: Chronological and Genealogical Tables with Historical Introductions* (London, 1894); see also the fuller Russian edition by V. Bartold (St Petersburg, 1899).

Lietzmann, H., *Zeitrechnung der römischen Kaiserzeit, des Mittelalters und der Neuzeit für die Jahre 1–2000 nach Christus*, 3rd ed. by D. K. Aland (Berlin, 1956).

Mas Latrie, J. M. J. L. de, *Trésor de chronologie, d'histoire, et de géographie pour l'étude et l'emploi des documents du moyen âge* (Paris, 1889).

Muralt, E. de, *Essai de chronographie byzantine* (*395–1057*) (St Petersburg, 1855).

Muralt, E. de, *Essai de chronographie byzantine* (*1057–1453*), 2 vols. (Basle and Geneva, 1871–3).

Neugebauer, P. V., *Hilfstafeln zur technischen Chronologie* [reprinted from *Astronomische Nachrichten*, Bd. 261] (Kiel, 1937).

Poole, R. L., *Medieval Reckonings of Time* (Helps for Students of History) (London, 1918).

Ruhl, F., *Chronologie des Mittelalters und der Neuzeit* (Berlin, 1897).

Schram, R., *Kalendariographische und chronologische Tafeln* (Leipzig, 1908).

Stokvis, A. M. H. J., *Manuel d'histoire de généalogie et de chronologie de tous les états du globe, depuis les temps les plus reculés jusqu'à nos jours*, 3 vols. (Leiden, 1888–93).

Wüstenfeld, H. F., *Wüstenfeld-Mahler'sche Vergleichungs-Tabellen zur muslimischen und iranischen Zeitrechnung mit Tafeln zur Umrechnung orient-christlicher Ären*, 3rd ed. by J. Mayr and B. Spuler (Wiesbaden, 1961).

Information may also be found in such works as Giry; and Philips [see I above]; and in Dölger, *Regesten*; Grumel; Gedeon; Le Quien; Ughelli [see IV below].

(B) EPIGRAPHY

Corpus der griechisch-christlichen Inschriften in Hellas, ed. N. A. Bees and others (Athens, 1941; in progress).

Grégoire, H., *Recueil des inscriptions grecques chrétiennes d'Asie Mineure*, I (Paris, 1922).

Jalabert, L. and Mouterde, R., *Inscriptions grecques et latines de la Syrie*, I–IV (Paris, 1929–55).

Michailov, G., *Inscriptiones graecae in Bulgaria repertae*, I: *Inscriptiones orae Ponti Euxini* (Sofia, 1956).

Millet, G., Pargoire, J. and Petit, L., *Recueil des inscriptions chrétiennes du Mont-Athos* (Bibliothèque des Ecoles françaises d'Athènes et de Rome, 91) (Paris, 1904).
See also the 'Bulletin épigraphique', in *REG* (e.g. J. and L. Robert, LVII (1944) and later vols.).

(c) NUMISMATICS

Adelson, H. L., *Lightweight Solidi and Byzantine Trade during the Sixth and Seventh Centuries* (*Num. Notes and Monographs*, 138) (New York, 1957); see the review by J. P. C. Kent, *Numismatic Chronicle*, XIX (1959), 237–40.
Bellinger, A. R., *The Anonymous Byzantine Bronze Coinage* (*Num. Notes and Monographs*, 35) (New York, 1928).
Bertelè, T., *L'imperatore alato nella numismatica bizantina* (Rome, 1951).
Breckenridge, J. D., *The Numismatic Iconography of Justinian II* (*Num. Notes and Monographs*, 144) (New York, 1959).
Codrington, O., *Manual of Musalman Numismatics* (Royal Asiatic Soc.) (London, 1904).
Corpus nummorum italicorum, vols. I–XV (Rome, 1910 ff., in progress).
Engel, A. and Serrure, R., *Traité de numismatique du moyen âge*, 2 vols. (Paris, 1891–4).
Goodacre, H., *A Handbook of the Coinage of the Byzantine Empire*, 3 vols. (London, 1928–33); new ed. (1957).
Grierson, P., *Coins and Medals; a Select Bibliography* (Historical Association, *Helps for Students of History*, 56) (London, 1954).
Grierson, P., 'Coinage and Money in the Byzantine Empire 498–c. 1090', *Settimane di studio del Centro italiano di studi sull'alto medioevo, Spoleto 1960*, VIII (1961), 411–53.
Konstantopoulos, K., Βυζαντιακὰ μολυβδόβουλλα (Athens, 1917).
Laurent, V., 'Bulletin de numismatique byzantine 1940–49', *REB*, IX (1951), 192–251.
Laurent, V., 'Bulletin de sigillographie byzantine', *B*, V (1929–30), 571–654; VI (1931), 771–829.
Laurent, V., *Documents de sigillographie byzantine; la collection C. Orghidan* (Bibliothèque byzantine, ed. P. Lemerle, Documents I) (Paris, 1952).
Longuet, H., *Introduction à la numismatique byzantine* (London, 1961).
Macdonald, G., *The Evolution of Coinage* (Cambridge, 1916).
Metcalf, D. M., 'The Byzantine Empire', *Congresso Internazionale di Numismatica*, I (Rome, 1961), 233–45.
Mosser, S. M., *A Bibliography of Byzantine Coin Hoards* (*Num. Notes and Monographs*, 67) (New York, 1935).
Pančenko, B. A., 'Katalog molivdovulov' ['Catalogue of lead seals'], *IRAIK*, VIII (1903), 199–246; IX (1904), 341–96; XIII (1908), 78–151.
Ratto, R., *Monnaies byzantines* (Lugano, 9 Dec. 1930; a sale catalogue, illustrated with a great deal of material; reprinted Amsterdam, 1959).
Sabatier, J., *Description générale des monnaies byzantines*, 2 vols. (Paris and London, 1862) (reprinted Leipzig, 1930 and Graz, 1955).
Schlumberger, G., *Numismatique de l'orient latin* (Société de l'Orient Latin), 2 vols. (Paris, 1878, 1882).
Schlumberger, G., *Sigillographie de l'empire byzantin* (Paris, 1884).
Schlumberger, G., Chalandon, F. and Blanchet, A., *Sigillographie de l'orient latin* (Paris, 1943).

Tolstoi, J., *Vizantijskie monety* [*Byzantine coins*], fasc. 1–7 (St Petersburg, 1912–14).

Wroth, W., *Catalogue of the Coins of the Vandals, Ostrogoths, and Lombards, and of the Empires of Thessalonica, Nicaea, and Trebizond in the British Museum* (London, 1911).

Wroth, W., *Catalogue of the Imperial Byzantine Coins in the British Museum*, 2 vols. (London, 1908).

(D) GENEALOGY

Argenti, P. P., *Libro d'Oro de la Noblesse de Chio:* I. *Notices historiques.* II. *Arbres généalogiques* (London, 1955).

Chatzes, A. C., Οἱ ʽΡαούλ, ʽΡάλ, ʽΡάλαι (*1080–1800*) (Kirchain, 1908).

Du Cange, C. du Fresne, *Familiae Augustae Byzantinae. Familiae Dalmaticae, Sclavonicae, Turcicae.* (*Historia Byzantina*, pt. 1. See below, v.)

Du Cange, C. du Fresne, *Les familles d'outre-mer*, ed. E. Rey (Paris, 1869). (Collection de documents inédits sur l'histoire de France.)

George, H. B., *Genealogical Tables illustrative of Modern History* (Oxford, 1873); 5th ed. J. R. H. Weaver, revised and enlarged (1916).

Grote, H., *Stammtafeln mit Anhang calendarium medii aevi* (vol. IX of Münz-studien) (Leipzig, 1877).

Hopf, K., *Chroniques gréco-romanes* [see below, IV].

Papadopulos, A., *Versuch einer Genealogie der Palaiologen, 1259–1453* (Diss., Munich, 1938).

Zambaur, E. K. M. von, *Manuel de généalogie et de chronologie pour l'histoire de l'Islam* (Hanover, 1927).

[See also *L'art de vérifier les dates* and S. Lane-Poole, *Mohammadan Dynasties* (III (A) above) and other works under III (A), (B), (C) and (E).]

(E) DEMOGRAPHY

Cahen, C., 'Le problème ethnique en Anatolie', *CHM*, II (1954), 347–62.

Charanis, P., 'The Armenians in the Byzantine Empire', *BS*, XXII (1961), 196–240.

Kyriakides, S. P. *The Northern Ethnological Boundaries of Hellenism* (Thessalonica, 1955); see also ʽΕτ. Μακ. Σπουδ., v (Thessalonica, 1946).

Lemerle, P., 'Invasions et migrations dans les Balkans depuis la fin de l'époque romaine jusqu'au VIIIᵉ siècle', *RH*, CXXI (1954), 265–308.

Mayer, R., *Byzantion-Konstantinopolis-Istanbul; eine genetische Stadtgeographie* (*Akademie der Wissenschaften, Wien, Philosoph.-Hist. Kl. Denkschriften*, 71) (Vienna, 1943).

Starr, J., *The Jews in the Byzantine Empire, 641–1204* (Athens, 1939).

Starr, J., *Romania: the Jewries of the Levant after the Fourth Crusade* (Paris, 1949).

Vryonis, S., Jr., 'Byzantium: the Social Basis of Decline in the Eleventh Century', *Greek, Roman and Byzantine Studies*, II (1959), 157–75.

See also Moravcsik (I above); Vasmer (and other works in II above); III (D) above; Barišič (IV below); and the bibliography on Anthropological and Demographic Studies by I. Ševčenko in the *American Historical Association's Guide* (I above).

IV. SOURCES AND COLLECTIONS OF SOURCES

Achéry, L. d', *Spicilegium sive collectio veterum aliquot scriptorum*, 13 vols. (Paris, 1655 (1665)–77); new ed. L. F. J. de la Barre, 3 vols. (Paris, 1723).

Acta Conciliorum Oecumenicorum, ed. E. Schwartz, 4 vols. in 12 (Berlin, 1914–40).

Acta Sanctorum Bollandiana (Brussels, 1643–1770; Paris and Rome, 1866, 1887; Brussels, 1894 ff., in progress). [*AASS.*]

Acts of Athos

> Chilandari: L. Petit and B. Korablev, *Actes de Chilandar*, I: *Actes grecs*, *VV*, XVII (1911); II: *Actes slaves*, *ib.* XIX (1912). V. Mošin and A. Sovre, *Supplementa ad acta graeca Chilandarii* (Ljubljana, 1948).
>
> Esphigmenou: L. Petit and W. Regel, *Actes d'Esphigménou*, *VV*, XII (1906).
>
> Kutlumus: P. Lemerle, *Actes de Kutlumus* (Archives de l'Athos, II) (Paris, 1937).
>
> Lavra: G. Rouillard and P. Collomp, *Actes de Lavra* (Archives de l'Athos, I) (Paris, 1937).
>
> Panteleimon: *Akty russkogo na svjatom Afone monastyrja sv. velikomučenika i celitelja Pantelejmona* [*Acts of the Russian Monastery of the Great Martyr and Healer St Panteleimon on the Holy Mt Athos*] (Kiev, 1873).
>
> Pantocrator: L. Petit, *Actes de Pantocrator*, *VV*, X (1903).
>
> Philotheou: W. Regel, E. Kurtz and B. Korablev, *Actes de Philothée*, *VV*, XX (1913).
>
> Zographou: W. Regel, E. Kurtz and B. Korablev, *Actes de Zographou*, *VV*, XIII (1907).
>
> See also V. Mošin, *Akti iz svetogorskih arhiva* [*Acts from the archives of the Holy Mountain*], Spomenik, XCI (Belgrade, 1939). T. Florinsky, *Afonskie akty* [*Acts of Athos*] (St Petersburg, 1880).

Amari, M., see under Muratori.

Archivio storico italiano. Cf. list of Abbreviations: *ASI.*

Barišič, F. and others (edd.), *Vizantiski izvori za istoriju narodna Jugoslavije* [*Byzantine sources for the history of the South Slavs*] (Belgrade, 1955 ff.).

Barker, E., *Social and Political Thought in Byzantium from Justinian I to the Last Palaeologus* (Oxford, 1957). [English transl. of passages from Byzantine writers and documents; see the review of this by R. J. H. Jenkins in *JTS*, n.s. X (1959), 418–21.]

Basilicorum libri LX, vols. I–VI, ed. W. E. Heimbach (Leipzig, 1833–70). With 2 supplts.: 1, ed. K. E. Zachariae von Lingenthal (Leipzig, 1846) [containing books XV–XIX]; and 2 (vol. VII), ed. E. C. Ferrini and J. Mercati (Leipzig, 1897); ed. H. J. Scheltema and others, series A: *Textus*; series B: *Scholia* (Groningen, 1953 ff., in progress).

Bataille, A., *Les Papyrus* (*Traité d'études byzantines*, ed. P. Lemerle, II) (Paris, 1955).

Bibliotheca hagiographica graeca (Subsidia hagiographica, 8ᵃ), 3rd ed. by F. Halkin, 3 vols. (Brussels, 1957). [*BHG.*]

Boissonade, J. F., *Anecdota graeca*, 5 vols. (Paris, 1829–33).

Boissonade, J. F., *Anecdota nova* (Paris, 1844).

Brightman, F. E., *Liturgies Eastern and Western.* I. *Eastern Liturgies* (Oxford, 1896).

Byzantine Texts, ed. J. B. Bury, 5 vols. (London, 1898–1904).

Christ, W. and Paranikas, M., *Anthologia graeca carminum christianorum* (Leipzig, 1871).

Codex Theodosianus, ed. T. Mommsen, P. M. Meyer and others (Berlin, 1905); transl. C. Pharr (Princeton, 1952).

Comnena, Anna, *Alexiad*, ed. A. Reifferscheid, 2 vols. (Leipzig, 1884); also L. Schopen and A. Reifferscheid, 2 vols. *CSHB* (1839–78); *MPG*, cxxxi (1864); and B. Leib (Budé with French transl.), 3 vols. (Paris, 1937–45); English transl. by E. A. S. Dawes (London, 1928).

Constantine Porphyrogenitus, *De cerimoniis aulae byzantinae*, ed. J. J. Reiske, *CSHB* (1829–40); new ed. of book I, c. 1–83 by A. Vogt, *Constantin VII Porphyrogénète: Le Livre des Cérémonies* (Paris, 1935, 1939–40); *De thematibus* and *De administrando imperio*, ed. I. Bekker, 3 vols. *CSHB* (1829–40); and *MPG*, cxii–cxiii; *De thematibus*, new ed. A. Pertusi, *Costantino Porfirogenito De thematibus* (Vatican, 1952); *De administrando imperio*, ed. (with English transl.) Gy. Moravcsik and R. J. H. Jenkins, 2 vols. (Budapest, 1949, and London, 1962). [*DAI*.]

Corpus scriptorum christianorum orientalium, ed. J. B. Chabot and others (Paris, Rome, etc., 1903 ff.). [*CSCO*.]

Corpus scriptorum ecclesiasticorum latinorum (Vienna, 1866 ff., in progress). [*CSEL*.]

Corpus scriptorum historiae Byzantinae (Bonn, 1828–97). [*CSHB*.]

Dimitrievsky, A., *Opisanie liturgičeskich rukopisej, chranjaščichsja v bibliotekach pravoslavnago vostoka* [*The liturgical manuscripts in the libraries of the Orthodox East*]. I: *Typica*, pt. I (Kiev, 1895); II: *Euchologia* (Kiev, 1901); III: *Typica*, pt. II (St Petersburg, 1917).

Dölger, F., *Aus den Schatzkammern des heiligen Berges*, 2 vols. (Munich, 1948).

Dölger, F., *Regesten der Kaiserurkunden des oströmischen Reiches* (*Corpus der griechischen Urkunden des Mittelalters und der neueren Zeit*, Reihe A, Abt. I), pt. I: 565–1025; II: 1025–1204; III: 1204–1282; IV: 1282–1341 (Munich–Berlin, 1924–60; in progress). [*DR*.]

Ehrhard, A., *Überlieferung und Bestand der hagiographischen und homiletischen Literatur der griechischen Kirche von den Anfängen bis zum Ende des 16. Jh.* (Texte und Untersuchungen zur Geschichte der altchristlichen Literatur, 50–2), 3 vols. (Leipzig, 1937–52).

Eparch, Book of the, ed. J. Nicole, Λέοντος τοῦ Σοφοῦ τὸ ἐπαρχικὸν βιβλίον (Geneva, 1893); reprinted in Zepos, *Jus graeco-romanum*, II; French transl. J. Nicole (Geneva, 1894); English transl. E. H. Freshfield, *Roman Law in the Later Roman Empire* (Cambridge, 1938), and A. E. R. Boak, *J. Econ. Business History*, I (1929), 600–19.

Fejér, G., *Codex diplomaticus Hungariae ecclesiasticus ac civilis* (chronological table by F. Knauz, index by M. Czinár), 45 vols. (Budapest, 1829–66).

Fonti per la storia d'Italia. Publ. Istituto storico italiano (Genoa, Leghorn and Rome, 1887 ff., in progress). [*Fonti*.]

Gedeon, M. J., Πατριαρχικοὶ Πίνακες (Constantinople, 1890).

Goar, J., *Euchologion sive rituale graecorum complectens ritus et ordines divinae liturgiae, officiorum, sacramentorum* (Paris, 1647).

Graevius, J. G. and Burmannus, P., *Thesaurus antiquitatum et historiarum Italiae, Siciliae, Sardiniae, Corsicae, etc.*, 45 vols. (Leiden, 1704–25).

Grumel, V., *Les Regestes des Actes du Patriarcat de Constantinople*, I: *Les Actes des Patriarches*, I: 381–715; II: 715–1043; III: 1043–1206 (Socii Assumptionistae Chalcedonenses, 1932, 1936, 1947). [In progress.] [*GR*.]

Haller, J., *Die Quellen zur Gesch. der Entstehung des Kirchenstaates* (Leipzig and Berlin, 1907). (In *Quellensammlung zur deutschen Geschichte*, ed. E. Brandenburger and G. Seeliger.)

Hergenröther, J., *Monumenta graeca ad Photium eiusque historiam pertinentia* (Regensburg, 1869).

Historiae patriae monumenta, see *Monumenta historiae patriae.*

Hopf, C., *Chroniques gréco-romanes inédites ou peu connues* (Berlin, 1873).

Jaffé, P., *Regesta Pontificum Romanorum ab condita ecclesia ad annum post Christum natum 1198* (Berlin, 1851); 2nd ed. W. Wattenbach, S. Loewenfeld, F. Kaltenbrunner and P. Ewald (Leipzig, 1885–8), 2 vols. [Jaffé.]

Justinian, *Codex Justinianus*, ed. P. Krueger (Berlin, 1877); also ed. P. Krueger in *Corpus juris civilis*, II; 9th ed. (Berlin, 1915).

Justinian, *Novellae*, ed. K. E. Zachariae von Lingenthal, 2 pts. and appendix (Leipzig, 1881–4); ed. R. Schoell and W. Kroll, in *Corpus juris civilis*, III; 4th ed. (Berlin, 1912).

Kehr, P. F., *Regesta Pontificum Romanorum. Italia Pontificia*, ed. P. F. Kehr, vol. I: *Rome*; II: *Latium*; III: *Etruria*; IV: *Umbria, etc.*; V: *Aemilia*; VI: *Liguria* (*Lombardy, Piedmont, Genoa*); VII: *Venetiae et Histria*; VIII: *Regnum Normannorum*; *Campania* (Berlin, 1906–35).

Le Quien, M., *Oriens Christianus*, 3 vols. (Paris, 1740).

Liber Censuum de l'église romaine, I, ed. P. Fabre and L. Duchesne (*EcfrAR*) (Paris, 1889–1910) (II in progress).

Liber Pontificalis, 3 vols. (Rome, 1724–55); ed. L. Duchesne, 2 vols. (*EcfrAR*) (Paris, 1884–92); ed. T. Mommsen, *Gesta Pontif. Romanorum*, I (to 715), *MGH* (1898).

Mai, A., ed., *Scriptorum veterum nova collectio*, 10 vols. (Rome, 1825–38).

Mai, A., ed., *Spicilegium romanum*, 10 vols. (Rome, 1839–44).

Mansi, J. D., *Sacrorum conciliorum nova et amplissima collectio*, 31 vols. (Florence and Venice, 1759–98); reprinted J. B. Martin and L. Petit, with continuation, vols. XXXII–L. (Paris, 1901 ff., in progress.) [Mansi.]

Migne, J. P., *Patrologiae cursus completus. Series graeco-latina*, 161 vols. in 166 (Paris, 1857–66). [*MPG.*] Indices, F. Cavallera (Paris, 1912). [This is the series containing Greek texts with Latin translations in parallel columns. The so-called *Series graeca* (81 vols. in 85, 1856–67) contains the Latin translations only.]

Migne, J. P., *Patrologiae cursus completus. Series latina*, 221 vols. (Paris, 1844–55). Index, 4 vols. (1862–4). [*MPL.*]

Miklosich, F. and Müller, J., *Acta et diplomata graeca medii aevi sacra et profana*, 6 vols. (Vienna, 1860–90). [MM.]

I, II. *Acta patriarchatus Constantinopolitani*, 2 vols. (1860, 1862).

III. *Acta et diplomata res graecas italasque illustrantia* (1865).

IV–VI. *Acta et diplomata monasteriorum et ecclesiarum*, 3 vols. (1870–90).

Mirbt, C., *Quellen zur Geschichte des Papsttums und des römischen Katholizismus*, 4th ed. (Tübingen, 1924).

Monumenta Germaniae historica, ed. G. H. Pertz, T. Mommsen and others (Hanover, 1826 ff.); new eds. in progress (Hanover and Berlin). [*MGH.*] [For a full list of this series to 1960 see *Repertorium Fontium Historiae Medii Aevi*, above, I; details to 1936 may be found in *CMH*, V and VIII, Gen. Bibl. IV.]

Monumenta historiae patriae, 19 vols. fol.; 2 vols. 4o (Turin, 1836 ff.). [*MHP.*]

Monumenta Hungariae historica (published by the Hungarian Academy). In four series, I: *Diplomataria*; II: *Scriptores*; III: *Monumenta comitialia*; IV: *Acta extera* (Budapest, 1857 ff.).

Monumenta musicae Byzantinae, ed. C. Höeg, H. J. W. Tillyard and E. Wellesz (Copenhagen, etc., 1935 ff.). [See bibliography to chapter XXIV.]

Monumenta spectantia historiam Slavorum meridionalium (Zagreb, 1868 ff.). [*MHSM.*]

Müller, C., *Fragmenta historicorum graecorum*, 5 vols. (Paris, 1841–83). [*FHG.*]

Muratori, L. A., *Rerum Italicarum scriptores*, 25 vols. (Milan, 1723–51). Supplements: J. M. Tartini, 2 vols. (Florence, 1748–70); and J. B. Mittarelli (Venice, 1771); and M. Amari, *Biblioteca arabo-sicula*, Italian transl. and Appendix (Turin, Rome, etc., 1880–1, 1889). *Indices chronolog.* (Turin, 1885). New enlarged ed. with the chronicles printed as separate parts by G. Carducci and others (Città di Castello and Bologna, 1900 ff., in progress). [*RISS.*]

Muratori, L. A., *Antiquitates italicae medii aevi*, 6 vols. (Milan, 1738–42). *Indices chronolog.* (Turin, 1885).

Nova Patrum Bibliotheca, vols. I–VII, ed. A. Mai (Rome, 1852–7); vols. VIII–X, ed. J. Cozza-Luzi (1871–1905).

Pauler, G. and Szilágyi, S., *A Magyar honfoglalás kútfői [Sources for the occupation of Hungary by the Magyars]* (Pest, 1900).

Pitra, J. B., *Juris ecclesiastici Graecorum historia et monumenta*, 2 vols. (Rome, 1864–8).

Pitra, J. B., *Analecta sacra et classica spicilegio Solesmensi parata*, 8 vols. (Paris, 1876–88).

Potthast, A., *Regesta Pontificum Romanorum inde ab anno 1198 ad annum 1304*, 2 vols. (Berlin, 1874–5). [*PR.*]

Prefect, Book of the, see above *Eparch, Book of the*.

Prochiron, ed. K. E. Zachariae von Lingenthal, Ὁ Πρόχειρος Νόμος. *Imperatorum Basilii, Constantini, et Leonis Prochiron, etc.* (Heidelberg, 1837); re-edited F. Brandileone (*Fonti*, 1895); Zepos, J. and P., *Jus graeco-romanum*, II (1931).

Recueil des historiens des croisades. AcadIBL (Paris, 1841 ff.). [*Rec.Hist.Cr.*]
    Documents arméniens, 2 vols. (1869, 1906).
    Historiens grecs, 2 vols. (1875, 1881).
    Historiens occidentaux, 5 vols. (1844–95).
    Historiens orientaux, 5 vols. (1872–1906).
    Lois, 2 vols. (1841, 1843).

Regesta chartarum Italiae, publ. by K. preuss. hist. Instit. and Istituto storico italiano (Rome, 1907 ff., in progress).

Rhalles, G. A. and Potles, M., Σύνταγμα τῶν θείων καὶ ἱερῶν κανόνων κτλ., 6 vols. (Athens, 1852–9). [*RP.*]

Sathas, K. N., Μεσαιωνικὴ βιβλιοθήκη. *Bibliotheca graeca medii aevi*, 7 vols. (Venice and Paris, 1872–94).

Sathas, K. N., Μνημεῖα Ἑλληνικῆς ἱστορίας. *Documents inédits relatifs à l'histoire de la Grèce au moyen âge*, 9 vols. (Paris, 1880–90).

Scriptores rerum Germanicarum in usum scholarum, see above, *Monumenta Germaniae Historica*. [*SGUS.*]

Scriptores rerum Hungaricarum tempore ducum regumque stirpis Arpadianae gestarum, ed. E. Szentpétery, I–II (Budapest, 1937). [*SRH.*]

Soloviev, A. and Mošin, V., *Grčke povelje srpskih vladara [Greek documents of the Serbian rulers]* (Belgrade, 1936).

Stritter, J. G., *Memoriae populorum olim ad Danubium, Pontum Euxinum, Paludem Maeotidem, Caucasum, Mare Caspium, et inde magis ad septentriones incolentium, e scriptoribus historiae Byzantinae erutae et digestae*, 4 vols. (St Petersburg, 1771–9).

Tafel, G. L. F. and Thomas, G. M., *Urkunden zur älteren Handels- und Staatsgeschichte der Republik Venedig*, pts. I–III (*Fontes Rerum Austriacarum*, Abt. II, vols. XII–XIV) (Vienna, 1856–7).

Thallóczy, L. de, Jireček, C. J. and Sufflay, E. de, *Acta et diplomata res Albaniae mediae aetatis illustrantia*, 2 vols. (Vienna, 1913–18).

Theiner, A., *Codex diplomaticus dominii temporalis S. Sedis*, 3 vols. (Rome, 1861–2).

Thiriet, F., *Régestes des délibérations du Sénat de Venise concernant la Romanie*, I–III (Paris, 1958–61).

Trinchera, F., *Syllabus Graecarum membranarum* (Naples, 1865).

Troya, C., *Codice diplomatico Longobardo dal 568 al 774* (Storia d'Italia del Medio-Evo, vol. IV, pts. 1–5), 5 vols. and index (Naples, 1852–9).

Ughelli, F., *Italia sacra*; 2nd ed. N. Coleti, 10 vols. (Venice, 1717–22).

Watterich, J. M., *Pontificum Romanorum qui fuerunt inde ab exeunte saeculo IX usque ad finem saeculi XII vitae*, 2 vols. (Leipzig, 1862).

Zachariae von Lingenthal, K. E., ᾿Ανέκδοτα (Leipzig, 1843).

   A. *Breviarium Novellarum Theodori Hermopolitani.*

   B. *Regulae Institutionum.*

   C. *Codicis per Stephanum graece conversi fragmenta.*

   D. *Fragmenta Epitomae graecae Novellarum ab Anonymo confectae.*

   E. *Edicta Praefectorum Praetorio.*

Zachariae von Lingenthal, K. E., *Collectio librorum juris graeco-romani ineditorum*. Ecloga Leonis et Constantini. Epanagoge Basilii, Leonis, et Alexandri (Leipzig, 1852). [Continued in *Jus graeco-romanum* below.]

Zachariae von Lingenthal, K. E., *Jus graeco-romanum*, 7 vols. (Leipzig, 1856–84).

   I. *Practica ex actis Eustathii Romani (= Pira).*

   II. *Synopsis minor; Ecloga.*

   III. *Novellae constitutiones Imperatorum post Justinianum.*

   IV. *Ecloga privata aucta; Ecloga ad Prochiron mutata; Epanagoge aucta.*

   V. *Synopsis maior.*

   VI. *Prochiron auctum.*

   VII. *Epitome legum.*

Zepos, J. and P., *Jus graeco-romanum*, 8 vols. (Athens, 1931). [Contains reprints of works edited by Zachariae von Lingenthal, Heimbach and others.]

   I. *Novellae Imperatorum post Justinianum*, ed. Zachariae and including some constitutions published elsewhere.

   II. *Ecloga*, ed. Zachariae; *Leges rusticae, militares, navales*, ed. Ashburner; *Prochiron, Epanagoge*, ed. Zachariae; *Eparchikon Leonis*, ed. Nicole.

   III. *Paraphrasis Theophili*, ed. Ferrini; *Rhopae*, ed. Zachariae; *Tract. de peculiis, Tract. de actionibus*, ed. Heimbach.

   IV. *Pira, Epitome*, ed. Zachariae.

   V. *Synopsis maior*, ed. Zachariae.

   VI. *Epanagoge aucta, Ecloga aucta, Ecloga ad Prochiron mutata, Synopsis minor*, ed. Zachariae.

   VII. *Prochiron auctum*, ed. Zachariae; *Meditatio de nudis pactis*, ed. Monnier and Platon; *Pselli synopsis*, ed. Bosquet; *Attaliatae Ponema*, ed. Zachariae; *Chomatiani Decisiones*, ed. Battandier.

   VIII. *Codices Moldaviae et Walachiae. Collectio consuetudinum.*

V. MODERN WORKS

Alexander, P. J., *The Patriarch Nicephorus of Constantinople: Ecclesiastical Policy and Image Worship in the Byzantine Empire* (Oxford, 1958).

Allen, W. E. D., *A History of the Georgian People* (London, 1932).

Amantos, K., Ἱστορία τοῦ Βυζαντινοῦ Κράτους, 2 vols. (Athens, 1939–47).

Amari, M., *Storia dei Musulmani di Sicilia*, 3 vols., 2nd ed. C. A. Nallino (Catania, 1933–9).

Ammann, A. M., *Abriss der ostslawischen Kirchengeschichte* (Vienna, 1950).

Arnold, T. W., *The Caliphate* (Oxford, 1924).

Atiya, A. S., *The Crusade in the Later Middle Ages* (London, 1938).

Atiya, A. S., *The Crusade of Nicopolis* (London, 1934).

Attwater, D., *The Christian Churches of the East*, 2 vols. (Milwaukee, 1948); new ed. (London, 1961).

Bank, A. V., *Iskusstvo Vizantii v sobranii gosudarstvennogo Ermitaža* [*Byzantine Art in the Hermitage Museum*] (Leningrad, 1960).

Baronius, C., *Annales Ecclesiastici una cum critica historico-chronologica P. A. Pagii, contin. O. Raynaldus*; ed. J. D. Mansi, 34 vols. (Lucca, 1738–46); Apparatus, 1 vol., Index, 4 vols. (1740, 1757–9); new ed. (Bar-le-Duc, 1864–83).

Baynes, N. H., *The Byzantine Empire* (London, 1925; revised ed. 1943).

Baynes, N. H., *Byzantine Studies and Other Essays* (London, 1955).

Beck, H.-G., *Kirche und theologische Literatur im byzantinischen Reich* (Munich, 1959). [Beck.]

Bertolini, O., *Roma di fronte a Bizanzio e ai Longobardi* (Rome, 1941).

Bon, A., *Le Péloponnèse byzantin jusqu'en 1204* (Paris, 1951).

Bratianu, G. I., *Études byzantines d'histoire économique et sociale* (Paris, 1938).

Bréhier, L., *L'Église et l'Orient au moyen âge. Les croisades*, 5th ed. (Paris, 1928).

Bréhier, L., *Le monde byzantin*, I: *Vie et mort de Byzance*; II: *Les institutions de l'empire byzantin*; III: *La civilisation byzantine* (Paris, 1947–50).

Bréhier, L., *La querelle des images (VIIIe–IXe siècles)* (Paris, 1904).

Bréhier, L., *Le schisme oriental du XIe siècle* (Paris, 1899).

Brockelmann, C., *Geschichte der arabischen Litteratur*, 2 vols. (Weimar and Berlin, 1898–1902).

Bryce, J., *The Holy Roman Empire*, enlarged ed. (London, 1907).

Bulgakov, S., *The Orthodox Church* (London, 1935).

Bury, J. B., *The Constitution of the Later Roman Empire* (Creighton Memorial Lecture) (Cambridge, 1910); reprinted in *Selected Essays* [see below].

Bury, J. B., *History of the Eastern Roman Empire from the Fall of Irene to the Accession of Basil I (802–867)* (London, 1912).

Bury, J. B., *History of the Later Roman Empire from Arcadius to Irene (395–800)*, 2 vols. (London, 1889); new ed. [395–565], 2 vols. (London, 1923).

Bury, J. B., *The Imperial Administrative System in the Ninth Century*. With revised text of the Kletorologion of Philotheos (British Academy. Supplemental papers, I) (London, 1911).

Bury, J. B., *Selected Essays of J. B. Bury*, ed. H. Temperley (Cambridge, 1930).

Bussell, F. W., *The Roman Empire: Essays on the Constitutional History... (81 A.D. to 1081 A.D.)*, 2 vols. (London, 1910).

Byzantium, ed. N. H. Baynes and H. St L. B. Moss (Oxford, 1948).

Caetani, L. C. (Duca di Sermoneta), *Annali dell'Islam*, 10 vols. in 12 (Milan, 1905–26).

Cahen, C., *La Syrie du nord à l'époque des croisades* (Paris, 1940).

Caspar, E., *Geschichte des Papsttums von den Anfängen bis zur Höhe der Weltherrschaft*, 2 vols. (Tübingen, 1930–3).

Cessi, R., *Storia della Repubblica di Venezia*, 2 vols. (Milan, 1944–6).

Chalandon, F., *Histoire de la domination normande en Italie et en Sicilie*, 2 vols. (Paris, 1907).

Chalandon, F., *Les Comnènes. Etudes sur l'empire byzantin aux XIe et XIIe siècles*, I: *Essai sur le règne d'Alexis Comnène (1081–1118)*; II: *Jean II Comnène (1118–1143) et Manuel I Comnène (1143–1180)* (Paris, 1900–13).

Chapman, C., *Michel Paléologue, restaurateur de l'empire byzantin* (Paris, 1926).

Charanis, P., 'The Monastic Properties and the State in the Byzantine Empire', *DOP*, IV (1948), 51–119.

Dalton, O. M., *Byzantine Art and Archaeology* (Oxford, 1911).

Dalton, O. M., *East Christian Art* (Oxford, 1925).

Demus, O., *Byzantine Mosaic Decoration* (London, 1948).

Dennis, G. T., *The Reign of Manuel II Palaeologus in Thessalonica, 1382–1387 (OCA, 159)* (Rome, 1960).

Der Nersessian, S., *Armenia and the Byzantine Empire* (Cambridge, Mass., 1945).

Diehl, C., *Byzance: grandeur et décadence* (Paris, 1919); English transl. by N. Walford, ed. P. Charanis, *Byzantium: Greatness and Decline* (New Brunswick, 1957).

Diehl, C., *Etudes byzantines* (Paris, 1905).

Diehl, C., *Figures byzantines*, 2 series (Paris, 1906–8, and later editions); English transl. by H. Bell, *Byzantine Portraits* (New York, 1927).

Diehl, C., *Histoire de l'empire byzantin* (Paris, 1930).

Diehl, C., *Manuel d'art byzantin* (Paris, 1910); 2nd ed. (Paris, 1925–6).

Diehl, C., *Les grands problèmes de l'histoire byzantine* (Paris, 1943).

Diehl, C. and Marçais, G., *Le monde oriental de 395 à 1081*, 2nd ed. (Paris, 1944).

Diehl, C., Guilland, R., Oeconomos, L. and Grousset, R., *L'Europe orientale de 1081 à 1453* (Paris, 1945).

Dölger, F., *Beiträge zur Geschichte der byzantinischen Finanzverwaltung besonders des 10. und 11. Jahrhunderts (BA, IX)* (Leipzig–Berlin, 1927); reprinted (Hildesheim, 1960, with addenda and corrigenda).

Dölger, F., *Byzanz und die europäische Staatenwelt* (Ettal, 1953).

Dölger, F., *Byzantinische Diplomatik* (Ettal, 1956).

Dölger, F., ΠΑΡΑΣΠΟΡΑ: *30 Aufsätze zur Geschichte, Kultur und Sprache des byzantinischen Reiches* (Ettal, 1961).

Du Cange, C. du Fresne, *Histoire de l'empire de Constantinople sous les emporours françois* (Paris, 1657); ed. J. A. Buchon, 2 vols. (Paris, 1826).

Du Cange, C. du Fresne, *Historia Byzantina duplici commentario illustrata*, 3 pts. (Paris, 1680).

Dvornik, F., *The Photian Schism* (Cambridge, 1948).

Dvornik, F., *Les Slaves, Byzance et Rome au IXe siècle* (Paris, 1926).

Dvornik, F., *The Making of Central and Eastern Europe* (London, 1949).

Ebersolt, J., *Orient et Occident. Recherches sur les influences byzantines et orientales en France avant et pendant les croisades*, 2nd ed. (Paris, 1954).

Every, G., *The Byzantine Patriarchate (451–1204)* (London, 1948); 2nd ed. (London, 1962).

Fallmerayer, J. P., *Geschichte des Kaiserthums von Trapezunt* (Munich, 1827).

Faris, Nabih Amin (ed.), *The Arab Heritage* (Princeton, 1946).

Finlay, G., *History of Greece*, B.C. *146 to* A.D. *1864*, ed. H. F. Tozer, 7 vols. (Oxford, 1877).

Fleury, Claude, *Histoire ecclésiastique*, 20 vols. (Paris, 1691–1720). [Continued to end of eighteenth century under O. Vidal. Many editions. (Orig. ed. to 1414). 4 additional vols. by Fleury to 1517, publ. Paris, 1836–7.]

Fliche, A. and Martin, V. (ed.), *Histoire de l'Eglise* (Paris, 1934 ff., in progress).

Fortescue, A. K., *The Orthodox Eastern Church* (London, 1927).

French, R. M., *The Eastern Orthodox Church* (London, 1951).

Gardner, A., *The Lascarids of Nicaea* (London, 1912).

Gaudefroy-Demombynes, M. and Platonov, S. F., *Le monde musulman et byzantin jusqu'aux croisades*, in E. Cavaignac, *Histoire du Monde*, VII, 1 (Paris, 1931).

Gay, J., *L'Italie méridionale et l'empire byzantin (867–1071)* (*EcfrAR*) (Paris, 1904).

Geanakoplos, D. J., *Emperor Michael Palaeologus and the West 1258–1282: a Study in Byzantine–Latin Relations* (Cambridge, Mass., 1959).

Gelzer, H., *Abriss der byzantinischen Kaisergeschichte*. In Krumbacher, K., *Geschichte d. byzant. Litteratur* [see below].

Gelzer, H., *Byzantinische Kulturgeschichte* (Tübingen, 1909).

Gelzer, H., *Ausgewählte kleine Schriften* (Leipzig, 1907).

Gerland, E., *Geschichte des lateinischen Kaiserreiches von Konstantinopel* (*Geschichte der Frankenherrschaft in Griechenland*, II, 1) (Homburg v.d. Höhe, 1905).

Gfrörer, A. F., *Byzantinische Geschichten*, ed. J. B. Weiss, 3 vols. (Graz, 1872–7).

Gibbon, E., *The History of the Decline and Fall of the Roman Empire* (London, 1776–81); ed. in 7 vols. by J. B. Bury (London, 1896–1900), and other editions. [Bury's notes essential, especially for bibliography.]

Gibbons, H. A., *The Foundation of the Ottoman Empire* (Oxford, 1916).

Gill, J., *The Council of Florence* (Cambridge, 1959).

Golubinsky, E. E., *Kratkij očerk istorii pravoslavnich cerkvi bolgarskij, serbskoj i ruminckoj ili moldo-valašskoj*. [*Short outline of the history of the Orthodox Churches of Bulgaria, Serbia and Rumania or Moldavia*] (Moscow, 1871).

Golubinsky, E. E., *Istorija russkoj cerkvi* [*History of the Russian Church*], 2 vols. in 4 (Moscow, 1900–11).

Goubert, P., *Byzance avant l'Islam*, I, II (1) (Paris, 1951, 1956).

Grabar, A., *L'empereur dans l'art byzantin. Recherches sur l'art officiel de l'Empire de l'Orient* (Paris, 1936).

Gregorovius, F., *Geschichte der Stadt Athen im Mittelalter*, 2 vols. (Stuttgart, 1889); Greek transl. with additions by S. P. Lampros, 3 vols. (Athens, 1904–6).

Gregorovius, F., *Geschichte der Stadt Rom im Mittelalter*, 8 vols. (Stuttgart, 1859–72). [Translated from 4th ed. by Mrs A. Hamilton (London, 1894–1902), 8 vols. in 13.]

Grousset, R., *L'empire du Levant. Histoire de la Question d'Orient* (Paris, 1949).

Grousset, R., *Histoire des croisades et du Royaume Franc de Jérusalem*, 3 vols. (Paris, 1934–6).

Grunebaum, G. E. von, *Medieval Islam. A Study in Cultural Orientation*, 2nd ed. (Chicago, 1953).

Guilland, R., *Etudes byzantines* (Paris, 1959).

Guilland, R., 'Etudes sur l'histoire administrative de l'empire byzantin'. [These articles are widely scattered in periodicals and a bibliography from 1938 to 1957 will be found in *B*, xxv–xxvii (1955–7, published 1957), 695–6.]

Hackett, J., *History of the Orthodox Church of Cyprus* (London, 1901).

Hammer Purgstall, J. von, *Geschichte des osmanischen Reiches*, 2 vols. (Pest, 1827–35) [with bibliography]; French transl. J. J. Hellert, 18 vols. and atlas (Paris, 1835–43).

Hartmann, L. M., *Geschichte Italiens im Mittelalter*, i–iv (Gotha, 1897–1915).

Hartmann, L. M., *Untersuchungen zur Geschichte der byzantinischen Verwaltung in Italien (540–750)* (Leipzig, 1889).

Hefele, C. J., contin. J. A. G. Hergenröther, *Conciliengeschichte*, 9 vols. (Freiburg-i.-B., 1855 ff.); revised in French transl. by H. Leclercq and others, *Histoire des Conciles* (Paris, 1907 ff.).

Hertzberg, G. F., *Geschichte der Byzantiner und des osmanischen Reiches bis gegen Ende des XVI^{en} Jahrhunderts* (Berlin, 1883). (Allgemeine Geschichte in Einzeldarstellungen.)

Hertzberg, G. F., *Geschichte Griechenlands seit dem Absterben des antiken Lebens bis zum Gegenwart*, 4 vols. (Gotha, 1876–9). (Geschichte der europäischen Staaten.)

Heyd, W., *Geschichte des Levantehandels im Mittelalter* (Stuttgart, 1879); French transl. F. Raynaud, *Histoire du commerce du Levant au moyen âge*, 2nd ed. (Leipzig, 1923); reprinted (1936).

Hill, Sir George, *A History of Cyprus*, vols. i–iii (Cambridge, 1940–8).

Hirsch, F., *Byzantinische Studien* (Leipzig, 1876).

Hitti, P. K., *History of the Arabs from the Earliest Times to the Present*, 6th ed. (London, 1956).

Hodgkin, T., *Italy and Her Invaders*, 8 vols. (Oxford, 1880–99), vols. vi (2nd ed. 1916) to viii.

Holl, K., *Gesammelte Aufsätze zur Kirchengeschichte. II. Der Osten* (Tübingen, 1928).

Honigmann, E., *Die Ostgrenze des byzantinischen Reiches von 363 bis 1071 nach griechischen, arabischen, syrischen und armenischen Quellen* (*Corpus Bruxellense Hist. Byz.* iii) (Brussels, 1935).

Hopf, K., *Geschichte Griechenlands vom Beginn des Mittelalters bis auf unsere Zeit* (Ersch–Gruber, vols. lxxxv and lxxxvi) (Leipzig, 1867, 1868).

Hussey, J. M., *Church and Learning in the Byzantine Empire 867–1185* (London, 1937).

Hussey, J. M., *The Byzantine World*, 2nd ed. (London, 1961).

Il Monachesimo Orientale: Atti del convegno di studi orientali che sul predetto tema si tenne a Roma, sotto la direzione del Pontifico Istituto Orientale, nei giorni 9–12 Aprile 1958. [*OCA*, 153.] (Rome, 1958.)

Jireček, C. J., *Geschichte der Bulgaren* (Prague, 1876).

Jireček, C. J., *Geschichte der Serben*, i, ii (all publ.) (Gotha, 1911–18).

Joannou, P., *Christliche Metaphysik in Byzanz. I. Die Illuminationslehre des Michael Psellos und Joannes Italos* (*Subsidia patristica et byzantina*, iii) (Ettal, 1956).

Jorga, N., *Brève histoire de la petite Arménie: l'Arménie cilicienne* (Paris, 1930).

Jorga, N., *Geschichte des osmanischen Reiches*, i–ii (Gotha, 1908–9).

Jorga, N., *Geschichte des rumänischen Volkes*, 2 vols. (Gotha, 1905).

Jorga, N., *Histoire de la vie byzantine. Empire et civilisation*, 3 vols. (Bucharest, 1934).

Jorga, N., *Histoire des Roumains et de la Romanité orientale*, I–IV in 5 vols. (Bucharest, 1937).

Jugie, M., *Le schisme byzantin. Aperçu historique et doctrinal* (Paris, 1941). [Cf. A. Michel's review in *BZ*, XLV (1952), 408–17, with important additions.]

Jugie, M., *Theologia dogmatica Christianorum orientalium ab ecclesia catholica dissidentium*, 5 vols. (Paris, 1926–35).

Kidd, B. J., *The Churches of Eastern Christendom* (London, 1927).

Köhler, G., *Die Entwicklung des Kriegswesen und der Kriegsführung in der Ritterzeit von der Mitte des 11. Jahrhunderts bis zu den Hussitenkriegen*, 3 vols. (Breslau, 1886–90).

Kondakoff (Kondakov), N. P., *Histoire de l'art byzantin*, French transl. F. Trawinski, 2 vols. (Paris, 1886–91).

Kornemann, E., *Doppelprinzipat und Reichsteilung in Imperium Romanum* (Leipzig and Berlin, 1930).

Kovačević, J., *Srednjovekovna nošnja balkanskich Slovena. Studija iz istorije srednjovekovne kulture Balkana* [*The Medieval Dress of the Balkan Slavs. A Study in the History of Medieval Culture in the Balkans*] (Belgrade, 1953).

Krekić, B., *Dubrovnik (Raguse) et le Levant au moyen-âge* (Paris, 1961).

Kretschmayr, H., *Geschichte von Venedig*, I–II (Gotha, 1905–20).

Krumbacher, K., *Geschichte der byzantinischen Litteratur (527–1453)*, 2nd ed. (*Handbuch d. klass. Altertums-Wissenschaft*, ed. I. von Müller, vol. IX, i) (Munich, 1897). [*GBL.*]

Kukules, Ph., Βυζαντινῶν Βίος καὶ Πολιτισμός, I–VI and supplts. in 8 vols. (Athens, 1947–57).

Kulakovsky, J., *Istorija Vizantii* [*History of Byzantium*], I–III (Kiev, 1913, 1912, 1915).

Lamma, P., *Comneni e Staufer: ricerche sui rapporti fra Bizanzio e l'Occidente nel secolo XII*, 2 vols. (Rome, 1955–7).

Lampros (Lambros), S. P., Ἱστορία τῆς Ἑλλάδος, I–VI (Athens, 1886–1908).

Lebeau, C., *Histoire du Bas-Empire*, ed. J. A. Saint-Martin and M. F. Brosset, 21 vols. (Paris, 1824–36).

Leib, B., *Rome, Kiev et Byzance à la fin du XIe siècle* (Paris, 1924).

Lemerle, P., *Philippes et la Macédoine orientale à l'époque chrétienne et byzantine* (*EcfrAR*, 158) (Paris, 1945).

Lemerle, P., 'Esquisse pour une histoire agraire de Byzance: les sources et les problèmes', *RH*, CCXIX (1958), 32–74, 254–84; CCXX (1958), 42–94.

Levčenko, M. V., *Istorija Vizantii* [*History of Byzantium*] (Moscow, Leningrad, 1940); French transl. *Byzance des origines à 1453* (Paris, 1949).

Lewis, B., *The Arabs in History*, 5th ed. (London, 1960).

Lombard, A., *Constantin V, empereur des Romains* (Paris, 1902).

Longnon, J., *L'empire latin de Constantinople et la principauté de Morée* (Paris, 1949).

Lot, F., *La fin du monde antique et le début du moyen âge* (Paris, 1927).

Lot, F., *L'art militaire et les armées au moyen âge en Europe et dans le Proche Orient*, 2 vols. (Paris, 1946).

Marquart, J., *Osteuropäische und ostasiatische Streifzüge* (Leipzig, 1903).

Martin, E. J., *History of the Iconoclastic Controversy* (London, n.d. [1930]).

Mathew, G., *Byzantine Aesthetics* (London, 1963).

Meliarakes, A., Ἱστορία τοῦ Βασιλείου τῆς Νικαίας καὶ τοῦ Δεσποτάτου τῆς Ἠπείρου *(1204–61)* (Athens, 1898).

Michel, A., *Die Kaisermacht in der Ostkirche (843–1204)* (Darmstadt, 1959). [A reprint of articles in *Ostkirch. Studien*, ɪɪ–ᴠ (1953–6).]

Miller, W., *Essays on the Latin Orient* (Cambridge, 1921).

Miller, W., *The Latins in the Levant: A History of Frankish Greece (1204–1566)* (London, 1908); enlarged Greek transl. Lampros (Lambros), S. P., Ἱστορία τῆς Φραγκοκρατίας ἐν Ἑλλάδι (Athens, 1909–10).

Miller, W., *Trebizond: the Last Greek Empire* (London, 1926).

Mosheim, J. L. von, *Institutionum historiae ecclesiasticae antiquae et recentioris libri* ɪᴠ, 4 vols. (Helmstedt, 1755); transl. J. Murdock, ed. H. Soames, 4 vols. (London, 1841); 2nd rev. ed. (1850).

Moss, H. St L. B., *The Birth of the Middle Ages, 395–814* (Oxford, 1935).

Muir, W., *The Caliphate: its Rise, Decline, and Fall*, revised ed. T. H. Weir (Edinburgh, 1924).

Muratori, L. A., *Annali d'Italia*, 12 vols. (Milan, 1744–9). [Also other editions and reprints.]

Mutafčiev, P., *Istorija na bŭlgarskija narod [History of the Bulgarian Nation]*, 2 vols., 3rd ed. (Sofia, 1948).

Neale, J. M., *History of the Holy Eastern Church*, pt. ɪ: *General Introduction*, 2 vols. (London, 1850).

Neumann, C., *Die Weltstellung des byzantinischen Reiches vor den Kreuzzügen* (Leipzig, 1894); French transl. Renauld and Kozlowski (Paris, 1905); and in *ROC*, x (1903–4), 56–171.

Nicol, D. M., *The Despotate of Epiros* (Oxford, 1957).

Niederle, L., *Manuel de l'antiquité slave*, ɪ: *L'histoire*; ɪɪ: *La civilisation* (Paris, 1923, 1926).

Norden, W., *Das Papsttum und Byzanz: die Trennung der beiden Mächte und das Problem ihrer Wiedervereinigung bis zum Untergange des byzantinischen Reichs (1453)* (Berlin, 1903); reprinted (1958).

Obolensky, D., *The Bogomils: a Study in Balkan Neomanichaeism* (Cambridge, 1948).

Ohnsorge, W., *Das Zweikaiserproblem im früheren Mittelalter* (Hildesheim, 1947).

Ohnsorge, W., *Abendland und Byzanz: Gesammelte Aufsätze zur Geschichte der byzantinisch-abendländischen Beziehungen und des Kaisertums* (Darmstadt, 1958).

Oman, C. W. C., *History of the Art of War in the Middle Ages* (London, 1898); 2nd ed., 2 vols. (London, 1924).

Ostrogorsky, G., *Studien zur Geschichte des byzantinischen Bilderstreites* (Breslau, 1929).

Ostrogorsky, G., 'Agrarian Conditions in the Byzantine Empire in the Middle Ages', *Cambridge Economic History of Europe*, ɪ (1942), 194–223, 579–83.

Ostrogorsky, G., *Pour l'histoire de la féodalité byzantine (Corpus Bruxellense Hist. Byz.*, Subsidia ɪ, Brussels, 1954).

Ostrogorsky, G., *Quelques problèmes d'histoire de la paysannerie byzantine (Corpus Bruxellense Hist. Byz.*, Subsidia ɪɪ, Brussels, 1956).

Ostrogorsky, G., *History of the Byzantine State* (Oxford, 1956).

Paparrhegopoulos, K., Ἱστορία τοῦ Ἑλληνικοῦ ἔθνους. 4th ed. P. Karolides, 5 vols. (Athens, 1903).

Pargoire, J., *L'église byzantine de 527 à 847* (Paris, 1905).

Pears, E., *The Destruction of the Greek Empire and the Story of the Capture of Constantinople by the Turks* (London, 1903).

Pears, E., *The Fall of Constantinople, being the Story of the Fourth Crusade* (London, 1885).

Pertile, A., *Storia del diritto italiano dalla caduta dell'impero Romano alla codificazione*, 2nd ed., 6 vols., P. Del Giudice (Turin, 1892–1902); Index, L. Eusebio (Turin, 1893).

Rambaud, A., *L'empire grec au dixième siècle: Constantin Porphyrogénète* (Paris, 1870).

Romano, G. and Solmi, A., *Le dominazioni barbariche in Italia (395–888)*, 3rd ed. (Milan, 1909).

Rouillard, G., *La vie rurale dans l'empire byzantin* (Paris, 1953).

Runciman, S., *The Emperor Romanus Lecapenus and his Reign. A Study of Tenth-Century Byzantium* (Cambridge, 1929).

Runciman, S., *A History of the First Bulgarian Empire* (London, 1930).

Runciman, S., *Byzantine Civilisation* (London, 1933).

Runciman, S., *A History of the Crusades*, 3 vols. (Cambridge, 1951–4).

Runciman, S., *The Eastern Schism: a Study of the Papacy and the Eastern Churches during the XIth and XIIth Centuries* (Oxford, 1955).

Runciman, S., *The Sicilian Vespers. A History of the Mediterranean World in the Late Thirteenth Century* (Cambridge, 1958).

Schaube, A., *Handelsgeschichte der romanischen Völker des Mittelmeergebiets bis zum Ende der Kreuzzüge* (Munich and Berlin, 1906).

Schenk, K., *Kaiser Leo III* (Halle, 1880).

Schlumberger, G., *Un empereur byzantin au Xe siècle: Nicéphore Phocas* (Paris, 1890).

Schlumberger, G., *L'épopée byzantine à la fin du Xe siècle.* I: *Jean Tzimiscès, Basile II (969–89)*; II: *Basile II (989–1025)*; III: *Les Porphyrogénètes, Zoé et Théodora (1025–57)* (Paris, 1896–1905).

Schupfer, F., *Manuale di storia del diritto italiano* (Città di Castello, 1904).

Schwarzlose, K., *Der Bilderstreit. Ein Kampf der griechischen Kirche um ihre Eigenart und um ihre Freiheit* (Gotha, 1890).

Setton, K. M. (editor-in-chief), *A History of the Crusades.* I: *The First Hundred Years*, ed. M. W. Baldwin; II: *The Later Crusades, 1189–1311*, ed. R. L. Wolff and H. W. Hazard (Philadelphia, 1955–62). [In progress.]

Setton, K. M., *Catalan Domination of Athens, 1311–1388* (Cambridge, Mass., 1948).

Šišić, F., *Geschichte der Kroaten* (Zagreb, 1917).

Skabalanovič, N., *Vizantijskoe gosudarstvo i cerkov' v XI v. [Byzantine State and Church in the Eleventh Century]* (St Petersburg, 1884).

Spinka, M., *A History of Christianity in the Balkans* (Chicago, 1933).

Stadtmüller, G., *Geschichte Südosteuropas* (Munich, 1950).

Stein, E., 'Untersuchungen zur spätbyzantinischen Verfassungs- und Wirtschaftsgeschichte', *Mitt. zur Osman. Gesch.* II (1923–5), 1–62; reprinted separately (Amsterdam, 1962).

Stein, E., *Geschichte des spätrömischen Reiches*, I: *Vom römischen zum byzantinischen Staate, 284–476* (Vienna, 1928); French ed. (Paris, 1959).

Stein, E., *Histoire du Bas-Empire*, II: *De la disparition de l'Empire d'Occident à la mort de Justinien, 476–565* (Paris, Brussels, Amsterdam, 1949).

Strzygowski, J., *Die Baukunst der Armenier und Europa*, 2 vols. (Vienna, 1919).

Tafrali, O., *Thessalonique au quatorzième siècle* (Paris, 1913).

Talbot Rice, D., *Byzantine Art* (Oxford, 1935); new ed. (London, 1954).

Talbot Rice, D., *The Beginnings of Christian Art* (London, 1957).

Talbot Rice, D., *The Art of Byzantium* (London, 1959).

Talbot Rice, D., *The Byzantines* (London, 1962).

Temperley, H. W. V., *History of Serbia* (London, 1917).

Thiriet, F., *La Romanie vénitienne au moyen âge. Le développement et l'exploitation du domaine colonial vénitien (XIIᵉ–XVᵉ siècles)* (*EcfrAR*, 193) (Paris, 1959).

Treitinger, O., *Die oströmische Kaiser- und Reichsidee nach ihrer Gestaltung im höfischen Zeremoniell* (Jena, 1938); reprinted (Darmstadt, 1956).

Uspensky, F. I., *Očerki po istorii vizantijskoj obrazovannosti* [*Studies in the History of Byzantine Civilisation*] (St Petersburg, 1891).

Uspensky, F. I., *Istorija vizantijskoj imperii* [*History of the Byzantine Empire*], I; II, 1; III (St Petersburg, 1913; Leningrad, 1927; Moscow, 1948).

Vasiliev, A. A., *History of the Byzantine Empire* (Madison, 1952).

Vasiliev, A. A., *Vizantija i Araby*, 2 vols. (St Petersburg, 1900–2) [the history from 813 with translation of passages from Arabic writers, but see now the French edition: *Byzance et les Arabes*, I: *La dynastie d'Amorium*, by H. Grégoire, M. Canard, etc. (Brussels, 1935); II: *La dynastie macédonienne*, by H. Grégoire and M. Canard, 2e partie: *Extraits des sources arabes*, by M. Canard (Brussels, 1950) covers the years 820–959, with translation of relevant passages from Arabic writers; the first part of vol. II has not yet appeared].

Vasilievsky, V. G., *Trudy* [*Works*], 4 vols. (St Petersburg and Leningrad, 1908–30).

Vinogradoff, P., *Roman Law in Mediaeval Europe* (London and New York, 1909).

Vogt, A., *Basile Iᵉʳ, empereur de Byzance et la civilisation byzantine à la fin du IXᵉ siècle* (Paris, 1908).

Weil, G., *Geschichte der Chalifen*, 3 vols. (Mannheim, 1846–51).

Weil, G., *Geschichte der islamitischen Völker von Mohammed bis zur Zeit des Sultans Selim* (Stuttgart, 1866).

Weitzmann, K., *Geistige Grundlagen und Wesen der Makedonischen Renaissance* (*Arbeitsgemeinschaft des Landes Nordrhein-Westfalen: Geisteswissenschaften*, Heft 107) (Cologne and Opladen, 1963).

Wellesz, E., *History of Byzantine Music and Hymnography*, 2nd ed. (Oxford, 1961).

Wittek, P., *The Rise of the Ottoman Empire* (*Royal Asiatic Soc. Monographs*, XXIII) (London, 1938).

Xénopol, A. D., *Histoire des Roumains de la Dacie Trajane… (513–1859)*, 2 vols. (Paris, 1896). [Abridged from the Rumanian edition.]

Xivrey, B. de, *Mémoire sur la vie et les ouvrages de l'empereur Manuel Paléologue* (Mém. de l'Inst. de France, *AcadIBL*, 19, 2) (Paris, 1853).

Zachariae von Lingenthal, K. E., *Geschichte des griechisch-römischen Rechts*, 3rd ed. (Berlin, 1892).

Zakythinos, D. A., *Le Despotat grec de Morée*, 2 vols. (Paris, 1932–53).

Zakythinos, D. A., *Crise monétaire et crise économique à Byzance du XIIIᵉ au XVᵉ siècle* (Athens, 1948).

Zernov, N., *Eastern Christendom: a Study of the Origin and Development of the Eastern Orthodox Church* (London, 1961).

Zlatarsky, V. N., *Istorija na bŭlgarskata dŭržava prez srednite vekove* [*History of the Bulgarian State in the Middle Ages*], 3 vols. (Sofia, 1918–40).

1054–1954. L'église et les églises, neuf siècles de douloureuse séparation entre l'orient et l'occident (Etudes et travaux offerts à Dom Lambert Beauduin), 2 vols. (Chevetogne, 1954–5).

Le Millénaire du Mont Athos 963–1963. Etudes et Mélanges, 2 vols. (Chevetogne and Venice, 1963–4).

CHAPTER XX. THE GOVERNMENT AND ADMINISTRATION OF THE BYZANTINE EMPIRE

See also the bibliographies for chapters I, III–V, XXI and XXIII

I. SOURCES

Basilicorum libri LX [see Gen. Bibl. IV].

Cecaumenus, *Strategicon. Cecaumeni strategicon et incerti scriptoris de officiis regiis libellus*, ed. B. Wassiliewsky and V. Jernstedt (St Petersburg, 1896); German transl. by H.-G. Beck (= *Byzantinische Geschichtsschreiber*, V, ed. E. von Ivánka) (Graz, 1956).

Codinus, George, Pseudo-, *De officiis*, ed. I. Bekker, *CSHB* (1839).

Constantine Porphyrogenitus, *De cerimoniis aulae byzantinae*; *De thematibus*; *De administrando imperio* [see Gen. Bibl. IV].

Dain, A., 'Memorandum inédit sur la défense des places', *REG*, LIII (1940), 123–36.

Dain, A., *L''Extrait Tactique' tiré de Léon VI* (Paris, 1942).

Dain, A. (ed.), *Sylloge Tacticorum quae olim 'Inedita Leonis Tactica' dicebantur* (Paris, 1938).

Dain, A., *Le Corpus Perditum* (Paris, 1939).

Dölger, F., *Regesten der Kaiserurkunden* [see Gen. Bibl. IV].

Eparch, Book of the ('Ἐπαρχικὸν βιβλίον) [see Gen. Bibl. IV].

Grumel, V., *Les regestes des actes du patriarcat* [see Gen. Bibl. IV].

    with French transl. (Bibliotheca Geographorum Arabicorum, VI) (Leyden, 1889), pp. 77 ff. [Translation and commentary by J. Barbier de Meynard, *JA*, sér. VI, vol. V (1865), 5 ff.]

Jus graeco-romanum, ed. K. E. Zachariae von Lingenthal [see Gen. Bibl. IV].

Jus graeco-romanum, ed. J. and P. Zepos [see Gen. Bibl. IV].

Justinian, *Codex, Novellae* [see Gen. Bibl. IV].

Khurdādbbih, ibn (Ibn Kordādbah), *Kitāb al Masālik* [Arab.], ed. M. J. Goeje

Kodāma (Qudāma), Kodāma ibn Dja'far, *Kitāb al Kharādj* (*Liber tributi*), ed. M. J. Goeje (Bibliotheca Geographorum Arabicorum, VI) (Leyden, 1889), pp. 197 ff.

Leo VI, *Novels*, ed. P. Noaille and A. Dain (Paris, 1944); also ed. H. Monnier (Bordeaux, 1923); and A. Spulber (Cernauţi, 1934).

Leo VI, *Problemata*, ed. A. Dain (Paris, 1935).

Leo VI, *Tactica*, *MPG*, CVII; ed. R. Vári, 2 vols. (Budapest, 1917 and 1922).

Liber de re militari (Incerti scriptoris Byzantini saeculi X), ed. R. Vári (Leipzig, 1901).

Liutprand of Cremona, *Relatio de legatione Constantinopolitana*, *SGUS*, 3rd ed. J. Becker (Hanover and Leipzig, 1915), pp. 175–212.

Maurice, Pseudo-, *Strategicon*, ed. J. Scheffer (Upsala, 1664).

'Naumachia' partim adhuc inedita in unum nunc primum congessit et indice auxit A. Dain (Paris, 1943).

Nicephorus Phocas, Pseudo-, Περὶ παραδρομῆς πολέμου (De velitatione bellica), ed. B. Hase, *CSHB* (with Leo Diaconus) (1828); also Y. A. Kulakovsky,

Στρατηγικὴ ἔκθεσις καὶ σύνταξις (Mém. Acad. Imp. de Pétersbourg), ser. 8, vol. VIII (1908).

Philotheos, *Kletorologion*, ed. J. B. Bury, *The Imperial Administrative System in the ninth century* (The British Academy Supplemental Papers, I) (London, 1911), pp. 131–79.

Schlumberger, G., *Sigillographie de l'empire byzantin* [see Gen. Bibl. III]. (For further bibliography on this subject see A. Pertusi, 'La formation des thèmes', cited below.)

Strategemata (Aetatis Byzantinae Tacticorum Collectio), ed. J.-A. de Foucault (Paris, 1949).

Tacticon Uspensky, F. Uspensky, 'Vizantijskaja tabel o rangach' ['Byzantine list of ranks'], *IRAIK*, III (1898), 98–137.

Tacticon Beneševič, V. N. Beneševič, 'Die byzantinischen Ranglisten nach dem *Kletorologion Philothei* und nach den Jerusalemer Handschriften', *BNJ*, V (1927), 97–167.

II. MODERN WORKS

Andréadès, A. M., 'The Economic Life of the Byzantine Empire', *Byzantium*, ed. N. H. Baynes and H. St L. B. Moss, pp. 51–70 [see Gen. Bibl. V].

Andréadès, A. M., 'La vénalité des offices est-elle d'origine byzantine?', *NRDF*, XLV (1921), 232–41.

Andréadès, A. M., 'Public Finances: Currency, Public Expenditure, Budget, Public Revenue', *Byzantium*, ed. N. H. Baynes and H. St L. B. Moss, pp. 71–85 [see Gen. Bibl. V].

Aussaresses, F., *L'armée byzantine à la fin du VIe siècle* (Paris, 1909).

Barker, E., *Social and Political Thought in Byzantium* [see Gen. Bibl. IV].

Baynes, N. H., *The Byzantine Empire* (London, 1926, and later reprints).

Baynes, N. H., 'The Emperor Heraclius and the Military Theme System', *EHR*, LXVII (1952), 380–1.

Boak, A. E. R., *The Master of the Offices in the Later Roman and Byzantine Empires* (Univ. of Michigan Studies, Humanistic Series, XIV) (New York, 1919).

Bréhier, L. and Batiffol, P., *Les survivances du culte impérial romain* (Paris, 1920).

Bréhier, L., *Le monde byzantin*, II [see Gen. Bibl. V].

Bréhier, L., 'Ἱερεὺς καὶ βασιλεύς', *Mémorial L. Petit, AOC*, I (1948), 41–5.

Bréhier, L., 'La marine de Byzance du VIIIe au XIe siècle', *B*, XIX (1949), 1–16.

Bréhier, L., 'L'investiture des patriarches de Constantinople au moyen âge', *Miscellanea G. Mercati*, III (Studi e Testi, 123) (Vatican, 1946), 368–72.

Brightman, F. E., 'Byzantine Imperial Coronations', *JTS*, II (1901), 319–92.

Brooks, F. W., 'Arabic Lists of the Byzantine Themes', *JHS*, XXI (1901), 67–77.

Bury, J. B., 'The Ceremonial Book of Constantine Pophyrogenitus', *EHR*, XXII (1907), 209–27, 417–39.

Bury, J. B., *The Constitution of the Later Roman Empire* (Cambridge, 1910); reprinted in *Selected Essays of J. B. Bury*, pp. 99–135 [see Gen. Bibl. V].

Bury, J. B., *The Imperial Administrative System in the Ninth Century* (The British Academy Supplemental Papers, I) (London, 1911).

Bury, J. B., 'The Naval Policy of the Roman Empire in Relation to the Western Provinces from the Seventh to the Ninth Century', *Centenario della nascita di M. Amari*, II (Palermo, 1900), 21–34.

Byzantium, ed. N. H. Baynes and H. St L. B. Moss [see Gen. Bibl. v].

Charanis, P., 'The Monastic Properties and the State' [see Gen. Bibl. v].

Christophilopoulos, A. P., Τὸ ἐπαρχικὸν βιβλίον Λέοντος τοῦ Σοφοῦ καὶ αἱ συντεχνίαι ἐν Βυζαντίῳ (Athens, 1935).

Christophilopoulos, A. P., Ἡ δικαιοδοσία τῶν ἐκκλησιαστικῶν δικαστηρίων κατὰ τὴν Βυζαντινὴν περίοδον', *EEBS*, XVIII (1948), 192–201.

Christophilopoulou, A. A., Ἡ Σύγκλητος εἰς τὸ Βυζαντινὸν Κράτος (Athens, 1949).

Dain, A., 'Appellations du feu grégeois', *Mélanges A. Ernout* (Paris, 1940), pp. 121–7.

Dain, A., 'Le partage du butin de guerre d'après les traités juridiques et militaires', *Actes du VIᵉ Congrès Intern. d'Etudes Byzantines: Paris, 1948*, I (Paris, 1950), 347–52.

Danstrup, J., 'Indirect Taxation at Byzantium', *CM*, VIII (1946), 139–67.

Darkó, E., 'La militarizzazione dell'Impero Bizantino', *SBN*, V (1939), 88–99.

Dawkins, R. M., 'Greeks and Northmen', *Custom is King: Essays presented to R. R. Marett* (London, 1936), pp. 35–47.

Dawkins, R. M., 'The Later History of the Varangian Guard', *JRS*, XXXVII (1947), 39–46.

Diehl, C., 'L'origine du régime des thèmes dans l'empire byzantin', *Etudes d'histoire du moyen âge dédiées à G. Monod* (Paris, 1896), 14 pp.; reprinted in *Etudes Byzantines* (Paris, 1905), pp. 276–92.

Diehl, C., 'Le sénat et le peuple byzantin au VIIᵉ et VIIIᵉ siècles', *B*, I (1924), 201–13.

Diehl, C., 'Un haut fonctionnaire byzantin: le Logothète', *Mélanges Nicolas Jorga* (Paris, 1933), pp. 217–27, and see *BZ*, XXXIV (1934), 373–9.

Diehl, C., *Les grands problèmes de l'histoire byzantine* (Paris, 1943).

Diehl, C., 'The Government and Administration of the Byzantine Empire', *Cambridge Medieval History*, IV (1923 ed.), 726–44.

Dieterich, K., *Hofleben in Byzanz* (Leipzig, n.d.) [1914?].

Dölger, F., *Byzanz und die europäische Staatenwelt* [see Gen. Bibl. v].

Dölger, F., 'Die Kaiserurkunde der Byzantiner als Ausdruck ihrer politischen Anschauungen', *HZ*, CLIX (1938/9), 229–50; reprinted in *Byzanz und die europäische Staatenwelt*, pp. 9–33.

Dölger, F., 'Die "Familie der Könige" im Mittelalter', *HJ*, LX (1940), 397–420; reprinted in *Byzanz und die europäische Staatenwelt*, pp. 34–69.

Dölger, F., 'Bulgarisches Zartum und byzantinisches Kaisertum', *Izvestija Bulgar. Arch. Inst.* IX (1935), 57–68; reprinted in *Byzanz und die europäische Staatenwelt*, pp. 140–58.

Dölger, F., *Beiträge zur Geschichte der byzantinischen Finanzverwaltung besonders des 10. und 11. Jahrhunderts* [see Gen. Bibl. v].

Dölger, F., 'Der Kodikellos des Christodulos von Palermo. Ein bisher unbekannter Typus der byzantinischen Kaiserurkunde', *Archiv für Urkundenforschung*, XI (1929), 1–65; reprinted in *Byzantinische Diplomatik*, pp. 1–74 [see Gen. Bibl. v].

Dölger, F., 'Rom in der Gedankenwelt der Byzantiner', *ZKG*, LVI (1937), 1–42; reprinted in *Byzanz und die europäische Staatenwelt*, pp. 70–115.

Dölger, F., 'Zum Gebührenwesen der Byzantiner', *Etudes dédiées à la mémoire d'André Andréadès* (Athens, 1939), pp. 34–9; reprinted in *Byzanz und die europäische Staatenwelt*, pp. 232–60.

Dölger, F., 'Der Bulgarenherrscher als geistlicher Sohn des byzantinischen Kaisers', *Sbornik dédié à la mémoire du professeur Peter Nikov = Izvestija Inst. Bulg. Hist.* xvi/xvii (1939), 219–32; reprinted in *Byzanz und die europäische Staatenwelt*, pp. 183–96.

Dvornik, F., 'The Circus Parties in Byzantium', *BM*, i, pt. 1 (1946), 119–33.

Ebersolt, J., 'Sur les fonctions et les dignités du Vestiarium byzantin', *Mélanges Charles Diehl*, i (Paris, 1930), 217–23.

Ensslin, W., *Gottkaiser und Kaiser von Gottes Gnaden. Sitzungsberichte der Bayerischen Akademie der Wissenschaften.* Philos.-Histor. Abteilung, vi (1943).

Ensslin, W., *Zur Frage nach der ersten Kaiserkrönung durch den Patriarchen und zur Bedeutung dieses Aktes im Wahlzeremoniell* (Würzburg, 1948). [Part of this is in *BZ*, xlii (1942), 101–15 and see also pp. 369–72 in the enlarged *BZ*, xlii (1942) which was re-issued in 1959.]

Ensslin, W., 'The Emperor and the Imperial Administration', *Byzantium*, ed. N. H. Baynes and H. St L. B. Moss, pp. 268–307 [see Gen. Bibl. v].

Ensslin, W., 'Der Kaiser Herakleios und die Themenverfassung', *BZ*, xlvi (1953), 362–8.

Ensslin, W., 'Staat und Kirche von Konstantin d. Gr. bis Theodosius d. Gr. Ein Beitrag zur Frage nach dem "Cäsaropapismus"', *Acta IX. Internat. Byz. Congr. Thessalonica 1953*, ii (=Ἑλληνικά, Παράρτημα ix, Athens, 1956), 404–15.

Fuchs, F., *Die höheren Schulen von Konstantinopel im Mittelalter* (Byzantinisches Archiv, Heft 8) (Leipzig/Berlin, 1926).

Gasquet, A. L., *Autorité impériale en matière religieuse à Byzance* (Paris, 1879).

Gelzer, H., *Die Genesis der byzantinischen Themenverfassung.* Abh. der K. Sächsischen Gesellschaft der Wissenschaften. Philol. Histor. Kl. 18, nr. 5 (Leipzig, 1899).

Gelzer, H., 'Das Verhältnis von Staat und Kirche in Byzanz', *HZ* (lxxxvi), n.s. l (1901), 195–252; reprinted in *Ausgewählte kleine Schriften* (Leipzig, 1907), pp. 57–141.

Gfrörer, F., *Byzantinische Geschichten*, ii, 401–36 ('Das byzantinische Seewesen') [see Gen. Bibl. v].

Glykatzi-Ahrweiler, H., *Recherches sur l'administration de l'empire byzantin aux IX–XI siècles* (= *Bull. de Correspondance hellénique*, lxxxiv) (Athens and Paris, 1960).

Glykatzi-Ahrweiler, H., 'Fonctionnaires et bureaux maritimes à Byzance', *REB*, xix (1961), 239–52.

Grabar, A., *L'empereur dans l'art byzantin* [see Gen. Bibl. v].

Guilland, R., 'Etudes sur l'histoire administrative de l'empire byzantin' [see Gen. Bibl. v].

Guilland, R., 'Sur quelques termes du Livre des Cérémonies de Constantin Porphyrogénète', *REG*, lvii (1945), 96–211; cf. lix (1946), 251–9.

Guilland, R., 'Le grand domesticat à Byzance', *EO*, xxxvii (1938), 53–64. On this see V. Laurent, 'Notes complémentaires', *ibid.* pp. 65–72.

Guilland, R., 'La collation et la perte ou la déchéance des titres nobiliaires à Byzance', *REB*, iv (1946), 24–69.

Guilland, R., 'Les eunuques dans l'empire byzantin', *EB*, i (1943), 197–238; ii (1944), 185–225; iii (1945), 179–214.

Guilland, R., 'Etudes sur l'histoire administrative de l'empire byzantin: le césarat', *OCP*, xiii (1947), 168–94.

Guilland, R., 'Le protovestiaire Georges Phrantzès', *REB*, VI (1948), 48–57.

Guilland, R., 'Etudes sur l'histoire administrative de l'empire byzantin: le grand connétable', *B*, XIX (1949), 99–111.

Guilland, R., 'Etudes de titulature et de prosopographie byzantines: le protostrator', *REB*, VII (1949), 156–79.

Guilland, R., 'Contribution à l'histoire administrative de l'empire byzantin: le drongaire et le grand drongaire de la veille', *BZ*, XLIII (1950), 340–65.

Guilland, R., 'Etudes de titulature et de prosopographie byzantines. Les chefs de la marine byzantine: Drongaire de la flotte, Grand drongaire de la flotte, Duc de la flotte, Mégaduc', *BZ*, XLIV (1951), 212–40.

Guilland, R., 'Etudes sur l'histoire administrative de l'empire byzantin: Proconsul, ἀνθύπατος', *REB*, XV (1957), 1–41.

Guilland, R., 'Etudes sur l'histoire administrative de l'empire Byzantin. Les fonctions des eunuques: le primicirius', *REB*, XIV (1956), 122–57.

Guilland, R., 'Etudes sur l'histoire administrative de l'empire byzantin: le despote', *REB*, XVII (1959), 52–89.

Guilland, R., 'Etudes sur l'histoire administrative de l'empire byzantin. Les fonctions des eunuques: le préposite', *BS*, XXII (1961), 241–301.

Heisenberg, A., 'Staat und Gesellschaft des byzantinischen Reiches', *Die Kultur der Gegenwart*, Teil II, Abt. IV, i (Leipzig, 1923), 364–414.

Karayannopulos, J., *Die Entstehung der byzantinischen Themenordnung* (Byzantinisches Archiv, X) (Munich, 1959).

Kolias, G., *Ämter- und Würdenkauf im früh- und mittelbyzantinischen Reich* (Texte und Forschungen zur byzantinisch-neugriechischen Philologie, 35) (Athens, 1939).

Kyriakides, S., Βυζαντιναὶ Μελέται II–V (Thessalonica, 1937) (cf. F. Dölger, *BZ*, XL (1940), pp. 180–91); VI (Thessalonica, 1937).

Laurent, V., 'L'idée de guerre sainte et la tradition byzantine', *RHSE*, XXIII (1946), 71–98.

Lemerle, P., 'Le juge général des Grecs et la réforme judiciaire d'Andronic III', *Mémorial L. Petit* (Bucharest, 1948), pp. 292–316.

Lemerle, P., 'Recherches sur les institutions judiciaires à l'époque des Paléologues. I: Le tribunal impérial', *Mélanges H. Grégoire*, I = *AIPHO*, IX (1949), 369–84.

Lemerle, P., 'Recherches sur les institutions judiciaires à l'époque des Paléologues. II: Le tribunal du patriarcat ou tribunal synodal', *Mélanges P. Peeters*, II = *AB*, LXVIII (1950), 318–33.

Lopez, R. S., 'Silk industry in the Byzantine Empire', *SP*, XX (1945), 1–42.

Lot, F., *L'art militaire* [see Gen. Bibl. V].

Manojlović, G., 'Le peuple de Constantinople', *B*, XI (1936), 617–716.

Maricq, A., 'La durée du régime des partis populaires à Constantinople', *Bull. Acad. Royale Belg., Cl. des Lettres*, XXXV (1949), 63–74.

Maricq, A., 'Factions de cirque et partis populaires', *Bull. Acad. Royale Belg., Cl. des Lettres*, XXXVI (1950), 396–421.

Michel, A., *Die Kaisermacht in der Ostkirche* [see Gen. Bibl. V].

Mickwitz, G., *Die Kartellfunktionen der Zünfte und ihre Bedeutung bei der Entstehung des Zunftwesens* (Helsingfors, 1936).

Mitard, M., 'Le pouvoir impérial au temps de Léon VI le Sage', *Mélanges Charles Diehl*, I (Paris, 1930), 81–9.

Moravcsik, Gy., *Byzantinoturcica* [see Gen. Bibl. I].

Müller, E., 'Die Anfänge der Königssalbung im Mittelalter und ihre historisch-politischen Auswirkungen', *HJ*, LVIII (1939), 317–60.

Neumann, C., 'Die byzantinische Marine', *HZ*, XLV (1898), 1–23.

Ohnsorge, W., *Das Zweikaiserproblem im früheren Mittelalter* (Hildesheim, 1947),

Oman, C. W. C., *The History of the Art of War. The Middle Ages*, 2 vols., 2nd ed. (London, 1924).

Ostrogorsky, G., 'Das Steuersystem im byzantinischen Altertum und Mittelalter', *B*, VI (1931), 229–40.

Ostrogorsky, G., 'Agrarian Conditions in the Byzantine Empire in the Middle Ages', *Cambridge Economic History of Europe*, I (1941), 194–223.

Ostrogorsky, G. and Stein, E., 'Die Krönungsordnungen des Zerimonienbuches', *B*, VII (1932), 185–233.

Ostrogorsky, G., 'Die byzantinische Staatenhierarchie', *Sem. Kond.* VIII (1936), 95–187.

Ostrogorsky, G., *Pronija. Prilog istoriji feudalizma u Vizantiji i u južnoslovenskim zemljama*; and French transl. *Pour l'histoire de la féodalité* [see Gen. Bibl. V].

Ostrogorsky, G., *Quelques problèmes d'histoire de la paysannerie byzantine* [see Gen. Bibl. V].

Ostrogorsky, G., 'The Byzantine Emperor and the Hierarchical World Order', *SEER*, XXXV (1956), 1–14.

Ostrogorsky, G., *History of the Byzantine State* [see Gen. Bibl. V].

Ostrogorsky, G., 'Sur la date de la composition du Livre des Thèmes et sur l'époque de la constitution des premiers thèmes d'Asie Mineure', *B*, XXIII (1953, published 1954), 31–66.

Ostrogorsky, G., 'Pour l'histoire de l'immunité à Byzance', *B*, XXVIII (1958, published 1959), 165–254.

Ostrogorsky, G., 'Korreferat zu A. Pertusi, "La formation des thèmes byzantins"', *Berichte zum XI. Int. Byz. Kongr.* (Munich, 1958), VII, 1–8.

Pertusi, A., 'La formation des thèmes byzantins', *Berichte zum XI. Int. Byz. Kongr.*, I (Munich, 1958), pp. 1–40 [with bibliography to 1957].

Pertusi, A., 'La Questione delle Origini dei Temi', *Costantino Porfirogenito De Thematibus*, pp. 103–11 [see Gen. Bibl. IV under Constantine Porphyrogenitus].

Runciman, S., *Byzantine Civilisation* [see Gen. Bibl. V].

Ševčenko, I., 'Léon Bardales et les juges généraux ou la corruption des incorruptibles', *B*, XIX (1949), 247–59.

Sickel, W., 'Das byzantinische Krönungsrecht bis zum 10. Jahrhundert', *BZ*, VII (1898), 511–57.

Stein, E., *Studien zur Geschichte des byzantinischen Reiches vornehmlich unter den Kaisern Justinian II. und Tiberius Constantinus* (Stuttgart, 1919), pp. 117–40 [on the themes].

Stein, E., 'Untersuchungen zur spätbyzantinischen Verfassungs- und Wirtschaftsgeschichte', *Mitteilungen zur Osmanischen Geschichte*, II (1923/5), pp. 1–62 (reprinted separately, Amsterdam, 1962).

Stöckle, A., *Spätrömische und byzantinische Zünfte. Untersuchungen zum sogenannten ἐπαρχικὸν βιβλίον Leos des Weisen* (*Klio*, Beiheft IX) (Leipzig, 1911).

Svoronos, N. G., *Recherches sur le cadastre byzantin et la fiscalité aux XIe et XIIe siècles: le cadastre de Thèbes* (= *Bull. de Correspondance hellénique*, LXXXIII) (Athens and Paris, 1959).

Treitinger, O., *Die oströmische Kaiser- und Reichsidee nach ihrer Gestaltung im höfischen Zeremoniell* [see Gen. Bibl. V].

Vasiliev, A. A., 'The Anglo-Saxon Immigration to Byzantium', *Annales de l'Institut Kondakov*, IX (1937), 39–70.

Voigt, K., *Staat und Kirche von Konstantin dem Grossen bis zum Ende der Karolingerzeit* (Stuttgart, 1936).

Ahrweiler, H., 'Fonctionnaires et bureaux maritimes à Byzance', *REB*, XIX (1961), 239–52.

CHAPTER XXI. BYZANTINE LAW

See also the bibliographies for chapters III, IV, XV, XX and XXIII

I. ORIGINAL AUTHORITIES

(A) COLLECTIONS OF TEXTS

Acta et diplomata Graeca medii aevi, ed. F. Miklosich and J. Müller, 6 vols. (Vienna, 1860–89) [cited below as MM].

Anecdota, ed. G. E. Heimbach, 2 vols. (Leipzig, 1838–40) [cited below as 'Hb., *Anecd.*'].

Anecdota, ed. K. E. Zachariae von Lingenthal (Leipzig, 1843) [cited below as 'Zach., *Anecd.*'].

Bibliotheca juris canonici veteris..., ed. G. Voelli and H. Justelli, 2 vols. (Paris, 1661) [cited below as 'Voelli'].

Dölger, F. (ed.), *Aus den Schatzkammern des Heiligen Berges* [i.e. Mt Athos]: *115 Urkunden und 50 Urkundensiegel aus 10 Jahrhunderten*, 2 vols. (Munich, 1948) [cited below as 'Dölger, *Schatzkammern*'].

Juris ecclesiastici Graecorum historia et monumenta, ed. J. B. Pitra, 2 vols. (Rome, 1864–8) [cited below as 'Pitra'].

Jus graeco-romanum, ed. K. E. Zachariae von Lingenthal, 7 vols. (Leipzig, 1856–84) [cited below as 'Zach., *JGR*'].

Jus graeco-romanum, ed. J. and P. Zepos, 8 vols. (Athens, 1931; reprinted Aalen, 1962) [cited below as 'Zepos, *JGR*'].

Rhalles, G. A. and Potles, M., Σύνταγμα τῶν θείων καὶ ἱερῶν κανόνων [see Gen. Bibl. IV; cited below as 'RP'].

Sathas, K. N., Μεσαιωνικὴ βιβλιοθήκη [see Gen. Bibl. IV; cited below as 'Sathas'].

(B) SEPARATE WORKS

Actionibus, Tractatus de, ed. G. E. Heimbach, *Observationes iuris graeco-romani*, I (Leipzig, 1830); reprinted by L. Sgoutas in Θέμις, I (Athens, 1846), pp. 117 ff. and in Zepos, *JGR*, III, pp. 361–9; ed. K. E. Zachariae von Lingenthal in *ZSR*, rom. Abt., XIV (1893), 88–97.

Anatolius, *Anecdota Laurentiana et Vaticana, in quibus praesertim Iustiniani Codicis summae ab Anatolio confectae plurima fragmenta...continentur*, in *Opere di C. Ferrini*, ed. V. Arangio-Ruiz, I (Milan, 1929), pp. 237–95.

Anonymus (the), *Anonymi Epitome Novellarum Iustiniani* (fragments) in Zach., *Anecd.* pp. 196–226.

Anonymus (the), see *Nomocanon XIV titulorum*.

Appendix Eclogae, in Zach., *Anecd.* pp. 184–95.

Ashburneri, Tractatus, ed. in F. Dölger, *Beiträge zur Geschichte der byzantinischen Finanzverwaltung* [see Gen. Bibl. v].

Athanasius, *Athanasii Emiseni Epitome Novellarum Justiniani*, in Hb., *Anecd.* I, pp. 1–259.

Attaliotes (=Attaleiates), *Michaelis Attaliotae* Ποίημα Νομικόν, in Zepos, *JGR*, VII, pp. 411–97.

Authenticum, ed. G. E. Heimbach, 2 vols. (Leipzig, 1846–51); ed. R. Schoell and G. Kroll in *Corpus Iuris Civilis*, ed. stereotypa, Berlin, III (Novellae).

Balsamon, Theodorus, *Commentary on the Nomocanon XIV titulorum*, in Voelli, II, pp. 785–1140; in RP, I, pp. 1–335.

Basilica, Basilicorum libri LX, ed. C. W. E. Heimbach, 6 vols. (Leipzig, 1833–70). Two supplements have been added to this edition: (1) *Supplementum editionis Basilicorum Heimbachianae...*, ed. K. E. Zachariae von Lingenthal (Leipzig, 1846); (2) *Basilicorum libri LX*, vol. VII—*Editionis Heimbachianae supplementum alterum*, ed. E. C. Ferrini and J. Mercati (Leipzig and Milan, 1897). The Greek text of this edition (including the supplements) has been reprinted without the Latin translation by J. Zepos, 5 vols. (Athens, 1910–12).

Basilica, Basilicorum libri LX, ed. H. J. Scheltema, D. Holwerda and N. van der Wal (Groningen, 1953 ff.; in progress).

Bestes, Theodorus, augmented version of the *Nomocanon XIV titulorum*, in Pitra, II, pp. 433–637.

Blastares, Matthaeus, *Syntagma alphabeticum canonum atque legum*, in RP, VI.

Book of the Eparch (=*Book of the Prefect*), see *Livre du préfet*.

Chomatianus, Demetrius, *Decisiones*, in *Analecta sacra et classica*, ed. J. B. Pitra, VII (Paris and Rome, 1891); extracts in Zepos, *JGR*, VII, pp. 501–48.

Chrysobulla, see *Novels* of the later Byzantine emperors.

Collectio XXV capitulorum, in Hb., *Anecd.* II, pp. 145–201; *variae lectiones* to this edition in Pitra, II, pp. 407–10.

Collectio LXXXVII capitulorum, in Hb., *Anecd.* II, pp. 202–34; *variae lectiones* to this edition in Pitra, II, pp. 385–407.

Collectio constitutionum ecclesiasticarum tripartita, in Voelli, II, pp. 1223–1376; *variae lectiones* to this edition in Pitra, II, pp. 410–16.

Collectio de tutoribus, in *Iuliani Epitome Novellarum*, ed. G. Haenel (Leipzig, 1873), pp. 201–2.

Constantine Porphyrogenitus, *Excerpta historica*, ed. U. P. Boissevain, C. De Boor and T. Büttner-Worbst, 4 vols. (Berlin, 1903–6) [see also Gen. Bibl. IV].

Creditis, Tractatus de, ed. K. E. Zachariae von Lingenthal, in *Heidelberger Jahrbücher*, XXXIV (1841), pp. 540 ff.

Dictatum de consiliariis, in *Iuliani Epitome Novellarum*, ed. G. Haenel (Leipzig, 1873), pp. 198–201.

Divisio, Brevis divisio Novellarum Iustiniani, in Hb., *Anecd.* II, pp. 234–7.

Ecloga (of the Isaurian emperors Leo III and Constantine V), ed. K. E. Zachariae von Lingenthal, in *Collectio librorum iuris graeco-romani Eclogam Leonis et Constantini, Epanagogen Basilii Leonis et Alexandri continens* (Leipzig, 1852), pp. 1–52 (reprinted in Zepos, *JGR*, II, pp. 1–62); C. A. Spulber, *L'Eclogue des Isauriens* (Cernauți, 1929), with a French translation; ed. A. G. Momferratus (Athens, 1889).

Ecloga privata aucta, in Zach., *JGR*, IV; reprinted in Zepos, *JGR*, VI, pp. 7–47.

Ecloga ad Prochiron mutata, in Zach., *JGR*, IV; reprinted in Zepos, *JGR*, VI, pp. 217–318.

Ecloga legum in Epitome expositarum, see *Epitome legum*.

Ecloga librorum I–X Basilicorum, edition of a fragment in H. J. Scheltema,
  Florilegium iurisprudentiae graeco-romanae (Leiden, 1950), pp. 59–60.

Edicta Iustiniani, ed. R. Schoell and G. Kroll in *Corpus Iuris Civilis*, ed.
  stereotypa, Berlin, III (Novellae), pp. 759–95.

Edicta praefectorum praetorio, in Zach., *Anecd.* pp. 265–78.

Enantiophanes, *see* Anonymus.

Epanagoge, ed. K. E. Zachariae von Lingenthal in *Collectio librorum iuris
  graeco-romani Eclogam Leonis et Constantini, Epanagogen Basilii Leonis
  et Alexandri continens* (Leipzig, 1852), pp. 53–217; reprinted in Zepos,
  JGR, II, pp. 229–368.

Epanagoge aucta, in Zach., *JGR*, IV; reprinted in Zepos, *JGR*, VI, pp. 49–216.

Eparchica, see *Edicta praefectorum praetorio* and *Livre du préfet*.

Epitome legum, in Zach., *JGR*, II (titles 1–23, under the name *Ecloga legum
  in Epitome expositarum*) and VII (titles 24–fin., under the name *Epitome
  legum*); reprinted together in Zepos, *JGR*, IV, pp. 261–585.

Epitome ad Prochiron mutata, (fragments) in Zach., *Anecd.* pp. 208–26.

Eustathius Romanus, *Eustathii Magistri tractatus de hypobolo*, ed. K. E.
  Zachariae von Lingenthal, *Geschichte des griechisch-römischen Rechts*,
  3rd ed. (Berlin, 1892), p. 96, n. 254.

Eustathius Romanus, *Pira Eustathii Romani*, see *Pira*.

Eustathius Romanus, (*pseudo-*)*Eustathii liber de temporum intervallis*, see Ῥοπαί.

Glossa Institutionum, see *Taurinensis*.

Harmenopulus, *Constantini Harmenopuli Manuale legum sive Hexabiblos...*,
  ed. G. E. Heimbach (Leipzig, 1851).

Hypobolo, tractatus de, see Eustathius and Phobenus.

Hypobolon, fragment on the, of cod. Vaticanus 845, ed. F. Brandileone,
  *Frammenti di legislazione normanna e di giurisprudenza bizantina nell'Italia
  meridionale, Rendiconti della R. Accademia dei Lincei* (1885–6).

Index Reginae, Novellarum Iustiniani index Reginae, in Hb., *Anecd.* II, pp.
  237–46.

John of Antioch, see *Collectio LXXXVII capitulorum* and *Nomocanon L
  titulorum*.

Julian, *Iuliani Epitome latina Novellarum Iustiniani...*, ed. G. Haenel
  (Leipzig, 1873).

Lex..., see Νόμος.

Livre du préfet, Le, Λέοντος τοῦ Σοφοῦ ἐπαρχικὸν βιβλίον, ed. J. Nicole (Geneva,
  1893); reprinted in Zepos, *JGR*, II, pp. 371–92 [see also Gen. Bibl. IV
  under *Eparch, Book of the*].

Lydus, John, *De magistratibus populi Romani*, ed. R. Wuensch (Leipzig, 1903).

Meditatio de nudis pactis, ed. H. Monnier and G. Platon in *Nouvelle revue
  historique de droit français et étranger*, XXXVII (1913), pp. 135–68, 311–36,
  474–510, 624–53, XXXVIII (1914), pp. 285–342, 709–59. Reprinted as a
  separate book, Paris, 1915; reprint of the Greek text without the commentary in Zepos, *JGR*, VII, pp. 365–75.

Nomocanon XIV titulorum, in Voelli, II, pp. 785–1140; in Pitra, II, pp. 433–
  637; in RP, I, pp. 1–335.

Nomocanon L titulorum, in Voelli, II, pp. 603–60.

Νόμος γεωργικός, ed. W. Ashburner, 'The farmers' law', *JHS*, XXX (1910),
  pp. 85–108 and XXXII (1912), pp. 68–95; reprinted in Zepos, *JGR*, II,
  pp. 65–71; ed. C. Ferrini, in *Opere di Contardo Ferrini*, ed. V. Arangio-
  Ruiz, I (Milan, 1929), pp. 375–95.

Νόμος ʿΡοδίων ναυτικός, ed. J. M. Pardessus, *Collection de lois maritimes*, I (Paris, 1828), ch. 6 (pp. 209–60); ed. C. Ferrini and J. Mercati, in *Basilicorum libri LX*, vol. VII (Leipzig and Milan, 1897), pp. 108–20 and 169–71; ed. R. Dareste, *Revue de Philologie*, XXIX (1905), pp. 1–29 and *Nouvelle revue historique de droit français et étranger*, XXIX (1905), pp. 428–49; ed. W. Ashburner, *The Rhodian Sea Law edited from the Manuscripts* (Oxford, 1909). Ashburner's text is reprinted in Zepos, *JGR*, II, pp. 75–9.

Νόμος στρατιωτικός, ed. K. E. Zachariae von Lingenthal, *BZ*, III (1894), pp. 450–5; ed. W. Ashburner, 'The Byzantine Mutiny-act', *JHS*, XLVI (1926), pp. 80–109 (reprinted in Zepos, *JGR*, II, pp. 93–103); ed. E. Korzenszky, 'Leges poenales militares', *Egypetemes Philologiae Közlöny* (1930), pp. 155–63 and 215–18 (reprinted in Zepos, *JGR*, II, pp. 80–9).

Novella Constantini Monomachi (Law of the year 1045, ordering the reopening of the law school in Constantinople), ed. P. de Lagarde, *Abhandlungen der Göttinger Gesellschaft der Wissenschaften*, hist.-phil. Kl., XXVIII (1881), pp. 195–202; reprinted by C. Ferrini with a Latin translation, *Archivio giuridico*, XXX (1884), 425–48 and in *Opere di Contardo Ferrini*, ed. V. Arangio-Ruiz, I (Milan, 1929), pp. 313–38.

Novellae imperatorum post Iustinianum, Zach., *JGR*, III; reprinted with additions in Zepos, *JGR*, I.

Novellae Iustiniani, Imp. Iustiniani Novellae quae vocantur..., ed. K. E. Zachariae von Lingenthal, 2 vols. (Leipzig, 1881), with two supplements: (1) *Appendix ad editionem Novellarum Iustiniani* (Leipzig, 1884); (2) *De diocesi Aegyptiaca lex* (Leipzig, 1891).

Novellae Iustiniani, Corpus Iuris Civilis, ed. T. Mommsen, P. Krüger, R. Schoell and W. Kroll, ed. stereotypa, Berlin, III.

Novellae Leonis Sapientis, Les Novelles de Léon VI le Sage, texte et traduction..., P. Noailles and A. Dain (Paris, 1944).

Novels of the later Byzantine emperors (chrysobulla, practica, prostagmata, etc.), see e.g. MM; Dölger, *Schatzkammern*; Sathas, I; Zepos, *JGR*, I; F. Dölger, *Sechs byzantinische Praktika für das Athoskloster Iberon* (Munich, 1949); G. Rouillard and P. Collomp, *Actes de Lavra*, I (Paris, 1937); for purposes of orientation consult F. Dölger, *Regesten der Kaiserurkunden* [see Gen. Bibl. IV].

Peculiis, Tractatus de, in Hb., *Anecd.* II, pp. 247–60; reprinted in Zepos, *JGR*, III, pp. 345–57.

Peira, see *Pira*.

Perusina, Iustiniani Codicis summa, in Hb., *Anecd.* II, pp. 1–144; ed. F. Patetta, *Bullettino dell'Istituto di diritto romano*, XII (1900).

Phobenus, George, *Tractatus de Hypobolo*, ed. K. E. Zachariae von Lingenthal, *Geschichte des griechisch-römischen Rechts*, 3rd ed. (Berlin, 1892), p. 96, n. 254.

Photius, (*pseudo*-) *Photii nomocanon*, see *Nomocanon XIV titulorum*.

Pira, Πεῖρα sive *Practica ex actis Eustathii Romani*, in Zach., *JGR*, I, pp. 1–300; reprinted in Zepos, *JGR*, IV, pp. 1–260.

Prochiron, Ὁ Πρόχειρος νόμος. *Imperatorum Basilii, Constantini et Leonis Prochiron*..., ed.... K. E. Zachariae von Lingenthal (Heidelberg, 1837); reprinted in Zepos, *JGR*, II, pp. 108–228.

Prochiron Vaticanum, Prochiron legum pubblicato secondo il codice Vaticano greco 845, ed. F. Brandileone and V. Puntoni (*Fonti*) (Rome, 1895).

Psellus, Michael, *Synopsis legum*, ed. F. Bosquet in G. Meermann, *Novus Thesaurus*... (The Hague, 1751), I, pp. 37–86; reprinted in Zepos, *JGR*, VII, pp. 379–407.

'Ροπαί, Aἱ, *oder die Schrift über die Zeitabschnitte...*, ed. K. E. Zachariae von Lingenthal (Heidelberg, 1836); reprinted in Zepos, *JGR*, III, pp. 273–342.

Stephanus, C. Ferrini, *Frammenti inediti della Somma del Codice di Stefano antecessore*, in *Opere di Contardo Ferrini*, ed. V. Arangio-Ruiz, I (Milan, 1929), pp. 307–12.

Stephanus, *Codicis per Stephanum antecessorem κατ' ἐπιτομήν graece conversi fragmenta ex cod. Bodleiano 3399*, in Zach., *Anecd.* pp. 176–95.

Synopsis Basilicorum, in Zach., *JGR*, V, pp. 1–714; reprinted in Zepos, *JGR*, V, pp. 1–598.

Synopsis minor, in Zach., *JGR*, II, pp. 1–264; reprinted in Zepos, *JGR*, VI, pp. 321–547.

Taurinensis, Glossa, Institutionum, ed. F. C. Savigny, *Geschichte des römischen Rechtes im Mittelalter*, 2nd ed., II (Heidelberg, 1834), pp. 429–75; ed. P. Krüger, *ZR*, VII (1868), 44–78; ed. A. Alberti, *Testi inediti e rari pubblicati sotto la direzione del prof. F. Patetta* (Turin, 1933).

Theodorus, *Theodori scholastici Breviarium Novellarum*, in Zach., *Anecd.* pp. 1–165.

Theophilus, Θεοφίλου ἀντικήνσωρος τὰ εὑρισκόμενα, *Theophili antecessoris paraphrasis graeca Institutionum...*, ed.... G. O. Reitz, 2 vols. (The Hague, 1751); *Institutionum graeca paraphrasis Theophilo antecessori vulgo tributa*, ed. C. Ferrini, 2 pts. (Berlin and Milan, 1884–97); reprinted in Zepos, *JGR*, III, pp. 1–271.

Theophilus, *Scolii inediti allo Pseudo-Teofilo contenuti nel manoscritto greco Parisino 1364*, in *Opere di Contardo Ferrini*, ed. V. Arangio-Ruiz, I (Milan, 1929), pp. 139–224.

Theoretron, Fragment on the Theoretron of cod. Vaticanus 845, ed. F. Brandileone, *Frammenti di legislazione normanna e di giurisprudenza bizantina nell'Italia meridionale, Rendiconti della R. Accademia dei Lincei* (1885–6).

Tipucitus, M. κριτοῦ τοῦ Πατζῆ Τιπούκειτος, I, ed. C. Ferrini and J. Mercati (Rome, 1914); II, ed. F. Dölger (Rome, 1929); III, IV, V, ed. S. Hörmann-von Stepski Doliwa and E. Seidl (Vatican, 1943, 1955, 1957).

II. MODERN WORKS

(A) BIBLIOGRAPHIES AND GENERAL SURVEYS

Albertoni, A., *Per una esposizione del diritto bizantino con riguardo all'Italia* (Imola, 1927).

Dölger, F., *Regesten der Kaiserurkunden* [see Gen. Bibl. IV, =*DR*].

Ferrari, G., 'Diritto bizantino', *Enciclopedia Italiana*, VII (Rome, 1930).

Heimbach, C. W. E., 'Griechisch-römisches Recht', Ersch–Gruber, LXXXVI, LXXXVII (Leipzig, 1868–9).

Heimbach, C. W. E., *Prolegomena et manuale Basilicorum*, in *Basilicorum libri LX*, ed. C. W. E. Heimbach, VI (Leipzig, 1870), 1–217 (reprinted separately, Amsterdam, 1962).

Krüger, P., *Geschichte der Quellen des römischen Rechts*, 2nd ed. (Munich, 1912).

Mortreuil, J. A. B., *Histoire du droit byzantin*, 3 vols. (Paris, 1843–6).

Siciliano-Villanueva, L., 'Diritto bizantino', *Enciclopedia giuridica Italiana* (Milan, 1906).

Wenger, L., *Die Quellen des römischen Rechts* (Vienna, 1953).

Zachariae von Lingenthal, K. E., *Historiae juris graeco-romani delineatio* (Heidelberg, 1839).

Zachariae von Lingenthal, K. E., review of Mortreuil, *Histoire du droit byzantin*, in Richter und Schneider's *Kritische Jahrbücher für die Rechtswissenschaft*, VIII (1844), 794–828 and 1083–7; XI (1847), 581–638.

Zachariae von Lingenthal, K. E., *Geschichte des griechisch-römischen Rechts*, 3rd ed. (Berlin, 1892).

Zepos, P. J., 'Die byzantinische Jurisprudenz zwischen Justinian und den Basiliken', *Berichte zum XI. Intern. Byz.-Kongr. Munich, 1958*, V, 1, with 'Korreferate' by H. J. Scheltema and J. de Malafosse, *ibid.* VII (Munich, 1958).

Zepos, P. J., *Greek Law* (Athens, 1948).

(B) ON THE SOURCES

Berger, A., 'The Emperor Justinian's Ban upon Commentaries to the Digest', *Bulletin of the Polish Institute of Arts and Sciences in America*, III (New York, 1945), 656–96; reprinted with additions in *Bullettino dell'Istituto di Diritto Romano*, LV–LVI (*Supplementum post-bellum*, 1951), 124–69.

Berger, A., 'On the so-called Tractatus de peculiis', *Scritti in onore di C. Ferrini* (Pubblicazioni dell'Università cattolica del Sacro cuore, XXIII), III (Milan, 1948), 174–210.

Berger, A., 'Studies in the Basilica. I. Τὸ κατὰ πόδας', *Bullettino dell'Istituto di Diritto Romano*, n.s. XIV–XV (1951), 65–184.

Berger, A., 'Procanon. Note on a rare term in the Scholia to the Basilica', *Festschrift F. Schultz*, II (Weimar, 1951), 9–21.

Biener, F. A., *Geschichte der Novellen Justinians* (Berlin, 1824).

Blagoev, N., *The Ecloga* (Universitetska Biblioteka, no. 122) (Sofia, 1932; in Bulgarian).

Brandileone, F., *Frammenti di legislazione normanna e di giurisprudenza bizantina nell'Italia meridionale, Rendiconti della R. Accademia dei Lincei* (1885–6).

Brandileone, F., 'Studio sul *Prochiron legum*', *Bullettino dell'Istituto Storico Italiano*, XVI (Rome, 1894), 93–126.

Christophilopoulos, A. P., Τὸ ἐπαρχικὸν βιβλίον Λέοντος τοῦ Σοφοῦ καὶ αἱ συντεχνίαι ἐν Βυζαντίῳ (Athens, 1935).

Christophilopoulos, A. P., 'Τὸ πρόβλημα τῆς Ecloga privata', Ἀρχεῖον ἰδιωτικοῦ δικαίου, IV (1937), 97–105.

Christophilopoulos, A. P., 'Ζητήματά τινα ἐκ τοῦ Ἐπαρχικοῦ βιβλίου', Ἑλληνικά, XI (1939), 125–36.

Christophilopoulos, A. P., 'Παρατηρήσεις εἰς τὴν Πεῖραν Εὐσταθίου τοῦ Ῥωμαίου', *BNJ*, XVII (1944), 82–91.

Cvetler, J., 'The Authorship of the Novel on the Reform of Legislative Education at Constantinople (about A.D. 1045)', *Symbolae Raphaeli Taubenschlag dedicatae*, II = *Eos, commentarii Societatis Philologiae Polonorum*, XLVIII, II (1957), 297–328.

Dain, A., 'La transcription des mots latins en grec dans les gloses nomiques', *Revue des études latines*, VIII (1930), 92–113.

Dain, A., 'Le second appendice de la *Synopsis Basilicorum*', *Mélanges Fernand de Visscher*, III (= *Revue Internationale des Droits de l'Antiquité*, IV, Brussels, 1950), 303–17.

Dölger, F., 'Ist der Nomos Georgikos ein Gesetz des Kaisers Justinian II.?', *Festschrift für Leopold Wenger*, II (Munich, 1945), 18–48.

Dölger, F., 'Harmenopulos und der Nomos Georgikos', Τόμος Κωνσταντίνου Ἀρμενοπούλου, ed. P. J. Zepos and others (Thessalonica, 1952), 151–61.

Ferrari (dalle Spade), G., *Scritti Giuridici*, I (Milan, 1953).

Ferrini, C., *Opere di Contardo Ferrini*, ed. V. Arangio-Ruiz, I (Milan, 1929).

Freshfield, E. H., *Les manuels officiels de droit romain publiés à Constantinople par les empereurs Léon III et Basile I 726–870* (Paris, 1929).

Freshfield, E. H., *A Manual of Roman Law: the Ecloga published by the Emperors Leo III and Constantine V of Isauria at Constantinople A.D. 726* (Cambridge, 1926).

Freshfield, E. H., *A revised Manual of Roman Law founded upon the Ecloga of Leo III and Constantine V of Isauria: Ecloga privata aucta* (Cambridge, 1927).

Freshfield, E. H., *A Manual of Later Roman Law: the Ecloga ad Procheiron mutata, founded upon the Ecloga of Leo III and Constantine V of Isauria, and on the Procheiros Nomos of Basil I of Macedonia, including the Rhodian Maritime Law* (Cambridge, 1927).

Freshfield, E. H., *A Manual of Eastern Roman Law: the Procheiros Nomos published by the Emperor Basil I at Constantinople between A.D. 867 and A.D. 879* (Cambridge, 1928).

Freshfield, E. H., *A Manual of Byzantine Law Compiled in the Fourteenth Century by George Harmenopoulos*: vol. VI. *On Torts and Crimes* (Cambridge, 1930).

Freshfield, E. H., *A Provincial Manual of Later Roman Law: the Calabrian Procheiron on Servitudes and Bye-laws incidental to the Tenure of Real Property* (Cambridge, 1931).

Freshfield, E. H., *Byzantine Guilds Professional and Commercial: Ordinances of Leo VI c. 895 from the Book of the Eparch* (Cambridge, 1938).

Grumel, V., 'La date de promulgation de l'Eclogue de Léon III', *EO*, XXXIV (1935), 327–31.

Grumel, V., 'Recherches récentes sur l'iconoclasme', *EO*, XXIX (1930), 92–100.

Holwerda, D., 'Le Code de Justinien et sa traduction grecque. La mise en page du texte du Code et de sa traduction κατὰ πόδας', *CM*, XXIII (1962), 274–92.

Krüger, P., 'Ueber eine neue Bearbeitung des Nomocanon in 14 Titeln', *ZR*, IX (1870), 185–95.

Lawson, F. H., 'The Basilica', *Law Quarterly Review*, XLIV (1930), 486–501 and XLV (1931), 536–56.

Lemerle, P., 'Recherches sur le régime agraire à Byzance: la terre militaire à l'époque des Comnènes', *Cahiers de Civilisation Médiévale*, II (1959), 265–81.

Lemerle, P., 'Esquisse pour une histoire agraire de Byzance' [see Gen. Bibl. v].

Malafosse, J. de, 'Les lois agraires à l'époque byzantine', *Recueil de l'Académie de Législation*, XIX (1949), 1–75.

Malafosse, J. de, 'L'Epanagogè', *DDC*, V (1950).

Malafosse, J. de, 'L'Ecloga ad Prochiron mutata', *Archives d'Histoire du Droit oriental*, V (1950), 1–24.

Malafosse, J. de, 'Le droit agraire au Bas-Empire et dans l'empire d'orient', *Rivista di diritto agrario*, I (1955), 35–73.

Malafosse, J. de, 'Le problème de l'édition des textes du "Jus Graeco-Romanum"', *Actes du premier Congrès de la Fédération Internationale des Associations d'Etudes classiques* (Paris, 1951), 251–4.

Maridakis, G. S., Τὸ ἀστικὸν δίκαιον ἐν ταῖς νεαραῖς τῶν Βυζαντινῶν αὐτοκρατόρων (Athens, 1922).

Maridakis, G. S., ''Ο 'Αρμενόπουλος καὶ ἡ τεχνικὴ τοῦ δικαίου', Τόμος Κωνσταντίνου 'Αρμενοπούλου, ed. P. J. Zepos and others (Thessalonica, 1952), 89–109.

Maridakis, G. S., 'Justinians Verbot der Gesetzeskommentierung', *ZSR*, rom. Abt., LXXIII (1956), 369–75.

Maschi, C. A., 'La parafrasi greca delle Istituzioni attribuita a Teofilo e le glosse a Gaio', *Scritti di diritto romano in onore di C. Ferrini pubblicati dalla R. Università di Pavia*, ed. G. G. Archi (Pavia, 1946), 321–42.

Mercati, G., 'Nuovi frammenti dei libri 58–9 dei Basilici in un palinsesto Vaticano', *Rendiconti dell'Istituto Lombardo di sc. e lett.*, ser. 2, vol. XXXIV (1901), 1003–7.

Mickwitz, G., *Die Kartellfunktionen der Zünfte und ihre Bedeutung bei der Entstehung des Zunftwesens* (Helsinki, 1936).

Monnier, H., 'Etudes de droit byzantin. Méditations sur la constitution ἑκατέρῳ et le *jus poenitendi*', *Nouvelle Revue historique de droit français et étranger*, XXIV (1900), 37–107, 169–211, 285–337; publ. sep.(Paris, 1900).

Monnier, H., 'Du "casus non existentium liberorum" dans les Novelles de Justinien', *Mélanges Gérardin* (Paris, 1907), 437–65.

Monnier, H., 'La novelle 20 de Léon le Sage', *Mélanges Fitting*, II (Montpellier, 1908), 121–60.

Monnier, H., 'La Novelle 50 de Léon le Sage', *Mélanges P. F. Girard*, II (Paris, 1912), 237–89.

Monnier, H., *Les Novelles de Léon le Sage* (Bordeaux, 1923).

Mortreuil, J. A. B., *Histoire du droit byzantin*, 3 vols. (Paris, 1843–6).

Müller, H., *Der 1. Titel des 20. Buches der Basiliken des Patzes in seinem Repertorium Tipucitus* (Würzburg, 1940).

Nallino, C. A., 'Libri giuridici bizantini in versioni arabe cristiane dei secoli XII–XIII', *Rendiconti della R. Accademia dei Lincei*, cl. Sc. mor., stor. e filol., ser. 6, vol. I, fasc. 3–4 (1925), 101–65 (= *Scritti*, I, 314–84).

Noailles, P., *Les collections de Novelles de l'empereur Justinien*. I. *Origine et formation sous Justinien* (Paris, 1912); II. *La Collection grecque des 168 Novelles* (Paris, 1914).

Noailles, P., 'L'inaliénabilité dotale et la Novelle 61', *Annales de l'Université de Grenoble*, XXX (1918), 451–509 and XXXI (1919), 161–218.

Noailles, P., 'La collection des cent treize Novelles de Léon le Sage et sa composition par l'empereur', *Comptes rendus de l'Académie des Inscriptions et Belles-Lettres* (1943), 249–63; reprinted in *Les Novelles de Léon VI le Sage*, by P. Noailles and A. Dain (Paris, 1944), 7–20.

Perry, B. E., 'A Manuscript Fragment of the Prochiron', *BZ*, XXXIII (1933), 362.

Peters, H., 'Die oströmischen Digestenkommentare und die Entstehung der Digesten', *Berichte über die Verhandlungen der Königl. Sächsischen Gesellschaft der Wissensch.*, phil.-hist. Kl., Bd. 65, Heft 1 (1913).

Pringsheim, F., 'Enantiophanes', *Seminar*, IV (1946), 21–44.

Pringsheim, F., 'Justinian's Prohibition of Commentaries to the Digest', *Mélanges F. de Visscher*, IV (= *Revue Internationale des Droits de l'Antiquité*, V, Brussels, 1950), 383–415.

Pringsheim, F., *Zum Plan einer neuen Ausgabe der Basiliken* (Verh. Berliner Akad. der Wissenschaft, 1937; revised reprint Berlin, 1956).

Riccoboni, S., 'Il proemio della parafrasi greca di Teofilo nella edizione del Ferrini', *Bullettino dell'Istituto di Diritto Romano*, XLV (1938), 1–11.

Scharf, J., 'Photius und die Epanagoge, *BZ*, XLIX (1956), 385–400.

Scheltema, H. J., 'Ueber den Ausdruck "Procanon"', *Tijdschrift voor Rechts-geschiedenis*, XXIII (1955), 83–92.

Scheltema, H. J., 'Ueber die Natur der Basiliken', *Tijdschrift voor Rechts-geschiedenis*, XXIII (1955), 287–310.

Scheltema, H. J., 'Ueber die angebliche Anonymuskatene', *Tijdschrift voor Rechtsgeschiedenis*, XXV (1957), 284–301.

Scheltema, H. J., 'Ueber die Werke des Stephanus', *Tijdschrift voor Rechts-geschiedenis*, XXVI (1958), 5–14.

Scheltema, H. J., 'Ueber die Scholienapparate der Basiliken', *Mnemosynon Bizoukides* (Thessalonica, 1960), 139–45.

Scheltema, H. J., 'The Nomoi of Julianus of Ascalon', *Symbolae...J. C. van Oven dedicatae* (Leiden, 1946), 349–60.

Scheltema, H. J., 'Les sources du droit de Justinien dans l'Empire d'Orient', *Revue historique de droit français et étranger*, XXX (1952), 1–17.

Scheltema, H. J., 'An den Wurzeln der mittelalterlichen Gesellschaft, das oströmische Reich', *Instituttet for sammenlignende Kulturforskning*, Serie A, XXIV (Oslo, 1958), 85–152.

Scheltema, H. J., 'Subseciva', *Tijdschrift voor Rechtsgeschiedenis*, XXX (1962) and XXXI (1963).

Scheltema, H. J., 'A propos de la prétendue préface des Basiliques', *Mélanges H. Lévy-Brühl* (Paris, 1959), 269–71.

Scheltema, H. J., 'Over de tijdsbepaling der vroeg-Byzantijnsche juristen', *Tijdschrift voor Geschiedenis*, LXXIV (1961), 277–84.

Scherillo, G., 'Sulle origine dell'Authenticum', *Atti del IV Congresso Nazionale di Studi Romani*, 4 (1938), 79–83.

Schmitt, L., 'Die Scholien zu Buch XII Titel 1 der Basiliken', *Tijdschrift voor Rechtsgeschiedenis*, XXIV (1956), 158–78.

Seidl, E., 'Il Tipukeitos e gli scolii dei Basilici', *Bullettino dell'Istituto di Diritto Romano*, LIX–LX, n.s. XVIII–XIX (1956), 229–32.

Seidl, E., 'Die Basiliken des Patzes', *Festschrift für P. Koschaker* (Weimar, 1939), 294–308.

Seidl, E., 'Die Basilikenscholien im Tipukeitos', *Festschrift F. Dölger* (= *BZ*, XLIV, 1951), 534–40.

Sontis, J. M., *Die Digestensumme des Anonymos. I. Zum Dotalrecht* (Heidel-berg, 1937).

Spulber, C. A., 'Qui fut Enantiophanès?', *Archives d'Histoire du Droit Oriental*, I (1937), 307–19.

Stöckle, A., *Spätrömische und byzantinische Zünfte* (Leipzig, 1911).

Tamassia, N., 'Per la storia dell'Autentico', *Atti del R. Istituto Veneto di scienze, lettere ed arti* (Venice, 1908).

Triantaphyllopoulos, C., Ἡ Ἑξάβιβλος τοῦ Ἀρμενοπούλου καὶ ἡ νομικὴ σκέψις ἐν Θεσσαλονίκῃ κατὰ τὸν ιδ' αἰῶνα (Thessalonica, 1960).

Wal, N. van der, 'La relation entre le "κατὰ πόδας" et le commentaire du Code justinien de Thalélée', *Revue historique de droit français et étranger*, XXX (1952), 546–52.

Wal, N. van der, *Les commentaires grecs du Code de Justinien* (Groningen, 1953).

Wal, N. van der, 'Spuren einer Einteilung in sechs Bände der Basiliken in den jüngeren Scholien', *Tijdschrift voor Rechtsgeschiedenis*, XXV (1957), 274–83.

Wal, N. van der, *Manuale Novellarum Justiniani* (Groningen, 1963).

Zachariae von Lingenthal, K. E., 'Interpretationen aus den Schriften der Justinianeischen Juristen', *Zeitschr. für geschichtliche Rechtswissenschaft,* XIV (1848), 95–135.

Zachariae von Lingenthal, K. E., 'Eine Verordnung Justinian's über den Seidenhandel aus den Jahren 540–547', *Mémoires de l'Acad. Imp. des Sciences de St Pétersbourg,* 7ᵉ série, tome IX, no. 6 (1865).

Zachariae von Lingenthal, K. E., 'Ueber die griechischen Bearbeitungen des Justinianeischen Codex', *ZR,* X (1872), 48–69.

Zachariae von Lingenthal, K. E., 'Beiträge zur Kritik und Restitution der Basiliken', *Mémoires de l'Acad. Imp. des Sciences de St Pétersbourg,* 7ᵉ série, tome XXIII, no. 6 (1877).

Zachariae von Lingenthal, K. E., 'Die griechischen Nomokanones', *Mémoires de l'Acad. Imp. des Sciences de St Pétersbourg,* 7ᵉ série, tome XXIII, no. 7 (1877).

Zachariae von Lingenthal, K. E., 'Die Handbücher des geistlichen Rechts aus den Zeiten des untergehenden byzantinischen Reiches und der türkischen Herrschaft', *Mémoires de l'Acad. Imp. des Sciences de St Pétersbourg,* 7ᵉ série, tome XXVIII, no. 7 (1881).

Zachariae von Lingenthal, K. E., 'Ueber eine lateinische Uebersetzung von Buch 53 der Basiliken', *Monatsberichte der Berliner Akad. der Wissenschaften,* philol.-philos. Kl., 10, 1 (1881), pp. 13–34.

Zachariae von Lingenthal, K. E., 'Zur Geschichte des Authenticum und der Epitome Novellarum des antecessor Julianus', *Sitzungsberichte der Berliner Akad. der Wissenschaften,* XLV (1882), 993–1003.

Zachariae von Lingenthal, K. E., 'Ueber den Verfasser und die Quellen des (pseudo-Photianischen) Nomokanon in 14 Titeln', *Mémoires de l'Acad. Imp. des Sciences de St Pétersbourg,* 7ᵉ série, tome XXXII, no. 16 (1885).

Zachariae von Lingenthal, K. E., 'Die Meinungsverschiedenheiten unter den Justinianischen Juristen', *ZSR,* rom. Abt., VI (1885), 1–55.

Zachariae von Lingenthal, K. E., 'Von den griechischen Bearbeitungen des Codex', *ZSR,* rom. Abt., VIII (1887), 1–75.

Zachariae von Lingenthal, K. E., 'Aus und zu den Quellen des römischen Rechts', *ZSR,* rom. Abt., VIII (1887), 206–47; X (1889), 252–95; XII (1891), 75–99; XIII (1892), 1–52; XV (1894), 365–73.

Zachariae von Lingenthal, K. E., 'Die Synopsis canonum', *Sitzungsberichte der Berliner Akad. der Wissenschaften,* LIII (1887), 1147–63.

Zachariae von Lingenthal, K. E., *Paralipomena ad Basilica* (Leipzig, 1893).

Zachariae von Lingenthal, K. E., 'Zum Militärgesetz des Leo', *BZ,* II (1893), 606–8.

Zachariae von Lingenthal, K. E., 'Wissenschaft und Recht für das Heer vom 6.–10. Jahrhundert', *BZ,* III (1894), 437–57.

Zoras, G., *Le corporazioni bizantine* (Rome, 1931).

(c) CIVIL LAW

Angeletopoulos, P. A., 'Τινὰ περὶ ἱερολογίας ἐπὶ γάμου καὶ ἐπὶ υἱοθεσίας', *BZ,* XXX (1930), 649–59.

Angeletopoulos, P. A., ''Ο κατὰ τὸ 'Ιουστινιανὸν καὶ Βυζαντινὸν δίκαιον τρόπος ὑπολογισμοῦ τῆς νομίμου μοίρας', *Studi in onore di Pietro Bonfante,* II (Milan, 1930), 647–67.

Bosdas (Μπόσδας), D. B., Περὶ τοῦ γάμου. Συμβολὴ εἰς τὴν μελέτην τοῦ γάμου κατὰ τὴν 'Εκλογὴν τῶν 'Ισαύρων (Athens, 1937).

Brandileone, F., *Sulla storia e sulla natura della donatio propter nuptias* (Bologna, 1892).

Bruck, E. F., 'Kirchlich-soziales Erbrecht in Byzanz. Johannes Chrysostomus und die mazedonischen Kaiser', *Studi in onore di S. Riccobono*, III (Palermo, 1936), 377–423.

Cassimatis, G., 'La notion du mariage de l'Eclogue des Isauriens', Μνημόσυνα Παππούλια, ed. P. G. Ballenda (Athens, 1934), 85–92.

Cassimatis, G., *Les intérêts dans la législation de Justinien et dans le droit byzantin* (Paris, 1931).

Christophilopoulos, A., Σχέσεις γονέων καὶ τέκνων κατὰ τὸ Βυζαντινὸν δίκαιον (Athens, 1946).

Christophilopoulos, A., ''Η ἐκποίησις τῶν προικῴων ἀκινήτων κατὰ τὸ Βυζαντινὸν δίκαιον', 'Αρχεῖον 'Ιδιωτικοῦ Δικαίου, VI (1939), 538–49.

Desminis, D. D., *Die Eheschenkung nach römischem und insbesondere nach byzantinischem Recht* (Athens, 1897).

Dyobuniates, G., 'Τὸ Φαλκίδιον τρίτον ἐν τῷ Βυζαντινῷ δικαίῳ', 'Επετηρὶς τοῦ Φιλολογικοῦ Συλλόγου Παρνασσοῦ, VI (1902), 219–56.

Ehrhardt, A., 'Byzantinische Kaufverträge in Ost und West', *ZSR*, rom. Abt., LI (1931), 126–87.

Herman, E., 'Die Schliessung des Verlöbnisses im Recht Justinians und der späteren byzantinischen Gesetzgebung', *Analecta Gregoriana*, VIII (1935), 79–107.

Herman, E., 'De benedictione nuptiali quid statuerit ius Byzantinum sive ecclesiasticum sive civile', *OCP*, IV (1938), 199–243.

Herman, E., 'Εὐχὴ ἐπὶ διγάμων', *OCP*, I (1935), 467–89.

Malafosse, J. de, 'Remarques sur le rôle de la volonté au Bas-Empire et à Byzance', *Mnemosynon Bizoukides* (Thessalonica, 1960), 347–62.

Michaelides-Nouaros, G., *Contribution à l'étude des pactes successoraux en droit byzantin (justinien et post-justinien)* (Paris, 1937).

Momferratos, A. G., Πραγματεία περὶ προγαμιαίας δωρεᾶς (Athens, 1884).

Nörr, D., *Die Fahrlässigkeit im byzantinischen Vertragsrecht* (Munich, 1960).

Ostrogorsky, G., 'The Peasants' Pre-emption Right', *JRS*, XXXVII (1947), 117–26.

Platon, G., *Observations sur le droit de προτίμησις en droit byzantin* (Paris, 1906) [a series of articles in the *Revue Générale du Droit*, XXVII (1903)–XXIX (1905) reprinted as a book].

Schupfer, F., 'La communità dei beni tra coniugi e l'Ecloga isaurica', *Rivista Italiana per le scienze giuridiche*, XXXVI (1904), 319 ff.

Tamassia, N., *L'affratellamento* (Turin, 1886).

Tornarites, J. C., 'Παλλακεία', 'Αρχεῖον Βυζαντινοῦ Δικαίου, I (1929–31), 404 ff.

Triantaphyllopoulos, K. D., 'Ο Φαλκίδιος νόμος ἐν τῷ Βυζαντινῷ δικαίῳ (Athens, 1912).

Triantaphyllopoulos, K. D., 'Die Novelle des Patriarchen Athanasios über die τριμοιρία', *BNJ*, VIII (1931), 136–46.

Triantaphyllopoulos, K. D., ''Επὶ τῇ συναινέσει μεταβάσεως κυριότητος ἐν τῷ μεταγενεστέρῳ Βυζαντινῷ δικαίῳ', Μνημόσυνα Παππούλια, ed. P. G. Ballenda (Athens, 1934), 263–9.

Zhishmann, H., *Das Eherecht der orientalischen Kirche* (Vienna, 1864).

(D) CIVIL PROCEDURE

Collinet, P., *Etudes historiques sur le droit de Justinien. IV. La procédure par libelle* (Paris, 1932).

Lemerle, P., 'Le juge général des Grecs et la réforme judiciaire d'Andronic III', *Mémorial L. Petit* (Bucharest, 1948), 292–316.

Lemerle, P., 'Recherches sur les institutions judiciaires à l'époque des Paléologues'; I, 'Le tribunal impérial', *Mélanges H. Grégoire*, I (= *AIPHO*, IX, 1949), 369–84; II, 'Le tribunal du patriarcat ou tribunal synodal', *Mélanges P. Peeters*, II (= *AB*, LXVIII, 1950), 318–33.

Ševčenko, I., 'Léon Bardales et les juges généraux ou la corruption des incorruptibles', *B*, XIX (1949), 247–59.

Steinwenter, A., 'Zur Gliederung des Verfahrens im Libellprozess', *Festschrift für Leopold Wenger*, I = *Münchener Beiträge zur Papyrusforschung und antiken Rechtsgeschichte*, XXXIV (Munich, 1944), 180–203.

Steinwenter, A., 'Das Verfahren sine scriptis im justinianischen Prozessrechte', *ZSR*, rom. Abt., LXXVI (1959), 306–23.

(E) CRIMINAL LAW

Ferrari, G., 'Il diritto penale nelle Novelle di Leone il Filosofo', *Rivista Penale*, LXVII, fasc. 4 (Turin, 1908), 3–29.

Herman, E., 'Zum Asylrecht im byzantinischen Reich', *OCP*, I (1935), 204–38.

Lampsides, O., Ἡ ποινὴ τῆς τυφλώσεως παρὰ Βυζαντινῶν (Athens, 1949).

Sinogowitz, B., *Studien zum Strafrecht der Ekloge* (Πραγματεῖαι τῆς Ἀκαδημίας Ἀθηνῶν, 21) (Athens, 1956).

Triantaphyllopoulos, K. D., 'Ἑλληνικαὶ νομικαὶ ἰδέαι ἐν τῷ Βυζαντινῷ ποινικῷ δικαίῳ', Ἀρχεῖον Ἰδιωτικοῦ Δικαίου, XVI (1953), 151–88.

Wenger, L., 'Ὅροι ἀσυλίας', *Philologus*, LXXXVI (1931), 427–54.

(F) ECCLESIASTICAL

Alivisatos, H. S., *Die kirchliche Gesetzgebung des Kaisers Justinian I.* (Berlin, 1913).

Granić, B., 'Die rechtliche Stellung und Organisation der griechischen Klöster nach dem justinianischen Recht', *BZ*, XXIX (1929/30), 6–35.

Granić, B., 'Die privatrechtliche Stellung der griechischen Mönche im V. und VI. Jahrhundert', *BZ*, XXX (1929/30), 669–76.

Granić, B., 'Das Klosterwesen in der Novellengesetzgebung Kaiser Leons des Weisen', *BZ*, XXXI (1931), 61–69.

Hagemann, H. R., *Die Stellung der piae causae nach justinianischem Recht* (Basel, 1953).

Herman, E., 'Ricerche sulle istituzioni monastiche bizantine', *OCP*, VI (1940), 293–375.

Herman, E., 'Chiese private e diritto di fondazione negli ultimi secoli dell'impero bizantino', *OCP*, XII (1946), 302–21.

Knecht, A., *System des Justinianischen Kirchenvermögensrecht* (Stuttgart, 1905).

Pfanmüller, G., *Die kirchliche Gesetzgebung Justinians, hauptsächlich auf Grund der Novellen* (Berlin, 1902).

Vernadsky, G. V., 'Vizantijskija učenija o vlasti carja i patriarcha' ['Byzantine teaching on the authority of the Emperor and the Patriarch'], *Recueil d'études déd. à la mémoire de N. P. Kondakov* (Prague, 1926), 143–54; see also 'Die kirchlichpolitische Lehre der Epanagoge', *BNJ*, VI (1928), 119–42.

Vismara, G., *Episcopalis audientia* (Milan, 1937).

(G) STATE AND GOVERNMENT. TAXATION

Bréhier, L., *Le monde byzantin*, II [see Gen. Bibl. v].

Bury, J. B., *The Constitution of the Later Roman Empire* [see Gen. Bibl. v].

Bury, J. B., *The Imperial Administrative System in the Ninth Century* [see Gen. Bibl. v].

Christophilopoulou, A. A., Ἡ σύγκλητος εἰς τὸ Βυζαντινὸν κράτος (᾽Επετηρὶς τοῦ ᾽Αρχείου τῆς ἱστορίας τοῦ ἑλληνικοῦ λαοῦ τῆς ᾽Ακαδημίας ᾽Αθηνῶν, II) (Athens, 1949).

Courtois, C., 'Exconsul. Observations sur l'histoire du consulat à l'époque byzantine', *B*, XIX (1949), 37–58.

Diehl, C., *Etudes sur l'administration byzantine dans l'exarchat de Ravenne* (Paris, 1888).

Dölger, F., *Beiträge zur Geschichte der byzantinischen Finanzverwaltung* [see Gen. Bibl. v].

Dölger, F., 'Das ἀερικόν', *BZ*, XXX (1929/30), 450–7.

Dölger, F., 'Die Frage des Grundeigentums in Byzanz', *Bulletin of the International Committee of Historical Sciences*, Vth Congress (Warsaw, 1933), 5–15.

Dölger, F., 'Das Fortbestehen der ἐπιβολή in mittel- und spätbyzantinischer Zeit', *Studi in memoria di A. Albertoni*, II (Padua, 1934), 5–11.

Dölger, F., 'Zum Gebührenwesen der Byzantiner', *Etudes Andréadès* (Athens, 1940), 35–59; reprinted in *Byzanz und die eur. Staatenwelt*, 232–60.

Gelzer, M., *Studien zur byzantinischen Verwaltung Aegyptens* (Leipzig, 1909).

Gelzer, M., 'Altes und Neues aus der ägyptischen Verwaltungsmisere', *Archiv für Papyrusforschung*, V (1913), 346–77.

Hartmann, L., *Untersuchungen zur Geschichte der byzantinischen Verwaltung in Italien (540–750)* (Leipzig, 1889).

Karayannopulos, J., 'Die Chrysoteleia der Iuga', *BZ*, XLIX (1956), 72–84.

Karayannopulos, J., 'Die kollektive Steuerverantwortung in der frühbyzantinischen Zeit', *Vierteljahrsschrift für Sozial- und Wirtschaftsgeschichte*, XLIII (1956), 289–322.

Karayannopulos, J., *Das Finanzwesen des frühbyzantinischen Staates* (Munich, 1958).

Monnier, H., 'Etudes de droit byzantin; l'ἐπιβολή', *Revue historique de droit français et étranger*, XVI (1892), 125–64; XVIII (1894), 433–86; XIX (1895), 59–103.

Ostrogorsky, G., *Pour l'histoire de la féodalité byzantine* [see Gen. Bibl. v].

Ostrogorsky, G., *Quelques problèmes d'histoire de la paysannerie byzantine* [see Gen. Bibl. v].

Ostrogorsky, G., 'Die ländliche Steuergemeinde des byzantinischen Reiches im 10. Jahrhundert', *Vierteljahrsschrift für Sozial- und Wirtschaftsgeschichte*, XX (1927), 1–108.

Ostrogorsky, G., 'Das Steuersystem im byzantinischen Altertum und Mittelalter', *B*, VI (1931), 229–40.

Ostrogorsky, G., 'Pour l'histoire de l'immunité à Byzance', *B*, xxviii (1958), 165–254.

Rouillard, G., *L'administration civile de l'Egypte byzantine* (2nd ed., Paris, 1928).

Rouillard, G., 'L'epibolè au temps d'Alexis I Comnène', *B*, x (1935), 81–9.

Spulber, C. A., *Le concept byzantin de la loi juridique* (Bucharest, 1938).

Stein, E., *Untersuchungen über das officium der Prätorianerpräfektur seit Diokletian* (Vienna, 1922).

Stein, E., 'Untersuchungen zum Staatsrecht des Bas-Empire', *ZSR*, rom. Abt., xli (1920), 195–251.

Stein, E., 'Untersuchungen zur spätbyzantinischen Verfassungs- und Wirtschaftsgeschichte' [see Gen. Bibl. v].

Stein, E., 'Justinian, Johannes der Kappadozier und das Ende des Konsulats', *BZ*, xxx (1929–30), 376–81.

Stein, E., 'Postconsulat et αὐτοκρατορία', *Mélanges Bidez* (= *AIPHO*, ii, 1934), 869–912.

Stein, E., 'La disparition du Sénat de Rome à la fin du VIme siècle', *Bulletin de la Classe des Lettres de l'Académie Royale de Belgique*, 5e série, tome xxv (1939), 308–22.

Tornarites, J. C., ''Αερικόν—aerarium—fiscus', 'Αρχεῖον Βυζαντινοῦ Δικαίου, i (1929–31), 307–66.

Zachariae von Lingenthal, K. E., 'Zur Kenntnis des römischen Steuerwesens in der Kaiserzeit', *Mémoires de l'Académie Imp. des Sciences de St Pétersbourg*, 7e série, tome vi, no. 9 (1863).

Zachariae von Lingenthal, K. E., 'Principii di un debito pubblico nell'impero bizantino' (transl. by C. Ferrini), *Rendiconti dell'Istituto Lombardo*, ser. 2, xvi, fasc. xviii (1883), 945–50; reprinted in *Opere di C. Ferrini*, ed. V. Arangio-Ruiz, i (Milan, 1929), 479–83.

CHAPTER XXII. SOCIAL LIFE IN THE BYZANTINE EMPIRE

I. SOURCES

Material for the history of Byzantine civilisation is derived from Byzantine sources as a whole, and only a select bibliography is given here, particularly of works bearing on the monuments and life of Constantinople. The bibliographies for the other chapters should also be consulted.

Lives of the Saints are too numerous to be cited individually. Of especial significance for this chapter are those of St Andrew the Fool (*MPG*, cxi, 627–888), St Irene (*AASS*, July, vi, 602–34), St Luke the Stylite (*PO*, xi (1915), 189–287), St Luke the Younger (*Phokika*, i (1874), 25–62), St Paul of Latros (*AB*, xi (1892), 19–74, 136–81), St Philaretus Eleemon (*B*, ix (1934), 112–67). For the evidence supplied by Lives of the Saints in general the reader should consult A. P. Rudakov, *Očerki vizantijskoj kul'tury po dannym grečeskoj agiografii* [*Byzantine civilisation from the evidence of Greek hagiography*] (Moscow, 1917). For an English transl. (with introduction and notes) of St Daniel the Stylite, St Theodore of Sykeon and St John the Almsgiver, see N. H. Baynes and E. Dawes, *Three Byzantine Saints* (Oxford, 1948).

Alexii Carmina, ed. P. Maas, 'Die Musen des Kaisers Alexios I.', *BZ*, XXII (1913), 348–69.

Anonymous, *De antiquitatibus Constantinopolitanis*, ed. A. Banduri (*Imperium orientale*, I) [see Gen. Bibl. II].

Anonymous, Περὶ τῶν τάφων τῶν βασιλέων τῶν ὄντων ἐν τῷ ναῷ τῶν ἁγίων ἀποστόλων, ed. A. Banduri (*Imperium orientale*, I) [see Gen. Bibl. II].

Ashburner Tract (so-called), ed. F. Dölger, *Beiträge zur Geschichte der byz. Finanzverwaltung*, pp. 113–23 [see Gen. Bibl. V].

Cecaumenus, *Strategicon*, ed. B. Wassiliewsky and V. Jernstedt (St Petersburg, 1896); German transl. by H.-G. Beck (= *Byzantinische Geschichtsschreiber*, V, ed. E. von Ivánka) (Graz, 1956). [For life in the provinces.]

Choniates, Nicetas, *De signis Constantinopolitanis*, ed. I. Bekker, *CSHB* (1835).

Constantine Porphyrogenitus, *De cerimoniis aulae byzantinae* [see Gen. Bibl. IV].

Constantine the Rhodian, 'Description of the works of art and of the church of the Holy Apostles at Constantinople', ed. E. Legrand and T. Reinach, *REG*, IX (1896), pp. 32–103.

De Velitatione Bellica, ed. C. B. Hase, *CSHB* (1828) (with *Leonis Diaconi Historia*).

Eparch, Book of the [see Gen. Bibl. IV].

Itinéraires russes en Orient, French transl. B. de Khitrovo (Geneva, 1889).

Kosminsky, E. A. (ed.), *Sbornik dokumentov po socialno-ekonomičeskoj istorii Vizantii* [*Documents for the social and economic history of Byzantium*] (Moscow, 1951).

Leo VI, *Tactica*, *MPG*, CXI, 671–1120.

Mesarites, Nicholas, *Description of the Church of the Holy Apostles*, ed. A. Heisenberg, *Grabeskirche und Apostelkirche*, II (Leipzig, 1908); ed. with transl. and commentary G. Downey, *Trans. Amer. Philosoph. Soc.*, n.s. XLVII (1957), 855–924.

Nicholas Muzalon, Archibishop of Cyprus, Στίχοι Νικολάου μοναχοῦ τοῦ Μουζάλωνος, ed. S. J. Doanides, Ἑλληνικά, VII (1934), 110–41. Cf. P. Maas and F. Dölger, 'Zu dem Abdankungsgedicht des Nikolaos Muzalon', *BZ*, XXXV (1935), 2–14.

Νόμος Γεωργικός = *The Farmers' Law*, ed. W. Ashburner, *JHS*, XXX (1910), 85–108; XXXII (1912), 68–83.

Notitia urbis Constantinopolitanae, ed. O. Seeck (*Notitia dignitatum*) (Berlin, 1876).

Pachymeres, George, Ἔκφρασις τοῦ Αὐγουστεῶνος, ed. A. Banduri (*Imperium orientale*, I) [see Gen. Bibl. II].

Paul the Silentiary, Ἔκφρασις τοῦ ναοῦ τῆς ἁγίας Σοφίας, ed. I. Bekker, *CSHB* (1837).

Paul the Silentiary, Ἔκφρασις τοῦ ἄμβωνος, *ibid.*

Photius, Ἔκφρασις τῆς ἐν τοῖς βασιλείοις νέας ἐκκλησίας, ed. A. Banduri (*Imperium orientale*, I) [see Gen. Bibl. II].

Procopius, *De aedificiis*, ed. J. Haury (*Opera Omnia*, III, 2) (Leipzig, 1913); English transl. H. B. Dewing (Loeb) (London, 1940).

Prodromus, Theodore, *Poèmes Prodromiques en grec vulgaire*, ed. D. C. Hesseling and H. Pernot (Amsterdam, 1910).

Psellus, Michael, Ἱστορικοὶ Λόγοι, Ἐπιστολαί, ed. K. N. Sathas, Μεσαιωνικὴ βιβλιοθήκη, V, 3–87 [see Gen. Bibl. IV].

Scriptores originum Constantinopolitanarum, ed. T. Preger, 2 vols. (Leipzig, 1901–7).

II. MODERN WORKS

Excellent general bibliographies are to be found in G. Ostrogorsky, *History of the Byzantine State* (Oxford, 1956) and A. A. Vasiliev, *History of the Byzantine Empire* (Madison, 1952).

On Byzantine art see the bibliography to chapter XXIX.

Andréadès, A., 'De la population de Constantinople sous les empereurs byzantins', *Metroon*, I (1920).

Antoniades, E. M., Ἔκφρασις τῆς ἁγίας Σοφίας (Paris, 1917).

Aristarches, S., ''Ἀρχαιολογικὸς χάρτης τῶν χερσαίων τειχῶν Κωνσταντινουπόλεως', Παράρτημα of the Ἑλληνικὸς Φιλολογικὸς Σύλλογος of Constantinople, XIV (1884), 1–15.

Banduri, A., *Imperium orientale* [see Gen. Bibl. II].

Baynes, N. H., 'The Hellenistic Civilisation and East Rome', in *Byzantine Studies* [see Gen. Bibl. V].

Baynes, N. H., 'The Thought World of East Rome', in *Byzantine Studies* [see Gen. Bibl. V].

Beylié, L. M. E. de, *L'habitation byzantine* (Paris, 1912).

Brătianu, G. I., *Etudes byzantines d'histoire économique et sociale* [see Gen. Bibl. V].

Bréhier, L., *Le monde byzantin*, III [see Gen. Bibl. V].

Brentano, L., *Die byzantinische Volkswirthschaft* (Munich, 1917).

Buckler, G. G., 'Byzantine Education', *Byzantium*, pp. 200–20 [see Gen. Bibl. V].

Bury, J. B., 'The Great Palace', *BZ*, XXI (1912), 210–25.

Constantius, Patriarch, Κωνσταντινιὰς παλαιὰ καὶ νεωτέρα (Vienna, 1824); 2nd ed. (Constantinople, 1844); French ed. *Constantiniade ou description de Constantinople ancienne et moderne* (Constantinople, 1846).

Diehl, C., *Byzance: grandeur et décadence* [see Gen. Bibl. V].

Diehl, C., *Figures byzantines* [see Gen. Bibl. V].

Diehl, C., 'La sagesse de Cécauménos', *Dans l'Orient byzantin* (Paris, 1917), pp. 149–66.

Diehl, C., 'La société byzantine', *Etudes byzantines*, pp. 131–52 [see Gen. Bibl. V].

Diehl, C., *Justinien et la civilisation byzantine au VIᵉ siècle* (Paris, 1901).

Dieterich, K., *Byzantinische Charakterköpfe* (Leipzig, 1908).

Dieterich, K., *Hofleben in Byzanz* (Leipzig, 1912).

Djelal Essad, *Constantinople* (Paris, 1909).

Dölger, F., *Beiträge zur Geschichte der byz. Finanzverwaltung* [see Gen. Bibl. V].

Dölger, F., *Aus den Schatzkammern des Heiligen Berges* [see Gen. Bibl. IV].

Dölger, F. and Schneider, A. M., *Byzanz* (Bern, 1952), pp. 108–24 [bibliography].

Du Cange, C. du Fresne, *Constantinopolis Christiana. Historia Byzantina*, pts. II and III [see Gen. Bibl. V].

Ebersolt, J., *Le Grand Palais de Constantinople et le livre des Cérémonies* (Paris, 1910).

Ebersolt, J., *Recherches dans les ruines du Grand Palais. Mission archéologique à Constantinople* (Paris, 1921).

Ebersolt, J., *Etudes sur la vie publique et privée à la cour byzantine. Mélanges d'histoire et d'archéologie byzantine* (Paris, 1917).

Ebersolt, J., *Constantinople byzantine et les voyageurs du Levant* (Paris, 1919).

Ebersolt, J., *Sainte Sophie de Constantinople* (Paris, 1910).

Ebersolt, J., *Sanctuaires de Constantinople* (Paris, 1921).

Ebersolt, J. and Thiers, A., *Les églises de Constantinople* (Paris, 1913).

Ferradou, A., *Les biens des monastères à Byzance* (Paris, 1897).

Gelzer, H., *Byzantinische Kulturgeschichte* [see Gen. Bibl. v].

Glück, H., *Das Hebdomon von Konstantinopel* (Vienna, 1920).

Grosvenor, E. A., *The Hippodrome of Constantinople* (London, 1889).

Guilland, R., 'La description des courses', *Mélanges O. et M. Merlier*, I (Athens, 1955), 31–47; reprinted in *Etudes byzantines* (Paris, 1959), pp. 89–107.

Gurlitt, C., *Die Baukunst Konstantinopels* (Berlin, 1907 ff.).

Gyllius, P., *De topographia Constantinopoleos* (Lyons, 1561).

Hammer-Purgstall, J. von, *Constantinopolis und der Bosporos*, 2 vols. (Pest, 1822).

Heisenberg, A., *Die Apostelkirche in Konstantinopel* (Leipzig, 1908).

Heyd, W., *Histoire du commerce du Levant* [see Gen. Bibl. v].

Hussey, J. M., *Church and Learning in the Byzantine Empire* [see Gen. Bibl. v].

Hussey, J. M., *The Byzantine World* [see Gen. Bibl. v].

Janin, R., *Constantinople byzantine* [see Gen. Bibl. II].

Každan, A. P., *Agrarnie otnošenija v Vizantii XIII–XIV vv.* [*Agrarian relations in Byzantium in the 13th and 14th centuries*] (Moscow, 1952).

Kukules, Ph., Βυζαντινῶν Βίος καὶ Πολιτισμός [see Gen. Bibl. v].

Krumbacher, K., *Geschichte der byzantinischen Litteratur* [see Gen. Bibl. v].

Labarte, J., *Le Palais impérial à Constantinople* (Paris, 1861).

Lethaby, W. R. and Swainson, H., *The Church of Sancta Sophia* (London, 1894).

Marin, E., *Les moines de Constantinople* (Paris, 1897).

Moravcsik, Gy., *Byzantinoturcica* [see Gen. Bibl. I].

Mordtmann, A., *Esquisse topographique de Constantinople* [see Gen. Bibl. II].

Neumann, C., *Die Weltstellung des byzantinischen Reiches vor den Kreuzzügen* [see Gen. Bibl. v].

Nissen, W., *Die Regelung des Klosterwesens im Rhomäerreiche* (Hamburg, 1897).

Oberhummer, E., *Constantinopolis* (Stuttgart, 1899).

Oeconomos, L., *La vie religieuse dans l'empire byzantin au temps des Comnènes et des Anges* (Paris, 1918).

Ostrogorsky, G., 'Agrarian Conditions in the Byzantine Empire', *Cambridge Econ. Hist.*, I, 194–223, 579–83 [see Gen. Bibl. v].

Ostrogorsky, G., *Pour l'histoire de la féodalité byzantine* [see Gen. Bibl. v].

Ostrogorsky, G., *Quelques problèmes d'histoire de la paysannerie byzantine* [see Gen. Bibl. v].

Papadopoulos, J., Αἱ Βλαχερναί (Constantinople, 1921).

Paparrhegopoulos, K., Ἱστορία τοῦ Ἑλληνικοῦ ἔθνους [see Gen. Bibl. v].

Paspates, A. G., Βυζαντιναὶ μελέται τοπογραφικαὶ καὶ ἱστορικαί (Constantinople, 1877).

Paspates, A. G., Τὰ βυζαντινὰ ἀνάκτορα (Athens, 1885).

Pulgher, D., *Les anciennes églises byzantines de Constantinople* [with atlas] (Vienna, 1878–80).

Rambaud, A., *L'empire grec au Xe siècle* (Paris, 1870).

Rambaud, A., 'Le sport et l'hippodrome à Constantinople', *Etudes sur l'histoire byzantine* (Paris, 1912), pp. 3–61.

Richter, J. P., *Quellen der byzantinischen Kunstgeschichte* (Vienna, 1897).

Roth, K., *Sozial- und Kulturgeschichte des byzantinischen Reichs* (Leipzig, 1917).

Rouillard, G., *La vie rurale dans l'empire byzantin* (Paris, 1953).

Runciman, S., *Byzantine Civilisation* [see Gen. Bibl. v].
Salzenberg, W., *Alt-christliche Baudenkmäler von Constantinopel* (Berlin, 1854).
Skabalanovič, N., *Vizantijskoe gosudarstvo i cerkov v XI v.* [see Gen. Bibl. v].
Skarlatos Byzantios, D. C., Ἡ Κωνσταντινούπολις, 3 vols. (Athens, 1851–69).
Strzygowski, J. and Forchheimer, P., *Die byzantinischen Wasserbehälter von Konstantinopel* (Vienna, 1897).
Testaud, G., *Des rapports des puissants et des petits propriétaires ruraux dans l'empire byzantin au Xᵉ siècle* (Bordeaux, 1898).
Turchi, N., *La civiltà bizantina* (Florence, 1915).
Uspensky, F. I., *Očerki po istorii vizantijskoj obrazovannosti* [*Studies in the history of Byzantine civilisation*] (St Petersburg, 1892).
Uspensky, F. I., 'Partii čirka i dimy v Konstantinopole' ['The Circus parties and demes in Constantinople'], *VV*, I (1894), 1–16.
Van Millingen, A., *Byzantine Churches in Constantinople* (London, 1912).
Van Millingen, A., *Byzantine Constantinople* [see Gen. Bibl. II].
Zakythinos, D. A., Βυζάντιον, Κράτος καὶ Κοινωνία (Athens, 1951).

CHAPTER XXIII. THE SECULAR CHURCH

I. GENERAL BIBLIOGRAPHY

For imperial legislation see Gen. Bibl. IV, under Justinian; K. E. Zachariae von Lingenthal; J. and P. Zepos; and also bibliography for chapter XXI. For ecclesiastical legislation see G. A. Rhalles and M. Potles, Gen. Bibl. IV. Some of these texts may also be found in the more accessible *MPG*. See also the bibliographies for chapters XX–XXI and XXIV–XXVI and the ecclesiastical dictionaries cited in Gen. Bibl. I.

Beck, H.-G., *Kirche und theologische Literatur im byzantinischen Reich* [see Gen. Bibl. v].
Bingham, J., *Origines sive antiquitates ecclesiasticae...*, 10 vols. (Halle, 1724–9).
Bréhier, L., *Le monde byzantin*, II [see Gen. Bibl. v].
Byzantium, ed. N. H. Baynes and H. St L. B. Moss [see Gen. Bibl. v].
Diehl, C., *Les grands problèmes de l'histoire byzantine* (Paris, 1943).
Diehl, C., *Byzance, grandeur et décadence* [see Gen. Bibl. v].
Dölger, F., *Regesten der Kaiserurkunden* [see Gen. Bibl. IV].
Dölger, F. and Schneider, A. M., *Byzanz* (Berne, 1952).
Gordillo, M., *Theologia orientalium cum latinorum comparata.* I: *Ab ortu nestorianismi usque ad expugnationem Constantinopoleos (431–1453)* (Rome, 1960).
Grumel, V., *Les regestes des actes du patriarcat de Constantinople* [see Gen. Bibl. IV].
Hausherr, I., *La direction spirituelle en Orient autrefois* (*OCA*, 144) (Rome, 1955).
Hausherr, I., *Noms du Christ et voies d'oraison* (*OCA*, 157) (Rome, 1960).
Hussey, J. M., *Church and Learning in the Byzantine Empire* [see Gen. Bibl. v].
Hussey, J. M., *The Byzantine World* [see Gen. Bibl. v].
Jugie, M., *Theologia dogmatica Christianorum orientalium* [see Gen. Bibl. v].
Jugie, M., *Le schisme byzantin* (Paris, 1941).

Lebedev, A. P., *Očerki vnutrennej istorii vizantijskovostočnoj cerkvi v IX, X, i XI v.* [*Studies in the internal history of the Byzantine Eastern Church in the IXth, Xth, and XIth centuries*] (Moscow, 1901).

Lebedev, A. P., *Duchovenstvo drevnej vselenskoj cerkvi ot vremen apostol'skich do IX v.* [*The clergy in the early universal church from apostolic times to the IXth century*] (Moscow, 1905).

Lebedev, A. P., *Istoričeskie očerki sostojanija viz.-vost. cerkvi ot konca XI-go do poloviny XV-go veka* [*Historical studies in the state of the Byzantine Eastern Church from the end of the XIth century to the middle of the XVth century*], 2nd ed. (Moscow, 1902).

Meester, P. de, *De Monachico Statu* [see Gen. Bibl. I].

Moravcsik, Gy., *Byzantinoturcica* [see Gen. Bibl. I].

Oeconomos, L., *La vie religieuse dans l'Empire byzantin au temps des Comnènes et des Anges* (Paris, 1918).

Ostrogorsky, G., *History of the Byzantine State* [see Gen. Bibl. v].

Pargoire, J., *L'Eglise byzantine de 527 à 847* [see Gen. Bibl. v].

Pilati, G., *Chiesa e Stato nei primi quindici secoli. Profilo dello sviluppo della teoria attraverso le fonti e la bibliografia* (Rome, 1961).

Runciman, S., *The Eastern Schism* [see Gen. Bibl. v].

Skabalanovič, N., *Vizantijskoe gosudarstvo i cerkov v XI veke* [see Gen. Bibl. v].

Thomassin, L., *Vetus et nova Ecclesiae disciplina circa beneficia et beneficiarios*, 3 vols. (Paris, 1688).

II. CHURCH AND EMPEROR

See also bibliography for chapter xx

Alivizatos, H. S., *Die kirchliche Gesetzgebung des Kaisers Justinian* (Berlin, 1913).

Baynes, N. H., *Constantine the Great and the Christian Church* (London, 1929).

Berkhof, H., *Kirche und Kaiser. Eine Untersuchung der Entstehung der byzantinischen und theokratischen Staatsauffassung im vierten Jahrhundert* (Zollikon–Zürich, 1947).

Beurlier, E., *Le culte impérial, son histoire et son organisation depuis Auguste jusqu'à Justinien* (Paris, 1891).

Bréhier, L. and Batiffol, P., *Les survivances du culte impérial romain* (Paris, 1920).

Bréhier, L., ' Ἱερεὺς καὶ βασιλεύς', *Mém. L. Petit* (Bucharest, 1948), pp. 41–5.

Charanis, P., 'Coronation and its Constitutional Significance in the Later Roman Empire', *B*, xv (1940/1), 49–66.

Charanis, P., 'The Imperial Crown Modiolus and its Constitutional Significance', *B*, xII (1937), 189–95.

Charanis, P., 'The Crown Modiolus Once More', *B*, xIII (1938), 377–83.

Dölger, F., 'Die Kaiserurkunde der Byzantiner als Ausdruck ihrer politischen Anschauungen', *HZ*, CLIX (1939), 229–50; reprinted in *Byzanz und die europäische Staatenwelt*, pp. 9–33 [see Gen. Bibl. v].

Ensslin, W., 'Zur Frage nach der ersten Kaiserkrönung durch den Patriarchen und zur Bedeutung dieses Aktes im Wahlzeremoniell', *BZ*, xLII (1942), 101–15, 369–72; published separately (Würzburg, 1948).

Ensslin, W., 'Das Gottesgnadentum des autokratischen Kaisertums der früh-byzantinischen Zeit', *Atti del V Congresso internazionale di studi Biz., Rome, 1936, SBN*, v (1939), 154–66.

Ensslin, W., 'Staat und Kirche von Konstantin d. Gr. bis Theodosius d. Gr. Ein Beitrag zur Frage nach dem "Cäsaropapismus"', *Acta IX. Internat. Byz. Congr. Thessalonica 1953*, II (= Ἑλληνικά, Παράρτημα IX, Athens, 1956), 404–15.

Gasquet, A., *De l'autorité impériale en matière religieuse à Byzance* (Paris, 1879).

Gelzer, H., 'Das Verhältnis von Staat und Kirche in Byzanz', *Ausgewählte kleine Schriften* (Leipzig, 1907), pp. 57–141.

Greenslade, S. L., *Church and State from Constantine to Theodosius* (London, 1954).

Herman, E., 'Zum Asylrecht im byzantinischen Reich', *OCP*, I (1935), 204–38.

Instinsky, H. U., *Bischofsstuhl und Kaiserthron* (Munich, 1955).

Janin, R., 'L'Empereur dans l'Eglise byzantine', *Nouvelle Revue Théologique*, LXXVII (1955), 49–60.

Kaden, E., 'L'église et l'état sous Justinien', *Mémoires publiés par la Faculté de Droit de Genève*, IX (1952), 109–44.

Karayanopulos, J., 'Der frühbyzantinische Kaiser', *BZ*, XLIX (1956), 369–84.

Kraft, H., 'Kaiser Konstantin und das Bischofsamt', *Saeculum*, VIII (1957), 32–42.

Lietzmann, H., *Die Anfänge des Problems Kirche und Staat*, *Sitz. Ber. d. Preuss. Akad. d. Wiss.* (1938), XXXVII–XLVI.

Martroye, F., 'L'asile et la législation impériale du IVᵉ au VIᵉ siècle', *Mém. de la Soc. nat. des antiquaires de France*, LXXV (1919), 159–246.

Michel, A., *Die Kaisermacht in der Ostkirche* [see Gen. Bibl. v].

Ostrogorsky, G., 'Otnošenie cerkvi i gosudarstva v Vizantii' ['Relations between church and state in Byzantium'], *Sem. Kond.* IV (1933), 121–34.

Pfannmüller, G., *Die kirchliche Gesetzgebung Justinians hauptsächlich auf Grund der Novellen* (Berlin, 1902).

Savagnone, F. G., *Studi sul diritto romano ecclesiastico*, *Annali del sem. giuridico di Palermo*, XIV (Cortona, 1929), 152 pp.

Stephanides, B., 'Τὰ ὅρια τῆς ἐκκλησιαστικῆς νομοθεσίας τῶν βυζαντινῶν αὐτοκρατόρων', *EEBS*, XXV (1955), 12–27.

Treitinger, O., 'Vom oströmischen Staats- und Reichsgedanken', *Leipziger Vierteljahrsschrift* (1940), pp. 1–26.

Treitinger, O., *Die oströmische Kaiser- und Reichsidee nach ihrer Gestaltung im höfischen Zeremoniell* [see Gen. Bibl. v].

Voigt, K., *Staat und Kirche von Konstantin dem Grossen bis zum Ende der Karolingerzeit* (Stuttgart, 1936).

Wenger, L., *Canon in den römischen Rechtsquellen und in den Papyri. Eine Wortstudie*, *Sitz. Akad. Wiss. in Wien*, Phil.-hist. Kl., 220, 2 (Vienna and Leipzig, 1942).

Ziegler, A. W., 'Die byzantinische Religionspolitik und der sogennante Cäsaropapismus', *Münchener Beiträge zur Slavenkunde. Festgabe P. Diels* (Munich, 1953), 81–97.

III. THE PATRIARCH

Alexander, P. J., *The Patriarch Nicephorus of Constantinople* [see Gen. Bibl. v].

Bréhier, L., 'L'investiture des patriarches de Constantinople au moyen âge', *Miscellanea G. Mercati*, III (Studi e Testi, 123) (Vatican, 1946), pp. 368–72.

Cotlarciuc, N., 'Die Besetzungsweise des Patriarchenstuhles von Konstantinopel', *Archiv f. kath. Kirchenrecht*, LXXXIII (1903), 3–40, 226–54.

Dvornik, F., *The Idea of Apostolicity in Byzantium and the Legend of the Apostle Andrew* (Cambridge, Mass., 1958).

Gelzer, H., 'Der Streit über den Titel des ökumenischen Patriarchen', *Jahrbücher f. prot. Theologie*, XIII (1887), 549–84.

Gelzer, H., 'Zur Zeitbestimmung der griechischen Notitiae Episcopatuum', *Jahrbücher f. prot. Theologie*, XII (1886), 337–72, 529–75.

Gelzer, H., 'Ungedruckte und ungenügend veröffentlichte Texte der Notitiae episcopatuum', *Abh. d. k. Bayer. Akad. d. Wiss.* 1. Klasse, Abt. III, Bd. XXI (Munich, 1901), pp. 529–641.

Gerland, E., 'Die Vorgeschichte des Patriarchats von Konstantinopel', *BNJ*, IX (1932), 215–30.

Gerland, E. and Laurent, V., *Corpus Notitiarum episcopatuum Ecclesiae Orientalis Graecae*, I (Kadikoi–Istanbul, 1931/6).

Hajjar, J., *Le synode permanent (Σύνοδος ἐνδημοῦσα) dans l'église byzantine des origines au XIe siècle* (*OCA*, 164) (Rome, 1962).

Janin, R., 'Formation du Patriarcat œcuménique de Constantinople', *EO*, XIII (1910), 213–18.

Joannou, P. P., *Pape, Concile et Patriarches dans la tradition canonique de l'église orientale jusqu'au IXe siècle* (Grottaferrata, 1962).

Konidares, G. D., *Αἱ μητροπόλεις καὶ ἀρχιεπισκοπαὶ τοῦ οἰκουμενικοῦ πατριαρχείου καὶ ἡ «τάξις» αὐτῶν* (Texte und Forschungen zur byz.-neugriech. Philologie, 13) (Athens, 1934).

Laurent, V., 'Les sources à consulter pour l'établissement des listes episcopales du patriarcat byzantin', *EO*, XXX (1931), 65–83.

Laurent, V., 'Le titre de patriarche œcuménique et Michel Cérulaire', *Miscellanea G. Mercati*, III (Studi e Testi, 123) (Vatican, 1946), pp. 373–86.

Laurent, V., 'Le rituel de l'investiture du patriarche byzantin au début du XVe siècle', *Bulletin Acad. Roum., Sect. Hist.* XXVIII (1947), 218–32.

Laurent, V., 'Le titre de patriarche œcuménique et la signature patriarcale', *REB*, VI (1948), 5–26.

Lübeck, K., *Reichseinteilung und kirchliche Hierarchie des Orients* (Münster i. W., 1901).

Sokolov, I. I., *Izbranie patriarchov v Vizantii (843–1451)* [*The election of the Patriarch in Byzantium*] (St Petersburg, 1907).

Stein, E., 'Le développement du pouvoir patriarcal du siège de Constantinople jusqu'au concile de Chalcédoine', *Le Monde Slave*, III (1926), 80–108.

Stephanides, B., 'Die geschichtliche Entwicklung der Synoden des Patriarchats von Konstantinopel', *ZKG*, LV (1936), 127–57.

Vailhé, S., 'Constantinople', *DTC*, III, 1307–1519.

Vailhé, S., 'Le titre de patriarche œcuménique avant S. Grégoire le Grand', *EO*, XI (1908), 65–9.

Vailhé, S., 'S. Grégoire le Grand et le titre de patriarche œcuménique', *ibid.* pp. 161–71.

Vailhé, S., 'Le droit d'appel en Orient et le Synode permanent de Constantinople', *EO*, XX (1921), 129–46.

Zhishman, J., *Die Synoden und die Episkopalämter in der morgenländischen Kirche* (Vienna, 1867).

IV. RIGHTS AND DUTIES OF METROPOLITANS
AND BISHOPS

Gillmann, F., *Das Institut der Chorbischöfe im Orient* (Munich, 1903).
Granić, B., 'Die Gründung des autokephalen Erzbistums von Justiniana Prima durch Kaiser Justinian I. im Jahre 535 n. Chr.', *B*, II (1925), 123–40.
Grumel, V., 'Titulature de métropolites byzantins. I. Les métropolites syncelles', *EB*, III (1945), 92–114.
Herman, E., 'Appunti sul diritto metropolitico nella Chiesa bizantina', *OCP*, XIII (1947), 522–50.
Ober, L., 'Die Translation der Bischöfe im Altertum', *Archiv f. kath. Kirchenrecht*, LXXXVIII (1908), 209–29, 441–65, 625–48; LXXXIX (1909), 3–33.
Rhalles, K., 'Περὶ τοῦ ἀξιώματος τῶν Μητροπολιτῶν', Πρακτικὰ τῆς 'Ακαδ. 'Αθηνῶν, XIII (1938), 755–67.
Sokolov, I. I., *Izbranie archijerejev v Vizantii IX–XV vv.* [*Episcopal election in Byzantium from the IXth to the XVth centuries*], *VV*, XXII (1915/16), 193–252.
Steinwenter, A., 'Die Stellung der Bischöfe in der byzantinischen Verwaltung Aegyptens', *Studi in onore di Pietro de Francisci*, I (Milan, 1956), 75–99.
Turner, C. H., 'Metropolitans and their Jurisdiction in Primitive Canon Law', *Studies in Early Church History* (Oxford, 1912), pp. 70–96.

V. DIGNITARIES OF CATHEDRAL CHURCHES

Athenagoras, Metropolitan, ''Ο θεσμὸς τῶν συγκέλλων ἐν τῷ Οἰκουμενικῷ Πατριαρχείῳ', *EEBS*, IV (1927), 3–38; V (1928), 169–92; VI (1929), 103–42.
Beurlier, E., 'Le chartophylax de la Grande Eglise de Constantinople', *Compte-Rendu du IIIᵉ Congrès scient. internat. des cath.* (Brussels, 1895), pp. 252–69.
Clugnet, L., 'Les offices et les dignités ecclésiastiques dans l'Eglise Grecque', *ROC*, III (1898), 142–50; 260–4; 452–7; and IV (1899), 116–28; publ. separately (Paris, 1899).
Demetriou, C. M. Οἱ ἐξωκατάκοιλοι ἄρχοντες τῆς ἐν Κωνσταντινουπόλει Μεγάλης τοῦ Χριστοῦ 'Εκκλησίας (Athens, 1927) (Texte und Forsch. z. byz.-neugriech. Phil., 7).
Zhishman, J., *Die Synoden und die Episkopalämter in der morgenländischen Kirche* (Vienna, 1867).

VI. THE LOWER CLERGY

Ferrari dalle Spade, G., *Immunità ecclesiastiche nel diritto romano imperiale* (Venice, 1939).
Funk, F. X., 'Handel und Gewerbe im christlichen Altertum', *Kirchengeschichtliche Abhandlungen und Untersuchungen*, II (Paderborn, 1899), 60–77.
Grashof, O., 'Die Gesetze der römischen Kaiser über die Immunitäten des Klerus', *Archiv f. kath. Kirchenrecht*, XXXVII (1877), 256–93.
Herman, E., 'Le professioni vietate al clero bizantino', *OCP*, X (1944), 23–44.
Knetes, Chr., 'Ordination and Matrimony in the Eastern Orthodox Church', *JTS*, XI (1910), 348–400, 481–513.

Panagiotakos, P. J., ʽΗ ἱερωσύνη καὶ αἱ ἐξ αὐτῆς νομοκανονικαὶ συνέπειαι κατὰ τὸ δίκαιον τῆς ᾽Ανατολικῆς ᾽Ορθοδόξου ᾽Εκκλησίας καὶ τὰ ἐν ῾Ελλάδι κρατοῦντα (Athens, 1951).
Panagiotakos, P. J., Σύστημα τοῦ ᾽Εκκλησιαστικοῦ Δικαίου κατὰ τὴν ἐν ῾Ελλάδι ἰσχὺν αὐτοῦ (Τὸ Δίκαιον τῶν Μοναχῶν, ιν) (Athens, 1957).

VII. ECCLESIASTICAL PROPERTY

Bruck, E. F., 'Kirchlich-soziales Erbrecht in Byzanz', *Studi in on. di S. Riccobono*, III (1933), 377–423.
Fourneret, P., *Ressources dont l'Eglise disposa pour reconstituer son patrimoine* (Paris, 1902).
Grashof, O., 'Die Gesetze der römischen Kaiser über die Verwaltung und Veräusserung des kirchlichen Vermögens', *Archiv f. kath. Kirchenrecht*, XXXVI (1876), 193–203.
Herman, E., 'Das bischöfliche Abgabenwesen im Patriarchat von Konstantinopel vom XI. bis zur Mitte des XIX. Jahrhunderts', *OCP*, V (1939), 434–513.
Herman, E., '"Chiese private" e diritto di fondazione negli ultimi secoli dell'impero bizantino', *OCP*, XII (1946), 302–21.
Iorgu, I. D., *Bunurile bisericeşti in primele 6 secole. Situaţia lor juridica şi canonica* (Bucharest, 1937).
Knecht, A., *System des Justinianischen Kirchenvermögensrechtes* (Stuttgart, 1905).
Kronts, G., ʽΗ ἐκκλησιαστικὴ περουσία κατὰ τοὺς ὀκτὼ πρώτους αἰῶνας (Athens, 1935).
Levčenko, M. V., 'Cerkovnye imuščestva V–VII vv. vostočno-rimskoj imperii' ['Ecclesiastical property in the Vth–VIIth centuries in the East Roman Empire'], *VV*, n.s. II (1949), 11–59.
Pétridès, S., 'Le chrysobulle de Manuel Comnène (1148) sur les biens de l'église', *ROC*, IV (XIV) (1909), 203–8.
Rhalles, K., Τὸ ἀναπαλλοτρίωτον τῆς ἐκκλησιαστικῆς περιουσίας (Athens, 1903).
Steinwenter, A., 'Die Rechtsstellung der Kirchen und Klöster nach den Papyri', *ZSR*, Kan. Abt. XIX (1930), 1–50.
Triantaphyllopoulos, C., 'Die Novelle des Patriarchen Athanasius über die "Trimoiria"', *BNJ*, VIII (1931), 136–46.
Troicky, S., 'Ktitorsko pravo u Vizantiji i u Nemanjičkoj Srbiji' ['The founder's rights in Byzantium and in Serbia under the Nemanići'], *Glas* ser. 2, LXXXVI (1935), 79–134.
Zhishman, J., *Das Stifterrecht in der morgenländischen Kirche* (Vienna, 1888).

VIII. MAINTENANCE OF THE CLERGY

Herman, E., 'Zum kirchlichen Benefizialwesen im byzantinischen Reich', *Atti del V Congresso Internaz. di Studi Biz., Rome, 1936, SBN*, V (1939), 657–71.
Herman, E., 'Die kirchlichen Einkünfte des byzantinischen Niederklerus', *OCP*, VIII (1942), 378–442.
Xanalatos, D., *Beiträge zur Wirtschafts- und Sozialgeschichte Makedoniens im Mittelalter, hauptsächlich auf Grund der Briefe des Erzbischofs Theophylakt von Achrida* (Speyer a. Rh., 1937).

IX. ECCLESIASTICAL JURISDICTION

Bell, N. J., 'The Episcopalis Audientia in Byzantine Egypt', *B*, I (1924), 139–44.

Busek, V., 'Episcopalis audientia, eine Friedens- und Schiedsgerichtbarkeit', *ZSR*, kan. Abt., xxviii (1934), 1–116.

Christophilopoulos, A., ''Η δικαιοδοσία τῶν ἐκκλησιαστικῶν δικαστηρίων κατὰ τὴν βυζαντινὴν περίοδον', *EEBS*, xviii (1948), 192–201.

Francisci, P. de, *Per la storia dell'episcopalis audientia fino alla Novella XXXV (XXXIV) di Valentiniano. Annali della facoltà di giurisprudenza della Univ. di Perugia*, xxx (1915).

Hinschius, P., *Kirchenrecht*, iv (Berlin, 1888), pp. 691–799.

Kober, F., *Der Kirchenbann*, 2nd ed. (Tübingen, 1863).

Kober, F., *Die Deposition und Degradation* (Tübingen, 1867).

Kober, F., *Die Suspension der Kirchendiener* (Tübingen, 1862).

Lammeyer, J., 'Die "audientia episcopalis" in Zivilsachen der Laien im römischen Kaiserrecht und in den Papyri', *Aegyptus*, xiii (1933), 193–202.

Laurent, V., 'Chronique de droit canonique byzantin. Dix années de recherches et d'études (1944–1953)', *L'Année Canon*, ii (1953), 258–75.

Milaš, N., *Das Kirchenrecht der morgenländischen Kirche* [see Gen. Bibl. i].

Petrakakos, D., Συμβολαὶ εἰς τὸ ποινικὸν δίκαιον τῆς 'Ορθ. 'Ανατ. 'Εκκλησίας (Leipzig, 1909).

Rhalles, K., Ποινικὸν δίκαιον τῆς 'Ορθ. 'Ανατ. 'Εκκλησίας (Athens, 1907).

Seriski, P. M., *Poenae in iure byzantino ecclesiastico ab initiis ad saec. XI (1054)* (Rome, 1941).

Steinwenter, A., 'Der antike christliche Rechtsgang und seine Quellen', *ZSR*, Kan. Abt. xxiii (1934), 1–116.

Sunorov, N., *Ob'em disciplinarnogo suda i jurisdikcii cerkvi v period vselenskich soborov* [*The disciplinary court and ecclesiastical jurisdiction in the period of the general councils*], 2nd ed. (Moscow, 1906).

Vismara, G., *Episcopalis audientia* (Milan, 1937).

Zachariae von Lingenthal, K. E., *Geschichte des griechisch–römischen Rechts*, pp. 381–4, 399–406 [see Gen. Bibl. v].

X. THE CHURCH AND THE PIETY OF THE FAITHFUL

Ammann, A. M., *Untersuchungen zur Geschichte der kirchlichen Kultur und des religiösen Lebens bei den Ostslawen*, i (Würzburg, 1955).

Baynes, N. H., 'The "Pratum Spirituale"', *OCP*, xiii (1947), 404–14.

Beck, H., *Vorsehung und Vorherbestimmung in der theologischen Literatur der Byzantiner* (*OCA*, 114) (Rome, 1937).

Cabasilas, Nicholas, *On Life in Christ*, *MPG*, cl; French transl. by S. Broussaleux, *La vie en Jésus-Christ*, *Irenikon*, ix (1932), Supplement, and 2nd ed. published separately (Chevetogne, 1961).

Cabasilas, Nicholas, *A Commentary on the Divine Liturgy*, transl. J. M. Hussey and P. A. McNulty (London, 1960).

Confirmation or the Laying on of Hands, by various writers, i (London, 1926).

Dauvillier, J., 'Extrême-Onction dans les églises orientales', *DDC*, v, 725–86.

Dauvillier, J. and De Clercq, C., *Le mariage en droit canonique oriental* (Paris, 1936).

Gass, W., *Die Mystik des Nikolaus Cabasilas von Leben in Christo* (Leipzig, 1899).

Hausherr, I., 'Les grands courants de la spiritualité orientale', *OCP*, I (1935), 114–38.

Hausherr, I., *Philautie. De la tendresse pour soi à la charité selon St Maxime le Confesseur* (*OCA*, 137) (Rome, 1952).

Hausherr, I., *Les leçons d'un contemplatif: le traité de l'Oraison d'Evagre le Pontique* (Paris, 1960).

Heiming, O., 'Orientalische Liturgie seit dem 4. Jahrhundert', *Archiv für Liturgiewissenschaft*, VII (1961), 233–66.

Herman, E., 'Confirmation dans l'Eglise orientale', *DDC*, IV, 109–28.

Herman, E., 'Baptême en Orient', *DDC*, II, 174–204.

Herman, E., 'Eucharistie en droit oriental', *DDC*, V, 499–556.

Hörmann, J., *Untersuchungen zur griechischen Laienbeicht* (Donauwörth, 1913).

Holl, K., *Enthusiasmus und Bussgewalt beim griechischen Mönchtum* (Leipzig, 1898).

Jugie, M., 'Mariage dans l'église gréco–russe', *DTC*, IX, 2317–31.

Kukules, Ph., Βυζαντινῶν Βίος καὶ Πολιτισμός [see Gen. Bibl. V]. [On religious teaching and schools.]

Lot-Borodine, M., 'La doctrine de la déification dans l'Eglise grecque jusqu'au XIe siècle', *Rev. de l'histoire des religions*, CV/CVI (1932/3).

Marongiu, A., 'La conclusione non formale del matrimonio nella novellistica e nella dottrina canonistica pre-tridentina', *Studi giuridici in memoria di Filippo Vassalli*, II (Turin, 1960), 1043–61.

Raes, A. and others, *Le Mariage: sa célébration et sa spiritualité dans les Eglises d'Orient* (Chevetogne, 1958).

Schultze, B., 'Die byzantinisch-slawische Theologie über den Dienst der Laien in der Kirche', *Ostkirchliche Studien*, V (1956), 243–84.

Schultze, B. and Chrysostomus, Johannes, *Die Glaubenswelt der orthodoxen Kirche* (Salzburg, 1961).

Viller, M. and Rahner, K., *Aszese und Mystik in der Väterzeit* (Freiburg i. Br., 1939).

Ware, T., *The Orthodox Church* (London, 1963).

Zhishman, J., *Das Eherecht der orientalischen Kirche* (Vienna, 1864).

CHAPTER XXIV. BYZANTINE MUSIC AND LITURGY

I. MUSIC IN CEREMONIES

Codinus (Pseudo-), George, *De officiis*, ed. I. Bekker, *CSHB* (1839); *MPG*, CLVII, 17–428.

Constantine Porphyrogenitus, *De cerimoniis aulae byzantinae* [see Gen. Bibl. IV].

Cottas, V., *Le Théâtre à Byzance* (Paris, 1931).

Grabar, A., *L'Empereur dans l'art byzantin* [see Gen. Bibl. V].

Handschin, J., *Das Zeremonienwerk Kaiser Konstantins und die sangbare Dichtung*. Rektoratsprogramm der Universität Basel (Basel, 1942).

Rambaud, A., *L'Empire grec au Xe siècle*, pp. 137–64 [see Gen. Bibl. v].
Rambaud, A., *Etudes sur l'histoire byzantine* (Paris, 1912).
Runciman, S., *Byzantine Civilisation* [see Gen. Bibl. v].
Sathas, K., Ἱστορικὸν δοκίμιον περὶ τοῦ θεάτρου καὶ τῆς μουσικῆς τῶν Βυζαντινῶν (Venice, 1878).
Tillyard, H. J. W., 'The Acclamation of Emperors in Byzantine Ritual', *Ann. Brit. School at Athens*, XVIII (1911–12), 239–60.
Wellesz, E., *History of Byzantine Music and Hymnography* [see Gen. Bibl. v].

II. THE ORIGINS OF
BYZANTINE ECCLESIASTICAL CHANT

Abert, H., 'Ein neu entdeckter frühchristlicher Hymnus mit antiken Musiknoten', *Zeit. für Musikwissenschaft*, IV (1921–2), 524–9.
Abert, H., 'Das älteste Denkmal der christlichen Kirchenmusik', *Die Antike*, II (1926), 282–90.
Attié, A., *La Divine Liturgie de St Jean Chrysostome* (Harissa (Lebanon), 1926).
Bardy, G., *La question des langues dans l'église ancienne*, I (Paris, 1948).
Baumstark, A., *Die Messe im Morgenland* (Sammlung Kösel, Munich, 1906).
Baumstark, A., *Festbrevier und Kirchenjahr der syrischen Jakobiten* (Paderborn, 1910).
Baumstark, A., *Liturgie comparée*, 3rd ed. (Prieuré d'Amay, 1953); English transl. by F. L. Cross (London, 1958).
Berthelot, M. and Ruelle, C. E., *Collection des anciens alchimistes grecs*, 3 vols. (Paris, 1887–8).
Bonner, C., 'The Homily on the Passion by Melito Bishop of Sardis', *Studies and Documents*, ed. K. and S. Lake, XII (London, 1940).
Borgia, N., 'Ὡρολόγιον, Diurno delle chiese di rito bizantino', *Orientalia Christiana*, XVI, 2 (Rome, 1929).
Brightman, F. E., *Liturgies Eastern and Western, I: Eastern Liturgies* (Oxford, 1896).
Couturier, A., *Cours de liturgie grecque–melkite*, 2 vols. (Jerusalem, 1912–14).
Delehaye, H., *Deux Typica byzantins de l'époque des Paléologues* (Brussels, 1921).
Dugmore, C. W., *The Influence of the Synagogue upon the Divine Office* (Oxford, 1944).
Emereau, C., *Saint Ephrem le Syrien* (Paris, 1919).
Eustratiades, S., Ἡ Θεοτόκος ἐν τῇ ὑμνογραφίᾳ (Paris, 1930).
Eustratiades, S., Θεοτοκάριον (Chennevières-sur-Marne, 1931).
Eustratiades, S., Εἱρμολόγιον (Chennevières-sur-Marne, 1932).
Gay, J., *L'Italie méridionale et l'empire byzantin* [see Gen. Bibl. v].
Gérold, T., *Les Pères de l'Eglise et la musique* (Paris, 1931).
Goar, J., Εὐχολόγιον sive *Rituale Graecorum* (Paris, 1647); 2nd ed. (Venice, 1730).
Hunt, A. S., 'A Christian Hymn with Musical Notation', *Oxyrhynchus Papyri*, pt. xv, no. 1786. [With a transcript of the music by H. Stuart Jones.]
Hussey, J. M., *Church and Learning in the Byzantine Empire 867–1185* [see Gen. Bibl. v].
Idelsohn, A. Z., *Jewish Music in its Historical Development* (New York, 1929); reprinted (1944).

Idelsohn, A. Z., 'Parallelen zwischen gregorianischen und hebräisch-orientalischen Gesangsweisen', *Zeit. für Musikwissenschaft*, IV (1921–22), 515–24.

Janin, R., *Les Eglises orientales et les rites orientaux* (Paris, 1926).

Jeannin, J., Puyade, J. and Lassalle, A. C., *Mélodies liturgiques Syriennes et Chaldéennes*, 2 vols. (Paris, 1924).

Meeser, P. de (ed.), Ἀκολουθία τοῦ Ἀκαθίστου ὕμνου, *Officio dell'Inno Acatisto* (Rome, 1903).

Nilles, N., *Kalendarium Manuale*, 2 vols. (Innsbruck, 1896–7).

Oesterley, W. O. E., *The Jewish Background of the Christian Liturgy* (Oxford, 1925).

Office-books (containing the hymns and texts of the Chants):

Horologion—Ὡρολόγιον τὸ μέγα περιέχον τὴν πρέπουσαν αὐτῷ ἀκολουθίαν.

Triodion—Τριῴδιον κατανυκτικὸν περιέχον ἅπασαν τὴν ἀνήκουσαν αὐτῷ ἀκολουθίαν τῆς ἁγίας καὶ μεγάλης Τεσσαρακοστῆς.

Pentecostarion—Πεντηκοστάριον χαρμόσυνον τὴν ἀπὸ τοῦ Πάσχα μέχρι τῆς τῶν ἁγίων πάντων κυριακῆς ἀνήκουσαν αὐτῷ ἀκολουθίαν περιέχον, ἐπὶ τέλους δὲ καὶ τὰ ἑωθινὰ εὐαγγέλια τὰ ἐν τῷ ὄρθρῳ ἑκάστης τῶν ἐν τῷ μεταξὺ τούτων ἑορτῶν ἀναγιγνωσκόμενα.

Paracletice—Παρακλητικὴ ἤτοι Ὀκτώηχος ἡ μεγάλη περιέχουσα πᾶσαν τὴν ἀνήκουσαν αὐτῇ ἀκολουθίαν μετὰ τῶν ἐν τῷ τέλει συνηθῶν προσθηκῶν.

Menaia—Μηναῖα τοῦ ὅλου ἐνιαυτοῦ.

[For details of printed editions see E. Wellesz, *History of Byzantine Music*, Gen. Bibl. v.]

Papadopoulos-Kerameus, A., Ἀνάλεκτα Ἱεροσολυμιτικῆς σταχυολογίας. II. Τυπικὸν τῆς ἐν Ἱεροσολύμοις ἐκκλησίας (St Petersburg, 1894).

Quasten, J., 'Musik und Gesang in den Kulten der heidnischen Antike und christlichen Frühzeit', *Liturgiegeschichtliche Quellen und Forschungen*, Heft 25 (Münster, 1930).

Raes, A., *Introductio in Liturgiam Orientalem* (Rome, 1947).

Salaville, S., *An Introduction to the Study of Eastern Liturgies* (London, 1932).

Salaville, S., *Studia Orientalia Liturgio-Theologica* (Rome, 1950).

Thibaut, J.-B., *Ordre des Offices de la Semaine Sainte à Jérusalem du IVe–Xe siècle* (Paris, 1926).

Trempela, P. N., Αἱ τρεῖς λειτουργίαι κατὰ τοὺς ἐν Ἀθήναις κώδικας (Athens, 1935).

Wellesz, E., 'Melito's Homily on the Passion: An Investigation into the Sources of Byzantine Hymnography', *JTS*, XLIV (1943), 41–52.

Wellesz, E., *A History of Byzantine Music and Hymnography* [see Gen. Bibl. v].

Werner, E., *The Sacred Bridge. The Interdependence of Liturgy and Music in Synagogue and Church during the First Millennium* (London, 1959).

III. BYZANTINE HYMNOGRAPHY

Cammelli, G., *Romano il Melode: Inni* (Florence, 1930).

Cantarella, R., *Poeti bizantini*, 2 vols. (Milan, 1948).

Christ, W. and Paranikas, M., *Anthologia graeca carminum christianorum* [see Gen. Bibl. IV].

Follieri, E., *Initia hymnorum Ecclesiae Graecae* (*Studi e Testi*, 211–14), 4 vols. (Vatican, 1960–3).

Grande, C. del, *L'Inno Acatisto* (Florence, 1948).

Kirchhoff, K., *Symeon, Licht vom Licht. Hymnen* (Hellerau, 1930).
Kirchhoff, K., *Die Ostkirche betet. Hymnen aus den Tagzeiten der byzantinischen Kirche*, 4 vols. (Hellerau, 1934–7).
Kirchhoff, K., *Osterjubel der Ostkirche*, 2 vols. (Münster, 1940).
Krumbacher, K., *Geschichte der byzantinischen Litteratur*, pp. 653–705 [see Gen. Bibl. v].
Krumbacher, K., 'Studien zu Romanos', *SBAW*, II (1898), 69–268.
Krumbacher, K., 'Die Akrostichis in der griechischen Kirchenpoesie', *ibid.* (1903), 551–691.
La Piana, G., *Le rappresentazioni sacre nella letteratura bizantina dalle origini al sec. X* (Grottaferrata, 1912).
La Piana, G., 'The Byzantine Theater', *SP*, XI (1936), 171–211.
Maas, P., 'Das Kontakion', *BZ*, XIX (1910), 258–309.
Mioni, E., *Romano il Melode* (Turin, 1937).
Neale, J. M., *A History of the Holy Eastern Church*, pt. I. *General Introduction*, 2 vols. (London, 1850).
Papadopoulos, G., Συμβολαὶ εἰς τὴν ἱστορίαν τῆς παρ' ἡμῖν ἐκκλησιαστικῆς μουσικῆς (Athens, 1904).
Papadopoulos-Kerameus, A., Ὁ Ἀκάθιστος ὕμνος. Βιβλιοθήκη Μαρασλῆ, CCXIV (Athens, 1903).
Papadopoulos-Kerameus, A., Πηγαὶ καὶ δάνεια τοῦ ποιήσαντος τὸν Ἀκάθιστον Ὕμνον, Βυζαντίς, I (1909), 517–40.
Pargoire, J., *L'Eglise byzantine de 527 à 847* [see Gen. Bibl. v].
Peeters, P., *Le Tréfonds Oriental de l'Hagiographie Byzantine* (Subsidia Hagiographica 26) (Brussels, 1950).
Pitra, J. B., *L'Hymnographie de l'Eglise grecque* (Rome, 1867).
Pitra, J. B., *Analecta sacra spicilegio Solesmensi parata*, I (Paris, 1876).
Simonetti, M., *Studi sull' innologia popolare cristiana dei primi secoli.* Atti d. Accad. Naz. dei Lincei, Memorie, ser. VIII, vol. IV, fasc. 6 (Rome, 1952).
Wellesz, E., 'Kontakion and Kanon', *Atti del Congresso Internazionale di Musica Sacra* (Rome, 1952), pp. 131–3.

IV. MUSICAL NOTATION AND THE STRUCTURE OF THE MELODIES

Bourgault-Ducoudray, L. A., *Etudes sur la musique ecclésiastique grecque. Mission musicale en Grèce et en Orient, janvier–mai 1875* (Paris, 1877).
Chrysanthus of Madytos, Θεωρητικὸν μέγα τῆς μουσικῆς (Trieste, 1832).
Clark, K. W., *Checklist of Manuscripts in St Catherine's Monastery, Mount Sinai, microfilmed for the Library of Congress 1950* (Washington, 1952).
Clark, K. W., *Checklist of Manuscripts in the Libraries of the Greek and Armenian Patriarchates in Jerusalem...* (Washington, 1953).
Fleischer, O., *Die spätgriechische Notenschrift. Neumenstudien*, III (Berlin, 1904).
Gaisser, H., 'Les "Hermoi" de Pâques dans l'Office grec, Etude rythmique et musicale', *OC*, III (1903).
Gastoué, A., *Catalogue des manuscrits de Musique byzantine. Publications de la Société Internationale de Musique, Section de Paris* (Paris, 1907).
Gastoué, A., *Introduction à la paléographie musicale byzantine. Catalogue des MSS. de musique byzantine* (Paris, 1907).
Gastoué, A., 'L'importance musicale, liturgique et philosophique du MS. Hagiopolites', *B*, v (1929–30), 347–55.

Laily, P.-A., *Analyse du Codex de Musique Grecque No. 19, Bibliothèque Vaticane* (*Fonds Borgia*) (Harissa, 1949).

Merlier, M., *Etudes de musique byzantine. Le premier mode et son plagal* (Paris, 1935).

Monumenta Musicae Byzantinae (Union Académique Internationale), ediderunt C. Høeg, H. J. W. Tillyard, Egon Wellesz.

Facsimilia:

Vol. I. *Sticherarium*, Codex Vindobonensis theol. gr. 181, ed. C. Høeg, H. J. W. Tillyard, E. Wellesz (Copenhagen, 1935).

Vol. II. *Hirmologium Athoum*, Codex Iviron 470, ed. C. Høeg (Copenhagen, 1938).

Vol. III. *Hirmologium Cryptense*, Codex Cryptensis E. γ. II, ed. Dom L. Tardo (Rome, 1951).

Vol. IV. *Contacarium Ashburnhamense*, ed. C. Høeg (Copenhagen, 1956).

Subsidia:

Vol. I. Fasc. 1. H. J. W. Tillyard, *Handbook of the Middle Byzantine Notation* (Copenhagen, 1935).

Vol. I. Fasc. 2. C. Høeg, *La Notation Ekphonétique* (Copenhagen, 1935).

Vol. II (= American Series no. 1). E. Wellesz, *Eastern Elements in Western Chant* (Boston (Mass.)–Copenhagen, 1947).

Vol. III. R. Palikarova-Verdeil, *La musique Byzantine chez les Bulgares et les Russes* (Copenhagen, 1953).

Vol. IV. M. Velimirović, *Byzantine Elements in Early Slavic Chant*, 2 vols. (Copenhagen, 1960).

Transcripta:

Vol. I. E. Wellesz, *Die Hymnen des Sticherarium für September* (Copenhagen, 1936).

Vol. II. H. J. W. Tillyard, *The Hymns of the Sticherarium for November* (Copenhagen, 1938).

Vol. III. H. J. W. Tillyard, *The Hymns of the Octoechus*, pt. I (Copenhagen, 1940).

Vol. IV. H. J. W. Tillyard, *Twenty Canons from the Trinity. Hirmologium* (= American Series no. 2) (Boston, (Mass.)–Copenhagen, 1951).

Vol. V. H. J. W. Tillyard, *The Hymns of the Octoechus*, pt. II (Copenhagen, 1949).

Vol. VI. C. Høeg, A. Ayoutanti and M. Stöhr, *The Hymns of the Hirmologium*, pt. II (Copenhagen, 1952).

Vol. VII. H. J. W. Tillyard, *The Hymns of the Pentecostarium* (Copenhagen, 1960).

Vol. VIII. A. Ayoutanti and H. J. W. Tillyard, *The Hymns of the Hirmologium*, pt. III, 2 (Copenhagen, 1956).

Vol. IX. E. Wellesz, *The Akathistos Hymn* (Copenhagen, 1957).

Lectionaria:

Vol. I. *Prophetologium*, ed. C. Høeg and G. Zuntz, fasc. I (Copenhagen, 1939); fasc. II, 1940; fasc. III, 1952; fasc. IV, 1955.

Papadopoulos-Kerameus, A., 'Βυζαντινῆς ἐκκλησιαστικῆς μουσικῆς ἐγχειρίδια', *BZ*, VIII (1899), 111–21.

Papadopoulos-Kerameus, A., ''Η τῆς Βυζαντινο-ἐκκλησιαστικῆς μουσικῆς σημαδοφωνίας γένεσις κατὰ πληροφορίας σλαβικῶν καὶ ἑλληνικῶν λειτουργικῶν μνημείων', *VV*, XV (1910), 49–70.

Petresco, J. D., *Les idiomèles et le canon de l'Office de Noël* (Paris, 1932).

Raasted, J., 'Some Observations on the Structure of the Stichera in Byzantine Rite', *B*, XXVIII (1958), 529–41.

Raasted, J., 'A Primitive Palaeobyzantine Musical Notation', *CM*, XXIII (1962), 302–10.

Rebours, J. B., 'Quelques manuscrits de musique byzantine', *ROC*, IX (1904), 299–309 and X (1905), 1–14.

Rebours, J. B., *Traité de psaltique. Théorie et pratique du chant dans l'Église grecque* (Paris, 1906).

Riemann, H., *Die byzantinische Notenschrift im 10.–15. Jahrhundert* (Leipzig, 1909).

Riemann, H., *Studien zur byzantinischen Musik. Byzantinische Notenschrift*, N.F. (Leipzig, 1915).

Sakkelion, I. and A., Κατάλογος τῶν χειρογράφων τῆς ἐθνικῆς βιβλιοθήκης τῆς Ἑλλάδος (Athens, 1892), ch. VI: Ἐκκλησιαστικὴ Μουσική, pp. 158–75.

Salvo, B. di, 'La trascrizione della notazione paleobizantina', *Bollettino della Badia Greca di Grottaferrata*, IV (1950), 114–30; V (1951), 92–110, 220–35.

Strunk, O., 'The Tonal System of Byzantine Music', *Musical Quart.*, XXVIII (1942), 339–55.

Strunk, O., 'Intonations and Signatures of the Byzantine Modes', *Musical Quart.*, XXXI (1945), 339–55.

Strunk, O., 'Some Notation of the Chartres Fragment', *Annales Musicologiques*, III (1955), 9–37.

Strunk, O., 'The Byzantine Office at Hagia Sophia', *DOP*, IX–X (1956), 177–202.

Strunk, O., 'The Antiphons of the Oktoechos', *Journal of the American Musicological Society*, XIII (1960), 50–67.

Tardo, L., *L'antica melurgia bizantina* (Grottaferrata, 1931).

Tardo, L., 'I codici melurgici della Vaticana e il contributo alla musica bizantina del monachismo greco della Magna Grecia', *Archivio storico per la Calabria e la Lucania*, I (1931), 1–24; 225–39.

Tardo, L., 'La musica bizantina e i codici di melurgia della Biblioteca di Grottaferrata', *Rivista d. Accademie e Biblioteche d'Italia*, IV (1931), 355–369.

Tardo, L., 'L'Ottoeco nei manoscritti melurgici', *Bollettino della Badia Greca di Grottaferrata*, n.s. I (1947), 26–38, 133–143; II (1948), 26–44 and published separately (Grottaferrata, 1955).

Thibaut, J. B., 'La notation de Saint Jean Damascène', *VV*, VI (1899), 1–12.

Thibaut, J. B., 'Etude de musique byzantine. La notation de Koukouzélès', *IRAIK*, VI (1900), 361–396.

Thibaut, J. B., *Origine byzantine de la notation neumatique de l'Eglise latine* (Paris, 1907).

Thibaut, J. B., *Monuments de la notation ekphonétique et hagiopolite de l'Eglise grecque* (St Petersburg, 1913).

Thibaut, J. B., *Le Panégyrique de l'Immaculée dans les chants hymnographiques de la liturgie grecque* (Paris, 1909).

Thibaut, J. B., 'La notation de Saint Jean Damascène ou Hagiopolite', *IRAIK*, III (1898), 138–79.

Thibaut, J. B., 'Etude de musique byzantine. Le chant ekphonétique', *BZ*, VIII (1899), 122–47.

Thodberg, C., *The Tonal System of the Kontakarium. Hist.-filos. Meddelser Kon. Videnskab. Selsbab.*, XXXVII, 7 (Copenhagen, 1960).

Tiby, O., *La musica bizantina. Teoria e storia* (Milan, 1938).

Tiby, O., 'I codici musicali Italo–Greci di Messina', *Rivista d. Accademie e Biblioteche d'Italia*, XI (1937), 14 ff.

Tillyard, H. J. W., *Byzantine Music and Hymnography* (London, 1923).

Tillyard, H. J. W., 'A Musical Study of the Hymns of Casia', *BA*, XX (1911), 420–85.

Tillyard, H. J. W., 'Fragment of a Byzantine Musical Handbook in the Monastery of Laura on Mt Athos', *Ann. Brit. School at Athens*, XIX (1912–13), 125–47.

Tillyard, H. J. W., 'The Modes in Byzantine Music', *Ann. Brit. School at Athens*, XXII (1916–18), 133–56.

Tillyard, H. J. W., 'Signatures and Cadences of the Byzantine Modes', *Ann. Brit. School at Athens*, XXVI (1923–5), 78–87.

Tillyard, H. J. W., 'Early Byzantine Neumes', *Laudate*, VIII (1930), 204–16.

Tillyard, H. J. W., 'Byzantine Neumes: The Coislin Notation', *BZ*, XXXVII (1937), 345–58.

Tillyard, H. J. W., 'Byzantine Music about A.D. 1100', *Musical Quart.*, XXXIX (1953), 223–31.

Tillyard, H. J. W., 'Gegenwärtiger Stand der byzantinischen Musikforschung', *Die Musikforschung*, VII (1954), 142–9.

Tillyard, H. J. W., 'The Byzantine Modes in the Twelfth Century', *Ann. Brit. School at Athens*, XLVIII (1953), 182–90.

Wellesz, E., *Aufgaben und Probleme auf dem Gebiet der byzantinischen und orientalischen Kirchenmusik. (Liturgiegeschichtliche Forschungen*, Heft 6) (Münster, 1923).

Wellesz, E., *Byzantinische Musik* (Breslau, 1927).

Wellesz, E., 'Das Problem der byzantinischen Notationen und ihrer Entzifferung', *B*, V (1929–30), 556–70.

Wellesz, E., *Trésor de musique byzantine* (Paris, 1934).

Wellesz, E., 'The Earliest Example of Christian Hymnody', *Classical Quart.*, XXXIX (1945), 34–45.

Wellesz, E., 'Early Byzantine Neumes', *Musical Quart.*, XXXVIII (1952), 68–79.

Wellesz, E., 'Das Prooemium des Akathistos', *Die Musikforschung*, VI (1953), 193–206.

Wellesz, E., 'Early Christian Music', *The New Oxford History of Music*, II (1954), 1–13.

Wellesz, E., 'Music of the Eastern Churches', *ibid.* pp. 14–53.

Wellesz, E., 'The Akathistos: a Study in Byzantine Hymnography', *DOP*, IX–X (1956), 143–74.

Wellesz, E., *History of Byzantine Music and Hymnography* [see Gen. Bibl. V].

CHAPTER XXV
BYZANTINE MONASTICISM

Additional bibliography may be found in chapters xx, xxi, xxiii, xxiv and xxvi, and in the following ecclesiastical dictionaries and works of reference: *DACL, DDC, DHGE, DS, DTC, LTK*, Beck and de Meester [see Gen. Bibl. i].

I. ORIGINAL AUTHORITIES

Acts of Athos [see Gen. Bibl. iv].

Balsamon, Theodore, *MPG*, cxxxvii–cxxxviii, *In canones SS. apostolorum, conciliorum, et in epistolas canonicas SS. patrum*.

Baynes, N. H. and Dawes, E. S. A., *Three Byzantine saints: contemporary biographies of St Daniel the Stylite, St Theodore of Sykeon and St John the Almsgiver* (Oxford, 1948).

Bezobrazov, P., *Unedierte Klosterregeln* [Russ.], *ZMNP*, cclivi (1887), 65–78.

Bibliotheca hagiographica graeca (for saints' lives which provide most valuable material but are too numerous to be cited individually) [see Gen. Bibl. iv].

Christodulus, *Diataxis*, MM, vi, 59–80 [see also below *Milet*].

Cyril of Scythopolis, *Vitae*, ed. E. Schwartz, *Kyrillos von Skythopolis* (Leipzig, 1939).

Delehaye, H., *Deux typica byzantins de l'époque des Paléologues* (Brussels, 1921).

Dimitrievsky, A., *Opisanie liturgičeskich rukopisej* [see Gen. Bibl. iv].

Dölger, F., *Regesten der Kaiserurkunden* [see Gen. Bibl. iv].

Dölger, F., *Aus den Schatzkammern des Heiligen Berges*, i (text) and ii (plates) (Munich, 1948).

Gregory Pacurianus, *Typicon*, ed. L. Petit, *VV*, xi (1904), supplement no. i, pp. i–xxxii, 1–63, *Typicon de Grégoire Pacourianos pour le monastère de Pétritzos (Bačkovo) en Bulgarie*; see also *CSCO*, cxliii (1953) and cxliv (1954).

Grumel, V., *Les Regestes des Actes du Patriarcat de Constantinople* [see Gen. Bibl. iv].

Irene Ducas, *Typicon*, ed. MM, v, pp. 327–91; also *MPG*, cxxvii.

Isaac Comnenus (brother of John II Comnenus), *Typicon*, ed. L. Petit, *IRAIK*, xiii (1908), 17–77.

John of Antioch, *MPG*, cxxxii, *Oratio de disciplina monastica et de monasteriis laicis non tradendis*.

John II Comnenus, *Typicon*, ed. A. Dimitrievsky, I: *Typica*, pt. i, pp. 656–702 [see Gen. Bibl iv].

Jus graeco-romanum, ed. K. E. Zachariae von Lingenthal; ed. J. and P. Zepos [see Gen. Bibl. iv].

Laurent, V., *La vie miraculeuse de St Pierre d'Atroa* († 837). (Subsidia Hagiographica, xxix) (Brussels, 1956).

Mansi, J. D., *Sacrorum conciliorum nova et amplissima collectio* [see Gen. Bibl. iv].

Meester, P. de, *De monachico statu juxta disciplinam byzantinam* [with bibliography] [see Gen. Bibl. i].

Meyer, P., *Die Haupturkunden für die Geschichte der Athosklöster* (Leipzig, 1894).

Miklosich, F. and Müller, J., *Acta et diplomata graeca* [see Gen. Bibl. IV].

Milet, Ergebnisse der Ausgrabungen und Untersuchungen seit dem Jahre 1899, ed. T. Wiegand (Königliche Museen zu Berlin), III, pt. I (Berlin, 1913): *Der Latmos*. See *Monumenta Latrensia Hagiographica*, ed. H. Delehaye, pp. 97 ff. (especially on Christodoulos).

Monastic *typica* [a full bibliography is given by P. de Meester, *De monachico statu*: see Gen. Bibl. I].

Peeters, P., 'Histoires monastiques géorgiennes', *AB*, XXXVI–XXXVII (1917–19, published 1922), 5–317.

Rhalles, G. A. and Potles, M., Σύνταγμα [see Gen. Bibl. IV].

II. MODERN WORKS

Alivisatos, H. S., *Die kirchliche Gesetzgebung des Kaisers Justinian I*. (Berlin, 1913).

Allatius, L., *Graecia orthodoxa*, 2 vols. (Rome, 1652–9).

Amand, D., *L'ascèse monastique de saint Basile* (Maredsous, 1948).

Amand de Mendieta, E., *La presqu'île des caloyers: le Mont Athos* (Bruges, 1955).

Bardy, G., 'Les origines des écoles monastiques en orient', *Mélanges J. Ghellinck* (Löwen, 1951), pp. 293–309.

Baston, B., 'Origin and Early History of Double Monasteries', *TRHS*, XXIII (1889).

Beck, H.-G., *Kirche und theologische Literatur im byzantinischen Reich* [with bibliography] [see Gen. Bibl. V].

Besse, J. M., *Les moines d'Orient antérieurs au concile de Chalcédoine* (Paris, 1900).

Besse, J. M., 'Les diverses sortes de moines en Orient avant le concile de Chalcédoine', *Revue Hist. Rel.* XL (1899), 159–202.

Byron, R., *The Station. Athos: Treasures and Men* (London, 1928).

Casey, R. P., 'Early Russian Monasticism', *OCP*, XIX (1953), 372–423.

Charanis, P., 'The Monastic Properties and the State' [see Gen. Bibl. V].

Clarke, W. K. L., *St Basil the Great. A Study in Monasticism* (Cambridge, 1913).

Corbo, V., 'L'ambiente materiale della vita dei monaci di Palestina nel periodo bizantino', *Il Monachesimo Orientale*, pp. 235–57 [see Gen. Bibl. V].

Curzon, R., *Visits to Monasteries in the Levant* (London, 1955; and earlier editions).

Dahm, C., *Athos, Berg der Verklärung* (Offenburg–Baden, 1959). [Excellent illustrations.]

Dalmais, J. H., 'Sacerdoce et monachisme dans l'Orient Chrétien', *Vie Spirituelle*, LXXIX (1948), 37–49.

Dawkins, R. M., *The Monks of Athos* (London, 1936).

Dawkins, R. M., 'Notes on Life in the Monasteries of Mt Athos', *HTR*, XLVI (1953), 217–31.

Delehaye, H., *Les saints stylites* (Subsidia hagiographia, XIV) (Paris and Brussels, 1923).

Delehaye, H., *Deux typica byzantins de l'époque des Paléologues* (Brussels, 1921). [This contains some discussion of the earlier typica.]

Dölger, F., *Sechs byzantinische Praktika des 14. Jahrhunderts für das Athos-*

kloster Iberon. Abh. Bay. Ak. Wiss., Cl. phil-hist. n.s. XXVIII (Munich, 1949).

Dölger, F., *Byzantinische Diplomatik* (Ettal, 1956).

Dumont, P., 'Vie cénobitique ou vie hésychaste dans quelques typica byzantins', *1054–1954. L'église et les églises*, II, pp. 3–13 [see Gen. Bibl. v *ad fin.*].

Ferradou, A., *Les biens des monastères à Byzance* (Bordeaux, 1896).

Granić, B., 'Das Klosterwesen in der Novellengesetzgebung Kaiser Leons des Weisen', *BZ*, XXXI (1931), 61–9.

Granić, B., 'Die rechtliche Stellung und Organisation der griechischen Klöster nach dem justinianischen Recht', *BZ*, XXIX (1929/30), 6–35.

Granić, B., 'L'acte de fondation d'un monastère dans les provinces grecques du Bas-Empire au Vᵉ et au VIᵉ siècles', *Mélanges Charles Diehl*, I (Paris, 1930), 101–5.

Granić, B., 'Die privatrechtliche Stellung der griechischen Mönche im V. und VI. Jahrhundert', *BZ*, XXX (1929/30), 669–76.

Hannay, J. O., *The Spirit and Origin of Christian Monasticism* (London, 1903).

Hasluck, F. W., *Athos and its Monasteries* (London, 1924).

Hausherr, I., *Direction spirituelle en Orient autrefois* (*OCA*, 144) (Rome, 1955).

Hausherr, I., 'Spiritualité monachale et unité chrétienne', *Il Monachesimo Orientale*, pp. 15–32 [see Gen. Bibl. v].

Heimbucher, M., *Die Orden und Kongregationen der katholischen Kirche*, I, 3rd ed. (Paderborn, 1933).

Hergès, A., 'Election et déposition des higoumènes au XIIᵉ siècle', *EO*, III (1899–1900), 40–9.

Herman, E., 'Ricerche sulle istituzioni monastiche bizantine. Typica ktetorika, caristicari e monasteri "liberi"', *OCP*, VI (1940), 293–375.

Herman, E., 'La "stabilitas loci" nel monachismo bizantino', *OCP*, XXI (1955), 115–42.

Herman, E., 'Die Regelung der Armut in den byzantinischen Klöstern', *OCP*, VII (1941), 406–60.

Heussi, K., *Der Ursprung des Mönchtums* (Tübingen, 1936).

Hilpisch, S., *Die Doppelklöster. Entstehung und Organisation* (= *Beiträge zur Geschichte des alten Mönchtums und des Benediktinerordens*, ed. I. Herwegen, Heft 15) (Münster, 1928).

Holl, K., 'Über das griechische Mönchtum', *Preussische Jahrbücher*, XCIV (1898), 407–24; reprinted in *Gesammelte Aufsätze zur Kirchengeschichte*, II. *Der Osten* (Tübingen, 1928), pp. 270–82.

Holl, K., *Enthusiasmus und Bussgewalt beim griechischen Mönchtum* (Leipzig, 1898).

Hussey, J. M., *Church and Learning in the Byzantine Empire, 867–1185* [see Gen. Bibl. v].

Hussey, J. M., 'Byzantine Monasticism', *History*, n.s. XXIV (1939), 56–62.

Hussey, J. M., *The Byzantine World* [see Gen. Bibl. v].

Il Monachesimo Orientale [see Gen. Bibl. v].

Janin, R., *La géographie ecclésiastique et l'empire byzantin*, pt. I: vol. III. *Les églises et les monastères* [see Gen. Bibl. II]. Further topographical bibliography will be found in H.-G. Beck, 'Notitia monasteriorum', *Kirche und theologische Literatur*, pp. 200–29 [see Gen. Bibl. v].

Janin, R., 'Les monastères nationaux et provinciaux à Byzance', *EO*, XXXVI (1933), 429–38.

Jeanselme, E. and Oeconomos, L., 'La satire contre les higoumènes', *B*, I (1924), 317–39.

Krivocheine, Archbishop Basil, 'The Most Enthusiastic Zealot, "Ζηλωτὴς μανικώτατος"', St Symeon the New Theologian as Abbot and Spiritual Instructor', *Ostkirchliche Studien* IV (1955), 108–28.

Krivocheine, Archbishop Basil, 'Mount Athos in the Spiritual Life of the Orthodox Church', *The Christian East*, II (1952), 35–50.

Krumbacher, K., *Geschichte der byzantinischen Litteratur* [see Gen. Bibl. v].

Kukules, Ph., Βυζαντινῶν Βίος καὶ Πολιτισμός, VI [see Gen. Bibl. v].

Kurth, J., 'Ein Stück Klosterinventar auf einem byzantinischen Papyrus', *BNJ*, I (1920), 144–8.

Lake, K., *The Early Days of Monasticism on Mount Athos* (Oxford, 1909).

Laurent, V., 'Charisticariat et commende à Byzance', *REB*, XII (1954), 100–13.

Leroy, J., 'La réforme studite', *Il Monachesimo Orientale*, pp. 181–214 [see Gen. Bibl. v].

Malone, E. E., 'The Monk and the Martyr', *Antonius Magnus Eremita* (= *Studia Anselmiana*, XXXVIII) (Rome, 1956), pp. 201–28.

Marin, E., *Les moines de Constantinople depuis la fondation de la Ville jusqu'à la mort de Photius* (Paris, 1897).

Meester, P. de, 'Le rasophorat dans le monachisme byzantin', *Sbornik P. Nikov = Isvestija Bulg. Hist. Soc.* 16/8 (Sofia, 1940), pp. 323–32.

Meester, P. de, 'Autour de quelques publications récentes sur les habits des moines en orient', *Ephemerides Liturgicae*, XLVII (1933), 446–58.

Meester, P. de, 'Les typica de fondation', *SBN*, VI (1940), 489–508.

Menthon, B., *Une terre de légende. L'Olympe de Bithynie* (Paris, 1935).

Milaš, N., *Das Kirchenrecht der morgenländischen Kirche* [see Gen. Bibl. I].

Minisci, T., 'Riflessi studitani nel monachesimo italo–greco', *Il Monachesimo Orientale*, pp. 215–33 [see Gen. Bibl. v].

Moravcsik, Gy., *Byzantinoturcica* [see Gen. Bibl. I].

Morrison, E. F., *St Basil and his Rule, a Study in Early Monasticism* (Oxford, 1912).

Nicol, D. M., 'The Meteora monasteries of Thessaly', *History Today*, V (1955), 602–11.

Nicol, D. M., *Meteora. The Rock Monasteries of Thessaly* (London, 1963).

Nissen, W., *Die Diataxis des Michael Attaleiates von 1077* (Jena, 1894).

Nissen, W., *Die Regelung des Klosterwesens im Rhomäerreich bis zum Ende des 9. Jahrhunderts* (Hamburg, 1897).

Oeconomos, L., *La vie religieuse dans l'empire byzantin au temps des Comnènes et des Anges* (Paris, 1918).

Österle, G., 'De monasterio stauropegiaco', *Il Diritto Eccles.*, LXIV (1953), 450–60.

Pančenko, B. A., 'Krestijanskaja sobstvennost v Vizantii' ['Peasant ownership in Byzantium'], *IRAIK*, IX (1904), 1–234.

Pargoire, J., 'Les débuts du monachisme à Constantinople', *RQH*, LXV (1899), 67–143.

Pargoire, J., 'Une loi monastique de S. Platon', *BZ*, VIII (1899), 98–106.

Pargoire, J., 'Les monastères doubles chez les Byzantins', *EO*, IX (1912), 21–5.

Řezáč, G., 'Le diverse forme di unione fra i monasteri orientali', *Il Monachesimo Orientale*, pp. 99–135 [see Gen. Bibl. v].

Robinson, N. F., *Monasticism in the Orthodox Churches* (London, 1916).

Rouillard, G., 'La politique de Michel VIII Paléologue à l'égard des monastères', *EB*, I (1943), 73–84.

Rousseau, O., 'Le rôle important du monachisme dans l'Eglise d'Orient', *Il Monachesimo Orientale*, pp. 33–55 [see Gen. Bibl. v].

Salaville, S., 'La vie monastique grecque au début du XIVe siècle d'après un discours inédit de Théolepte de Philadelphie', *EB*, II (1944), 119–25.

Salaville, S., 'Une lettre et un discours inédits de Théolepte de Philadelphie', *REB*, v (1947), 101–15.

Schäfer, T., 'Justinianus I et vita monachica', *Acta Congr. Jur. Internat.* (Rome, 1934/5), pp. 175–88.

Schiwietz (Siwiec), S., *Das morgenländische Mönchtum*, 3 vols. (Mainz and Mödling, 1904–38).

Skabalanovič, N., *Vizantijskoe gosudarstvo i cerkov* [see Gen. Bibl. v].

Sokolov, I., *Sostojanie monašestva v vizantijskoj cerkvi v polovine IX do načala XIII veka (842–1204)* [*The state of monasticism in the Byzantine Church from the middle of the IXth century to the beginning of the XIIIth century*] (Kazan, 1894).

Souarn, R., 'La profession religieuse, empêchement canonique du mariage chez les Grecs', *EO*, VII (1904), 194–8.

Strzygowski, J., 'Nea Moni auf Chios', *BZ*, v (1896), 140–57.

Tafel, G. L. F., *Betrachtungen über den Mönchsstand. Eine Stimme des zwölften Jahrhunderts* (Berlin, 1847). [On Eustathius of Thessalonica with a translation of his *De emendanda vita monachica*.]

Ueding, L., 'Die Kanones von Chalkedon in ihrer Bedeutung für Mönchtum und Klerus', *Das Konzil von Chalkedon*, II, ed. A. Grillmeier and H. Bacht (Würzburg, 1953), pp. 569–676.

Vailhé, S., 'Les premiers monastères de la Palestine', *Bess.* III (1897–8), 39–58.

Vailhé, S., 'Les monastères de la Palestine', *ibid.* pp. 209–25, 334–56; IV (1898–9), 193–210.

Volk, O., *Die byzantinischen Klösterbibliotheken Griechenlands, Konstantinopels und Kleinasiens* (Diss., Munich, 1955).

Zhishman, J., *Das Stifterrecht in der morgenländischen Kirche* (Vienna, 1888).

Zöckler, O., *Aszese und Mönchtum*, I (Frankfurt, 1887).

Zöckler, O., 'Zur Mönchsgeschichte des Orients', *Theol. Literaturblatt*, XXIX (1898), 337–40.

Le Millénaire du Mont Athos [see Gen. Bibl. v *ad fin.*].

CHAPTER XXVI. BYZANTINE THEOLOGICAL SPECULATION AND SPIRITUALITY

Further bibliography may be found in ecclesiastical dictionaries such as *DACL, DDC, DHGE, DS, DTC, LTK* and in works of reference, particularly Altaner, Beck, Cross, Ghellinck, Krumbacher and Moravcsik [see Gen. Bibl. I and v]. See also the bibliography for chapters II, x, XXIII and xxv.

I. ORIGINAL AUTHORITIES

Baynes, N. H. and Dawes, E. S. A., *Three Byzantine Saints: Contemporary Biographies of St Daniel the Stylite, St Theodore of Sykeon and St John the Almsgiver* (Oxford, 1948).

Bibliotheca hagiographica graeca (for saints' lives) [see Gen. Bibl. IV].

Cabasilas, Nicholas, *Commentary on the Divine Liturgy*, *MPG*, CL; French transl. S. Salaville (Sources chrét. IV) (Paris, 1943); English transl. J. M. Hussey and P. A. McNulty (London, 1960).

Cabasilas, Nicholas, *On Life in Christ*, *MPG*, CL; French transl. S. Broussaleux, *La vie en Jésus-Christ, Irénikon* IX (1932), Supplement, and 2nd ed. published separately (Chevetogne, 1961).

Climacus, John, *The Ladder of Divine Ascent*, *MPG*, LXXXVIII; ed. with Italian transl. P. Trevisan, 2 vols. (Turin, 1941); English transl. Archimandrite Lazarus Moore (London, 1959).

Cyril of Scythopolis, *Vitae*, ed. E. Schwartz, *Kyrillos von Skythopolis* (Leipzig, 1939).

Dölger, F., *Regesten der Kaiserurkunden* [see Gen. Bibl. IV].

Grumel, V., *Les Regestes des Actes du Patriarcat de Constantinople* [see Gen. Bibl. IV].

Holl, K., 'Die Sacra Parallela des Johannes Damascenus', *Texte und Untersuchungen*, N.F. 1 (= 16), 1 (Leipzig, 1897).

John of Damascus, *Works*, *AASS*, 6 May, II, 723–61, 3rd ed. I–XXXVI; *MPG*, XCIV–XCVI; *MPG*, CXL, 812–84; W. Christ and M. Paranikas, pp. 117–21, 205–36 [see Gen. Bibl. IV]; three orations on the Holy Icons, transl. M. H. Allies (London, 1898). [For bibliography see B. Studer, and for work in progress see F. Dölger and J. M. Hoeck, cited below under Modern Works.]

Italus, John, *Quaestiones quodlibetales* ('Ἀπορίαι καὶ Λύσεις), ed. P. Joannou (Ettal, 1956).

Italus, John, *Opuscula selecta*, ed. G. Cereteli, 2 vols. (Tiflis, 1924–6).

Italus, John, *Trial of John Italus for Heresy*, ed. T. Uspensky, *IRAIK*, II (1897), 1–66.

Mansi, J. D., *Sacrorum conciliorum nova et amplissima collectio* [see Gen. Bibl. IV].

Maximus the Confessor, *Works*, *MPG*, XC; *The Ascetic Life: The Four Centuries on Charity*, transl. with commentary by P. Sherwood (London, 1955); *Centuries sur la charité*, French transl. by J. Pegon (Sources chrét. IX) (Paris, 1943).

Michel, A., *Humbert und Kerullarios. Quellen und Studien zum Schisma des XI. Jahrhunderts* (Quellen und Forschungen aus dem Gebiete der Geschichte der Görresgesellschaft, XXI and XXIII), 2 vols. (Paderborn, 1924–30).

Nicetas Byzantius, *Capita syllogistica*, ed. J. Hergenröther, *Monumenta graeca* [see Gen. Bibl. IV].

Nicetas Stethatus, *MPG*, CXX, *De salutatione manuale. Libellus contra Latinos* (Latin only; the Greek is given by A. Michel, *Humbert und Kerullarios*, II, 322 ff., see above).

Nicetas Stethatus, *Dialexis*, ed. A. Michel, *op. cit.* II, 320–1.

Nicetas Stethatus, *De azymis et sabbatorum jejuniis, et nuptiis sacerdotum* (*Antidialogus*), ed. A. Michel, *op. cit.* II, 322–42.

Nicetas Stethatus, *Altera synthesis contra Latinos de Filioque*, ed. A. Michel, *op. cit.* II, 371–409.

Nicetas Stethatus, *Vie de Syméon le nouveau théologien*, ed. with French transl. I. Hausherr and G. Horn (*Orientalia Christiana*, XII) (Rome, 1928).

Nicetas Stethatus, *Tres centuriae asceticae*, *MPG*, CXX.

Nicetas Stethatus, Μυστικὰ συγγράμματα, ed. P. K. Chrestou, S. Sakkos and G. Mantzarides (Thessalonica, 1957).

Nicetas Stethatus, *Opuscules et lettres*, ed. with French transl. by J. Darrouzès (Sources chrét. LXXXI) (Paris, 1961).

Nicholas of Methone, *Orationes duae contra haeresim dicentium sacrificium pro nobis salutare non trishypostatae divinitati, sed patri soli esse*, ed. A. K. Demetracopulos (Leipzig, 1865).

Nicholas of Methone, *Theological Orations*, ed. A. K. Demetracopulos, *Bibliotheca ecclesiastica* (Leipzig, 1866).

Nicholas of Methone, *Refutation of Proclus's Elements of Theology*, ed. J. T. Vomel (Frankfurt, 1825).

Palamas, Gregory, *Works*, *MPG*, CL–CLI; *Triads*, ed. with French transl. J. Meyendorff, *Défense des saints hésychastes* (Spic. Sacr. Lovan. Etudes et documents, 30–1), 2 vols. (Louvain, 1959).

Petit, L. (ed.), *Documents relatifs au Concile de Florence*, *PO*, XV, XVII (Paris, 1920–3).

Φιλοκαλία τῶν ἱερῶν νηπτικῶν, ed. Nicodemus the Hagiorite, 3 vols. (Venice, 1782); reprinted (Athens, 1957–60); part of this collection of Byzantine ascetical writings is transl. (from the Russian transl. of the original) by E. Kadloubovsky and G. E. H. Palmer, *Writings from the Philokalia on Prayer of the Heart* (London, 1951); and *Early Fathers from the Philokalia* (London, 1954); *Petite Philocalie de la prière du cœur*, selected and transl. J. Gouillard (Paris, 1953).

Photius, *Orations* and *Homilies*, 2 vols., ed. S. Aristarches (Constantinople, 1900); English transl. C. A. Mango (Cambridge, Mass., 1958).

Photius, *Mystagogia*, and other writings, *MPG*, CI–CIV (for full bibliography see above chapter X).

Pseudo-Dionysius the Areopagite, *Works*, *MPG*, III; French transl. M. de Gaudillac (Paris, 1943).

Pseudo-Dionysius the Areopagite, *De coelesti hierarchia*, text and French transl. by G. Heil, R. Roques and M. de Gaudillac (Sources chrét. LVIII) (Paris, 1958).

Symeon the New Theologian, *Sermons*, *Loves of the Divine Hymns* (both in Latin transl. only) and *Capita*, *MPG*, CXX; *Capita*, ed. with French transl. J. Darrouzès (Sources chrét. 51)(Paris, 1957); German transl. of the *Hymns* by K. Kirchhoff, 2nd ed. (Hellerau, 1952); the Greek text of four of these hymns is edited by P. Maas, 'Aus der Poesie des Mystikers Symeon', in *Festgabe Albert Ehrhard*, ed. A. M. Königer (Bonn, 1927), pp. 327–41. For a group of the sermons see the critical edition by B. Krivocheine, *Catéchèses* I–III (Sources chrét. 96, 104, 113) (Paris, 1963–5).

Symeon the New Theologian, *Epistola de confessione*, ed. K. Holl, *Enthusiasmus und Bussgewalt* (Leipzig, 1898), pp. 110–27; also *MPG*, XCV, where it is wrongly attributed to John of Damascus.

Symeon the New Theologian, *Letter* to Stephen of Nicomedia, ed. I. Hausherr and G. Horn, *Orientalia Christiana*, XII (1928), no. 45, pp. lxiii–lxv.

Theodore the Studite, *Opera*, *MPG*, XCIX; eds. A. Mai and G. Cozza-Luzi, *Nova Patrum Bibliotheca*, VIII, no. 1 (Rome, 1871); *Parva catechesis*, ed. E. Auvray (Paris, 1891); Μεγάλη Κατήχησις (Βιβλίον δεύτερον ἐκδοθὲν ὑπὸ τῆς Αὐτοκρατορικῆς Ἀρχαιογραφικῆς Ἐπιτροπῆς), ed. A. Papadopulos-Kerameus (St Petersburg, 1904).

Zigabenus, John, *Panoplia dogmatica* and other works, *MPG*, CXXX–CXXXI.

II. MODERN WORKS

Allatius, L., *De ecclesiae occidentalis atque orientalis perpetua consensione* (Cologne, 1648).

Altaner, B., *Patrologie* [see Gen. Bibl. I].

Amand de Mendieta, E., *La presqu'île des caloyers : le Mont Athos* (Bruges, 1955).

Anastos, M. V., *The Mind of Byzantium* (New York, 1961).

Anastos, M. V., 'Some Aspects of Byzantine Influence on Latin Thought', *Twentieth-Century Europe and the Foundations of Modern Europe*, ed. M. Clagett, G. Post and R. Reynolds (Madison, 1961), pp. 131–87.

Angelov, D., *Der Bogomilismus auf dem Gebiete des byzantinischen Reiches*, 2 pts. (Sofia, 1948–51).

Bacht, H., 'Das "Jesus-Gebet"—seine Geschichte und seine Problematik', *Geist und Leben*, XXIV (1951), 326–38.

Beck, H.-G., 'Humanismus und Palamismus', *XII Congr. Intern. Et. Byz.: Ochride, 1961, Rapports*, III, pp. 63–82.

Beck, H.-G., *Kirche und theologische Literatur im byzantinischen Reich* (with bibliography) [see Gen. Bibl. V].

Biedermann, H. M., *Das Menschenbild bei Symeon dem Jüngeren dem Theologen (949–1022)* (Würzburg, 1949).

Brianchaninov, I., *On the Prayer of Jesus* (London, 1952).

Cavarnos, C., *Anchored in God : an inside account of Life, Art, and Thought on the Holy Mountain of Athos* (Athens, 1959).

Delehaye, H., *Les saints stylites* (Subsidia hagiographia, XIV) (Paris and Brussels, 1923).

Dölger, F., 'Die Johannes-Damaskenos-Ausgabe des byzantinischen Institutes Scheyern', *B*, XX (1950), 303–14.

Fina, K., 'Anselm von Havelberg. Untersuchungen zur Kirchen- und Geistesgeschichte des 12. Jh.', *Anal. Praemonstrat.*, XXXII (1956), 69–101, 193–227; XXXIII (1957), 5–39, 268–301 (to be cont.).

Gardner, A., *Theodore of Studium : His Life and Times* (London, 1905).

Ghellinck, J. de, *Patristique et moyen-âge* [see Gen. Bibl. I].

Gill, J., *The Council of Florence* [see Gen. Bibl. V].

Gouillard, J., 'Autour du palamisme', *EO*, XXXVII (1938), 424–64 (bibliography).

Hart, T. A., 'Nicephorus Gregoras: Historian of the Hesychast Controversy', *JEH*, II (1951), 169–80.

Hausherr, I., *La direction spirituelle en Orient autrefois* (*OCA*, CXLIV) (Rome, 1955).

Hausherr, I., 'Dogme et spiritualité orientale', *Rev. Ascét. et Myst.*, XXIII (1947), 3–37.

Hausherr, I., 'L'hésychasme', *OCP*, XXII (1956), 5–40, 247–85.

Hausherr, I., 'Les grands courants de la spiritualité orientale', *OCP*, I (1935), 114–38; 'The great currents of eastern spirituality', *ECQ*, II (1937), 111–21, 175–85.

Hausherr, I., *Saint Théodore Studite : l'homme et l'ascète (d'après ses catéchèses)*, *Orientalia Christiana*, VI (Rome, 1926).

Hausherr, I., 'Spiritualité monachale et unité chrétienne', *Il Monachesimo Orientale*, pp. 15–32 [see Gen. Bibl. V].

Hausherr, I., *Les leçons d'un contemplatif : le traité d'Oraison d'Evagre le Pontique* (Paris, 1960).

Hausherr, I., *Noms du Christ et voies d'oraison* (Rome, 1960).
Hefele, C. J. and Leclercq, H., *Histoire des Conciles* [see Gen. Bibl. v].
Heppell, M., 'Slavonic Translations of early Byzantine Ascetical Literature', *JEH*, v (1954), 86–100.
Hoeck, J. M., 'Stand und Aufgaben der Damaskenos-Forschung', *OCP*, xvii (1951), 5–60.
Holl, K., *Enthusiasmus und Bussgewalt beim griechischen Mönchtum* (Leipzig, 1898).
Holl, K., 'Über das griechische Mönchtum', *Preussische Jahrbücher*, xciv (1898), 407–24; reprinted in *Gesammelte Aufsätze zur Kirchengeschichte*, ii. *Der Osten* (Tübingen, 1928), 270–82.
Hussey, J. M., *Church and Learning in the Byzantine Empire, 867–1185* [see Gen. Bibl. v].
Hussey, J. M., *Ascetics and Humanists in Eleventh-century Byzantium* (Heffer, Cambridge, 1960).
Hussey, J. M., *The Byzantine World* [see Gen. Bibl. v].
Il Monachesimo Orientale [see Gen. Bibl. v].
Ivánka, E. von, 'Palamismus und Vätertradition', *1054–1954. L'Eglise et les Eglises*, ii, 29–46 [see Gen. Bibl. v *ad fin.*].
Joannou, P., *Christliche Metaphysik in Byzanz* [see Gen. Bibl. v].
Joannou, P., 'Die Definition des Seins bei Eustratios von Nikaia: die Universalienlehre in der byzantinischen Theologie im XI. Jh.', *BZ*, xlvii (1954), 358–68.
Jugie, M., *Theologia dogmatica* [see Gen. Bibl. v].
Jugie, M., *Le schisme byzantin* [see Gen. Bibl. v].
Karmiris, J., Τὰ δογματικὰ καὶ συμβολικὰ μνημεῖα τῆς ὀρθοδόξου καθολικῆς Ἐκκλησίας, 2 vols. (Athens, 1952–3).
Krivocheine, Archbishop Basil, 'Mount Athos in the spiritual life of the Orthodox Church', *The Christian East*, ii (1952), 35–50.
Krivocheine, Archbishop Basil, 'The Most Enthusiastic Zealot, "Ζηλωτὴς μανικώτατος", St Symeon the New Theologian as Abbot and Spiritual Instructor', *Ostkirchliche Studien*, iv (1955), 108–28.
Krivocheine, Archbishop Basil, 'The Writings of St Symeon the New Theologian', *OCP*, xx (1954), 298–328.
Krivocheine, Archbishop Basil, 'The Brother-loving Poor Man (Πτωχὸς φιλάδελφος). The mystical autobiography of St Symeon the New Theologian (949–1022)', *The Christian East*, n.s. ii (1953–4), 216–77.
Krumbacher, K., *Geschichte der byzantinischen Litteratur* [see Gen. Bibl. v].
La prière de Jésus avec un chapitre sur l'usage de la prière, par un moine de l'Eglise d'Orient, 3rd ed. (Chevetogne, 1960); see also *Irénikon*, xx (1947), 244–73, 381–421; xxv (1952), 371–82.
Laurent, V., 'La direction spirituelle à Byzance. La correspondance d'Irène Eulogie Choumnaina Paléologina avec son second directeur', *REB*, xiv (1956), 48–86.
Lemaître, J. and others, 'Contemplation', *DS*, ii, cols. 1643–1911.
Lossky, V., *Essai sur la théologie mystique de l'église d'orient* (Paris, 1944); English transl. (London, 1957).
Lot-Borodine, M., *Un maître de la spiritualité byzantine au XIVᵉ siècle, Nicolas Cabasilas* (Rech. Sc. Relig. 49) (Paris, 1961).
Meyendorff, J., *Introduction à l'étude de Grégoire Palamas* (Paris, 1959).
Moravcsik, Gy., *Byzantinoturcica* [see Gen. Bibl. i].
Obolensky, D., *The Bogomils* [see Gen. Bibl. v].

Oeconomos, L., *La vie religieuse dans l'empire byzantin au temps des Comnènes et des Anges* (Paris, 1918).

Orthodox Spirituality by a Monk of the Eastern Church (London, 1945).

Quasten, J., *Patrology* [see Gen. Bibl. I].

Roques, R., *L'univers dionysien* (Paris, 1954).

Rousseau, O., 'Le rôle important du monachisme dans l'Eglise d'Orient', *Il Monachesimo Orientale*, pp. 33–55 [see Gen. Bibl. v].

Runciman, S., *The Eastern Schism* [see Gen. Bibl. v].

Salaville, S., 'Philosophie et théologie ou épisodes scolastiques à Byzance de 1059 à 1117', *EO*, xxix (1930), 132–56.

Salaville, S., 'De la spiritualité patristique et byzantine à la théologie russe', *EB*, iii (1945), 215–44 (bibliographical survey).

Schreiber, G., 'Anselm von Havelberg und die Ostkirche', *ZKG*, lx (1942), 354–411.

Schultze, F., 'Untersuchungen über das Jesusgebet', *OCP*, xviii (1952), 319–43.

Stephanou, P. E., *Jean Italos, philosophe et humaniste* (*OCA*, cxxxiv) (Rome, 1949).

Stephanou, P. E., 'Jean Italos: l'immortalité de l'âme et la résurrection', *EO*, xxxii (1933), 413–28.

Studer, B., *Die theologische Arbeitsweise des Johannes von Damaskus* (Ettal, 1956).

Thomas, C., *Theodor von Studion und sein Zeitalter* (Osnabrück, 1892).

Vast, H., *Le Cardinal Bessarion: Etude sur la chrétienté et la renaissance vers le milieu du XVᵉ siècle* (Paris, 1878) (see also the periodical *Bessarione*, Rome).

Völker, W., *Kontemplation und Ekstase bei Pseudo-Dionysius Areopagita* (Wiesbaden, 1958).

Wenger, A., 'Bulletin de spiritualité et de théologie byzantine', *REB*, xiii (1955), 140–96 [a bibliographical survey of work published from July 1952–December 1954, including sections on texts and manuscripts, Gregory of Nyssa and the pseudo-Macarius, Evagrius of Pontus, the pseudo-Dionysius, John of Damascus, Symeon the New Theologian, Palamas, as well as various aspects of Byzantine spirituality, e.g. the Jesus Prayer].

Zervos, C., *Un philosophe néoplatonicien du XIᵉ siècle: Michel Psellos* (Paris, 1919).

CHAPTER XXVII
BYZANTINE LITERATURE

I. GENERAL WORKS

(Details of these works are not repeated in the bibliography which follows.)

FOURTH TO SIXTH CENTURIES

Christ, W. von, Schmid, W. and Stählin, O., *Geschichte der griechischen Litteratur*, 6th ed., pt. II: *Die nachklassische Periode der griechischen Litteratur*, 2. Hälfte: A.D. 100–530 (Handbuch der Altertumswissenschaft, vii, ii, 2, Munich, 1924), pp. 943–1104, 1372–1492.

Wright, F. A., *A History of Later Greek Literature: from the Death of Alexander in 323 B.C. to the Death of Justinian in 565 A.D.* (London, 1932).

SIXTH TO FIFTEENTH CENTURIES

Beck, H.-G., *Kirche und theologische Literatur im byzantinischen Reich* [see Gen. Bibl. i].

Dawkins, R. M., 'Greek Language in the Byzantine Period', in *Byzantium*, ed. N. H. Baynes and H. St L. B. Moss, pp. 252–67 [see Gen. Bibl. v].

Hunger, H., *Byzantinische Geisteswelt von Konstantin dem Grossen bis zum Fall Konstantinopels* (Baden-Baden, 1958) [German translations of selections from a wide range of Byzantine works].

Krumbacher, K., *Geschichte der byzantinischen Litteratur* [see Gen. Bibl. v].

Marshall, F. H., 'Byzantine Literature', in *Byzantium*, ed. N. H. Baynes and H. St L. B. Moss, pp. 221–51 with bibliography, pp. 410–14 [see Gen. Bibl. v].

Moravcsik, Gy., *Byzantinoturcica* [see Gen. Bibl. i].

Sajdak, J., *Literatura Bizantinska* (Warsaw, 1933) [in Polish, with extracts].

For works published between 1938 and 1962, see F. Dölger, 'Forschungen zur byzantinischen Geschichte, Literatur und Sprache 1938–1950', in *Byzanz*, ed. F. Dölger and A. M. Schneider, pp. 17–31, 175–233 [see Gen. Bibl. i]; 'Bibliographie 1919–1951', *BZ*, xliv (1951) (=*Festschrift F. Dölger*), 1*–50*; for 1952–1956 see 'Note bibliografiche', *Convegno di Scienze Mor. Stor. e Filol., Atti* 12 (1957), 473–6; for 1952–1960 see *ΠΑΡΑΣΠΟΡΑ* (Ettal, 1961), pp. xiv–xx.

See also 'Bibliographische Notizen und Mitteilungen' appearing annually in *BZ*, pt. iii: 1 a, Gelehrte Literatur; 1 b, Volksliteratur; 1 c, Sagen; Volkskunde; 3 a, Sprache; 3 b, Metrik und Musik; 4, Theolog. Literatur; Hagiographie.

II. RELIGIOUS LITERATURE

Altaner, B., *Patrologie* [fourth to eighth centuries] [see Gen. Bibl. i].

Bardenhewer, O., *Geschichte der altchristlichen Literatur*, iii (4. Jahrhundert), 1912 (new ed. with additions, 1923); iv (5. Jahrhundert), 1924; v (6.–8. Jahrhunderte), Freiburg im Breisgau, 1932.

Beck, H.-G., *Vorsehung und Vorbestimmung in der theologischen Literatur der Byzantiner* (Rome, 1937). [A number of Byzantine theologians of all centuries are here appraised from a literary standpoint, with bibliography.]

Beck, H.-G., *Kirche und theologische Literatur im byzantinischen Reich* [sixth to fifteenth centuries].

Cassamassa, A. and Mannucci, U., *Istituzioni di Patrologia*, 6th ed., pt. ii, *Epoca postnicena* (Rome, 1950) [fourth to eighth centuries].

Christ-Schmid-Stählin [see above], pp. 1372–492 [fourth to sixth centuries].

Courcelle, P., *Les lettres grecques en occident. De Macrobe à Cassiodore*, 2nd ed. (Paris, 1948) [for the influence of Greek patristic literature of the fourth to sixth centuries on the West].

Dölger, F., *Byzanz*, pp. 175–97.

Ehrhard, A., 'Theologie' in K. Krumbacher, *Geschichte der byzantinischen Litteratur*, pp. 37–218 [sixth to fifteenth centuries].

Quasten, J. and Plumpe, J. C. (edd.), *Ancient Christian Writers* (Washington, 1946 ff., in progress) [English translations of some of the Fathers, including Athanasius' *Vita Antonii*].

For most of the original texts the reader is referred to Migne, *Patrologia Graeca* [Gen. Bibl. IV]. But there have been numerous later editions, for which the works mentioned above should be consulted. For lives of the saints see *Bibliotheca hagiographica graeca* [Gen. Bibl. IV].

III. SECULAR PROSE IN THE 'KATHAREUOUSA'

(A) GENERAL WORKS

Christ-Schmid-Stählin, pp. 943–1104 [fourth to sixth centuries].
Dölger, F., *Byzanz*, pp. 17–31, 197–201, 208–13, 219 f., 230 f.
Krumbacher, pp. 219–786 [sixth to fifteenth centuries].

(B) SPECIAL WORKS

(i) *Histories and Chronicles*

Colonna, M. E., *Gli storici Bizantini dal IV al XV secolo*. I. *Storici profani* (Naples, 1956) [but see review by Gy. Moravcsik, *BZ*, L (1957), 439–42].
Moravcsik, Gy., *Byzantinoturcica* I: *Die byzantinischen Quellen zur Geschichte der Türkvölker* [short notices of almost all Byzantine historians and chroniclers with details of editions and full bibliography] [see Gen. Bibl. I].

The last general edition of Byzantine historians and chroniclers was the *Corpus Scriptorum Historiae Byzantinae* (the so-called 'Bonn Corpus'), 50 vols. (Bonn, 1829–92), but critical editions of some of the texts that appear in these volumes have since been published; see details in Gy. Moravcsik.
Excerpts critically edited in G. Soyter, *Byzantinische Geschichtsschreiber und Chronisten*: Ausgewählte Texte mit Einleitung, kritischem Apparat und Kommentar (Heidelberg, 1929).
Some texts have been translated into German in the series *Byzantinische Geschichtsschreiber*, gen. ed. E. V. Ivánka (Graz, Vienna, Cologne, 1954 ff.).

(ii) *Rhetoric and Satire*

Christ-Schmid-Stählin, pp. 985–1034 [fourth to sixth centuries].
Friedländer, P., *Johannes von Gaza und Paulus Silentiarius* (Berlin-Leipzig, 1912) [on the ἔκφρασις].
Krumbacher, pp. 450–98 [sixth to fifteenth centuries].

(iii) *Philosophy*

Christ-Schmid-Stählin, pp. 1050–74 [fourth to sixth centuries].
Geyer, P., 'Die patristische und scholastische Philosophie', in F. Ueberweg, *Grundriss der Philosophie*, pt. II, 12th ed. [reprint of 11th ed.] (Tübingen, 1951), pp. 74–94, 117–31, 281–7.
Krumbacher, pp. 428–49 [sixth to fifteenth centuries].
Tatakis, B., *La philosophie byzantine* (Paris, 1949).

(iv) *Philology and Grammar*

Christ-Schmid-Stählin, pp. 1075–94 [fourth to sixth centuries].

Krumbacher, pp. 466–905 [sixth to fifteenth centuries].

For bibliography on scientific topics (including geography) see below chapter XXVIII.

IV. POETRY IN THE 'KATHAREUOUSA'

(A) GENERAL

Cantarella, R., *Poeti bizantini.* I: *Testi; Introduzione, traduzione e commento* (Milan, 1948) [wide selection of texts from both 'kathareuousa' and demotic, with Italian translation and introduction in vol. II].

Christ-Schmid-Stählin, pp. 956–85, 1046–50 [fourth to sixth centuries].

Dölger, F., *Byzanz*, pp. 202–8.

Dölger, F., *Die byzantinische Dichtung in der Reinsprache* (Handbuch der griechischen und lateinischen Philologie, Byzantinische Literatur), 2nd ed., in *Eucharisterion, F. Dölger z. 70. Geburtstag* (Thessalonica, 1961), pp. 1–64.

Krumbacher, pp. 639–786 [sixth to fifteenth centuries].

La Piana, G., 'The Byzantine Theater', *SP*, XI (1936), 171–211.

Soyter, G. (ed.), *Byzantinische Dichtung* (Athens, 1938) [a selection of poetry in both 'kathareuousa' and demotic from the fourth to the fifteenth century; Greek text with German translation in the metres of the originals].

Trypanis, C. A. (ed.), *Medieval and Modern Greek Poetry. An Anthology* (Oxford, 1951) [selections from both 'kathareuousa' and demotic, without translation but with notes and introduction].

(B) RELIGIOUS

Bardenhewer, O., *Geschichte der altchristlichen Literatur*, V, pp. 158–73 [down to eighth century].

Christ, W. and Paranikas, M., *Anthologia graeca carminum christianorum* (Leipzig, 1871) [includes textual criticism].

Christ-Schmid-Stählin, pp. 1374 ff. [fourth to sixth centuries].

Dölger, F., *Byzanz*, pp. 158–63.

Dölger, F., *Die byzantinische Dichtung in der Reinsprache*, pp. 1–64.

Emereau, E., 'Hymnographi Graeci', *EO*, XXI (1922), 158–279; XXII (1923), 11 25, 420–39; XXIII (1924), 196–200, 276–85, 408–14; XXIV (1925), 164–79; XXV (1926), 178–84.

Follieri, E., *Initia hymnorum Ecclesiae Graecae* (*Studi e Testi* 211–14), 4 vols. (Vatican, 1960–3).

Krumbacher, pp. 653–705 [sixth to fifteenth centuries].

Pitra, J. B. (ed.), *Analecta Sacra Spicilegio Solesmensi parata*, I (Paris, 1876) [alphabetical list of Byzantine church poets, with editions].

See also the collections of R. Cantarella, G. Soyter and C. A. Trypanis listed under IV (A) above.

V. VERNACULAR POETRY

Artelt, W., *Index zur Geschichte der Mathematik, Naturwissenschaft und Technik*, ɪ (Munich and Berlin, 1953).

Dieterich, K., *Geschichte der byzantinischen und neugriechischen Litteratur* (Die Litteraturen des Ostens in Einzeldarstellungen, ɪv), 2nd ed., Leipzig, 1909), pp. v–x, 1–120 [emphasises continuity of modern Greek literature].

Dölger, F., *Byzanz*, pp. 214–19.

Grégoire, H., Ὁ Διγενὴς Ἀκρίτας. Ἡ Βυζαντινὴ Ἐποποιία στὴν Ἱστορία καὶ στὴν Ποίηση (New York, 1942) [and many other writings by this scholar on the popular epic].

Impellizzeri, S., *Il Digenis Akritas. L'Epopea di Bizanzio* (Florence, 1940).

Kalonaros, P. P., Βασίλειος Διγενὴς Ἀκρίτας, 2 vols. (Athens, 1941) [edition of the Greek text, with detailed introduction].

Krumbacher, pp. 787–910.

Mavrogordato, J., *Digenes Akrites* (Oxford, 1956).

Wagner, W. (ed.), *Carmina Graeca Medii Aevi* (Leipzig, 1874) [contains most of the popular verse-romances].

See also the collections of R. Cantarella, G. Soyter and C. A. Trypanis listed under ɪv (A) above.

For information on individual authors, see also articles in the larger encyclopaedias, especially Pauly-Wissowa and the *Lexikon für Theologie und Kirche* [see Gen. Bibl. ɪ].

CHAPTER XXVIII
BYZANTINE SCIENCE

I. GENERAL WORKS

(Details of these works are not repeated in the bibliography which follows.)

Andreeva, M. A., *Očerki po kul'ture vizantijskogo dvora v XIII v.* [*Studies in the culture of the Byzantine Court in the XIIIth century*] (Prague, 1927) [especially pp. 128–78].

Byzantinische Zeitschrift [*BZ*]. [Useful bibliographical reviews.]

Delatte, A., *Anecdota Atheniensia* ɪ: *Textes grecs inédits relatifs à l'histoire des religions*; ɪɪ: *Textes grecs relatifs à l'histoire des sciences* (Liège, 1927 and 1939).

Dölger, F. and Schneider, A. M., *Byzanz* (= Wissenschaftliche Forschungsberichte, v) (Berne, 1952). [Contains a detailed bibliography for the years 1938–50.]

Haskins, C. H., *Studies in the History of Mediaeval Science* (Cambridge, Mass., 1924).

Heiberg, J. L., *Geschichte der Mathematik und Naturwissenschaften im Altertum* (= Handbuch der Altertumswissenschaften, v, 1. Teil, 2. Hälfte) (Munich, 1925).

Isis. [Useful bibliographical reviews.]

Krumbacher, K., *Geschichte der byzantinischen Litteratur* [see Gen. Bibl. v]. [Indispensable though now needing revision.]

Kukules, Ph., Βυζαντινῶν Βίος καὶ Πολιτισμός [see Gen. Bibl. v].

Moravcsik, Gy., *Byzantinoturcica*. [This contains full bibliography on a number of Byzantine authors. See Gen. Bibl. I.]

Ohnsorge, W., 'Byzanz und das Abendland im 9. und 10. Jahrhundert', *Saeculum*, v (1954), 194–200; reprinted in *Abendland und Byzanz* [see Gen. Bibl. v].

Sarton, G., *Guide to the History of Science* (Waltham: Mass., 1952) [for bibliography on the various branches of science].

Sarton, G., *Introduction to the History of Science*, I–III (Baltimore, 1927–48). [An account of Byzantine science up to and including the fourteenth century; this should be consulted for bibliography.]

Singer, C., *From Magic to Science* (London, 1928).

Tannery, P., *Sciences exactes chez les Byzantins. Mémoires scientifiques* IV (Paris, 1920).

Thorndike, L., *A History of Magic and Experimental Science. I–II. The First Thirteen Centuries of our Era. III–IV. The Fourteenth and Fifteenth Centuries* (New York, 1923–34).

For Byzantine schools and education see also:

Bréhier, L., 'Notes sur l'histoire de l'enseignement supérieur à Constantinople', *B*, III (1927), 73–94; IV (1929), 13–28.

Browning, R., 'The Patriarchal School at Constantinople in the Twelfth Century', *B*, XXXII (1962), 166–202 (to be cont.).

Browning, R., 'Byzantinische Schulen und Schulmeister', *Das Altertum*, IX (1963), 105–18.

Diller, A., 'The Byzantine Quadrivium', *Isis*, XXXVI (1945/6), 132.

Dvornik, F., 'Photius et la réorganisation de l'académie patriarcale', *Mélanges P. Peeters*, II = *AB*, LXVIII (1950), 108–25. [Describes the secular instruction available even at the patriarchal school.]

Fuchs, F., *Die höheren Schulen von Konstantinopel im Mittelalter* (Leipzig-Berlin, 1926) (cf. H. Grégoire, *B*, IV (1929), 771–8).

Hussey, J. M., *Church and Learning in the Byzantine Empire 867–1185* [see Gen. Bibl. v].

Laurent, V., 'Le quadrivium et la formation intellectuelle sous les Paléologues'. This is the preface (pp. xvii–xliii) to P. Tannery, *Quadrivium de Georges Pachymère* (*Studi e Testi* 94) (Vatican, 1940).

II. SPECIAL TOPICS

(A) MATHEMATICS AND ASTRONOMY

(i) *General works*

Cantor, M., *Vorlesungen über Geschichte der Mathematik*, I, 3rd ed. (Leipzig, 1907), 500–17.

Heiberg, J. L., *Geschichte der Mathematik und Naturwissenschaften im Altertum* (Munich, 1925).

Mogenet, J., 'Une scholie inédite du Vat. gr. 1594 sur les rapports entre l'astronomie arabe et Byzance', *Osiris*, XIV (1962), 198–221.

Neugebauer, O., *The Exact Sciences in Antiquity*, 2nd ed. (Providence, 1957).

Neugebauer, O., *Studies in Byzantine Astronomical Terminology* (*Trans. American Philos. Society*, n.s. 50, II) (Philadelphia, 1960).

Sarton, G., *Guide to the History of Science*, pp. 150 ff. (mathematics); pp. 156 f. (astronomy); pp. 170 f. (chronometry).

Stephanides, M., 'Τὰ Μαθηματικὰ τῶν Βυζαντινῶν', Ἀθηνᾶ, xxxv (1923), 206–18.

Van der Waerden, B., 'Eine byzantinische Sonnentafel', *SBAW*, Math. Naturw. Kl. (1954), 159–68.

Zinner, E., *Die Geschichte der Sternkunde* (Berlin, 1931), pp. 150 ff.

The prolegomena to the mathematical texts in the Teubner editions also contain some historical information.

(ii) *Individual authors*

John Philoponus

Delatte, A., *Anecdota Atheniensia*, II, 133–87, new edition of the commentary on the 'Introductio arithmetica'. [For the various editions of the commentary on Nicomachus made by Proclus, Philoponus, Asclepius of Tralles (sixth century) and Arsenius Olbiodorus (fourteenth century) see pp. 129 ff., Astrolabica, pp. 189–271 (see above Gen. Works).]

Heath, T., *Mathematics in Aristotle* (Oxford, 1949), pp. 45 f. and 48 f.

Kroll, W., Pauly-Wissowa, IX, 2, cols. 1764–95.

Neugebauer, O., 'The Early History of the Astrolabe', *Isis*, XL (1949), 240–56.

Anthemius of Tralles

Huxley, G. L., *Anthemius of Tralles: a Study in Later Greek Geometry* (Cambridge: Mass., 1959).

Leo the Mathematician

Lipšic, E. E., 'Vizantijskij učenij Lev Matematik (iz istorii viz. kul'tury v IX v.)' ['The Byzantine scholar Leo the Mathematician—from the history of Byzantine learning in the IXth century'], *VV*, n.s. II (1949), 106–49.

Michael Psellus

De omnifaria doctrina, ed. L. G. Westerink (Utrecht, 1948), cap. 120ff. (pp. 64 ff.). [Contains much of Psellus' treatise on astronomy.]

Περὶ τῶν ἰδεῶν ἃς ὁ Πλάτων λέγει, ed. C. G. Linder, *Philologus*, XVI (1860), 523–6 and E. Kurtz–F. Drexl, *M. Pselli Scripta Minora*, I (Milan, 1936), 433–6; transl. J. M. Hussey, *Church and Learning*, pp. 226–9 [see Gen. Bibl. v].

Renauld, E., *Etude de la langue et du style de Michel Psellos* (Paris, 1920). [This gives a full bibliography up to 1920.]

Soterichi ad Nicomachi Geraseni introductionem arithmeticam de Platonis Psychogonia scholia, ed. R. Hoche (Elberfeld, 1871).

Symeon Seth (and others)

Anastos, M. V., 'Ὑπόγειος, a Byzantine Term for Perigee and some Byzantine Views of the Date of Perigee and Apogee', *OCP*, XIII (1947), 385–403.

Adelard of Bath

Bliemetzrieder, F., *Adelhard von Bath* (Munich, 1935).

Haskins, C. H., *Studies in the History of Mediaeval Science* (Cambridge, 1924).

Nicephorus Blemmydes

Codellas, P. S., 'Nikephoros Blemmydes' Philosophical Works and Teachings', *Proc. Xth Internat. Congr. of Phil.* (Amsterdam, 1949), pp. 1117 f.

George Pachymeres

Heiberg, J. L., 'Mathematisches zu Aristoteles', *Abh. zur Gesch. der mathe-matischen Wissenschaften*, XVIII (1904), 1–49 (esp. pp. 37 ff.). [A student's notes on a lecture on the Organon.]

Tannery, P., *Quadrivium de Georges Pachymère (Studi e Testi* 94) (Vatican, 1940).

Tannery, P., 'Georgii Pachymerae arithmetices capitula viginti', *Diophanti Alexandrini opera*, II (Leipzig, 1895), 78–122.

Maximus Planudes

Scholia in Diophantum (Liber I et Liber II): Maximi quae feruntur Planudis, ed. P. Tannery, *Diophanti opera*, II (Leipzig, 1895), 125–255.

Wendel, C., Pauly-Wissowa (new ed.), XX, 2 (1950), cols. 2202–53.

Theodore Metochites

Beck, H.-G., *Theodoros Metochites* (Munich, 1952).

Codellas, P. S., 'Theodoros Metochites', *Actes du VIe Congrès internat. d'études byzantines (Paris, 1948)* (Paris, 1950), I, 385–8.

Hunger, H., 'Theodoros Metochites als Vorläufer des Humanismus in Byzanz', *BZ*, XLV (1952), 4–19.

Sarton, G., 'The Astronomical Summary of Theodoros Metochites', *Isis*, XXXII (1940), 120.

Ševčenko, I., *Etudes sur la polémique entre Théodore Métochite et Nicéphore Choumnos* (Brussels, 1962).

The Elements of Astronomy. An edition by I. Ševčenko is in preparation; cf. *Isis*, XLI (1950), 52; see also Ševčenko cited above.

Isaac Argyrus

Heiberg, J. L., *Literargeschichtliche Studien über Euklid* (Leipzig, 1882), pp. 171 f. [For the scholia on Euclid, which were published by Dasy-podius in 1579.]

John Cabasilas

Heiberg, J. L., 'Den graeske Mathematiks Overleveringshistorie', *Overs. over D.K. Danske Vidensk. Selsk. Forh.* (Copenhagen, 1896), p. 84.

(B) PHYSICS

(i) *General works*

The standard works on the history of physics (cited by G. Sarton, *Guide to the History of Science*, pp. 157 ff.) have little information on Byzantium. For further references see J. L. Heiberg, *Geschichte der Mathematik und Naturwissenschaften* (Munich, 1925).

Stephanides, M., Συμβολαὶ εἰς τὴν Ἱστορίαν τῶν Φυσικῶν Ἐπιστήμων καὶ ἰδίως τῆς χημείας (Athens, 1914).

Stephanides, M., 'Αἱ φυσικαὶ ἐπιστῆμαι τῶν Βυζαντινῶν', Ἡμερολόγιον τῆς μεγάλης Ἑλλάδος (Athens, 1924), pp. 269–77. [Some detailed information on Byzantine physics.]

(ii) *Individual authors*

Michael Psellus

Bidez, J., *Catalogue des manuscrits alchimiques grecs*, vol. 6. *Michel Psellus* (Brussels, 1928). [For meteorological writings.]

Camotius, J. B., *In Physicen Aristotelis commentarii* (Venice, 1554). [A Latin translation of the commentary on Aristotle's *Physics*; the Greek text has not been published.]
De omnifaria doctrina, ed. G. Westerink (Utrecht, 1948). [Reference to writings on physics pp. 51 ff., 57 f., 60 and *passim.*]

Symeon Seth
Brief Solutions of Problems in Physics, ed. D. G. Seebode (Wiesbaden, 1857). [The text given comprises the introduction, last part of the second book and the whole of the third book of a work by Seth.]
Delatte, A., *Anecdota Atheniensia*, II, 2, 16–89 [see above Gen. Works].
Gianelli, C., 'Di alcune versioni e rielaborazioni serbe delle Solutiones breves questionum naturalium, attribuite a Michele Psello', *Atti V Congr. Intern. di Studi Biz.* I = *SBN*, V (1939), 445–68.

Nicephorus Chumnus
Verpeaux, J., *Nicéphore Choumnos: homme d'état et humaniste byzantin (ca. 1250/1255–1327)* (Paris, 1959).

(C) OPTICS

General works

In addition to the works on the history of physics, see

Hoppe, E., *Geschichte der Optik* (Leipzig, 1926).
Mach, E., *Die Prinzipien der physikalischen Optik* (Leipzig, 1921); English transl. (London, 1926).
Pla, C., *La enigma de la luz* (Buenos Aires, 1949).
Priestley, J., *The History and Present State of Discoveries relating to Vision, Light and Colours*, 2 vols. (London, 1772).
Sambursky, S., 'Philoponus' Interpretation of Aristotle's Theory of Light', *Osiris*, XIII (1958), 114–26.
Sarton, G., *Guide to the History of Science*, p. 162.
Wilde, E., *Geschichte der Optik*, 2 vols. (Berlin, 1838 and 1843).

(D) ACOUSTICS

(i) General works

Lang, P. H., *Music in Western Civilisation* (New York, 1941).
Reese, G., *Music in the Middle Ages* (New York, 1940).
[On both these histories see G. Sarton, in *Isis*, XXXIV (1942), 182–6.]
Wellesz, E., *History of Byzantine Music and Hymnography*, 2nd ed. (Oxford, 1961). [Detailed bibliography.]

(ii) Individual authors

Michael Psellus
On the Sound Hall in Nicomedia, ed. J. F. Boissonade, *Psellus* (Nuremberg, 1838), pp. 58–62.

Nicephorus Gregoras
Guilland, R., *Essai sur Nicéphore Grégoire* (Paris, 1926), pp. 270 ff.
Høeg, C., 'La théorie de la musique byzantine', *REG*, XXXV (1922), 321–54.

(E) ZOOLOGY

(i) *General works*

Heichelheim, F. M., 'Byzantine Silks', *Ciba Review*, LXXV (Basel, 1949) [with bibliography], pp. 2742–67].

Henning, R., 'Die Einführung der Seidenraupenzucht ins Byzantinerreich', *BZ*, XXXIII (1933), 295–312 [on silkworms].

Kukules, Ph., ''Η μελισσοκομία παρὰ Βυζαντινοῖς', *BZ*, XLIV (1951), 347–57 [on bees].

Sarton, G., *Guide to the History of Science*, pp. 171 ff. [detailed bibliography of works dealing with the history of biology, natural history, zoology, botany and agriculture].

Singer, C., *A History of Biology*, 2nd ed. (New York, 1950), pp. 14 ff.

Théodoridès, J., 'Introduction à l'étude de la zoologie byzantine', *Actes du VIIe Congr. Intern. d'hist. des sciences (Jerusalem, 1953)* (Paris, 1953), pp. 601–9.

(ii) *Individual authors or works*

Epitome of Aristotle's *Zoology*, ed. S. Lampros, *Excerptorum Constantini de natura animalium libri duo* (Berlin, 1885) (= Supplementum Aristotelicum, I, 1). [Two of the four original books.]

Geoponica. This is from Constantine VII's collection of excerpts and is based on the much better work of Cassianus Bassus (sixth century), ed. H. Beckh, *Geoponica sive Cassiani Bassi scholastici de re rustica eclogae* (Leipzig, 1895). For the history of the text see A. D. Wilson, 'A Greek Treatise on Agriculture', *Brit. Mus. Quart.* XIII (1939), 10 f.

Timothy of Gaza

Bodenheimer, F. S. and Rabinowitz, A., 'Timothy of Gaza περὶ ζῴων', *Coll. de travaux de l'Acad. Intern. Hist. Sciences*, III (1949) [translation and commentary based on the edition by E. Haupt in *Hermes*, III (1869), 1–30, 174].

Cosmas Indicopleustes

See under GEOGRAPHY.

The Physiologus

Delatte, A., *Anecdota Atheniensia*, I, 358 (for the various editions of the *Physiologus*) [see above Gen. Works].

Pauly-Wissowa, XX, 1 (1941), cols. 1074–129.

Thorndike, L., *History of Magic and Experimental Science*, I, 497–503 [see above Gen. Works].

(F) BOTANY

(i) *General works*

Delatte, A., *Anecdota Atheniensia*, II, *Glossaires de botanique*, pp. 273–454 [see above Gen. Works].

Hohlwein, N., 'Palmiers et palmériers dans l'Egypte romaine', *Etudes de Papyrologie*, V (1939), 1–74. [On the cultivation of palm trees in the Byzantine period.]

Jeanselme, E. and Oeconomos, L., 'Aliments et recettes culinaires des By-
    zantins', *Proc. of the Third Intern. Congr. of the Hist. of Medicine, London,
    1922* (Antwerp, 1923), pp. 155–68.
Jessen, K. F. W., *Botanik der Gegenwart und Vorzeit* (Leipzig, 1864; reprinted
    Waltham, 1948).
Kukules, Ph., "Η ἀμπελουργία παρὰ Βυζαντινοῖς', *EEBS*, xx (1950), 17–32.
Langkavel, B., *Botanik der späteren Griechen vom dritten bis dreizehnten Jahr-
    hundert* (Berlin, 1866).
Meyer, E. H. F., *Geschichte der Botanik*, 4 vols. (Königsberg, 1854–7).
Sarton, G., *Guide to the History of Science*, pp. 173 ff.
Thomson, M. H., 'Catalogue des manuscrits grecs à Paris contenants des
    traités anonymes de botanique', *REG*, xLvi (1933), 334–8. [On botanical
    manuscripts in Paris.]
See also *Geoponica* (above, under Zoology), caps. 2–12, pp. 31–384.

(ii) *Individual authors*

Michael Psellus

De omnifaria doctrina, ed. G. Westerink (Utrecht, 1948), pp. 87 ff. (nos. 172,
    186, 187, 188, 193). Cf. Meyer, *op. cit.* iii, 352 ff.
Περὶ γεωργικῶν, ed. J. F. Boissonade, *Anecdota Graeca*, i (Paris, 1829), pp. 242–7.
    [Also deals with the husbandry of grain, wine and fruit and with grafting.
    Manuel II's (1391–1425) curriculum included agriculture among school
    subjects.]

Pedanius Dioscorides

For the manuscripts of Dioscorides see Pauly-Wissowa, v (1905), cols. 1131–42
    and C. Singer, 'The Herbal in Antiquity and its Transmission to Later
    Ages', *JHS*, xLvii (1927), 1–62.

(g) MINERALOGY

(i) *General works*

Sarton, G., *Guide to the History of Science*, pp. 178 f.

(ii) *Individual authors*

Michael Psellus

Περὶ λίθων δυνάμεων, ed. J. L. Ideler, *Physici et medici graeci minores* (Berlin,
    1841), i, 244–7. [The still unpublished work Περὶ λίθων of Neilus Dias-
    sorinus (†after 1375) is similar in content.]

(h) CHEMISTRY

General works

Berthelot, M., *Les origines de l'alchémie* (Paris, 1885).
Faerber, E., *Die geschichtliche Entwicklung der Chemie* (Berlin, 1921).
Farber (formerly Faerber), E., *The Evolution of Chemistry* (New York, 1952).
Lippmann, E. O. von, *Entstehung und Ausbreitung der Alchemie*, i (Berlin,
    1919).
Sarton, G., *Guide to the History of Science*, pp. 163 ff.

(I) MEDICINE, DENTISTRY AND VETERINARY SCIENCE

(i) *General works*

(a) *Medicine*

For general accounts of the history of medicine see

Laignel-Lavastine, M., *Histoire générale de la médecine, de la pharmacie, de l'art dentaire et de l'art vétérinaire*, I (Paris, 1936).

Sarton, G., *Guide to the History of Science*, pp. 180–1, 184–90.

Castiglioni, A., *A History of Medicine*, transl. E. B. Krumbhaar, 2nd ed. (New York, 1947).

Creutz, R. and Steudel, J., *Einführung in die Geschichte der Medizin* (Iserlohn, 1948).

Diepgen, P., *Geschichte der Medizin* (Berlin, 1949), I, especially pp. 162–74.

Garrison, F. H., *Introduction to the History of Medicine*, 4th ed., revised and enlarged (Philadelphia, 1929), especially pp. 110–16. [Covers only the period 476–732.]

Haeser, H., *Lehrbuch der Geschichte der Medizin und der epidemischen Krankheiten*, 3rd ed. (Jena, 1875), I, *Altertum und Mittelalter*, especially pp. 445–86.

Neuburger, M. and Pagel, J., *Handbuch der Geschichte der Medizin* (originated by T. Puschmann), I (Jena, 1902), especially pp. 492–588.

Neuburger, M., *Geschichte der Medizin*, 2 vols. (Stuttgart, 1906 and 1911).

Temkin, O., 'Byzantine Medicine: Tradition and Empiricism', *DOP*, XVI (1962), 97–115.

Treatment of diseases of the eyes

Hirschberg, J., *Geschichte der Augenheilkunde* (Leipzig, 1899) (= Graefe-Saemisch, *Handbuch der gesamten Augenheilkunde*, XII), pp. 361–7.

Specialist works on Byzantine medicine

Byzantine medical texts are published in the *Corpus medicorum graecorum* and in J. Ideler, *Physici et medici Graeci minores*, vols. I and II (Berlin, 1841/2). See also K. Krumbacher, *Geschichte der byz. Litteratur*, p. 616 [see Gen. Bibl. v].

Bariety, M., 'La médecine byzantine dans l'Alexiade d'Anne Comnène', *Mém. de la Soc. française d'histoire de la médecine*, III (1947), 17–21. For medicine under the Comneni [inaccessible to the author].

Brunet, F., 'Alexander de Tralles et la médecine byzantine', *Œuvres médicales d'Alexandre de Tralles*, I (Paris, 1933).

Codellas, P. S., 'The Pantocrator, the Imperial Byzantine Medical Center of XIIth century A.D. in Constantinople', *Bull. Hist. Med.* XII (1942), 392–410, with pictures of Byzantine doctors and ground plans of the buildings.

Diepgen, P., 'Zur Frauenheilkunde im byzantinischen Kulturkreis des Mittelalters', *Abhandlung d. geistes- und sozialwiss. Kl. der Akademie der Wiss. und d. Liter.* (Mainz, 1950), pp. 3–14.

Dmitrievsky, A., *Opisanie liturgičeskich rukopisej chranjaščichsja v bibliotekach pravoslavnago vostoka* [*The liturgical manuscripts in the libraries of the Orthodox East*] (Kiev, 1895), *Typika*, I, pp. 656–702. [The Typikon of the Pantocrator monastery.]

Dölger, F., 'Streiflichter aus der sanitären und hygienischen Kultur im byzantinischen Reiche', *Münchner mediz. Wochenschrift*, LXXVII (1930), 810 f. [Notes that the Pantocrator monastery had its own master apothecary.]

Grumel, V., 'La profession médicale à Byzance à l'époque des Comnènes', *REB*, VII (1949), 42–6.

Jeanselme, E. and Oeconomos, L., 'Les œuvres d'assistance et les hôpitaux byzantins au siècle des Comnènes', *Communication to the First Congress of the History of Medicine (Antwerp, 1920)* (Antwerp, 1921).

Jorga, N., 'La continuation des hôpitaux byzantins par des hôpitaux roumains', *RHSE*, IX (1932), 345–50. [Later influence of the Pantocrator monastery.]

Kukules, Ph., 'Διὰ τὴν ἱστορίαν τῆς ἰατρικῆς κατὰ τοὺς βυζαντινοὺς χρόνους', Ἀκαδημαϊκὴ Ἰατρική, XVI (1952), 3–24.

Purnopulos, G. K., Ἱστορία τῆς Βυζαντινῆς ἰατρικῆς (Athens, 1942).

Schmidt, A., 'Über den Ursprung der Apotheken', *Pharmazeutische Zeit.* LXXII (1927), 1107 ff.

(b) Dentistry

Boissier, R., 'L'art dentaire dans l'antiquité', in Laignel-Lavastine, pp. 609–16 [see above, under Medicine].

Sarton, G., *Guide to the History of Science*, p. 189.

Sudhoff, K., *Geschichte der Zahnheilkunde*, 2nd ed. (Leipzig, 1926).

Weinberger, B. W., *An Introduction to the History of Dentistry*, I (St Louis, 1948).

(c) Veterinary science

Belitz, W., 'Wiederkäuer und ihre Krankheiten im Altertum', *Abhand. aus d. Geschichte d. Veterinärmedizin* (Leipzig, 1924), Heft 12.

Leclainche, E., 'La médecine vétérinaire dans l'antiquité', in Laignel-Levastine [see above, under Medicine], pp. 617–66. See also p. 665 for further bibliography.

Sarton, G., *Guide to the History of Science*, p. 191 for bibliography.

(ii) Individual authors

Oribasius

Corpus of Medicine (Ἰατρικαὶ συναγωγαί), ed. U. C. Bussemaker and C. Daremberg, *Œuvres d'Oribase* (Paris, 1851–62), vols. I–IV (with French transl.). See also *Corpus medicorum Graecorum*, ed. J. Raeder, VI, 1–2 (1928–33); and VI, 3 (1926), for *Synopsis*. The subjects dealt with are dietetics, hygiene, therapeutics, drugs, anatomy and special pathology.

Schröder, H. O., Pauly-Wissowa, supplt. VII (1940), cols. 797–812.

Aëtius of Amida

Medicine, ed. A. Olivieri, Aetii Amideni Libri Medicinales, I–IV (*Corp. med. Graec.* VIII, 1, 1935) and V–VIII (*ibid.* VIII, 2, 1950). Book VII is devoted to ophthalmics: Aëtius does not mention the operation for cataract, which was known to Paul of Aegina. Books IX, XII, XIII, XV and XVI have also been published, see G. Sarton in *Isis*, XLII (1951), 150 ff.

Ricci, J. V., *Aëtios of Amida: the Gynaecology and Obstetrics of the sixth century A.D.* (Philadelphia, 1950). Contains an English translation of Book XVI which follows a Latin transl. of 1542.

Metrodora

Ἐκ τῶν Μητροδώρας περὶ τῶν γυναικείων παθῶν τῆς μήτρας, ed. A. Kuses, *Praktika Akad. Athen.* xx (1945: appeared 1949), pp. 46–68 (edited from a twelfth-century manuscript). [It is the oldest Greek work on gynaecology (sixth century).]

Alexander of Tralles

Θεραπευτικά, ed. T. Puschmann (with German transl.), 2 vols. (Vienna, 1878–9).

Œuvres médicales d'Alexandre de Tralles, ed. F. Brunet (with French transl.), 4 vols. (Paris, 1933–7).

Περὶ ὀφθαλμῶν, ed. T. Puschmann, 'Nachträge zu Alexander Trallianus', *Berliner Studien für classische Philologie und Archäologie*, v, Heft 2 (Berlin, 1887), 134–79.

Περὶ ἐλμίνθων, ed. J. L. Ideler, *Physici et medici Graeci minores*, I (Berlin, 1841), 305–11; also in T. Puschmann (see above), II, 586–599.

Paul of Aegina

Ὑπόμνημα, also known as Ἐπιτομῆς ἰατρικῆς βιβλία ἑπτά. For translations see G. Sarton in *Isis*, XLII (1951), 150.

Sophronius

Nissen, T., 'Sophronius Studien III', *BZ*, XXXIX (1939), 349–81.

Leo

Kuses, A. P., 'The Written Tradition of the Works of Leo the Iatrosophist', *Praktika Akad. Athen.* XIX (1944; published 1949), 170–7. [On the treatise *On the Peculiarities of Human Beings*. On the identity of this Leo see above, E. E. Lipšic (under (A) Leo the Mathematician).]

Mercurius

Τοῦ λογιωτάτου μοναχοῦ Κύρου Μερκουρίου ἀναγκαιοτάτη διδασκαλία περὶ σφυγμῶν, ed. J. L. Ideler, *Physici et medici Graeci minores*, II, 254–6.

Symeon Seth

Brunet, M., *Syméon Seth, médecin de l'Empereur Michel Ducas, sa vie, son œuvre* (Bordeaux, 1939).

Theodore Prodromus

Codellas, P. S., 'The Case of Smallpox of Theodorus Prodromus (XIIth Century A.D.)', *Bull. Hist. Med.* xx (1946), 207–15.

Nicephorus Blemmydes

Kuses, A. P., 'Les œuvres médicales de Nicéphore Blemmydès selon les manuscrits existants', *Praktika Akad. Athen.* XIX (1944; published 1949), 56–75.

Constantine Meliteniotes

Dölger, F., 'Die Abfassungszeit des Gedichtes "Auf die Enthaltsamkeit" des Meliteniotes', *AIPHO*, II (1934), 315–30 (= *Mélanges Bidez*).

Kuses, A. P., 'Quelques considérations sur les traductions en grec des œuvres médicales orientales et principalement sur les deux manuscrits de la traduction d'un traité persan par Constantine Melitiniotis', *Praktika Akad. Athen.* XIV (1939), 205–20.

Nicholas of Reggio

Thorndike, L., 'Translation of Works of Galen from the Greek by Niccolò da Reggio', *BM*, ɪ (1946), 213–35.

Alexander of Tralles

Monzlinger, E., *Zahnheilkundliches bei Alexander von Tralles und späteren Ärzten der Byzantinerzeit*. Diss. (Leipzig, 1922).

Hippiatrica

Hippiatrica, ed. E. Oder and K. Hoppe, *Corpus hippiatricorum Graecorum*, 2 vols. (Leipzig, 1924 and 1927).

Hoppe, K., 'J. du Rueil's Übersetzung der griechischen Hippiatriker', *Abh. aus d. Gesch. d. Veterinärmed.* (1926), Heft 9.

Sevilla, H. J., 'L'hippiatrique byzantine au quatrième siècle', *Recueil de Médec. Véter.* cɪɪɪ (1927), 154–65.

Sevilla, H. J., 'L'art vétérinaire antique (le syndrome "coliques") dans l'hippiatrie grecque', *Proc. of the Third Intern. Congr. of the Hist. of Medicine, London, 1922* (Antwerp, 1923), pp. 274–87.

Simon, F., *Das Corpus Hippiatricorum Graecorum von E. Oder und K. Hoppe in seiner Bedeutung als Sammelwerk griechisch–römischer Überlieferungen in griechischer Sprache über Heilbehandlung von Tieren in den nachchristlichen Jahrhunderten unter besonderer Berücksichtigung des damaligen Standes der Veterinär-Chirurgie*. Diss. (Munich, 1929).

Apsyrtus

Björck, G., 'Apsyrtus Julius Africanus et l'hippiatrique grecque', *Universitets Årsskrift*, ɪv (Uppsala, 1944).

Oder, E., 'Apsyrtus. Lebensbild des bedeutendsten altgriechischen Veterinärs', *Vetinärhistorisches Jahrbuch*, ɪɪ (1926), 121–36.

Mulomedicina Chironis

Heiberg, J. L., *Geschichte der Mathematik und Naturwissenschaften*, p. 118 [see above Gen. Works].

Hoppe, K., 'Zur Mulomedizina Chironis', *Abh. aus d. Gesch. d. Veterinärmedizin* (1925), Heft 3.

(J) PHARMACOLOGY

(i) *General works*

Bouvet, M., 'La pharmacie dans l'antiquité', in Laignel-Lavastine (see above, under Medicine), pp. 555–608, esp. pp. 593 f.

Delatte, A., *Anecdota Atheniensia*, ɪɪ. Traités alimentaires, pp. 455–99 [see above Gen. Works].

Jeanselme, E., 'Sels médicamenteux et aromatiques pris par les Byzantins au cours des repas', *Bull. soc. franç. hist. méd.* (1922), pp. 324–34.

Jeanselme, E. and Oeconomos, L., 'Aliments et recettes culinaires des Byzantins', *Proc. of the Third Intern. Congr. of the Hist. of Medicine, London, 1922* (Antwerp, 1923), pp. 155–68.

Kremers, E. and Urdang, G., *History of Pharmacy* (Philadelphia, 1951).

Sarton, G., *Guide to the History of Science*, p. 191.

Schelenz, H., *Geschichte der Pharmazie* (Berlin, 1904).

Schmidt, A., *Drogen und Drogenhandel in Altertum* (Leipzig, 1924).

(ii) *Individual authors*

Hierophilus

Oeconomos, L., 'Le calendrier de régime d'Hierophile d'après des manuscrits plus complets que le Parisinus 396', *Actes du VIe Congr. Intern. d'études byz.* (Paris, 1948 (1950)), I, 169–79.

Πῶς ὀφείλει διαιτᾶσθαι ἄνθρωπος ἐφ' ἑκάστῳ μηνί, ed. A. Delatte, *Anecdota Atheniensia*, II, 456–66 [see above Gen. Works].

(K) GEOGRAPHY

(i) *General works*

Diller, A., *The Tradition of the Minor Greek Geographers* (Lancaster, 1952). A few texts revised and re-edited (e.g. Periplus Ponti Euxini, edited from an eleventh-century Athos MS.). See also *Isis*, XLIV (1953), 75 and *BZ*, XLVII (1954), 156 ff.

Günther, S., *Geschichte der Erdkunde* (Leipzig–Vienna, 1904), esp. pp. 14, 37–9.

Müller, C., *Geographi graeci minores*, 2 vols. (Paris, 1855 and 1861). For texts, including Byzantine ones.

Sarton, G., *Guide to the History of Science*, pp. 177 ff.

Schütte, G., 'Der Ursprung der handschriftlichen Ptolemäus-Karten', *Mitteilungen zur Geschichte der Medizin und Naturwissenschaften*, XIII (1914), 573–7.

Tozer, H. F., *A History of Ancient Geography* (Cambridge, 1897), esp. pp. 363 f. on the continuing influence of Ptolemy (and of his errors).

(ii) *Individual authors*

Anonymous

Delatte, A., 'Un manuel byzantin de cosmologie et de géographie', *Acad. royale de Belgique, Bull. de la classe des lettres et des sc. moral. et pol.* XVIII (1932), 189–222. [On geographical errors in an anonymous manuscript (later than seventh century).]

Cosmas Indicopleustes

Anastos, M. V., 'The Alexandrian Origin of the Christian Topography of Cosmas Indicopleustes', *DOP*, III (1946), 73–80. [Anastos takes the view that Cosmas did not compose his work while living on Mount Sinai. It is also doubtful whether he was a monk.]

Wolska, W., *La topographie chrétienne de Cosmas Indicopleustès: théologie et science au VIe siècle* (Paris, 1962) [with bibliography].

Periplus Ponti Euxini

Diller, A., *The Tradition of the Minor Greek Geographers* [see above].

Portolani

Delatte, A. (ed.), *Les portulans grecs* (Paris, 1947).

Delatte, A., 'Les difficultés de l'édition des Portulans grecs', *Acad. royale de Belgique, Bull. de la classe des lettres et des sc. moral. et pol.* XXXIII (1947), 445–58.

Hierocles

Honigmann, E., *Le synecdèmos d'Hiéroclès et l'opuscule géographique de Georges de Chypre* (Brussels, 1939).

George Chrysococces

Lampsides, U., 'Georges Chrysococcis, le médecin, et son œuvre', *BZ*, XXXVIII (1938), 312–22.

(L) SUPERSTITION AND PSEUDO-SCIENCES

(i) *General*

Pauly-Wissowa: the following articles: 'Aberglaube'; 'Mageia'; 'Alchemie'; 'Astrologie'; 'Planeten'; 'Iatromathematike'; 'Mantike'; 'Onomato-manteia'; *see also* the following on soothsaying: 'Aleuromanteia'; 'Alphitomanteia'; 'Hydromanteia'; 'Kapnomanteia'; 'Katoptroman-teia'; 'Krithomanteia'; 'Lecanomanteia'; 'Traumdeutung'.

Krumbacher gave a detailed guide to the almost impossibly vast literature on the subject of soothsaying (pp. 627–31). Since his time many new texts have been published, especially by A. Delatte, *Anecdota Atheniensia*, I, and in the *Catalogus codicum astrologorum graecorum*. See also the general works of L. Thorndike, Ph. Kukules and A. Delatte.

Bárány-Oberschall, M., 'Nouvelles données concernant l'histoire des amulettes magiques byzantins' [Hungarian with French summary], *Folia Archaeol.* III–IV (1941), 268–71.
Berthelot, M. and Ruelle, C. E., *Collection des anciens alchimistes grecs*, I–III (Paris, 1887–8). French translations in vol. III.
Berthelot, M., *Les origines de l'alchimie* (Paris, 1885).
Biro, B., 'A Byzantine bronze amulet' [in Hungarian with a French sum-mary], *Erdély Nemzeti Museum*, II (1942), 242–57.
Björck, G., 'Heidnische und christliche Orakel mit fertigen Antworten', *Symbolae Osloenses*, XIX (1939), 86–98.
Boll, F. and Bezold, C., *Sternglaube und Sterndeutung*, 4th ed. (Leipzig–Berlin, 1931).
Catalogus codicum astrologorum graecorum, ed. F. Cumont and others, I–XII (Brussels, 1898–1953).
Catalogue des manuscrits alchimiques grecs, ed. J. Bidez, O. Lagercrantz and others, I–VIII (Brussels, 1924–32).
Delatte, A., *Anecdota Atheniensia*, I [these religious texts are largely concerned with magic] [see above Gen. Works].
Delatte, A., 'Herbarius, Recherches sur le cérémoniel usité chez les anciens pour la cueillette des simples et des herbes magiques' (Paris, 1936) (= *Bull. Acad. royale de Belgique, Classe d. lettres*, XXII (1931), 227–348).
Delatte, A., 'Le traité des plantes planétaires d'un manuscrit de Leningrad', *Mélanges H. Grégoire* (= *AIPHO*, IX, 1949), pp. 145–77. [The connection of plants and minerals with the planets.]
Delatte, A. and L., 'Un traité byzantin de géomancie (C. Paris. 2419)', *Mélanges F. Cumont* (= *AIPHO*, IV, 1936), pp. 575–658.
Delatte, A. and L., 'Un chapitre de géomancie du Codex Vaticanus Palatinus 312', *Mélanges Desrousseaux* (Paris, 1937), pp. 131–43.
Dölger, F., 'Antike Zahlenmystik in einer byzantinischen Klosterregel', Προσφορὰ εἰς Στ. Κυριακίδην, Ἑλληνικά, Παράρτημα IV (1953), 183–9.
Drexl, F., 'Ein griechisches Losbuch', *BZ*, XLI (1941), 311–18.
Dubs, H. H., 'The Beginning of Alchemy', *Isis*, XXXVIII (1947/8), 62–85.

Laurent, V., 'Amulettes byzantines et formulaires magiques', *BZ*, xxxvi (1936), 300–95.

Neugebauer, O. and van Hoesen, H. B., *Greek Horoscopes* (Philadelphia, 1959).

Nie, H. de, 'Een koptisch-christlijke orakelfrag', *Jaarbericht van 'In Oriente Lux'*, viii (1942), 615–18.

Papadopulos, I., 'Περὶ τῶν ἀποφράδων ἡμερῶν', *EEBS*, xviii (1948), 238–44.

Rehm, A., 'Zur Übersetzungsgeschichte der griechischen Alchemisten', *BZ*, xxxix (1939), 394–434.

Stephanides, M., 'Μουσικὴ καὶ χρυσοποιΐα κατὰ τοὺς Βυζαντινοὺς χυμευτάς', *EEBS*, iv (1927), 39–45.

Thorndike, L., 'The True Place of Astrology in the History of Science', *Isis*, xlvi (1955), 273–8.

Zinner, E., *Sternglaube und Sternforschung* (Freiburg–Munich, 1953) [with full bibliography, pp. 145–60].

Journal of the Warburg and Courtauld Institutes (Warburg Institute, London) contains a good deal of relevant information.

(ii) *Individual authors*

Ptolemy

Tetrabiblos, ed. and transl. (together with Manetho) by R. E. Robbins, 2nd ed., Loeb Classical Library (London, 1948).

Stephen of Alexandria

On Making Gold (apocryphal), ed. F. Sherwood Taylor (with transl. and commentary): 'The Alchemical Work of Stephanos of Alexandria', *Ambix*, i (1937–8), 116–39.

Goldschmidt, G., 'Ein Beitrag zur Ursprungsgeschichte der Alchemie', *Cahiers de Frontenex* (Geneva, 1947), pp. 101–26. [For New Testament influences on Stephen's works.]

Michael Psellus

On Making Gold, ed. J. Bidez, *Catalogue des manuscrits alchimiques grecs*, vi (1928), 26–47.

Ruelle, C. E., 'La Chrysopée de Psellus', *REG*, ii (1889), 260–6. [On the manuscripts.]

(M) TECHNICS AND TECHNOLOGY

(i) *General works*

Blümmer, H., *Technologie und Terminologie der Gewerbe und Künste bei Griechen und Römern*, i–iv (Leipzig, 1875–87), 2nd ed. of vol. i (1912) [with numerous illustrations].

Diels, H., *Antike Technik*, 3rd ed. (Leipzig and Berlin, 1924).

Feldhaus, F. M., *Die Maschine im Leben der Völker* (Basel, 1954).

Feldhaus, F. M., *Die Technik der Antike und des Mittelalters* (Potsdam, 1931), esp. pp. 219–56.

Forbes, R. J., *Man the Maker, a History of Technology and Engineering* (New York, 1950).

Forbes, R. J., *Studies in Ancient Technology*, i–vi (Leiden, 1958).

Klemm, F., *Technik, Eine Geschichte ihrer Probleme* (Freiburg–Munich, 1954).

Merckel, C., *Die Ingenieurtechnik im Altertum* (Berlin, 1899).

Rickard, J. A., *Man and Metals*, I (New York–London, 1932).

Russo, Fr., *Histoire des sciences et des techniques. Bibliographie* (Paris, 1954); supplt. (1955).

Sarton, G., *Guide to the History of Science*, pp. 175 f.

Singer, C., Holmyard, E. J., Hall, A. R. and Williams, T. I., *A History of Technology*, II (Oxford, 1956).

Stemplinger, E., *Antike Technik* (Munich, 1924).

Ucelli, A., *Storia della tecnica dal medio evo ai nostri giorni*, 2nd ed. (Milan, 1945).

Ucelli, A., *Enciclopedia storica delle scienze e delle loro applicazioni*, II, tom. 1 (Milan, 1942), 427–806.

(ii) On particular topics

Alföldi, A., 'Die Geschichte des Throntabernakels', *La nouv. Clio*, 1/2 (1949/50), 537–66.

Bagatti, B., 'Bombe a "fuoco greco" in Palestina (VIII–XIII secolo)', *Faenza*, XXXIX (1953), 35–8 (see *Isis*, XIX (1933), 225).

Berriman, A. E., *Historical Metrology* (New York, 1953).

Brett, G., 'The Automata in the Byzantine "Throne of Salomon"', *SP*, XXIX (1954), 477–87, 8 plates.

Brunov, N. O., 'Architektura Konstantinopolja v IX–XII vv.' ['Architecture in Constantinople in the 9th to 12th centuries'], *VV*, II (27) (1949), 150–214 (with plans and illustrations).

Dain, A., 'Le partage du butin de guerre d'après les traités juridiques et militaires', *Actes du VIᵉ Congr. Intern. d'études Byz. (Paris, 1948)*, I (1950), 347–52.

Dain, A., 'Appellations grecques du feu grégeois', *Mélanges A. Ernout* (Paris, 1940), pp. 121–7.

Dain, A., 'La tradition des stratégistes byzantins', *B*, XX (1950), 315–16 [a survey of the whole development of military strategy from Aineias to Nicephorus Uranus].

Die Landmauer von Konstantinopel, I, F. Krischen (Berlin, 1938), and II, B. Beyer, A. M. Plath, and A. M. Schneider (Berlin, 1943) (= *Denkmäler antiker Architektur*, VI and VIII). [Vol. III contains plates.]

Downey, G., 'Byzantine Architects, their Training and Methods', *B*, XVIII (1948), 99–118.

Forbes, R. J., *Short History of the Art of Distillation* (Leiden, 1948) [chapter II, 'The Alexandrian Chemists'].

Forbes, R. J., *Notes on the History of Ancient Roads and their Construction* (Amsterdam, 1934).

Forbes, R. J., 'Bibliography of Road Building, c. 300–1840', *Roads, Road Construction* (London, 17 June 1938).

Guilland, R., 'The Hippodrome at Byzantium', SP, XXIII (1948), 676–82.

Guilland, R., 'Μελέται περὶ τοῦ Ἱπποδρόμου τῆς Κωνσταντινουπόλεως', *EEBS*, XX (1950), 33–5.

Gunther, R., *The Astrolabes of the World*, 2 vols. (Oxford, 1932).

Hadjinicolaou-Marava, A., *Recherches sur la vie des esclaves dans le monde byzantin* (Collection de l'Institut Français d'Athènes 45) (Athens, 1950).

Heichelheim, F. M., 'Byzantine Silks', *Ciba Rev.* LXXV (1949), 2753–59, 2761–7 (illustrated).

Hultsch, F., *Griechische und römische Metrologie* (Berlin, 1883). [Gives a list of the ancient measures.]

Huuri, K., 'Zur Geschichte des mittelalterlichen Geschützwesens aus orientalischen Quellen', *Studia Orientalia ed. Societas Orient. Fennica*, IX, 3 (Helsingfors, 1941), 71–93.

Ibel, T., *Die Wage im Altertum und Mittelalter*, Diss. (Erlangen, 1908).

Irigoin, J., 'Les débuts de l'emploi du papier à Byzance', *BZ*, XLVI (1953), 314–19.

Jähns, M., *Geschichte der Kriegswissenschaften*, I (Munich–Leipzig, 1889).

Lammert, F., 'Suda, Die Kriegsschriftsteller und Suidas', *BZ*, XXXVIII (1938), 23–35.

Lefebvre des Noëttes, R., 'Le système d'attelage du cheval et du bœuf à Byzance et les conséquences de son emploi', *Mélanges Ch. Diehl*, I (1930), 183–90.

Lopez, R. S., 'Silk Industry in the Byzantine Empire', *SP*, XX (1945), 1–42.

Machabey, A., *Mémoire sur l'histoire de la balance et de la balancerie* (Paris, 1949).

Mercier, M., *Le feu grégeois* (Paris, 1952).

Müfid, A., *Stockwerkbau der Griechen und Römer* (= Istanbuler Forschungen, I) (Berlin–Leipzig, 1932).

Neumann, B., 'Antike Gläser', *Zeitschr. f. angewandte Chemie*, XXXVIII (1925), 776–80 and 857–64.

Partington, J. R., *History of Greek Fire and Gunpowder* (Cambridge, 1960).

Pauly-Wissowa: see articles on 'Geschütze'; 'Kriegskunst'; 'Poliorketiker'; 'Pons'.

Pigulevskaja, N. V., 'Bizantijskaja diplomatija i torgovlja šelkom v V–VII vv.' ['Byzantine diplomacy and the silk trade from the 5th to the 7th centuries'], *VV*, I (XXVI) (1947), 184–214.

Sauvaget, J., 'Flacons à vin ou grenades à feu grégeois', *Mélanges H. Grégoire*, I (= *AIPHO*, IX (1949)), 525–30.

Schmidt, F., *Geschichte der geodätischen Instrumente und Verfahren im Altertum und Mittelalter* (= Veröffentlichungen der Pfälzischen Gesell. zur Förderung der Wiss. XXIV) (Neustadt a. d. H., 1935).

Singer, C., *The Earliest Chemical Industry. An Essay in the Historical Relations of Economics and Technology Illustrated from the Alum Trade* (London, 1948).

Talbot Rice, D., *Byzantine Glazed Pottery* (Oxford, 1930).

The Great Palace of the Byzantine Emperors. A First Report on the Excavations carried out in Istanbul on behalf of the Walker Trust, 1935–1938 (The University of St Andrews), 2nd ed. (London, 1949). Second Report, ed. D. Talbot Rice (Edinburgh, 1958).

Treue, W., *Kulturgeschichte der Schraube* (Munich, 1954), pp. 108 ff. [On screws.]

Ucelli, A., *Storia della tecnica dal medio evo ai nostri giorni*. 2nd ed. (Milan, 1945), pp. 307–10 [on the construction of the dome of St Sophia]; pp. 177 f. [on military techniques].

Underwood, P. A., 'Some Principles of Measure in the Architecture of the Period of Justinian', *Cahiers Archéologiques*, III (1948), 64–74.

Vári, R., 'Zur Überlieferung mittelgriechischer Taktiker', *BZ*, XV (1906), 47–87.

Weigand, E., 'Die Helladisch–Byzantinische Seidenweberei', Εἰς μνήμην Σπ. Λάμπρος (Athens, 1935), pp. 503–14.

Zaloziecky, W., *Das byzantinische Kunstgewerbe in der mittelalterlichen und spätmittelalterlichen Periode* (= Geschichte des Kunstgewerbes aller Zeiten und Völker, v) (Berlin, 1932), pp. 192–6.

Zaloziecky, W., *Die Sophienkirche in Konstantinopel und ihre Stellung in der Geschichte der abendländischen Architektur* (Rome, 1936). [See also under *Account of the Building of St Sophia*.]

(iii) *Individual authors*

Pappus of Alexandria

Downey, G., 'Pappus of Alexandria on Architectural Studies', *Isis*, XXXVIII (1947/8), 197–200.

Downey, G., 'On some Post-classical Greek Architectural Terms', *Trans. Amer. Philol. Ass.* LXXVII (1946), 22–34.

Painter's Handbook of Mt Athos

Papadopulos-Kerameus, A. (ed.), Διονυσίου τοῦ ἐκ Φουρνᾶ Ἑρμηνεία τῆς ζωγραφικῆς τέχνης καὶ αἱ κύριαι αὐτῆς ἀνέκδοτοι πηγαί (St Petersburg, 1900). [The first book (introduction to painting) deals with materials (brushes, colours, varnish, size); painting on paper, fabrics and walls; gilding; mother of pearl; gold lettering; restorations, etc.]; French transl. A. N. Didron, *Manuel d'iconographie chrétienne* (Paris, 1845); English transl. of Didron by M. Stokes, *Christian Iconography*, 2 vols. (London, 1886–91) with summary of the *Painter's Handbook*.

Partington, J. R., 'Chemical Arts in the Mount Athos Manual of Christian Iconography', *Isis*, XXII (1934/5), 136–49.

Schäfer, G., *Das Handbuch der Malerei vom Berge Athos* (Trier, 1885).

Account of the Building of St Sophia (eighth or ninth century)

Emerson, W. and van Nice, R. L., 'A Unique Architectural Achievement of the 6th century', *Bull. Amer. Acad. of Arts and Science*, IV (1950), 2–3.

Preger, T. (ed.), in *Scriptores originum Constantinopolitanarum*, I (Leipzig, 1901), 74–108.

Preger, T., 'Die Erzählung vom Bau der Hagia Sophia', *BZ*, X (1901), 455–76. [With a description of the church's ornamentation and valuable furnishings.]

Würthle, P., *Die Monodie auf den Einsturz der Hagia Sophia* (Paderborn, 1917).

Zaloziecky, W., *Die Sophienkirche in Konstantinopel und ihre Stellung in der Geschichte der abendländischen Architektur* (Rome, 1936).

Procopius

Downey, G., 'The Composition of Procopius, De aedificiis', *Trans. Amer. Philol. Ass.* LXXVIII (1947), 171–83.

Hero of Alexandria

Drachmann, A. G., 'Ktesebios, Philon and Heron, a Study in ancient Pneumatics', *Acta historica scientiarum naturalium et medicinalium*, IV (Copenhagen, 1948).

Drachmann, A. G., 'Heron und Ptolemaios', *Centaurus*, I (1950/1), 117–31 [deals with the use of the analemma, dioptra and theodolite in ancient astronomy].

Leontius

On preparing a sphere of Arateia, ed. (with a French transl.) by N. Halma, *Les phénomènes d'Aratus de Soles, et de Germanicus César; avec les Scholies de Théon, les catastérismes d'Eratosthène et la sphère de Leontius* (Paris, 1821), pp. 65–73.

Stevenson, E. L., *Terrestrial and Celestial Globes*, I (New Haven, 1921), 21–3 and 25. [Leontius mechanicus.]

Susemihl, F., *Geschichte der griechischen Litteratur in der Alexandrinerzeit* (Leipzig, 1891), I, 293 f.

'De rebus bellicis' and other military texts

Dain, A. (ed.), *La 'Tactique' de Nicéphore Ouranos* (Paris, 1937).

Dain, A., *Le 'Corpus perditum'* (Collection de Philologie Classique) (Paris, 1939).

Dain, A., 'Memorandum inédit sur la défense des places', *REG*, LIII (1940), 123–36.

Delatte, E., 'L'armement d'une caravelle grecque au XVI siècle d'après un manuscrit de Vienne', *Miscellanea Mercati*, III (*Studi e Testi* 123), pp. 490–508 (Rome, 1946).

Incerti scriptoris byzantini saeculi X liber de re militari, ed. R. Vári (Leipzig–Berlin, 1901) [anonymous writing].

Strategemata, ed. J. A. Foucault (Paris, 1949).

Thompson, E. A., *A Roman Reformer and Inventor, being the New Text of the Treatise 'De rebus bellicis'* (Oxford, 1952).

Treatise on poliorcetics [siege-warfare], ed. R. Schneider, 'Griechische Poliorketiker II (Text, Übersetzung und Abbildungen)', *Abhandlung d. k. Gesellschaft der Wiss. zu Göttingen, phil.-hist. Kl.* N.F. XI, 1 (1908). Part I (X, 1) contains Apollodorus' 'art of siege-warfare' in a Byzantine paraphrase.

Strategicon of 'Maurice'

Arriani tactica et Mauricii ars militaris, ed. with Latin transl. J. Scheffer (Uppsala, 1664).

A Related Strategicon, ed. K. K. Müller, 'Ein griechisches Fragment über Kriegswesen', *Festschrift L. Urlichs* (Würzburg, 1880), pp. 106–38.

Tactica and other writings

Dain, A., *L''Extrait Tactique' tiré de Léon VI le Sage* (Bibliothèque de l'Ecole des Hautes Etudes 284) (Paris, 1942).

Dolley, R. H., 'Naval Tactics in the Heyday of the Byzantine Thalassocracy', *Atti VIII Congr. Intern. di Studi Bizant.* (*1951*), I (= *SBN*, VII, 1953), 324–39.

Eickhoff, E., *Seekrieg und Seepolitik zwischen Islam und Abendland bis zum Aufstiege Pisas und Genuas (650–1040)* (*Schriften der Universität des Saarlandes*) (Saarbrücken, 1953).

Lammert, F., 'Die älteste erhaltene Schrift über Seetaktik und ihre Beziehung zum Anonymus Byzantinus des 6. Jahrhunderts', *Klio*, XXXIII (1940), 271–88.

Leonis imperatoris tactica, ed. R. Vári, I (Budapest, 1917); II, 1 (1922). [The first 14 Constitutiones together with the references to Leo's sources and those of Maurice.]

Naumachica partim adhuc inedita, in unum nunc primum congessit et indice auxit, ed. A. Dain (Paris, 1943).

Problemata, ed. A. Dain, *Leonis VI Sapientis problemata* (Paris, 1935).
Sylloge (apocryphal work of tenth century), ed. A. Dain, *Sylloge tacticorum quae olim 'inedita Leonis tactica' dicebantur* (Paris, 1938).
Tactica, *MPG*, cvii, 669–1120.

See also Moravcsik, *Byzantinoturcica* under 'Leon Sophos' and 'Maurikios'.

CHAPTER XXIX. BYZANTINE ARCHITECTURE AND ART

I. GENERAL WORKS

Beckwith, J., *The Art of Constantinople: an introduction to Byzantine Art 330–1453* (London, 1961).
Bréhier, L., *Le monde byzantin*, iii, 504–70 [see Gen. Bibl. v].
Dalton, O. M., *Byzantine Art and Archaeology* (Oxford, 1911).
Dalton, O. M., *East Christian Art* (Oxford, 1925).
Diehl, C., *Manuel d'art byzantin*, 2 vols., 2nd ed. (Paris, 1925–6).
Kitzinger, E., 'Byzantine Art in the period between Justinian and Iconoclasm', *Berichte zum XI. Intern. Byz.-Kongress* (Munich, 1958), iv (1).
Mathew, G., *Byzantine Aesthetics* (London, 1963).
Millet, G., *L'art byzantin*, in A. Michel, *Histoire de l'art*, i and iii (Paris, 1905, 1908).
Sotiriou, G., Χριστιανικὴ καὶ Βυζαντινὴ Ἀρχαιολογία (Athens, 1942).
Talbot Rice, D., *Byzantine Art* (Oxford, 1935); revised ed. (Pelican Books, 1954).
Talbot Rice, D., *The Art of Byzantium* (London, 1959).
Talbot Rice, D., *Art of the Byzantine Era* (London, 1963).
Wulff, O., *Altchristliche und byzantinische Kunst*, 2 vols. (Berlin, 1916–18).

II. ARCHITECTURE

Antoniades, E. M., Ἔκφρασις τῆς Ἁγίας Σοφίας (Paris, 1917).
Beylié, L. de, *L'habitation byzantine* (Paris, 1903).
Brockhaus, H., *Die Kunst in den Athos–Klöstern* (Leipzig, 1891).
Chatzidakis, M., Μυστρᾶς (Athens, 1948).
Choisy, A., *L'art de bâtir chez les Byzantins* (Paris, 1884).
Diehl, C., Le Tourneau, M. and Saladin, H., *Les monuments chrétiens de Salonique* (Paris, 1918).
Ebersolt, J., *Monuments d'architecture byzantine* (Paris, 1934).
Ebersolt, J. and Thiers, A., *Les églises de Constantinople* (Paris, 1913).
George, W. S. and others, *The Church of Saint Eirene at Constantinople* (Oxford, 1912).
Gurlitt, C., *Die Baukunst Konstantinopels* (Berlin, 1912).
Hamilton, J. A., *Byzantine Architecture and Decoration*, 2nd ed. (London, 1956).
Jerphanion, G. de, *Les églises rupestres de Cappadoce* (text 2 vols.; plates 3 vols.) (Paris, 1925–42).
Macdonald, W. L., *Early Christian and Byzantine Architecture* (New York, 1962).
Millet, G., *Le monastère de Daphni* (Paris, 1899).

Millet, G., *Monuments byzantins de Mistra* (Paris, 1910).
Millet, G., *L'école grecque dans l'architecture byzantine* (Paris, 1916).
Orlandos, A. K., Μοναστηριακὴ 'Αρχιτεκτονική, 2nd ed. (Athens, 1958).
Salzenberg, W., *Alt-Christliche Baudenkmäler von Constantinopel* (Berlin, 1854).
Schneider, A. M., *Byzanz* (Berlin, 1936).
Schneider, A. M., *Die Hagia Sophia zu Konstantinopel* (Berlin, 1939).
Schultz, R. W. and Barnsley, S. H., *The Monastery of Saint Luke of Stiris in Phocis* (London, 1901).
The Great Palace of the Byzantine Emperors. First Report on the Excavations carried out in Istanbul on behalf of the Walker Trust, 1935–1938 (The University of St Andrews), 2nd ed. (London, 1949). Second Report, ed. D. Talbot Rice (Edinburgh, 1958).
Van Millingen, A., *Byzantine Constantinople* [see Gen. Bibl. II].
Van Millingen, A., *Byzantine Churches in Constantinople* (London, 1912).
Wulzinger, K., *Byzantinische Baudenkmäler zu Konstantinopel* (Hanover, 1925).

III. PAINTING

(See also works cited under I and II.)

Buberl, P., *Die byzantinischen Handschriften der Nationalbibliothek in Wien*, I (Leipzig, 1937).
Buchthal, H., *The Miniatures of the Paris Psalter. A Study in Middle Byzantine Painting* (London, 1938).
Chatzidakis, M., Μυστρᾶς (Athens, 1948).
Demus, O., *Die Mosaiken von San Marco in Venedig, 1100–1300* (Vienna, 1935).
Demus, O., *The Mosaics of Norman Sicily* (London, 1949).
Demus, O., *Byzantine Mosaic Decoration* (London, 1948).
Demus, O., 'Die Entstehung des Paläologenstils in der Malerei', *Berichte zum XI. Intern. Byz.-Kongress* (Munich, 1958), IV (2).
Demus, O., *The Church of San Marco in Venice* (Cambridge, Mass., 1960).
Der Nersessian, S., *L'illustration du Roman de Barlaam et Joasaph* (Paris, 1937).
Diez, E. and Demus, O., *Byzantine Mosaics in Greece. Hosios Lucas and Daphni* (Cambridge, Mass., 1931).
Drevnosti Gosudarstva Rossijskago [*Antiquities of the Russian State. Cathedral of St Sophia of Kiev*]. I. Tolstoi and N. P. Kondakov, *Russkija Drevnosti* [*Russian antiquities*], IV–VI (St Petersburg, 1891–9).
Ebersolt, J., *La miniature byzantine* (Paris, 1926).
Gerstinger, H., *Die griechische Buchmalerei* (Vienna, 1926).
Grabar, A., *Miniatures byzantines de la Bibl. Nat.*, Album (Paris, 1939).
Grabar, A., *Les Miniatures de Grégoire de Nazianze de l'Ambrosienne*, Album (Paris, 1943).
Grabar, A., *Byzantine Painting* (London and Geneva, 1953).
Grabar, A. and Chatzidakis, M., *Greece. Byzantine Mosaics* (Unesco, Paris, 1959).
Grabar, A. and Mijatev, K., *Bulgaria. Medieval Wall-paintings* (Unesco, 1962).
Grabar, I., *Die Freskomalerei der Dimitrikathedrale in Wladimir* (Berlin, 1926).
Hesseling, D. C., *Miniatures de l'octateuque grec de Smyrne* (Leyden, 1919).

Jerphanion, G. de, *Les églises rupestres de Cappadoce* [see above, under Architecture].

Lassus, J., 'Les miniatures byzantines du Livre des Rois', *Mélanges d'archéologie et d'histoire*, xLv (Paris, 1928), 38–74.

Lazarev, V., *Istorija vizantijskoj živopisi* [*History of Byzantine painting*], 2 vols. (Moscow, 1947, 1948).

Mango, C., 'The Date of the Narthex Mosaics of the Church of the Dormition at Nicaea', *DOP*, xIII (1959), 245–52.

Menologio di Basilio II (Cod. Vat. gr. 1613) (Codices e Vaticanis selecti, VIII) (Turin, 1907).

Millet, G., *Le monastère de Daphni* (Paris, 1899).

Millet, G., *Les monuments de Mistra* (Paris, 1910).

Millet, G., *Monuments de l'Athos*, i (Paris, 1910).

Millet, G., *Recherches sur l'iconographie de l'Evangile* (Paris, 1916).

Miniature della Bibbia cod. Vat. Regin. gr. 1 e del Salterio cod. Vat. Palat. gr. 381 (Collezione paleografica Vaticana, fasc. 1) (Milan, 1905).

Morey, C. R., 'Notes on East Christian Miniatures', *The Art Bulletin*, xi (1929) (cf. *Speculum*, xIV, 1939).

Mjasojedov, V. K., *Les fresques byzantines de Spas-Nereditsa* [in Russian] (Leningrad, 1925); French transl. (Paris, 1927).

Omont, H., *Miniatures dans les plus anciens ms. grecs de la Bibl. Nat.*, 2nd ed. (Paris, 1929).

Orlandos, A. C., *Monuments byzantins de Chios*, 2 vols. (Athens, 1930–1).

Pächt, O., *Byzantine Illumination* (Oxford, 1952).

Painter's Handbook, compiled by Dionysius of Fourna (fl. end fourteenth century), ed. A. Papadopoulos-Kerameus, Διονυσίου τοῦ ἐκ Φουρνᾶ Ἑρμηνεία τῆς ζωγραφικῆς τέχνης (St Petersburg, 1900); French transl. by A. N. Didron, *Manuel d'iconographie chrétienne* (Paris, 1845); English transl. of Didron by M. Stokes, *Christian Iconography*, 2 vols. (London, 1886–91), with a summary of the *Painter's Handbook*.

Pelekanidis, G., Καστορία [*Castoria, Wall-paintings*, in Greek] (Thessalonica, 1953).

Schmit, F., *Die Koimesis-kirche von Nikaia* (Berlin–Leipzig, 1927).

Schultz, R. W. and Barnsley, S. H., *The Monastery of Saint Luke of Stiris in Phocis* (London, 1901).

Stornajolo, C., *Le miniature della Topografia Cristiana di Cosma Indicopleuste, etc.* (*Codices e Vaticanis selecti*, x) (Milan, 1908).

Talbot Rice, D. and Radojčić, S., *Yugoslavia. Medieval Frescoes* (Unesco, 1955).

The Great Palace [see above, II].

Tikkanen, J. J., *Die Psalterillustration im Mittelalter* (Helsingfors, 1903).

Underwood, P. A., 'Preliminary Reports on the Restoration of the Frescoes in the Kariye Camii at Istanbul' may be found in *DOP*, Ix–x (1956) to xIII (1959).

Underwood, P. A., 'The Evidence of Restorations in the Sanctuary Mosaics of the Church of the Dormition at Nicaea', *DOP*, xIII (1959).

Wald, E. de, *The Illustrations in the Manuscripts of the Septuagint*, III, 1 and 2 (Princeton, 1941, 1942).

Weitzmann, K., *Die byzantinische Buchmalerei des 9. und 10. Jahrhunderts* (Berlin, 1935).

Weitzmann, K., *Illustration in Roll and Codex. A Study of the Origin and Method of Text-Illustration* (Princeton, 1947).

Weitzmann, K., *The Joshua Roll* (Princeton, 1948).

Weitzmann, K., *Greek Mythology in Byzantine Art* (Princeton, 1951).

Whittemore, T., *The Mosaics of St Sophia at Istanbul*, I–IV (Oxford, 1933–52).

Wilpert, J., *Die römischen Mosaiken und Malereien der kirchlichen Bauten vom IV. bis XIII. Jahrhundert*, 4 vols., 2nd ed. (Freiburg, 1917).

Wulff, O., *Die Koimesiskirche in Nicäa und ihre Mosaiken* (Strasbourg, 1903).

Wulff, O. and Alpatov, M., *Denkmäler der Ikonenmalerei* (Hellerau, 1925).

Xyngopoulos, A., Ἡ ψηφιδωτὴ διακόσμησις τοῦ ναοῦ τῶν Ἁγίων Ἀποστόλων Θεσσαλονίκης (Thessalonica, 1953).

IV. CARVING, GOLD WORK AND OTHER ARTS

Bank, A. V., *Iskusstvo vizantii v sobranii gosudarstvennogo Ermitaža* [*Byzantine art in the state collection in the Hermitage*] (Leningrad, 1960).

Bárány-Oberschall, M., *The Crown of the Emperor Constantine Monomachos* (Budapest, 1937).

Bettini, S., *La scultura bizantina*, fascicules 89 and 90 of the *Nov. Enciclop. Monografica illustrata* (Florence, n.d.).

Bréhier, L., *La sculpture et les arts mineurs byzantins* (Paris, 1936).

Chatzidakis, E., *Broderies d'église* (Athens, 1953).

Cruikshank Dodd, E., *Byzantine Silver Stamps* (Washington, 1961).

Ebersolt, J., *Les arts somptuaires de Byzance* (Paris, 1923).

Falke, O. von, *Kunstgeschichte der Seidenweberei*, new ed. (Berlin, 1921).

Goldschmidt, R. and Weitzmann, K., *Die byzantinischen Elfenbeinskulpturen des X.–XIII. Jahrhunderts*, 2 vols. (Berlin, 1930, 1934).

Grisar, H. S. J., *Die römische Kapelle Sancta Sanctorum* (Freiburg, 1908).

Kondakov, N., *Histoire et monuments des émaux byzantins* (Frankfurt, 1892).

Kondakov, N., *Les monuments de l'art chrétien au Mont-Athos* (St Petersburg, 1902).

Lauer, Ph., 'Le trésor du Sancta Sanctorum à Rome', *Monuments Piot*, XII (1906).

Lessing, J., *Die Gewebesammlung des K. Kunstgewerbe-Museums* (Berlin, 1900–).

Maculevič, L., *Byzantinische Antike. Studien auf Grund der Silbergefässe der Ermitage* (Berlin and Leipzig, 1929).

Millet, G., *Broderies religieuses de style byzantin*, 2 vols. (Paris, 1938, 1947).

Millet, G., *La dalmatique du Vatican* (Paris, 1945).

Molinier, E., *Histoire générale des arts appliqués à l'industrie*, IV, *L'Orfèvrerie* (Paris, 1901).

Molinier, E., *Le trésor de la basilique de Saint-Marc à Venise* (Venice, 1888).

Morgan, C. H., *Corinth, XI. The Byzantine Pottery* (Amer. School Class. Stud. in Athens) (Harvard Univ. Press, 1942).

Muñoz, A., *L'art byzantin à l'exposition de Grottaferrata* (Rome, 1906).

Pasini, A., *Il tesoro di San Marco* (Venice, 1885).

Rosenberg, A., *Zellenschmelz* (Frankfurt, 1920).

Schlumberger, G.—a number of articles in *Monuments Piot*, I (1894); VI (1900); IX (1903); and *Mélanges d'Archéologie byzantine* (Paris, 1895).

Talbot Rice, D., *Byzantine Glazed Pottery* (Oxford, 1930).

CHAPTER XXX. THE PLACE OF BYZANTIUM IN THE MEDIEVAL WORLD

(This should be supplemented by the General Bibliography and by the bibliographies to the other chapters, especially I–II, X–XXII and XXIX.)

Åberg, N., *The Occident and the Orient in the Art of the seventh century*: Pt. I, *The British Isles*. Pt. II, *Lombard Italy*. Pt. III, *Merovingian empire*. *Kungl. Vitterhets Historie och Antikvitets Akademeins Handlingar*, LVI, 1–3 (Stockholm, 1943–7).

Baynes, N. H. and Baron Meyendorff, 'The Byzantine Inheritance in Russia', *Byzantium*, ed. N. H. Baynes and H. St L. B. Moss, pp. 369–91 [see Gen. Bibl. v].

Bischoff, B., 'Das griechische Element in der abendländischen Bildung des Mittelalters', *BZ*, XLIV (1951), 27–55.

Bloch, H., 'Monte Cassino, Byzantium and the West in the earlier Middle Ages', *DOP*, III (1946), 163–224.

Boase, T. S. R., *English Art, 1100–1216* (Oxford, 1953).

Bolgar, R. B., *The Classical Heritage and its Beneficiaries* (Cambridge, 1954).

Bréhier, L., 'Les Colonies d'Orientaux en Occident au commencement du moyen-âge', *BZ*, XII (1903), 1–39.

Buchthal, H., *Miniature Painting in the Latin Kingdom of Jerusalem* (Oxford, 1957).

Byron, R. and Talbot Rice, D., *The Birth of Western Painting* (London, 1930).

Charanis, P., 'On the Question of the Hellenization of Sicily and Southern Italy during the Middle Ages', *AHR*, LII (1946), 74–86.

Clapham, A. W., *Romanesque Architecture in Western Europe* (Oxford, 1950).

Dawkins, R. M., 'The Later History of the Varangian Guard: Some Notes', *JRS*, XXXVII (1947), 39–46.

Demus, O., *The Mosaics of Norman Sicily* (London, 1950).

Demus, O., 'Die Entstehung des Paläologenstils in der Malerei', *Berichte zum XI. Intern. Byz.-Kongress* (Munich, 1958), IV (2).

Demus, O., *The Church of San Marco in Venice* (Cambridge, Mass., 1960).

Der Nersessian, S., *Armenia and the Byzantine Empire* (Cambridge, Mass., 1945).

Dölger, F., 'Byzanz als weltgeschichtliche Potenz', *Wort und Wahrheit*, IV (1949), 249–63; reprinted in ΠΑΡΑΣΠΟΡΑ [see Gen. Bibl. v], pp. 1–19.

Dölger, F., *Byzanz und die europäische Staatenwelt* [see Gen. Bibl. v].

Dölger, F., 'Byzanz und das Abendland vor den Kreuzzügen', *X Congr. Intern. di Scienze Storiche, Roma, 1955. Relazioni*, III (Florence, 1956), 67–112; reprinted in ΠΑΡΑΣΠΟΡΑ (Ettal, 1961), 73–106 [with bibliography].

Dvornik, F., *Les Slaves, Byzance et Rome au IXᵉ siècle* (Paris, 1926).

Ebersolt, J., *Orient et Occident. Recherches sur les influences byzantines et orientales en France pendant les Croisades*, 2nd ed. (Paris, 1954).

Gardner, A., *French Church Architecture* (Oxford, 1938).

Geanakoplos, D. J., *Greek Scholars in Venice. Studies in the Dissemination of Greek Learning from Byzantium to Western Europe* (Cambridge, Mass., 1962).

Giunta, F., *Bizantini e Bizantinismo nella Sicilia Normanna* (Palermo, 1950).

Heilig, K. J., *Ostrom und das deutsche Reich um die Mitte des 12. Jahrhunderts*, in T. Mayer, K. J. Heilig and C. Erdmann, *Kaisertum und Herzogsgewalt im Zeitalter Friedrichs I.* (Leipzig, 1944).

Heyd, W., *Histoire du commerce du Levant* [see Gen. Bibl. v].

Hinks, R. P., *Carolingian Art* (London, 1935).

Hinks, R. P., *El Greco* (London, 1954).

Huxley, M. (ed.), *The Root of Europe* (London, 1952).

Jantzen, H., *Ottonische Kunst* (Munich, 1947).

Jenkins, R. J. H., *Byzantium and Byzantinism* (University of Cincinnati, 1963).

Koehler, W., 'Byzantine Art in the West', *DOP*, I (1941), 61–87.

Lamma, P., *Comneni e Staufer: ricerche sui rapporti fra Bisanzio e l'Occidente nel secolo XII*, 2 vols. (Rome, 1955–7).

Laurent, V., 'Byzance et l'Angleterre au lendemain de la conquête normande. A propos d'un sceau byzantin trouvé à Winchester', *Numismatic Circular*, LXXI (1963), 93–6.

Leib, B., *Rome, Kiev et Byzance à la fin du XIe siècle (1088–1099)* (Paris, 1924).

Lopez, R. S., 'Le problème des relations Anglo-Byzantines du septième au dixième siècle', *B*, XVIII (1948), 139–62.

Lopez, R. S., 'The Trade of Medieval Europe: the South', *Cambridge Economic History*, II (Cambridge, 1952), 257–354.

Lopez, R. S., 'East and West in the early Middle Ages: Economic Relations', *X Congr. Intern. di Scienze Storiche, Rome, 1955. Relazioni*, III (Florence, 1956), 113–63 [with bibliography].

Moravcsik, Gy., *Die byzantinische Kultur und das mittelalterliche Ungarn. Sitzungsberichte der Deutschen Akademie der Wissenschaft zu Berlin*, Kl. f. Philos. Gesch., etc. (Berlin, 1955), Nr. 4.

Muntz, E., 'Les artistes byzantins dans l'Europe latine du Ve au XVe siècle', *Revue de l'art chrétien*, XXXVI (1893), 181–90.

Oakeshott, W., *The Artists of the Winchester Bible* (London, 1945).

Oakeshott, W., *Classical Inspiration in Medieval Art* (London, 1959).

Ohnsorge, W., *Das Zweikaiserproblem im früheren Mittelalter. Die Bedeutung des byzantinischen Reiches für die Entwicklung der Staatsidee in Europa* (Hildesheim, 1947).

Ohnsorge, W., *Abendland und Byzanz* (Darmstadt, 1958).

Riant, P., *Les expéditions et pèlerinages des Scandinaves en Terre Sainte au temps des croisades* (Paris, 1865).

Riant, P., *Exuviae Sacrae Constantinopolitanae*, I–II (Geneva, 1877–8); III by F. de Mély (Paris, 1904).

Runciman, S., 'Byzantine Trade and Industry', *Cambridge Economic History*, II (Cambridge, 1952), 89–118.

Saxl, F. and Wittgower, R., *British Art and the Mediterranean* (Oxford, 1948).

Schramm, P. E., *Kaiser, Rom und Renovatio*, 2 vols. (Leipzig, 1929).

Setton, K. M., 'The Byzantine Background to the Italian Renaissance', *Proc. Amer. Philosoph. Soc.* C (1956), 1–76.

Stender-Petersen, A., 'Das Problem der ältesten byzantinisch-russisch-nordischen Beziehungen', *X Congr. Intern. di Scienze Storiche, Roma, 1955. Relazioni*, III (Florence, 1956), 165–88.

Talbot Rice, D., *The Byzantine Element in Late Saxon Art* (Charlton Lecture, 1946) (Oxford, 1947).

Talbot Rice, D., *Byzantine Painting and Developments in the West before A.D. 1200* (London, 1948).

Talbot Rice, D., *English Art, 871–1100* (Oxford, 1951).

Talbot Rice, D., *The Beginnings of Christian Art* [see Gen. Bibl. v].

Vaccari, A., *La Grecia nell'Italia meridionale* (*Orientalia Christiana*, III, no. 13) (Rome, 1925).

Vasiliev, A. A., 'Quelques remarques sur les voyageurs du moyen-âge à Constantinople', *Mélanges Charles Diehl*, I (Paris, 1930), 293–8.

Vasiliev, A. A., 'The Opening Stages of the Anglo-Saxon Immigration to Byzantium in the Eleventh Century', *Sem. Kond.* IX (1937), 39–70.

Weiss, R., 'The Greek Culture of South Italy in the Later Middle Ages', *Proc. Brit. Acad.* XXXVII (1951), 23–50.

Weitzmann, K., *The Fresco Cycle of Santa Maria di Castelseprio* (Princeton, 1951).

Zaloziecky, W., *Byzanz und Abendland im Spiegel ihrer Kunsterscheinungen* (Salzburg and Leipzig, 1936).

INDEX

Bold figures denote a major entry.